青が散る
宮本
Italo Calvino
А.С. ПУШКИН
CAMINHO
Saramago
英汉对照
新译
围城
D0830940

THE top10 OF EVERYTHING 2001

THE top10 OF EVERYTHING 2001

RUSSELL ASH

DK
A Dorling Kindersley Book

Contents

Dorling Kindersley

LONDON, NEW YORK, SYDNEY, DELHI,
PARIS, MUNICH, and JOHANNESBURG

Project Editor David Tombesi-Walton
Senior Designer Tracy Hambleton-Miles

DTP Designer Jason Little
Production Silvia La Greca, Elizabeth Cherry
Picture Research Anna Grapes

Managing Editor Stephanie Jackson
Managing Art Editor Nigel Duffield

Produced for Dorling Kindersley by
Cooling Brown, 9–11 High Street,
Hampton, Middlesex TW12 2SA

Editor Alison Bolus
Designers Tish Mills, Elaine Hewson
Creative Director Arthur Brown

Author's Research Manager Aylla Macphail

Published in Great Britain in 2000 by
Dorling Kindersley Limited,
9 Henrietta Street,
London WC2E 8PS

2 4 6 8 10 9 7 5 3 1

Copyright © 2000 Dorling Kindersley Limited, London
Text copyright © 2000 Russell Ash

The right of Russell Ash to be identified as Writer of this Work has been asserted by him in accordance with the Copyright, Designs and Patents Act 1988.

All rights reserved. No part of this publication may be reproduced, stored in a retrieval system, or transmitted in any form or by any means, electronic, mechanical, photocopying, recording, or otherwise, without the prior permission of the copyright holder.

A CIP catalogue record of this book is available from the British Library.

0 7513 0468 9

Reproduction by Colourpath, London
Printed and bound by L.Rex Printing Company Ltd, China

See our complete catalogue at
www.dk.com

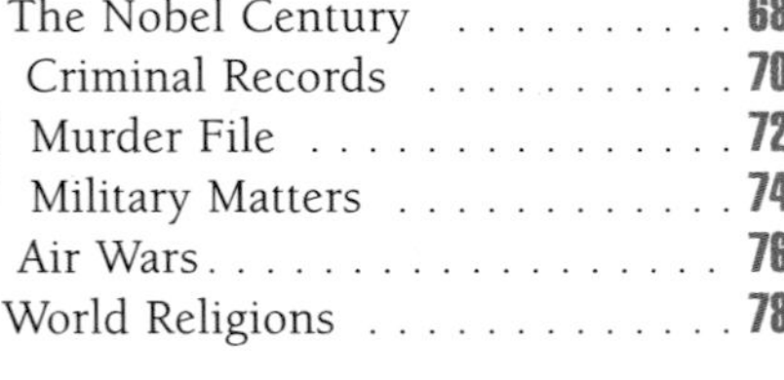

THE Sun SOUVENIR MILLENNIUM EDITION
THE YEAR 2000

Culture & Learning

Music

Stage & Screen

The Commercial World

On the Move

Sports

Introduction

Looking Back

This is the 12th annual edition of *The Top 10 of Everything* and the first to be published in the new century and the new millennium. We start with a look back at the 20th century in A Century of Change before moving on to chart many of the developments of the 1990s.

Information Overload?

The Internet is a mixed blessing: on the one hand, it gives increased access to information, especially official figures; on the other, we are increasingly overwhelmed by the sheer volume of data. Perhaps today more than ever the value of *The Top 10 of Everything* is that it distils down all this available information to a manageable level, which is why, despite the Internet, books like this still have a place.

Listomania

During the past dozen years, the number of published lists has increased inexorably, and the 20th century ended with a tidal wave of lists of the best films, books, and recordings of all time. Scarcely a day goes by when I am not inspired with an idea for a new list, such as the top advertising campaigns, leading fat consumers, latest assassinated monarchs, deadliest serial killers, fastest rollercoasters, largest molluscs, and champion cowboys, as featured here.

Not Just the Best

The book focuses on superlatives in numerous categories and also contains a variety of "firsts" or "latests", which recognize the pioneers and the most recent achievers in various fields of endeavour. Lists of films are based on worldwide box-office income, and those on recorded music, videos, and books are based on sales, unless otherwise stated.

History in the Making

The Top 10 of Everything now spans three decades and has become a historical resource. Schools use back numbers when undertaking projects on social changes, while others buy *Top 10* to commemorate births and other family events, as a "time capsule" of the year.

A Never-ending Task

While I endeavour to ensure that all the information is as up to date as possible, certain statistics are slow to be collated and published. At the same time, lists relating to bestsellers and sporting achievements can change almost daily. Even lists that one would not expect to alter do: a revised height for Everest was published while I was at work on this book.

The Research Network

Compiling *The Top 10 of Everything* has been a pleasure and a revelation to me: in the course of my work on it and the associated television series, and through publicity tours in the UK and US, I have discovered numerous interesting facts, increased my library, and, in particular, met many people who have become consultants on the book. My thanks to all of them and to everyone who has contacted me with helpful information.

Keep in Touch

If you have any list ideas or comments, please write to me c/o the publishers or e-mail me direct at ash@pavilion.co.uk.

Other Dorling Kindersley books by Russell Ash:
The Factastic Book of Comparisons
The Factastic Book of 1,001 Lists
Factastic Millennium Facts
Great Wonders of the World

Special Features

- More than 1,000 lists make this the most wide-ranging *Top 10 of Everything* ever.
- A Century of Change surveys some of the fascinating Top 10s of the 20th century.
- Double the number of pages have been devoted to some of the most popular subjects.
- Illustrated SnapShots add extra information to many lists.
- "Did You Know?" entries offer unusual sidelights on the subjects explored.
- "Why Do We Say?" features explain the origins of popular words and phrases.
- Quiz questions with multi-choice answers appear throughout the book.
- Dramatic vertical format spreads add to the visual appeal.

A Century of Change

TOP 10

MOST HIGHLY POPULATED COUNTRIES, 1900–2000

	1900	1950	2000
1	China	China	China
2	India	India	India
3	Russia	USSR	USA
4	USA	USA	Indonesia
5	Germany	Japan	Brazil
6	Austria	Indonesia	Russia
7	Japan	Germany	Pakistan
8	UK	UK	Bangladesh
9	Turkey	Brazil	Japan
10	France	Italy	Nigeria

TEEMING MILLIONS

China began the 20th century with some 400 million inhabitants and ended it with 1.2 billion, about one-fifth of the world's population.

TOP 10

MOST HIGHLY POPULATED CITIES, 1900

	CITY/LOCATION	POPULATION*
1	**London**, UK	6,581,000
2	**New York**, USA	3,437,000
3	**Paris**, France	2,714,000
4	**Berlin**, Germany	1,889,000
5	**Chicago**, USA	1,699,000
6	**Vienna**, Austria	1,675,000
7	**Wuhan**, China	1,500,000
8	**Tokyo**, Japan	1,440,000
9	**Philadelphia**, USA	1,294,000
10	**St. Petersburg**, Russia	1,265,000

* *Including adjacent suburban areas*

Censuses and population estimates conducted around 1900 indicated that these cities, plus just three others (Constantinople in Turkey, Moscow in Russia, and Xian in China), were the only ones with populations in excess of 1 million. As we enter the 21st century, there are over 400 world cities with million-plus populations.

A CENTURY OF SPEED: THE PROGRESSION OF THE LAND SPEED RECORD

DECADE*	DRIVER	COUNTRY	SPEED KM/H	SPEED MPH
1900	Camille Jenatzy	Belgium	105.882	65.792
1910	Barney Oldfield	USA	211.267	131.275
1920	Tommy Milton	USA	250.000	155.343
1930	Henry Segrave	UK	372.671	231.567
1940	John Cobb	UK	595.041	369.741
1950	John Cobb	UK	633.803	393,827
1960	Mickey Thompson	USA	654.359	406,600#
1970	Gary Gabelich	USA	1,014.513	630,389
1980	Gary Gabelich	USA	1,014.513	630,389
1990	Richard Noble	UK	1,020.408	634.052
2000	Andy Green	UK	1,227.985	763.035

* *As at the first year of each decade*

\# *Based on flying mile; all others over flying km*

A CENTURY OF US POPULATION

(Year/population)

1900 75,994,575 **1910** 91,972,266 **1920** 105,710,620 **1930** 122,775,046 **1940** 131,669,275 **1950** 150,697,361 **1960** 179,323,175 **1970** 203,302,031 **1980** 226,542,199 **1990** 248,709,873 **2000*** 274,634,000

* *Estimated*

The greatest rate of increase in the US population within a decade occurred not in this century but in the first decade of the 19th century, when it expanded by 36.4 per cent. The lowest growth rate during the past 200 years was registered in the 1930s, at just 7.2 per cent.

A CENTURY OF UK POPULATION

(Year/population)

1901 38,237,000 **1911** 42,082,000 **1921*** 44,027,000 **1931*** 46,038,000 **1941** 48,216,000 **1951** 50,225,000 **1961** 52,709,000 **1971** 55,928,000 **1981** 56,352,000 **1991** 57,808,000, **2001#** 59,994,000

* *Figures for Northern Ireland estimated*

\# *Estimated*

Did You Know? United Nations estimates for world population in 2050 predict a 50 per cent increase on today's 6 billion, bringing the total to about 9 billion.

FRANKLY, MY DEAR...

Gone With the Wind, starring Clark Gable and Vivien Leigh, was the most expensive film ever made, allowing for inflation. It was also the most successful.

TOP 10

SUCCESSIVE HOLDERS OF THE TITLE "WORLD'S TALLEST HABITABLE BUILDING" IN THE 20TH CENTURY

	BUILDING/LOCATION	YEAR	STOREYS	M	FT
1	**City Hall**, Philadelphia	1901	7	156	512
2	**Singer Building***, New York	1908	34	200	656
3	**Metropolitan Life**, New York	1909	50	212	700
4	**Woolworth Building**, New York	1913	59	241	792
5	**40 Wall Street**, New York	1929	71	260	854
	with spire			282	927
6	**Chrysler Building**, New York	1930	77	282	925
	with spire			319	1,046
7	**Empire State Building**, New York	1931	102	381	1,250
	with spire			449	1,472
8	**World Trade Center**, New York	1973	110	415	1,362
	with spire			521	1,710
9	**Sears Tower**, Chicago	1974	110	443	1,454
	with spires			520	1,707
10	**Petronas Towers**, Kuala Lumpur, Malaysia	1996	96	452	1,482

* *Demolished 1970*

TOP 10

MOST EXPENSIVE FILMS OF THE 20TH CENTURY

	DECADE	FILM/YEAR	COST $
1	1900–09	*For the Term of His Natural Life** (1908)	34,000
2	1910–19	*A Daughter of the Gods* (1916)	1,000,000
3	1920–29	*Ben-Hur* (1925)	3,900,000
4	1930–39	*Gone With the Wind* (1939)	4,250,000
5	1940–49	*Joan of Arc* (1948)	8,700,000
6	1950–59	*Ben-Hur* (1959)	15,000,000
7	1960–69	*Cleopatra* (1963)	44,000,000
8	1970–79	*Superman* (1978)	55,000,000
9	1980–89	*Who Framed Roger Rabbit* (1988)	70,000,000
10	1990–99	*Titanic* (1997)	200,000,000

* *Australian; all others US*

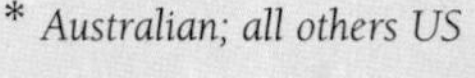

UNBEATEN CITY HALL

Once the world's tallest building, Philadelphia City Hall remains the largest and most expensive municipal building in the US.

The Universe & The Earth

Star Gazing

TOP 10 STARS NEAREST TO THE EARTH*

	STAR	LIGHT YEARS	KM (MILLIONS)	MILES (MILLIONS)
1	Proxima Centauri	4.22	39,923,310	24,792,500
2	Alpha Centauri	4.35	41,153,175	25,556,250
3	Barnard's Star	5.98	56,573,790	35,132,500
4	Wolf 359	7.75	73,318,875	45,531,250
5	Lalande 21185	8.22	77,765,310	48,292,500
6	Luyten 726-8	8.43	79,752,015	49,526,250
7	Sirius	8.65	81,833,325	50,818,750
8	Ross 154	9.45	89,401,725	55,518,750
9	Ross 248	10.40	98,389,200	61,100,000
10	Epsilon Eridani	10.80	102,173,400	63,450,000

* *Excluding the Sun*

A spaceship travelling at 40,237 km/h (25,000 mph) – which is faster than any human has yet reached in space – would take more than 113,200 years to reach the Earth's closest star, Proxima Centauri. While the nearest stars in this list lie just over four light years away from the Earth, others within the Milky Way lie at a distance of 2,500 light years.

CLOSE TO THE EARTH

The name of Proxima Centauri, a red dwarf star in the constellation of Centaurus, means literally "nearest of Centaurus", and it is indeed the Earth's closest star beyond the Sun.

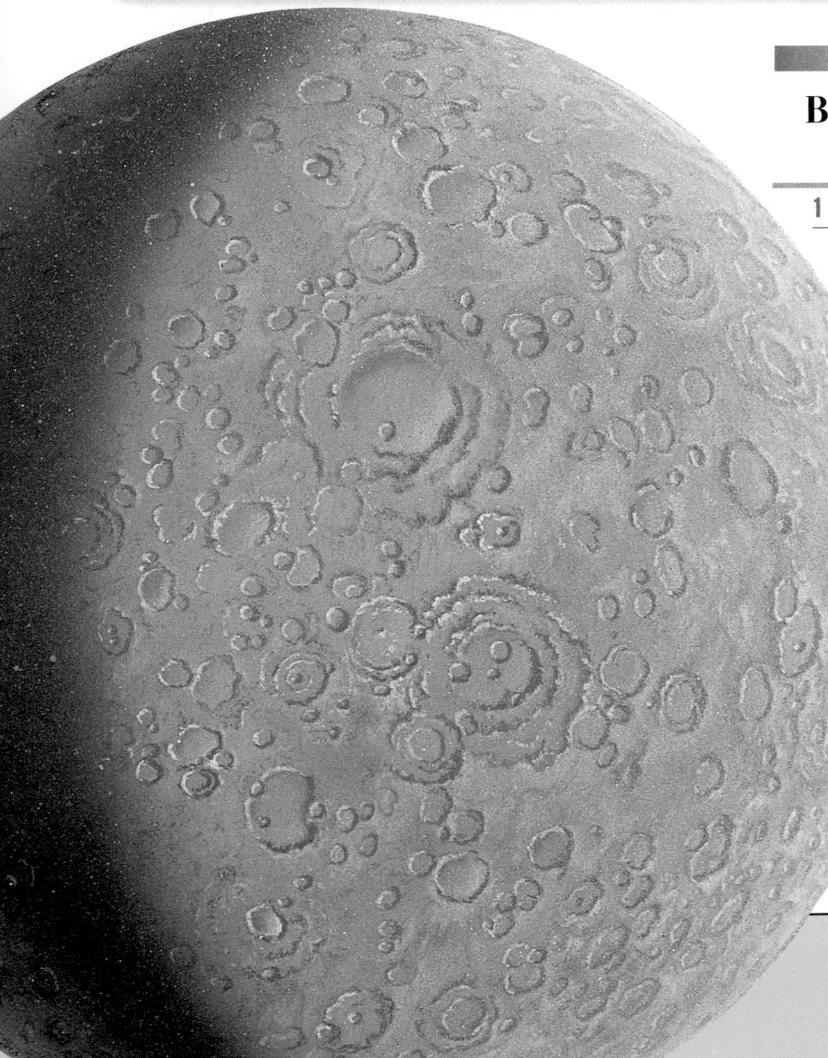

TOP 10 BODIES FURTHEST FROM THE SUN*

	BODY	AVERAGE DISTANCE FROM THE SUN KM	MILES
1	Pluto	5,914,000,000	3,675,000,000
2	Neptune	4,497,000,000	2,794,000,000
3	Uranus	2,871,000,000	1,784,000,000
4	Chiron	2,800,000,000	1,740,000,000
5	Saturn	1,427,000,000	887,000,000
6	Jupiter	778,300,000	483,600,000
7	Mars	227,900,000	141,600,000
8	Earth	149,600,000	92,900,000
9	Venus	108,200,000	67,200,000
10	Mercury	57,900,000	36,000,000

* *In the Solar System, excluding satellites and asteroids*

Chiron, a "mystery object" that may be either a comet or an asteroid, was discovered on 1 November 1977 by American astronomer Charles Kowal. It measures 200–300 km (124–186 miles) in diameter.

AMERICAN DISCOVERY

The Solar System's smallest planet, Pluto, found in 1930, is the only planet to have been discovered by an American – Clyde Tombaugh.

TOP 10 ★

BRIGHTEST STARS*

	STAR/CONSTELLATION	APPARENT MAGNITUDE#
1	**Sirius**, Canis Major	-1.46
2	**Canopus**, Carina	-0.73
3	**Alpha Centauri**, Centaurus	-0.27
4	**Arcturus**, Boötes	-0.04
5	**Vega**, Lyra	+0.03
6	**Capella**, Auriga	+0.08
7	**Rigel**, Orion	+0.12
8	**Procyon**, Canis Minor	+0.38
9	**Achernar**, Eridanus	+0.46
10	**Beta Centauri**, Centaurus	+0.61

* *Excluding the Sun*

\# *Based on apparent visual magnitude as viewed from the Earth – the lower the number, the brighter the star*

At its brightest, the star Betelgeuse is brighter than some of these, but its variability disqualifies it from the Top 10. More distant stars naturally appear fainter. To compensate for this effect, absolute magnitude estimates the brightness of a star at an imaginary fixed distance of 10 parsecs, or 32.6 light years, enabling comparison between the "true" brightness of different stars.

RINGS OF ICE

Saturn's ring system was not discovered until 1656. Composed of ice, the rings are up to 270,000 km (167,770 miles) in diameter.

TOP 10 ★

LARGEST BODIES IN THE SOLAR SYSTEM

	BODY	MAXIMUM DIAMETER KM	MILES
1	**Sun**	1,392,140	865,036
2	**Jupiter**	142,984	88,846
3	**Saturn**	120,536	74,898
4	**Uranus**	51,118	31,763
5	**Neptune**	49,532	30,778
6	**Earth**	12,756	7,926
7	**Venus**	12,103	7,520
8	**Mars**	6,794	4,222
9	**Ganymede**	5,269	3,274
10	**Titan**	5,150	3,200

Most of the planets are visible with the naked eye and have been observed since ancient times. The exceptions are Uranus, discovered on 13 March 1781 by British astronomer Sir William Herschel; Neptune, found by German astronomer Johann Galle on 23 September 1846; and, outside the Top 10, Pluto, located using photographic techniques by American astronomer Clyde Tombaugh. Its discovery was announced on 13 March 1930; its diameter is uncertain but is thought to be about 2,302 km (1,430 miles).

TOP 10 ★

LONGEST DAYS IN THE SOLAR SYSTEM

	BODY	LENGTH OF DAY* DAYS	HOURS	MINS
1	**Venus**	244	0	0
2	**Mercury**	58	14	0
3	**Sun**	25#	0	0
4	**Pluto**	6	9	0
5	**Mars**		24	37
6	**Earth**		23	56
7	**Uranus**		17	14
8	**Neptune**		16	7
9	**Saturn**		10	39
10	**Jupiter**		9	55

* *Period of rotation, based on 23-hour, 56-minute sidereal day*

\# *Variable*

TOP 10 ★

GALAXIES NEAREST TO THE EARTH

	GALAXY	DISTANCE LIGHT YEARS
1	**Large Cloud of Magellan**	169,000
2	**Small Cloud of Magellan**	190,000
3	**Ursa Minor dwarf**	250,000
4	**Draco dwarf**	260,000
5	**Sculptor dwarf**	280,000
6	**Fornax dwarf**	420,000
7	=**Leo I dwarf**	750,000
	=**Leo II dwarf**	750,000
9	**Barnard's Galaxy**	1,700,000
10	**Andromeda Spiral**	2,200,000

These and other galaxies are members of the so-called "Local Group", although with vast distances such as these, "local" is a relative term.

TOP 10 ★

MOST MASSIVE BODIES IN THE SOLAR SYSTEM*

	BODY	MASS#
1	**Sun**	332,800.000
2	**Jupiter**	317.828
3	**Saturn**	95.161
4	**Neptune**	17.148
5	**Uranus**	14.536
6	**Earth**	1.000
7	**Venus**	0.815
8	**Mars**	0.10745
9	**Mercury**	0.05527
10	**Pluto**	0.0022

* *Excluding satellites*

\# *Compared with the Earth = 1; the mass of the Earth is approximately 73,500,000 trillion tonnes*

When was Halley's Comet last seen?

see p.14 for the answer

A 1976
B 1986
C 1996

Asteroids, Meteorites & Comets

TOP 10

MOST RECENT OBSERVATIONS OF HALLEY'S COMET

1 1986
The Japanese Suisei *probe passed within 151,000 km (93,827 miles) of its 15-km (9-mile) nucleus on 8 March 1986, revealing a whirling nucleus within a hydrogen cloud emitting 22–55 tonnes of water per second. The Soviet probes* Vega 1 *and* Vega 2 *passed within 8,890 km (5,524 miles) and 8,030 km (4,990 miles) respectively. The European Space Agency's* Giotto *passed as close as 596 km (370 miles) on 14 March of the same year. All were heavily battered by dust particles, and it was concluded that Halley's comet is composed of dust bonded by water and carbon dioxide ice.*

2 1910
Predictions of disaster were widely published, with many people convinced that the world would come to an end. Mark Twain, who had been born at the time of the 1835 appearance and who believed that his fate was linked to that of the comet, died when it reappeared in this year.

3 1835
Widely observed but noticeably dimmer than in 1759.

4 1759
The comet's first return, as predicted by Halley, thus proving his calculations correct.

5 1682
Observed in Africa and China and extensively in Europe, where it was observed on 5–19 September by Edmund Halley, who predicted its return.

6 1607
Seen extensively in China, Japan, Korea, and Europe, described by German astronomer Johannes Kepler and its position accurately measured by amateur Welsh astronomer Thomas Harriot.

7 1531
Observed in China, Japan, Korea, and in Europe on 13–23 August by Peter Appian, German geographer and astronomer, who noted that comets' tails point away from the Sun.

8 1456
Observed in China, Japan, Korea, and by the Turkish army that was threatening to invade Europe. When the Turks were defeated by Papal forces, it was seen as a portent of the latter's victory.

9 1378
Observed in China, Japan, Korea, and Europe.

10 1301
Seen in Iceland, parts of Europe, China, Japan, and Korea.

Before Edmund Halley (1656–1742) studied and foretold the return of the famous comet that now bears his name, no one had succeeded in proving that comets travel in predictable orbits. The dramatic return in 1759 of the comet Halley had observed in 1682 established the science of cometary observation. There have been about 30 recorded appearances of Halley's comet. The most famous occurred in 1066, when William (later known as William the Conqueror) regarded it as a sign of his imminent victory over King Harold at the Battle of Hastings; it is clearly shown in the Bayeux Tapestry.

TOP 10

COMETS COMING CLOSEST TO THE EARTH

	COMET	DATE*	DISTANCE AU#
1	Lexell	1 July 1770	2.3
2	Tempel-Tuttle	26 Oct 1366	3.4
3	Halley	10 Apr 837	5.0
4	Biela	9 Dec 1805	5.5
5	Grischow	8 Feb 1743	5.8
6	Pons-Winnecke	26 June 1927	5.9
7	La Hire	20 Apr 1702	6.6
8	Schwassmann-Wachmann	31 May 1930	9.3
9	Cassini	8 Jan 1760	10.2
10	Schweizer	29 Apr 1853	12.6

* *Of closest approach to the Earth*

\# *Astronomical Units: 1 AU = mean distance from the Earth to the Sun (149,598,200 km/92,955,900 miles)*

TOP 10 MOST FREQUENTLY SEEN COMETS

(Comet/years between appearances)

1 Encke, 3.302 **2 Grigg-Skjellerup**, 4.908 **3 Honda-Mrkós-Pajdusáková**, 5.210 **4 Tempel 2**, 5.259 **5 Neujmin 2**, 5.437 **6 Brorsen**, 5.463 **7 Tuttle-Giacobini-Kresák**, 5.489 **8 Tempel-L. Swift**, 5.681 **9 Tempel 1**, 5.982 **10 Pons-Winnecke**, 6.125

ROCK OF AGES

Visitors are encouraged to touch the 3.4-m (11-ft) Ahnighito, the largest meteorite on public display, and to appreciate that it is as old as the Solar System – some 4.5 billion years.

THE 10

FIRST ASTEROIDS TO BE DISCOVERED

	ASTEROID/DISCOVERER	DISCOVERED
1	**Ceres**, Giuseppe Piazzi	1 Jan 1801
2	**Pallas**, Heinrich Olbers	28 Mar 1802
3	**Juno**, Karl Ludwig Harding	1 Sep 1804
4	**Vesta**, Heinrich Olbers	29 Mar 1807
5	**Astraea**, Karl Ludwig Hencke	8 Dec 1845
6	**Hebe**, Karl Ludwig Hencke	1 July 1847
7	**Iris**, John Russell Hind	13 Aug 1847
8	**Flora**, John Russell Hind	18 Oct 1847
9	**Metis**, Andrew Graham	25 Apr 1848
10	**Hygeia**, Annibale de Gasparis	12 Apr 1849

Asteroids, sometimes known as "minor planets", are fragments of rock orbiting between Mars and Jupiter. There are perhaps 45,000 of them, but fewer than 10 per cent have been named.

ASTEROIDS

Since the discovery of Ceres, the first and largest asteroid, over 6,000 have been found, 26 of them larger than 200 km (120 miles) in diameter. Gaspra, pictured here, measures only 20 x 12 km (12 x 7 miles), but was closely studied by the *Galileo* spacecraft in 1991. The total mass of all the asteroids is less than that of the Moon. It is believed that, on average, one asteroid larger than 0.4 km (¼ mile) strikes the Earth every 50,000 years. As recently as 1994, a small asteroid with the temporary designation 1994XM, measuring a modest 18 m (33 ft) in diameter, came within 112,600 km (69,594 miles) of the Earth – making it the closest recorded near-miss.

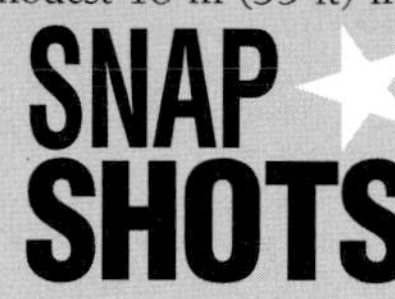

TOP 10

LARGEST METEORITES EVER FOUND

	SITE/LOCATION	ESTIMATED WEIGHT TONNES
1	**Hoba West**, Grootfontein, Namibia	more than 60.0
2	**Ahnighito ("The Tent")**, Cape York, West Greenland	57.3
3	**Campo del Cielo**, Argentina	41.4
4	**Canyon Diablo***, Arizona, USA	30.0
5	**Sikhote-Alin**, Russia	27.0
6	**Chupaderos**, Mexico	24.2
7	**Bacuberito**, Mexico	22.0
8	**Armanty**, Western Mongolia	20.0
9	**Mundrabilla#**, Western Australia	17.0
10	**Mbosi**, Tanzania	16.0

* *Formed Meteor Crater; fragmented – total in public collections is around 11.5 tonnes*

\# *In two parts – 11.5 and 6.1 tonnes*

The Hoba meteorite was found on a farm in 1920. A 2.73 x 2.43 m (9 x 8 ft) slab, it consists of 82 per cent iron and 16 per cent nickel. In 1989, 36 Malaysian soldiers with the UN Peacekeeping Force attempted to hack pieces off it as souvenirs, causing an outcry. "The Tent", known by its original Inuit name of Ahnighito, was discovered in 1894 by the American Arctic explorer Admiral Robert Peary. Now in the Hayden Planetarium at the New York Museum of Natural History, it is the largest meteorite in the world on exhibition.

TOP 10

LARGEST METEORITES EVER FOUND IN THE UK

	SITE/LOCATION	DATE FOUND	WEIGHT KG	WEIGHT LB
1	**Barwell**, Leicestershire	24 Dec 1965	44.0	97.0
2	**Wold Cottage**, Yorkshire	13 Dec 1795	25.4	56.0
3	**Appley Bridge**, Lancashire	13 Oct 1914	15.0	33.0
4	**Strathmore**, Tayside	3 Dec 1917	13.0	28.7
5	**Bovedy**, Londonderry, N. Ireland	25 Apr 1969	5.4	11.9
6	**High Possil**, Strathclyde	5 Apr 1804	4.5	9.9
7	**Crumlin**, Antrim, N. Ireland	13 Sep 1902	4.3	9.5
8	**Rowton**, Shropshire	20 Apr 1876	3.5	7.7
9	**Middlesbrough**, Cleveland	14 Mar 1881	1.6	3.5
10	**Ashdon**, Essex	9 Mar 1923	1.3	2.9

There have been only 17 definite meteorites found in the UK, all of which are held in public collections. Most broke up on impact – that from Barwell, the largest of all, consists of many fragments, while the Strathmore meteorite comprises four stones.

Did You Know? A car damaged by a 10-kg (22-lb) meteorite in Peekskill, New York, in 1992 was sold to the Montana Meteorite Lab for $69,000 – complete with the meteorite.

TOP 10 ★

FIRST WOMEN IN SPACE

	NAME/SPACECRAFT	DATE
1	**Valentina V. Tereshkova**, *Vostok 6*	16–19 June 1963
2	**Svetlana Savitskaya**, *Soyuz T7*	19 Aug 1982
3	**Sally K. Ride**, *Challenger STS-7*	18–24 June 1983
4	**Judith A. Resnik**, *Discovery STS-41-D*	30 Aug–5 Sep 1984
5	**Kathryn D. Sullivan**, *Challenger STS-41-G*	5–13 Oct 1984
6	**Anna L. Fisher**, *Discovery STS-51-A*	8–16 Nov 1984
7	**Margaret R. Seddon**, *Discovery STS-51-D*	12–19 Apr 1985
8	**Shannon W. Lucid**, *Discovery STS-51-G*	17–24 June 1985
9	**Bonnie J. Dunbar**, *Challenger STS-61-A*	30 Oct–6 Nov 1985
10	**Mary L. Cleave**, *Atlantis STS-61-B*	26 Nov–3 Dec 1985

On 18 May 1991, Helen Sharman, a 27-year-old chemist, became Britain's first astronaut and the 15th woman in space when she went on a seven-day mission on *Soyuz TM12* to the *Mir* space station.

TOP 10 ★

FIRST MOONWALKERS

	ASTRONAUT/SPACECRAFT	TOTAL EVA* HR:MIN	MISSION DATES
1	**Neil A. Armstrong**, *Apollo 11*	2:32	16–24 July 1969
2	**Edwin E. ("Buzz") Aldrin**, *Apollo 11*	2:15	16–24 July 1969
3	**Charles Conrad, Jr.**, *Apollo 12*	7:45	14–24 Nov 1969
4	**Alan L. Bean**, *Apollo 12*	7:45	14–24 Nov 1969
5	**Alan B. Shepard**, *Apollo 14*	9:23	31 Jan–9 Feb 1971
6	**Edgar D. Mitchell**, *Apollo 14*	9:23	31 Jan–9 Feb 1971
7	**David R. Scott**, *Apollo 15*	19:08	26 July–7 Aug 1971
8	**James B. Irwin**, *Apollo 15*	18:35	26 July–7 Aug 1971
9	**John W. Young**, *Apollo 16*	20:14	16–27 Apr 1972
10	**Charles M. Duke**, *Apollo 16*	20:14	16–27 Apr 1972

* *Extra Vehicular Activity (i.e. time spent out of the lunar module on the Moon's surface)*

MOON ROCKET

Apollo 11 *blasts off from Cape Canaveral on 16 July 1969. Aboard are Americans Neil Armstrong and "Buzz" Aldrin, destined to be the first men to walk on the Moon.*

THE 10 ★

FIRST BODIES TO HAVE BEEN VISITED BY SPACECRAFT

	BODY	SPACECRAFT	COUNTRY	YEAR
1	**Moon**	*Pioneer 4*	USA	1959
2	**Venus**	*Mariner 2*	USA	1962
3	**Mars**	*Mariner 4*	USA	1965
4	**Sun**	*Pioneer 7*	USA	1966
5	**Jupiter**	*Pioneer 10*	USA	1973
6	**Mercury**	*Mariner 10*	USA	1974
7	**Saturn**	*Pioneer 11*	USA	1979
8	**Comet Giacobini-Zinner**	*International Sun–Earth Explorer 3 (International Cometary Explorer)*	Europe/ USA	1985
9	**Uranus**	*Voyager 2*	USA	1986
10	**Halley's Comet**	*Giotto*	Europe	1986

THE 10 ★

FIRST ANIMALS IN SPACE

	NAME/ANIMAL	COUNTRY	DATE
1	**Laika**, dog	USSR	3 Nov 1957
2=	**Laska and Benjy**, mice	USA	13 Dec 1958
4=	**Able and Baker**, female rhesus monkey, and female squirrel monkey	USA	28 May 1959
6=	**Otvazhnaya**, female Samoyed husky, and an unnamed rabbit	USSR	2 July 1959
8	**Sam**, male rhesus monkey	USA	4 Dec 1959
9	**Miss Sam**, female rhesus monkey	USA	21 Jan 1960
10=	**Belka and Strelka**, female Samoyed huskies	USSR	19 Aug 1960

TOP 10

FIRST PEOPLE TO ORBIT THE EARTH

	NAME/SPACECRAFT	COUNTRY OF ORIGIN	DATE
1	**Yuri A. Gagarin**, *Vostok I*	USSR	12 Apr 1961
2	**Gherman S. Titov**, *Vostok II*	USSR	6–7 Aug 1961
3	**John H. Glenn**, *Friendship 7*	USA	20 Feb 1962
4	**M. Scott Carpenter**, *Aurora 7*	USA	24 May 1962
5	**Andrian G. Nikolayev**, *Vostok III*	USSR	11–15 Aug 1962
6	**Pavel R. Popovich**, *Vostok IV*	USSR	12–15 Aug 1962
7	**Walter M. Schirra**, *Sigma 7*	USA	3 Oct 1962
8	**L. Gordon Cooper**, *Faith 7*	USA	15–16 May 1963
9	**Valeri F. Bykovsky**, *Vostok V*	USSR	14–19 June 1963
10	**Valentina V. Tereshkova**, *Vostok VI*	USSR	16–19 June 1963

Yuri Gagarin, at the age of 27, orbited the Earth once, taking 1 hour 48 minutes. Titov, the youngest-ever astronaut at 25 years 329 days, performed 17 orbits during 25 hours. The first American to orbit the Earth, John Glenn, is the oldest on this list at 40; he has since gone on to become the oldest astronaut of all time.

FIRST IN SPACE

In 1961, Soviet cosmonaut Yuri Gagarin became the first human to enter space and orbit the Earth. His flight aboard Vostok 1 *lasted just 108 minutes. After receiving his country's highest honours, Gagarin was killed in a MiG-15 plane crash in 1968.*

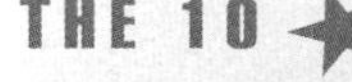

THE 10

FIRST COUNTRIES TO HAVE ASTRONAUTS OR COSMONAUTS IN ORBIT

	COUNTRY/ASTRONAUT OR COSMONAUT	DATE*
1	**USSR**, Yuri Alekseyivich Gagarin	12 Apr 1961
2	**USA**, John H. Glenn	20 Feb 1962
3	**Czechoslovakia**, Vladimir Remek	2 Mar 1978
4	**Poland**, Miroslaw Hermaszewski	27 June 1978
5	**East Germany**, Sigmund Jahn	26 Aug 1978
6	**Bulgaria**, Georgi I. Ivanov	10 Apr 1979
7	**Hungary**, Bertalan Farkas	26 May 1980
8	**Vietnam**, Pham Tuan	23 July 1980
9	**Cuba**, Arnaldo T. Mendez	18 Sep 1980
10	**Mongolia**, Jugderdemidiyn Gurragcha	22 Mar 1981

* *Of first space entry of a national of that country*

THE 10

FIRST SPACEWALKERS

	ASTRONAUT	SPACECRAFT	EVA* HR:MIN	EVA DATE
1	Alexei Leonov	*Voskhod 2*	0.23	18 Mar 1965
2	Edward H. White	*Gemini 4*	0:36	3 June 1965
3	Eugene A. Cernan	*Gemini 9*	2:07	3 June 1966
4	Michael Collins	*Gemini 10*	0:50	19 July 1966
5	Richard F. Gordon	*Gemini 11*	0:33	13 Sep 1966
6	Edwin E. ("Buzz") Aldrin	*Gemini 12*	2:29	12 Nov 1966
7	=Alexei Yeleseyev	*Soyuz 5*	0:37	16 Jan 1969
	=Yevgeny Khrunov	*Soyuz 5*	0:37	16 Jan 1969
9	=Russell L. Schweickart	*Apollo 9*	0:46	6 Mar 1969
	=David R. Scott	*Apollo 9*	0:46	6 Mar 1969

* *Extra Vehicular Activity*

Leonov's first spacewalk almost ended in disaster when his spacesuit "ballooned" and he was unable to return through the air-lock into the capsule until he had reduced the pressure in his suit to a dangerously low level. Edward H. White was killed in the *Apollo* spacecraft fire of 27 January 1967.

Space Explorers

SPACELINK

In 1995, the USA's 100th crewed flight, Atlantis *STS-71, linked up with Russian space station* Mir *for the first time, exchanging astronauts and cosmonauts between the two spacecraft.*

TOP 10

MOST EXPERIENCED SPACEMEN*

	SPACEMAN	MISSIONS	TOTAL DURATION OF MISSIONS DAYS	HOURS	MINS	SECS
1	Sergei V. Avdeyev	3	747	14	22	47
2	Valeri V. Polyakov	2	678	16	33	18
3	Anatoli Y. Solovyov	5	651	0	11	25
4	Viktor M. Afanasyev	3	545	2	34	41
5	Musa K. Manarov	2	541	0	29	38
6	Alexander S. Viktorenko	4	489	1	35	17
7	Sergei K. Krikalyov	4#	483	9	37	26
8	Yuri V. Romanenko	3	430	18	21	30
9	Alexander A. Volkov	3	391	11	52	14
10	Vladimir G. Titov	5#	387	0	51	03

* *To 1 January 2000*

\# *Including flights aboard US space shuttles*

All the missions listed were undertaken by the USSR (and, latterly, Russia). In recent years, a number of US astronauts have added to their space logs by spending time on board the Russian *Mir* space station, but none has matched the records set by Russian cosmonauts. While Valeri Polyakov holds the record for the longest continuous space flight, Sergei Avdeyev exceeded Polyakov's cumulative record on 20 June 1999, by spending his 679th day in space.

TOP 10

MOST EXPERIENCED SPACEWOMEN*

	SPACEWOMAN#	MISSIONS	TOTAL DURATION OF MISSIONS DAYS	HOURS	MINS	SECS
1	Shannon W. Lucid	5	223	2	52	26
2	Yelena V. Kondakova	2	178	10	41	31
3	Tamara E. Jernigan	5	63	1	25	40
4	Bonnie J. Dunbar	5	50	8	24	44
5	Marsha S. Ivins	4	43	0	27	43
6	Kathryn C. Thornton	4	40	15	15	18
7	Janice E. Voss	4	37	21	10	18
8	Wendy B. Lawrence	3	37	5	23	20
9	Susan J. Helms	3	33	20	16	31
10	Nancy J. Currie	3	30	17	23	46

* *To 1 January 2000*

\# *All US except 2 (Russian)*

Shannon Lucid became both America's most experienced astronaut and the world's most experienced female astronaut in 1996. She took off in US space shuttle *Atlantis STS-76* on 22 March, and transferred to the Russian *Mir* space station, returning on board *Atlantis STS-79* on 26 September after travelling 121 million km (75.2 million miles) in 188 days, 4 hours, 0 minutes, 14 seconds – also a record duration for a single mission by a US astronaut.

Did You Know? The greatest number of people in space at the same time was 13, when, on 14 March 1995, a space shuttle, a Russian spacecraft, and the *Mir* space station orbited simultaneously.

TOP 10

OLDEST US ASTRONAUTS*

	ASTRONAUT	LAST FLIGHT	AGE#
1	John H. Glenn	6 Nov 1998	77
2	F. Story Musgrave	7 Dec 1996	61
3	Vance D. Brand	11 Dec 1990	59
4	Karl G. Henize	6 Aug 1985	58
5	Roger K. Crouch	17 July 1997	56
6	William E. Thornton	6 May 1985	56
7	Don L. Lind	6 May 1985	54
8	Henry W. Hartsfield	6 Nov 1988	54
9	John E. Blaha	7 Dec 1996	54
10	William G. Gregory	18 Mar 1995	54

* *Including payload specialists, etc., to 1 January 2000*

\# *Those of apparently identical age have been ranked according to their precise age in days at the time of their last flight.*

At 53, Shannon Lucid (born 14 January 1943, last flight 31 March 1996) holds the record as the oldest woman in space.

TOP 10

YOUNGEST US ASTRONAUTS*

	ASTRONAUT	FIRST FLIGHT	AGE#
1	Kenneth D. Bowersox	25 June 1984	28
2	Sally K. Ride	18 June 1983	32
3	Tamara E. Jernigan	5 June 1991	32
4	Eugene A. Cernan	3 June 1966	32
5	Koichi Wakata	11 Jan 1996	32
6	Steven A. Hawley	30 Aug 1984	32
7	Mary E. Weber	13 July 1995	32
8	Kathryn D. Sullivan	5 Oct 1984	33
9	Ronald E. McNair+	3 Feb 1984	33
10	George D. Nelson	6 Apr 1984	33

* *To 1 January 2000*

\# *Those of apparently identical age have been ranked according to their precise age in days at the time of their first flight.*

\+ *Killed in* Challenger *disaster, 28 January 1986*

TOP 10

LONGEST SPACE MISSIONS*

	NAME/MISSION DATES	DAYS
1	Valeri V. Polyakov 8 Jan 1994–22 Mar 1995	437.7
2	Sergei V. Avdeyev 13 Aug 1998–28 Aug 1999	379.6
3	=Musa K. Manarov 21 Dec 1987–21 Dec 1988	365.9
	=Vladimir G. Titov 21 Dec 1987–21 Dec 1988	365.9
5	Yuri V. Romanenko 5 Feb–5 Dec 1987	326.5
6	Sergei K. Krikalyov 18 May 1991–25 Mar 1992	311.8
7	Valeri V. Polyakov 31 Aug 1988–27 Apr 1989	240.9
8	=Oleg Y. Atkov 8 Feb–2 Oct 1984	237.0
	=Leonid D. Kizim 8 Feb–2 Oct 1984	237.0
	=Anatoli Y. Solovyov 8 Feb–2 Oct 1984	237.0

* *To 1 January 2000*

Space medicine specialist Valeri V. Polyakov (born 27 April 1942) spent his 52nd birthday in space during his record-breaking mission aboard the *Mir* space station.

"ASTRONAUT"

In a pioneering science-fiction novel, *Across the Zodiac*, published in 1880, British writer Percy Greg (1836–89) presented the first fictional account of interplanetary travel by space ship, calling his vessel *Astronaut* (from the Greek for "star sailor"). By the late 1920s, the word had become used to mean a space *traveller*, rather than his ship, and, once the space age began, it was this sense that became established in the West, with *cosmonaut* as the Russian equivalent.

WHY DO WE SAY?

SPACE-AGE WOMAN

With three further missions since her first flight aboard space shuttle Endeavor STS-57 *in 1993, NASA astronaut Janice Voss has earned a place among the world's most experienced spacewomen.*

Waterworld

TOP 10 DEEPEST OCEANS AND SEAS

	OCEAN OR SEA	GREATEST DEPTH M	GREATEST DEPTH FT	AVERAGE DEPTH M	AVERAGE DEPTH FT
1	Pacific Ocean	10,924	35,837	4,028	13,215
2	Indian Ocean	7,455	24,460	3,963	13,002
3	Atlantic Ocean	9,219	30,246	3,926	12,880
4	Caribbean Sea	6,946	22,788	2,647	8,685
5	South China Sea	5,016	16,456	1,652	5,419
6	Bering Sea	4,773	15,659	1,547	5,075
7	Gulf of Mexico	3,787	12,425	1,486	4,874
8	Mediterranean Sea	4,632	15,197	1,429	4,688
9	Japan Sea	3,742	12,276	1,350	4,429
10	Arctic Ocean	5,625	18,456	1,205	3,953

The deepest point in the deepest ocean is the Marianas Trench in the Pacific at a depth of 10,924 m (35,837 ft). The Pacific is so vast that it contains more water than all the world's other seas and oceans put together.

TOP 10 LONGEST RIVERS

	RIVER	LOCATION	LENGTH KM	LENGTH MILES
1	Nile	Tanzania/Uganda/Sudan/Egypt	6,670	4,145
2	Amazon	Peru/Brazil	6,448	4,007
3	Yangtze–Kiang	China	6,300	3,915
4	Mississippi–Missouri–Red Rock	USA	5,971	3,710
5	Yenisey–Angara–Selenga	Mongolia/Russia	5,540	3,442
6	Huang Ho (Yellow River)	China	5,464	3,395
7	Ob'-Irtysh	Mongolia/Kazakhstan/Russia	5,410	3,362
8	Congo	Angola/Dem. Rep. of Congo	4,700	2,920
9	Lena–Kirenga	Russia	4,400	2,734
10	Mekong	Tibet/China/Myanmar (Burma)/ Laos/Cambodia/Vietnam	4,350	2,703

TOP 10 LONGEST GLACIERS

	GLACIER	LOCATION	LENGTH KM	LENGTH MILES
1	Lambert-Fisher	Antarctica	515	320
2	Novaya Zemlya	Russia	418	260
3	Arctic Institute	Antarctica	362	225
4	Nimrod-Lennox-King	Antarctica	290	180
5	Denman	Antarctica	241	150
6	=Beardmore	Antarctica	225	140
	=Recovery	Antarctica	225	140
8	Petermanns	Greenland	200	124
9	Unnamed	Antarctica	193	120
10	Slessor	Antarctica	185	115

TOP 10 LARGEST FRESHWATER LAKES IN THE US*

	LAKE	LOCATION	APPROX. AREA SQ KM	APPROX. AREA SQ MILES
1	Michigan	Illinois/Indiana/ Michigan/Wisconsin	58,016	22,400
2	Iliamna	Alaska	2,590	1,000
3	Okeechobee	Florida	1,813	700
4	Becharof	Alaska	1,186	458
5	Red	Minnesota	1,168	451
6	Teshepuk	Alaska	816	315
7	Naknek	Alaska	627	242
8	Winnebago	Wisconsin	557	215
9	Mille Lacs	Minnesota	536	207
10	Flathead	Montana	510	197

* *Excluding those partly in Canada*

TOP 10 DEEPEST DEEP-SEA TRENCHES

(Trench/ocean/deepest point in m/ft)

❶ **Marianas**, Pacific, 10,924/35,837 ❷ **Tonga***, Pacific, 10,800/35,430 ❸ **Philippine**, Pacific, 10,497/34,436 ❹ **Kermadec***, Pacific, 10,047/32,960 ❺ **Bonin**, Pacific, 9,994/32,786 ❻ **New Britain**, Pacific, 9,940/32,609 ❼ **Kuril**, Pacific, 9,750/31,985 ❽ **Izu**, Pacific, 9,695/31,805 ❾ **Puerto Rico**, Atlantic, 8,605/28,229 ❿ **Yap**, Pacific, 8,527/27,973

* *Some authorities consider these parts of one feature*

JUNGLE FEEDER

It was not until 1953 that the source of the Amazon was identifed as a stream called Huarco flowing from the Misuie glacier in the Peruvian Andes mountains. It joins the Amazon's main tributary at Ucayali, Peru.

TOP 10 ★ COUNTRIES WITH THE GREATEST AREAS OF INLAND WATER

	COUNTRY	PERCENTAGE OF TOTAL AREA	WATER AREA SQ KM	WATER AREA SQ MILES
1	**Canada**	7.60	755,170	291,573
2	**India**	9.56	314,400	121,391
3	**China**	2.82	270,550	104,460
4	**USA**	2.20	206,010	79,541
5	**Ethiopia**	9.89	120,900	46,680
6	**Colombia**	8.80	100,210	38,691
7	**Indonesia**	4.88	93,000	35,908
8	**Russia**	0.47	79,400	30,657
9	**Australia**	0.90	68,920	26,610
10	**Tanzania**	6.25	59,050	22,799

Large areas of some countries are occupied by major rivers and lakes. Lake Victoria, for example, raises the water area of Uganda to 15.39 per cent of its total. In Europe, three Scandinavian countries have considerable percentages of water: Sweden 8.68 per cent, Finland 9.36 per cent, and Norway 5.05 per cent.

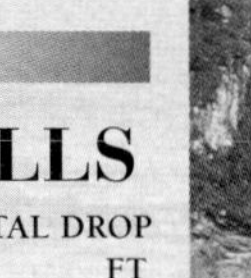

TOP 10 ★ HIGHEST WATERFALLS

	WATERFALL	LOCATION	TOTAL DROP M	TOTAL DROP FT
1	**Angel**	Venezuela	979	3,212*
2	**Tugela**	South Africa	947	3,107
3	**Utigård**	Norway	800	2,625
4	**Mongefossen**	Norway	774	2,540
5	**Yosemite**	California	739	2,425
6	**Østre Mardøla Foss**	Norway	656	2,152
7	**Tyssestrengane**	Norway	646	2,120
8	**Cuquenán**	Venezuela	610	2,000
9	**Sutherland**	New Zealand	580	1,904
10	**Kjellfossen**	Norway	561	1,841

* *Longest single drop 807 m (2,648 ft)*

FALL AND ANGEL

Angel Falls in Venezuela were discovered in 1933 by American adventurer James Angel, after whom they are named. Their overall height is equivalent to two-and-a-half Empire State Buildings.

TOP 10 ★ DEEPEST FRESHWATER LAKES

	LAKE	LOCATION	GREATEST DEPTH M	GREATEST DEPTH FT
1	**Baikal**	Russia	1,637	5,371
2	**Tanganyika**	Burundi/ Tanzania/Dem. Rep. of Congo/ Zambia	1,471	4,825
3	**Malawi**	Malawi/ Mozambique/Tanzania	706	2,316
4	**Great Slave**	Canada	614	2,015
5	**Matana**	Celebes, Indonesia	590	1,936
6	**Crater**	Oregon, USA	589	1,932
7	**Toba**	Sumatra, Indonesia	529	1,736
8	**Hornindals**	Norway	514	1,686
9	**Sarez**	Tajikistan	505	1,657
10	**Tahoe**	California/ Nevada, USA	501	1,645

TOP 10 ★ LARGEST LAKES

	LAKE	LOCATION	APPROX. AREA SQ KM	APPROX. AREA SQ MILES
1	**Caspian Sea**	Azerbaijan/ Iran/Kazakhstan/ Russia/Turkmenistan	371,000	143,205
2	**Superior**	Canada/USA	82,413	31,820
3	**Victoria**	Kenya/ Tanzania/Uganda	68,800	26,570
4	**Huron**	Canada/USA	59,596	23,010
5	**Michigan**	USA	58,016	22,400
6	**Aral Sea**	Kazakhstan/ Uzbekistan	40,000	15,444
7	**Tanganyika**	Burundi/ Tanzania/Dem. Rep. of Congo/Zambia	32,900	13,860
8	**Great Bear**	Canada	31,150	12,030
9	**Baikal**	Russia	30,500	11,775
10	**Great Slave**	Canada	28,570	11,030

TOP 10 ★ LARGEST LAKES IN THE UK

	LAKE	LOCATION	APPROX. AREA SQ KM	APPROX. AREA SQ MILES
1	**Lough Neagh**	N. Ireland	381.74	147.39
2	**Lower Lough Erne**	N. Ireland	105.08	40.57
3	**Loch Lomond**	Scotland	71.22	27.50
4	**Loch Ness**	Scotland	56.64	21.87
5	**Loch Awe**	Scotland	38.72	14.95
6	**Upper Lough Erne**	N. Ireland	31.73	12.25
7	**Loch Maree**	Scotland	28.49	11.00
8	**Loch Morar**	Scotland	26.68	10.30
9	**Loch Tay**	Scotland	26.39	10.19
10	**Loch Shin**	Scotland	22.53	8.70

Where in the Solar System does a day last 244 Earth days?
see p.13 for the answer

A Pluto
B Neptune
C Venus

Islands of the World

TOP 10 LARGEST VOLCANIC ISLANDS

	ISLAND/LOCATION	TYPE	APPROX. AREA SQ KM	SQ MILES
1	**Sumatra**, Indonesia	Active volcanic	443,065.8	171,068.7
2	**Honshu**, Japan	Volcanic	225,800.3	87.182.0
3	**Java**, Indonesia	Volcanic	138,793.6	53.588.5
4	**North Island**, New Zealand	Volcanic	111,582.8	43.082.4
5	**Luzon**, Philippines	Active volcanic	109,964.9	42.457.7
6	**Iceland**	Active volcanic	101,826.0	39,315.2
7	**Mindanao**, Philippines	Active volcanic	97,530.0	37,656.5
8	**Hokkaido**, Japan	Active volcanic	78,719.4	30,394.7
9	**New Britain**, Papua New Guinea	Volcanic	35,144.6	13,569.4
10	**Halmahera**, Indonesia	Active volcanic	18,039.6	6,965.1

Source: *United Nations*

TOP 10 LARGEST ISLANDS

	ISLAND/LOCATION	APPROX. AREA* SQ KM	SQ MILES
1	**Greenland**	2,175,600	840,070
2	**New Guinea**, Papua New Guinea/Indonesia	800,000	309,000
3	**Borneo**, Indonesia/ Malaysia/Brunei	744,100	287,300
4	**Madagascar**	587,041	226,657
5	**Baffin Island**, Canada	507,450	195,875
6	**Sumatra**, Indonesia	424,760	164,000
7	**Honshu**, Japan	230,966	89,176
8	**Great Britain**	229,957	88,787
9	**Victoria Island**, Canada	217,206	83,896
10	**Ellesmere Island**, Canada	196,160	75,767

* *Mainlands, including areas of inland water, but excluding offshore islands*

Australia is regarded as a continental land mass rather than an island; otherwise it would rank first at 7,618,493 sq km (2,941,517 sq miles), or 35 times the size of Great Britain. The largest US island is Hawaii, which measures 10,456 sq km (4,037 sq miles), and the largest off mainland USA is Kodiak, Alaska, at 9,510 sq km (3,672 sq miles).

TOP 10 LARGEST ISLANDS IN EUROPE

	ISLAND/LOCATION	AREA SQ KM	SQ MILES
1	**Great Britain**, North Atlantic	229,957	88,787
2	**Iceland**, North Atlantic	103,000	39,769
3	**Ireland**, North Atlantic	83,766	32,342
4	**West Spitsbergen**, Arctic Ocean	39,368	15,200
5	**Sicily**, Mediterranean Sea	25,400	9,807
6	**Sardinia**, Mediterranean Sea	23,800	9,189
7	**North East Land**, Barents Sea	15,000	5,792
8	**Cyprus**, Mediterranean Sea	9,251	3,572
9	**Corsica**, Mediterranean Sea	8,720	3,367
10	**Crete**, Mediterranean Sea	8,260	3,189

Great Britain became an island only after the end of the last ice age, some 8,000 years ago, when the land bridge that had previously existed was inundated and the North Sea became connected with the English Channel. Until then the Dogger Bank, now a notable fishing ground, was land, and the River Thames was a tributary of the Rhine.

TOP 10 LARGEST ISLANDS IN THE UK

	ISLAND/ LOCATION	POPULATION	AREA SQ KM	SQ MILES
1	**Lewis and Harris**, Outer Hebrides	23,390	2,225.30	859.19
2	**Skye**, Inner Hebrides	8,139	1,666.08	643.27
3	**Mainland**, Shetland	22,184	967.00	373.36
4	**Mull**, Inner Hebrides	2,605	899.25	347.20
5	**Anglesey**, Wales	69,800	713.80	275.60
6	**Islay**, Inner Hebrides	3,997	638.79	246.64
7	**Isle of Man**, England	69,788	571.66	220.72
8	**Mainland**, Orkney	14,299	536.10	206.99
9	**Arran**, Inner Hebrides	4,726	435.32	168.08
10	**Isle of Wight**, England	126,600	380.99	147.10

Did You Know? The volcanic island of Surtsey emerged from the sea to the south of Iceland in 1963. It was named after the Norse god Surtur.

UNDER THE VOLCANO

Volcanic Sumatra's tallest peak, Gunung Kerinici, is a 3,805-m (12,484-ft) active volcano that was first climbed in 1877. Southeast Asia has more active volcanoes than any other part of the world.

TOP 10 HIGHEST ISLANDS

(Island/location/highest elevation in m/ft)

❶ **New Guinea**, Papua New Guinea/Indonesia, 5,030/16,503 ❷ **Akutan**, Alaska, USA, 4,275/14,026 ❸ **Borneo**, Indonesia/Malaysia/Brunei, 4,175/13,698 ❹ **Hawaii**, USA, 4,169/13,678 ❺ **Formosa**, China, 3,997/13,114 ❻ **Sumatra**, Indonesia, 3,804/12,480 ❼ **Ross**, Antarctica, 3,794/12,448 ❽ **Honshu**, Japan, 3,776/12,388 ❾ **South Island**, New Zealand, 3,764/12,349 ❿ **Lombok**, Lesser Sunda Islands, Indonesia, 3,726/12,224

Source: *United Nations*

TOP 10 LARGEST LAKE ISLANDS

	ISLAND	LAKE/LOCATION	AREA SQ KM	AREA SQ MILES
1	**Manitoulin**	Huron, Ontario, Canada	2,766	1,068
2	**Vozrozhdeniya**	Aral Sea, Uzbekistan/ Kazakhstan	2,300	888
3	**René-Lavasseur**	Manicouagan Reservoir, Quebec, Canada	2,020	780
4	**Olkhon**	Baykal, Russia	730	282
5	**Samosir**	Toba, Sumatra, Indonesia	630	243
6	**Isle Royale**	Superior, Michigan, USA	541	209
7	**Ukerewe**	Victoria, Tanzania	530	205
8	**St. Joseph**	Huron, Ontario, Canada	365	141
9	**Drummond**	Huron, Michigan, USA	347	134
10	**Idjwi**	Kivu, Dem. Rep. of Congo	285	110

Not all islands are surrounded by sea: many sizeable islands are situated in lakes. The second largest in this list, Vozrozhdeniya, is growing as the Aral Sea contracts, and is set to link up with the surrounding land as a peninsula.

TOP 10 LARGEST ISLANDS IN THE US

(Island/location/area in sq km/sq miles)

❶ **Hawaii**, Hawaii 10,456/4,037 ❷ **Kodiak**, Alaska, 9,510/3,672 ❸ **Prince of Wales**, Alaska, 6,700/2,587 ❹ **Chicagof**, Alaska, 5,400/2,085 ❺ **Saint Lawrence**, Alaska, 4,430/1,710 ❻ **Admiralty**, Alaska, 4,270/1,649 ❼ **Baranof**, Alaska, 4,237/1,636 ❽ **Nunivak**, Alaska, 4,210/1,625 ❾ **Unimak**, Alaska, 4,160/1,606 ❿ **Long Island**, New York, 3,269/1,401

MALTESE SQUEEZE

Close-packed high-rise housing in the capital, Valetta, exemplifies Malta's status as the world's most densely populated island country. Over 383,000 people are packed into just 316 sq km (122 sq miles).

TOP 10 MOST DENSELY POPULATED ISLAND COUNTRIES

	ISLAND	AREA SQ KM	AREA SQ MILES	POPULATION*	POPULATION PER SQ KM	POPULATION PER SQ MILE
1	**Malta**	316	122	383,285	1,213	3,142
2	**Bermuda**	53	21	62,912	1,187	2,996
3	**Maldives**	298	115	310,425	1,042	2,699
4	**Bahrain**	694	268	641,539	924	2,394
5	**Mauritius**	1,865	720	1,196,172	642	1,661
6	**Taiwan**	35,742	13,800	22,319,222	624	1,617
7	**Barbados**	430	166	259,248	603	1,562
8	**Tuvalu**	25	10	10,730	429	1,073
9	**Marshall Islands**	181	70	68,088	376	973
10	**Japan**	372,801	143,939	126,434,470	339	878

* *Estimated for the year 2000*

Source: *United Nations*

The Face of the Earth

TOP 10 DEEPEST DEPRESSIONS

	DEPRESSION/LOCATION	MAXIMUM DEPTH BELOW SEA LEVEL M	FT
1	**Dead Sea**, Israel/Jordan	400	1,312
2	**Turfan Depression**, China	154	505
3	**Qattâra Depression**, Egypt	133	436
4	**Poluostrov Mangyshlak**, Kazakhstan	132	433
5	**Danakil Depression**, Ethiopia	117	383
6	**Death Valley**, USA	86	282
7	**Salton Sink**, USA	72	235
8	**Zapadny Chink Ustyurta**, Kazakhstan	70	230
9	**Prikaspiyskaya Nizmennost'**, Kazakhstan/Russia	67	220
10	**Ozera Sarykamysh**, Turkmenistan/Uzbekistan	45	148

LYING LOW

The shore of the Dead Sea is the lowest exposed ground below sea level, but the bed of the sea actually reaches 728 m (2,388 ft) below sea level. Much of Antarctica is also below sea level.

TOP 10 HIGHEST ACTIVE VOLCANOES

	VOLCANO	LOCATION	LATEST ACTIVITY	HEIGHT M	FT
1	**Guallatiri**	Chile	1987	6,060	19,882
2	**Lááscar**	Chile	1991	5,990	19,652
3	**Cotopaxi**	Ecuador	1975	5,897	19,347
4	**Tupungatito**	Chile	1986	5,640	18,504
5	**Popocatépetl**	Mexico	1995	5,452	17,887
6	**Ruiz**	Colombia	1992	5,400	17,716
7	**Sangay**	Ecuador	1988	5,230	17,159
8	**Guagua Pichincha**	Ecuador	1988	4,784	15,696
9	**Purace**	Colombia	1977	4,755	15,601
10	**Kliuchevskoi**	Russia	1995	4,750	15,584

This list includes all volcanoes that have been active at some time during the 20th century. The tallest currently active volcano in Europe is Mt. Etna.

TOP 10 LARGEST DESERTS

	DESERT	LOCATION	APPROX. AREA SQ KM	SQ MILES
1	**Sahara**	North Africa	9,000,000	3,500,000
2	**Australian**	Australia	3,800,000	1,470,000
3	**Arabian**	Southwest Asia	1,300,000	502,000
4	**Gobi**	Central Asia	1,036,000	400,000
5	**Kalahari**	Southern Africa	520,000	201,000
6	**Turkestan**	Central Asia	450,000	174,000
7	**Takla Makan**	China	327,000	125,000
8	=**Namib**	Southwest Africa	310,000	120,000
	=**Sonoran**	USA/Mexico	310,000	120,000
10	=**Somali**	Somalia	260,000	100,000
	=**Thar**	Northwest India/Pakistan	260,000	100,000

Did You Know? Analysis of the latest data concerning Everest indicates that the mountain is growing higher and moving north-east at a rate of 6 cm (2.4 in) per annum.

TOP 10 LONGEST CAVES

	CAVE/LOCATION	TOTAL KNOWN LENGTH KM	MILES
1	**Mammoth cave system**, Kentucky, USA	567	352
2	**Optimisticeskaja**, Ukraine	201	125
3	**Jewel Cave**, South Dakota, USA	174	108
4	**Hölloch**, Switzerland	166	103
5	**Lechuguilla Cave**, New Mexico, USA	161	100
6	**Siebenhengsteholen-system**, Switzerland	140	87
7=	**Fisher Ridge cave system**, Kentucky, USA	126	78
=	**Wind Cave**, South Dakota, USA	126	78
9	**Ozernay**, Ukraine	111	69
10	**Gua Air Jernih**, Malaysia	109	68

Source: *Tony Waltham, BCRA, 1999*

TOP 10 DEEPEST CAVES

	CAVE SYSTEM/ LOCATION	TOTAL KNOWN DEPTH M	FT
1	**Lampreschtsofen**, Austria	1,632	5,354
2	**Gouffre Mirolda**, France	1,610	5,282
3	**Réseau Jean Bernard**, France	1,602	5,256
4	**Shakta Pantjukhina**, Georgia	1,508	4,948
5	**Sistema Huautla**, Mexico	1,475	4,839
6	**Sistema del Trave**, Spain	1,444	4,737
7	**Boj Bulok**, Uzbekistan	1,415	4,642
8	**Puerto di Illamina**, Spain	1,408	4,619
9	**Lukina Jama**, Croatia	1,392	4,567
10	**Sistema Cheve**, Mexico	1,386	4,547

Source: *Tony Waltham, BCRA, 1999*

TOP 10 HIGHEST MOUNTAINS

	MOUNTAIN/LOCATION	HEIGHT* M	FT
1	**Everest**, Nepal/Tibet	8,846	29,022
2	**K2**, Kashmir/China	8,611	28,250
3	**Kangchenjunga**, Nepal/Sikkim	8,598	28,208
4	**Lhotse**, Nepal/Tibet	8,501	27,890
5	**Makalu I**, Nepal/Tibet	8,470	27,790
6	**Dhaulagiri I**, Nepal	8,172	26,810
7	**Manaslu I**, Nepal	8,156	26,760
8	**Cho Oyu**, Nepal	8,153	26,750
9	**Nanga Parbat**, Kashmir	8,126	26,660
10	**Annapurna I**, Nepal	8,078	26,504

* *Height of principal peak; lower peaks of the same mountain are excluded*

In November 1999 it was announced that an analysis of data beamed from sensors on Everest's summit to GPS satellites had claimed a new height of 8,850 m (29,035 ft). This height has been accepted by the National Geographic Society but awaits confirmation as the official figure.

TOP 10 COUNTRIES WITH THE HIGHEST ELEVATIONS*

	COUNTRY/PEAK	HEIGHT M	FT
1	**Nepal**#, Everest	8,846	29,022
2	**Pakistan**, K2	8,611	28,250
3	**India**, Kangchenjunga	8,598	28,208
4	**Bhutan**, Khula Kangri	7,554	24,784
5	**Tajikistan**, Mt. Garmo (formerly Kommunizma)	7,495	24,590
6	**Afghanistan**, Noshaq	7,490	24,581
7	**Kyrgystan**, Pik Pobedy	7,439	24,406
8	**Kazakhstan**, Khan Tengri	6,995	22,949
9	**Argentina**, Cerro Aconcagua	6,960	22,834
10	**Chile**, Ojos del Salado	6,885	22,588

* *Based on the tallest peak in each country*

\# *Everest straddles Nepal and Tibet, which, now known as Xizang, is a province of China*

TOP 10 LARGEST METEORITE CRATERS

(Crater/location/diameter in km/miles)

1 = **Sudbury**, Ontario, Canada, 140/87; = **Vredefort**, South Africa, 140/87 3 **Manicouagan**, Quebec, Canada, 100/62; = **Popigai**, Russia, 100/62 5 **Puchezh-Katunki**, Russia, 80/50 6 **Kara**, Russia, 60/37 7 **Siljan**, Sweden, 52/32 8 **Charlevoix**, Quebec, Canada, 46/29 9 **Araguainha Dome**, Brazil, 40/25 10 **Carswell**, Saskatchewan, Canada, 37/23

METEORITE CRATERS

Unlike on the Solar System's other planets and moons, many astroblemes (collision sites) on the Earth have been weathered over time. Geologists are thus unsure whether or not certain crater-like structures are of meteoric origin or are the remnants of extinct volcanoes. The Vredefort Ring, for example, was thought to be volcanic but has since been claimed as a definite meteor crater. Barringer Crater in Arizona (1.265 km/0.79 miles) is, however, the largest that all scientists agree is an astrobleme. The original diameter of many craters, such as Manicouagan (seen from a Space Shuttle), has been reduced by erosion.

SNAP SHOTS

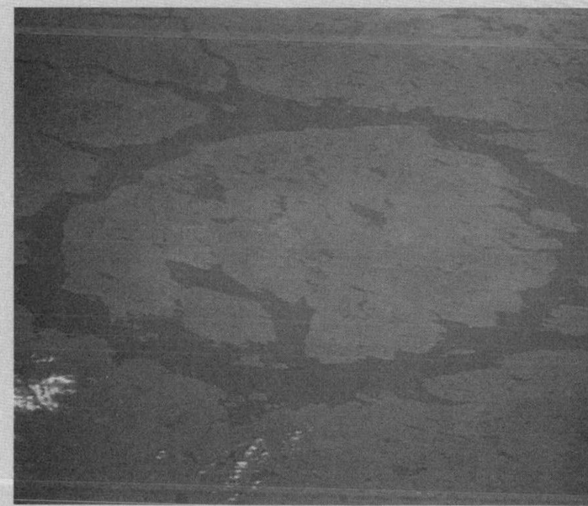

Background image: **NAMIB DESERT**

World Weather

TOP 10 ★

HOTTEST YEARS IN THE UK

	YEAR	AVERAGE TEMPERATURE* °C	°F
1	1990	10.63	51.13
2	1949	10.62	51.12
3	=1995	10.55	50.99
	=1997	10.55	50.99
5	1989	10.50	50.90
6	1959	10.48	50.86
7	=1733	10.47	50.85
	=1834	10.47	50.85
	=1921	10.47	50.85
10	1779	10.40	50.72

* *Since 1659, based on Central England averages*

TOP 10 ★

WARMEST PLACES IN GREAT BRITAIN

	WEATHER STATION/LOCATION	AVERAGE ANNUAL TEMPERATURE* °C	°F
1	**St. Mary's**, Isles of Scilly	11.5	52.7
2	**Penzance**, Cornwall	11.1	52.0
3	**Ilfracombe**, Devon	11.0	51.8
4	=**Central London**	10.9	51.6
	=**Southampton**, Hampshire	10.9	51.6
	=**Southsea (Portsmouth)**, Hampshire	10.9	51.6
	=**Torbay and Teignmouth**, Devon	10.9	51.6
8	=**Herne Bay**, Kent	10.8	51.4
	=**Lizard**, Cornwall	10.8	51.4
	=**Ryde and Sandown**, Isle of Wight	10.8	51.4

* *Based on The Meteorological Office's 30-year averages for the period 1961–90*

COLD COMFORT

Yakutsk, Siberia, a port with a population of 200,000, experiences some of the world's coldest winters, but receives surprisingly little precipitation – just 213 mm (8.39 in) a year.

TOP 10 ★

COLDEST PLACES IN GREAT BRITAIN

	WEATHER STATION/LOCATION	AVERAGE ANNUAL TEMPERATURE* °C	°F
1	**Dalwhinnie**, Highland	6.0	42.8
2	=**Leadhills**, Highland	6.3	43.3
	=**Braemar**, Aberdeenshire	6.3	43.3
	=**Balmoral**, Aberdeenshire	6.3	43.3
5	**Tomatin**, Highland	6.4	43.5
6	**Grantown-on-Spey**, Highland	6.5	43.7
7	**Lagganlia, nr. Kingraig**, Highland	6.6	43.9
8	**Crawfordjohn**, Lanarkshire	6.7	44.1
9	**Eskdalemuir**, Dumfries and Galloway	6.8	44.2
10	**Lerwick**, Shetland	6.9	44.4

* *Based on The Meteorological Office's 30-year averages for the period 1961–90*

On two occasions (11 Feb 1895 and 10 Jan 1982) Braemar has experienced -27°C (-17°F), the coldest temperature officially recorded in Britain.

TOP 10 ★

COLDEST INHABITED PLACES

	WEATHER STATION/LOCATION	AVERAGE TEMPERATURE °C	°F
1	**Norilsk**, Russia	–10.9	12.4
2	**Yakutsk**, Russia	–10.1	13.8
3	**Yellowknife**, Canada	–5.4	22.3
4	**Ulan-Bator**, Mongolia	–4.5	23.9
5	**Fairbanks**, Alaska, USA	–3.4	25.9
6	**Surgut**, Russia	–3.1	26.4
7	**Chita**, Russia	–2.7	27.1
8	**Nizhnevartovsk**, Russia	–2.6	27.3
9	**Hailar**, Mongolia	–2.4	27.7
10	**Bratsk**, Russia	–2.2	28.0

TOP 10 COLDEST YEARS IN THE UK

(Year/average temperature in °C/°F)*

❶ **1740**, 6.86/44.35 ❷ **1695**, 7.29/45.12 ❸ **1879**, 7.44/45.39 ❹ = **1694**, 7.67/45.81; = **1698**, 7.67/45.81 ❻ **1692**, 7.73/45.91 ❼ **1814**, 7.78/46.00 ❽ **1784**, 7.85/46.13 ❾ **1688**, 7.86/46.15 ❿ **1675**, 7.88/46.18

* *Since 1659, based on Central England averages*

TOP 10

HOTTEST INHABITED PLACES

	WEATHER STATION/LOCATION	AVERAGE TEMPERATURE °C	°F
1	**Djibouti**, Djibouti	30.0	86.0
2	=**Timbuktu**, Mali	29.3	84.7
	=**Tirunelevi**, India	29.3	84.7
	=**Tuticorin**, India	29.3	84.7
5	=**Nellore**, India	29.2	84.6
	=**Santa Marta**, Colombia	29.2	84.6
7	=**Aden**, South Yemen	28.9	84.0
	=**Madurai**, India	28.9	84.0
	=**Niamey**, Niger	28.9	84.0
10	=**Hudaydah**, North Yemen	28.8	83.8
	=**Ouagadougou**, Burkina Faso	28.8	83.8
	=**Thanjavur**, India	28.8	83.8
	=**Tiruchirapalli**, India	28.8	83.8

HOT SPOT

A small town at the end of a Saharan caravan route, Timbuktu in Mali is one of the world's hottest places, coming second only to Djibouti.

TOP 10

WETTEST INHABITED PLACES

	WEATHER STATION/LOCATION	AVERAGE ANNUAL RAINFALL MM	IN
1	**Buenaventura**, Colombia	6,743	265.47
2	**Monrovia**, Liberia	5,131	202.01
3	**Pago Pago**, American Samoa	4,990	196.46
4	**Moulmein**, Myanmar	4,852	191.02
5	**Lae**, Papua New Guinea	4,645	182.87
6	**Baguio**, Luzon Island, Philippines	4,573	180.04
7	**Sylhet**, Bangladesh	4,457	175.47
8	**Conakry**, Guinea	4,341	170.91
9	=**Padang**, Sumatra Island, Indonesia	4,225	166.34
	=**Bogor**, Java, Indonesia	4,225	166.34

The total annual rainfall of the Top 10 wettest places is equivalent to more than 26 1.83-m (6-ft) adults standing on top of each other. The greatest rainfall in a 12-month period was 26,461 mm (1,041.75 in) at Cherrapunji, India.

TOP 10

DRIEST INHABITED PLACES

	WEATHER STATION/LOCATION	AVERAGE ANNUAL RAINFALL MM	IN
1	**Aswan**, Egypt	0.5	0.02
2	**Luxor**, Egypt	0.7	0.03
3	**Arica**, Chile	1.1	0.04
4	**Ica**, Peru	2.3	0.09
5	**Antofagasta**, Chile	4.9	0.19
6	**Minya**, Egypt	5.1	0.20
7	**Asyut**, Egypt	5.2	0.21
8	**Callao**, Peru	12.0	0.47
9	**Trujilo**, Peru	14.0	0.54
10	**Fayyum**, Egypt	19.0	0.75

The total annual rainfall of the Top 10 driest inhabited places, as recorded over long periods, is just 64.8 mm (2½ in) – the average length of an adult little finger. The Atacama Desert often receives virtually no rain for years on end.

Did You Know? The highest temperatures recorded in the US and Europe are 47.8°C (118°F) (Phoenix, Arizona), and 47.2°C (117°F) (Seville, Spain).

Out of This World

TOP 10 ★ HEAVIEST ELEMENTS

	ELEMENT	DISCOVERER/COUNTRY	YEAR DISCOVERED	DENSITY*
1	**Osmium**	S. Tennant, UK	1804	22.59
2	**Iridium**	S. Tennant	1804	22.56
3	**Platinum**	J. C. Scaliger#, Italy/France	1557	21.45
4	**Rhenium**	W. Noddack *et al.*, Germany	1925	21.01
5	**Neptunium**	Edwin M. McMillan/ Philip H. Abelson, USA	1940	20.47
6	**Plutonium**	G. T. Seaborg *et al.*, USA	1940	20.26
7	**Gold**	–	Prehistoric	19.29
8	**Tungsten**	J. J. and F. Elhuijar, Spain	1783	19.26
9	**Uranium**	M. J. Klaproth, Germany	1789	19.05
10	**Tantalum**	A. G. Ekeberg, Sweden	1802	16.67

* *Grams per cu cm at 20°C*
\# *Earliest reference to this element*

TOP 10 ★ LIGHTEST ELEMENTS*

	ELEMENT	DISCOVERER/COUNTRY	YEAR DISCOVERED	DENSITY#
1	**Lithium**	J. A. Arfvedson, Sweden	1817	0.533
2	**Potassium**	Sir Humphry Davy, UK	1807	0.859
3	**Sodium**	Sir Humphry Davy	1807	0.969
4	**Calcium**	Sir Humphry Davy	1808	1.526
5	**Rubidium**	R. W. Bunsen/G. Kirchoff, Germany	1861	1.534
6	**Magnesium**	Sir Humphry Davy	1808+	1.737
7	**Phosphorus**	Hennig Brandt, Germany	1669	1.825
8	**Beryllium**	F. Wöhler, Germany/ A. A. B. Bussy, France	1828★	1.846
9	**Caesium**	R. W. Bunsen/G. Kirchoff	1860	1.896
10	**Sulphur**	–	Prehistoric	2.070

* *Solids only* # *Grams per cu cm at 20°C* + *Recognized by Joseph Black, 1755, but not isolated* ★ *Recognized by Nicholas Vauquelin, 1797, but not isolated*

TOP 10 MOST EXTRACTED METALLIC ELEMENTS

(Element/estimated annual extraction in tonnes)

❶ **Iron**, 716,000,000 ❷ **Aluminium**, 15,000,000 ❸ **Copper**, 6,540,000 ❹ **Manganese**, 6,220,000 ❺ **Zinc**, 5,020,000 ❻ **Lead**, 2,800,000 ❼ **Nickel**, 510,000 ❽ **Magnesium**, 325,000 ❾ **Sodium**, 200,000 ❿ **Tin**, 165,000

Certain metallic minerals are extracted in relatively small quantities, whereas compounds containing these elements are major industries: contrasting with 200,000 tonnes of metallic sodium, 168 million tonnes of salt are extracted annually; metallic calcium is represented by about 2,000 tonnes, contrasting with some 112 million tonnes of lime (calcium carbonate), and 200 tonnes of the metal potassium contrast with 51 million tonnes of potassium salts.

TOP 10 ★ METALLIC ELEMENTS WITH THE GREATEST RESERVES

	ELEMENT	ESTIMATED GLOBAL RESERVES (TONNES)
1	**Iron**	110,000,000,000
2	**Magnesium**	20,000,000,000
3	**Potassium**	10,000,000,000
4	**Aluminium**	6,000,000,000
5	**Manganese**	3,600,000,000
6	**Zirconium**	over 1,000,000,000
7	**Chromium**	1,000,000,000
8	**Barium**	450,000,000
9	**Titanium**	440,000,000
10	**Copper**	310,000,000

This list includes accessible reserves of commercially mined metallic elements, but excludes two, calcium and sodium, that exist in such vast quantities that their reserves are considered "unlimited" and unquantifiable.

COPPER TO SPARE

Copper is among the world's most extracted elements. Bingham Copper Mine, Utah, USA, is the largest man-made excavation in the world.

TOP 10

MOST COMMON ELEMENTS IN THE EARTH'S CRUST

	ELEMENT	PARTS PER MILLION*
1	Oxygen	474,000
2	Silicon	277,100
3	Aluminium	82,000
4	=Iron	41,000
	=Calcium	41,000
6	=Magnesium	23,000
	=Sodium	23,000
8	Potassium	21,000
9	Titanium	5,600
10	Hydrogen	1,520

* *mg per kg*

TOP 10

MOST COMMON ELEMENTS IN THE UNIVERSE

	ELEMENT	PARTS PER MILLION
1	Hydrogen	739,000
2	Helium	240,000
3	Oxygen	10,700
4	Carbon	4,600
5	Neon	1,340
6	Iron	1,090
7	Nitrogen	970
8	Silicon	650
9	Magnesium	580
10	Sulphur	440

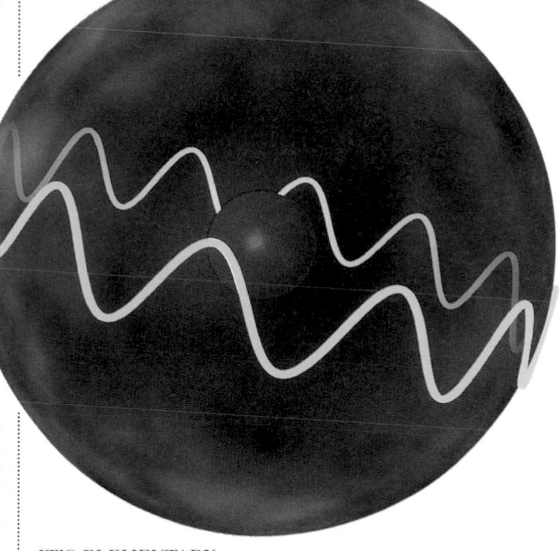

IT'S ELEMENTARY

The gas hydrogen is the simplest and most abundant element. This computer-generated image shows a hydrogen atom with a nucleus and orbiting electron.

TOP 10 PRINCIPAL COMPONENTS OF AIR

(Component/volume per cent)

❶ **Nitrogen**, 78.110 ❷ **Oxygen**, 20.953 ❸ **Argon**, 0.934 ❹ **Carbon dioxide**, 0.01–0.10 ❺ **Neon**, 0.001818 ❻ **Helium**, 0.000524 ❼ **Methane**, 0.0002 ❽ **Krypton**, 0.000114 ❾ = **Hydrogen**, 0.00005; = **Nitrous oxide**, 0.00005

THE 10 DEGREES OF HARDNESS*

(Substance)

❶ Talc ❷ Gypsum ❸ Calcite ❹ Fluorite ❺ Apatite ❻ Orthoclase ❼ Quartz ❽ Topaz ❾ Corundum ❿ Diamond

* *According to the Mohs Scale, in which No. 1 is the softest mineral and No. 10 is the hardest*

THE GOLD RUSH

In August 1896, 35-year-old George Washington Carmack struck gold while panning the Rabbit (later Bonanza) Creek, south of the Yukon at Klondike near the Canadian/Alaskan border. When news of his discovery reached the outside world, it sparked the world's biggest gold rush since the California stampede of 1849. More than 100,000 prospectors travelled to the inhospitable region to seek their fortunes, and in the first year alone some $22 million worth of Klondike gold was shipped out. Most of the gold-seekers failed, however, with many dying from the freezing winter conditions or else returning home empty-handed. In 1976 much of the area was designated as the Klondike Gold Rush Historical Park.

SNAP SHOTS

TOP 10

MOST EXTRACTED NON-METALLIC ELEMENTS

	ELEMENT	ESTIMATED ANNUAL EXTRACTION (TONNES)
1	Hydrogen	350,000,000,000
2	Carbon*	16,200,000,000
3	Chlorine	168,000,000
4	Phosphorus	153,000,000
5	Oxygen	100,000,000
6	Sulphur	54,000,000
7	Nitrogen	44,000,000
8	Silicon#	3,885,000
9	Boron	1,000,000
10	Argon	700,000

* *Carbon, natural gas, oil, and coal*

\# *Various forms*

CRYSTAL BOMB

Known since ancient times, sulphur is extracted in large quantities for use in many industrial and chemical processes, including making explosives.

Which is the world's highest island?

see p.23 for the answer

A Sumatra
B Hawaii
C New Guinea

Natural Disasters

THE 10 ★

WORST EARTHQUAKES OF THE 20TH CENTURY

	LOCATION	DATE	ESTIMATED NO. KILLED
1	**Tang-shan**, China	28 July 1976	242,419
2	**Nan-Shan**, China	22 May 1927	200,000
3	**Kansu**, China	16 Dec 1920	180,000
4	**Messina**, Italy	28 Dec 1908	160,000
5	**Tokyo/Yokohama**, Japan	1 Sep 1923	142,807
6	**Kansu**, China	25 Dec 1932	70,000
7	**Yungay**, Peru	31 May 1970	66,800
8	**Quetta**, India*	30 May 1935	50–60,000
9	**Armenia**	7 Dec 1988	over 55,000
10	**Iran**	21 June 1990	over 40,000

* *Now Pakistan*

Reaching 7.2 on the Richter scale, the earthquake that struck Kobe, Japan, on 17 January 1995 was exceptionally precisely monitored by the rescue authorities. It left a total of 3,842 dead and 14,679 injured.

THE 10 

WORST AVALANCHES AND LANDSLIDES OF THE 20TH CENTURY*

	LOCATION	INCIDENT	DATE	ESTIMATED NO. KILLED
1	**Yungay**, Peru	Landslide	31 May 1970	17,500
2	**Italian Alps**	Avalanche	13 Dec 1916	10,000
3	**Huarás**, Peru	Avalanche	13 Dec 1941	5,000
4	**Nevada Huascaran**, Peru	Avalanche	10 Jan 1962	3,500
5	**Medellin**, Colombia	Landslide	27 Sep 1987	683
6	**Chungar**, Peru	Avalanche	19 Mar 1971	600
7	**Rio de Janeiro**, Brazil	Landslide	11 Jan 1966	550
8	=**Northern Assam**, India	Landslide	15 Feb 1949	500
	=**Grand Rivière du Nord**, Haiti	Landslide	13/14 Nov 1963	500
10	**Blons**, Austria	Avalanche	11 Jan 1954	411

* *Excluding those where most deaths resulted from flooding, earthquakes, etc., associated with landslides*

The worst incident of all, the destruction of Yungay, Peru, in May 1970, was only part of a much larger cataclysm that left a total of up to 70,000 dead. Following an earthquake and flooding, the town was wiped out by an avalanche that left just 2,500 survivors out of a population of 20,000.

One of the most tragic landslide disasters of this century occurred at Aberfan, Wales, on 20 October 1966. Weakened by the presence of a spring, a huge volume of slurry from a 244-m (800-ft) high heap of coal mine waste suddenly flowed down and engulfed the local school, killing 144 people.

TURKISH EARTHQUAKE

The earthquake that occurred in Turkey on 17 August 1999 was the second worst of the decade, resulting in a death toll unofficially estimated at between 30,000 and 40,000. It lasted only 45 seconds but measured 7.4 on the Richter scale. Its epicentre was 11 km (7 miles) southeast of Izmit, an industrial area 90 km (50 miles) east of Istanbul, where many multistorey concrete apartment buildings collapsed into rubble. Most had been poorly constructed with inferior materials and little regard for the area's known vulnerability to earthquakes. In this and the surrounding area, some 20,000 structures were destroyed or damaged, while the country's industrial infrastructure was severely damaged. The Tüpras oil refinery in Korfez was set ablaze, Turkey's electricity supply cut, and water and road networks disrupted.

THE 10

COSTLIEST HURRICANES TO STRIKE THE USA

	HURRICANE	YEAR	DAMAGE ($)*
1	Andrew	1992	30,475,000,000
2	Hugo	1989	8,491,561,181
3	Agnes	1972	7,500,000,000
4	Betsy	1965	7,425,340,909
5	Camille	1969	6,096,287,313
6	Diane	1955	4,830,580,808
7	Frederic	1979	4,328,968,903
8	New England	1938	4,140,000,000
9	Fran	1996	3,200,000,000
10	Opal	1995	3,069,395,018

* *Adjusted to 1996 dollars*

Source: *The National Hurricane Center*

THE 10 WORST EPIDEMICS OF ALL TIME

	EPIDEMIC	LOCATION	DATE	ESTIMATED NO. KILLED
1	Black Death	Europe/Asia	1347–51	75,000,000
2	Influenza	Worldwide	1918–20	21,640,000
3	Plague	India	1896–1948	12,000,000
4	AIDS	Worldwide	1981–present	11,700,000
5	Typhus	Eastern Europe	1914–15	3,000,000
6	= "Plague of Justinian"	Europe/Asia	541–90	millions*
	= Cholera	Worldwide	1846–60	millions*
	= Cholera	Europe	1826–37	millions*
	= Cholera	Worldwide	1893–94	millions*
10	Smallpox	Mexico	1530–45	>1,000,000

* *No precise figures available*

THE 10

WORST VOLCANIC ERUPTIONS OF ALL TIME

LOCATION/DATE/INCIDENT — EST. NO. KILLED

1 **Tambora**, Indonesia, 5–12 Apr 1815 — 92,000

The eruption on the island of Sumbawa killed about 10,000 islanders immediately, with a further 82,000 dying subsequently from disease and famine resulting from crops being destroyed. An estimated 1,700,000 tons of ash was hurled into the atmosphere, blocking out the sunlight.

2 **Miyi-Yama**, Java, 1793 — 53,000

The volcano dominating the island of Kiousiou erupted, engulfing all the local villages in mudslides and killing most of the rural population.

3 **Mont Pelée**, Martinique, 8 May 1902 — 40,000

After lying dormant for centuries, Mont Pelée began to erupt in April 1902.

4 **Krakatoa**, Sumatra/Java, 26–27 Aug 1883 — 36,380

Krakatoa exploded with what may have been the biggest bang ever heard by humans, audible up to 4,800 km (3,000 miles) away.

5 **Nevado del Ruiz**, Colombia, 13 Nov 1985 — 22,940

The hot steam, rocks, and ash ejected from Nevado del Ruiz melted its icecap, resulting in a mudslide that completely engulfed the town of Armero.

6 **Mount Etna**, Sicily, 11 Mar 1669 — over 20,000

Europe's largest volcano has erupted frequently, but the worst instance occurred in 1669, when the lava flow engulfed the town of Catania.

7 **Laki**, Iceland, Jan–June 1783 — 20,000

An eruption on the Laki volcanic ridge culminated on 11 June with the largest ever recorded lava flow. It engulfed many villages in a river of lava up to 80 km (50 miles) long and 30 m (100 ft) deep, releasing poisonous gases that killed those who escaped.

8 **Vesuvius**, Italy, 24 Aug 79 — 16–20,000

The Roman city of Herculaneum was engulfed by a mud flow, while Pompeii was buried under a vast and preserving layer of pumice and volcanic ash.

9 **Vesuvius**, Italy, 16–17 Dec 1631 — up to 18,000

The next major cataclysm was almost as disastrous, when lava and mudflows gushed down onto the surrounding towns, including Naples.

10 **Mount Etna**, Sicily, 1169 — over 15,000

Large numbers died in Catania cathedral, where they believed they would be safe, and more were killed when a tidal wave caused by the eruption hit the port of Messina.

THE 10

WORST FLOODS AND STORMS OF THE 20TH CENTURY

	LOCATION	DATE	ESTIMATED NO. KILLED
1	Huang He River, China	Aug 1931	3,700,000
2	Bangladesh	13 Nov 1970	300–500,000
3	Henan, China	Sep 1939	over 200,000
4	Bangladesh	30 Apr 1991	131,000
5	Chang Jiang River, China	Sep 1911	100,000
6	Bengal, India	15–16 Nov 1942	40,000
7	Bangladesh	1–2 June 1965	30,000
8	Bangladesh	28–29 May 1963	22,000
9	Bangladesh	11–12 May 1965	17,000
10	Morvi, India	11 Aug 1979	5–15,000

No. 4 was omitted previously because the total number of fatalities combines the effects of storm, flood and tidal wave, and it is impossible to isolate the figures for just those deaths attributable to the storm and flood aspects of the disaster. On balance, I think it deserves to be recorded.

Background image: INFLUENZA VIRUSES

Where is the world's highest waterfall?
see p.21 for the answer

A Venezuela
B India
C China

TOP 10

Life on Earth

Extinct & Endangered

COME INTO MY PARLOUR ...

Listed as "vulnerable" by the International Union for the Conservation of Nature, the distinctive Dolomedes *Great raft or Fishing spider can sit on water as it awaits its prey.*

THE 10 MOST ENDANGERED BIG CATS*

1	Amur leopard
2	Anatolian leopard
3	Asiatic cheetah
4	Eastern puma
5	Florida cougar
6	North African leopard
7	Siberian tiger
8	South Arabian leopard
9	South China tiger
10	Sumatran tiger

* *In alphabetical order*

Source: *International Union for the Conservation of Nature*

All 10 of these big cats are classed by the International Union for Conservation of Nature as being "critically endangered", that is, facing an extremely high risk of extinction in the wild in the immediate future.

THE 10 MOST ENDANGERED SPIDERS

	SPIDER	COUNTRY
1	Kauai cave wolf spider	USA
2	Doloff cave spider	USA
3	Empire cave pseudoscorpion	USA
4	Glacier Bay wolf spider	USA
5	Great raft spider	Europe
6	Kocevje subterranean spider (*Troglohyphantes gracilis*)	Slovenia
7	Kocevje subterranean spider (*Troglohyphantes similis*)	Slovenia
8	Kocevje subterranean spider (*Troglohyphantes spinipes*)	Slovenia
9	Lake Placid funnel wolf spider	USA
10	Melones cave harvestman	USA

Source: *International Union for the Conservation of Nature*

The first spider on this list is considered by the IUCN as "endangered" (facing a very high risk of extinction in the wild in the near future), and the others as "vulnerable" (facing a high risk of extinction in the wild in the medium-term future). Some exist exclusively in one habitat, making them especially susceptible to environmental threats.

THE 10 COUNTRIES WITH THE MOST ASIAN ELEPHANTS

	COUNTRY	NUMBER*
1	India	24,000
2	Myanmar	6,000
3	Indonesia	4,500
4	Laos	4,000
5	Sri Lanka	3,000
6	=Thailand	2,000
	=Cambodia	2,000
8	=Borneo	1,000
	=Malaysia	1,000
10	Vietnam	400

* Based on maximum estimates

The total numbers of Asian elephants is put at anything from a minimum of 37,860 to a maximum 48,740. Estimates of populations of Asian elephants are notoriously unreliable as this species is exclusively a forest animal and its numbers cannot be sampled using aerial survey techniques.

Source: *International Union for the Conservation of Nature*

THE 10 MOST RECENTLY EXTINCT ANIMAL SPECIES

1	Partula Tree Snails from Hawaii
2	Palos Verde Blue Butterfly
3	Canary Islands Blackfly
4	Lord Howe Islands Phasmid Fly
5	Dusky Seaside Sparrow
6	Colombian Grebe and Atitlan Grebe
7	Glaucous Macaw
8	Hawaiian Honey Creeper
9	Pohmpei (Caroline Island bird)
10	Bali Tiger

The saddest thing about this list is that by the time you read it, it will be out of date because yet another species will have become extinct, usually as a direct result of man's intervention.

Did You Know? Once thought extinct but later rediscovered, the Kakapo parrot cannot fly, but instead climbs trees and glides down to the ground.

"AS DEAD AS A DODO'

When Portuguese sailors first encountered a large, flightless bird on the island of Mauritius, they were struck by its ludicrous clumsy appearance and the ease with which they were able to catch it; so they christened it the "doudo", the Portuguese word for "stupid". Even its Latin name emphasizes its silliness – *Didus ineptus*. As doudos, or dodos, tasted delicious, they were hunted down, and by 1681, when the last was seen by English naturalist Benjamin Harry, they were completely extinct – hence the expression, "as dead as a dodo".

WHY DO WE SAY?

THE 10

MOST ENDANGERED MAMMALS

	MAMMAL	ESTIMATED NO.
1	=Tasmanian wolf	?
	=Halcon fruit bat	?
	=Ghana fat mouse	?
4	Javan rhinoceros	50
5	Iriomote cat	60
6	Black lion tamarin	130
7	Pygmy hog	150
8	Kouprey	100–200
9	Tamaraw	200
10	Indus dolphin	400

The first three mammals on the list have not been seen for many years and may well be extinct.

THE 10

COUNTRIES WITH THE MOST THREATENED SPECIES

	COUNTRY	MAMMALS	BIRDS	REPTILES	AMPHIBIANS	FISH	INVERTEBRATES	TOTAL
1	USA	35	50	28	24	123	594	854
2	Australia	58	45	37	25	37	281	483
3	Indonesia	128	104	19	0	60	29	340
4	Mexico	64	36	18	3	86	40	247
5	Brazil	71	103	15	5	12	34	240
6	China	75	90	15	1	28	4	213
7	South Africa	33	16	19	9	27	101	205
8	Philippines	49	86	7	2	26	18	188
9	India	75	73	16	3	4	22	193
10	=Japan	29	33	8	10	7	45	132
	=Tanzania	33	30	4	0	19	46	132

TOP 10 COUNTRIES WITH THE MOST AFRICAN ELEPHANTS

(Country/elephants)

1 **Tanzania**, 73,459* **2** **Dem. Rep. of Congo**, 65,974# **3** **Botswana**, 62,998* **4** **Gabon**, 61,794+ **5** **Zimbabwe**, 56,297* **6** **Congo**, 32,563# **7** **Zambia**, 19,701* **8** **Kenya**, 13,834* **9** **South Africa**, 9,990* **10** **Cameroon**, 8,824#

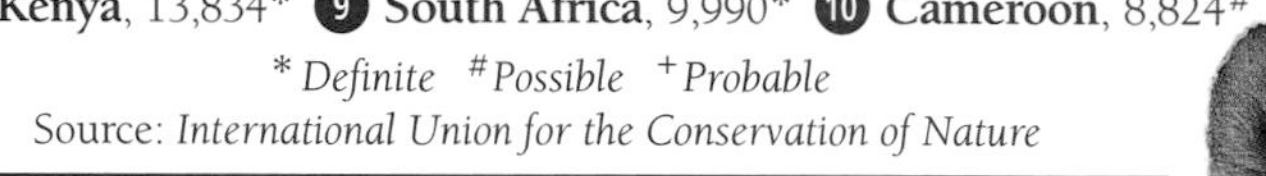

* *Definite* # *Possible* + *Probable*

Source: *International Union for the Conservation of Nature*

LONE WOLF

Although officially declared extinct in 1936, the marsupial Thylacine, *or Tasmanian wolf, remains the subject of frequent alleged sightings.*

Land Animals 1

TOP 10 ★ HEAVIEST TERRESTRIAL MAMMALS

	MAMMAL	LENGTH* M	FT	WEIGHT KG	LB
1	African elephant	7.3	24	7,000	14,432
2	White rhinoceros	4.2	14	3,600	7,937
3	Hippopotamus	4.0	13	2,500	5,512
4	Giraffe	5.8	19	1,600	3,527
5	American bison	3.9	13	1,000	2,205
6	Arabian camel (dromedary)	3.5	12	690	1,521
7	Polar bear	2.6	8	600	1,323
8	Moose	3.0	10	550	1,213
9	Siberian tiger	3.3	11	300	661
10	Gorilla	2.0	7	220	485

* *Head to toe or head to tail*

The list excludes domesticated cattle and horses. It also avoids comparing close kin, such as the African and Indian elephants.

TOP 10 ★ SLEEPIEST ANIMALS*

	ANIMAL	AVERAGE HOURS OF SLEEP PER DAY
1	Koala	22
2	Sloth	20
3	=Armadillo	19
	=Opossum	19
5	Lemur	16
6	=Hamster	14
	=Squirrel	14
8	=Cat	13
	=Pig	13
10	Spiny anteater	12

* *Excluding periods of hibernation*

SLEEPYHEAD

The eastern Australian koala (which is actually a marsupial, not a bear), sleeps almost constantly to conserve the little energy it has.

TOP 10 ★ HEAVIEST PRIMATES

	PRIMATE	LENGTH* CM	IN	WEIGHT KG	LB
1	Gorilla	200	79	220	485
2	Man	177	70	77	170
3	Orang-utan	137	54	75	165
4	Chimpanzee	92	36	50	110
5	=Baboon	100	39	45	99
	=Mandrill	95	37	45	99
7	Gelada baboon	75	30	25	55
8	Proboscis monkey	76	30	24	53
9	Hanuman langur	107	42	20	44
10	Siamung gibbon	90	35	13	29

* *Excluding tail*

The longer, skinnier, and lighter forms of the langurs, gibbons, and monkeys, designed for serious monkeying around in trees, contrast sharply with their heavier great ape cousins.

GENTLE GIANT

The largest of all primates, the gorilla has a menacing appearance that has been exploited in such films as King Kong. *In fact, gorillas are usually docile.*

TOP 10

HEAVIEST CARNIVORES

	CARNIVORE	LENGTH M	LENGTH FT	WEIGHT KG	WEIGHT LB
1	Southern elephant seal	6.5	21	3,500	7,716
2	Walrus	3.8	12	1,200	2,646
3	Steller sea lion	3.0	9	1,100	2,425
4	Grizzly bear	3.0	9	780	1,720
5	Polar bear	2.6	8	600	1,323
6	Tiger	2.8	9	300	661
7	Lion	1.9	6	250	551
8	American black bear	1.8	6	227	500
9	Giant panda	1.5	5	160	353
10	Spectacled bear	1.8	6	140	309

Of the 273 mammal species in the order *Carnivora*, or meat-eaters, many (including its largest representatives on land, the bears) are in fact omnivorous, and around 40 specialize in eating fish or insects. All, however, share a common ancestry indicated by the butcher's-knife form of their canine teeth. As the Top 10 would otherwise consist exclusively of seals and related marine carnivores, only three have been included in order to enable the terrestrial heavyweight division to make an appearance. The polar bear is probably the largest land carnivore if shoulder height (when the animal is on all fours) is taken into account: it tops an awesome 1.6 m (5.3 ft), compared with the 1.2 m (4 ft) of its nearest rival, the grizzly.

TOP BEAR

Although among the heaviest carnivores, many records of giant grizzlies have been exaggerated by hunters and showmen for prestige.

"GORILLA"

"Gorilla" was adopted in 1847 as part of the original scientific name for the large ape, *Troglodytes gorilla*. The word was coined by Dr. Thomas Staughton Savage, an American missionary in Africa, who had heard of the Gorillai, a mythical African tribe of hairy women, imaginatively described in a 5th- or 6th-century BC Greek account of the voyages of Hanno the Carthaginian.

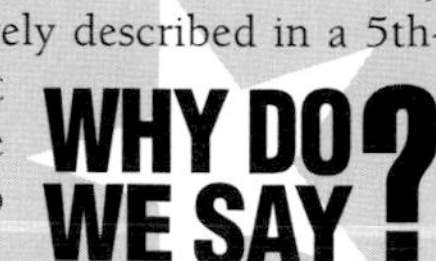

Did You Know? Giant pandas spend up to 15 hours a day eating, consuming as much as 45 kg (99 lb) of bamboo shoots a day.

Land Animals 2

"WHITE ELEPHANT"

The rare albino or white elephant was considered sacred to the people of Siam (now Thailand). Legend has it that the king would sometimes present such an elephant to an unpopular courtier. Decorum would have meant that the courtier could not refuse the gift, but the immense cost of looking after the beast would have ruined him financially. A "white elephant" thus became a synonym for a burdensome gift that one could not dispose of.

WHY DO WE SAY?

TOP 10 MOST INTELLIGENT MAMMALS

1 Man **2** Chimpanzee **3** Gorilla **4** Orang-utan **5** Baboon **6** Gibbon **7** Monkey **8** Smaller toothed whale **9** Dolphin **10** Elephant

This list is based on research conducted by Edward O. Wilson, Professor of Zoology at Harvard University, who defined intelligence as speed and extent of learning performance over a wide range of tasks, also taking account of the ratio of the animal's brain size to its body bulk.

TOP 10 ★ MOST PROLIFIC WILD MAMMALS

	ANIMAL	AVERAGE LITTER
1	Malagasy tenrec	25.0
2	Virginian opossum	22.0
3	Golden hamster	11.0
4	Ermine	10.0
5	Prairie vole	9.0
6	Coypu	8.5
7=	European hedgehog	7.0
=	African hunting dog	7.0
9=	Meadow vole	6.5
=	Wild boar	6.5

The prairie vole probably holds the world record for most offspring produced in a season. It has up to 17 litters in rapid succession, bringing up to 150 young into the world.

DEADLY CHARM

Traditionally used by Indian snake charmers, the enacingly hooded Indian cobra's venom is sufficiently powerful to kill an elephant.

TOP 10 ★ MOST VENOMOUS CREATURES

	CREATURE*	TOXIN	FATAL AMOUNT MG#
1	Indian cobra	Peak V	0.009
2	Mamba	Toxin 1	0.02
3	Brown snake	Texilotoxin	0.05
4=	Inland taipan	Paradotoxin	0.10
=	Mamba	Dendrotoxin	0.10
6	Taipan	Taipoxin	0.11
7=	Indian cobra	Peak X	0.12
=	Poison arrow frog	Batrachotoxin	0.12
9	Indian cobra	Peak 1X	0.17
10	Krait	Bungarotoxin	0.50

* *Excluding bacteria*

\# *Quantity required to kill one average-sized human adult*

The venom of these creatures is almost unbelievably powerful: 1 milligram of Mamba Toxin 1 would be sufficient to kill 50 people. Such creatures as scorpions (0.5 mg) and black widow spiders (1.0 mg) fall just outside the Top 10.

PENSIVE PRIMATE

Numbered among the most intelligent mammals, and noted for its use of tools, the forest-dwelling orang-utan's name derives from the Malay words for "man of the woods".

TOP 10 LONGEST LAND ANIMALS

	ANIMAL*	LENGTH# M	FT
1	Royal python	10.7	35
2	Tapeworm	10.0	33
3	African elephant	7.3	24
4	Estuarine crocodile	5.9	19
5	Giraffe	5.8	19
6	White rhinoceros	4.2	14
7	Hippopotamus	4.0	13
8	American bison	3.9	13
9	Arabian camel (dromedary)	3.5	12
10	Siberian tiger	3.3	11

* Longest representative of each species

\# Head to toe or head to tail

GROWING FAST

The giraffe is the tallest of all living animals. In 1937 a calf giraffe that measured 1.58 m (5 ft 2 in) at birth was found to be growing at an astonishing 1.3 cm (0.5 in) per hour.

TOP 10 FASTEST MAMMALS

	MAMMAL	MAXIMUM RECORDED SPEED KM/H	MPH
1	Cheetah	105	65
2	Pronghorn antelope	89	55
3	=Mongolian gazelle	80	50
	=Springbok	80	50
5	=Grant's gazelle	76	47
	=Thomson's gazelle	76	47
7	Brown hare	72	45
8	Horse	69	43
9	=Greyhound	68	42
	=Red deer	68	42

QUICK OFF THE MARK

The speedy cheetah can accelerate to 96 km/h (60 mph) in just three seconds.

TOP 10 DEADLIEST SNAKES

	SNAKE	MAXIMUM DEATHS PER BITE	MORTALITY RATE RANGE (PER CENT)
1	Black mamba	200	75–100
2	Forest cobra	50	70–95
3	Russell's viper	150	40–92
4	Taipan	26	10–90
5	Common krait	60	70–80
6	Jararacussa	100	60–80
7	Terciopelo	40	Not known
8	Egyptian cobra	35	50
9	Indian cobra	40	30–35
10	Jararaca	30	25–35

What is special about Kitti's hognosed bat?

see p.42 for the answer

A It is the rarest
B It is the lightest
C It is the fastest

TOP 10 HEAVIEST MARINE MAMMALS

	MAMMAL	LENGTH M	FT	WEIGHT TONNES
1	Blue whale	33.5	110.0	130.0
2	Fin whale	25.0	82.0	45.0
3	Right whale	17.5	57.4	40.0
4	Sperm whale	18.0	59.0	36.0
5	Grey whale	14.0	46.0	32.7
6	Humpback whale	15.0	49.2	26.5
7	Baird's whale	5.5	18.0	11.0
8	Southern elephant seal	6.5	21.3	3.6
9	Northern elephant seal	5.8	19.0	3.4
10	Pilot whale	6.4	21.0	2.9

Probably the largest animal that ever lived, the blue whale dwarfs the other whales listed here, all but one of which far outweigh the biggest land animal, the elephant.

TOP 10 ★ HEAVIEST SHARKS

	SHARK	WEIGHT KG	LB
1	Whale shark	21,000	46,297
2	Basking shark	14,515	32,000
3	Great white shark	3,314	7,300
4	Greenland shark	1,020	2,250
5	Tiger shark	939	2,070
6	Great hammerhead shark	844	1,860
7	Six-gill shark	590	1,300
8	Grey nurse shark	556	1,225
9	Mako shark	544	1,200
10	Thresher shark	500	1,100

As well as specimens that have been caught, estimates have been made of beached examples, but such is the notoriety of sharks that many accounts of their size are exaggerated, and this list should be taken as an approximate ranking based on the best available evidence.

TOP 10 ★ HEAVIEST TURTLES

	TURTLE	WEIGHT KG	LB
1	Pacific leatherback turtle	865	1,908
2	Atlantic leatherback turtle	454	1,000
3	Green sea turtle	408	900
4	Loggerhead turtle	386	850
5	Alligator snapping turtle	183	403
6	Black sea turtle	126	278
7	Flatback turtle	84	185
8	Hawksbill turtle	68	150
9=	Kemps ridley turtle	50	110
=	Olive ridley turtle	50	110

TOP 10 FISHING COUNTRIES

(Country/annual catch in tonnes)

❶ **China**, 33,166,640 ❷ **Peru**, 9,521,960 ❸ **Chile**, 7,590,947 ❹ **Japan**, 6,758,829 ❺ **USA**, 5,614,534 ❻ **India**, 5,260,420 ❼ **Indonesia**, 4,401,940 ❽ **Russia**, 4,373,827 ❾ **Thailand**, 3,647,900 ❿ **Norway**, 2,807,551

MARINE MONSTER

There are several species of right whale, with exceptional specimens reputedly exceeding 70 tonnes.

Background image: **SHOAL OF MACKEREL**

TOP 10 HEAVIEST SPECIES OF FRESHWATER FISH CAUGHT

	SPECIES	ANGLER/LOCATION/DATE	WEIGHT KG	LB	OZ
1	White sturgeon	Joey Pallotta III, Benicia, California, USA, 9 July 1983	212.28	468	0
2	Alligator gar	Bill Valverde, Rio Grande, Texas, USA, 2 Dec 1951	126.55	279	0
3	Beluga sturgeon	Merete Lehne, Guryev, Kazakhstan, 3 May 1993	101.97	224	13
4	Nile perch	Adrian Brayshaw, Lake Nasser, Egypt, 18 Dec 1997	96.62	213	0
5	Flathead catfish	Ken Paulie, Withlacoochee River, Florida, USA, 14 May 1998	56.05	123	9
6	Blue catfish	William P. McKinley, Wheeler Reservoir, Tennessee, USA, 5 July 1996	50.35	111	0
7	Chinook salmon	Les Anderson, Kenai River, Alaska, USA, 17 May 1985	44.11	97	4
8	Giant tigerfish	Raymond Houtmans, Zaire River, Zaire, 9 July 1988	44.00	97	0
9	Smallmouth buffalo	Randy Collins, Athens Lake, Arkansas, USA, 6 June 1993	37.28	82	3
10	Atlantic salmon	Henrik Henrikson, Tana River, Norway (date unknown) 1928	35.89	79	2

Source: *International Game Fish Association*

TOP 10 HEAVIEST SPECIES OF SALTWATER FISH CAUGHT

	SPECIES	ANGLER/LOCATION/DATE	WEIGHT KG	LB	OZ
1	Great white shark	Alfred Dean, Ceduna, South Australia, 21 Apr 1959	1,208.39	2,664	0
2	Tiger shark	Walter Maxwell, Cherry Grove, California, USA, 14 June 1964	807.41	1,780	0
3	Greenland shark	Terje Nordtvedt, Trondheimsfjord, Norway, 18 Oct 1987	775.0	1,708	9
4	Black marlin	A. C. Glassell, Jr., Cabo Blanco, Peru, 4 Aug 1953	707.62	1,560	0
5	Bluefin tuna	Ken Fraser, Aulds Cove, Nova Scotia, Canada, 26 Oct 1979	678.59	1,496	0
6	Atlantic blue marlin	Paulo Amorim, Vitoria, Brazil, 29 Feb 1992	635.99	1,402	2
7	Pacific blue marlin	Jay W. de Beaubien, Kaaiwi Point, Kona, 31 May 1982	624.15	1,376	0
8	Swordfish	L. Marron, Iquique, Chile, 7 May 1953	536.16	1,182	0
9	Mako shark	Patrick Guillanton, Black River, Mauritius, 16 Nov 1988	505.76	1,115	0
10	Hammerhead shark	Allen Ogle, Sarasota, Florida, USA, 20 May 1982	449.52	991	0

Source: *International Game Fish Association*

TOP 10 SPECIES OF FISH MOST CAUGHT

	SPECIES	TONNES CAUGHT PER ANNUM
1	Anchoveta	11,896,808
2	Alaska pollock	4,298,619
3	Chilean jack mackerel	4,254,629
4	Silver carp	2,333,669
5	Atlantic herring	1,886,105
6	Grass carp	1,821,606
7	South American pilchard	1,793,425
8	Common carp	1,627,198
9	Chubb mackerel	1,507,497
10	Skipjack tuna	1,462,637

Some 3 million tonnes of shrimps and prawns, and a similar amount of squid, cuttlefish, and octopuses, are caught annually.

SPEEDY SWIMMER

The highly streamlined sailfish is acknowledged as the fastest over short distances, with anglers reporting them capable of unreeling 91 m (300 ft) of line in three seconds.

TOP 10 FASTEST FISH

(Fish/recorded speed in km/h/mph)

1 **Sailfish**, 110/68 2 **Marlin**, 80/50 3 **Bluefin tuna**, 74/46 4 **Yellowfin tuna**, 70/44 5 **Blue shark**, 69/43 6 **Wahoo**, 66/41 7 = **Bonefish**, 64/40; = **Swordfish**, 64/40 9 **Tarpon**, 56/35 10 **Tiger shark**, 53/33

Flying fish have a top speed in the water of only 37 km/h (23 mph), but airborne they can reach 56 km/h (35 mph). Many sharks qualify for the list; only two are listed here to prevent the list becoming overly shark-infested.

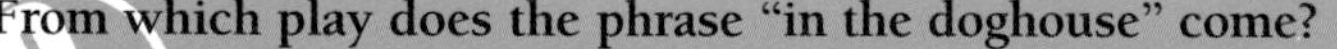

From which play does the phrase "in the doghouse" come?

see p.45 for the answer

A *Peter Pan*
B *A Midsummer Night's Dream*
C *The Importance of Being Earnest*

Flying Animals

TOP 10 ISLANDS WITH THE MOST ENDEMIC BIRD SPECIES*

(Island/species)

1 **New Guinea**, 195 **2** **Jamaica**, 26 **3** **Cuba**, 23 **4** **New Caledonia**, 20 **5** **Rennell Solomon Islands**, 15 **6** **São Tomé**, 14 **7** = **Aldabra, Seychelles**, 13; = **Grand Cayman, Cayman Islands**, 13 **9** **Puerto Rico**, 12 **10** **New Britain, Papua New Guinea**, 11

* *Birds that are found uniquely on these islands*
Source: *United Nations*

TOP 10 MOST COMMON NORTH AMERICAN GARDEN BIRDS

(Bird/percentage of feeders visited)

1 **Dark-eyed junco**, 83 **2** **House finch**, 70 **3** = **American goldfinch**, 69; = **Downy woodpecker**, 69 **5** **Blue jay**, 67 **6** **Mourning dove**, 65 **7** **Black-capped chickadee**, 60 **8** **House sparrow**, 59 **9** **Northern cardinal**, 56 **10** **European starling**, 52

Source: *Project FeederWatch/ Cornell Lab of Ornithology*

These are the birds that watchers are most likely to see at their feeders in North America.

TINSELTOWN BIRD

One of the most common garden birds, finches were spread from the western American states in the 1940s by dealers who sold them as "Hollywood Finches".

TOP 10 LIGHTEST BATS

	BAT/HABITAT	LENGTH CM	LENGTH IN	WEIGHT G	WEIGHT OZ
1	**Kitti's hognosed bat** (*Craseonycteris thonglongyai*), Thailand	2.9	1.10	2.0	0.07
2	**Proboscis bat** (*Rhynchonycteris naso*), Central and South America	3.8	1.50	2.5	0.09
3	=**Banana bat** (*Pipistrellus nanus*), Africa	3.8	1.50	3.0	0.11
	=**Smoky bat** (*Furiptera horrens*), Central and South America	3.8	1.50	3.0	0.11
5	=**Little yellow bat** (*Rhogeessa mira*), Central America	4.0	1.57	3.5	0.12
	=**Lesser bamboo bat** (*Tylonycteris pachypus*), Southeast Asia	4.0	1.57	3.5	0.12
7	**Disc-winged bat** (*Thyroptera tricolor*), Central and South America	3.6	1.42	4.0	0.14
8	**Lesser horseshoe bat** (*Rhynolophus hipposideros*), Europe and Western Asia	3.7	1.46	5.0	0.18
9	**California myotis** (*Myotis californienses*), North America	4.3	1.69	5.0	0.18
10	**Northern blossom bat** (*Macroglossus minimus*), Southeast Asia to Australia	6.4	2.52	15.0	0.53

This list focuses on the smallest example of 10 different bat families. The weights shown are typical, rather than extreme – and since a bat can eat more than half its own weight, the weights of individual examples may vary considerably. The smallest of all weighs less than a table-tennis ball, and even the heaviest listed here weighs less than an empty aluminium drink can. Length is of head and body only, since tail lengths vary from zero (as in Kitti's hognosed bat and the Northern blossom bat) to long (as in the Proboscis bat and Lesser horseshoe bat).

TOP 10 FASTEST BIRDS

	BIRD	RECORDED SPEED KM/H	MPH
1	**Spine-tailed swift**	171	106
2	**Frigate bird**	153	95
3	**Spur-winged goose**	142	88
4	**Red-breasted merganser**	129	80
5	**White-rumped swift**	124	77
6	**Canvasback duck**	116	72
7	**Eider duck**	113	70
8	**Teal**	109	68
9	=**Mallard**	105	65
	=**Pintail**	105	65

This list picks out star performers among the medium- to large-sized birds that can hit their top speed without help from wind or gravity. Fastest among swimming birds is the gentoo penguin at 35 km/h (22.3 mph), while the speediest of flightless birds is the ostrich at 72 km/h (45 mph).

TOP 10 LARGEST BIRDS IN THE UK

	BIRD	BEAK-TO-TAIL LENGTH CM	IN
1	=**Mute swan**	145–160	57–63
	=**Whooper swan**	145–160	57–63
3	**Bewick's swan**	116–128	46–50
4	**Canada goose**	up to 110	up to 43
5	**Grey heron**	90–100	35–39
6	**Cormorant**	84–98	33–39
7	**Gannet**	86–96	34–38
8	**Golden eagle**	76–91	30–36
9	**White-tailed sea eagle**	69–91	27–36
10	**Capercaillie (male)**	82–90	32–35

Because of its size, the mute swan (which weighs up to 12 kg/26 lb) needs very strong and long feathers to power its flight: its outer wing feathers can be up to 45 cm (18 in) long, but even so each feather weighs only 15 g (½ oz).

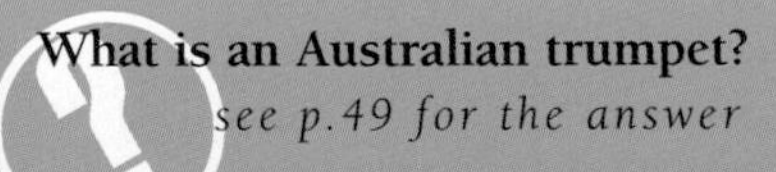

What is an Australian trumpet?
see p.49 for the answer

A A swan
B A marine snail
C A venomous spider

OCEAN FLYER

The subject of Coleridge's poem The Rime of the Ancient Mariner, *the albatross has a massive wingspan and is able to soar over the oceans for days at a time.*

TOP 10 BIRDS WITH THE LARGEST WINGSPANS

(Bird/wingspan in m/ft)

❶ **Marabou stork**, 4.0/13 ❷ **Albatross**, 3.7/12 ❸ **Trumpeter swan**, 3.4/11 ❹ = **Mute swan**, 3.1/10; = **Whooper swan**, 3.1/10; = **Grey pelican**, 3.1/10; = **California condor**, 3.1/10; = **Black vulture**, 3.1/10 ❾ = **Great bustard**, 2.7/9; = **Kori bustard**, 2.7/9

TOP 10 HEAVIEST FLIGHTED BIRDS

	BIRD	WINGSPAN M	FT	WEIGHT KG	LB	OZ
1	Great bustard	2.7	9	20.9	46	1
2	Trumpeter swan	3.4	11	16.8	37	1
3	Mute swan	3.1	10	16.3	35	15
4	=Albatross	3.7	12	15.8	34	13
	=Whooper swan	3.1	10	15.8	34	13
6	Manchurian crane	2.1	7	14.9	32	14
7	Kori bustard	2.7	9	13.6	30	0
8	Grey pelican	3.1	10	13.0	28	11
9	Black vulture	3.1	10	12.5	27	8
10	Griffon vulture	2.1	7	12.0	26	7

Wing size does not necessarily correspond to weight in flighted birds. The 4-m (13-ft) wingspan of the marabou stork beats all the birds listed here, yet its body weight is normally no heavier than any of these. When laden with a meal of carrion, however, the marabou can double its weight and may fail to take off.

"A LITTLE BIRD TOLD ME"

This phrase is often used to announce that one has information but may not be willing to reveal the source of it. Birds as messengers are legendary, but this expression, like so many others, has its origin in the Bible. In the Book of Ecclesiastes (9:20), the writer warns those who complain against kings and the rich and powerful that "a bird of the air shall carry the voice, and that which hath wings shall tell the matter".

WHY DO WE SAY?

TOP 10 MOST COMMON BIRDS IN THE UK

	BIRD	ESTIMATED NO. OF PAIRS
1	Wren	7,600,000
2	Chaffinch	5,800,000
3	Robin	4,500,000
4	Blackbird	4,200,000
5	Blue tit	3,500,000
6	=House sparrow	2,700,000
	=Woodpigeon	2,700,000
8	Willow warbler	2,300,000
9	Dunnock	1,900,000
10	Meadow pipit	1,800,000

Source: *Royal Society for the Protection of Birds*

SWANNING AROUND

A heavyweight among flighted birds, exceptional specimens of the mute swan may top 22.5 kg (49 lb 10 oz) and have wingspans of up to 3.7 m (12 ft).

Cats, Dogs & Pets

TOP 10 ★ FILMS STARRING DOGS

	FILM	YEAR
1	*101 Dalmatians*	1996
2	*One Hundred and One Dalmatians**	1961
3	*Lady and the Tramp**	1955
4	*Oliver & Company**	1988
5	*Turner & Hooch*	1989
6	*The Fox and the Hound**	1981
7	*Beethoven*	1992
8	*Homeward Bound II: Lost in San Francisco*	1996
9	*Beethoven's 2nd*	1993
10	*K-9*	1991

* *Animated*

Man's best friend has been stealing scenes since the earliest years of film-making, with the 1905 low-budget *Rescued by Rover* outstanding as one of the most successful productions of the pioneer period. The numerous silent era films starring Rin Tin Tin, an ex-German army dog who emigrated to the US, and his successor Lassie, whose long series of feature and TV films date from the 1940s onwards, are among the most enduring in cinematic history.

TOP 10 ★ DOG BREEDS IN THE UK

	BREED	NO. REGISTERED BY KENNEL CLUB
1	Labrador retriever	33,398
2	German shepherd (Alsatian)	17,905
3	West Highland white terrier	14,419
4	Cocker spaniel	13,378
5	Golden retriever	12,730
6	English springer spaniel	12,409
7	Cavalier King Charles spaniel	11,577
8	Staffordshire bull terrier	9,900
9	Boxer	9,894
10	Yorkshire terrier	7,339

The 10 principal breeds of dogs registered by the Kennel Club in 1999 remained identical to those of the previous year. Independent surveys of dog ownership present a similar picture, though with certain other popular breeds (among them the Jack Russell, border collie and poodle) making a stronger showing than in the Kennel Club's list.

TOP 10 ★ PEDIGREE CAT BREEDS IN THE UK

	BREED	NO. REGISTERED BY CAT FANCY
1	Persian long hair	7,815
2	Siamese	4,596
3	British short hair	4,563
4	Burmese	3,190
5	Birman	2,207
6	Bengal	1,503
7	Maine coon	1,390
8	Oriental short hair	1,321
9	Ragdoll	933
10	Exotic short hair	744

This is based on a total of 32,327 cats registered with the Governing Council of the Cat Fancy .

TOP 10 ★ MOST INTELLIGENT DOG BREEDS

1 Border collie
2 Poodle
3 German shepherd (Alsatian)
4 Golden retriever
5 Doberman pinscher
6 Shetland sheepdog
7 Labrador retriever
8 Papillon
9 Rottweiler
10 Australian cattle dog

Source: *Stanley Coren, The Intelligence of Dogs*

TOP 10 DOGS' NAMES IN THE UK

1 Max 2 Ben 3 Charlie 4 Molly 5 Holly 6 Sam 7 Barney 8 Jake 9 Lucy 10 Rosie

Source: *PetPlan Pet Insurance*

TOP DOGS

Labrador retrievers are the most popular pedigree dogs in both the US and the UK, where they were first bred as gundogs in the 19th century.

Background image: **GUINEA PIGS**

TOP 10 CATS' NAMES IN THE UK

1 Charlie 2 Molly 3 Oscar 4 Tigger 5 Jasper 6 Poppy 7 Smudge 8 Lucy 9 Rosie 10 Sophie

Source: *PetPlan Pet Insurance*

WHAT'S NEW, PUSSYCAT?

Although their role as household mouse exterminators is less significant today, cats maintain their place among the world's favourite animals.

TOP 10 PETS IN THE UK

	PET	NO. OWNED, 1999
1	Goldfish	16,800,000
2	Tropical fish	9,100,000
3	Cat	7,700,000
4	Dog	6,700,000
5	Rabbit	1,500,000
6	Bird (excluding budgerigar)	1,300,000
7	=Budgerigar	1,000,000
	=Hamster	1,000,000
9	Guinea pig	800,000
10	Marine fish	700,000

Source: *Pet Food Manufacturers' Association*

Half of the households in the UK own a pet, ranging from dogs, cats, and rabbits to more exotic snakes and spiders.

"IN THE DOGHOUSE"

In J. M. Barrie's famous children's play, *Peter Pan* (1904), irascible Mr. Darling mistreats the dog-nursemaid, Nana, as a result of which the Darling children – Wendy, John, and Michael – leave home. As a penance, Mr. Darling lives in the doghouse until the children return. Mr. Darling was based on Arthur Llewelyn Davies, the real-life father of the boys on whom Barrie based the story, and Nana was Barrie's own dog, Luath.

WHY DO WE SAY?

TOP 10 RABBITS' NAMES IN THE UK

1 Thumper 2 Flopsy 3 Charlie 4 Fudge 5 Rosie 6 Smokey 7 Snowy 8 Daisy 9 George 10 Molly

Source: *PetPlan Pet Insurance*

FURRY FAVOURITES

Although Flopsy is second choice, Beatrix Potter's more famous creations of Peter and Benjamin are surprisingly absent from the Top 10 rabbits' names.

Creepy Crawlies 1

TOP 10

FASTEST FLYING INSECTS

	SPECIES	KM/H	MPH
1	**Hawkmoth** (*Sphingidaei*)	53.6	33.3
2	=**West Indian butterfly** (*Nymphalidae prepona*)	48.0	30.0
	=**Deer bot fly** (*Cephenemyia pratti*)	48.0	30.0
4	**Deer bot fly** (Chrysops)	40.0	25.0
5	**West Indian butterfly** (*Hesperiidae* sp.)	30.0	18.6
6	**Dragonfly** (*Anax parthenope*)	28.6	17.8
7	**Hornet** (*Vespa crabro*)	21.4	13.3
8	**Bumble bee** (*Bombus lapidarius*)	17.9	11.1
9	**Horsefly** (*Tabanus bovinus*)	14.3	8.9
10	**Honey bee** (*Apis millefera*)	11.6	7.2

Few accurate assessments of these speeds have been attempted, and this list reflects only the results of those scientific studies recognized by entomologists.

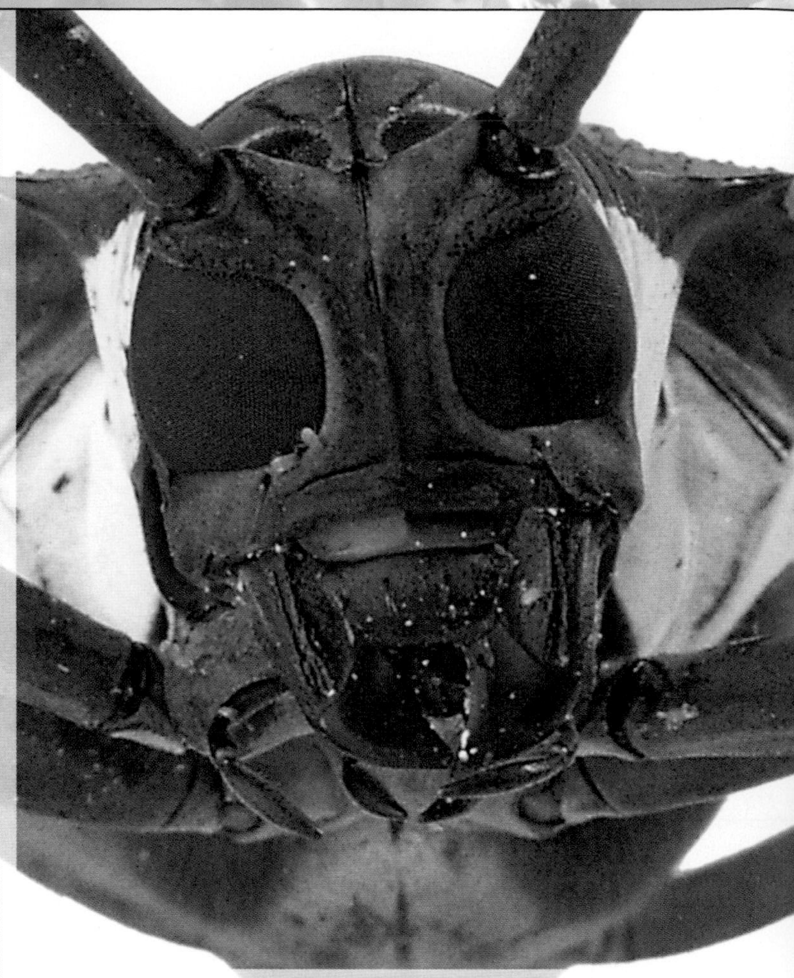

BEETLE BEATS ALL

This Red-spotted longhorn beetle is one of about 400,000 beetles identified so far. This makes the beetle the most common known species of insect.

TOP 10

LARGEST MOTHS

	MOTH	WINGSPAN MM	IN
1	**Atlas moth** (*Attacus atlas*)	300	11.8
2	**Owlet moth** (*Thysania agrippina*)*	290	11.4
3	***Haematopis grataria***	260	10.2
4	**Hercules emperor moth** (*Coscinocera hercules*)	210	8.3
5	**Malagasy silk moth** (*Argema mitraei*)	180	7.1
6	***Eacles imperialis***	175	6.9
7	=**Common emperor moth** (*Bunaea alcinoe*)	160	6.3
	=**Giant peacock moth** (*Saturnia pyri*)	160	6.3
9	**Gray moth** (*Brahmaea wallichii*)	155	6.1
10	=**Black witch** (*Ascalapha odorata*)	150	5.9
	=**Regal moth** (*Citheronia regalis*)	150	5.9
	=**Polyphemus moth** (*Antheraea polyphemus*)	150	5.9

* *Exceptional specimen measured at 308 mm (12¼ in)*

TOP 10

MOST COMMON INSECTS*

	SPECIES	APPROXIMATE NO. OF KNOWN SPECIES
1	**Beetles** (*Coleoptera*)	400,000
2	**Butterflies and moths** (*Lepidoptera*)	165,000
3	**Ants, bees, and wasps** (*Hymenoptera*)	140,000
4	**True flies** (*Diptera*)	120,000
5	**Bugs** (*Hemiptera*)	90,000
6	**Crickets, grasshoppers, and locusts** (*Orthoptera*)	20,000
7	**Caddisflies** (*Trichoptera*)	10,000
8	**Lice** (*Phthiraptera/Psocoptera*)	7,000
9	**Dragonflies and damselflies** (*Odonata*)	5,500
10	**Lacewings** (*Neuroptera*)	4,700

* *By number of known species*

This list includes only species that have been discovered and named: it is surmised that many thousands of species still await discovery.

Did You Know? The heaviest of all insects is the Goliath beetle, which can weigh up to 100 g (3½ oz), or more than twice the weight of a golf ball.

LEGGING IT TO THE TOP

The Haplophilus subterraneus *centipede measures up to 70 mm (2¾ in) and has 89 pairs of legs. It is interesting to note that all centipedes always have an odd number of body segments (although the number of legs is, of course, always even!).*

TOP 10

CREATURES WITH THE MOST LEGS

	CREATURE	AVERAGE NO. OF LEGS
1	Millipede *Illacme plenipes*	750
2	Centipede *Himantarum gabrielis*	354
3	Centipede *Haplophilus subterraneus*	178
4	Millipedes*	30
5	Symphylans	24
6	Caterpillars*	16
7	Woodlice	14
8	Crabs, shrimps	10
9	Spiders	8
10	Insects	6

* *Most species*

Because "centipede" means 100 feet and "millipede" 1,000 feet, many people believe that centipedes have 100 legs and millipedes 1,000. However, despite their names and depending on their species, centipedes, have anything from 28 to 354 legs and millipedes up to 400, with the record standing at more than 700. The other principal difference between them is that each body segment of a centipede has two legs, whereas that of a millipede has four.

BIG WING

The male African giant swallowtails, Papilio antimachus, *are Africa's largest butterflies, with wingspans of up to an impressive 230 mm (9⅛ in).*

TOP 10

LARGEST BUTTERFLIES

	BUTTERFLY	WINGSPAN MM	WINGSPAN IN
1	Queen Alexandra's birdwing	280	11.0
2	African giant swallowtail	230	9.1
3	Goliath birdwing	210	8.3
4	=*Trogonoptera trojana*	200	7.9
	=Buru opalescent birdwing	200	7.9
	=*Troides hypolitus*	200	7.9
7	=*Ornithoptera lydius*	190	7.5
	=Chimaera birdwing	190	7.5
	=*Troides magellanus*	190	7.5
	=*Troides miranda*	190	7.5

Creepy Crawlies 2

TOP 10 LARGEST SNAILS

(Species/length in mm/in)

1 Australian trumpet *(Syrinx aruanus)*, 770/30¼ **2 Horse conch** *(Pleuroploc filamentosa)*, 580/22¼ **3 = Baler shell** *(Voluta amphora)*, 480/18¾; = **Triton's trumpet** *(Charonia tritonis)*, 480/18¾ **5 Beck's volute** *(Voluta becki)*, 470/18½ **6 Umbilicate volute** *(Voluta umbilicalis)*, 420/16½ **7 Madagascar helmet** *(Cassis madagascariensis)*, 409/16 **8 Spider conch** *(Lambis truncata)*, 400/15¾ **9 Knobbly trumpet** *(Charonia nodifera)*, 390/15¼ **10 Goliath conch** *(Strombus goliath)*, 380/15

TOP 10 DEADLIEST SPIDERS

	SPIDER/LOCATION
1	**Banana spider** *(Phonenutria nigriventer)*, Central and South America
2	**Sydney funnel web** *(Atrax robustus)*, Australia
3	**Wolf spider** *(Lycosa raptoria/erythrognatha)*, Central and South America
4	**Black widow** (Latrodectus species), worldwide
5	**Violin spider/Recluse spider**, worldwide
6	**Sac spider**, Southern Europe
7	**Tarantula** *(Eurypelma rubropilosum)*, Neotropics
8	**Tarantula** *(Acanthoscurria atrox)*, Neotropics
9	**Tarantula** *(Lasiodora klugi)*, Neotropics
10	**Tarantula** *(Pamphobeteus species)*, Neotropics

This list ranks spiders according to their "lethal potential" – their venom yield divided by their venom potency. The Banana spider, for example, yields 6 mg of venom, with 1 mg the estimated lethal dose in man. However, few spiders are capable of killing humans – there were just 14 recorded deaths caused by Black widows in the US in the whole of the 19th century.

TOP 10 MOST POPULAR US STATE INSECTS

	INSECT/STATES	NO.
1	**Honey bee**, Arkansas, Georgia, Kansas, Louisiana, Maine, Mississippi, Missouri, Nebraska, New Hampshire, New Jersey, North Carolina, South Dakota, Utah, Vermont, Wisconsin	15
2	**Swallowtail butterfly**, Florida (giant/zebra longwing), Georgia (tiger), Mississippi (spicebush), Ohio (tiger), Oklahoma (black), Oregon (Oregon), Virginia (tiger), Wyoming (western)	8
3	**Ladybird beetle/ladybug**, Delaware (convergent), Iowa, Massachusetts, New York (nine-spotted), New Hampshire (two-spotted), Ohio, Tennessee (ladybug)	7
4	**Monarch butterfly**, Alabama, Idaho, Illinois, Texas, Vermont	5
5	**Firefly**, Pennsylvania, Tennessee	2
6	=**Baltimore checkerspot butterfly**, Maryland	1
	=**California dogface butterfly**, California	1
	=**Carolina mantis**, South Carolina	1
	=**Colorado hairstreak butterfly**, Colorado	1
	=**European praying mantis**, Connecticut	1
	=**Four-spotted skimmer dragonfly**, Alaska	1
	=**Green darner dragonfly**, Texas	1
	= **Karner blue butterfly**, New Hampshire	1
	= **Tarantula hawk wasp**, New Mexico	1
	= **Viceroy butterfly**, Kentucky	1

READY TO STRIKE

Found only in New South Wales, male Sydney funnel web spiders are, unusually, more dangerous than the females.

SNAIL'S PACE

Although exceeded by marine species, the Giant African land snail is the largest terrestrial mollusc. Exceptional specimens may reach almost 400 mm (15.5 in) in length and weigh 900 g (2 lb).

THE 10 COUNTRIES WITH THE MOST THREATENED INVERTEBRATES

(Country/threatened invertebrate species)

1 **USA**, 594 2 **Australia**, 281 3 **South Africa**, 101 4 **Portugal**, 67 5 **France**, 61 6 **Spain**, 57 7 **Tanzania**, 46 8 = **Japan**, 45; = **Dem. Rep. of Congo**, 45 10 = **Austria**, 41; = **Italy**, 41

Source: *International Union for the Conservation of Nature*

TOP 10 LARGEST MOLLUSCS*

	SPECIES	CLASS	LENGTH MM	LENGTH IN
1	**Giant squid** *(Architeuthis sp.)*	Cephalopod	16,764	660#
2	**Giant clam** *(Tridacna gigas)*	Marine bivalve	1,300	51
3	**Australian trumpet**	Marine snail	770	30
4	***Hexabranchus sanguineus***	Sea slug	520	20
5	***Carinaria cristata***	Heteropod	500	19
6	**Steller's coat of mail shell** *(Cryptochiton stelleri)*	Chiton	470	18
7	**Freshwater mussel** *(Cristaria plicata)*	Freshwater bivalve	300	11
8	**Giant African snail** *(Achatina achatina)*	Land snail	200	7
9	**Tusk shell** *(Dentalium vernedi)*	Scaphopod	138	5
10	**Apple snail** *(Pila werneri)*	Freshwater snail	125	4

* *Largest species within each class*

\# *Estimated; actual length unknown*

Which breed of dog is regarded as the most intelligent?

see p.44 for the answer

A Border collie
B Saint Bernard
C Afghan hound

TOP 10 TALLEST TREES IN THE UK*

	TREE	LOCATION	HEIGHT M	HEIGHT FT
1	= Douglas fir	The Hermitage, Dunkeld, Tayside	64.5	212
	= Douglas fir	Dunans, Strathclyde	64.5	212
3	Sitka spruce	Private estate, Strathearn, Tayside	61.5	202
4	Grand fir	Ardkinglass Arboretum, Strathclyde	60.0	197
5	Giant sequoia	Castle Leod, Strathpeffer, Highland	53.0	174
6	= Noble fir	Ardkinglass House, Strathclyde	52.0	171
	= Norway spruce	Moniac Glen, Highland	52.0	171
	= Japanese larch	Diana's Grove, Blair Castle, Tayside	52.0	171
9	Western hemlock	Benmore Younger Botanic Gardens, Argyll, Strathclyde	51.0	167
10	Caucasian fir	Cragside, Northumberland	50.0	164

* *The tallest known example of each of the 10 tallest species*

Source: *The Tree Register of the British Isles*

ON TAP

In the 20th century, annual world demand for natural rubber, especially from the automotive industry, increased from under 50,000 to over 6 million tonnes.

TOP 10 ★ RUBBER-PRODUCING COUNTRIES

	COUNTRY	1998 PRODUCTION TONNES
1	Thailand	2,162,411
2	Indonesia	1,564,324
3	Malaysia	1,082,400
4	India	542,000
5	China	450,000
6	Philippines	200,000
7	Vietnam	180,700
8	Côte d'Ivoire	115,668
9	Sri Lanka	105,783
10	Nigeria	90,000
	World total	6,780,089

Source: *Food and Agriculture Organization of the United Nations*

TOP 10 ★ TIMBER-PRODUCING COUNTRIES

	COUNTRY	1998 PRODUCTION CU M	CU FT
1	USA	494,937,000	17,478,536,826
2	China	313,017,000	11,054,092,059
3	India	306,455,000	10,822,357,195
4	Brazil	220,313,000	7,780,280,892
5	Indonesia	202,988,500	7,168,471,891
6	Canada	191,178,000	6,751,387,981
7	Nigeria	117,387,000	4,145,483,167
8	Russia	83,968,000	2,965,302,211
9	Sweden	60,224,000	2,126,790,686
10	Ethiopia	52,310,000	1,847,310,388
	World total	3,385,623,000	119,562,158,989

Source: *Food and Agriculture Organization of the United Nations*

TREE TOPS

The USA leads the world in timber production, supplying the requirements of industries such as construction and paper manufacture.

TOP 10

MOST COMMON TREES IN THE UK

	TREE	PERCENTAGE OF TOTAL FOREST AREA
1	Sitka spruce	28
2	Scots pine	13
3	Oak	9
4	Lodgepole pine	7
5=	Larch	6
=	Norway spruce	6
7=	Ash	4
=	Beech	4
=	Birch	4
10	Sycamore	3

Source: *Forestry Commission*

TOP 10

COUNTRIES WITH THE LARGEST AREAS OF FOREST

	COUNTRY	AREA SQ KM	SQ MILES
1	Russia	7,659,120	2,957,203
2	Canada	4,940,000	1,907,345
3	Brazil	4,880,000	1,884,179
4	USA	2,959,900	1,142,824
5	Dem. Rep. of Congo	1,738,000	671,046
6	Australia	1,450,000	559,848
7	China	1,304,960	503,848
8	Indonesia	1,117,740	431,562
9	Peru	848,000	327,415
10	India	685,000	264,480
	World total	41,380,090	15,976,944

The world's forests occupy some 28 per cent of the total land area of the planet. Almost 45 per cent of the area of Russia is forested, representing a total area that is almost the size of Australia.

NATURAL BEAUTY

The largest National Forest in the US, the Tongass in Alaska, is a magnificent wilderness that encompasses mountains, rivers, glaciers, and islands. This vast forest is over three times the size of the next forest in the Top 10.

TOP 10

LARGEST NATIONAL FORESTS IN THE US

	FOREST	LOCATION	AREA SQ KM	SQ MILES
1	Tongass National Forest	Sitka, Alaska	67,177	25,937
2	Chugach National Forest	Anchorage, Alaska	21,448	8,281
3	Toiyabe National Forest	Sparks, Nevada	12,950	5,000
4	Tonto National Forest	Phoenix, Arizona	11,735	4,531
5=	Boise National Forest	Boise, Idaho	10,925	4,218
=	Gila National Forest	Silver City, New Mexico	10,925	4,218
7=	Humboldt National Forest	Elko, Nevada	10,116	3,906
=	Challis National Forest	Challis, Idaho	10,116	3,906
9=	Shoshone National Forest	Cody, Wyoming	9,712	3,750
=	Flathead National Forest	Kalispell, Montana	9,712	3,750

The list's No. 1 is actually larger than all 10 of the smallest states in the United States and the District of Columbia. Even the much smaller No. 2 is larger than Connecticut.

Did You Know? A vast area of the Tunguska Forest of Siberia was flattened in an instant on 30 June 1908 when a meteorite – or perhaps part of Encke's comet – exploded in the sky above it.

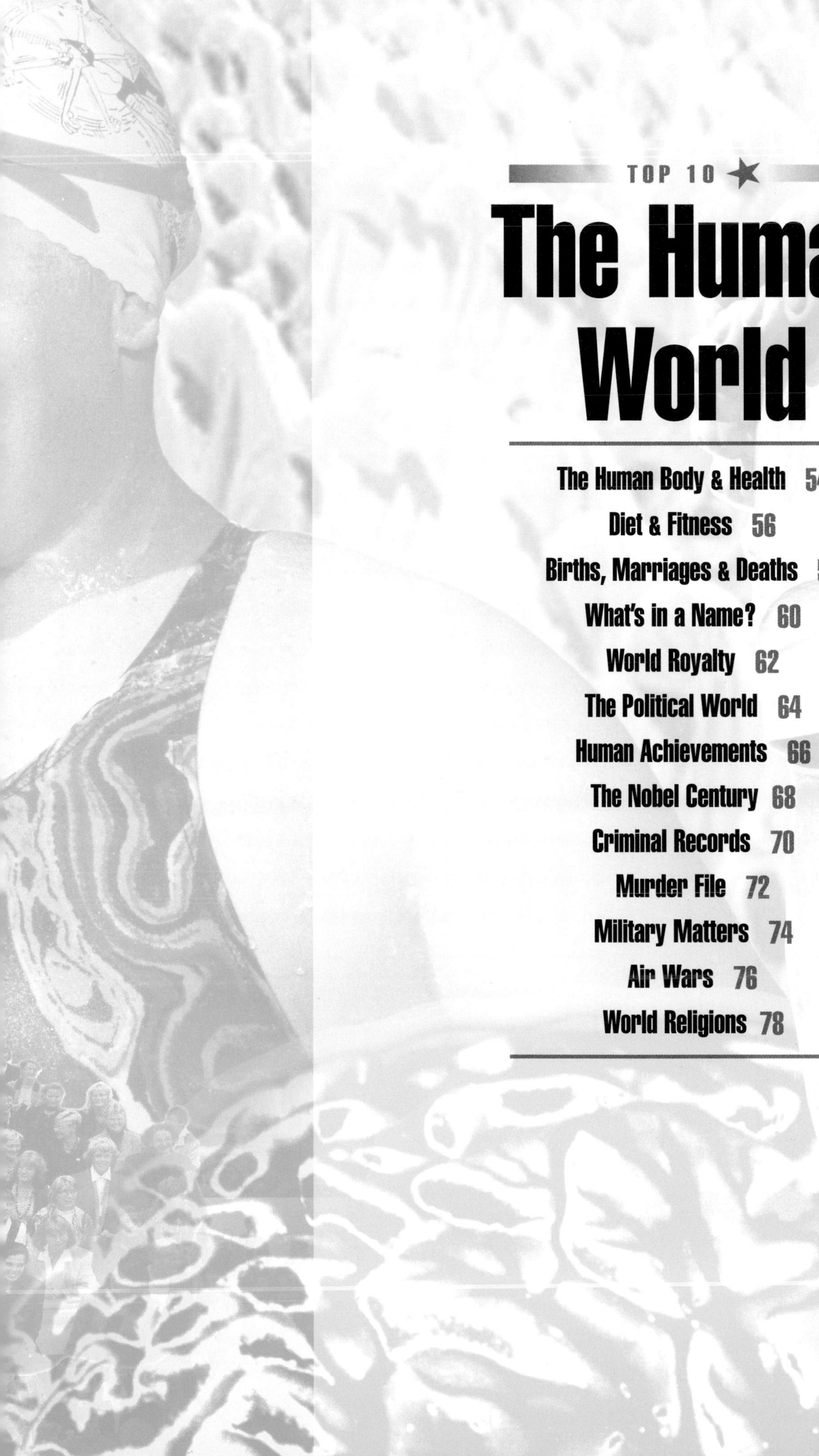

TOP 10 ★

The Human World

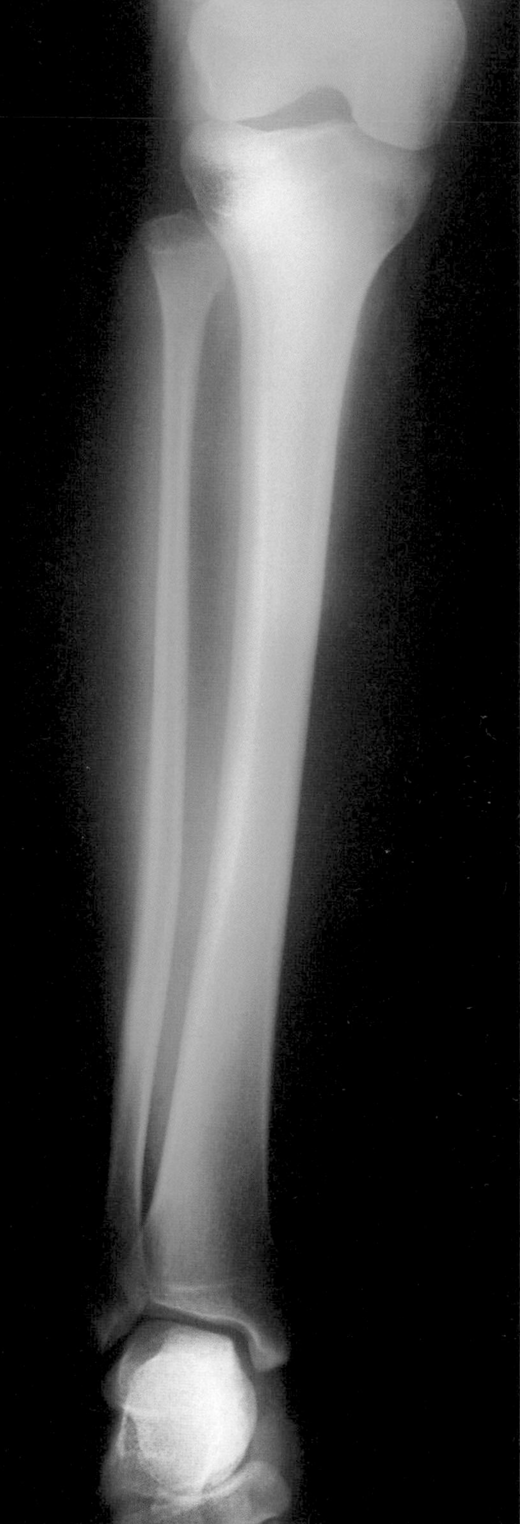

THE WINNING LEG

The second longest bone, the tibia is named after the Latin word for a flute, which it resembles in shape and length. The three longest bones are all in the leg.

TOP 10

COUNTRIES THAT SPEND THE MOST ON HEALTH CARE

	COUNTRY	HEALTH SPENDING PER CAPITA ($)
1	USA	4,093
2	Switzerland	3,603
3	Germany	2,677
4	Norway	2,622
5	Japan	2,442
6	Denmark	2,388
7	France	2,349
8	Sweden	2,222
9	Austria	2,012
10	Netherlands	1,978
	UK	1,454

Source: *World Bank,* World Development Indicators 1999

TOP 10

LONGEST BONES IN THE HUMAN BODY

	BONE	AVERAGE LENGTH CM	IN
1	**Femur** (thighbone – upper leg)	50.50	19.88
2	**Tibia** (shinbone – inner lower leg)	43.03	16.94
3	**Fibula** (outer lower leg)	40.50	15.94
4	**Humerus** (upper arm)	36.46	14.35
5	**Ulna** (inner lower arm)	28.20	11.10
6	**Radius** (outer lower arm)	26.42	10.40
7	**7th rib**	24.00	9.45
8	**8th rib**	23.00	9.06
9	**Innominate bone** (hipbone – half pelvis)	18.50	7.28
10	**Sternum** (breastbone)	17.00	6.69

These are average dimensions of the bones of an adult male measured from their extremities (ribs are curved, and the pelvis is measured diagonally). The same bones in the female skeleton are usually 6 to 13 per cent smaller, with the exception of the sternum, which is virtually identical.

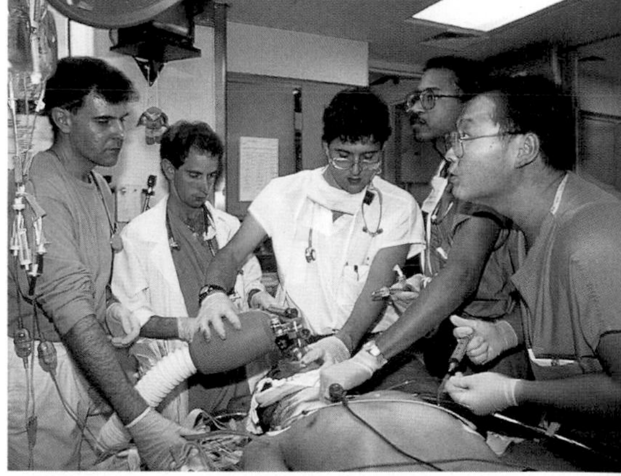

ER, USA

The world's hospital emergency rooms have to be equipped to treat victims of everything from minor injuries to the major traumas of vehicle accidents, natural disasters, and terrorist activities.

TOP 10

MOST COMMON REASONS FOR VISITS TO THE DOCTOR

	COMPLAINT	RATE*
1	**Acute upper respiratory infections**	772
2	**Acute bronchitis and bronchitis**	719
3	**Asthma**	425
4	**Disorders of conjunctiva** (eye)	415
5	**Hypertension** (high blood pressure)	412
6=	**Disorders of external ear**	409
=	**Acute pharyngitis** (sore throat)	409
8	**Acute tonsillitis**	407
9	**Ill-defined intestinal infections**	394
10	**Various unspecified disorders of back**	372

* *Annually, per 10,000 patients*

TOP 10 MOST COMMON HOSPITAL CASUALTY COMPLAINTS

1 Cuts 2 Bruises 3 Dog bites 4 Sprained ankles 5 Eye injuries 6 Head injuries 7 Minor burns 8 Fractures 9 Upper respiratory tract infections 10 Gastroenteritis

TOP 10

MOST COMMON TYPES OF ILLNESS

	TYPE	NEW CASES ANNUALLY
1	Diarrhoea (including dysentery)	4,002,000,000
2	Malaria	up to 500,000,000
3	Acute lower respiratory infections	395,000,000
4	Occupational injuries	350,000,000
5	Occupational diseases	217,000,000
6	Trichomoniasis	170,000,000
7	Mood (affective) disorders	122,865,000
8	Chlamydial infections	89,000,000
9	Alcohol dependence syndrome	75,000,000
10	Gonococcal (bacterial) infections	62,000,000

Source: *World Health Organization*

TOP 10

MOST COMMON PHOBIAS

	OBJECT OF PHOBIA	MEDICAL TERM
1	Spiders	Arachnephobia or arachnophobia
2	People and social situations	Anthropophobia or sociophobia
3	Flying	Aerophobia or aviatophobia
4	Open spaces	Agoraphobia, cenophobia or kenophobia
5	Confined spaces	Claustrophobia, cleisiophobia, cleithrophobia, or clithrophobia
6	=Vomiting	Emetophobia or emitophobia
	=Heights	Acrophobia, altophobia, hypsophobia, or hypsiphobia
8	Cancer	Carcinomaphobia, carcinophobia, carcinomatophobia, cancerphobia, or cancerophobia
9	Thunderstorms	Brontophobia or keraunophobia
10	=Death	Necrophobia or thanatophobia
	=Heart disease	Cardiophobia

TOP 10

MOST COMMON ELEMENTS IN THE HUMAN BODY

	ELEMENT	AVERAGE WEIGHT* G	OZ
1	Oxygen	45,500	1,608
2	Carbon	12,600	445
3	Hydrogen	7,000	247
4	Nitrogen	2,100	74
5	Calcium	1,050	37
6	Phosphorus	700	25
7	Sulphur	175	6
8	Potassium	140	5
9	=Chlorine	105	4
	=Sodium	105	4

* *Average in 70-kg (154-lb) person*

The Top 10 elements account for more than 99 per cent of the total, with the balance comprising minute quantities of metallic elements including iron, zinc, tin, and aluminium. Each has one or more specific functions: oxygen is essential for energy production, carbon and hydrogen are major cell components, while nitrogen is vital for DNA and most body functions.

TOP 10

LARGEST HUMAN ORGANS

	ORGAN		AVERAGE WEIGHT G	OZ
1	Skin		10,886	384.0
2	Liver		1,560	55.0
3	Brain	male	1,408	49.7
		female	1,263	44.6
4	Lungs	right	580	20.5
		left	510	18.0
		total	1,090	38.5
5	Heart	male	315	11.1
		female	265	9.3
6	Kidneys	right	140	4.9
		left	150	5.3
		total	290	10.2
7	Spleen		170	6.0
8	Pancreas		98	3.5
9	Thyroid		35	1.2
10	Prostate (male only)		20	0.7

This list is based on average immediate post-mortem weights, as recorded by St. Bartholemew's Hospital, London, and other sources during a 10-year period. Various instances of organs far in excess of the average have been recorded, including male brains of over 2,000 g (70.6 oz). The Victorians believed that the heavier the brain, the greater the intelligence, and were impressed by the recorded weights of 1,658 g (58 oz) for author William Makepeace Thackeray.

WEIGHTY MATTER

The modern technique of Magnetic Resonance Imaging (MRI) enables us to view the human brain, the human body's third-largest organ.

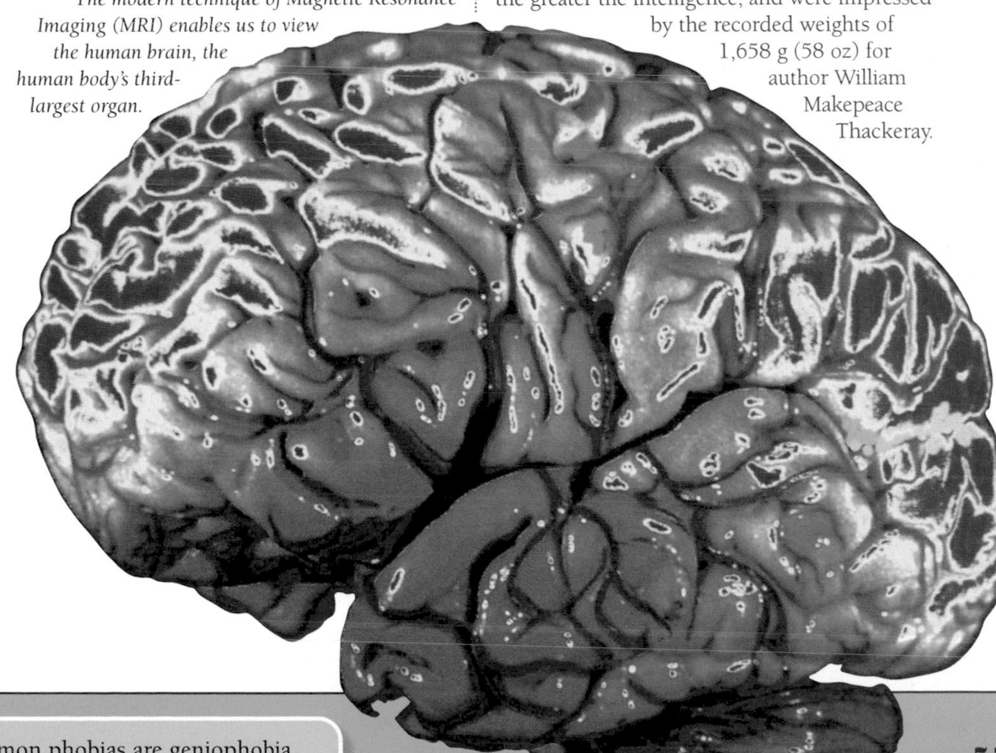

Did You Know? Among the least-common phobias are geniophobia (fear of eggshells,) barophobia (gravity), apeirophobia (infinity), and linonophobia (string).

Diet & Fitness

TOP 10 ★

FOODS WITH THE BIGGEST INCREASE IN CONSUMPTION IN THE UK*

	PRODUCT	CONSUMPTION PER CAPITA PER WEEK (G) 1988	1998	INCREASE %
1	Skimmed milk	542	1,143	110
2	Low-fat and reduced-fat spreads	38	69	81
3	Pickles and sauces	63	96	52
4	Processed potatoes, frozen	76	111	46
5	Processed potatoes, not frozen	62	89	43
6	Yoghurt and fromage frais	91	129	41
7	Buns, scones, and tea-cakes	32	41	28
8	Vegetable and salad oils	41	50	22
9	Cakes and pastries	73	88	20
10	Fresh fruit	595	716	20

* *Based on Ministry of Agriculture, Fisheries and* Food National Food Survey

TOP 10 ACTIVITIES FOR WEIGHT MANAGEMENT

❶ Walking ❷ Cycling ❸ Swimming ❹ Active hobbies (gardening, DIY, etc.) ❺ Low-impact aerobics ❻ Jogging ❼ Weight training ❽ Vigorous sports ❾ Housework ❿ Switching off the television

Source: Slimming World

TOP 10 ★

PROTEIN CONSUMERS

	COUNTRY	PROTEIN CONSUMPTION PER CAPITA PER DAY GM	OZ
1	Greece	114.9	4.05
2	Portugal	113.5	4.00
3	Iceland	113.3	3.99
4	France	113.1	3.98
5	USA	112.3	3.96
6	Ireland	110.6	3.90
7	Malta	110.0	3.88
8	Cyprus	109.3	3.85
9	Italy	108.6	3.83
10	New Zealand	108.1	3.81
	UK	94.8	3.34
	World average	73.9	2.60

Source: *Food and Agricultural Organization of the UN*

TOP 10 ★

LEAST PROTEIN CONSUMERS

	COUNTRY	PROTEIN CONSUMPTION PER CAPITA PER DAY GM	OZ
1	Dem. Rep. of Congo	28.1	0.99
2	Mozambique	34.9	1.23
3	Liberia	36.5	1.28
4	Angola	40.5	1.42
5	Haiti	41.0	1.44
6	Comoros	42.9	1.51
7	Republic of Congo	43.1	1.52
8	Sierra Leone	43.6	1.53
9	Djibouti	43.7	1.54
10	Central African Republic	43.8	1.54

Source: *Food and Agricultural Organization of the UN*

TOP 10 ★

FOODS WITH THE BIGGEST DECREASE IN CONSUMPTION IN THE UK*

	PRODUCT	CONSUMPTION PER CAPITA PER WEEK (G) 1988	1998	DECREASE %
1	Margarine	108	26	76
2	Whole milk	1,557	713	54
3	Flour	103	55	46
4=	Beef and veal	180	109	39
=	Sugar	196	119	39
6	Oatmeal and oat products	18	11	38
7=	Eggs	160	104	35
=	Wholemeal and brown bread	233	150	35
9	Butter	57	39	31
10=	Honey, preserves, syrup, and treacle	53	37	30
=	Fresh potatoes	1,033	715	30

* *Based on Ministry of Agriculture, Fisheries and* Food National Food Survey

TOP 10 ★

LEAST FAT CONSUMERS

	COUNTRY	FAT CONSUMPTION PER CAPITA PER DAY GM	OZ
1	Burundi	11.0	0.38
2	Eritrea	19.5	0.68
3	Bangladesh	22.0	0.77
4	Rwanda	22.4	0.79
5	Ethiopia	22.7	0.80
6	Afghanistan	24.0	0.84
7	Laos	25.7	0.90
8	Dem. Rep. of Congo	27.7	0.95
9	Uganda	28.0	0.98
10	Zambia	29.7	1.04

Source: *Food and Agricultural Organization of the UN*

SINK OR SWIM

Swimming promotes all-round fitness with reduced danger of muscle-strain, and is thus considered one of the most valuable activities for slimmers.

Background image: **LETTUCE**

TOP 10

MOST FATTENING FOODS*

	FOOD	ENERGY DENSITY KCALS PER 100G
1	Cooking oils/fats#	891–899
2	Butter/margarine+	739
3	Hollandaise sauce	707
4	Mayonnaise	691
5	Creamed coconut	669
6	French dressing	651
7	Nuts★	630
8	Peanut butter	623
9	Tahini paste	607
10	Pork scratchings	606

* *Based on most concentrated source of Calories*

\# *Including coconut, cod liver, olive, lard, and dripping*

\+ *Margarine 737 kcals*

★ *Average*

Source: Slimming World

TOP 10

LEAST FATTENING FOODS*

	FOOD	ENERGY DENSITY KCALS PER 100G
1	=Celery	7
	=Rhubarb	7
	=Chicory, boiled	7
4	=Globe artichoke, boiled	8
	=Oyster mushrooms	8
6	Marrow, boiled	9
7	=Cucumber	10
	=Canned beansprouts, drained	10
9	=Mushrooms, boiled	11
	=Fennel, boiled	11
	=Swede, boiled	11
	=Canned bamboo shoots	11

* *Based on least concentrated source of Calories*

Source: Slimming World

TOP 10

FAT CONSUMERS

	COUNTRY	FAT CONSUMPTION PER CAPITA PER DAY GM	OZ
1	France	164.0	5.78
2	Austria	161.4	5.69
3	Belgium and Luxembourg	159.6	5.63
4	Greece	153.4	5.41
5	Italy	146.8	5.18
6	Cyprus	146.7	5.17
7	Spain	144.7	5.10
8	Germany	144.4	5.09
9	Switzerland	143.6	5.06
10	USA	142.8	5.03
	UK	141.0	4.97
	World average	71.7	2.53

Source: *Food and Agricultural Organization of the UN*

TOP 10

CALORIE CONSUMERS

	COUNTRY	AVERAGE DAILY PER CAPITA CONSUMPTION
1	USA	3,699.1
2	Portugal	3,667.0
3	Greece	3,648.6
4	Belgium and Luxembourg	3,619.2
5	Ireland	3,565.1
6	Austria	3,535.8
7	Turkey	3,524.7
8	France	3,518.4
9	Italy	3,506.9
10	Cyprus	3,429.2
	UK	3,276.0

Source: *Food and Agricultural Organization of the UN*

The Calorie requirement of the average man is 2,700 and that of the average woman is 2,500. Inactive people need less, while those engaged in heavy labour might require to increase, perhaps even to double, these figures. Calories that are not consumed as energy turn to fat.

PORTUGUESE PLATTER

This traditional beef, egg, and fried potato dish is a component of Portugal's high per capita Calorie consumption.

TOP 10

COUNTRIES WITH THE HIGHEST FEMALE LIFE EXPECTANCY

	COUNTRY	LIFE EXPECTANCY AT BIRTH (YEARS), 1998
1	Japan	83.59
2	Switzerland	81.90
3	France	81.86
4	Sweden	81.53
5	Norway	81.07
6	Australia	81.05
7	Canada	80.89
8	Italy	80.74
9	Belgium	80.61
10	Iceland	80.59
	UK	79.48

Source: UN Demographic Yearbook

TOP 10

COUNTRIES WITH THE HIGHEST MALE LIFE EXPECTANCY

	COUNTRY	LIFE EXPECTANCY AT BIRTH (YEARS), 1998
1	Luxembourg	77.87
2	Japan	77.01
3	Sweden	76.51
4	Iceland	76.20
5	Switzerland	75.70
6	Greece	75.62
7	Norway	75.37
8	Israel	75.30
9	Australia	75.22
10	Malta	74.94
	UK	74.31

Source: UN Demographic Yearbook

Half a century ago, the vast majority of the global population died before the age of 50. Today, the great majority survive well beyond that age. Between 1980 and 1995, global average life expectancy increased by an average of 4.6 years and is now 64 years for men, 67 for women.

YOUNG AT HEART

In the past century, female life expectancy in Japan has increased by almost 40 years, from 44.3 years in 1900 to its present 83.59.

THE 10 COUNTRIES WITH THE HIGHEST DEATH RATE

(Country/1998 death rate per 100,000)

1 **Rwanda**, 44.6 **2** **Sierra Leone**, 29.6 **3** **Liberia**, 27.9 **4** **Malawi**, 22.4 **5** = **Guinea Bissau**, 21.8; = **Uganda**, 21.8 **7** **Afghanistan**, 21.7 **8** **Guinea**, 20.3 **9** **Burundi**, 19.6 **10** **The Gambia**, 19.2

UK, 10.7

Source: UN Demographic Yearbook

THE 10 COUNTRIES WITH THE MOST DEATHS FROM HEART DISEASE

(Country/1998 death rate per 1,000)

1 **Ukraine**, 534.1 **2** **Estonia**, 438.8 **3** **Lithuania**, 418.3 **4** **Belarus**, 382.7 **5** **Moldova**, 381.0 **6** **Russia**, 356.4 **7** **Georgia**, 328.1 **8** **Hungary**, 304.4 **9** **Bulgaria**, 267.9 **10** **Finland**, 267.7

Source: UN Demographic Yearbook

TOP 10

COUNTRIES WITH THE LOWEST BIRTH RATE

	COUNTRY	1998 LIVE BIRTHS PER 1,000
1	Bulgaria	7.4
2	Latvia	7.9
3	Estonia	8.6
4	Ukraine	8.7
5	=Belarus	8.8
	=Czech Republic	8.8
7	Spain	9.0
8	Russia	9.2
9	Hong Kong	9.3
10	=Italy	9.4
	=Slovenia	9.4
	UK	12.5

Source: UN Demographic Yearbook

TOP 10

COUNTRIES WITH THE HIGHEST BIRTH RATE

	COUNTRY	1998 LIVE BIRTHS PER 1,000
1	Niger	52.5
2	=Angola	50.8
	=Mali	50.8
	=Uganda	50.8
5	=Guinea	50.6
	=Malawi	50.6
7	Afghanistan	49.7
8	Sierra Leone	49.0
9	Ethiopia	48.9
10	Yemen	48.7
	UK	12.5

Source: UN Demographic Yearbook

The countries with the highest birth rates are amongst the poorest countries in the world. In these countries, people often want to have large families so that the children can help to earn income for the family when they are older. The 10 countries with the highest birth rate therefore correspond very closely with those countries with the highest fertility rate.

THE 10

MOST COMMON CAUSES OF DEATH

	CAUSE	APPROXIMATE NO. OF DEATHS PER ANNUM
1	Ischaemic heart disease	7,375,000
2	Cancers*	7,229,000
3	Cerebrovascular disease	5,106,000
4	Acute lower respiratory infection	3,452,000
5	HIV/AIDS	2,285,000
6	Chronic obstructive pulmonary disease	2,249,000
7	Diarrhoea (including dysentery)	2,219,000
8	Childhood diseases#	1,651,000
9	Tuberculosis	1,498,000
10	Road traffic accidents	1,171,000

* *Lung cancer deaths alone number 1,244,000*

\# *Including pertussis, polio, diptheria, measles and tetanus*

Source: WHO World Health Report 1999

TOP 10

COUNTRIES WITH THE HIGHEST DIVORCE RATE

	COUNTRY	1998 DIVORCE RATE PER 1,000
1	Maldives	10.75
2	=Belarus	4.63
	=China	4.63
4	Russia	4.51
5	USA	4.33
6	Surinam	4.26
7	Estonia	3.85
8	Cuba	3.72
9	Ukraine	3.71
10	Puerto Rico	3.49
	UK	2.89

Source: UN Demographic Yearbook

The UK has the highest divorce rate in Europe (excluding republics of the former Soviet Union).

TOP 10

PROFESSIONS OF COMPUTER-DATING MEMBERS IN THE UK

WOMEN'S PROFESSIONS	PERCENTAGE OF THOSE REGISTERED		PERCENTAGE OF THOSE REGISTERED	MEN'S PROFESSIONS
Teachers/lecturers	7.8	1	6.1	Engineers
Nurses	5.2	2	5.3	Computer professionals
Women at home	4.8	3	4.8	Teachers/lecturers
Secretaries	4.5	4	4.5	Company directors
Civil servants	3.9	5	4.3	Accountants
Social workers	3.8	6	4.2	Doctors
Solicitors	3.5	7	4.0	Managers
Accountants	3.1	8	3.7	Civil servants
Doctors	2.8	9	2.5	Architects
Students	1.3	10	1.4	Farmers

Source: *Dateline International*

TOP 10 COUNTRIES WITH THE HIGHEST MARRIAGE RATE

(Country/1998 marriages per 1,000)

1 **Antigua and Barbuda**, 21.0 **2** **Maldives**, 19.7 **3** **Bermuda**, 15.7 **4** **Barbados**, 13.5 **5** **Liechtenstein**, 12.9 **6** **Seychelles**, 11.4 **7** **Bangladesh**, 9.7 **8** **Mauritius**, 9.5 **9** = **Bahamas**, 9.3; = **Sri Lanka**, 9.3

UK, 5.5 Source: UN Demographic Yearbook

The highest marriage rates in the world are actually recorded in places that are not independent countries. Gibraltar, for example, has a marriage rate of 26.7 per 1,000.

WEDDED BLISS?

Cuba once featured prominently among countries with a high marriage rate, but today ranks among the world's foremost countries for divorce.

Did You Know? In Rwanda, the death rate at 44.6 per 1,000 people is actually greater than the birth rate, which is 43.9 per 1,000 people.

What's in a Name?

TOP 10 FIRST NAMES IN ENGLAND & WALES

GIRLS		BOYS
Chloe	1	Jack
Emily	2	Thomas
Megan	3	James
Olivia	4	Joshua
Sophie	5	Daniel
Charlotte	6	Matthew
Lauren	7	Samuel
Jessica	8	Joseph
Rebecca	9	Callum
Hannah	10	William

TOP 10 FIRST NAMES IN SCOTLAND

BOYS		GIRLS
Jack	1	Chloe
Lewis	2	Rebecca
Ryan	3	Lauren
Cameron	4	Emma
Ross	5	Amy
James	6	Megan
Andrew	7	Caitlin
Liam	8	Rachel
Scott	9	Erin
Connor	10	Sophie

As in England and Wales, Jack and Chloe remained the top names in Scotland in 1999. Among boys' names, Liam experienced the greatest increase in popularity, rising seven places on the previous year to enter the Top 10, while Lauren underwent the greatest rise among girls, moving up five places. Outside the Top 10, the unisex name Morgan rose by a remarkable 32 places among boys and seven places among girls, reaching nos. 73 and 18 respectively. It should be noted that there are considerable variations between regions.

TOP 10 FIRST NAMES IN IRELAND

GIRLS		BOYS
Chloe	1	Conor
Ciara	2	Sean
Sarah	3	Jack
Aoife	4	James
Emma	5	Adam
Niamh	6	Aaron
Rachel	7	Dylan
Megan	8	David
Rebecca	9	Michael
Lauren	10	Daniel

TOP 10 FIRST NAMES IN NORTHERN IRELAND

GIRLS		BOYS
Chloe	1	Matthew
Emma	2	Ryan
Rebecca	3	James
Amy	4	Jack
Lauren	5	Conor
Hannah	6	Adam
Shannon	7	Jordan
Sarah	8	Michael
Rachel	9	David
Megan	10	Christopher

A comparative survey of names recorded in both 1975 and 1998 showed that none of the Top 10 1998 girls' names appeared in the earlier list, while three boys' names (James, Michael, and David) were in both.

TOP 10 SURNAMES IN SCOTLAND*

1. Smith 2. Brown 3. Wilson 4. Thomson 5. Robertson 6. Campbell 7. Stewart 8. Anderson 9. Macdonald 10. Scott

* *Based on a survey of names appearing on birth and death registers, and both names on marriage registers*

TOP 10 SURNAMES IN THE UK

(Surname/number)

1. **Smith**, 538,369 2. **Jones**, 402,489 3. **Williams**, 279,150 4. **Brown**, 260,652 5. **Taylor**, 251,058 6. **Davies/Davis**, 209,584 7. **Wilson**, 191,006 8. **Evans**, 170,391 9. **Thomas**, 152,945 10. **Johnson**, 146,535

This survey of British surnames is based on an analysis of almost 50 million names appearing on the British electoral rolls.

TOP 10 FIRST NAMES IN WALES

GIRLS		BOYS
Chloe	1	Thomas
Megan	2	Jack
Emily	3	Joshua
Sophie	4	Daniel
Lauren	5	Callum
Jessica	6	James
Georgina	7	Liam
Ffion	8	Samuel
Hannah	9	Ryan
Rebecca	10	Matthew

TOP 10 FIRST NAMES IN AUSTRALIA*

GIRLS		BOYS
Emily	1	Joshua
Jessica	2	Matthew
Sarah	3	Daniel
Emma	4	James
Hannah	5	Jake
Samantha	6	Benjamin
Georgia	7	Lachlan
Rebecca	8	Nicholas
Amy	9	Jack
Sophie	10	Thomas

* *Based on births registered in New South Wales*

"WENDY"

Like Pamela, Lorna, Thelma, and Mavis, Wendy is one of a group of girls' names invented by authors. Margaret, the infant daughter of writer W. E. Henley, called family friend J. M. Barrie her "friendy", pronouncing it as "wendy", a nickname she then acquired. Margaret died aged 5 in 1894, but her name lived on as Wendy Darling in Barrie's 1904 play *Peter Pan*. The popularity of the play and 1911 book ensured that Wendy became a common first name in both the UK and US.

WHY DO WE SAY ?

TOP 10 FIRST NAMES IN CANADA*

GIRLS		BOYS
Emily	1	Matthew
Sarah	2	Joshua
Emma	3	Nicholas
Jessica	4	Ryan
Taylor	5	Alexander
Hannah	6	Tyler
Megan	7	Michael
Samantha	8	Brandon
Ashley	9	Jacob
Nicole	10	Kyle

* *Based on births in British Columbia*

TOP 10 FIRST NAMES IN NORWAY

GIRLS		BOYS
Ingrid	1	Andreas
Ida	2	Markus
Marte	3	Kristian
Karoline	4	Martin
Silje	5	Kristoffer
Julie	6	Thomas
Camila	7	Jonas
Kristine	8	Fredrik
Maria	9	Daniel
Vilde	10	Marius

TOP 10 SURNAMES IN THE MANHATTAN TELEPHONE DIRECTORY

1 Smith 2 Brown 3 Williams 4 Cohen 5 Lee 6 Johnson 7 Rodriguez 8 Green 9 Davis 10 Jones

TOP 10 MOST COMMON SURNAMES IN THE US

	NAME	% OF ALL US NAMES
1	Smith	1.006
2	Johnson	0.810
3	Williams	0.699
4	=Brown	0.621
	=Jones	0.621
6	Davis	0.480
7	Miller	0.424
8	Wilson	0.339
9	Moore	0.312
10	=Anderson	0.311
	=Taylor	0.311
	=Thomas	0.311

The Top 10 (or, in view of those in equal 10th place, 12) US surnames together make up over 6 per cent of the entire US population – in other words, one American in every 16 bears one of these names. Extending the list, some 28 different names comprise 10 per cent of the entire population, 115 names 20 per cent, 315 names 30 per cent, 755 names 40 per cent, 1,712 names 50 per cent, and 3,820 names 60 per cent.

TOP 10 TERMS OF ENDEARMENT USED IN THE US

1 Honey 2 Baby 3 Sweetheart 4 Dear 5 Lover 6 Darling 7 Sugar 8 = Angel; = Pumpkin 10 = Beautiful; = Precious

A survey of romance conducted by a US champagne company concluded that 26 per cent of American adults favoured "honey" as their most frequently used term of endearment. Curiously, identical numbers were undecided whether to call their loved one an angel or a pumpkin....

TOP 10 BOYS' NAMES IN THE US, 1989–99

1989		1999
Michael	1	Jacob
Christopher	2	Michael
Joshua	3	Matthew
Matthew	4	Nicholas
David	5	Christopher
Daniel	6	Joshua
Andrew	7	Austin
Joseph	8	Tyler
Justin	9	Brandon
John	10	Joseph

TOP 10 GIRLS' NAMES IN THE US, 1989–99

1989		1999
Jessica	1	Emily
Ashley	2	Sarah
Amanda Brittany	=3 =	Brianna
	4	Samantha
Sarah	5	Hailey
Jennifer	6	Ashley
Stephanie	7	Kaitlyn
Samantha	8	Madison
Elizabeth	9	Hannah
Lauren	10	Alexis

TOP 10 SURNAMES IN CHINA

1 Zhang 2 Whang 3 Li 4 Zhao 5 Chen 6 Yang 7 Wu 8 Liu 9 Huang 10 Zhou

Which country was the first to ratify the UN Charter?
see p.64 for the answer

A USA
B Nicaragua
C China

World Royalty

TOP 10

LONGEST-REIGNING BRITISH MONARCHS

	MONARCH	REIGN	AGE AT ACCESSION	AGE AT DEATH	REIGN YEARS
1	Queen Victoria	1837–1901	18	81	63
2	King George III	1760–1820	22	81	59
3	King Henry III	1216–72	9	64	56
4	King Edward III	1327–77	14	64	50
5	Queen Elizabeth II	1952–	25	—	48
6	Queen Elizabeth I	1558–1603	25	69	44
7	King Henry VI	1422–61*	8 months	49	38
8	King Henry VIII	1509–47	17	55	37
9	King Charles II	1649–85	19	54	36
10	King Henry I	1100–35	31–32#	66–67#	35

** Henry VI was deposed; he died in 1471.*

 # Henry I's birthdate is unknown, so his age at accession and death are uncertain.

This list excludes the reigns of monarchs before 1066, so omits such rulers as Ethelred II, who reigned for 37 years.

THE 10

FIRST IN LINE TO THE BRITISH THRONE

	SUCCESSOR	BORN
1	HRH The Prince of Wales (Prince Charles Philip Arthur George)	14 Nov 1948
2	HRH Prince William of Wales (Prince William Arthur Philip Louis)	21 June 1982
3	HRH Prince Henry of Wales (Prince Henry Charles Albert David)	15 Sep 1984
4	HRH The Duke of York (Prince Andrew Albert Christian Edward)	19 Feb 1960
5	HRH Princess Beatrice of York (Princess Beatrice Elizabeth Mary)	8 Aug 1988
6	HRH Princess Eugenie of York (Princess Eugenie Victoria Helena)	23 Mar 1990
7	HRH Prince Edward (Prince Edward Antony Richard Louis)	10 Mar 1964
8	HRH The Princess Royal (Princess Anne Elizabeth Alice Louise)	15 Aug 1950
9	Master Peter Mark Andrew Phillips	15 Nov 1977
10	Miss Zara Anne Elizabeth Phillips	15 May 1981

TOP 10

LONGEST-REIGNING QUEENS*

	QUEEN	COUNTRY	REIGN	REIGN YEARS
1	Victoria	Great Britain	1837–1901	63
2	Wilhelmina	Netherlands	1890–1948	58
3	Wu Chao	China	655–705	50
4	Elizabeth II	UK	1952–	48
5	Salote Tubou	Tonga	1918–65	47
6	Elizabeth I	England	1558–1603	44
7	Maria Theresa	Hungary	1740–80	40
8	Maria I	Portugal	1777–1816	39
9	Joanna I	Italy	1343–81	38
10=	Suiko Tenno	Japan	593–628	35
=	Isabella II	Spain	1833–68	35

** Queens and empresses who rule (or ruled) in their own right, not as consorts of kings or emperors*

LONG TO REIGN OVER US

If Queen Elizabeth II is on the throne on 11 September 2015, she will have beaten Queen Victoria's record by one day to become the world's longest-reigning queen.

THE 10

LATEST WORLD MONARCHS TO COME TO POWER

	MONARCH/COUNTRY	ACCESSION
1	**King Sayyidi Muhammad VI ibn al-Hasan**, Morocco	23 July 1999
2	**Sultan Tuanku Salehuddin Abdul Aziz Shah ibni al-Marhum Hisamuddin Alam Shah**, Malaysia	26 Apr 1999
3	**Emir Sheikh Hamad ibn 'Isa al-Khalifah**, Bahrain	6 Mar 1999
4	**King Abdallah (II) ibn al-Hussein al-Hashimi**, Jordan	7 Feb 1999
5	**King Letsie III**, Lesotho	7 Feb 1996
6	**Emir Sheikh Ahmad ibn Khalifa al-Thani**, Qatar	27 June 1995
7	**King Albert II**, Belgium	9 Aug 1993
8	**King Preah Baht Samdach Preah Norodom Sihanuk Varmn**, Cambodia	24 Sep 1993*
9	**King Harald V**, Norway	17 Jan 1991
10	**Prince Hans Adam II**, Liechtenstein	13 Nov 1989

** Elected king*

TOP 10

LONGEST-REIGNING LIVING MONARCHS*

	MONARCH/COUNTRY	DATE OF BIRTH	ACCESSION
1	**King Bhumibol Adulyadej**, Thailand	5 Dec 1927	9 June 1946
2	**Prince Rainier III**, Monaco	31 May 1923	9 May 1949
3	**Queen Elizabeth II**, UK	21 Apr 1926	6 Feb 1952
4	**King Malietoa Tanumafili II**, Western Samoa	4 Jan 1913	1 Jan 1962#
5	**Grand Duke Jean**, Luxembourg	5 Jan 1921	12 Nov 1964
6	**King Taufa'ahau Tupou IV**, Tonga	4 July 1918	16 Dec 1965
7	**King Haji Hassanal Bolkiah**, Brunei	15 July 1946	5 Oct 1967
8	**Sultan Sayyid Qaboos ibn Said al-Said**, Oman	18 Nov 1942	23 July 1970
9	**Queen Margrethe II**, Denmark	16 Apr 1940	14 Jan 1972
10	**King Birendra Bir Bikram Shah Dev**, Nepal	28 Dec 1945	31 Jan 1972

** Including hereditary rulers of principalities, dukedoms, etc.*

 # Sole ruler since 15 April 1963

There are 29 countries that have emperors, kings, queens, princes, dukes, sultans, or other hereditary rulers as their heads of state. The current Sultan of Oman took control of the country by ousting his own father in a palace coup.

THE 10

LATEST WORLD MONARCHS TO BE ASSASSINATED

	MONARCH/COUNTRY	DATE OF DEATH
1	**King Faisal ibn Abdul Aziz**, Saudi Arabia *Murdered by his nephew during an audience with the Kuwaiti oil minister.*	25 Mar 1975
2	**King Faisal II**, Iraq *Murdered with his entire household; their bodies were paraded through Baghdad as part of a military coup.*	14 July 1958
3	**King Abdullah ibn al-Hussein**, Jordan *Gunned down on a visit to his father's tomb in Jerusalem by Mustafa Ashu, a young Palestinian nationalist.*	20 July 1951
4	**King Ananda Mahidol, Rama VIII**, Thailand *Assassinated in the palace, having been conspired against by his personal secretary and others.*	9 June 1946
5	**King Alexander I**, Yugoslavia *Shot in Marseilles by an assassin sent by Croat leader Ante Paveilic.*	9 Oct 1934
6	**King Sardar Mohammad Nadir Khan**, Afghanistan *Shot while giving out prizes at a school.*	8 Nov 1933
7	**King George I**, Greece *Killed in Salonika by Schinas, a Greek revolutionary.*	18 Mar 1913
8	**King Carlos I**, Portugal *Ambushed and murdered, together with Luis Philippe, the crown prince, by anti-royalists.*	1 Feb 1908
9	**King Alexander Obrenovich**, Serbia *Shot to death and hacked with sabres, together with his wife, Draga, by military conspirators.*	11 July 1903
10	**King Umberto I**, Italy *Murdered in Monza by anarchist Gaetano Bresci.*	29 July 1900

TOP 10

LONGEST-REIGNING MONARCHS

	MONARCH/COUNTRY	REIGN	AGE AT ACCESSION	REIGN YEARS
1	**King Louis XIV**, France	1643–1715	5	72
2	**King John II**, Liechtenstein	1858–1929	18	71
3	**Emperor Franz-Josef**, Austria-Hungary	1848–1916	18	67
4	**Queen Victoria**, Great Britain	1837–1901	18	63
5	**Emperor Hirohito**, Japan	1926–89	25	62
6	**Emperor Kangxi**, China	1662–1722	8	61
7	**Emperor Qianlong**, China	1736–96	25	60
8	**King Christian IV**, Denmark	1588–1648	11	59*
9	**King George III**, Great Britain	1760–1820	22	59*
10	**Prince Honore III**, Monaco	1733–93	13	59*

** Those with the same number of reign years are ranked according to days.*

Did You Know? Despite being pregnant 17 times, British Queen Anne produced only one child – William, Duke of Gloucester – who survived infancy, although he died at the age of 11.

Background image: EMPEROR AND EMPRESS HIROHITO

THE 10

FIRST COUNTRIES TO RATIFY THE UN CHARTER

	COUNTRY	DATE
1	Nicaragua	6 July 1945
2	USA	8 Aug 1945
3	France	31 Aug 1945
4	Dominican Republic	4 Sep 1945
5	New Zealand	19 Sep 1945
6	Brazil	21 Sep 1945
7	Argentina	24 Sep 1945
8	China	28 Sep 1945
9	Denmark	9 Oct 1945
10	Chile	11 Oct 1945

In New York on 26 June 1945, barely weeks after the end of World War II in Europe (the Japanese did not surrender until 3 September), 50 nations signed the World Security Charter, thereby establishing the United Nations as an international peacekeeping organization. The UN came into effect on 24 October, which has since been celebrated as United Nations Day.

KEEPING THE PEACE

Since its formation in 1945, the United Nations has deployed forces to maintain the peace in the world's troublespots. Here, peace-keeping troops enter East Timor in September 1999.

TOP 10

LONGEST-LIVED BRITISH PRIME MINISTERS

	PRIME MINISTER	PARTY	OFFICE	BORN	DIED	AGE YEARS	AGE DAYS
1	Harold Macmillan	Con	1957–63	10 Feb 1894	29 Dec 1986	92	322
2	Sir Alec Douglas-Home	Con	1963–64	2 July 1903	9 Oct 1995	92	98
3	Winston S. Churchill	Co Con	1940–45 1951–55	30 Nov 1874	24 Jan 1965	90	45
4	William E. Gladstone	Lib	1868–74 1880–85, 1886 1892–94	29 Dec 1809	19 May 1898	88	141
5	James Callaghan	Lab	1976–79	27 Mar 1912	–	88*	
6	Henry Addington	T	1801–04	30 May 1757	15 Feb 1844	86	261
7	Earl Russell	W Lib	1846–52 1865–66	18 Aug 1792	28 May 1878	85	273
8	Clement R. Attlee	Lab	1945–51	3 Jan 1883	8 Oct 1967	84	279
9	Duke of Wellington	T	1828–30	1 May 1769	14 Sep 1852	83	136
10	Edward Heath	Con	1970–74	9 Jul 1916	–	84*	

* *Alive at time of going to press*

Co = Coalition; Con = Conservative; Lab = Labour; Lib = Liberal; T = Tory; W = Whig

THE 10

FIRST COUNTRIES TO GIVE WOMEN THE VOTE

	COUNTRY	YEAR
1	**New Zealand**	1893
2	**Australia,** (South Australia, 1894; Western Australia, 1898; Australia united, 1901)	1902
3	**Finland** (a Grand Duchy under the Russian Crown)	1906
4	**Norway** (restricted franchise; all women over 25 in 1913)	1907
5	**Denmark and Iceland** (a Danish dependency until 1918)	1915
6	=**Netherlands**	1917
	=**USSR**	1917
8	=**Austria**	1918
	=**Canada**	1918
	=**Germany**	1918
	=**Great Britain and Ireland** (Ireland part of the United Kingdom until 1921; women over 30 – lowered to 21 in 1928)	1918
	=**Poland**	1918

TOP 10

LONGEST-SERVING PRESIDENTS TODAY

	PRESIDENT	COUNTRY	TOOK OFFICE
1	**General Gnassingbé Eyadéma**	Togo	14 Apr 1967
2	**El Hadj Omar Bongo**	Gabon	2 Dec 1967
3	**Colonel Mu'ammar Gadhafi***	Libya	1 Sep 1969
4	**Lt.-General Hafiz al-Asad**	Syria	22 Feb 1971
5	**Zayid ibn Sultan al-Nuhayyan**	United Arab Emirates	2 Dec 1971
6	**Fidel Castro**	Cuba	2 Nov 1976
7	**France-Albert René**	Seychelles	5 June 1977
8	**Daniel Teroitich arap Moi**	Kenya	14 Oct 1978
9	**Saddam Hussein**	Iraq	16 July 1979
10	**Teodoro Obiang Nguema Mbasogo**	Equatorial Guinea	3 Aug 1979

* *Since a reorganization in 1979, Colonel Gadhafi has held no formal position but continues to rule under the ceremonial title of "Leader of the Revolution".*

TOP 10

YOUNGEST BRITISH PRIME MINISTERS

	PRIME MINISTER	LIFESPAN	YEAR ELECTED	AGE ON TAKING OFFICE* YEARS	DAYS
1	**William Pitt**	1759–1806	1783	24	205
2	**Duke of Grafton**	1735–1811	1768	33	16
3	**Marquess of Rockingham**	1730–82	1765	35	61
4	**Duke of Devonshire**	1720–64	1756	c.36	–
5	**Lord North**	1732–92	1770	37	290
6	**Earl of Liverpool**	1770–1828	1812	42	1
7	**Henry Addington**	1757–1844	1801	43	291
8	**Tony Blair**	b. 6 May 1953	1997	43	360
9	**Sir Robert Walpole**	1676–1745	1721	44	107
10	**Viscount Goderich**	1782–1859	1827	44	305

* *Where a prime minister served in more than one ministry, only the first ministry is listed.*

THE 10

FIRST FEMALE PRIME MINISTERS AND PRESIDENTS

	PRIME MINISTER OR PRESIDENT/COUNTRY	PERIOD IN OFFICE
1	**Sirimavo Bandaranaike**, (PM), Sri Lanka	1960–65/ 1970–77/ 1994–
2	**Indira Gandhi** (PM), India	1966–77/ 1980–84
3	**Golda Meir** (PM), Israel	1969–74
4	**Maria Estela Perón** (P), Argentina	1974–76
5	**Elisabeth Domitien** (PM), Central African Republic	1975–76
6	**Margaret Thatcher** (PM), UK	1979–90
7	**Dr. Maria Lurdes Pintasilgo** (PM), Portugal	1979–80
8	**Vigdís Finnbogadóttir** (P), Iceland	1980–
9	**Mary Eugenia Charles** (PM), Dominica	1980–95
10	**Gro Harlem Brundtland** (PM), Norway	Feb–Oct 1981/ 1986–89/ 1990–96

WOMEN IN POWER

The Swedish parliament has a high proportion of women members. Worldwide, women MPs today comprise 13 per cent of all MPs.

TOP 10

PARLIAMENTS WITH THE HIGHEST PERCENTAGE OF WOMEN MEMBERS*

	PARLIAMENT/ ELECTION	WOMEN MEMBERS	TOTAL MEMBERS	% WOMEN
1	**Sweden**, 1998	149	349	42.7
2	**Denmark**, 1998	67	179	37.4
3	**Finland**, 1999	74	200	37.0
4	**Norway**, 1997	60	165	36.4
5	**Netherlands**, 1998	54	150	36.0
6	**Iceland**, 1999	22	63	34.9
7	**Germany**, 1998	207	669	30.9
8	**South Africa**, 1999	120	400	30.0
9	**New Zealand**, 1996	35	120	29.2
10	**Cuba**, 1998	166	601	27.6
	UK (1997)	121	659	18.4

* *As at 25 December 1999*

Source: *Inter-Parliamentary Union*

This information is based on the most recent general election results available for all democratic countries.

Did You Know? Félix Houhouët-Boigny, President of the Côte d'Ivoire until his death in 1993 at the age of 88, was the world's oldest president.

Human Achievements

THE 10 NORTH POLE FIRSTS

1 First to reach the Pole?
American adventurer Frederick Albert Cook claimed that he had reached the Pole, accompanied by two Inuits, on 21 April 1908, but his claim is disputed. It is more likely that Robert Edwin Peary, Matthew Alexander Henson (both Americans), and four Inuits were first at the Pole on 6 April 1909.

2 First to fly over the Pole in an airship
A team of 16, led by Roald Amundsen, the Norwegian explorer who first reached the South Pole in 1911, flew across the North Pole on 12 May 1926 in the Italian-built airship Norge.

3 First to land at the Pole in an aircraft
Soviets Pavel Afanaseyevich Geordiyenko, Mikhail Yemel'yenovich Ostrekin, Pavel Kononovich Sen'ko, and Mikhail Mikhaylovich Somov arrived at and departed from the Pole by air on 23 April 1948.

4 First solo flight over the Pole in a single-engined aircraft
Capt. Charles Francis Blair, Jr. of the US flew a single-engined Mustang fighter, Excalibur III, *on 29 May 1951, crossing from Bardufoss, Norway, to Fairbanks, Alaska.*

5 First submarine to surface at the Pole
USS Skate *surfaced at the Pole on 17 March 1959.*

6 First confirmed overland journey to the Pole
American Ralph S. Plaisted, with companions Walter Pederson, Gerald Pitzel, and Jean Luc Bombardier, reached the Pole on 18 April 1968, using snowmobiles.

7 First solo overland journey to the Pole
Japanese explorer Naomi Uemura reached the Pole on 1 May 1978, travelling by dog sled, and was then picked up by an aeroplane.

8 First to reach the Pole on skis
A team of seven, led by Dimitry Shparo (USSR), was the first to reach the North Pole on 31 May 1979.

9 First crossing on a Pole-to-Pole expedition
Sir Ranulph Fiennes and Charles Burton walked over the North Pole on 10 April 1982, having crossed the South Pole on 15 December 1980.

10 First woman to walk to the Pole
Along with five male companions, American physical education teacher Ann Bancroft reached the Pole on 1 May 1986.

Lt.-Cdr. Richard Byrd and Floyd Bennett claimed to have traversed the Pole on 9 May 1926 in an aircraft, but recent analysis of Byrd's diary indicates that they turned back some 241 km (150 miles) short of the Pole, thereby disqualifying their entry.

POLE TO POLE

The 1979–82 Transglobe Expedition led by Sir Ranulph Fiennes, here at Scott Base, South Pole, was the first to traverse both Poles.

THE 10 CIRCUMNAVIGATION FIRSTS

	CIRCUMNAVIGATION/CRAFT	VOYAGER(S)	RETURN DATE
1	**First**, *Vittoria*	Juan Sebastian de Elcano*	6 Sep 1522
2	**First in less than 80 days**, various	"Nellie Bly"#	25 Jan 1890
3	**First solo**, *Spray*	Capt. Joshua Slocum	3 July 1898
4	**First by air**, *Chicago, New Orleans*	Lt. Lowell Smith, Lt. Leslie P. Arnold	28 Sep 1924
5	**First non-stop by air**, *Lucky Lady II*	Capt. James Gallagher	2 Mar 1949
6	**First underwater**, *Triton*	Capt. Edward L. Beach	25 Apr 1960
7	**First non-stop solo**, *Suhaili*	Robin Knox-Johnston	22 Apr 1969
8	**First helicopter**, *Spirit of Texas*	H. Ross Perot Jr. and Jay Coburn	30 Sep 1982
9	**First air without refuelling**, *Voyager*	Richard Rutan and Jeana Yeager	23 Dec 1986
10	**First by balloon**, *Breitling Orbiter 3*	Brian Jones and Bertrand Piccard	21 Mar 1999

* *The expedition was led by Ferdinand Magellan, but he did not survive the voyage.*

\# *Real name Elizabeth Cochrane. This US journalist set out to beat the fictitious "record" established in Jules Verne's novel,* Around the World in 80 Days.

THE 10 FIRST MOUNTAINEERS TO CLIMB EVEREST

(Mountaineer/nationality/date)

1 **Edmund Hillary**, New Zealander, 29 May 1953 2 **Tenzing Norgay**, Nepalese, 29 May 1953 3 **Jürg Marmet**, Swiss, 23 May 1956 4 **Ernst Schmied**, Swiss, 23 May 1956 5 **Hans-Rudolf von Gunten**, Swiss, 24 May 1956 6 **Adolf Reist**, Swiss, 24 May 1956 7 **Wang Fu-chou**, Chinese, 25 May 1960 8 **Chu Ying-hua**, Chinese, 25 May 1960 9 **Konbu**, Tibetan, 25 May 1960 10 **= Nawang Gombu**, Indian, 1 May 1963; **= James Whittaker**, American, 1 May 1963

Nawang Gombu and James Whittaker are 10th equal because they ascended the last feet to the summit side by side.

The citizens of which country have won the most Nobel Prizes for Literature?

A US
B UK
C France

see p.69 for the answer

THE 10

FIRST SUCCESSFUL HUMAN DESCENTS OVER NIAGARA FALLS

	NAME/METHOD	DATE
1	**Annie Edson Taylor**, Wooden barrel	24 Oct 1901
2	**Bobby Leach**, Steel barrel	25 Jul 1911
3	**Jean Lussier**, Steel and rubber ball fitted with oxygen cylinders	4 Jul 1928
4	**William Fitzgerald** (a.k.a. Nathan Boya), Steel and rubber ball fitted with oxygen cylinders	15 Jul 1961
5	**Karel Soucek**, Barrel	3 Jul 1984
6	**Steven Trotter**, Barrel	18 Aug 1985
7	**Dave Mundy**, Barrel	5 Oct 1985
8	=**Peter deBernardi**, Metal container	28 Sep 1989
	=**Jeffrey Petkovich**, Metal container	28 Sep 1989
10	**Dave Mundy**, Diving bell	26 Sep 1993

Source: *Niagara Falls Museum*

TOP 10

FASTEST CROSS-CHANNEL SWIMMERS

	SWIMMER/NATIONALITY	YEAR	TIME HRS:MINS
1	**Chad Hundeby**, American	1994	7:17
2	**Penny Lee Dean**, American	1978	7:40
3	**Tamara Bruce**, Australian	1994	7:53
4	**Philip Rush**, New Zealander	1987	7:55
5	**Hans van Goor**, Dutch	1995	8:02
6	**Richard Davey**, British	1988	8:05
7	**Irene van der Laan**, Dutch	1982	8:06
8	**Paul Asmuth**, American	1985	8:12
9	**Anita Sood**, Indian	1987	8:15
10	**John van Wisse**, Australian	1994	8:17

Source: *Channel Swimming Association*

The first person to swim the Channel was Matthew Webb (British), who on 24–25 August 1875 made the crossing in what now seems a rather leisurely time of 21 hours 45 minutes.

NIAGARA FALLS

Annie Edson Taylor, a Michigan schoolteacher, celebrated her 43rd birthday in 1901 by being the first to plunge over Niagara Falls and survive. She was followed in 1911 by 69-year-old Bobby Leach (who later died when he slipped on a piece of orange peel!). On 4 July 1928, watched by an excited crowd of 100,000, Jean Lussier (seen here), a circus acrobat from Springfield, Massachusetts, travelled over the Falls in a 344-kg (758-lb) steel-reinforced rubber sphere. In 1920, barber Charles Stephens became one of many killed in the attempt. Other failed efforts include those of George Stathakis (1930) and William Hill, Jr. (1951).

SNAP SHOTS

THE 10 LATEST WINNERS OF *TIME* MAGAZINE'S "PERSON OF THE YEAR" AWARD

(Year/recipient)

1 1999, **Jeffrey T. Bezos**, founder of Amazon.com **2** 1998, **Bill Clinton**, US President/**Kenneth Starr**, Independent Counsel **3** 1997, **Andrew S. Grove**, CEO of Intel, microchip company **4** 1996, **David Ho**, AIDS researcher **5** 1995, **Newt Gingrich**, US politician **6** 1994, **Pope John Paul II** **7** 1993, **Yasser Arafat**, **F. W. de Klerk**, **Nelson Mandela**, **Yitzhak Rabin**, "peacemakers" **8** 1992, **Bill Clinton**, US President **9** 1991, **George Bush**, US President **10** 1990, **Ted Turner**, US businessman

CHANNEL NO. 3

In 1994, 17-year-old Australian Tamara Bruce achieved the third-fastest Channel swim of all time, becoming the 487th person to swim from England to France.

The Nobel Century

THE 10 ★

LATEST WINNERS OF THE NOBEL PRIZE FOR PHYSICS

	WINNER	COUNTRY	YEAR
1	=Gerardus 't Hooft	Netherlands	1999
	=Martinus J. G. Veltman	Netherlands	1999
3	=Robert B. Laughlin	USA	1998
	=Horst L. Störmer	Germany	1998
	=Daniel C. Tsui	USA	1998
6	=Steven Chu	USA	1997
	=William D. Phillips	USA	1997
	=Professor Claude Cohen-Tannoudji	France	1997
9	=David M. Lee	USA	1996
	=Douglas D. Osheroff	USA	1996
	=Robert C. Richardson	USA	1996

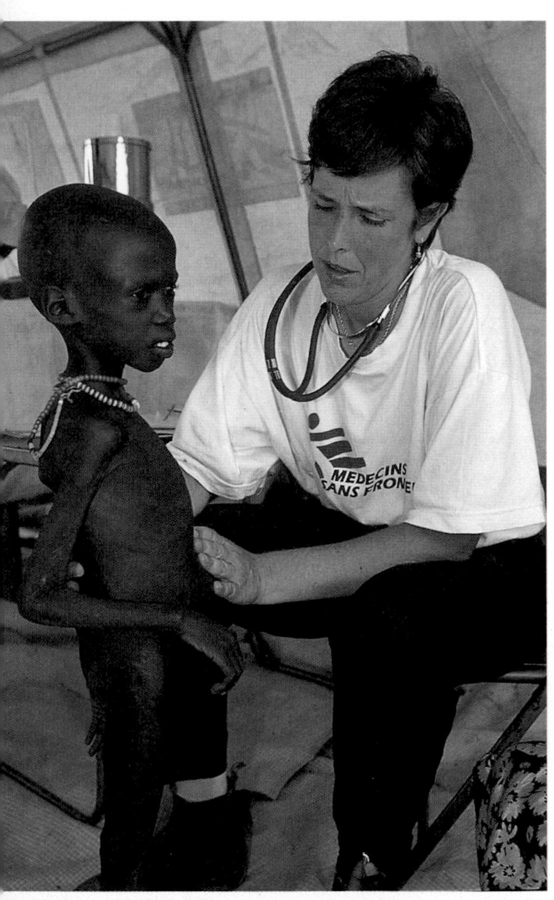

TOP 10 ★

NOBEL PRIZE-WINNING COUNTRIES*

	COUNTRY	PHY	CHE	PH/MED	LIT	PCE	ECO	TOTAL
1	USA	67	43	78	10	18	25	241
2	UK	21	25	24	8	13	7	98
3	Germany	20	27	16	7	4	1	75
4	France	12	7	7	12	9	1	48
5	Sweden	4	4	7	7	5	2	29
6	Switzerland	2	5	6	2	3	–	18
7	USSR	7	1	2	3	2	1	16
8	Netherlands	8	3	2	–	1	1	15
9	Italy	3	1	3	6	1	–	14
10	Denmark	3	–	5	3	1	–	12

Phy – Physics; Che – Chemistry; Ph/Med – Physiology or Medicine; Lit – Literature; Pce – Peace; Eco – Economic Sciences. Germany includes the united country before 1948, West Germany to 1990 and the united country since 1990

** In addition, institutions including the Red Cross have been awarded 17 Nobel Peace Prizes*

THE 10 ★

LATEST WINNERS OF THE NOBEL PEACE PRIZE

	WINNER	COUNTRY	YEAR
1	Médecins Sans Frontières	Belgium	1999
2	=John Hume	UK	1998
	=David Trimble	UK	1998
4	=International Campaign to Ban Landmines	–	1997
	=Jody Williams	USA	1997
6	=Carlos Filipe Ximenes Belo	East Timor	1996
	=José Ramos-Horta	East Timor	1996
8	Joseph Rotblat	UK	1995
9	=Yasir Arafat	Palestine	1994
	=Shimon Peres	Israel	1994
	=Itzhak Rabin	Israel	1994

COMPASSION WITHOUT LIMITS

Brussels-based Médecins Sans Frontières, which has provided emergency medical aid worldwide since 1971, won the Peace Prize in 1999. International organizations have been awarded the prize 17 times.

TOP 10 NOBEL PHYSICS PRIZE-WINNING COUNTRIES

(Country/prizes)

1 **USA**, 67 2 **UK**, 21 3 **Germany**, 20 4 **France**, 12 5 **Netherlands**, 8 6 **USSR**, 7 7 **Sweden**, 4 8 = **Austria**, 3; = **Denmark**, 3; = **Italy**, 3; = **Japan**, 3

TOP 10 ★

NOBEL PEACE PRIZE-WINNING COUNTRIES

	COUNTRY	PRIZES
1	USA	18
2	International institutions	17
3	UK	13
4	France	9
5	Sweden	5
6	=Belgium	4
	=Germany	4
	=South Africa	4
9	=Israel	3
	=Switzerland	3

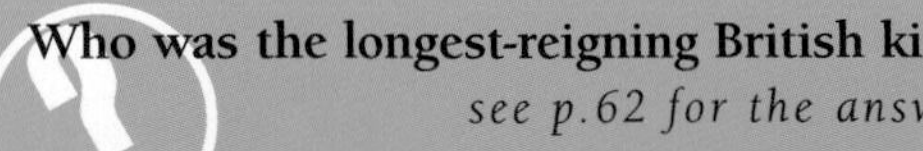

Who was the longest-reigning British king?

see p.62 for the answer

A Henry VIII
B Charles II
C George III

THE 10 ★

LATEST WINNERS OF THE NOBEL PRIZE FOR LITERATURE

	WINNER	COUNTRY	YEAR
1	Günter Grass	Germany	1999
2	José Saramago	Portugal	1998
3	Dario Fo	Italy	1997
4	Wislawa Szymborska	Poland	1996
5	Seamus Heaney	Ireland	1995
6	Kenzaburo Oe	Japan	1994
7	Toni Morrison	USA	1993
8	Derek Walcott	Saint Lucia	1992
9	Nadine Gordimer	South Africa	1991
10	Octavio Paz	Mexico	1990

TOP 10 NOBEL LITERATURE PRIZE-WINNING COUNTRIES

(Country/prizes)

❶ **France**, 12 ❷ **USA**, 10 ❸ **UK**, 8 ❹ = **Sweden**, 7; = **Germany**, 7 ❻ **Italy**, 6 ❼ **Spain**, 5 ❽ = **Denmark**, 3; = **Ireland**, 3; = **Norway**, 3; = **Poland**, 3; = **USSR**, 3

LITERARY LAUREATE

German novelist Günter Grass, the most famous of whose darkly humorous stories is The Tin Drum, *won the 1999 Nobel Prize for Literature.*

LATEST WINNERS OF THE NOBEL PRIZE FOR PHYSIOLOGY OR MEDICINE

	WINNER	COUNTRY	YEAR
1	Günter Blobel	Germany	1999
2	=Robert F. Furchgott	USA	1998
	=Louis J. Ignarro	USA	1998
	=Ferid Murad	USA	1998
5	Stanley B. Prusiner	USA	1997
6	=Peter C. Doherty	Australia	1996
	=Rolf M. Zinkernagel	Switzerland	1996
8	=Christiane Nüsslein-Volhard	Germany	1995
	=Eric F. Wieschaus	USA	1995
	=Edward B. Lewis	USA	1995

THE 10 ★

LATEST WINNERS OF THE NOBEL PRIZE FOR CHEMISTRY

	WINNER/COUNTRY	YEAR
1	**Ahmed Zewail**, Egypt	1999
2	=**Walter Kohn**, USA	1998
	=**John A. Pople**, UK	1998
4	=**Paul D. Boyer**, USA	1997
	=**John E. Walker**, UK	1997
	=**Jens C. Skou**, Denmark	1997
7	=**Sir Harold W. Kroto**, UK	1996
	=**Richard E. Smalley**, USA	1996
9	=**Paul Crutzen**, Netherlands	1995
	=**Mario Molina**, Mexico	1995
	=**Frank Sherwood Rowland**, USA	1995

TOP 10 NOBEL CHEMISTRY PRIZE-WINNING COUNTRIES

(Country/prizes)

❶ **USA**, 43 ❷ **Germany**, 27 ❸ **UK**, 25 ❹ **France**, 17 ❺ **Switzerland**, 5 ❻ **Sweden**, 4 ❼ = **Canada**, 3; = **Netherlands**, 3 ❾ = **Argentina**, 1; = **Austria**, 1; = **Belgium**, 1; = **Czechoslovakia**, 1; = **Egypt**, 1; = **Finland**, 1; = **Hungary**, 1; = **Italy**, 1; = **Japan**, 1; = **Mexico**, 1; = **Norway**, 1; = **USSR**, 1

TOP 10 ★

NOBEL PHYSIOLOGY OR MEDICINE PRIZE-WINNING COUNTRIES

	COUNTRY	PRIZES
1	USA	78
2	UK	24
3	Germany	16
4	=France	7
	=Sweden	7
6	Switzerland	6
7	Denmark	5
8	=Austria	4
	=Belgium	4
10	=Australia	3
	=Italy	3

TOP 10

TYPES OF OFFENCE REMAND PRISONERS ARE CHARGED WITH IN ENGLAND AND WALES

	OFFENCE	PRISONERS*
1	Violence against the person	2,410
2	Burglary	2,280
3	Theft and handling	1,960
4	=Drugs offences	1,770
	=Other offences	1,770
6	Robbery	1,070
7	Sexual offences	710
8	Offence not recorded	460
9	Motoring offences	320
10	Fraud and forgery	180

* *As at end September 1999*

Source: *Home Office* Prison Population Brief

TOP 10

COUNTRIES WITH THE HIGHEST PRISON POPULATION RATES

	COUNTRY	TOTAL PRISON POPULATION*	PRISONERS PER 100,000
1	Russia	1,009,863	685
2	USA	1,725,842	645
3	Belarus	52,033	505
4	Kazakhstan	82,945	495
5	Belize	1,118	490
6	Bahamas	1,401	485
7	Singapore	15,746#	465
8	Kyrgyzstan	19,857	440
9	Ukraine	211,568	415
10	Latvia	10,070	410
	UK	73,545	125

* *Including pre-trial detainees*

\# *Almost half the detainees are held in drug rehabilitation centres*

Source: *Home Office*

HARD CELL

The USA ranks second in the world for its total prison population, which rises annually. Here inmates move through the cell blocks of the Ellis II prison unit at Huntsville Prison, Texas.

TOP 10

LARGEST PRISONS IN THE UK

	PRISON/LOCATION	INMATES
1	**Walton**, Liverpool	1,500
2	**Wandsworth**, London	1,340
3	**Armley**, Leeds	1,257
4	**Strangeways**, Manchester	1,157
5	**Doncaster**	1,106
6	**Winson Green**, Birmingham	1,097
7	**Pentonville**, London	1,091
8	**Barlinnie**, Glasgow	1,015
9	**Durham**	907
10	**Elmley**	892

Did You Know? Marie-Augustin, the 22-year-old Marquis de Pélier, was jailed in 1786 for whistling at Queen Marie Antoinette. Forgotten, he was not released unil 1832.

THE 10

FIRST COUNTRIES TO ABOLISH CAPITAL PUNISHMENT

	COUNTRY	DATE ABOLISHED
1	Russia	1826
2	Venezuela	1863
3	Portugal	1867
4	=Brazil	1882
	=Costa Rica	1882
6	Ecuador	1897
7	Panama	1903
8	Norway	1905
9	Uruguay	1907
10	Colombia	1910
	UK	1965

Some countries abolished capital punishment in peacetime only, or for all crimes except treason, generally abolishing it totally at a more recent date, although several later reinstated it. Some countries retained capital punishment on their statute books but effectively abolished it.

THE 10

COUNTRIES WITH THE HIGHEST CRIME RATES

	COUNTRY	RATE*
1	Gibraltar	18,316
2	Surinam	17,819
3	St. Kitts and Nevis	15,468
4	Finland	14,799
5	Rwanda	14,550
6	New Zealand	13,854
7	Sweden	12,982
8	Denmark	10,525
9	Canada	10,451
10	US Virgin Islands	10,441
	England and Wales	9,980

* *Reported crime per 100,000 population*

TOP 10

COUNTRIES WITH THE MOST POLICE OFFICERS

	COUNTRY	POPULATION PER POLICE OFFICER*
1	Russia	81
2	Singapore	93
3	Uruguay	120
4	Kazakhstan	128
5	Bahamas	134
6	Croatia	149
7	Saint Vincent and Grenadines	167
8	Lithuania	183
9	Cyprus	191
10	Malta	197

* *In latest year for which figures available*

Source: Fifth United Nations Survey of Crime Trends and Operation of Criminal Justice Systems

Police manpower figures generally include only full-time paid officials, and exclude clerical and volunteer staff.

TOP 10

COUNTRIES WITH THE FEWEST POLICE OFFICERS

	COUNTRY	POPULATION PER POLICE OFFICER*
1	Mexico	21,691
2	Madagascar	4,692
3	Costa Rica	2,751
4	Egypt	2,691
5	Morocco	996
6	Zambia	936
7	Spain	777
8	India	745
9	Nicaragua	688
10	Philippines	645
	UK	252

* *In latest year for which figures available*

Source: Fifth United Nations Survey of Crime Trends and Operation of Criminal Justice Systems

MOUNTING GUARD

Canada is one of only a handful of countries with a crime rate of more than 10,000 reported crimes per 100,000 inhabitants.

TOP 10

MOST COMMON MURDER WEAPONS AND METHODS IN ENGLAND AND WALES

	WEAPON OR METHOD	VICTIMS (1998/99)
1	Sharp instrument	207
2	Hitting and kicking	101
3	Strangulation and asphyxiation	81
4	Blunt instrument	68
5	Poison or drugs	56
6	Shooting	47
7	Burning	30
8	Motor vehicle	15
9	Drowning	7
10	Explosion	2

TOP 10

MOST COMMON MURDER WEAPONS AND METHODS IN THE US

	WEAPON OR METHOD	VICTIMS (1998)
1	Handguns	7,361
2	Knives or cutting instruments	1,877
3	Firearms (type not stated)	609
4	"Personal weapons" (hands, feet, fists, etc.)	949
5	Blunt objects (hammers, clubs, etc.)	741
6	Shotguns	619
7	Rifles	538
8	Strangulation	211
9	Fire	130
10	Asphyxiation	99

Source: FBI Uniform Crime Reports

TOP 10

RELATIONSHIPS OF MURDER VICTIMS TO PRINCIPAL SUSPECTS IN ENGLAND AND WALES

	RELATIONSHIP	VICTIMS (1998/99)
1	Male friend or acquaintance	172
2	Male stranger	120
3	Current or former wife, female cohabitant, or lover	75
4	Son	41
5	Current or former husband, male cohabitant, or lover	37
6	Female friend or acquaintance	36
7	Daughter	28
8	Female stranger	20
9	Father	8
10	Mother	7

Source: *Home Office Criminal Statistics England and Wales 1998*

In addition to these offences, the Home Office statistics record that, in 1998/99, 10 homicide victims were unspecified male and 10 female family members, while 19 men and 19 women were described as "other person in course of employment", such as security guards killed during hold-ups.

THE 10

MOST PROLIFIC SERIAL KILLERS OF THE 20TH CENTURY

	NAME/COUNTRY/CRIMES AND PUNISHMENT	VICTIMS*
1	**Pedro Alonso López**, Colombia *Captured in 1980, López, nicknamed the "Monster of the Andes", led police to 53 graves, but probably murdered at least 300 in Colombia, Ecuador, and Peru. He was sentenced to life.*	300
2	**Henry Lee Lucas**, USA *Lucas admitted in 1983 to 360 murders. He remains on Death Row in Huntsville Prison, Texas.*	200
3	**Luis Alfredo Gavarito**, Colombia *Gavarito confessed in 1999 to a spate of murders, which are still the subject of investigation.*	140
4	**Dr. Harold Shipman**, UK *In January 2000, Manchester doctor Shipman was found guilty of the murder of 15 women patients, but police believe his total number of victims to be at least 131, and perhaps over 150.*	131
5=	**Donald Henry "Pee Wee" Gaskins**, USA *Gaskins was executed in 1991 for a series of murders that may have reached 200.*	100
=	**Javed Iqbal**, Pakistan *Iqbal and two accomplices were found guilty in March 2000 of murdering boys in Lahore. He was sentenced to be publicly strangled, dismembered and his body dissolved in acid.*	100
7	**Delfina and Maria de Jesús Gonzales**, Mexico *In 1964 the Gonzales sisters were sentenced to 40 years' imprisonment for killing 80 women and 11 men.*	91
8	**Bruno Lüdke**, Germany *Lüdke confessed to murdering 86 women in 1928–43. He died in hospital after a lethal injection.*	86
9	**Daniel Camargo Barbosa**, Ecuador *Barbosa was sentenced to just 16 years in prison for a catalogue of crimes.*	71
10	**Kampatimar Shankariya**, India *Caught after a two-year killing spree, Shankariya was hanged in Jaipur, India, in 1979.*	70

* *Estimated minimum; includes individual and partnership murderers; excludes mercy killings by doctors, murders by bandits and by groups, such as political and military atrocities, and gangland slayings.*

THE 10

WORST CITIES FOR MURDER IN THE US

	CITY	MURDERS (1998)*
1	Chicago	703
2	New York	633
3	Detroit	430
4	Los Angeles	426
5	Philadelphia	338
6	Baltimore	312
7	Washington, D.C.	260
8	Houston	254
9	Dallas	252
10	New Orleans	230

* *Murders and non-negligent manslaughter*

Source: FBI Uniform Crime Reports

THE 10 ★ COUNTRIES WITH THE HIGHEST MURDER RATES

	COUNTRY	ANNUAL MURDERS PER 100,000 POPULATION
1	Swaziland	88.1
2	Colombia	81.9
3	Namibia	72.4
4	South Africa	56.9
5	Lesotho	33.9
6	Belize	33.2
7	Philippines	30.1
8	Jamaica	27.6
9	Guatemala	27.4
10	French Guiana	27.2
	England and Wales	1.4

TOP 10 ★ COUNTRIES WITH THE LOWEST MURDER RATES

	COUNTRY	ANNUAL MURDERS PER 100,000 POPULATION
1	=Argentina	0.1
	=Brunei	0.1
3	=Burkina Faso	0.2
	=Niger	0.2
5	=Guinea	0.5
	=Guinea-Bissau	0.5
	=Iran	0.5
8	=Finland	0.6
	=Saudi Arabia	0.6
10	=Cameroon	0.7
	=Ireland	0.7
	=Mongolia	0.7

Among countries that report to international monitoring organizations, some 18 record murder rates of fewer than one per 100,000. It should be borne in mind, however, that some countries do not report, and there are a number of places that, having had no murders in recent years, could claim a murder rate of zero.

FIREPOWER

While handguns are the most common murder weapons in the US and certain other countries, restrictions on their use elsewhere relegates them to a less significant position.

TOP 10 ★ CIRCUMSTANCES FOR MURDER IN THE US

	REASON	MURDERS (1998)
1	**Argument** (unspecified)	4,080
2	**Robbery**	1,232
3	**Narcotic drug laws violation**	679
4	**Juvenile gang killing**	627
5	**Felony** (unspecified)	268
6	**Argument over money or property**	240
7	**Brawl due to influence of alcohol**	206
8	**Romantic triangle**	184
9	**Brawl due to influence of narcotics**	116
10	**Suspected felony**	104

Source: FBI Uniform Crime Reports

A total of 14,088 murders were reported in 1998, including 1,560 without a specified reason, and 4,358 for which the reasons were unknown.

THE 10 ★ WORST STATES FOR MURDER IN THE US

	STATE	FIREARMS USED	TOTAL MURDERS (1998)
1	California	1,469	2,171
2	Texas	899	1,346
3	New York	521	898
4	Illinois*	537	701
5	Michigan	439	684
6	Pennsylvania	424	611
7	North Carolina	373	607
8	Louisiana	415	540
9	Georgia	329	519
10	Maryland	331	405

* *Provisional figures*

Source: FBI Uniform Crime Reports

Of the 8,482 murders committed in the Top 10 states in 1998, 5,737 (or 67 per cent) involved firearms. New Hampshire had just four murders.

What was Richard Bong's claim to fame?
see p.77 for the answer

A He won the Nobel Prize for Physics
B He was the leading US air ace of World War II
C He held the Olympic long-jump record

Military Matters

CHINESE ARMED FORCES

Members of the Chinese army, the largest military force in the world, parade in the now infamous Tiananmen Square, Beijing.

TOP 10 LARGEST ARMED FORCES

	COUNTRY	ARMY	ESTIMATED ACTIVE FORCES NAVY	AIR	TOTAL
1	China	1,830,000	230,000	420,000	2,480,000
2	USA	469,300	369,800	361,400	1,371,500*
3	India	980,000	53,000	140,000	1,173,000
4	North Korea	950,000	46,000	86,000	1,082,000
4	Russia	348,000	171,500	184,600	1,004,100#
6	South Korea	560,000	60,000	52,000	672,000
7	Turkey	525,000	51,000	63,000	639,000
8	Pakistan	520,000	22,000	45,000	587,000
9	Iran	350,000	20,600	50,000	545,600+
10	Vietnam	412,000	42,000	30,000★	484,000
	UK	113,500	43,700	52,200	212,400♦

* *Includes 171,000 Marine Corps*

\# *Includes Strategic Deterrent Forces, Paramilitary, National Guard, etc.*

\+ *Includes 125,000 Revolutionary Guards*

★ *15,000 air force/15,000 air defence* ♦ *Includes 1,900 Strategic Forces*

"BAZOOKA"

American radio comedian Bob Burns (1893–1956) invented a bizarre trombone-like musical instrument to which he gave the name "bazooka". Bazoo was a slang word for the mouth, and Burns added the *ka* suffix to make it sound like an instrument, such as a harmonica. When the anti-tank rocket-launcher was demonstrated during World War II, a soldier commented that it "looks just like Bob Burns' bazooka".

WHY DO WE SAY?

THE 10 YEARS WITH THE MOST NUCLEAR EXPLOSIONS

(Year/explosions)

1 **1962**, 178 2 **1958**, 116 3 **1968**, 79 4 **1966**, 76 5 **1961**, 71 6 **1969**, 67 7 **1978**, 66 8 = **1967**, 64; = **1970**, 64 10 **1964**, 60

TOP 10

COUNTRIES WITH THE LARGEST DEFENCE BUDGETS

	COUNTRY	BUDGET ($ MILLION)
1	USA	270,200
2	Japan	41,100
3	UK	34,600
4	Russia	31,000
5	France	29,500
6	Germany	24,700
7	Saudi Arabia	18,400
8	Italy	16,200
9	China	12,600
10	South Korea	11,600

The so-called "peace dividend" – the savings made as a consequence of the end of the Cold War between the West and the former Soviet Union – means that both the numbers of personnel and the defence budgets of many countries have been cut.

TOP 10 SMALLEST ARMED FORCES*

(Country/estimated total active forces)

1 **Antigua and Barbuda**, 150 **2** **Seychelles**, 450 **3** **Barbados**, 610 **4** **Luxembourg**, 768 **5** **The Gambia**, 800 **6** **Bahamas**, 860 **7** **Belize**, 1,050 **8** **Cape Verde**, 1,100 **9** **Equatorial Guinea**, 1,320 **10** **Guyana**, 1,600

** Excluding countries not declaring a defence budget*

TOP 10 COUNTRIES WITH THE MOST SUBMARINES

	COUNTRY	SUBMARINES
1	USA	76
2	China	71
3	Russia (and associated states)	over 70
4	North Korea	26
5	South Korea	19
6	=India	16
	=Japan	16
8	=Turkey	15
	=UK	15
10	Germany	14

TOP 10 COUNTRIES WITH THE LARGEST NAVIES

	COUNTRY	MANPOWER (1999)*
1	USA	369,800
2	China	230,000
3	Russia	171,500
4	Taiwan	68,000
5	France	62,600
6	South Korea	60,000
7	India	53,000
8	Turkey	51,000
9	Indonesia	47,000
10	North Korea	46,000

** Including naval air forces and marines*

CRUISE SHIP

The US Navy is the world's largest. Here, the destroyer USS Merrill launches a Tomahawk cruise missile.

THE 10 20TH-CENTURY WARS WITH THE MOST MILITARY FATALITIES

	WAR	YEARS	MILITARY FATALITIES
1	World War II	1939–45	15,843,000
2	World War I	1914–18	8,545,800
3	Korean War	1950–53	1,893,100
4	=Sino-Japanese War	1937–41	1,000,000
	=Biafra–Nigeria Civil War	1967–70	1,000,000
6	Spanish Civil War	1936–39	611,000
7	Vietnam War	1961–73	546,000
8	=India–Pakistan War	1947	200,000
	=USSR invasion of Afghanistan	1979–89	200,000
	=Iran–Iraq War	1980–88	200,000

The statistics of warfare have always been an imperfect science. Not only are battle deaths seldom recorded accurately, but figures are often deliberately inflated by both sides in a conflict. These figures thus represent military historians' "best guesses" – and fail to take into account civilian deaths.

TOP 10 COUNTRIES WITH THE MOST CONSCRIPTED PERSONNEL

(Country/conscripts)

1 **China**, 1,275,000 **2** **Turkey**, 528,000 **3** **Russia**, 330,000 **4** **Egypt**, 320,000 **5** **Iran**, 250,000 **6** **South Korea**, 159,000 **7** **Germany**, 142,000 **8** **Poland**, 141,600 **9** **Italy**, 126,000 **10** **Israel**, 107,500

Most countries have abolished peacetime conscription (the UK did so in 1960 and the USA in 1973), and now recruit their forces on an entirely voluntary basis.

TOP 10 COUNTRIES WITH THE HIGHEST MILITARY/CIVILIAN RATIO

(Country/ratio in 1999)*

1 **North Korea**, 503 **2** **Israel**, 289 **3** **United Arab Emirates**, 243 **4** **Singapore**, 228 **5** **Jordan**, 207 **6** **Syria**, 193 **7** **Iraq**, 180 **8** **Bahrain**, 176 **9** = **Taiwan**, 173; = **Qatar**, 173

UK, 36

** Military personnel per 10,000 population*

Did You Know? The first submarine attack to destroy a warship took place on 17 February 1864, when the Confederate submarine *H. L. Hunley* sunk the Union sloop *Housatonic* off Charleston, South Carolina.

THE 10 ★ AREAS OF EUROPE MOST BOMBED BY ALLIED AIRCRAFT* IN WORLD WAR II

	AREA	BOMBS DROPPED (IMPERIAL TONS)
1	Germany	1,350,321
2	France	583,318
3	Italy	366,524
4	Austria, Hungary, and the Balkans	180,828
5	Belgium and Netherlands	88,739
6	Southern Europe and Mediterranean	76,505
7	Czechoslovakia and Poland	21,419
8	Norway and Denmark	5,297
9	Sea targets	564
10	British Channel Islands	93

* *British and US*

Between Aug 1942 and May 1945 alone, Allied air forces (Bomber Command plus 8 and 15 US Air Forces) flew 731,969 night sorties (and Bomber Command a further 67,598 day sorties), dropping a total of 1,850,919 imperial tons of bombs.

THE 10 ★ COUNTRIES SUFFERING THE GREATEST AIRCRAFT LOSSES IN WORLD WAR II

	COUNTRY	AIRCRAFT LOST
1	Germany	116,584
2	USSR	106,652
3	USA	59,296
4	Japan	49,485
5	UK	33,090
6	Australia	7,160
7	Italy	5,272
8	Canada	2,389
9	France	2,100
10	New Zealand	684

Reports of aircraft losses vary considerably from country to country, some of them including aircraft damaged, lost due to accidents, or scrapped, as well as those destroyed during combat. Very precise combat loss figures exist for the Battle of Britain: during the period 10 July to 31 Oct 1940, 1,065 RAF aircraft were destroyed, compared with 1,922 Luftwaffe fighters, bombers, and other aircraft.

THE 10 ★ CITIES MOST BOMBED BY THE RAF AND USAF IN WORLD WAR II

	CITY	ESTIMATED CIVILIAN FATALITIES
1	Dresden	over 100,000
2	Hamburg	55,000
3	Berlin	49,000
4	Cologne	20,000
5	Magdeburg	15,000
6	Kassel	13,000
7	Darmstadt	12,300
8	=Heilbronn	7,500
	=Essen	7,500
10	=Dortmund	6,000
	=Wuppertal	6,000

The high level of casualties in Dresden resulted principally from the saturation bombing and the firestorm that ensued after Allied raids on the lightly defended city. Although the main objective was to destroy the railway marshalling yards, the scale of the raids was massive: 775 British bombers took part in the first night's raid on 13 Feb 1945, followed the next day by 450 US bombers, with a final attack by 200 US bombers on 15 Feb.

TOP 10 ★ GERMAN AIR ACES OF WORLD WAR II

	PILOT	KILLS CLAIMED
1	Major Eric Hartmann	352
2	Major Gerhard Barkhorn	301
3	Major Günther Rall	275
4	Oberlt. Otto Kittel	267
5	Major Walther Nowotny	258
6	Major Wilhelm Batz	237
7	Major Erich Rudorffer	222
8	Oberst. Heinz Bär	220
9	Oberst. Hermann Graf	212
10	Major Heinrich Ehrler	209

Many of these figures relate to kills on the Eastern Front, where the Luftwaffe was undoubtedly superior to its Soviet opponents.

TOP 10 ★ JAPANESE AIR ACES OF WORLD WAR II

	PILOT	KILLS CLAIMED
1	W. O. Hiroyoshi Nishizawa	87
2	Lt. Tetsuzo Iwamoto	80
3	Petty Officer 1st Class Shoichi Sugita	70
4	Lt. Saburo Sakai	64
5	Petty Officer 1st Class Takeo Okumura	54
6	Petty Officer 1st Class Toshio Ohta	34
7	W. O. Kazuo Sugino	32
8	Petty Officer 1st Class Shizuo Ishii	29
9	Ensign Kaeneyoshi Muto	28
10	=Lt. Sadaaki Akamatsu	27
	=Lt. Junichi Sasai	27

TOP 10 ★ US AIR ACES OF THE KOREAN WAR

	PILOT	KILLS CLAIMED*
1	Capt. Joseph McConnell Jr.	16
2	Major James Jabara	15
3	Capt. Manuel J. Fernandez	14.5
4	Major George A. Davis Jr.	14
5	Col. Royal N. Baker	13
6	=Major Frederick C. Blesse	10
	=Lt. Harold H. Fischer	10
	=Lt. Col. Vermont Garrison	10
	=Col. James K. Johnson	10
	=Capt. Lonnie R. Moore	10
	=Capt. Ralph S. Parr Jr.	10

* *Decimals refer to kills shared across groups such as flying squadrons*

Background image: **BOMB-DAMAGED DRESDEN**

TOP GUNS

Majors Richard I. Bong (left) and Thomas B. McGuire (right), the leading US air aces of World War II, are shown here in Leyte, the Philippines, in 1944. After achieving a total of 78 kills between them, they were both killed in crashes the following year.

TOP 10 US AIR ACES OF WORLD WAR II

(Pilot/kills claimed)*

❶ **Major Richard I. Bong**, 40 ❷ **Major Thomas B. McGuire**, 38 ❸ **Cdr. David S. McCampbell**, 34 ❹ = **Col. Francis S. Gabreski**#, 28; = **Lt-Col. Gregory Boyington**, 28 ❻ = **Major Robert S. Johnson**, 27; = **Col. Charles H. MacDonald**, 27 ❽ = **Major George E. Preddy**, 26; = **Major Joseph J. Foss**, 26 ❿ **Lt. Robert M. Hanson**, 25

* *Decimals refer to kills shared across groups such as flying squadrons*

\# *Also 6.5 kills in Korean War*

TOP 10 COUNTRIES WITH THE MOST COMBAT AIRCRAFT*

(Country/combat aircraft)

❶ **Russia**, 3,966 ❷ **China**, 3,520 ❸ **USA**, 2,598 ❹ **India**, 774 ❺ **Taiwan**, 598 ❻ **North Korea**, 593 ❼ **Egypt**, 583 ❽ **France**, 531 ❾ **Ukraine**, 521 ❿ **South Korea**, 488

UK, 462

* *Air force only, exluding long-range strike/attack aircraft*

TOP 10

BRITISH AND COMMONWEALTH AIR ACES OF WORLD WAR II

	PILOT/COUNTRY	KILLS CLAIMED*
1	**Sqd. Ldr. Marmaduke Thomas St John Pattle**, South Africa	over 40
2	**Gp. Capt. James Edgar "Johnny" Johnson**, Great Britain	33.91
3	**Wing Cdr. Brendan "Paddy" Finucane**, Ireland	32
4	**Flt. Lt. George Frederick Beurling**, Canada	31.33
5	**Wing Cdr. John Randall Daniel Braham**, Great Britain	29
6	**Gp. Capt. Adolf Gysbert "Sailor" Malan**, South Africa	28.66
7	**Wing Cdr. Clive Robert Caldwell**, Australia	28.5
8	**Sqd. Ldr. James Harry "Ginger" Lacey**, Great Britain	28
9	**Sqd. Ldr. Neville Frederick Duke**, Great Britain	27.83
10	**Wing Cdr. Colin F. Gray**, New Zealand	27.7

* *Decimals refer to kills shared across groups such as flying squadrons*

TOP 10

FASTEST FIGHTER AIRCRAFT OF WORLD WAR II

	AIRCRAFT/COUNTRY	MAXIMUM SPEED KM/H	MPH
1	**Messerschmitt Me 163**, Germany	959	596
2	**Messerschmitt Me 262**, Germany	901	560
3	**Heinkel He 162A**, Germany	890	553
4	**P-51-H Mustang**, USA	784	487
5	**Lavochkin La-11**, USSR	740	460
6	**Spitfire XIV**, UK	721	448
7	**Yakovlev Yak-3**, USSR	719	447
8	**P-51-D Mustang**, USA	708	440
9	**Tempest VI**, UK	705	438
10	**Focke-Wulf Fw 190D**, Germany	700	435

Also known as the Komet, the Messerschmitt Me 163 was a short-range rocket-powered interceptor brought into service in 1944–45, during which time this aircraft scored a number of victories over its slower Allied rivals. The Messerschmitt Me 262 was the first jet in operational service. The jet engine of the Soviet Yakovlev Yak-3 was mounted centrally under the cockpit. To avoid the danger of setting the tail-wheel tyre on fire, it was replaced with an all-steel wheel, making landings a somewhat noisy affair.

TOP COMBAT AIRCRAFT

Following its debut in 1976, the F-16 Fighting Falcon proved to be one of the most versatile fighter aircraft of the 20th century. Although designed for air-to-air fighting, it is equally valued for air-to-ground attack, and is available in both one- and two-seater versions. In military terms, it has a relatively low cost (some $20 million each), a considerable range of some 3,220 km (2,000 miles), and is strongly built. It is highly manoeuvrable, has a top speed of 2,170 km/h (1,350 mph), and is capable of achieving Mach 2.05 at 12,190 m (40,000 ft), with a ceiling of 15,240 m (50,000 ft). Its US makers, Lockheed Martin, have produced over 2,000 F-16s, while a similar number are on order, making it the world's most extensively flown combat aircraft.

SNAP SHOTS

Did You Know? The highest "score" by a night-fighter pilot was the total of 121 kills credited to World War II pilot Major Heinz-Wolfgang Schnauffer.

World Religions

TOP 10 LARGEST JEWISH POPULATIONS

	COUNTRY	TOTAL JEWISH POPULATION
1	USA	6,122,462
2	Israel	4,354,900
3	France	640,156
4	Russia	460,266
5	Ukraine	424,136
6	UK	345,054
7	Canada	342,096
8	Argentina	253,666
9	Brazil	107,692
10	Belarus	107,350
	World total	15,050,000

The Diaspora – the scattering of the Jewish people – has been in progress for nearly 2,000 years, and Jewish communities are found in virtually every country in the world. In 1939 the total world Jewish population was around 17 million. Some 6 million fell victim to Nazi persecution, but numbers have now topped 15 million.

JEWISH PRAYERS

The Wailing Wall, Jerusalem, was part of the temple erected by King Herod. Jews traditionally pray here, lamenting the destruction of the temple in AD *70.*

TOP 10 LARGEST CHRISTIAN DENOMINATIONS

	DENOMINATION	MEMBERS
1	Roman Catholic	912,636,000
2	Orthodox	139,544,000
3	Pentecostal	105,756,000
4	Lutheran	84,521,000
5	Baptist	67,146,000
6	Anglican	53,217,000
7	Presbyterian	47,972,000
8	Methodist	25,599,000
9	Seventh-Day Adventist	10,650,000
10	Churches of Christ	6,400,000

Source: *Christian Research*

Although Christian communities are found in almost every country in the world, it is difficult to put a precise figure on nominal membership (a declared religious persuasion) rather than active participation (regular attendance at a place of worship). For example, the total Christian population of the UK was estimated to be 37,394,000 in 1995, but it is estimated that the population who regularly attend church services (who could be classified as practising Christians) is just over 6 million.

TOP 10 LARGEST HINDU POPULATIONS

	COUNTRY	TOTAL HINDU POPULATION
1	India	814,632,942
2	Nepal	21,136,118
3	Bangladesh	14,802,899
4	Indonesia	3,974,895
5	Sri Lanka	2,713,900
6	Pakistan	2,112,071
7	Malaysia	1,043,500
8	USA	798,582
9	South Africa	649,980
10	Mauritius	587,884
	World total	865,000,000

More than 99 per cent of the world's Hindu population lives in Asia, with 94 per cent in India.

TOP 10 RELIGIOUS BELIEFS

	RELIGION	MEMBERS*
1	Christianity	2,015,743,000
2	Islam	1,215,693,000
3	Hinduism	865,000,000
4	Non-religions	774,693,000
5	Buddhism	362,245,000
6	Tribal religious	255,950,000
7	Atheism	151,430,000
8	New religions	102,174,000
9	Sikhism	23,102,000
10	Judaism	15,050,000

* *Estimated total projections to mid-1998*

Outside the Top 10, several other religions have members numbering in millions, among them some 7 million Bahaists, 6 million Confucians, 4 million Jains, and 3 million Shintoists.

TOP 10 LARGEST CHRISTIAN POPULATIONS

	COUNTRY	TOTAL CHRISTIAN POPULATION
1	USA	182,674,000
2	Brazil	157,973,000
3	Mexico	88,380,000
4	China	73,300,000
5	Philippines	65,217,000
6	Germany	63,332,000
7	Italy	47,403,000
8	France	45,624,000
9	Nigeria	38,969,000
10	Dem. Rep. of Congo	37,922,000
	World total	2,015,743,000

Source: *Christian Research*

Did You Know? Britain is to introduce a new remembrance day in 2001 to honour the millions of Jews killed during the Holocaust.

TOP 10 LARGEST MUSLIM POPULATIONS

	COUNTRY	TOTAL MUSLIM POPULATION
1	**Pakistan**	157,349,290
2	**Indonesia**	156,213,374
3	**Bangladesh**	133,873,621
4	**India**	130,316,250
5	**Iran**	74,087,700
6	**Turkey**	66,462,107
7	**Russia**	64,624,770
8	**Egypt**	57,624,098
9	**Nigeria**	46,384,120
10	**Morocco**	33,542,780
	World total	1,215,693,000

Historically, Islam spread as a result of conquest, missionary activity, and through contacts with Muslim traders. In such countries as Indonesia, its appeal lay in part in its opposition to Western colonial influences, which, along with the concept of Islamic community and other tenets, has attracted followers worldwide.

BOWING TO MECCA

Islam places many strictures on its female members but is nonetheless the world's fastest-growing religion. Here, hundreds of Muslim women unite in prayer.

TOP 10 LARGEST BUDDHIST POPULATIONS

	COUNTRY	TOTAL BUDDHIST POPULATION
1	**China**	104,000,000
2	**Japan**	90,510,000
3	**Thailand**	57,450,000
4	**Vietnam**	50,080,000
5	**Myanmar**	41,880,000
6	**Sri Lanka**	12,540,000
7	**South Korea**	11,110,000
8	**Cambodia**	9,870,000
9	**India**	7,000,000
10	**Malaysia**	3,770,000
	World total	362,245,000

HEAD OF THE FAITH

Although India now features in ninth place among countries with high Buddhist populations, the religion originated there in the 6th century BC.

ILD SPONSORSHIP

TOP 10 ★

Town & Country

Countries of the World

TOP 10 LARGEST COUNTRIES

	COUNTRY	AREA SQ KM	AREA SQ MILES
1	Russia	17,070,289	6,590,876
2	Canada	9,970,599	3,849,670
3	China	9,596,961	3,705,408
4	USA	9,169,389	3,540,321
5	Brazil	8,511,965	3,286,488
6	Australia	7,686,848	2,967,909
7	India	3,287,590	1,269,346
8	Argentina	2,780,400	1,073,512
9	Kazakhstan	2,717,300	1,049,156
10	Sudan	2,505,813	967,500
	UK	244,101	94,247
	World total	135,807,000	52,435,381

TOP 10 COUNTRIES IN WHICH WOMEN MOST OUTNUMBER MEN

(Country/women per 100 men)

1 **Latvia**, 120 **2** = **Cape Verdi**, 115; = **Ukraine**, 115 **4** **Russia**, 114 **5** = **Belarus**, 112; = **Estonia**, 112; = **Lithuania**, 112 **8** = **Hungary**, 109; = **Antigua and Barbuda**, 109; = **Georgia**, 109; = **Moldova**, 109

Source: *United Nations*

TOP 10 SMALLEST COUNTRIES

	COUNTRY	AREA SQ KM	AREA SQ MILES
1	Vatican City	0.44	0.17
2	Monaco	1.95	0.77
3	Gibraltar	6.47	2.50
4	Macao	16.06	6.20
5	Nauru	21.23	8.20
6	Tuvalu	25.90	10.00
7	Bermuda	53.35	20.60
8	San Marino	59.57	23.00
9	Liechtenstein	157.99	61.00
10	Antigua	279.72	108.00

The "country" status of several of these micro-states is questionable, since their government, defence, currency, and other features are often intricately linked with those of larger countries, such as the Vatican City with Italy's.

TOP 10 LONGEST BORDERS

	COUNTRY	BORDERS KM	BORDERS MILES
1	China	22,143	13,759
2	Russia	20,139	12,514
3	Brazil	14,691	9,129
4	India	14,103	8,763
5	USA	12,248	7,611
6	Dem. Rep. of Congo	10,271	6,382
7	Argentina	9,665	6,006
8	Canada	8,893	5,526
9	Mongolia	8,114	5,042
10	Sudan	7,697	4,783

This list represents the total length of borders, compiled by adding together the lengths of individual land borders.

RUSSIAN SURVIVORS

The disproportionately high number of women in Russia and other former Soviet countries is the result of high mortality rates among the region's men, caused in part by poor diet and excessive consumption of alcohol and tobacco.

TOP 10 COUNTRIES IN WHICH MEN MOST OUTNUMBER WOMEN

(Country/men per 100 women)

1 **Qatar**, 189 **2** **United Arab Emirates**, 174 **3** **Bahrain**, 133 **4** **Saudi Arabia**, 124 **5** = **Oman**, 113; = **Andorra**, 113 **7** = **Guam**, 112; = **Hong Kong**, 112 **9** **Brunei**, 110 **10** **Kuwait**, 109

Source: *United Nations*

Did You Know? The USA's 6,416-km (3,987-mile) frontier with Canada is the longest continuous frontier in the world.

TOP 10 MOST DENSELY POPULATED COUNTRIES

	COUNTRY	AREA (SQ KM)	ESTIMATED POPULATION*	POPULATION PER SQ KM
1	**Monaco**	1.95	32,231	16,528.7
2	**Singapore**	618	3,571,710	5,779.5
3	**Malta**	316	383,285	1,212.9
4	**Maldives**	298	310,425	1,041.7
5	**Bahrain**	694	641,539	924.4
6	**Bangladesh**	143,998	129,146,695	896.9
7	**Mauritius**	1,865	1,196,172	641.4
8	**Barbados**	430	259,248	602.9
9	**South Korea**	99,274	47,350,529	476.9
10	**San Marino**	61	25,215	413.4
	UK	244,101	59,247,439	242.7
	World	135,807,000	6,073,098,801	44.7

* *For the year 2000*

Source: *US Bureau of the Census/United Nations*

TOP 10 LARGEST COUNTRIES IN EUROPE

	COUNTRY	AREA SQ KM	AREA SQ MILES
1	**Russia** (in Europe)	4,710,227	1,818,629
2	**Ukraine**	603,700	233,090
3	**France**	547,026	211,208
4	**Spain***	504,781	194,897
5	**Sweden**	449,964	173,732
6	**Germany**	356,999	137,838
7	**Finland**	337,007	130,119
8	**Norway**	324,220	125,182
9	**Poland**	312,676	120,725
10	**Italy**	301,226	116,304

* *Including offshore islands*

The UK falls just outside the Top 10 at 244,101 sq km (94,247 sq miles). Excluding the Isle of Man and the Channel Islands, its area comprises England (130,410 sq km/50,351 sq miles), Scotland (78,789 sq km/30,420 sq miles), Wales (20,758 sq km/8,015 sq miles), and Northern Ireland (14,144 sq km/5,461 sq miles).

TOP 10 COUNTRIES WITH THE OLDEST POPULATIONS

(Country/percentage over 65)

1 **Sweden**, 17.3 2 = **Italy**, 16.6; = **Greece**, 16.6 4 **Portugal**, 16.1 5 **Belgium**, 16.0 6 **Spain**, 15.9 7 **UK**, 15.8 8 **Norway**, 15.7 9 = **Germany**, 15.5; = **Japan**, 15.5

Source: *World Bank*

Nine of the ten countries with the oldest populations are in western Europe, implying that this region has lower death rates and a higher life expectancy than the rest of the world.

TOP 10 COUNTRIES WITH THE YOUNGEST POPULATIONS

(Country/percentage under 15)

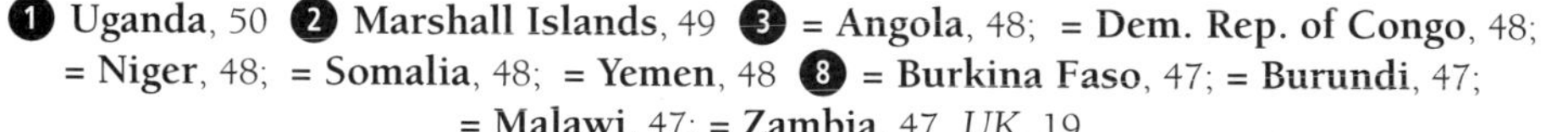

1 **Uganda**, 50 2 **Marshall Islands**, 49 3 = **Angola**, 48; = **Dem. Rep. of Congo**, 48; = **Niger**, 48; = **Somalia**, 48; = **Yemen**, 48 8 = **Burkina Faso**, 47; = **Burundi**, 47; = **Malawi**, 47; = **Zambia**, 47 *UK*, 19

Source: *United Nations*

Countries with high proportions of their people under the age of 15 are usually characterized by high birth rates and high death rates.

LOOKING TO THE FUTURE

Soaring birth rates in many African countries have created broad-based population pyramids, with up to half their populations aged under 15.

World Cities

TOP 10 ★ MOST DENSELY POPULATED CITIES*

	CITY/COUNTRY	POPULATION PER SQ KM	SQ MILE
1	**Hong Kong**, China	98,053	253,957
2	**Lagos**, Nigeria	67,561	174,982
3	**Dhaka**, Bangladesh	63,900	165,500
4	**Jakarta**, Indonesia	56,650	146,724
5	**Bombay**, India	54,997	142,442
6	**Ahmadabad**, India	50,676	131,250
7	**Ho Chi Minh City** (Saigon), Vietnam	50,617	131,097
8	**Shenyang**, China	44,125	114,282
9	**Bangalore**, India	43,583	112,880
10	**Cairo**, Egypt	41,413	107,260

* *Includes only cities with populations of over 2 million*

Source: *US Bureau of the Census*

RUSH HOUR – NIGERIAN STYLE

Nigeria's former capital and still its most important city, Lagos is also one of the world's densest and fastest-growing cities, as a result of which it suffers from traffic congestion, overcrowding, and slum dwellings.

TOP 10 ★ FASTEST-GROWING CITIES

	CITY/COUNTRY	EST. INCREASE, 1995-2010 (%)*
1	**Hangzhou**, China	171.1
2	**Addis Ababa**, Ethiopia	170.7
3	**Kabul**, Afghanistan	156.3
4	**Handan**, China	141.6
5	**Isfahan**, Iran	141.3
6	**Maputo**, Mozambique	139.9
7	**Lagos**, Nigeria	139.5
8	**Luanda**, Angola	138.8
9	**Nairobi**, Kenya	133.6
10	**Qingdao**, China	132.4

* *Urban agglomerations of over 1 million population only*

Source: *United Nations*

TOP 10 ★ LARGEST CITIES IN NORTH AMERICA

	CITY/COUNTRY	EST. POPULATION, 2015*
1	**Mexico City**, Mexico	19,200,000
2	**New York**, USA	17,600,000
3	**Los Angeles**, USA	14,200,000
4	**Chicago**, USA	7,500,000
5	**Toronto**, Canada	5,200,000
6	**Philadelphia**, USA	4,800,000
7	**Santo Domingo**, Dominican Republic	4,700,000
8	=**Guadalajara**, Mexico	4,500,000
	=**San Francisco**, USA	4,500,000
10	=**Dallas**, USA	4,400,000
	=**Washington, DC**, USA	4,400,000

* *Of urban agglomeration*

Source: *United Nations*

TOP 10 ★ HIGHEST CITIES

	CITY/COUNTRY	HEIGHT M	FT
1	**Wenchuan**, China	5,099	16,730
2	**Potosí**, Bolivia	3,976	13,045
3	**Oruro**, Bolivia	3,702	12,146
4	**Lhasa**, Tibet	3,684	12,087
5	**La Paz**, Bolivia	3,632	11,916
6	**Cuzco**, Peru	3,399	11,152
7	**Huancayo**, Peru	3,249	10,660
8	**Sucre**, Bolivia	2,835	9,301
9	**Tunja**, Colombia	2,820	9,252
10	**Quito**, Ecuador	2,819	9,249

Lhasa was formerly the highest capital city in the world, a role now occupied by La Paz, capital of Bolivia. Wenchuan is situated at more than half the elevation of Everest, and even the cities at the foot of this list are more than one-third as high.

Did You Know? Ein Bokek, beside the Dead Sea, is the world's lowest inhabited place at 393.5 m (1,291 ft) below sea level.

TOP 10

LARGEST CITIES

	CITY/COUNTRY	EST. POPULATION, 2015*
1	**Tokyo**, Japan	28,900,000
2	**Bombay**, India	26,200,000
3	**Lagos**, Nigeria	24,600,000
4	**São Paulo**, Brazil	20,300,000
5	**Dhaka**, Bangladesh	19,500,000
6	**Karachi**, Pakistan	19,400,000
7	**Mexico City**, Mexico	19,200,000
8	**Shanghai**, China	18,000,000
9	**New York**, USA	17,600,000
10	**Calcutta**, India	17,300,000

* *Of urban agglomeration*

Source: *United Nations*

The definition taken in the above and other city lists is the United Nations definition of "urban agglomeration", which comprises the city or town proper and also the suburban fringe or thickly settled territory lying outside of, but adjacent to, the city boundaries.

TOP 10

LARGEST CITIES IN THE US*

	CITY/STATE	POPULATION
1	**New York**, New York	7,420,166
2	**Los Angeles**, California	3,597,556
3	**Chicago**, Illinois	2,802,079
4	**Houston**, Texas	1,786,691
5	**Philadelphia**, Pennsylvania	1,436,287
6	**San Diego**, California	1,220,666
7	**Phoenix**, Arizona	1,198,064
8	**San Antonio**, Texas	1,114,130
9	**Dallas**, Texas	1,075,894
10	**Detroit**, Michigan	970,196

* *Estimated figures up to 1 July 1999*

Source: *US Bureau of the Census*

These are estimates for central city areas only, not for the total metropolitan areas that surround them, which may be several times as large.

TOP 10

LARGEST CITIES IN EUROPE

	CITY/COUNTRY	EST. POPULATION, 2015*
1	**Paris**, France	9,700,000
2	**Moscow**, Russia	9,300,000
3	**London**, UK	7,600,000
4	**Essen**, Germany	6,600,000
5	**St. Petersburg**, Russia	5,100,000
6	**Milan**, Italy	4,300,000
7	**Madrid**, Spain	4,100,000
8=	**Frankfurt**, Germany	3,700,000
=	**Katowice**, Poland	3,700,000
10	**Dusseldorf**, Germany	3,400,000

* *Of urban agglomeration*

Source: *United Nations*

PARISIAN GRANDEUR

A population of 9.5 million, a central position, and cultural and other attractions have led to the inexorable growth of Paris to its present rank as Europe's largest city.

TOP 10

LARGEST NON-CAPITAL CITIES

	CITY/COUNTRY/CAPITAL CITY	POPULATION
1	**Shanghai**, China *Beijing*	13,584,000 *11,299,000*
2	**Bombay**, India *New Delhi*	15,138,000 *8,419,000*
3	**Calcutta***, India *New Delhi*	11,923,000 *8,419,000*
4	**Lagos**, Nigeria *Abuja*	10,287,000 *378,671*
5	**Sâo Paulo**, Brazil *Brasília*	10,017,821 *1,864,000*
6	**Karachi***, Pakistan *Islamabad*	9,733,000 *350,000*
7	**Tianjin**, China *Beijing*	9,415,000 *11,299,000*
8	**Istanbul***, Turkey *Ankara*	8,274,921 *2,937,524*
9	**New York**, USA *Washington, DC*	7,420,166 *523,124*
10	**Madras**, India *New Delhi*	6,002,000 *8,419,000*

* *Former capital*

TOP 10

MOST POPULATED FORMER CAPITAL CITIES

	CITY/COUNTRY	CEASED TO BE CAPITAL	POPULATION*
1	**Calcutta**, India	1912	11,021,918
2	**Istanbul**, Turkey	1923	7,774,169
3	**Karachi**, Pakistan	1968	7,183,000
4	**Rio de Janeiro**, Brazil	1960	5,547,033
5	**St. Petersburg**, Russia	1980	4,273,001
6	**Berlin**, Germany	1949	3,472,009
7	**Alexandria**, Egypt	c.641	3,380,000
8	**Melbourne**, Australia	1927	3,189,200
9	**Nanjiang**, China	1949	2,610,594
10	**Philadelphia**, USA	1800	1,524,249

* *Within administrative boundaries*

TOP 10 LARGEST REGIONS IN THE UK

	REGION	LOCATION	AREA SQ KM	AREA SQ MILES
1	**Highland**	Scotland	25,784	9,952
2	**North Yorkshire**	England	8,038	3,208
3	**Argyll and Bute**	Scotland	6,930	2,676
4	**Cumbria**	England	6,824	2,635
5	**Devon**	England	6,560	2,533
6	**Dumfries and Galloway**	Scotland	6,439	2,486
7	**Aberdeenshire**	Scotland	6,318	2,439
8	**Lincolnshire**	England	5,921	2,286
9	**Norfolk**	England	5,372	2,074
10	**Perth and Kinross**	Scotland	5,311	2,051

The largest region in Wales is the Unitary Authority of Powys, covering 5,196 sq km (2,006 sq miles), and in Ireland, Derry, which covers 1,699 sq km (644 sq miles).

TOP 10 MOST HIGHLY POPULATED COUNTIES IN THE UK*

	COUNTY#	POPULATION
1	**Essex**	1,288,000
2	**Lancashire**	1,135,000
3	**Tyne and Wear**	1,121,000
4	**Surrey**	1,057,000
5	**Hertfordshire**	1,025,000
6	**Staffordshire**	807,000
7	**West Sussex**	747,000
8	**Nottinghamshire**	745,000
9	**Derbyshire**	730,000
10	**Devon**	686,000

* *Excluding metropolitan counties and city regions*

\# *All in England*

The shifting of county boundaries and the creation of new Unitary Authorities makes it difficult to provide comparative figures across the UK. The metropolitan counties and city regions have been excluded here in order to avoid a list dominated by cities; nevertheless, all the most populated in the UK are in England.

TOP 10 LEAST POPULATED REGIONS IN THE UK

	REGION/LOCATION	POPULATION
1	**Moyle**, Northern Ireland	16,000
2	**Orkney Islands**, Scotland	20,000
3	**Shetland Islands**, Scotland	23,000
4	**Ballymoney**, Northern Ireland	25,000
5	**Eilean Siar** (Western Isles), Scotland	28,000
6=	**Larne**, Northern Ireland	31,000
=	**Limavady**, Northern Ireland	31,000
8	**Cookstown**, Northern Ireland	32,000
9	**Rutland**, England	36,000
10=	**Carrickfergus**, Northern Ireland	37,000
=	**Strabane**, Northern Ireland	37,000

The traditional counties of Northern Ireland have been replaced by Unitary Authorities, which are considerably smaller than most regions in the rest of Britain, and hence feature prominently in this list. While national population figures have grown, those of some of these regions have declined in the past 100 years: that of Orkney was 28,609 at the 1901 Census, and that of Shetland 28,166.

TOP 10 MOST DENSELY POPULATED COUNTIES IN ENGLAND*

	COUNTY	POPULATION PER SQ KM	POPULATION PER SQ MILE
1	**Tyne and Wear**	2,076	5,377
2	**Surrey**	630	1,632
3	**Hertfordshire**	625	1,620
4	**Lancashire**	392	1,014
5	**West Sussex**	376	974
6	**Kent**	374	969
7	**Essex**	371	961
8	**Nottinghamshire**	357	925
9	**Hampshire**	334	865
10	**Cheshire**	322	834

* *Excluding metropolitan counties and cities*

The most densely populated areas of England are excluded from this list because they are not numbered within what can properly be called counties. Outside London, the 40 sq km (15.4 sq mile) area covered by the Unitary Authority of Portsmouth is the most densely populated, with 4,750 people per sq km (1,834 people per sq mile).

TOP 10 LEAST DENSELY POPULATED COUNTIES IN ENGLAND

	COUNTY	POPULATION PER SQ KM	POPULATION PER SQ MILE
1	**Northumberland**	61	158
2	**North Yorkshire**	70	181
3	**Cumbria**	72	186
4	**Shropshire**	87	225
5=	**Devon**	105	272
=	**Lincolnshire**	105	272
7	**Wiltshire**	130	337
8	**Cornwall and the Isles of Scilly**	137	355
9	**Somerset**	141	365
10	**Norfolk**	146	378

TOP 10 MOST DENSELY POPULATED REGIONS IN NORTHERN IRELAND

	UNITARY AUTHORITY	POPULATION PER SQ KM	SQ MILE
1	Belfast	2,620	6,786
2	North Down	936	2,424
3	Castlereagh	783	2,028
4	Newtownabbey	531	1,375
5	Carrickfergus	460	1,191
6	Craigavon	278	720
7	Lisburn	249	645
8	Ards	184	477
9	Fermanagh	149	386
10	Ballymena	118	306

Although heading this list, Belfast is the only region of Northern Ireland to have experienced a population decrease: in the period from 1981 to 1997 it went down by 8.9 per cent. By contrast, that of Lisburn increased by a massive 30.7 per cent, making it the region with the greatest population increase in the province. It was closely followed by Carrickfergus (29.7 per cent) and Banbridge (28.7 per cent).

TOP 10 MOST DENSELY POPULATED REGIONS IN SCOTLAND

	COUNCIL AREA	POPULATION PER SQ KM	SQ MILE
1	Glasgow City	3,494	9,049
2	Dundee City	2,286	5,921
3	City of Edinburgh	1,716	4,444
4	Aberdeen City	1,162	3,010
5	North Lanarkshire	689	1,785
6	Renfrewshire	682	1,766
7	East Dunbartonshire	645	1,671
8	West Dunbartonshire	590	1,528
9	Inverclyde	535	1,386
10	East Renfrewshire	513	1,329

Despite being the most densely populated, most of the regions listed here actually declined in population during the period 1981 to 1997. Inverclyde suffered the greatest decrease with a 14.5 per cent drop. East Renfrewshire was the only one in the Top 10 to show an increase in double figures, with a rise of 10.4 per cent. Although heading this list, Glasgow City's population similarly declined, by 14.1 per cent.

TOP 10 MOST DENSELY POPULATED REGIONS IN WALES

	UNITARY AUTHORITY	POPULATION PER SQ KM	SQ MILE
1	Cardiff	2,273	5,887
2	Newport	722	1,870
3	Torfaen	718	1,860
4	Blaenau Gwent	668	1,730
5	=Caerphilly	609	1,577
	=Swansea	609	1,577
7	Rhondda, Cynon, Taff	569	1,474
8	Bridgend	531	1,375
9	Merthyr Tydfil	516	1,336
10	The Vale of Glamorgan	357	925

While following a pattern of depopulation similar to that of Scotland, a number of densely populated regions of Wales underwent expansion in the period from 1981 to 1997. Cardiff, No. 1 on this list, grew by a healthy 11.0 per cent, which is the highest rate of increase among those in the Top 10. Outside this list, Ceredigion experienced the greatest population increase, at 15.1 per cent.

TOP 10 LEAST DENSELY POPULATED REGIONS IN NORTHERN IRELAND

	UNITARY AUTHORITY	POPULATION PER SQ KM	SQ MILE
1	Moyle	31	80
2	Omagh	42	109
3	Strabane	43	111
4	Limavady	54	140
5	=Ballymoney	61	158
	=Dungannon	61	158
7	=Cookstown	62	161
	=Derry	62	161
9	Magherafelt	68	176
10	Armagh	81	210

TOP 10 LEAST DENSELY POPULATED REGIONS IN SCOTLAND

	COUNCIL AREA	POPULATION PER SQ KM	SQ MILE
1	Highland	8	21
2	Eilean Siar (Western Isles)	9	23
3	Argyll and Bute	13	34
4	Shetland Islands	16	41
5	Orkney Islands	20	52
6	The Scottish Borders	22	57
7	Dumfries and Galloway	23	60
8	Perth and Kinross	25	65
9	Aberdeenshire	36	93
10	=Moray	38	98
	=Stirling	38	98

TOP 10 LEAST DENSELY POPULATED REGIONS IN WALES

	UNITARY AUTHORITY	POPULATION PER SQ KM	SQ MILE
1	Powys	24	62
2	Ceredigion	39	101
3	Gwynedd	46	119
4	=Carmarthenshire	71	184
	=Pembrokeshire	71	184
6	Isle of Anglesey	93	241
7	Conwy	98	254
8	Monmouthshire	103	268
9	Denbighshire	107	277
10	Neath Port Talbot	315	816

Did You Know? The most overcrowded piece of land in England is Kensington and Chelsea in London, where each of its 12 sq km (4.6 sq miles) accommodates the incredible figure of 13,667 people.

Place Names

TOP 10 LONGEST PLACE NAMES IN THE UK*

	NAME/LOCATION	LETTERS
1	**Gorsafawddachaidraigddanheddogled-dollônpenrhynareurdraethceredigion** (see Top 10 Longest Place Names)	67
2	**Llanfairpwllgwyngyllgogerychwyrndrobwll-llantysiliogogogoch** (see Top 10 Longest Place Names)	58
3	**Sutton-under-Whitestonecliffe**, North Yorkshire	27
4	**Llanfihangel-yng-Ngwynfa**, Powys	22
5	=**Llanfihangel-y-Creuddyn**, Dyfed	21
	=**Llanfihangel-y-Traethau**, Gwynedd	21
7	**Cottonshopeburnfoot**, Northumberland	19
8	=**Blakehopeburnhaugh**, Northumberland	18
	=**Coignafeuinternich**, Inverness-shire	18
10	=**Claddach-baleshare**, North Uist, Outer Hebrides	17
	=**Claddach-knockline**, North Uist, Outer Hebrides	17

* *Single and hyphenated words only*

Runners up include Combeinteignhead, Doddiscombsleigh, Moretonhampstead, Stokeinteignhead and Woolfardisworthy (pronounced "Woolsery"), all of which are in Devon and have 16 letters.

TOP 10 COUNTRIES WITH THE LONGEST OFFICIAL NAMES

	OFFICIAL NAME*	COMMON ENGLISH NAME	LETTERS
1	**al-Jamāhīrīyah al-Arabīya al-Lībīyah ash-Sha bīyah al-Ishtirākīyah**	Libya	56
2	**al-Jumhūrīyah al-Jazā'irīyah ad-Dīmuqrāṭīyah ash-Sha bīyah**	Algeria	49
3	**United Kingdom of Great Britain and Northern Ireland**	United Kingdom	45
4	**Sri Lankā Prajathanthrika Samajavadi Janarajaya**	Sri Lanka	43
5	**Jumhurīyat al-Qumur al-Ittihādīyah al-Islāmīyah**	The Comoros	41
6	=**al-Jumhūrīyah al-Islāmīyah al-Mūrītānīyah**	Mauritania	36
	=**The Federation of St. Christopher and Nevis**	St. Kitts and Nevis	36
8	**Jamhuuriyadda Dimuqraadiga Soomaaliya**	Somalia	35
9	**al-Mamlakah al-Urdunnīyah al-Hāshimīyah**	Jordan	34
10	**Repoblika Demokratika n'i Madagaskar**	Madagascar	32

* *Some official names have been transliterated from languages that do not use the Roman alphabet; their length may vary according to the method used.*

TOP 10 MOST COMMON PLACE NAMES IN GREAT BRITAIN

	NAME	OCCURRENCES
1	Newton	150
2	Blackhill/Black Hill	141
3	Mountpleasant/Mount Pleasant	130
4	Castlehill/Castle Hill	127
5	Woodside/Wood Side	116
6	Newtown/New Town	111
7	Greenhill/ Green Hill	108
8	Woodend/Wood End	106
9	Burnside	105
10	Beacon Hill	94

These entries include the names of towns, villages, woods, hills, and other named locations, but exclude combinations of these names with others. (Newton Abbot and Newton-le-Willows, for example, are not counted with the Newtons.)

TOP 10 MOST COMMON STREET NAMES IN THE US

1. 2nd/Second Street 2. 3rd/Third Street 3. 1st/First Street 4. 4th/Fourth Street 5. Park Street 6. 5th/Fifth Street 7. Main Street 8. 6th/Sixth Street 9. Oak Street 10. 7th/Seventh Street Source: *US Bureau of the Census*

TOP 10 MOST COMMON STREET NAMES IN THE UK

1. High Street
2. Station Road
3. Church Road
4. Park Road
5. The Drive
6. Station Approach
7. Green Lane
8. The Avenue
9. London Road
10. Church Lane

TOP 10 MOST COMMON HOUSE NAMES IN THE UK

1. The Cottage
2. The Bungalow
3. Rose Cottage
4. The Lodge
5. The Coach House
6. The School House
7. The White House
8. Woodlands
9. Hill Crest
10. The Gables

Did You Know? 1st/First Street is the third most common street name in the US only because many streets that would be so designated are instead called Main Street.

TOP 10 ★

LONGEST PLACE NAMES*

NAME	LETTERS
1 Krung thep mahanakhon bovorn ratanakosin mahintharayutthaya mahadilok pop noparatratchathani burirom udomratchanivetmahasathan amornpiman avatarnsathit sakkathattiyavisnukarmprasit	167
When the poetic name of Bangkok, capital of Thailand, is used, it is usually abbreviated to "Krung Thep" (city of angels).	
2 Taumatawhakatangihangakoauauotamateaturipukakapikimaungahoronukupokaiw-henuakitanatahu	85
This is the longer version (the other has a mere 83 letters) of the Maori name of a hill in New Zealand. It translates as "The place where Tamatea, the man with the big knees, who slid, climbed and swallowed mountains, known as land-eater, played on the flute to his loved one".	
3 Gorsafawddachaidraigddanheddogleddollônpenrhynareurdraethceredigion	67
A name contrived by the Fairbourne Steam Railway, Gwynedd, North Wales, for publicity purposes and in order to outdo its rival, No. 4. It means "The Mawddach station and its dragon teeth at the Northern Penrhyn Road on the golden beach of Cardigan Bay".	
4 Llanfairpwllgwyngyllgogerychwyrndrobwllllantysiliogogogoch	58
This is the place in Gwynedd famed especially for the length of its railway tickets. It means "St Mary's Church in the hollow of the white hazel near to the rapid whirlpool of Llantysilio of the Red Cave". Questions have been raised about its authenticity, since its official name comprises only the first 20 letters, and the full name appears to have been invented as a hoax in the 19th century by a local poet, John Evans, known as Y Bardd Cocos. It also has Britain's longest Internet site name: http://www.llanfairpwllgwyngyllgogerychwyrndrobwllllantysiliogogogoch.wales.com/llanfair	
5 El Pueblo de Nuestra Señora la Reina de los Angeles de la Porciuncula	57
The site of a Franciscan mission and the full Spanish name of Los Angeles; it means "the town of Our Lady the Queen of the Angels of the Little Portion". Nowadays it is customarily known by its initial letters, "LA", making it also one of the shortest-named cities in the world.	
6 Chargoggagoggmanchauggagoggchaubunagungamaugg	45
America's second longest place name, a lake near Webster, Massachusetts. Its Indian name, loosely translated, means "You fish on your side, I'll fish on mine, and no one fishes in the middle". It is said to be pronounced "Char-gogg-a-gogg (pause) man-chaugg-a-gogg (pause) chau-bun-a-gung-amaugg". It is, however, an invented extension of its real name (Chagungungamaug Pond, or "boundary fishing place"), devised in the 1920s by Larry Daly, the editor of the Webster Times.	
7=Lower North Branch Little Southwest Miramichi	40
Canada's longest place name – a short river in New Brunswick.	
=Villa Real de la Santa Fe de San Francisco de Asis	40
The full Spanish name of Santa Fe, New Mexico, translates as, "Royal city of the holy faith of St. Francis of Assisi".	
9 Te Whakatakanga-o-te-ngarehu-o-te-ahi-a-Tamatea	38
The Maori name of Hammer Springs, New Zealand; like the second name in this list, it refers to a legend of Tamatea, explaining how the springs were warmed by "the falling of the cinders of the fire of Tamatea". Its name is variously written either hyphenated or as a single word.	
10 Meallan Liath Coire Mhic Dhubhghaill	32
The longest multiple name in Scotland, a place near Aultanrynie, Highland, this is alternatively spelled Meallan Liath Coire Mhic Dhughaill (30 letters).	

* *Including single-word, hyphenated, and multiple-word names*

CITY OF ANGELS

The original 57-letter Spanish name of Los Angeles contrasts dramatically with its more common designation as "LA".

The Tallest Buildings

TOP 10 ★ TALLEST HABITABLE BUILDINGS

	BUILDING/YEAR/LOCATION	STOREYS	HEIGHT M	HEIGHT FT
1	**Petronas Towers**, 1996, Kuala Lumpur, Malaysia	96	452	1,482
2	**Sears Tower**, 1974, Chicago, USA	110	443	1,454
	with spires		*520*	*1,707*
3	**World Trade Center***, 1972, New York, USA	110	417	1,368
4	**World Finance Center**, 2001, Hong Kong, China	88	400	1,312
5	**Jin Mao Building**, 1997, Shanghai, China	93	382	1,255
	with spire		*420*	*1,378*
6	**Empire State Building**, 1931, New York, USA	102	381	1,250
	with spire		*449*	*1,472*
7	**T & C Tower**, 1997, Kao-hsiung, Taiwan	85	348	1,142
8	**Amoco Building**, 1973, Chicago, USA	80	346	1,136
9	**John Hancock Center**, 1969, Chicago, USA	100	343	1,127
	with spires		*449*	*1,470*
10	**Shun Hing Square**, 1996, Shenzen, China	80	330	1,082
	with spires		*384*	*1,260*

* *Twin towers; the second tower, completed in 1973, has the same number of storeys but is slightly smaller at 415m (1,360 ft), although its spire takes it up to 521 m (1,710 ft).*

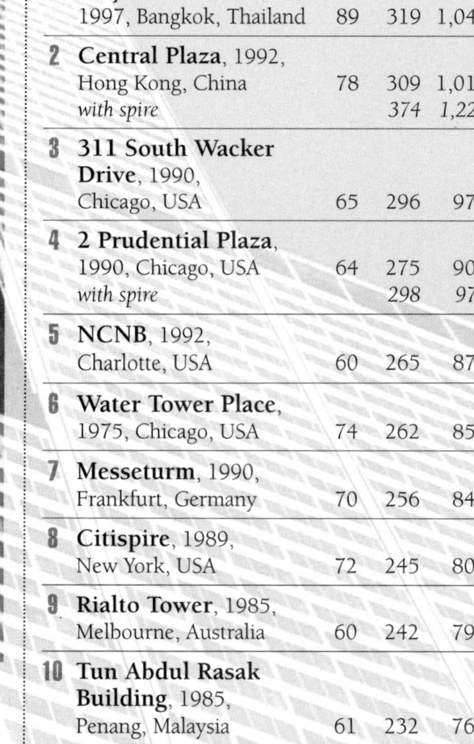

CHICAGO GIANT

Chicago's tallest skyscraper weighs 201,848 tonnes (222,500 tons). It has 16,100 windows and contains 69,000 km (43,000 miles) of telephone cable.

TOP 10 ★ TALLEST REINFORCED CONCRETE BUILDINGS

	BUILDING/YEAR/LOCATION	STOREYS	HEIGHT M	HEIGHT FT
1	**Baiyoke II Tower**, 1997, Bangkok, Thailand	89	319	1,046
2	**Central Plaza**, 1992, Hong Kong, China	78	309	1,015
	with spire		*374*	*1,228*
3	**311 South Wacker Drive**, 1990, Chicago, USA	65	296	970
4	**2 Prudential Plaza**, 1990, Chicago, USA	64	275	901
	with spire		*298*	*978*
5	**NCNB**, 1992, Charlotte, USA	60	265	871
6	**Water Tower Place**, 1975, Chicago, USA	74	262	859
7	**Messeturm**, 1990, Frankfurt, Germany	70	256	841
8	**Citispire**, 1989, New York, USA	72	245	802
9	**Rialto Tower**, 1985, Melbourne, Australia	60	242	794
10	**Tun Abdul Rasak Building**, 1985, Penang, Malaysia	61	232	761

Reinforced concrete was patented in France on 16 March 1867 by Joseph Monier (1823–1906) and was later developed by another Frenchman, François Hennebique (1842–1921). The first American buildings constructed from it date from a century ago, since when it has become one of the most important of all building materials. It is constructed from concrete slabs containing steel bars that expand and contract at the same rate as the concrete. This provides great tensile strength and fire resistance. These qualities make it the ideal construction material for bridge spans and skyscrapers.

TOP 10 CITIES WITH THE MOST SKYSCRAPERS*

(City/country/skyscrapers)

1 **New York City**, USA, 162 2 **Chicago**, USA, 72 3 **Hong Kong**, China, 41 4 **Shanghai**, China, 38 5 **Tokyo**, Japan, 29 6 **Houston**, USA 27 7 **Singapore**, 25 8 **Los Angeles**, USA, 21 8 **Dallas**, USA, 19 10 **Sydney**, Australia, 18

* *Habitable buildings of more than 152 m (500 ft)*

TOP 10 TALLEST TELECOMMUNICATIONS TOWERS

	TOWER/YEAR/LOCATION	HEIGHT M	HEIGHT FT
1	**CN Tower**, 1975, Toronto, Canada	555	1,821
2	**Ostankino Tower**, 1967, Moscow, Russia	537	1,762
3	**Oriental Pearl Broadcasting Tower**, 1995, Shanghai, China	468	1,535
4	**Menara Telecom Tower**, 1996, Kuala Lumpur, Malaysia	421	1,381
5	**Tianjin TV and Radio Tower**, 1991, Tianjin, China	415	1,362
6	**Central Radio and TV Tower**, 1994, Beijing, China	405	1,328
7	**TV Tower**, 1983, Tashkent, Uzbekistan	375	1,230
8	**Liberation Tower**, 1998, Kuwait City, Kuwait	372	1,220
9	**Alma-Ata Tower**, 1983, Kazakhstan	370	1,214
10	**TV Tower**, 1969, Berlin, Germany	365	1,198

TOP 10 TALLEST MASTS

	MAST/LOCATION	HEIGHT M	HEIGHT FT
1	**KVLY Channel 11 TV Tower** (formerly KTHI-TV), Blanchard/Fargo, North Dakota, USA	629	2,063
2	**KSLA-TV Mast**, Shreveport, Louisiana, USA	579	1,898
3	=**WBIR-TV Mast**, Knoxville, Tennessee, USA	533	1,749
	=**WTVM & WRBL TV Mast**, Columbus, Georgia, USA	533	1,749
5	**KFVS TV Mast**, Cape Girardeau, Missouri, USA	511	1,676
6	**WPSD-TV Mast**, Paducah, Kentucky, USA	499	1,638
7	**WGAN TV Mast**, Portland, Maine, USA	493	1,619
8	**KWTV TV Mast**, Oklahoma City, Oklahoma, USA	479	1,572
9	**BREN Tower**, Area 25, Nevada Test Site, Nevada, USA	465	1,530
10	**Omega Base Navigational Mast**, Gippsland, Victoria, Australia	426	1,400

TOP 10 HIGHEST PUBLIC OBSERVATORIES

	BUILDING/LOCATION	OBSERVATORY	YEAR	HEIGHT M	HEIGHT FT
1	**CN Tower**, Toronto, Canada	Space deck	1975	447	1,465
2	**World Trade Center**, New York City, USA	Rooftop Tower B	1973	415	1,360
3	**Sears Tower**, Chicago, USA	103rd floor	1974	412	1,353
4	**Empire State Building**, New York, USA	102nd floor Outdoor observatory	1931	381 320	1,250 1,050
5	**Ostankino Tower**, Moscow, Russia	5th floor turret	1967	360	1,181
6	**Oriental Pearl Broadcasting Tower**, Shanghai, China	VIP observation level Public observation level	1995	350 263	1,148 863
7	**Jin Mao Building**, Shanghai, China	88th floor	1997	340	1,115
8	**John Hancock Center**, Chicago, USA	94th floor	1968	314	1,030
9	**Sky Central Plaza**, Guanghshou, China	90th floor	1996	310	1,016
10	**KL Tower**, Kuala Lumpur, Malaysia	Revolving restaurant Public observation level	1995	282 276	925 907

TALLEST BY FAR

The world's tallest free-standing structure, the CN Tower in Toronto, Canada, attracts almost 2 million visitors a year to its space deck level at 447 m (1,465 ft).

Bridges & Other Structures

TOP 10 ★ LONGEST ROAD TUNNELS

	TUNNEL/YEAR	LOCATION	LENGTH KM	MILES
1	**Laerdal**, 2000	Norway	24.50	15.22
2	**St. Gotthard**, 1980	Switzerland	16.32	10.14
3	**Arlberg**, 1978	Austria	13.98	8.69
4	=**Fréjus**, 1980	France/Italy	12.90	8.02
	=**Pinglin Highway**, U/C	Taiwan	12.90	8.02
6	**Mont Blanc**, 1965	France/Italy	11.60	7.21
7	**Gudvangen**, 1992	Norway	11.43	7.08
8	**Folgefonn**, 2001	Norway	11.10	6.90
9	**Kan-Etsu II**, 1991	Japan	11.06	6.87
10	**Kan-Etsu I**, 1986	Japan	10.93	6.79

U/C = under construction

TOP 10 ★ LONGEST STEEL ARCH BRIDGES

	BRIDGE/YEAR/LOCATION	LONGEST SPAN M	FT
1	**New River Gorge**, 1977, Fayetteville, West Virginia, USA	518	1,700
2	**Kill Van Kull**, 1931, Bayonne, New Jersey/ Staten Island, New York, USA	504	1,654
3	**Sydney Harbour**, 1932, Australia	503	1,650
4	**Fremont**, 1973, Portland, Oregon, USA	383	1,257
5	**Port Mann**, 1964, Vancouver, Canada	366	1,200
6	**Thatcher Ferry**, 1962, Panama Canal	344	1,128
7	**Laviolette**, 1967, Quebec, Canada	335	1,100
8	=**Runcorn–Widnes**, 1961, UK	330	1,082
	=**Zdákov**, 1967, Lake Orlik, Czech Republic	330	1,082
10	=**Birchenough**, 1935, Fort Victoria, Zimbabwe	329	1,080
	=**Roosevelt Lake**, 1990, Arizona, USA	329	1,080

TOP 10 ★ LARGEST SPORTS STADIUMS

	STADIUM/LOCATION	CAPACITY
1	**Strahov Stadium**, Prague, Czech Republic	240,000
2	**Maracaña Municipal Stadium**, Rio de Janeiro, Brazil	220,000
3	**Rungnado Stadium**, Pyongyang, South Korea	150,000
4	**National Stadium of Iran**, Azadi, Iran	128,000
5	**Estádio Maghalaes Pinto**, Belo Horizonte, Brazil	125,000
6	=**Estádio Morumbi**, São Paulo, Brazil	120,000
	=**Estádio da Luz**, Lisbon, Portugal	120,000
	=**Senayan Main Stadium**, Jakarta, Indonesia	120,000
	=**Yuba Bharati Krirangan**, Nr Calcutta, India	120,000
10	**Estádio Castelão**, Fortaleza, Brazil	119,000

These figures represent maximum capacities. In fact, new safety regulations introduced in many countries mean that actual audiences for most events are smaller. The Aztec Stadium, Mexico City, holds 107,000, with most of the seats under cover. The New Orleans Superdome is the largest indoor stadium, with a capacity of 97,365. The largest stadium in the United Kingdom is Wembley Stadium, with a capacity of 80,000. This is being replaced with a new National Stadium, with a capacity of 90,000, scheduled for completion for the 2003 Cup Final.

TOP 10 ★ LONGEST CABLE-STAYED BRIDGES

	BRIDGE/YEAR/LOCATION	LENGTH OF MAIN SPAN M	FT
1	**Tatara**, 1999, Onomichi–Imabari, Japan	890	2,920
2	**Pont de Normandie**, 1994, Le Havre, France	856	2,808
3	**Qinghzhou Minjiang**, 1996, Fozhou, China	605	1,985
4	**Yang Pu**, 1993, Shanghai, China	602	1,975
5	=**Meiko–Chuo**, 1997, Nagoya, Japan	590	1,936
	=**Xu Pu**, 1997, Shanghai, China	590	1,936
7	**Skarnsundet**, 1991, Trondheim Fjord, Norway	530	1,739
8	**Tsurumi Tsubasa**, Yokohama, Japan	510	1,673
9	=**Ikuchi**, 1994, Onomichi–Imabari, Japan	490	1,608
	=**Öresund**, 2000, Copenhagen–Malmö, Denmark/Sweden)	490	1,608

SHANGHAI SURPRISE

One of the world's longest cable-stayed bridges, Shanghai's Yang Pu was built to ease traffic congestion on the city's busy inner ring road.

TOP 10 LONGEST CANTILEVER BRIDGES

	BRIDGE/YEAR/ LOCATION	LONGEST SPAN M	FT
1	**Pont de Québec**, 1917, Canada	549	1,800
2	**Firth of Forth**, 1890, Scotland	521	1,710
3	**Minato**, 1974, Osako, Japan	510	1,673
4	**Commodore John Barry**, 1974, New Jersey/ Pennsylvania, USA	494	1,622
5	=**Greater New Orleans 1**, 1958, Louisiana, USA	480	1,575
	=**Greater New Orleans 2**, 1988, Louisiana, USA	480	1,575
7	**Howrah**, 1943, Calcutta, India	457	1,500
8	**Gramercy**, 1995, Louisiana, USA	445	1,460
9	**Transbay**, 1936, San Francisco, USA	427	1,400
10	**Baton Rouge**, 1969, Louisiana, USA	376	1,235

TOP 10 LONGEST UNDERWATER TUNNELS

	TUNNEL/YEAR/ LOCATION	LENGTH KM	MILES
1	**Seikan**, 1988, Japan	53.90	33.49
2	**Channel Tunnel**, 1994, France/England	49.94	31.03
3	**Dai–Shimizu**, 1982, Japan	22.17	13.78
4	**Shin–Kanmon**, 1975, Japan	18.68	11.61
5	**Great Belt Fixed Link** (Eastern Tunnel), 1997, Denmark	8.00	4.97
6	**Bømlafjord***, 2000, Norway	7.82	4.86
7	**Oslofjord***, 2000, Norway	7.39	4.59
8	**Severn**, 1886, UK	7.01	4.36
9	**Magerøysund***, 1999, Norway	6.87	4.27
10	**Haneda**, 1971, Japan	5.98	3.72

* *Road; others rail*

The need to connect the Japanese islands of Honshu, Kyushu, and Hokkaido has resulted in a wave of undersea tunnel building in recent years, with the Seikan the most ambitious project of all. Connecting Honshu and Hokkaido, 23.3 km (14.4 miles) of the tunnel is 100 m (328 ft) below the seabed. It took 24 years to complete.

TOP 10 HIGHEST DAMS

	DAM/RIVER/LOCATION	YEAR	HEIGHT M	FT
1	**Rogun**, Vakhsh, Tajikistan	U/C	335	1,099
2	**Nurek**, Vakhsh, Tajikistan	1980	300	984
3	**Grande Dixence**, Dixence, Switzerland	1961	285	935
4	**Inguri**, Inguri, Georgia	1980	272	892
5	**Vajont**, Vajont, Italy	1960	262	860
6	=**Manuel M. Torres (Chicoasén)**, Grijalva, Mexico	1980	261	856
	=**Tehri**, Bhagirathi, India	U/C	261	856
8	**Alvaro Obregon (El Gallinero)**, Tenasco, Mexico	1946	260	853
9	**Mauvoisin**, Drance de Bagnes, Switzerland	1957	250	820
10	**Alberto Lleras C.**, Guavio, Colombia	1989	243	797

U/C = under construction

Source: *International Commission on Large Dams (ICOLD)*

TOP 10 LONGEST SUSPENSION BRIDGES

	BRIDGE/YEAR/LOCATION	LENGTH OF MAIN SPAN M	FT
1	**Akashi–Kaiko**, 1998, Kobe–Naruto, Japan	1,990	6,529
2	**Great Belt**, 1997, Denmark	1,624	5,328
3	**Humber Estuary**, 1981, UK	1,410	4,626
4	**Jiangyin**, 1998, China	1,385	4,544
5	**Tsing Ma**, 1997, Hong Kong, China	1,377	4,518
6	**Verrazano Narrows**, 1964, New York, USA	1,298	4,260
7	**Golden Gate**, 1937, San Francisco, USA	1,280	4,200
8	**Höga Kusten**, 1997, Veda, Sweden	1,210	3,970
9	**Mackinac Straits**, 1957, Michigan, USA	1,158	3,800
10	**Minami Bisan-seto**, 1988, Kojima–Sakaide, Japan	1,100	3,609

The Messina Strait Bridge between Sicily and Calabria, Italy, remains a speculative project but, if constructed according to plan, it will have by far the longest centre span of any bridge at 3,320 m (10,892 ft). At 3,910 m (12,828 ft), however, Japan's Akashi–Kaiko bridge, completed in 1998 and with a main span of 1,990 m (6,528 ft), is the world's longest overall.

DAM RECORD BUSTER

An incongruous mural depicting Lenin celebrates this Soviet engineering accomplishment, the building of the world's second highest dam, the Nurek, Tajikistan.

Background image: PONT DE QUÉBEC CANADA

Where is the tallest mast outside the USA?

see p.91 for the answer

A Germany
B Australia
C China

青が散る
宮本輝

TOP 10 ★

Culture & Learning

Word Power

TOP 10 ★ LONGEST WORDS IN THE ENGLISH LANGUAGE*

WORD/MEANING — LETTERS

1 Ornicopytheobibliopsychocrystarroscioaerogenethliometeoroaustrohieroanthropoichthyopyrosiderochpnomyoalectryoophiobotanopegohydrorhabdocrithoaleuroalphitohalomolybdoclerobeloaxinocoscinodactyliogeolithopessopsephocatoptrotephraoneirochiroonychodactyloarithstichooxogeloscogastrogyrocerobletonooenoscapulinaniac — 310

Medieval scribes used this word to refer to "A deluded human who practises divination or forecasting by means of phenomena, interpretation of acts, or other manifestations related to the following animate or inanimate objects and appearances: birds, oracles, Bible, ghosts, crystal gazing, shadows, air appearances, birth stars, meteors, winds, sacrificial appearances, entrails of humans and fishes, fire, red-hot irons, altar smoke, mice, grain picking by rooster, snakes, herbs, fountains, water, wands, dough, meal, barley, salt, lead, dice, arrows, hatchet balance, sieve, ring suspension, random dots, precious stones, pebbles, pebble heaps, mirrors, ash writing, dreams, palmistry, nail rays, finger rings, numbers, book passages, name letterings, laughing manners, ventriloquism, circle walking, wax, susceptibility to hidden springs, wine, and shoulder blades."

2 Lopadotemachoselachogaleokranioleipsanodrimhypotrimmatosilphioparaomelitokatakechymenokichlepikossyphophattoperisteralektryonoptekephalliokigklopeleiolagoiosiraiobaphetraganopterygon — 182

The English transliteration of a 170-letter Greek word that appears in The Ecclesiazusae *(a comedy by the Greek playwright Aristophanes, c.448–380 BC). It is used as a description of a 17-ingredient dish.*

3 Aequeosalinocalcalinosetaceoaluminosocupreovitriolic — 52

Invented by a medical writer, Dr. Edward Strother (1675–1737), to describe the spa waters at Bath.

4 Osseocarnisanguineoviscericartilaginonervomedullary — 51

Coined by writer and East India Company official Thomas Love Peacock (1785–1866), and used in his satire Headlong Hall *(1816) as a description of the structure of the human body.*

5 Pneumonoultramicroscopicsilicovolcanoconiosis — 45

It first appeared in print (though ending in "-koniosis") in F. Scully's Bedside Manna *[sic] (1936), then found its way into* Webster's Dictionary *and is now in the* Oxford English Dictionary. *It is said to mean a lung disease caused by breathing fine dust.*

6 Hepaticocholecystostcholecystenterostomies — 42

Surgical operations to create channels of communication between gall bladders and hepatic ducts or intestines.

7 Praetertranssubstantiationalistically — 37

The adverb describing the act of surpassing the act of transubstantiation; the word is found in Mark McShane's novel Untimely Ripped *(1963).*

8 = Pseudoantidisestablishmentarianism — 34

A word meaning "false opposition to the withdrawal of state support from a Church", derived from that perennial favourite long word, antidisestablishmentarianism (a mere 28 letters).

= Supercalifragilisticexpialidocious — 34

An invented word, but perhaps now eligible since it has appeared in the Oxford English Dictionary. *It was popularized by the song of this title in the film* Mary Poppins *(1964), where it is used to mean "wonderful", but it was originally written in 1949 in an unpublished song by Parker and Young who spelt it "supercalafajalistickespialadojus" (32 letters).*

10 = Encephalomyeloradiculoneuritis — 30

A syndrome caused by a virus associated with encephalitis.

= Hippopotomonstrosesquipedalian — 30

Appropriately, the word that means "pertaining to an extremely long word".

= Pseudopseudohypoparathyroidism — 30

First used (hyphenated) in the US in 1952 and (unhyphenated) in Great Britain in The Lancet *in 1962 to describe a medical case in which a patient appeared to have symptoms of pseudohypoparathyroidism, but with "no manifestations suggesting hypoparathyroidism".*

* *Excluding names of chemical compounds*

TOP 10 ★ MOST USED LETTERS IN WRITTEN ENGLISH

SURVEY*		#MORSE
e	1	e
t	2	t
a	3	a
o	4	i
i	5	n
n	6	o
s	7	s
r	8	h
h	9	r
l	10	d

* *The order as indicated by a survey across approximately 1 million words appearing in a wide variety of printed texts, ranging from newspapers to novels.*

\# *The order estimated by Samuel Morse, the inventor in the 1830s of Morse code, based on his calculations of the respective quantities of type used by a printer. The number of letters in the printer's type trays ranged from 12,000 for "e" to 4,400 for "d", with only 200 for "z".*

TOP 10 ★ MOTHER TONGUES MOST SPOKEN BY LONDON SCHOOL CHILDREN

	LANGUAGE	SPEAKERS
1	English	608,500
2	Bengali and Silheti	40,400
3	Punjabi	29,800
4	Gujarati	28,600
5	Hindi/Urdu	26,000
6	Turkish	15,600
7	Arabic	11,000
8	English-based Creole	10,700
9	Yoruba	10,400
10	Somali	8,300

Source: *University of Westminster*

Did You Know? Honorificabilitudinitatibus (27 letters), which means "honourably", is the longest word used by Shakespeare; it appears in *Love's Labour's Lost* (Act V, Scene i).

TOP 10 COUNTRIES WITH THE MOST ENGLISH-LANGUAGE SPEAKERS*

	COUNTRY	APPROXIMATE NO. OF SPEAKERS
1	USA	232,910,000
2	UK	57,520,000
3	Canada	18,655,000
4	Australia	15,204,000
5	South Africa	3,900,000
6	Ireland	3,590,000
7	New Zealand	3,309,000
8	Jamaica	2,400,000
9	Trinidad and Tobago	1,199,000
10	Guyana	749,000

* *Inhabitants for whom English is their mother tongue*

The Top 10 represents the countries with the greatest numbers of inhabitants who speak English as their mother tongue. After the 10th entry, the figures dive to around or under 260,000, in the case of the Bahamas, Barbados, and Zimbabwe. In addition to these and others that make up a world total that is probably in excess of 500 million, there are perhaps as many as 1 billion who speak English as a second language: a large proportion of the population of the Philippines, for example, speaks English, and there are many countries, such as India, Nigeria, and other former British colonies in Africa, where English is either an official language or is widely understood.

TOP 10 MOST WIDELY SPOKEN LANGUAGES

	LANGUAGE	APPROXIMATE NO. OF SPEAKERS
1	Chinese (Mandarin)	1,075,000,000
2	English	514,000,000
3	Hindustani	496,000,000
4	Spanish	425,000,000
5	Russian	275,000,000
6	Arabic	256,000,000
7	Bengali	215,000,000
8	Portuguese	194,000,000
9	Malay-Indonesian	176,000,000
10	French	129,000,000

According to mid-1999 estimates by Emeritus Professor Sidney S. Culbert of the University of Washington, in addition to those languages appearing in the Top 10, there are three further languages that are spoken by more than 100 million individuals: German (128 million), Japanese (126 million), and Urdu (105 million). A further 13 languages are spoken by 50–100 million people: Punjabi (94), Korean (78), Telugu (76), Tamil (74), Marathi (71), Cantonese (71), Wu (70), Vietnamese (67), Javanese (64), Italian (63), Turkish (61), Tagalog (58), and Thai (52).

TOP 10 MOST STUDIED FOREIGN LANGUAGES IN THE UK

1 Spanish 2 Danish 3 Swedish 4 Italian 5 Czech 6 Finnish 7 Turkish 8 Polish 9 Greek 10 French

This ranking is based on language courses studied at the School of Languages at the University of Westminster (formerly the Polytechnic of Central London). The largest source of language teaching in the state sector in the whole of Europe, it offers courses in 28 different languages.

TOP 10 LANGUAGES OFFICIALLY SPOKEN IN THE MOST COUNTRIES

	LANGUAGE	COUNTRIES
1	English	57
2	French	33
3	Arabic	23
4	Spanish	21
5	Portuguese	8
6	= Dutch	4
	= German	4
8	= Chinese (Mandarin)	3
	= Danish	3
	= Italian	3
	= Malay	3

There are many countries in the world with more than one official language – both English and French are recognized officially in Canada, for example. English is used in numerous countries as the lingua franca – the common language that enables people who speak mutually unintelligible languages to communicate with each other.

THE ROSETTA STONE

Made in Egypt in about 200 BC and discovered in 1799 during the French occupation of Egypt, the Rosetta Stone was taken to England in 1801 and is now in the British Museum, London. It has the same inscription in three different alphabets – Egyptian hieroglyphics at the top, demotic Egyptian in the middle, and Greek below. After a painstaking study of the relationship between the different alphabets, French scholar Jean François Champollion (1790–1832) was able to decipher the hieroglyphics, all knowledge of which had previously been lost. The Rosetta Stone thus provided the key to our understanding of this ancient language.

SNAP SHOTS

Children at School

TOP 10 COUNTRIES WITH THE LONGEST SCHOOL YEARS

(Country/school year in days)

1 **China**, 251 2 **Japan**, 243 3 **Korea**, 220 4 **Israel**, 215 5 = **Germany**, 210; = **Russia**, 210 7 **Switzerland**, 207 8 = **Netherlands**, 200; = **Scotland**, 200; = **Thailand**, 200

England, 192

THE 10 ★ COUNTRIES WITH THE MOST PRIMARY SCHOOL PUPILS PER TEACHER

	COUNTRY	PRIMARY SCHOOL PUPILS PER TEACHER*
1	Central African Republic	77
2	Congo	70
3	Mali	70
4	Chad	67
5	Malawi	59
6	Bangladesh	63
7	=Afghanistan	58
	=Mozambique	58
	=Rwanda	58
	=Senegal	58
	UK	19

* *In latest year for which figures available*

Source: *UNESCO*

TOP 10 ★ A LEVEL SUBJECTS STUDIED BY PUPILS IN ENGLAND, WALES, AND NORTHERN IRELAND

	SUBJECT	TOTAL TAKING EXAM (1999)
1	English	90,340
2	General Studies	85,338
3	Mathematics	69,945
4	Biology	56,036
5	Geography	42,181
6	Chemistry	41,727
7	History	38,482
8	Business Studies	37,926
9	Art*	37,385
10	Physics	33,880

* *Includes a range of related subjects*

Source: *Associated Examining Board*

EASTERN PROMISE

China has the most children at school and the world's longest school year, but spends just 2 per cent of its GNP on education – less than half that of Western countries.

TOP 10 ★ COUNTRIES SPENDING THE MOST ON EDUCATION

	COUNTRY	EXPENDITURE AS PERCENTAGE OF GNP*
1	Kiribati	11.4
2	Moldova	9.4
3	Namibia	8.4
4	Botswana	7.8
5	Denmark	7.7
6	South Africa	7.5
7	Barbados	7.3
8	=Finland	7.2
	=Zimbabwe	7.2
10	Sweden	7.1
	UK	4.7

* *Gross National Product in latest year for which data available*

Source: *UNESCO*

A number of other countries rank high in this list, but there are insufficient recent data to include them. In 1980, French Guiana spent 16.5 per cent of its GNP on education, Martinique 14.5 per cent, and Guadeloupe 13.6 per cent. The UK and USA do not make it into the Top 20.

"ACADEMY"

Fabled queen Helen of Troy ("the face that launched a thousand ships") was kidnapped from Sparta by Theseus and later rescued by her brothers, Castor and Pollux. They were assisted in their task by an Athenian named Academus. A grove or public garden called the Grove of Academus was planted in Athens to commemorate this event. It was here that the Greek philosopher Plato founded his school of philosphy, where like-minded scholars could gather to listen to his orations and discuss moral issues. This school was called the Academia, from which we have the word "academy".

WHY DO WE SAY?

EDUCATING THE MASSES

Indian culture places a high value on education, and consequently some 7 percent of the country's entire population attends secondary school.

TOP 10 COUNTRIES WITH THE MOST SECONDARY SCHOOL PUPILS

	COUNTRY	SECONDARY SCHOOL PUPILS
1	China	69,155,538
2	India	68,872,393
3	USA	21,473,692
4	Russia	13,732,000
5	Indonesia	12,223,753
6	Japan	9,878,568
7	Iran	8,776,792
8	Germany	8,260,674
9	Mexico	7,589,414
10	Egypt	6,726,738
	UK	6,696,772

The UK is No. 11 on the list, followed by France with 5,980,518 pupils. In the US, about 8 per cent of the population attends secondary school – a figure that shows how impressive is India's rate of 7 per cent.

Source: *UNESCO*

THE 10 COUNTRIES WITH THE HIGHEST ILLITERACY RATES*

COUNTRY	FEMALE ILLITERACY RATE (%)		MALE ILLITERACY RATE (%)	COUNTRY
Niger	93.4	1	79.1	Niger
Burkina Faso	90.8	2	71.7	Nepal
Guinea-Bissau	85.5	3	70.5	Burkina Faso
Afghanistan	85.0	4	60.6	Mali
Yemen	82.8	5	59.3	Guinea-Bissau
Sierra Leone	81.8	6	57.0	Senegal
= Central African Republic	79.7	7	54.6	Sierra Leone
= Nepal	79.7	8	54.5	Ethiopia
Guinea	78.1	9	52.8	Afghanistan
Liberia	77.6	10	52.0	Central African Republic

* *Age over 15; figures estimated where no recent data available*

Source: *UNESCO*

The United Nations defines an illiterate person as someone who cannot, with understanding, both read and write a short, simple statement on his or her daily life. Literacy is a good measure of educational achievement in developing regions, because it reflects successful schooling, not just attendance at school as is measured by enrolment figures. The Top 10 list shows that in some countries of the world, the majority of the population cannot read or write.

TOP 10 COUNTRIES WITH THE HIGHEST PERCENTAGE OF MALE SECONDARY SCHOOL TEACHERS

	COUNTRY	SECONDARY SCHOOL TEACHERS	MALE PER CENT*
1	Chad	2,598	96
2	=Bangladesh	128,389	90
	=Dem. Rep. of Congo	59,325	90
	=Mauritania	1,600	90
5	= Ethiopia	25,075	89
	=Togo	4,736	89
7	=Burkina Faso	3,346	88
	=Equatorial Guinea	466	88
	=Guinea	4,690	88
	=Nepal	25,357	88
	UK	317,266	54

* *In latest year for which figures available*

Whose notebooks are known as *The Codex Hammer*?

see p.102 for the answer

A Mozart
B Leonardo da Vinci
C Marco Polo

Higher Education

TOP 10 ★ COUNTRIES WITH THE HIGHEST PERCENTAGE OF FEMALE UNIVERSITY STUDENTS

	COUNTRY	PERCENTAGE OF FEMALE STUDENTS*
1	Cyprus	75
2	US Virgin Islands	74
3	Qatar	73
4	United Arab Emirates	72
5	Kuwait	66
6	Namibia	65
7	Myanmar	64
8	Barbados	62
9	Mongolia	61
10=	Bulgaria	60
=	Cuba	60
=	Panama	60

* *In latest year for which data available*

Source: *UNESCO*

CRÈME DE LA CRÈME

Between the late 1960s and 1970, the University of Paris was split into 13 separate establishments, which comprise the world's largest higher education body.

TOP 10 ★ LARGEST UNIVERSITIES

	UNIVERSITY/LOCATION	STUDENTS
1	**University of Paris**, France	311,163
2	**University of Calcutta**, India	300,000
3	**University of Mexico**, Mexico	269,000
4	**University of Bombay**, India	262,350
5	**University of Guadalajara**, Mexico	214,986
6	**University of Rome**, Italy	189,000
7	**University of Buenos Aires**, Argentina	183,397
8	**University of Rajasthan**, India	175,000
9	**University of California**, USA	157,331
10	**Gujarat University**, Italy	153,379

The huge number of university institutions in India reflects not only the country's massive population and the high value placed on education in Indian culture, but also the inclusion of many "Affiliating and Teaching" colleges attached to universities. It should be noted that the University of Paris is divided into numerous separate centres, and that the figure is for the total of all the centres.

THE 10 ★ COUNTRIES WITH THE LOWEST PERCENTAGE OF FEMALE UNIVERSITY STUDENTS

	COUNTRY	PERCENTAGE OF FEMALE STUDENTS*
1	Equatorial Guinea	4
2=	Central African Republic	9
=	Guinea	9
4	Chad	12
5=	Eritrea	13
=	Yemen	13
7	Mali	14
8	Mauritania	15
9	Cambodia	16
10=	Ethiopia	17
=	Tanzania	17
=	Togo	17

* *In latest year for which data available*

Source: *UNESCO*

WOMAN'S WORK

Women study separately but in large numbers at the United Arab Emirates University in Al-Ain, which was founded in 1976.

TOP 10 COUNTRIES OF ORIGIN OF FOREIGN STUDENTS STUDYING IN THE UK

(Country/students)

1 Malaysia, 18,539 2 Ireland, 17,160 3 Greece, 17,073 4 Germany, 12,402 5 France, 11,312 6 Hong Kong, 11,298 7 USA, 8,600 8 Spain, 7,261 9 Singapore, 6,787 10 China, 5,496

TOP 10 HOST COUNTRIES FOR UK FOREIGN STUDENTS

(Country/students)

1 USA, 7,799 2 France, 4,194 3 Germany, 3,171 4 Spain, 1,948 5 Ireland, 1,810 6 Canada, 1,334 7 Netherlands, 612 8 Australia, 526 9 Norway, 482 10 Sweden, 422

TOP 10

COUNTRIES WITH THE MOST UNIVERSITY STUDENTS

	COUNTRY	PERCENTAGE FEMALE	UNIVERSITY STUDENTS*
1	USA	53	8,529,132
2	India	32	4,425,247
3	China	36	3,170,936
4	Russia	53	2,587,510
5	Japan	29	2,311,618
6	Philippines	57	2,017,972
7	Indonesia	31	1,889,408
8	Germany	42	1,857,906
9	Brazil	53	1,716,263
10	Korea	32	1,556,949

* *In latest year for which data available*

Source: *UNESCO*

TOP 10

OLDEST UNIVERSITIES IN THE UK

	UNIVERSITY	YEAR FOUNDED
1	Oxford	1160
2	Cambridge	1209
3	St. Andrews	1411
4	Glasgow	1451
5	Aberdeen	1495
6	Edinburgh	1583
7	Durham*	1832
8	London#	1836
9	Manchester	1851
10	University of Wales+	1893

* *A short-lived Cromwellian establishment was set up in 1657*

\# *Constituent colleges founded earlier: University College 1826, King's College 1828*

\+ *Constituent colleges founded earlier: Lampeter 1822, Aberystwyth 1872, Cardiff 1883, Bangor 1884*

TOP 10

COUNTRIES WITH THE HIGHEST PROPORTION OF ADULTS IN HIGHER EDUCATION

	COUNTRY	TOTAL ADULT STUDENTS	ADULT STUDENTS PER 100,000*
1	Canada	1,763,105	5,997
2	Korea	2,541,659	5,609
3	Australia	1,002,476	5,552
4	USA	14,261,778	5,339
5	New Zealand	162,350	4,508
6	Finland	213,995	4,190
7	Norway	180,383	4,164
8	Spain	1,591,863	4,017
9	Ireland	47,955	3,618
10	France	2,091,688	3,600
	UK	1,820,489	3,135

* *In latest year for which data available*

Source: *UNESCO*

GRADUATION DAY

Decked in their traditional tasselled mortar boards and gowns, more students graduate from US universities than from those of any other country.

Where would you find the 82-m (270-ft) statue of Motherland?

see p.110 for the answer

A Volgograd, Russia
B Kiev, Ukraine
C Prague, Czech Republic

Book Firsts & Records

TOP 10 MOST CITED AUTHORS OF ALL TIME

(Author/country/dates)

1. **William Shakespeare**, UK, 1564–1616 2. **Charles Dickens**, UK, 1812–70 3. **Sir Walter Scott**, UK, 1771–1832 4. **Johann Goethe**, Germany, 1749–1832 5. **Aristotle**, Greece, 384–322 BC 6. **Alexandre Dumas (père)**, France, 1802–70 7. **Robert Louis Stevenson**, UK, 1850–94 8. **Mark Twain**, USA, 1835–1910 9. **Marcus Tullius Cicero**, Italy, 106–43 BC 10. **Honoré de Balzac**, France, 1799–1850

This Top 10 is based on a search of a major US library computer database, Citations, which includes books both by and about the author, with a total of more than 15,000 for Shakespeare.

TOP 10 LARGEST LIBRARIES

	LIBRARY	LOCATION	FOUNDED	BOOKS
1	Library of Congress	Washington, DC, USA	1800	29,000,000
2	National Library of China	Beijing, China	1909	20,000,000
3	National Library of Canada	Ottawa, Canada	1953	16,000,000
4	Deutsche Bibliothek*	Frankfurt, Germany	1990	15,997,000
5	British Library#	London, UK	1753	15,000,000
6	Harvard University Library	Cambridge, Massachusetts, USA	1638	13,143,330
7	Vernadsky Central Scientific Library of the National Academy of Sciences	Kiev, Ukraine	1919	13,000,000
8	Russian State Library+	Moscow, Russia	1862	11,750,000
9	New York Public Library★	New York, USA	1895	11,300,000
10	Bibliothèque Nationale de Paris	Paris, France	1701	11,000,000

* *Formed in 1990 through the unification of the Deutsche Bibliothek, Frankfurt (founded 1947), and the Deutsche Bucherei, Leipzig*

\# *Founded as part of the British Museum, 1753; became an independent body in 1973*

\+ *Founded 1862 as Rumyantsev Library, formerly State V. I. Lenin Library*

★ *Astor Library founded 1848, consolidated with Lenox Library and Tilden Trust to form New York Public Library in 1895*

TOP 10 TYPES OF BOOK PUBLISHED IN THE UK

(Subject/new titles published in 1999)

1. **Fiction**, 9,800 2. **Children's**, 9,099 3. **History**, 5,193 4. **Economics**, 4,670 5. **Religion**, 4,595 6. **Social sciences**, 4,495 7. **Computers/computer games**, 4,100 8. **Medicine**, 4,093 9. **School textbooks**, 3,963 10. **Art**, 3,842

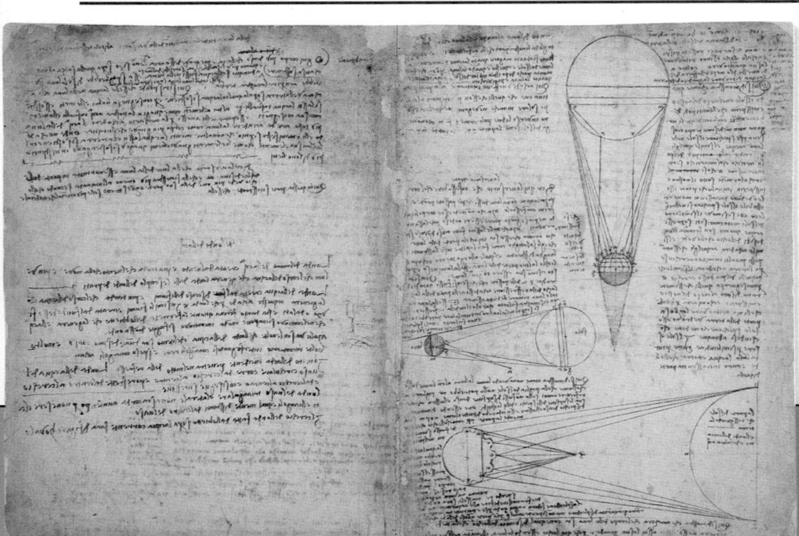

UNDER THE HAMMER

The Codex Hammer, a collection of Leonardo da Vinci's scientific writings, was compiled in the early 16th century. It has over 350 drawings that illustrate the artist's scientific theories. In 1994 it achieved a record price at auction when bought by Bill Gates.

TOP 10 MOST EXPENSIVE BOOKS AND MANUSCRIPTS EVER SOLD AT AUCTION

	BOOK OR MANUSCRIPT/SALE	PRICE (£)*
1	***The Codex Hammer***, c.1508–10, Christie's, New York, 11 Nov 1994 ($30,800,000)	19,230,000
	This Leonardo da Vinci notebook was bought by Bill Gates, the billionaire founder of Microsoft.	
2	***The Gospels of Henry the Lion***, c.1173–75, Sotheby's, London, 6 Dec 1983	7,400,000
	At the time of its sale, this became the most expensive manuscript or book ever sold.	
3	***The Birds of America*, John James Audubon**, 1827–38, Christie's, New York, 10 Mar 2000 ($8,000,000)	5,187,731
	This holds the record for any natural history book.	
4	***The Canterbury Tales*, Geoffrey Chaucer**, c.1476–77, Christie's, London, 8 July 1998	4,600,000
	Printed by William Caxton and bought by Paul Getty.	
5	***The Gutenberg Bible***, 1455, Christie's, New York, 22 Oct 1987 ($5,390,000)	2,934,131
	This is one of the first books ever printed, by Johann Gutenberg and Johann Fust in 1455.	
6	***The Northumberland Bestiary***, c.1250–60, Sotheby's, London, 29 Nov 1990	2,700,000
	This holds the record for an English manuscript.	
7	***The Burdett Psalter and Hours***, 1282–86, Sotheby's, London, 23 June 1998	2,500,000
	This is the third most expensive illustrated manuscript ever sold.	
8	**Autograph manuscript of nine symphonies by Wolfgang Amadeus Mozart**, c.1773–74, Sotheby's, London, 22 May 1987	2,350,000
	This holds the record for any music manuscript.	
9	***The Birds of America*, John James Audubon**, 1827–38, Sotheby's, New York, 6 June 1989 ($3,600,000)	2,292,993
10	***The Hours of Saint-Lô***, 1470, Sotheby's, New York, 21 Apr 1998 ($3,300,000)	1,980,000

* *Excluding premiums*

THE 10

FIRST PUBLICATIONS PRINTED IN ENGLAND

	AUTHOR/BOOK
1	*Propositio ad Carolum ducem Burgundiae**
2	Cato, *Disticha de Morbidus*
3	Geoffrey Chaucer, *The Canterbury Tales*
4	*Ordinale seu Pica ad usem Sarum* ("*Sarum Pie*")
5	John Lydgate, *The Temple of Glass*
6	John Lydgate, *Stans puer mensam*
7	John Lydgate, *The Horse, the Sheep and the Goose*
8	John Lydgate, *The Churl and the Bird*
9	*Infanta Salvatoris*
10	William Caxton, advertisement for "Sarum Pie"

* *This work was printed before September 1476; all the others were printed in either 1476 or 1477.*

THE 10 FIRST POCKET BOOKS*

(Author/title)

❶ James Hilton, *Lost Horizon* ❷ Dorothea Brande, *Wake Up and Live!* ❸ William Shakespeare, *Five Great Tragedies* ❹ Thorne Smith, *Topper* ❺ Agatha Christie, *The Murder of Roger Ackroyd* ❻ Dorothy Parker, *Enough Rope* ❼ Emily Brontë, *Wuthering Heights* ❽ Samuel Butler, *The Way of All Flesh* ❾ Thornton Wilder, *The Bridge of San Luis Rey* ❿ Felix Salten, *Bambi*

* *All published in 1939*

"BLURB"

American humorist Frank Gelett Burgess (1866–1951), best known as the author of the nonsense poem *I Never Saw a Purple Cow*, was also the inventor of the word "blurb" – the effusive text used on book jackets to describe the book within. In his book *Are You a Bromide?*, Burgess claimed that its author was Miss Belinda Blurb, whose work was said to be the sensation of the year.

WHY DO WE SAY?

BEST RED AUTHOR

During the Cultural Revolution, Chinese leader Mao Tse-Tung (Zedong) became the subject of a personality cult, with his bestselling Quotations ... (Little Red Book) its most potent symbol.

TOP 10

LARGEST REFERENCE LIBRARIES IN THE UK

	LIBRARY/LOCATION/FOUNDED	BOOKS
1	**British Library**, London, 1753	15,000,000
2	=**Bodleian Library**, Oxford, 1602	6,500,000
	=**National Library of Scotland**, Edinburgh, 1682	6,500,000
4	**University Library**, Cambridge, *c*.1400	6,050,000
5	**National Library of Wales**, Aberystwyth, 1907	5,000,000
6	**British Library of Political and Economic Science**, London School of Economics, 1894	4,000,000
7	**John Rylands University Library**, Manchester, 1972*	3,500,000
8	**University of Edinburgh**, 1580	2,700,000
9	**University of Leeds**, 1874	2,500,000
10	**University of Birmingham**, 1880	2,100,000

* *In 1972 the John Rylands Library (founded in 1900) was amalgamated with Manchester University Library (founded 1851).*

TOP 10

BESTSELLING BOOKS OF ALL TIME

	BOOK/AUTHOR	FIRST PUBLISHED	APPROX. SALES
1	*The Bible*	*c*.1451–55	over 6,000,000,000
2	*Quotations from the Works of Mao Tse-tung* (dubbed *Little Red Book* by the Western press)	1966	900,000,000
3	*American Spelling Book* by Noah Webster	1783	up to 100,000,000
4	*The Guinness Book of Records*	1955	over 85,000,000*
5	*World Almanac*	1868	73,500,000*
6	*The McGuffey Readers* by William Holmes McGuffey	1836	60,000,000
7	*The Common Sense Book of Baby and Child Care* by Benjamin Spock	1946	over 50,000,000
8	*A Message to Garcia* by Elbert Hubbard	1899	up to 40,000,000
9	=*In His Steps: "What Would Jesus Do?"* by Rev. Charles Monroe Sheldon	1896	over 30,000,000
	=*Valley of the Dolls* by Jacqueline Susann	1966	over 30,000,000

* *Aggregate sales of annual publication*

Which language is not among the world's Top 10? A Japanese B Spanish C French

see p.97 for the answer

THE 10

LATEST WINNERS OF THE NATIONAL BOOK AWARD FOR FICTION

YEAR	AUTHOR/TITLE
1999	Ha Jin, *Waiting*
1998	Alice McDermott, *Charming Billy*
1997	Charles Frazier, *Cold Mountain*
1996	Andrea Barrett, *Ship Fever and Other Stories*
1995	Philip Roth, *Sabbath's Theater*
1994	William Gaddis, *A Frolic of His Own*
1993	E. Annie Proulx, *The Shipping News*
1992	Cormac McCarthy, *All the Pretty Horses*
1991	Norman Rush, *Mating*
1990	Charles Johnson, *Middle Passage*

The National Book Award is presented by the National Book Foundation as part of its program to foster reading in the US. Award winners are announced each November, and receive $10,000.

THE WRITE STUFF

Michael Cunningham made his debut as a novelist in 1990 and rounded off the decade in 1999 by winning the Pulitzer Prize for Fiction.

TOP 10

NON-FICTION TITLES OF THE 1990s IN THE UK

	TITLE/AUTHOR	SALES
1	***Diana: Her True Story***, Andrew Morton	1,600,000
2	***Notes from a Small Island***, Bill Bryson	1,370,000
3	***Fever Pitch***, Nick Hornby	1,300,000
4	***Wild Swans***, Jung Chang	1,250,000
5	***Bravo Two Zero***, Andy McNab	1,100,000
6	***A Brief History of Time***, Stephen Hawking	1,050,000
7	***Angela's Ashes***, Frank McCourt	903,000
8	***The Little Book of Calm***, Paul Wilson	900,000
9	***Toujours Provence***, Peter Mayle	800,000
10	***Men Are from Mars, Women Are from Venus***, John Gray	790,000

Source: *Bookwatch*

The Top 10 non-fiction titles of the 1990s – a mixture of titles by a cosmopolitan group of authors from the UK, US, and other countries – sold more than 11 million copies between them.

THE 10

LATEST WINNERS OF THE PULITZER PRIZE FOR FICTION

YEAR	AUTHOR/TITLE
1999	Michael Cunningham, *The Hours*
1998	Philip Roth, *American Pastoral*
1997	Steven Millhauser, *Martin Dressler: The Tale of an American Dreamer*
1996	Richard Ford, *Independence Day*
1995	Carol Shields, *The Stone Diaries*
1994	E. Annie Proulx, *The Shipping News*
1993	Robert Olen Butler, *A Good Scent from a Strange Mountain: Stories*
1992	Jane Smiley, *A Thousand Acres*
1991	John Updike, *Rabbit at Rest*
1990	Oscar Hijuelos, *The Mambo Kings Play Songs of Love*

TOP 10 GENERAL NON-FICTION TITLES OF 1999 IN THE UK

(Title/author/sales)

1 ***Angela's Ashes***, Frank McCourt, 212,000 2 ***Managing My Life***, Alex Ferguson, 192,000 3 ***Notes from a Small Island***, Bill Bryson, 177,000 4 ***Men Are from Mars, Women Are from Venus***, John Gray, 152,000 5 ***Stalingrad***, Antony Beevor, 139,000 6 ***Notes from a Big Country***, Bill Bryson, 133,000 7 ***'Tis***, Frank McCourt, 121,000 8 ***Walking With Dinosaurs***, Tim Haines, 120,000 9 ***Georgiana, Duchess of Devonshire***, Amanda Foreman, 107,000 10 ***If Only***, Geri Halliwell, 105,000

Source: *Bookwatch*

THE 10

LATEST WINNERS OF THE WHITBREAD "BOOK OF THE YEAR" AWARD

YEAR	AUTHOR/TITLE
1999	Seamus Heaney, *Beowulf*
1998	Ted Hughes, *Birthday Letters*
1997	Ted Hughes, *Tales from Ovid*
1996	Seamus Heaney, *The Spirit Level*
1995	Kate Atkinson, *Behind the Scenes at the Museum*
1994	William Trevor, *Felicia's Journey*
1993	Joan Brady, *Theory of War*
1992	Jeff Torrington, *Swing Hammer Swing!*
1991	John Richardson, *A Life of Picasso*
1990	Nicholas Mosley, *Hopeful Monsters*

Winning his second Whitbread Award, in 1999 for his translation of the Anglo-Saxon poem *Beowulf*, Seamus Heaney controversially only narrowly defeated J. K. Rowling, whose *Harry Potter and the Prisoner of Azkaban* went on to win the "Children's Book of the Year" Award.

Did You Know? Before being filmed, *Gone With the Wind* was the bestselling US novel of both 1936 and 1937, in the latter year winning the Pulitzer prize for Fiction.

TOP 10

CHILDREN'S TITLES OF 1999 IN THE UK

	TITLE/AUTHOR	SALES
1	*Harry Potter and the Philosopher's Stone*, *J. K. Rowling*	502,000
2	*Harry Potter and the Chamber of Secrets*, *J. K. Rowling*	416,000
3	*Harry Potter and the Prisoner of Azkaban*, *J. K. Rowling*	343,000
4	*Children's Book of Books*	246,000
5	*The Beano Book 2000*	174,000
6	*Star Wars: The Phantom Menace* Junior Novelisation	123,000
7	*A Bug's Life*	73,000
8	*The Dandy Book 2000*	70,000
9	*Girls in Love*, *Jacqueline Wilson*	64,000
10	*Buried Alive!*, *Jacqueline Wilson*	63,000

Source: *Bookwatch*

TOP 10

FICTION TITLES OF 1999 IN THE UK

	TITLE/AUTHOR	SALES
1	*Harry Potter and the Philosopher's Stone*, J. K. Rowling	502,000
2	*Harry Potter and the Chamber of Secrets*, J. K. Rowling	416,000
3	*Harry Potter and the Prisoner of Azkaban*, J. K. Rowling	343,000
4	*Tara Road*, Maeve Binchy	287,000
5	*Hannibal*, Thomas Harris	286,000
6	*Charlotte Gray*, Sebastian Faulks	228,000
7	*About a Boy*, Nick Hornby	227,000
8	*Bridget Jones: The Edge of Reason*, Helen Fielding	226,000
9	*Point of Origin*, Patricia D. Cornwell	212,000
10	*The Long Road Home*, Danielle Steele	206,000

Source: *Bookwatch*

THE 10 LATEST WINNERS OF THE BOOKER PRIZE

(*Year/author/title*)

1 1999 J. M. Coetzee, *Disgrace* 2 1998 Ian McEwan, *Amsterdam* 3 1997 Arundhati Roy, *The God of Small Things* 4 1996 Graham Swift, *Last Orders* 5 1995 Pat Barker, *The Ghost Road* 6 1994 James Kelman, *How Late It Was, How Late* 7 1993 Roddy Doyle, *Paddy Clarke Ha Ha Ha* 8 1992 = Michael Ondaatje, *The English Patient*; = Barry Unsworth, *Sacred Hunger* 10 1991 Ben Okri, *Famished Road*

The South African writer J. M. Coetzee is the only person to have won the Booker prize twice (*Life and Times of Michael K* in 1983).

FIRST THINGS FIRST

Bengal-born Arundhati Roy achieved fame and fortune with her Booker prize-winning The God of Small Things.

TOP 10

FICTION TITLES OF THE 1990s IN THE UK

	TITLE/AUTHOR	SALES
1	*The Silence of the Lambs*, Thomas Harris	1,500,000
2	*Bridget Jones's Diary*, Helen Fielding	1,300,000
3	*High Fidelity*, Nick Hornby	1,100,000
4	*Birdsong*, Sebastian Faulks	1,030,000
5	*Jurassic Park*, Michael Crichton	1,000,000
6	*Captain Corelli's Mandolin*, Louis de Bernières	980,000
7	*Schindler's List*, Thomas Keneally	850,000
8	*The Chamber*, John Grisham	800,000
9	*The Glass Lake*, Maeve Binchy	780,000
10	*The Client*, John Grisham	770,000

Source: *Bookwatch*

THE 10

LATEST WINNERS OF THE WHITBREAD "CHILDREN'S BOOK OF THE YEAR" AWARD

YEAR	AUTHOR/TITLE
1999	J. K. Rowling, *Harry Potter and the Prisoner of Azkaban*
1998	David Almond, *Skellig*
1997	Andrew Norris, *Aquila*
1996	Anne Fine, *The Tulip Touch*
1995	Michael Morpurgo, *The Wreck of the Zanzibar*
1994	Geraldine McCaughrean, *Gold Dust*
1993	Anne Fine, *Flour Babies*
1992	Gillian Cross, *The Great Elephant Chase*
1991	Diana Hendry, *Harvey Angell*
1990	Peter Dickinson, *AK*

The Press

TOP 10 TEEN MAGAZINES IN THE UK*

(Magazine/average circulation per issue)

1 *Sugar*, 430,217 2 *Top of the Pops*, 368,700 3 *More!*, 300,194 4 *It's Bliss*, 287,796 5 *Smash Hits*, 241,530 6 *J17*, 230,190 7 *TV Hits*, 205,372 8 *Live & Kicking*, 165,720 9 *Mizz*, 160,426 10 *Looks*, 137,091

* *Actively purchased magazines only*

Source: *Audit Bureau of Circulation Ltd.*

TOP 10 BESTSELLING BRITISH COMICS OF ALL TIME*

	PUBLICATION	YEARS
1	*Beano*	1938–
2	*Comic Cuts*	1890–1953
3	*Dandy*	1937–
4	*Eagle*	1950–69; revived 1982
5	*Film Fun*	1920–62
6	*Illustrated Chips*	1890–1953
7	*Mickey Mouse Weekly*	1936–57
8	*Radio Fun*	1938–61
9	*Rainbow*	1914–56
10	*School Friend*	1950–65

* *In alphabetical order*

All 10 comics featured here (in alphabetical order) achieved very high circulation figures, with *Eagle*, *Film Fun*, *Rainbow*, and *School Friend* perhaps hitting 1 million at their peak.

TOP 10 CONSUMER MAGAZINES IN THE UK*

	MAGAZINE	AVERAGE CIRCULATION PER ISSUE
1	*What's on TV*	1,741,157
2	*Radio Times*	1,337,036
3	*Take a Break*	1,230,758
4	*Reader's Digest*	1,142,130
5	*TV Times*	790,999
6	*FHM*	702,514
7	*Woman*	670,241
8	*TV Quick*	638,855
9	*Bella*	572,151
10	*Woman's Own*	569,019

* *Actively purchased magazines only*

Source: *Audit Bureau of Circulation Ltd.*

TOP 10 WOMEN'S MONTHLY MAGAZINES IN THE UK*

(Magazine/average circulation per issue)

1 *Cosmopolitan*, 470,280 2 *Candis*, 450,443 3 *Marie Claire*, 450,213 4 *Prima*, 421,412 5 *Good Housekeeping*, 400,094 6 *Yours*, 311,025 7 *Woman & Home*, 295,225 8 *New Woman*, 276,285 9 *Essentials*, 262,269 10 *Slimming World Magazine*, 255,726

* *Actively purchased magazines only*

Source: *Audit Bureau of Circulation Ltd.*

"TABLOID"

The British drug company Burroughs, Wellcome & Co. registered "tabloid" as a trade name on 14 March 1884. Derived from the word "tablet", it was applied to concentrated types of drugs marketed by the firm. By the end of the nineteenth century, "tabloid" was used to describe anything compressed and small. The phrase "tabloid journalism", which described the content of small-format newspapers, soon became so established in the language that the company could no longer claim the word as their trademark.

WHY DO WE SAY?

TOP 10 NEWSPAPER-READING COUNTRIES

(Country/daily newspapers per 1,000 people)

1 **Norway**, 593 2 **Japan**, 580 3 **Finland**, 455 4 **Sweden**, 446 5 **South Korea**, 394 6 **Kuwait**, 376 7 **UK**, 332 8 **Switzerland**, 330 9 **Singapore**, 324 10 **Denmark**, 311

Source: *World Bank*

TOP 10 DAILY NEWSPAPERS IN THE UK, 1999

	NEWSPAPER	AVERAGE CIRCULATION*
1	*The Sun*	3,596,212
2	*Daily Mail*	2,367,315
3	*Daily Mirror*	2,317,459
4	*The Express*	1,058,900
5	*The Daily Telegraph*	1,035,688
6	*The Times*	721,160
7	*Daily Star*	614,106
8	*Financial Times*	414,469
9	*The Guardian*	391,387
10	*The Independent*	224,391

* *For the six month period July–December 1999*

SNAP HAPPY

Despite the growth of television, newspaper photographers continue to provide images to feed the insatiable demands of the world's press, often going to extraordinarily intrusive lengths to gain their shots.

RISING SUN

Launched in 1964 as a revamped Daily Herald, *British tabloid* The Sun *has become the world's bestselling English-language daily newspaper.*

TOP 10

OLDEST NATIONAL NEWSPAPERS PUBLISHED IN THE UK

	NEWSPAPER	FIRST PUBLISHED
1	*London Gazette*	16 Nov 1665
2	*Lloyd's List*	1726
3	*The Times*	1 Jan 1785
4	*The Observer*	4 Dec 1791
5	*The Licensee*	8 Feb 1794
6	*The Scotsman*	25 Jan 1817
7	*The Sunday Times*	Feb 1821
8	*The Guardian*	5 May 1821
9	*The News of the World*	1 Oct 1843
10	*The Daily Telegraph*	29 June 1855

1 *Originally published in Oxford as the* Oxford Gazette, *while the royal court resided there during an outbreak of the plague. After 23 issues, it moved to London with the court and changed its name.*

2 *Providing shipping news, first on a weekly basis (as* Lloyd's News), *but since 1734 as Britain's oldest daily.*

3 *First published as the* Daily Universal Register, *it changed its name to* The Times *on 1 March 1788.*

4 The Observer *is the longest-running Sunday paper.*

5 *Britain's oldest trade newspaper (a daily established by the Licensed Victuallers Association to earn income for its charity) and the first national paper on Fleet Street, the* Morning Advertiser *changed its name to* The Licensee *and became a twice-weekly news magazine in 1994, at the time of its 200th anniversary.*

6 *Originally published weekly, the* Daily Scotsman *was published from July 1855 to December 1859, and retitled* The Scotsman *in January 1860.*

7 *Issued as the* New Observer *until March 1821 and the* Independent Observer *from April 1821 until 22 October 1822, when it changed its name to* The Sunday Times. *On 4 February 1962 it became the first British newspaper to issue a colour supplement.*

8 *A weekly until 1855 (and called* The Manchester Guardian *until 1959).*

9 *In April 1951, sales peaked at 8,480,878 copies – the highest-ever circulation of any British newspaper.*

10 *The first issues were published as the* Daily Telegraph and Courier, *but from 20 August 1855,* Courier *was dropped from the title.*

TOP 10

ENGLISH-LANGUAGE DAILY NEWSPAPERS

	NEWSPAPER	COUNTRY	AVERAGE DAILY CIRCULATION
1	*The Sun*	UK	3,592,000
2	*Daily Mail*	UK	2,300,000
3	*The Mirror*	UK	2,290,000
4	*Wall Street Journal*	USA	1,740,000
5	*USA Today*	USA	1,653,000
6	*Times of India*	India	1,296,000
7	*The Express*	UK	1,096,000
8	*Los Angeles Times*	USA	1,068,000
9	*The New York Times*	USA	1,067,000
10	*The Daily Telegraph*	UK	1,026,000

TOP 10

DAILY NEWSPAPERS

	NEWSPAPER	COUNTRY	AVERAGE DAILY CIRCULATION
1	*Yomiuri Shimbun*	Japan	14,533,000
2	*Asahi Shimbun*	Japan	12,601,000
3	*Mainichi Shimbun*	Japan	5,846,000
4	*Chunichi Shimbun*	Japan	4,704,000
5	*Bild-Zeitung*	Germany	4,409,000
6	*The Sun*	UK	3,592,000
7	*Daily Mail*	UK	2,300,000
8	*The Mirror*	UK	2,290,000
9	*Wall Street Journal*	USA	1,740,000
10	*USA Today*	USA	1,653,000

Source: *World Association of Newspapers*

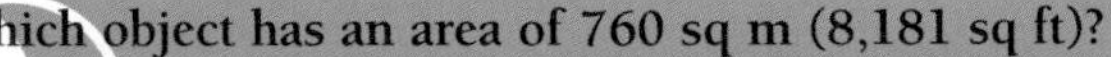

Which object has an area of 760 sq m (8,181 sq ft)?

see p.111 for the answer

A The largest painting in the Louvre Museum, Paris
B The robes of the Statue of Liberty
C The pages of the world's biggest newspaper

TOP 10 TOYS OF THE 20TH CENTURY IN THE UK*

1 The teddy bear 2 Beanie Babies 3 Monopoly 4 Scrabble 5 Lego 6 Action Man 7 Mastermind 8 Yo-yo 9 Trivial Pursuit 10 Barbie doll

* *As voted by the British Association of Toy Retailers, together with public Internet poll*

TOP 10 LEISURE ACTIVITIES AMONG ADULTS IN THE UK

	ACTIVITY	PER CENT PARTICIPATING*
1	Watching television	99
2	Visiting/entertaining	96
3	Listening to the radio	88
4	Listening to records/tapes/CDs	78
5	=Reading books	65
	=Visiting a pub	65
7	Meal in a restaurant (not fast food)	62
8	Gardening	49
9	Driving for pleasure	47
10	Walking	45

* *Based on percentage of people over 16 years old participating in each activity in the three months prior to interview for activities away from the home, or in the four weeks prior to interview for activities in the home*

TOP 10 TOYS AND GAMES OF 1999 IN THE UK*

1 Furby 2 Baby Furby 3 Bounce Around Tigger 4 Mountain Bike Extreme 5 Baby Annabell 6 Lovable Bears (talking) 7 Monopoly 8 First Steps Plus Baby Walker 9 Action Man Hovercraft 10 Jenga

* *Ranked by value of retail sales*
Source: *NPD Group Worldwide*

THE 10 LATEST TOYS OF THE YEAR

YEAR	TOY
1999	Furby Babies
1998	Furby
1997	Teletubbies
1996	Barbie
1995	POGS
1994	Power Rangers
1993	Thunderbirds' Tracey Island
1992	WWF Wrestlers
1991	Nintendo Game Boy
1990	Teenage Mutant Turtles

The British Association of Retailers' Toy of the Year Award was started in 1965, when it was awarded to the James Bond Aston Martin die-cast car.

TOP 10 MOST LANDED-ON SQUARES IN MONOPOLY®*

US GAME		UK GAME
Illinois Avenue	1	Trafalgar Square
Go	2	Go
B. & O. Railroad	3	Fenchurch Street Station
Free Parking	4	Free Parking
Tennessee Avenue	5	Marlborough Street
New York Avenue	6	Vine Street
Reading Railroad	7	King's Cross Station
St. James Place	8	Bow Street
Water Works	9	Water Works
Pennsylvania Railroad	5	Marylebone Station

* *Based on a computer analysis of the probability of landing on each square*

Monopoly® is a registered trade mark of Parker Brothers division of Tonka Corporation, USA, under licence to Waddington Games Ltd.

TOP 10 HIGHEST-SCORING SCRABBLE® WORDS

	WORD/PLAY	SCORE
1	QUARTZY *(i) Play across a triple-word-score (red) square with the Z on a double-letter-score (light blue) square* *(ii) Play across two double-word-score (pink) squares with Q and Y on pink squares*	164/162
2	=BEZIQUE *(i) Play across a red square with either the Z or the Q on a light blue square* *(ii) Play across two pink squares with the B and second E on two pink squares*	161/158
	=CAZIQUE *(i) Play across a red square with either the Z or the Q on a light blue square* *(ii) Play across two pink squares with the C and E on two pink squares*	161/158
4	ZINKIFY *Play across a red square with the Z on a light blue square*	158
5	=QUETZAL *Play across a red square with either the Q or the Z on a light blue square*	155
	=JAZZILY *(Using a blank as one of the Zs) Play across a red square with the non-blank Z on a light blue square*	155
	=QUIZZED *(Using a blank as one of the Zs) Play across a red square with the non-blank Z or the Q on a light blue square*	155
8	=ZEPHYRS *Play across a red square with the Z on a light blue square*	152
	=ZINCIFY *Play across a red square with the Z on a light blue square*	152
	=ZYTHUMS *Play across a red square with the Z on a light blue square*	152

All the Top 10 words contain seven letters and therefore earn the premium of 50 for using all the letters in the rack. Being able to play them depends on there already being suitable words on the board to which they can be added. In an actual game, the face values of the perpendicular words to which they are joined would also be counted, but these are discounted here as the total score variations would be infinite. Scrabble was invented in the US during the Depression by an unemployed architect, Alfred Butts, and developed in the 1940s by James Brunot.

Background image: **BEANIE BABIES**

TOP 10 ★

MOST EXPENSIVE TOYS SOLD AT AUCTION IN THE UK*

	TOY/SALE	PRICE (£)
1	**Roullet et Decamps musical automaton of a snake charmer**, Sotheby's, London, 17 Oct 1996	155,500
2	***Titania's Palace*, a doll's house with 2,000 items of furniture**, Christie's, London, 10 Jan 1978	135,000
3	**Roullet et Decamps musical automaton of a mask seller**, Sotheby's, London, 17 Oct 1996	122,500
4	**Silver mounted set of carved, boxwood chessmen**, Sotheby's, London, 23 May 1996	96,100
5	**Gustave Vichy automaton of a bird trainer**, Sotheby's, London, 20 Nov 1996	84,000
6	**Hornby 00-gauge train set** (the largest ever sold at auction), Christies, London, 27 Nov 1992	80,178
7	**Russian carousel** (tinplate Ferris wheel), *c.*1904, Sotheby's, London, 10 Feb 1993	62,500
8=	**Tinplate carousel by Märklin**, *c.*1910, Sotheby's, London, 23 Jan 1992	47,300
=	**Set of Märklin horse-drawn fire appliances**, *c.*1902, Sotheby's, London, 23 Jan 1992	47,300
10	**Machine Man**, Sotheby's, London, 7 Nov 1996	42,500

* *Excluding dolls and teddy bears*

TOP 10 ★

MOST EXPENSIVE TEDDY BEARS SOLD AT AUCTION IN THE UK

	BEAR/SALE	PRICE (£)*
1	**"Teddy Girl", a 1904 Steiff bear**, Christie's, London, 5 Dec 1994 *This bear precisely doubled the previous world record for a teddy bear when it was acquired by Yoshiro Sekiguchi for a museum near Tokyo.*	110,000
2	**"Happy", a dual-plush Steiff teddy bear**, 1926, Sotheby's, London, 19 Sep 1989 *Although estimated at £700–£900, competitive bidding pushed the price up to the then world record, when it was acquired by collector Paul Volpp.*	55,000
3	**"Elliot", a blue Steiff bear**, 1908, Christie's, London, 6 Dec 1993 *Produced as a sample for Harrods.*	49,500
4	**"Teddy Edward", a golden mohair teddy bear**, Christie's, London, 9 Dec 1996 *Star of* Watch With Mother.	38,500
5	**Black Steiff teddy bear**, *c.*1912, Sotheby's, London, 18 May 1990	24,200
6	**Steiff, blank button, brown teddy bear**, *c.*1905, Christie's, London, 8 Dec 1997	23,000
7	**"Albert", a Steiff teddy bear**, *c.*1910, Christie's, London, 9 Dec 1996	18,400
8	**Steiff teddy bear**, Christie's, London, 9 Dec 1996	17,250
9	**"Theodore", a miniature Steiff teddy bear, 9 cm (3½ in) tall**, *c.*1948, Christie's, London, 11 Dec 1995	14,625
10=	**"Black Jack", black Steiff teddy bear**, Christie's, London, 22 May 1997	13,800
=	**Cinnamon Steiff teddy bear**, *c.*1905, Christie's, London, 23 May 1997	13,800

* *Prices include buyer's premium*

"TEDDY BEAR"

While on a hunting trip, US President Theodore ("Teddy") Roosevelt refused to shoot a young bear. This became the subject of a famous cartoon by Clifford K. Berryman, published in the *Washington Post*. Immediately afterwards, Morris Michtom, a New York shopkeeper, made stuffed bears and, with Roosevelt's permission, advertised them as "Teddy's Bears". Margarete Steiff, a German toymaker, soon began making her toy bears, exporting them to the US to meet demand.

WHY DO WE SAY?

TOP 10 ★

MOST EXPENSIVE DOLLS SOLD AT AUCTION IN THE UK

	DOLL/SALE	PRICE (£)
1	**Kämmer and Reinhardt doll**, Sotheby's, London, 8 Feb 1994	188,500
2	**Kämmer and Reinhardt bisque character doll**, German, *c.*1909, Sotheby's, London, 17 Oct 1996 *(Previously sold at Sotheby's, London, 16 Feb 1989 for £90,200)*	108,200
3	**Kämmer and Reinhardt bisque character doll**, *c.*1909, Sotheby's, London, 17 Oct 1996	91,700
4	**Albert Marque bisque character doll**, Sotheby's, London, 17 Oct 1996	71,900
5=	**William and Mary wooden doll**, English, *c.*1690, Sotheby's, London, 24 Mar 1987	67,000
=	**Wooden doll, Charles II**, 17th century, Christie's, London, 18 May 1989	67,000
7	**Albert Marque bisque character doll**, Sotheby's, London, 17 Oct 1996	58,700
8=	**Albert Marque bisque character doll**, Christie's, London, 23 May 1997	56,500
=	**Mulatto pressed bisque swivel-head Madagascar doll**, Sotheby's, London, 17 Oct 1996	56,500
10	**Shellacked pressed bisque swivel-head doll**, Sotheby's, London, 17 Oct 1996	45,500

TOP 10 BESTSELLING COMPUTER GAMES AT W. H. SMITH, 1999

(Game/publisher)

1 **Tomb Raider: Last Revelation**, Eidos 2 **Pokémon Blue**, Nintendo 3 **FIFA 2000**, EA 4 **Pokémon Red**, Nintendo 5 **Medal of Honour**, EA 6 **Final Fantasy VIII**, Sony 7 **James Bond: Tomorrow Never Dies**, EA 8 **Pokémon Pikachu**, Nintendo 9 **Lego Racers**, Lego Media 10 **Crash Team Racing**, Sony

Which comic book superhero first appeared in 1938?
see p.119 for the answer
A Batman
B Spider-Man
C Superman

HIGH AND MIGHTY

The statue of Christ the Redeemer, Rio de Janeiro, Brazil, is 30 m (100 ft) tall and stands on a 7-m (22-ft) pedestal with a chapel inside. It was unveiled in 1931 by the radio pioneer Guglielmo Marconi.

TOP 10 ★

TALLEST FREE-STANDING STATUES

	STATUE/LOCATION	HEIGHT M	FT
1	**Chief Crazy Horse**, Thunderhead Mountain, South Dakota, USA *Started in 1948 by Polish-American sculptor Korczak Ziolkowski, and continued after his death in 1982 by his widow and eight of his children, this gigantic equestrian statue is even longer than it is high (195 m/641 ft). It is being carved out of the granite mountain by dynamiting and drilling.*	172	563
2	**Buddha**, Tokyo, Japan *This Japanese–Taiwanese project, unveiled in 1993, took seven years to complete and weighs 1,000 tonnes.*	120	394
3	**The Indian Rope Trick**, Riddersberg Säteri, Jönköping, Sweden *Sculptor Calle Ornemark's 144-tonne wooden sculpture depicts a long strand of "rope" held by a fakir, while another figure ascends.*	103	337
4	**Motherland**, 1967, Volgograd (formerly Stalingrad), Russia *This concrete statue of a woman with a raised sword, designed by Yevgeniy Vuchetich, commemorates the Soviet victory at the Battle of Stalingrad (1942–43).*	82	270
5	**Buddha**, Bamian, Afghanistan *This dates from the 3rd–4th centuries* AD.	53	173
6	**Kannon**, Otsubo-yama, near Tokyo, Japan *The vast statue of the goddess of mercy was unveiled in 1961 in honour of the dead of World War II.*	52	170
7	**Statue of Liberty**, New York, USA *Designed by Auguste Bartholdi and presented to the US by the people of France, the statue was shipped in sections to Liberty (formerly Bedloes) Island, where it was assembled before being unveiled on 28 October 1886 It was restored on 4 July 1986.*	46	151
8	**Christ**, Rio de Janeiro, Brazil *The work of sculptor Paul Landowski and engineer Heitor da Silva Costa, the figure of Christ was unveiled in 1931.*	38	125
9	**Tian Tan (Temple of Heaven) Buddha**, Po Lin Monastery, Lantau Island, Hong Kong *This was completed after 20 years' work and was unveiled on 29 December 1993.*	34	112
10	**Quantum Cloud**, Greenwich, London, UK *This gigantic steel human figure surrounded by a matrix of steel struts was created in 1999.*	29	95

TOP 10 OLDEST MUSEUMS AND ART GALLERIES IN THE UK

(Museum or art gallery/location/founded)

❶ **Ashmolean Museum**, Oxford, 1683 ❷ **British Museum**, London, 1753 ❸ **National Museum of Antiquities**, Edinburgh, 1780 ❹ **Hunterian Museum**, Glasgow, 1807 ❺ = **Museum of Antiquities**, Newcastle upon Tyne, 1813; = **Royal College of Surgeons Museum**, London, 1813 ❼ **Dulwich Picture Gallery**, London, 1814 ❽ **Fitzwilliam Museum**, Cambridge, 1816 ❾ **Leeds City Museum**, 1820 ❿ **Manchester Museum**, 1821

TOP 10

LARGEST PAINTINGS IN THE LOUVRE MUSEUM, PARIS

	PAINTING/ARTIST	SIZE (HEIGHT X WIDTH) M	FT
1	*Interior of Westminster Abbey*, Jean-Pierre Alaux	19.0 x 40.0	62 x 131
2	*Interior of St. Peter's, Rome*, Jean-Pierre Alaux	17.5 x 40.0	57 x 131
3	*Palace Ceiling*, Francesco Fontebasso	8.0 x 10.0	26 x 33
4	*The Marriage Feast at Cana*, Paolo Veronese	6.7 x 9.9	22 x 32
5	*The Coronation of Napoleon*, Jacques-Louis David	6.2 x 9.8	20 x 32
6	*The Battle of Arbela*, Charles Lebrun	4.7 x 12.7	15 x 42
7	*Alexander and Porus*, Charles Lebrun	4.7 x 12.6	15 x 41
8	*Crossing the Granicus*, Charles Lebrun	4.7 x 12.1	15 x 40
9	*The Battle of Eylau*, Antoine-Jean Gros	5.2 x 7.8	17 x 26
10	*Napoleon Visiting the Plague Victims of Jaffa*, Antoine-Jean Gros	5.2 x 7.2	17 x 24

TOP 10 ART EXHIBITIONS, 1999

(Exhibition/venue/total attendance)

1 ***Van Gogh's van Goghs***, Los Angeles County Museum, 821,004 2 ***Monet in the 20th Century***, The Royal Academy, London, 739,324 3 ***The Maya***, Palazzo Grassi, Venice, 700,000 4 ***Richard Serra***, Bilbao Guggenheim, 675,071 5 ***Millet, van Gogh***, Musée d'Orsay, Paris, 661,568 6 ***Eduardo Chillida***, Bilbao Guggenheim, 542,770 7 ***Van Gogh's van Goghs***, National Gallery of Art, Washington, D.C. 480,496 8 ***Egyptian Art in the Age of Pyramids***, Metropolitan Museum of Fine Art, New York City, 473,234 9 ***John Singer Sargent***, National Gallery of Art, Washington, D.C. 453,937 10 ***Cézanne to van Gogh: Doctor Gachet Collection***, Metropolitan Museum of Fine Art, New York City, 429,024

Source: The Art Newspaper

TOP 10 ★ MOST EXPENSIVE PAINTINGS EVER SOLD AT AUCTION

	PAINTING/ARTIST/SALE	PRICE (£)
1	*Portrait of Dr. Gachet*, Vincent van Gogh (Dutch; 1853–90), Christie's, New York, 15 May 1990	44,378,696 ($75,000,000)
2	*Au Moulin de la Galette*, Pierre-Auguste Renoir (French; 1841–1919), Sotheby's, New York, 17 May 1990	42,011,832 ($71,000,000)
3	*Portrait de l'Artiste Sans Barbe*, Vincent van Gogh, Christie's, New York, 19 Nov 1998	39,393,940 ($65,000,000)
4	*Rideau, Cruchon et Compotier*, Paul Cézanne (French; 1839–1906), Sotheby's, New York, 10 May 1999	33,950,616 ($55,000,000)
5	*Les Noces de Pierrette, 1905*, Pablo Picasso (Spanish; 1881–1973), Binoche et Godeau, Paris, 30 Nov 1989	33,123,028 (F.Fr315,000,000)
6	*Irises*, Vincent van Gogh, Sotheby's, New York, 11 Nov 1987	28,000,000 ($49,000,000)
7	*Femme Assise Dans un Jardin*, Pablo Picasso, Sotheby's, New York, 10 Nov 1999	27,950,310 ($45,000,000)
8	*Self Portrait: Yo Picasso*, Pablo Picasso, Sotheby's, New York, 9 May 1989	26,687,116 ($43,500,000)
9	*Le Rêve*, Pablo Picasso, Christie's, New York, 10 Nov 1997	26,035,502 ($44,000,000)
10	*Nu au Fauteuil Noir*, Pablo Picasso, Christie's, New York, 9 Nov 1999	25,465,838 ($41,000,000)

TOP 10 ★ ARTISTS WITH MOST WORKS SOLD FOR MORE THAN ONE MILLION POUNDS

	ARTIST	TOTAL VALUE OF WORKS SOLD (£)	NO. OF WORKS SOLD
1	Pablo Picasso (Spanish; 1881–1973)	661,180,934	178
2	Claude Monet (French; 1888–1926)	469,260,341	147
3	Pierre Auguste Renoir (French; 1841–1919)	306,660,875	105
4	Edgar Degas (French; 1834–1917)	165,984,914	58
5	Paul Cézanne (French; 1839–1906)	218,114,972	51
6	Amedeo Modigliani (Italian; 1884–1920)	138,987,464	44
7	=Henri Matisse (French; 1869–1954)	129,059,168	43
	=Vincent van Gogh (Dutch; 1853–90)	316,089,235	43
9	Camille Pissaro (French; 1830–1903)	45,831,652	31
10	Paul Gauguin (French; 1848–1903)	83,345,360	28

RAGS TO RICHES

The impoverished van Gogh painted this self-portrait, Portrait de l'Artist Sans Barbe, *at Arles in September 1888. Just over a century later, it fetched $65 million at auction, making it the third most expensive painting sold at auction.*

TOP 10 ★ MOST EXPENSIVE PAINTINGS BY 20TH-CENTURY ARTISTS*

	PAINTING/ARTIST/SALE	PRICE (£)
1	*Paysage, Île de la Grane Jatte*, George Seurat (French; 1859–91), Sotheby's, New York, 10 May 1999	19,753,086 ($32,000,000)
2	*Interchange*, Willem de Kooning (American/ Dutch; 1904–97), Sotheby's, New York, 8 Nov 1989	11,898,735 ($18,800,000)
3	*Fugue*, Wassily Kandinsky (Russian; 1866–1944), Sotheby's, New York, 17 May 1990	11,242,604 ($19,000,000)
4	*Orange Marilyn*, Andy Warhol (American; 1928–87), Sotheby's, New York, 14 May 1998	9,722,223 ($15,750,000)
5	*Nu Assiss Sur un Divan*, Amedeo Modigliani (Italian; 1884–1920), Sotheby's, New York, 11 Nov 1999	9,472,051 ($15,250,001)
6	*Harmonie jaune*, Henri Matisse (French; 1869–1954), Christie's, New York, 11 Nov 1992	8,741,723 ($13,200,000)
7	*False Start*, Jasper Johns (American; b.1930), Sotheby's, New York, 10 Nov 1988	8,611,112 ($15,500,000)
8	*La Pose Hindoue*, Henri Matisse, Sotheby's, New York, 8 May 1995	8,598,727 ($13,500,000)
9	*Contrastes de Formes*, Fernand Léger (French; 1881–1955), Christie's, London, 27 Nov 1989	8,500,000
10	*La Mulatresse Fatma*, Henri Matisse, Sotheby's, New York, 11 May 1993	8,496,733 ($13,000,000)

* *Excluding Picasso, who would otherwise completely dominate the list*

Did You Know? Vincent van Gogh did not cut off his ear, as is popularly believed. He lopped off only part of his left ear lobe.

TOP 10 ★ MOST EXPENSIVE OLD MASTER PAINTINGS EVER SOLD AT AUCTION

	PAINTING/ARTIST/SALE	PRICE (£)
1	*Portrait of Duke Cosimo I de Medici*, **Jacopo da Carucci (Pontormo)** (Italian; 1493–1558), Christie's, New York, 31 May 1989	20,253,164 ($32,000,000)
2	*The Old Horse Guards, London, from St James's Park*, **Canaletto** (Italian; 1697–1768), Christie's, London, 15 Apr 1992	9,200,000
3	*View of the Giudecca and the Zattere, Venice*, **Francesco Guardi** (Italian; 1712–93), Sotheby's, Monaco, 1 Dec 1989	8,937,960 (F.Fr85,000,000)
4	*Le Retour du Bucentaure le Jour de l'Ascension*, **Canaletto**, Ader Tajan, Paris, 15 Dec 1993	7,594,937 (F.Fr66,000,000)
5	=*Adoration of the Magi*, **Andrea Mantegna** (Italian; 1431–1506), Christie's, London, 18 Apr 1985	7,500,000
	=*Tieleman Roosterman in Black Doublet, White Ruff*, **Frans Hals** (elder, Dutch; *c.*1580–1666), Christie's, London, 8 July 1999	7,500,000
7	*Venus and Adonis*, **Titian** (Italian; *c.*1488–1576), Christie's, London, 13 Dec 1991	6,800,000
8	*Portrait of a Girl Wearing a Gold-trimmed Cloak*, **Rembrandt** (Dutch; 1606–69), Sotheby's, London, 10 Dec 1986	6,600,000
9	*View of Molo from Bacino di San Marco, Venice* and *View of the Grand Canal Facing East from Campo di Santi, Venice* (pair), **Canaletto**, Sotheby's, New York, 1 June 1990	5,988,024 ($10,000,000)
10	*Portrait of Bearded Man in Red Coat*, **Rembrandt**, Sotheby's, New York, 30 Jan 1998	5,061,350 ($8,250,000)

THERE'S SOMETHING ABOUT MARY

Six paintings by Mary Cassatt, such as her Mother, Sara and the Baby, *are numbered among the 10 highest priced paintings by a woman.*

TOP 10 ★ MOST EXPENSIVE PAINTINGS BY WOMEN ARTISTS EVER SOLD AT AUCTION

	PAINTING/ARTIST/SALE	PRICE (£)
1	*In the Box*, **Mary Cassatt** (American; 1844–1926), Christie's, New York, 23 May 1996	2,450,331 ($3,700,000)
2	*The Conversation*, **Mary Cassatt**, Christie's, New York, 11 May 1988	2,180,850 ($4,100,000)
3	*Cache-cache*, **Berthe Morisot** (French; 1841–95), Sotheby's, New York, 10 May 1999	2,160,494 ($3,500,000)
4	*Mother, Sara and the Baby*, **Mary Cassatt**, Christie's, New York, 10 May 1989	2,147,239 ($3,500,000)
5	*From the Plains*, **Georgia O'Keeffe** (American; 1887–1986), Sotheby's, New York, 3 Dec 1997	2,000,000 ($3,300,000)
6	*Après le Déjeuner*, **Berthe Morisot**, Christie's, New York, 14 May 1997	1,993,865 ($3,250,000)
7	*Autoretrato con Chango y Loro*, **Frida Kahlo** (Mexican; 1907–54), Sotheby's, New York, 17 May 1995	1,847,134 ($2,900,000)
8	*Augusta Reading to Her Daughter*, **Mary Cassatt**, Sotheby's, New York, 9 May 1989	1,717,790 ($2,800,000)
9	*Children Playing With Cat*, **Mary Cassatt**, Sotheby's, New York, 3 Dec 1998	1,626,506 ($2,700,000)
10	*Young Lady in a Loge, Gazing to the Right*, **Mary Cassatt**, Sotheby's, New York, 10 Nov 1992	1,523,179 ($2,300,000)

TOP 10 ★ MOST EXPENSIVE PAINTINGS BY ANDY WARHOL

	PAINTING*/SALE	PRICE (£)
1	***Orange Marilyn***, Sotheby's, New York, 14 May 1998	9,722,223 ($15,750,000)
2	***Marilyn X 100***, Sotheby's, New York, 17 Nov 1992	2,251,656 ($3,400,000)
3	***Shot Red Marilyn***, Sotheby's, New York, 3 May 1989	2,228,916 ($3,700,000)
4	***Shot Red Marilyn***, Sotheby's, New York, 2 Nov 1994	2,062,500 ($3,300,000)
5	***Marilyn Monroe, Twenty Times***, Sotheby's, New York, 10 Nov 1988	2,000,000 ($3,600,000)
6	***Big Torn Campbell's Soup Can***, Christie's, New York, 7 May 1997	1,987,578 ($3,200,000)
7	***Orange Marilyn***, Christie's, New York, 19 Nov 1998	1,515,152 ($2,500,000)
8	***Big Electric Chair***, Christie's, London, 30 June 1999	1,500,000
9	***Marion,*** Sotheby's, New York, 18 May 1999	1,481,482 ($2,400,000)
10	***Self Portrait***, Christie's, New York, 12 May 1998	1,358,025 ($2,200,000)

* *Including silkscreen works*

"FAMOUS FOR 15 MINUTES"

Andy Warhol's own fame has outlived his famous phrase, his works continuing to attain considerable prices at auction.

HIGH FIGURES

The distinctive elongated figures created by Swiss sculptor Alberto Giacometti (1901–66), shown at work in his studio in 1958, command high prices at auction.

TOP 10 ★ MOST EXPENSIVE SCULPTURES BY ALBERTO GIACOMETTI

	SCULPTURE/SALE	PRICE (£)
1	***La Forêt – Sept Figures et Une Tête***, Sotheby's, New York, 16 Nov 1998	4,121,212 ($6,800,000)
2	***L'Homme Qui Marche I***, Christie's, London 28 Nov 1988	3,400,000
3	***Trois Hommes Qui Marchent I***, Sotheby's, New York, 11 Nov 1999	3,229,814 ($5,200,000)
4	***Grande Femme Debout I***, Christie's, New York, 14 Nov 1989	2,903,226 ($4,500,000)
5	***Grande Femme Debout II***, Christie's, New York, 12 May 1987	2,000,000 ($3,300,000)
6	***Trois Hommes Qui Marchent II***, Christie's, New York, 14 May 1997	1,963,190 ($3,200,000)
7	***Trois Hommes Qui Marchent***, Christie's, New York, 11 May 1988	1,861,702 ($3,500,000)
8	***Grande Femme Debout I***, Christie's, New York, 14 Nov 1990	1,827,410 ($3,600,000)
9	***Grande Femme Debout I***, Christie's, New York, 12 May 1987	1,696,970 ($2,800,000)
10	***L'Homme Qui Marche III – Walking Man III***, Christie's, New York, 12 May 1998	1,666,667 ($2,700,000)

Did You Know? Between 18 October and 4 December 1961, Henri Matisse's painting *Le Bateau* hung upside down in the Museum of Modern Art, New York. An estimated 116,000 people passed through the gallery before anyone noticed.

TOP 10 ★ MOST EXPENSIVE SCULPTURES BY HENRY MOORE

	SCULPTURE/SALE	PRICE (£)
1	***Two-piece Reclining Figure, Points***, Christie's, New York, 9 Nov 1999	2,298,137 ($3,700,000
2	***Reclining Figure***, Christies, New York, 13 May 1999	2,283,951 ($3,700,000)
3	***Working Model for UNESCO Reclining Figure***, Christie's, New York, 15 May 1990	2,189,349 ($3,700,000)
4	***Reclining Figure, Angles***, Christie's, New York, 13 Nov 1996	1,445,783 ($2,400,000)
5	***Draped Reclining Woman***, Sotheby's, New York, 13 Nov 1997	1,390,533 ($2,350,000)
6	***Reclining Connected Forms***, Sotheby's, New York, 17 May 1990	1,301,775 ($2,200,000)
7	***Festival Reclining Figure***, Sotheby's, New York, 11 May 1994	1,233,333 ($1,850,000)
8	***Reclining Figure, Bone Skirt***, Sotheby's, New York, 13 May 1997	1,226,994 ($2,000,000)
9	***Working Model for Three Way Piece No. 3 Vertebrae***, Sotheby's, New York, 17 May 1990	1,183,432 ($2,000,000)
10	***Reclining Figure – Festival***, Sotheby's, New York, 18 Nov 1986	1,118,880 ($1,600,000)

British sculptor Henry Spencer Moore (1898–1986) was a war artist before achieving international fame for his sculptures. Many of these were commissioned for public buildings, but those that have entered the marketplace have achieved consistently high prices.

TOP 10 ★ MOST EXPENSIVE PAINTINGS BY ROY LICHTENSTEIN

	PAINTING/SALE	PRICE (£)
1	***Kiss II***, Christie's, New York, 7 May 1990	3,273,810 ($5,500,000)
2	***Torpedo...Los***, Christie's, New York, 7 Nov 1989	3,164,557 ($5,000,000)
3	***Tex!***, Christie's, New York, 20 Nov 1996	2,142,857 ($3,600,000)
4	***Blang!***, Christie's, New York, 7 May 1997	1,614,907 ($2,600,000)
5	***Kiss II***, Christie's, New York, 3 May 1995	1,437,500 ($2,300,000)
6	***I...I'm Sorry!***, Sotheby's, New York, 1 Nov 1994	1,406,250 ($2,250,000)
7	***The Ring***, Sotheby's, New York, 19 Nov 1997	1,190,476 ($2,000,000)
8	***Forest Scene***, Sotheby's, New York, 19 Nov 1996	1,130,952 ($1,900,000)
9	***Girl With Piano***, Sotheby's, New York, 17 Nov 1992	1,092,715 ($1,650,000)
10	***I Can See the Whole Room... And There's Nobody In It***, Christie's, New York, 9 Nov 1988	1,055,556 ($1,900,000)

TOP 10 ★ MOST EXPENSIVE PAINTINGS BY JACKSON POLLOCK

	PAINTING*/SALE	PRICE (£)
1	***Number 8, 1950***, Sotheby's, New York, 2 May 1989	6,325,302 ($10,500,000)
2	***Frieze***, Christie's, New York, 9 Nov 1988	2,888,889 ($5,200,000)
3	***Search***, Sotheby's, New York, 2 May 1988	2,352,940 ($4,400,000)
4	***Number 19, 1949***, Sotheby's, New York, 2 May 1989	2,168,675 ($3,600,000)
5	***Number 31, 1949***, Christie's, New York, 3 May 1988	1,711,230 ($3,200,000)
6	***Number 26, 1950***, Sotheby's, New York, 4 May 1987	1,506,025 ($2,500,000)
7	***Something of the Past***, Christie's, New York, 7 May 1996	1,447,369 ($2,200,000)
8	***Number 19, 1948***, Christies, New York, 4 May 1993	1,437,909 ($2,200,000)
9	***Number 13***, Christie's, New York, 7 Nov 1990	1,428,570 ($2,800,000)
10	***Number 20***, Sotheby's, New York, 8 May 1990	1,309,524 ($2,200,000)

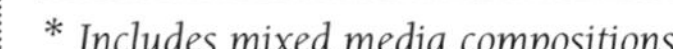

* *Includes mixed media compositions*

SECOND KISS

Kiss II *by pop artist Roy Lichtenstein (1923–97) gained a record $5.5 million at auction, followed closely at $5 million by* Torpedo...Los. *His work was partly inspired by images from comic strips.*

THE 10 ★ MOST EXPENSIVE WATERCOLOURS

	WATERCOLOUR/ARTIST/SALE	PRICE (£)
1	*La Moisson en Provence*, **Vincent van Gogh**, (Dutch; 1853–90), Sotheby's, London, 24 June 1997	8,000,000
2	*Les Toits – 1882*, **Vincent van Gogh**, Ader Picard & Tajan, Paris, 20 Mar 1990	2,900,107 (F.Fr 27,000,000)
3	*Die Sangerin L. Ais Fiordiligi*, **Paul Klee**, (Swiss; 1879–1940), Sotheby's, London, 28 Nov 1989	2,400,000
4	*Nature Morte au Melon Vert*, **Paul Cézanne**, (French; 1839–1906), Sotheby's, London, 4 Apr 1989	2,300,000
5	*John Biglin in Single Scull*, **Thomas Eakins**, (American; 1844–1916), Christie's, New York, 23 May 1990	1,893,490 ($3,200,000)
6	*Au Moulin Rouge*, *La Fille du Roi d'Egypte*, **Pablo Picasso**, (Spanish; 1881–1973), Sotheby's, London, 29 Nov 1994	1,650,000
7	*Coral Divers*, **Winslow Homer** (American; 1836–1910), Christie's, New York, 2 Dec 1998	1,445,783 ($2,400,000)
8	*Two Girls in Boat*, *Tynemouth*, *England*, **Winslow Homer**, Christie's, New York, 2 Dec 1998	1,385,542 ($2,300,000)
9	*La Montagne Sainte-Victoire Vue des Lauves*, **Paul Cézanne**, Christie's, London, 30 Nov 1992	1,300,000
10	*Buste de Femme*, **Pablo Picasso**, Sotheby's, New York, 11 Nov 1999	1,242,236 ($2,000,000)

TOP 10 ★ MOST EXPENSIVE PRINTS

	PRINT/ARTIST/SALE	PRICE (£)
1	*Diehard*, **Robert Rauschenberg** (American; b.1925), Sotheby's, New York, 2 May 1989	963,855 ($1,600,000)
2	*Mao*, **Andy Warhol** (American; 1928–87), Sothebys, London, 26 June 1996	610,000
3	*Elles*, **Henri de Toulouse-Lautrec** (French; 1864–1901), Sotheby's, New York, 10 May 1999	493,097 ($800,000)
4	*Famille Tahitienne*, **Paul Gauguin** (French; 1848–1903), Francis Briest, Paris, 4 Dec 1998	486,097 (F.Fr 4,545,010)
5	*Glider*, **Robert Rauschenberg**, Christie's, New York, 14 Nov 1995	483,871 ($750,000)
6	*Elles*, **Henri de Toulouse-Lautrec**, Sotheby's, New York, 7 Nov 1997	411,243 ($695,000)
7	*La Suite Vollard*, **Pablo Picasso** (Spanish;1881–1973), Christie's, New York, 2 Nov 1999	401,235 ($650,000)
8	*Suicide*, **Andy Warhol**, Sotheby's, New York, 18 May 1999	401,235 ($650,000)
9	*Les Saltimbanques*, **Pablo Picasso**, Sotheby's, New York, 3 May 1996	400,000 ($600,000)
10	*Head of Marilyn Monroe*, **Andy Warhol**, Beijers, Stockholm, 21 May 1990	379,372 (SKR 3,900,000)

Included within the classification of prints are silkscreens, lithographs, monotypes, aquatints, woodcuts, engravings, and etchings.

TOP 10 ★ MOST EXPENSIVE DRAWINGS*

	TITLE/ARTIST/SALE	PRICE (£)
1	*Famille de l'Arlequin*, **Pablo Picasso** (Spanish; 1881–1973), Christie's, New York, 14 Nov 1989	9,032,259 ($14,000,000)
2	=*Study for Head and Hand of an Apostle*, **Raphael** (Italian; 1483–1520), Christie's, London, 13 Dec 1996	4,800,000
	=*Oliviers avec les Alpilles au Fond*, **Vincent van Gogh** (Dutch; 1853–90), Sotheby's, London, 7 Dec 1999	4,800,000
4	*Corpse and Mirror*, **Jasper Johns** (American: b.1930), Christie's, New York, 10 Nov 1997	4,497,042 $7,600,000
5	*Rebus*, **Robert Rauschenberg** (American, b.1925), Sotheby's, New York, 30 Apr 1991	3,905,325 ($6,600,000)
6	*Jardin de Fleurs*, **Vincent van Gogh**, Christie's, New York, 14 November 1990	3,857,868 ($7,600,000)
7	*Study of a Man's Head and Hand*, **Raphael**, Christie's, London, 3 July 1984	3,300,000
8	*Rebus*, **Robert Rauschenberg**, Sotheby's, New York, 10 Nov 1988	3,194,445 ($5,750,000)
9	**Page from Vasari's *Libro de'Disegni*, Raffaellino del Garbo and Filippino Lippi** (Italian; 16th century), Christie's, London, 3 July 1984	3,000,000
10	**Untitled oil crayon canvas, Cy Twombly** (American; b.1929), Sotheby's, New York, 8 May 1990	2,976,190 ($5,000,000)

* *Media include pencil, pen, ink, drawing, crayon*

AHEAD OF THE FIELD

Van Gogh's harvest scene, La Moisson en Provence *(1888), sold for £8 million in 1997, making it the world's most expensive watercolour.*

TRIBAL RECORD

Edward S. Curtis's magnficent 20-volume set of photographs recording the life of North American Indians in the early twentieth century is the costliest ever sold at auction.

TOP 10 ★ MOST EXPENSIVE PHOTOGRAPHS

	PHOTOGRAPH/PHOTOGRAPHER/SALE	PRICE ($)
1	*The North American Indian** (1907–30), **Edward S. Curtis** (American; 1868–1952), Sotheby's, New York, 7 Oct 1993	441,519 ($662,500)
2	*Egypte et Nubie: Sites et monuments les plus intéressants pour l'étude de l'art et de l'histoire** (1858), **Félix Teynard** (French; 1817–92), Laurin Guilloux Buffetaud Tailleur, Paris, 21 Dec 1990	377,469 (F.Fr3,700,000)
3	*Noir et Blanche* (1926), **Man Ray** (American; 1890–1976), Christie's, New York, 4 Oct 1998	363,076 ($607,500)
4	*The North American Indian** (1907–30), **Edward S. Curtis**, Christie's, New York, 6 Apr 1995	299,194 ($464,500)
5	*Georgia O'Keeffe: A Portrait – Hands with Thimble* (1930), **Alfred Stieglitz** (American; 1864–1946), Christie's, New York, 8 Oct 1993	265,578 ($398,500)
6	*Equivalents (21)** (1920s), **Alfred Stieglitz**, Christie's, New York, 30 Oct 1989	254,826 ($396,000)
7	*Mondrian's Pipe and Glasses* (1926), **André Kertész** (Hungarian-American; 1894–1985), Christie's, New York, 17 Apr 1997	237,464 ($376,500)
8	*Noir et Blanche* (1926), **Man Ray**, Christie's, New York, 21 Apr 1994	229,479 ($354,500)
9	*The North American Indian** (1907–30), **Edward S. Curtis**, Christie's, New York, 13 Oct 1992	199,798 ($396,000)
10	*Self-Portrait*, **Herbert Bayer** (Austrian; 1900–85), Christie's, New York, 5 Oct 1999	172,370 ($277,500)

* *Collections; all others are single prints*

TOP 10 ★ MOST COLLECTED FOSSILS IN THE UK

1 **Shark's teeth** Found in London clay at Sheppey, Kent; *c.*55 million years old.

2 **Crinoid ossicles and stem fragments** Single and multiple rounded plates of sea-lily stems, *c.*340 million years old.

3 **Gryphaea** Known as "Devil's toenail", an unusal bivalve with unequal-sized valves, found in Lias of England; *c.*200 million years old.

4 **Belemnites** Called "Devil's thunderbolts", bullet-shaped skeletal parts of cephalopods; *c.*100–200 million years old.

5 **Productus** The curved, ribbed shell of a bivalve; *c.*300 million years old.

6 **Ammonites** Coiled shells of cephalopod molluscs; 65–210 million years old.

7 **Trilobites** Locally known as "Dudley bugs", jointed skeletons of extinct arthropods.

8 **Micraster** Heart-shaped sea urchin with a star pattern on top; *c.*80 million years old.

9 **Lithostrotion** Compound or colonial coral with star-like cross-section; star-like arrangement of large pores on upper surface *c.*300 million years old.

10 **Rhynchonella** Strongly ribbed, small and drop shaped or triangular trachiopod; *c.*180 million years old.

MOST EXPENSIVE ITEMS OF ENGLISH FURNITURE

	ITEM/SALE	PRICE (£)
1	**The Anglesey Desk**, Regency bronze-mounted and brass-inlaid ebony and mahogany library desk, attributed to Marsh & Tatbam, Christie's, London, 8 July 1993	1,761,500
2	**The Dundas Armchairs**, pair of George III giltwood armchairs, designed by Robert Adam and made by Thomas Chippendale, Christie's, London, 3 July 1997	1,706,500
3	**The Warwick Tables**, supplied to Queen Anne for St. James's Palace in 1704–05, by Gerrit Jensen probably in association with Thomas Pelletier, Sotheby's, London, 10 July 1998	1,651,500
4	**The Dundas Sofas**, pair of George III giltwood sofas designed by Robert Adam and made by Thomas Chippendale, Christie's, London, 3 July 1997	1,541,500
5	**The Lonsdale Langlois Commode**, a George III ormolu-mounted rosewood, fruitwood, and marquetry bombe commode, Christie's, New York, 24 Nov 1998	1,519,500 ($2,532,500)
6	**The St. Giles's Dining-Chairs**, set of 17 George II mahogany dining-chairs, attributed to William Hallett Senior, Christie's, London, 8 July 1999	1,211,500
7	**A George II ormolu-mounted mahogany dressing and writing-commode**, attributed to John Channon, Christie's, London, 6 July 1989	1,100,000
8	**A pair of George II mahogany commodes**, attributed to Vile & Cobb, Sotheby's, London, 18 Nov 1993	991,500
9	**The Stowe Apollo Tables**, pair of George II gilt-gesso side tables, attributed to Benjamin Goodison, Christie's, London, 9 July 1998	936,500
10	**A George III mahogany commode**, attributed to Thomas Chippendale, Christie's, London, 5 Dec 1991	935,000

TOP 10

MOST EXPENSIVE ITEMS OF AMERICAN FURNITURE

	ITEM/SALE	PRICE (£)
1	**The Nicholas Brown Chippendale mahogany block and shell desk and bookcase**, *c.*1760–70, attributed to John Goddard, Christie's, New York, 3 June 1989	7,539,510 ($12,100,000)
2	**Richard Edwards Chippendale carved mahogany pier table**, by Thomas Tufft, *c.*1775–76, Christie's, New York, 20 Jan 1990	2,817,276 ($4,620,000)
3	**The Samuel Whitehorne Queen Anne block-and-shell carved mahogany kneehole desk**, attributed to Edmund Townsend, *c.*1780, Sotheby's, New York, 20 Jan 1996	2,397,450 ($3,632,500)
4	**Chippendale carved mahogany tea-table**, *c.*1760–80, Christie's, New York, 28 May 1987	1,526,175 ($2,422,500)
5	**The Edwards-Harrison family Chippendale carved mahogany high chest-of-drawers**, dressing table and pair of side chairs, by Thomas Tufft, *c.*1775–76, Christie's, New York, 28 May 1987	1,073,600 ($1,760,000)
6	**The Edward Jackson parcel gilt inlaid and figured mahogany mirrored bonnet-top secretary bookcase**, *c.*1738–48, Sotheby's, New York, 20 Jan 1996	945,450 ($1,432,500)
7	**Chippendale carved mahogany tea-table**, *c.*1760–80, Christie's, New York, 25 Jan 1986	746,428 ($1,045,000)
8	**Cornelius Stevenson Chippendale carved mahogany tea-table** attributed to Thomas Affleck, carving attributed to Nicholas Bernard & Martin Jugiez, *c.*1760–80, Christie's, New York, 20 Jan 1990	737,858 ($1,210,000)
9	**Chipppendale carved mahogany tea-table**, *c.*1770, Christie's, New York, 26 Jan 1995	463,667 ($695,500)
10	**Chippendale mahogany serpentine back sofa**, *c.*1760–85, Christie's, New York, 18 Oct 1986	423,500 ($605,000)

TOP 10

MOST EXPENSIVE MINIATURES

	MINIATURE/ARTIST/SALE	PRICE (£)
1	***Two Orientals*, Francisco José de Goya y Lucientes** (Spanish; 1746–1828), Christie's, London, 3 Dec 1997	580,000
2	***Maja and Celestina*, Francisco José de Goya y Lucientes**, Sotheby's, New York, 30 May 1991	294,118 ($500,000)
3	***Portrait of George Villiers, Duke of Buckingham*, Jean Petitot** (French; 1607–91), Christie's, London, 30 Apr 1996	250,000
4	***Man Clasping Hand from Cloud*, possibly Lord Thomas Howard, Nicholas Hilliard**, (British; 1547–1619), Christie's, London, 3 Mar 1993	160,000
5	***King George III when Prince of Wales Wearing Order of Garter*, Jean-Etienne Liotard**, (Swiss; 1702–89), Christie's, London, 21 Oct 1997	115,000
6	***Portrait of Henry Stuart, Earl of Ross and 1st Duke of Albany*, attributed to Lievine Teerling-Bening** (Flemish; 16th century), Bonhams, London, 20 Nov 1997	110,000
7	***Portrait of Tsar Nicholas II in Uniform with Orders*, Russian School** (Russian; 20th century), Christie's, New York, 1 Dec 1995	91,503 ($140,000)
8	***Bacchic Scenes*, Jean Jacques de Gault** (French?; *c.*1738–1812), Sotheby's, Geneva, 13 Nov 1995	590,909 (S.Fr 160,000)
9	***Landscape with Saint Jerome*, Hans Bol** (Dutch; 1534–93), Sotheby's, London, 11 Feb 1999	90,000
10	***Lady Wearing Rust Coloured Dress with Lace Collar and Jewels*, Samuel Cooper** (British; 1609–72), Sotheby's, London, 11 Oct 1994	80,000

Background image: JIMI HENDRIX'S FENDER STRATOCASTER ELECTRIC GUITAR

SUPER HERO

Created by writer Jerry Siegel (American, 1914–96) and artist Joe Shuster (Canadian, 1914–92), Superman made his debut in the June 1938 first issue of Action Comics*, now the most prized of all comic books.*

TOP 10 ★

MOST VALUABLE AMERICAN COMICS

COMIC	VALUE ($)*
1 *Action Comics* No. 1 *Published in June 1938, the first issue of* Action Comics *marked the original appearance of Superman.*	185,000
2 *Detective Comics* No. 27 *Issued in May 1939, it is prized as the first comic book to feature Batman.*	165,000
3 *Superman* No. 1 *The first comic book devoted to Superman, reprinting the original* Action Comics *story, was published in summer 1939.*	130,000
4 *Marvel Comics* No. 1 *The Human Torch and other heroes were first introduced in the issue dated October 1939.*	115,000
5 *All American Comics* No. 16 *The Green Lantern made his debut in the issue dated July 1940.*	65,000
6 =*Batman* No. 1 *Published in spring 1940, this was the first comic book devoted to Batman.*	63,000
=*Whizz Comics* No. 2 *Published in February 1940 – and confusingly numbered "2" when it was in fact the first issue – it was the first comic book to feature Captain Marvel.*	63,000
8 *Flash Comics* No. 1 *Dated January 1940, and featuring The Flash, it is rare because it was produced in small numbers for promotional purposes, and was unique since issue 2 was retitled* Whizz Comics.	57,000
9 *Captain America Comics* No. 1 *Published in March 1941, this was the original comic book in which Captain America appeared.*	56,000
10 *Detective Comics* No. 1 *Published in March 1937, it was the first in a long-running series.*	50,000

Source: The Overstreet Comic Book Price Guide, #30, 2000. *©2000 Gemstone Publishing, Inc.*

All rights reserved.

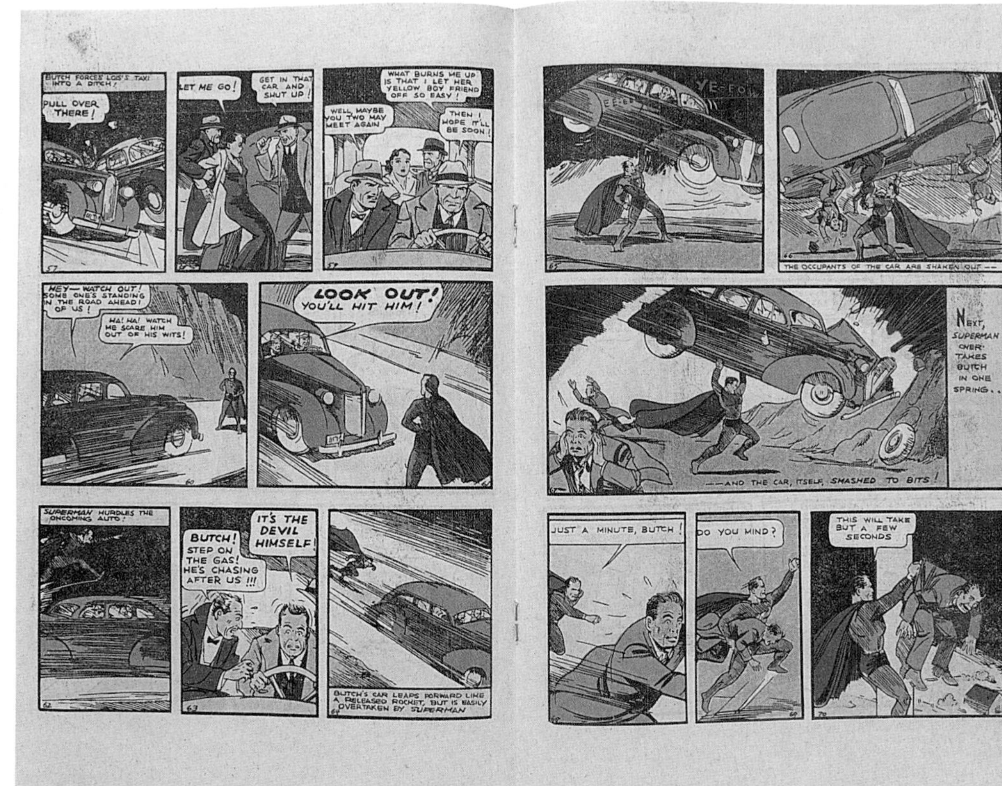

TOP 10 ★

MOST EXPENSIVE MUSICAL INSTRUMENTS

INSTRUMENT*/SALE	PRICE (£)
1 **"Kreutzer" violin by Antonio Stradivari**, Christies, London, 1 Apr 1998	946,000
2 **"Cholmondeley" violoncello by Antonio Stradivari**, Sotheby's, London, 22 June 1998	682,000
3 **Accoustic guitar owned by David Bowie, Paul McCartney, and George Michael**, Christie's, London, 18 May 1994	220,000
4 **Jimi Hendrix's Fender Stratocaster electric guitar**, Sotheby's, London, 25 Apr 1990	198,000
5 **Steinway grand piano, decorated by Lawrence Alma-Tadema and Edward Poynter for Henry Marquand**, 1884–87, Sotheby Parke Bernet, New York, 26 Mar 1980	163,000 ($390,000)
6 **Double bass by Domenico Montagnana**, Sotheby's, London, 16 Mar 1999	155,500
7 **Viola by Giovanni Paolo Maggini**, Christie's, London, 20 Nov 1984	129,000
8 **Verne Powell's platinum flute**, Christie's, New York, 18 Oct 1986	126,200 ($187,000)
9 **English double-manual harpsichord by Burkat Shudi and John Broadwood**, Sotheby's, London, 27 Oct 1999	106,000
10 **Seven-keyed bugle by Charles-Joseph Sax**, Brussels, 1842, Sotheby's, London, 18 Nov 1993	5,200

* *Most expensive example only given per category of instrument*

In which country is the bestselling English-language newspaper published?

see p.107 for the answer

A USA
B India
C UK

TOP 10 ★

Music

Chart Hits

TOP 10 ALBUMS OF ALL TIME

(*Title/artist or group*)

❶ ***Thriller***, Michael Jackson ❷ ***Dark Side of the Moon***, Pink Floyd ❸ ***Their Greatest Hits 1971–1975***, Eagles ❹ ***The Bodyguard***, Soundtrack ❺ ***Rumours***, Fleetwood Mac ❻ ***Sgt. Pepper's Lonely Hearts Club Band***, The Beatles ❼ ***Led Zeppelin IV***, Led Zeppelin ❽ ***Greatest Hits***, Elton John ❾ ***Jagged Little Pill***, Alanis Morissette ❿ ***Bat out of Hell***, Meat Loaf

Total worldwide sales of albums have traditionally been notoriously hard to gauge, but even with the huge expansion of the album market during the 1980s, and multiple million sales of many major releases, this Top 10 is still élite territory.

TOP 10 ALBUMS OF ALL TIME IN THE UK

(*Title/artist or group/year*)

❶ ***Sgt. Pepper's Lonely Hearts Club Band***, The Beatles, 1967 ❷ ***(What's the Story) Morning Glory?***, Oasis, 1995 ❸ ***Bad***, Michael Jackson, 1987 ❹ ***Brothers in Arms***, Dire Straits, 1985 ❺ ***Stars***, Simply Red, 1991 ❻ ***Thriller***, Michael Jackson, 1982 ❼ ***Greatest Hits***, Queen, 1981 ❽ ***Spice***, Spice Girls, 1996 ❾ ***The Immaculate Collection***, Madonna, 1990 ❿ ***Talk on Corners***, The Corrs, 1997

Source: *BPI*

ARTISTS WITH THE MOST CONSECUTIVE UK TOP 10 HITS

	ARTIST OR GROUP/PERIOD	HITS
1	**Madonna**, Nov 1984–Dec 1994	35
2	**Cliff Richard**, June 1960–Mar 1965	21
3	=**The Beatles**, July 1964–Mar 1976	18
	=**Abba**, Sep 1975–Dec 1981	18
5	**Boyzone**, Dec 1994–Dec 1999	16
6	**The Rolling Stones**, Feb 1964–Apr 1971	14
6	=**Kylie Minogue**, Jan 1988–June 1991	13
8	=**The Shadows**, July 1960–May 1964	12
	=**Slade**, Oct 1971–Oct 1974	12
	=**Take That**, Oct 1992–Mar 1996	12

Source: *The Popular Music Database*

TOP 10

SINGLES THAT STAYED LONGEST IN THE UK CHARTS

	TITLE/ARTIST OR GROUP/ FIRST CHART ENTRY	WEEKS IN CHART
1	***Release Me***, Engelbert Humperdinck, 1967	56
2	***Stranger on the Shore***, Mr. Acker Bilk, 1961	55
3	***Relax***, Frankie Goes to Hollywood, 1984	48
4	***My Way***, Frank Sinatra, 1969	47
5	***Rivers of Babylon***, Boney M, 1978	40
6	=***I Love You Because***, Jim Reeves, 1964	39
	=***Tie a Yellow Ribbon Round the Old Oak Tree***, Dawn featuring Tony Orlando, 1973	39
8	=***A Scottish Soldier***, Andy Stewart, 1961	38
	=***White Lines (Don't Don't Do It)***, Grandmaster Flash and Melle Mel, 1983	38
10	***Love Is All Around***, Wet Wet Wet, 1994	37

Source: *The Popular Music Database*

TOP 10

ARTISTS WITH THE MOST WEEKS ON THE UK SINGLES CHART*

	ARTIST OR GROUP	TOTAL WEEKS
1	**Elvis Presley**	1,155
2	**Cliff Richard**	1,129
3	**Elton John**	566
4	**Madonna**	507
5	**Michael Jackson**	479
6	**Rod Stewart**	466
7	**The Beatles**	456
8	**Frank Sinatra**	440
9	**David Bowie**	436
10	**Diana Ross**	433

* *Up to 1 January 2000*

Source: *The Popular Music Database*

SOARING LIKE EAGLES

One of the world's bestselling albums, the Eagles' Their Greatest Hits 1971–1975, *was also the first to be certified platinum.*

TOP 10 ★ SINGLES OF ALL TIME

#	TITLE/ARTIST OR GROUP/YEAR	SALES EXCEED
1	*Candle in the Wind (1997)/ Something About the Way You Look Tonight*, Elton John, 1997	37,000,000
2	*White Christmas*, Bing Crosby, 1943	30,000,000
3	*Rock Around the Clock*, Bill Haley and His Comets, 1954	17,000,000
4	*I Want to Hold Your Hand*, The Beatles, 1963	12,000,000
5	=*Hey Jude*, The Beatles, 1968	10,000,000
	=*It's Now or Never*, Elvis Presley, 1960	10,000,000
	=*I Will Always Love You*, Whitney Houston, 1993	10,000,000
8	=*Hound Dog/Don't Be Cruel*, Elvis Presley, 1956	9,000,000
	=*Diana*, Paul Anka, 1957	9,000,000
10	=*I'm a Believer*, The Monkees, 1966	8,000,000
	=*(Everything I Do) I Do it for You*, Bryan Adams, 1991	8,000,000

TOP 10 ★ SINGLES OF ALL TIME IN THE UK

#	TITLE/ARTIST OR GROUP/YEAR	EST. UK SALES
1	*Candle in the Wind (1997)/ Something About the Way You Look Tonight*, Elton John, 1997	4,800,000
2	*Do They Know It's Christmas?*, Band Aid, 1984	3,510,000
3	*Bohemian Rhapsody*, Queen, 1975/91	2,130,000
4	*Mull of Kintyre*, Wings, 1977	2,050,000
5	*Rivers of Babylon/ Brown Girl in the Ring*, Boney M, 1978	1,995,000
6	*Relax*, Frankie Goes to Hollywood, 1984	1,910,000
7	*She Loves You*, The Beatles, 1963	1,890,000
8	*You're the One That I Want*, John Travolta and Olivia Newton-John, 1978	1,870,000
9	*Unchained Melody*, Robson Green and Jerome Flynn, 1995	1,820,000
10	*Mary's Boy Child/Oh My Lord*, Boney M, 1978	1,790,000

Source: *BPI*

More than 50 singles have sold over 1 million copies apiece in the UK during the last 40 years, and these are the cream of that crop. The Band Aid single had a host of special circumstances surrounding it, and it took the remarkable response to the death of Diana, Princess of Wales, to generate sales capable of overtaking it. The only act to appear twice is Boney M, a group masterminded by German producer Frank Farian.

TEEN TRIUMPH

Paul Anka's song Diana, *released when he was just 16 years old, remains one of the bestselling singles of all time.*

OLD BLUE EYES

Frank Sinatra is one of only two septuagenarians to achieve a Top 10 hit in the UK. His single, New York, New York, *remains a highly popular classic.*

TOP 10 ★ OLDEST SINGERS TO HAVE A TOP 10 HIT IN THE UK

#	ARTIST/TITLE	AGE YRS	AGE MTHS
1	**Frank Sinatra**, *New York, New York*	70	4
2	**Andy Williams**, *Music to Watch Girls By*	70	3
3	**Louis Armstrong**, *What a Wonderful World*	68	0
4	**Honor Blackman**, *Kinky Boots*	64	0
5	**Tom Jones***, *Mama Told Me Not to Come*	59	10
6	**Cliff Richard**, *The Millennium Prayer*	59	2
7	**James Brown**, *Living in America*	56	10
8	**Ted Heath**, *Swingin' Shepherd Blues*	56	2
9	**Petula Clark**, *Downtown '88 Remix*	56	0
10	**Diana Ross**, *Not Over You Yet*	55	7

* *With Stereophonics*

The ages listed are those of the artists at the end of the Top 10 run of their most recent (to date) Top 10 hit. Posthumous Top 10 entries – such as two by Bing Crosby – are not counted. With several of the artists here still actively and successfully recording, some may have further Top 10 hits yet to deliver.

Record Firsts

THE 10 FIRST BRITISH SOLO ARTISTS TO HAVE A NO. 1 SINGLE IN THE US

	ARTIST/SINGLE	DATE AT NO. 1
1	**Mr. Acker Bilk**, *Stranger on the Shore*	26 May 1962
2	**Petula Clark**, *Downtown*	23 Jan 1965
3	**Donovan**, *Sunshine Superman*	3 Sep 1966
4	**Lulu**, *To Sir With Love*	21 Oct 1967
5	**George Harrison**, *My Sweet Lord*	26 Dec 1970
6	**Rod Stewart**, *Maggie May*	2 Oct 1971
7	**Gilbert O'Sullivan**, *Alone Again Naturally*	29 July 1972
8	**Elton John**, *Crocodile Rock*	3 Feb 1973
9	**Ringo Starr**, *Photograph*	24 Nov 1973
10	**Eric Clapton**, *I Shot the Sheriff*	14 Sep 1974

Source: *The Popular Music Database*

THE 10 FIRST AMERICAN SOLO ARTISTS TO HAVE A NO. 1 SINGLE IN THE UK

	ARTIST/SINGLE	DATE AT NO. 1
1	**Al Martino**, *Here in My Heart*	14 Nov 1952
2	**Jo Stafford**, *You Belong to Me*	16 Jan 1953
3	**Kay Starr**, *Comes A-Long A-Love*	23 Jan 1953
4	**Eddie Fisher**, *Outside of Heaven*	30 Jan 1953
5	**Perry Como**, *Don't Let the Stars Get in Your Eyes*	6 Feb 1953
6	**Guy Mitchell**, *She Wears Red Feathers*	13 Mar 1953
7	**Frankie Laine**, *I Believe*	24 Apr 1953
8	**Doris Day**, *Secret Love*	16 Apr 1954
9	**Johnnie Ray**, *Such a Night*	30 Apr 1954
10	**Kitty Kallen**, *Little Things Mean a Lot*	10 Sep 1954

Source: *The Popular Music Database*

THE 10 FIRST UK CHART SINGLES

(Single/artist)

1 ***Here in My Heart***, Al Martino 2 ***You Belong to Me***, Jo Stafford 3 ***Somewhere Along the Way***, Nat "King" Cole 4 ***Isle of Innisfree***, Bing Crosby 5 ***Feet Up***, Guy Mitchell 6 ***Half as Much***, Rosemary Clooney 7 = ***High Noon***, Frankie Laine; = ***Forget Me Not***, Vera Lynn 9 = ***Sugarbush***, Doris Day and Frankie Laine; = ***Blue Tango***, Ray Martin

Source: New Musical Express *(for week ending 15 November 1952)*

THE 10 FIRST AMERICAN GROUPS TO HAVE A NO. 1 SINGLE IN THE UK

	GROUP/SINGLE	DATE AT NO. 1
1	**Bill Haley and His Comets**, *Rock Around the Clock*	25 Nov 1955
2	**Dream Weavers**, *It's Almost Tomorrow*	16 Mar 1956
3	**Teenagers featuring Frankie Lymon**, *Why Do Fools Fall in Love?*	20 July 1956
4	**The Crickets**, *That'll Be the Day*	1 Nov 1957
5	**Platters**, *Smoke Gets in your Eyes*	20 Mar 1959
6	**Marcels**, *Blue Moon*	4 May 1961
7	**Highwaymen**, *Michael*	12 Oct 1961
8	**B. Bumble and the Stingers**, *Rocker*	17 May 1962
9	**Supremes**, *Baby Love*	19 Nov 1964
10	**Byrds**, *Mr. Tambourine Man*	22 July 1965

Source: *The Popular Music Database*

SUPREME SUPREMES

Nine years after their first US No. 1, the Supremes became only the ninth US group to top the UK charts – the song was Baby Love.

THE 10

FIRST BRITISH GROUPS TO HAVE A NO. 1 SINGLE IN THE US

	GROUP/SINGLE	DATE AT NO. 1
1	**Tornados**, *Telstar*	22 Dec 1962
2	**The Beatles**, *I Want to Hold Your Hand*	1 Feb 1964
3	**The Animals**, *House of the Rising Sun*	5 Sep 1964
4	**Manfred Mann**, *Do Wah Diddy Diddy*	17 Oct 1964
5	**Freddie and the Dreamers**, *I'm Telling You Now*	10 Apr 1965
6	**Wayne Fontana and the Mindbenders**, *The Game of Love*	24 Apr 1965
7	**Herman's Hermits**, *Mrs. Brown You've Got a Lovely Daughter*	1 May 1965
8	**The Rolling Stones**, *(I Can't Get No) Satisfaction*	10 July 1965
9	**Dave Clark Five**, *Over and Over*	25 Dec 1965
10	**Troggs**, *Wild Thing*	30 July 1966

Source: *The Popular Music Database*

THE 10

FIRST MILLION-SELLING UK SINGLES

	SINGLE/ARTIST	YEAR
1	***Rock Around the Clock***, Bill Haley and His Comets	1954
2	***Mary's Boy Child***, Harry Belafonte	1957
3	***Diana***, Paul Anka	1957
4	***It's Now or Never***, Elvis Presley	1960
5	***Stranger on the Shore***, Mr. Acker Bilk	1961
6	***The Young Ones***, Cliff Richard	1962
7	***I Remember You***, Frank Ifield	1962
8	***She Loves You***, The Beatles	1963
9	***I Want to Hold Your Hand***, The Beatles	1963
10	***Can't Buy Me Love***, The Beatles	1964

HIT MANN

Do Wah Diddy Diddy, a cover version of a US-written song, became British group Manfred Mann's debut No. 1 US chart hit.

THE 10

FIRST UK CHART ALBUMS

	ALBUM	ARTIST OR GROUP
1	***South Pacific***	Soundtrack
2	***Come Fly With Me***	Frank Sinatra
3	***Elvis' Golden Records***	Elvis Presley
4	***King Creole***	Elvis Presley
5	***My Fair Lady***	Broadway Cast
6	***Warm***	Johnny Mathis
7	***The King and I***	Soundtrack
8	***Dear Perry***	Perry Como
9	***Oklahoma!***	Soundtrack
10	***Songs by Tom Lehrer***	Tom Lehrer

Source: Melody Maker

The first album chart was printed in *Melody Maker* for the week ending 8 November 1958, and represents a time capsule of the popular music of the era, a transitional period when crooners, comedy singers, and musicals rubbed shoulders with up-and-coming rock artists.

THE 10

FIRST FEMALE SINGERS TO HAVE A NO. 1 SINGLE IN THE UK

	ARTIST/SINGLE	DATE AT NO. 1
1	**Jo Stafford**, *You Belong to Me*	16 Jan 1953
2	**Kay Starr**, *Comes A-Long A-Love*	23 Jan 1953
3	**Lita Roza**, *(How Much is That) Doggie in the Window?*	17 Apr 1953
4	**Doris Day**, *Secret Love*	16 Apr 1954
5	**Kitty Kallen**, *Little Things Mean a Lot*	10 Sep 1954
6	**Vera Lynn**, *My Son, My Son*	5 Nov 1954
7	**Rosemary Clooney**, *This Ole House*	26 Nov 1954
8	**Ruby Murray**, *Softly Softly*	18 Feb 1955
9	**Alma Cogan**, *Dreamboat*	15 July 1955
10	**Anne Shelton**, *Lay Down Your Arms*	21 Sep 1956

Source: *The Popular Music Database*

Did You Know? The Tornados' *Telstar*, the first ever US No. 1 by a British group, was inspired by the 10 July 1962 launch of the first satellite to transmit TV signals between Europe and the USA. It sold over 5 million copies worldwide.

TOP 10 ARTISTS WITH THE MOST NO. 1 SINGLES IN THE UK

	ARTIST OR GROUP	NO. 1 SINGLES*
1	=The Beatles	17
	=Elvis Presley	17
3	Cliff Richard	14
4	Abba	9
5	=The Rolling Stones	8
	=Take That	8
	=Madonna	8
	=Spice Girls	8
9	George Michael	7
10	=Slade	6
	=Rod Stewart	6
	=Boyzone	6

* As at 1 January 2000

Source: *The Popular Music Database*

BIG BROTHER

In 1972, Donny Osmond and his younger brother Jimmy became the UK's two youngest chart toppers. At just 9, Jimmy is the youngest by far in this list.

TOP 10 YOUNGEST SOLO ARTISTS TO HAVE A NO. 1 SINGLE IN THE UK*

	ARTIST/TITLE/YEAR	AGE# YRS	MTHS
1	**Little Jimmy Osmond**, *Long Haired Lover from Liverpool*, 1972	9	8
2	**Donny Osmond**, *Puppy Love*, 1972	14	6
3	**Helen Shapiro**, *You Don't Know*, 1961	14	10
4	**Billie**, *Because We Want To*, 1998	15	9
5	**Paul Anka**, *Diana*, 1957	16	0
6	**Tiffany**, *I Think We're Alone Now*, 1988	16	3
7	**Nicole**, *A Little Peace*, 1982	17	0
8	**Britney Spears**, *...Baby One More Time*, 1999	17	2
9	**Sandie Shaw**, *(There's) Always Something There to Remind Me*, 1964	17	7
10	**Glenn Medeiros**, *Nothing's Gonna Change My Love*, 1988	18	0

* To 1 January 2000

\# During first week of debut No. 1 UK single

Source: *The Popular Music Database*

TOP 10 ALBUMS LONGEST AT NO. 1 IN THE UK

(Title/artist or group/weeks at No. 1)

❶ ***South Pacific***, Soundtrack, 115 ❷ ***The Sound of Music***, Soundtrack, 70 ❸ ***Bridge Over Troubled Water***, Simon and Garfunkel, 41 ❹ ***Please Please Me***, The Beatles, 30 ❺ ***Sgt. Pepper's Lonely Hearts Club Band***, The Beatles, 27 ❻ ***G.I. Blues***, Elvis Presley/Soundtrack, 22 ❼ **=** ***With The Beatles***, The Beatles, 21; **=** ***A Hard Day's Night***, The Beatles/Soundtrack, 21 ❾ **=** ***Blue Hawaii***, Elvis Presley/Soundtrack, 18; **=** ***Saturday Night Fever***, Soundtrack, 18

Source: *The Popular Music Database*

TOP 10 LONGEST GAPS BETWEEN NO. 1 HIT SINGLES IN THE UK

	ARTIST OR GROUP/PERIOD	GAP YRS	MTHS
1	**The Righteous Brothers**, 11 Feb 1965–28 Oct 1990	25	8
2	**The Hollies**, 15 July 1965–18 Sep 1988	23	2
3	**Blondie**, 22 Nov 1980–13 Feb 1999	18	3
4	**Queen**, 24 Jan 1976–20 Jan 1991	15	0
5	**Diana Ross**, 11 Sep 1971–2 Mar 1986	14	6
6	**Frank Sinatra**, 1 Oct 1954–27 May 1966	11	7
7	**Cliff Richard**, 17 Apr 1968–19 Aug 1979	11	4
8	**Bee Gees**, 4 Sep 1968–23 Apr 1978	9	7
9	**Cliff Richard**, 15 Sep 1979–4 Dec 1988	9	3
10	**Cliff Richard**, 29 Dec 1990–4 Dec 1999	8	11

TOP 10 ALBUMS WITH THE MOST CONSECUTIVE WEEKS AT NO. 1 IN THE UK

	TITLE/ARTIST OR GROUP	WEEKS AT NO. 1
1	***South Pacific***, Soundtrack	70
2	***Please Please Me***, The Beatles	30
3	***Sgt. Pepper's Lonely Hearts Club Band***, The Beatles	23
4	=***With The Beatles***, The Beatles	21
	=***A Hard Day's Night***, The Beatles/Soundtrack	21
6	***South Pacific***, Soundtrack	19
7	=***The Sound of Music***, Soundtrack	18
	=***Saturday Night Fever***, Soundtrack	18
9	***Blue Hawaii***, Elvis Presley/Soundtrack	17
10	***Summer Holiday***, Cliff Richard and the Shadows/Soundtrack	14

Source: *The Popular Music Database*

SATCHMO SINGS

Louis Armstrong topped the UK charts just once in his singing career, in 1968, when he was aged 67. His hit, What a Wonderful World, *sold over 1 million copies worldwide.*

TOP 10 OLDEST ARTISTS TO HAVE A NO. 1 SINGLE IN THE UK*

	ARTIST OR GROUP/TITLE	AGE# YRS	MTHS
1	**Louis Armstrong**, *What a Wonderful World*	67	10
2	**Cliff Richard**, *The Millennium Prayer*	59	1
3	**Cher**, *Believe*	52	7
4	**Elton John**, *Candle in the Wind (1997)/Something About the Way You Look Tonight*	51	7
5	**Frank Sinatra**, *Somethin' Stupid*	51	4
6	**Telly Savalas**, *If*	51	1
7	**The Righteous Brothers**, *Unchained Melody*	50 / 50	2/ 1
8	**Charles Aznavour**, *She*	50	1
9	**Clive Dunn**, *Grandad*	49	0
10	**Ben E. King**, *Stand by Me*	48	5

* *To 1 January 2000*

\# *Those of apparently identical age have been ranked according to their precise age in days*

Source: *The Popular Music Database*

The ages listed are those of the artists during the final week of their last (to date) No. 1 hit. Seven of the 10 are still alive, so there is room for further improvement.

TOP 10 SINGLES WITH THE MOST WEEKS AT NO. 1 IN THE UK

	TITLE/ARTIST OR GROUP/YEAR	WEEKS AT NO. 1*
1	***I Believe***, Frankie Laine, 1953	18
2	***(Everything I Do) I Do It for You***, Bryan Adams, 1991	16
3	***Love Is All Around***, Wet Wet Wet, 1994	15
4	***Bohemian Rhapsody***, Queen, 1975/91	14
5	***Rose Marie***, Slim Whitman, 1955	11
6	=***Cara Mia***, David Whitfield, 1954	10
	=***I Will Always Love You***, Whitney Houston, 1993	10
8	=***Diana***, Paul Anka, 1957	9
	=***Here in My Heart***, Al Martino, 1952	9
	=***Mull of Kintyre***, Wings, 1977	9
	=***Oh Mein Papa***, Eddie Calvert, 1954	9
	=***Secret Love***, Doris Day, 1954	9
	=***Two Tribes***, Frankie Goes To Hollywood, 1984	9
	=***You're the One That I Want***, John Travolta and Olivia Newton-John, 1978	9

* *For consecutive chart-topping weeks, except for Nos. 1 and 4, where the totals are cumulative*

Source: *The Popular Music Database*

TOP 10 SLOWEST UK ALBUM CHART RISES TO NO. 1

(Title/artist or group/weeks to reach No. 1)

1 **Tyrannosaurus Rex**, *My People Were Fair and Had Sky in Their Hair... But Now They're Content to Wear Stars on Their Brows*, 199 2 **Elvis Presley**, *40 Greatest Hits*, 114 3 **Various artists**, *Fame (Original Soundtrack)*, 98 4 **Cranberries**, *Everybody Else Is Doing it, So Why Can't We?*, 67 5 **Mike Oldfield**, *Tubular Bells*, 65 6 **Ace of Base**, *Happy Nation*, 54 7 **Fleetwood Mac**, *Rumours*, 49 8 **Bob Dylan**, *The Freewheelin' Bob Dylan*, 48 9 **Celine Dion**, *The Colour of My Love*, 47 10 = **Elton John**, *Sleeping With the Past*, 44; = **Madonna**, *Like a Virgin*, 44

Source: *The Popular Music Database*

BROTHERS IN WAITING

A gap of almost a decade separates the Bee Gees' No. 1 hits: I've Gotta Get a Message to You *in September 1968 and* Tragedy *in April 1978.*

TOP 10 ★ SINGLES OF THE 1990s IN THE UK

	SINGLE/ARTIST OR GROUP	YEAR RELEASED
1	***Candle in the Wind (1997)/Something About the Way You Look Tonight***, Elton John	1997
2	***Unchained Melody/The White Cliffs of Dover***, Robson and Jerome	1995
3	***Love Is All Around***, Wet Wet Wet	1994
4	***Barbie Girl***, Aqua	1997
5	***Believe***, Cher	1998
6	***Perfect Day***, Various artists	1997
7	***(Everything I Do) I Do It for You***, Bryan Adams	1991
8	***...Baby One More Time***, Britney Spears	1999
9	***I'll Be Missing You***, Puff Daddy and Faith Evans	1997
10	***I Will Always Love You***, Whitney Houston	1992

TOP 10 ★ SINGLES OF THE 1990s IN THE UK (MALE)

	SINGLE/ARTIST	YEAR RELEASED
1	***Candle in the Wind (1997)/Something About the Way You Look Tonight***, Elton John	1997
2	***(Everything I Do) I Do It for You***, Bryan Adams	1991
3	***Angels***, Robbie Williams	1998
4	***I'd Do Anything for Love (But I Won't Do That)***, Meat Loaf	1991
5	***Earth Song***, Michael Jackson	1996
6	***Ice Ice Baby***, Vanilla Ice	1990
7	***Sacrifice/Healing Hands***, Elton John	1990
8	***Baby Come Back***, Pato Banton	1994
9	***Men in Black***, Will Smith	1997
10	***The One and Only***, Chesney Hawkes	1991

TOP 10 SINGLES OF THE 1990s IN THE UK (FEMALE)

(Single/artist/year released)

❶ ***Believe***, Cher, 1998 ❷ ***My Heart Will Go on,*** Celine Dion, 1998 ❸ ***I Will Always Love You,*** Whitney Houston, 1992 ❹ ***...Baby One More Time***, Britney Spears, 1999 ❺ ***How Do I Live***, LeAnn Rimes, 1998 ❻ ***Think Twice***, Celine Dion, 1995 ❼ ***Saturday Night***, Whigfield, 1994 ❽ ***The Shoop Shoop Song (It's in His Kiss)***, Cher, 1991 ❾ ***Without You***, Mariah Carey, 1994 ❿ ***Vogue***, Madonna, 1990

FANTASY FIGURES

Mariah Carey's 1995 single Fantasy *became the first ever by a female artist to debut at US No. 1, becoming one of the top sellers of the decade.*

TOP 10 SINGLES OF EACH YEAR IN THE 1990s IN THE UK

YEAR	SINGLE/ARTIST OR GROUP
1990	*Unchained Melody*, Righteous Brothers
1991	*(Everything I Do) I Do It for You*, Bryan Adams
1992	*I Will Always Love You*, Whitney Houston
1993	*I'd Do Anything for Love (But I Won't Do That)*, Meat Loaf
1994	*Love Is All Around*, Wet Wet Wet
1995	*Unchained Melody/The White Cliffs of Dover*, Robson and Jerome
1996	*Killing Me Softly*, The Fugees
1997	*Candle in the Wind (1997)/Something About the Way You Look Tonight*, Elton John
1998	*Believe*, Cher
1999	*...Baby One More Time*, Britney Spears

TOP 10 SINGLES OF EACH YEAR IN THE 1980s IN THE UK

YEAR	SINGLE/ARTIST OR GROUP
1980	*Don't Stand So Close to Me*, Police
1981	*Don't You Want Me*, Human League
1982	*Come on Eileen*, Dexy's Midnight Runners
1983	*Karma Chameleon*, Culture Club
1984	*Do They Know It's Christmas?*, Band Aid
1985	*The Power of Love*, Jennifer Rush
1986	*Every Loser Wins*, Nick Berry
1987	*Never Gonna Give You Up*, Rick Astley
1988	*Mistletoe and Wine*, Cliff Richard
1989	*Ride on Time*, Black Box

Jennifer Rush is the sole US entrant in this Top 10. She and fellow singer Stevie Wonder were the only Americans to have UK million-selling singles during this decade.

TOP 10 SINGLES OF THE 1980s IN THE UK

	SINGLE/ARTIST OR GROUP	YEAR RELEASED
1	*Do They Know It's Christmas?*, Band Aid	1984
2	*Relax*, Frankie Goes to Hollywood	1984
3	*I Just Called to Say I Love You*, Stevie Wonder	1984
4	*Two Tribes*, Frankie Goes to Hollywood	1984
5	*Don't You Want Me*, Human League	1981
6	*Last Christmas*, Wham!	1984
7	*Karma Chameleon*, Culture Club	1983
8	*Careless Whisper*, George Michael	1984
9	*The Power of Love*, Jennifer Rush	1985
10	*Come on Eileen*, Dexy's Midnight Runners	1982

Singles from the boom year of 1984 dominate the UK 1980s Top 10, two of them by newcomers Frankie Goes to Hollywood. Nos. 1, 6, and 8 feature the vocal talents of George Michael.

TOP 10 SINGLES OF THE 1970s IN THE UK

	SINGLE/ARTIST OR GROUP	YEAR RELEASED
1	*Mull of Kintyre*, Wings	1977
2	*Rivers of Babylon/Brown Girl in the Ring*, Boney M	1978
3	*You're the One That I Want*, John Travolta and Olivia Newton-John	1978
4	*Mary's Boy Child/Oh My Lord*, Boney M	1978
5	*Summer Nights*, John Travolta and Olivia Newton-John	1978
6	*Y.M.C.A.*, Village People	1979
7	*Bohemian Rhapsody*, Queen	1975
8	*Heart of Glass*, Blondie	1979
9	*Merry Xmas Everybody*, Slade	1973
10	*Don't Give up on Us*, David Soul	1977

Most of the biggest sellers of the 1970s occurred in an 18-month period between December 1977 and May 1979. *Mull of Kintyre* was the first-ever record in Britain to top 2 million copies.

QUEEN RULES

Queen's Bohemian Rhapsody *was one of the UK's top sellers of the 1970s, while* Another One Bites the Dust *was a US smash of the 1980s.*

TOP 10 SINGLES OF THE 1960s IN THE UK

	SINGLE/ARTIST OR GROUP	YEAR RELEASED
1	*She Loves You*, The Beatles	1963
2	*I Want to Hold Your Hand*, The Beatles	1963
3	*Tears*, Ken Dodd	1965
4	*Can't Buy Me Love*, The Beatles	1964
5	*I Feel Fine*, The Beatles	1964
6	*We Can Work It Out/Day Tripper*, The Beatles	1965
7	*The Carnival Is Over*, The Seekers	1965
8	*Release Me*, Engelbert Humperdinck	1967
9	*It's Now or Never*, Elvis Presley	1960
10	*Green, Green Grass of Home*, Tom Jones	1966

Which female group has had the most UK and US hits?
see p.134 for the answer

A Spice Girls
B The Supremes
C Bangles

Hit Albums of the Decades

BRIDGING THE ATLANTIC

Simon and Garfunkel's single and album Bridge over Troubled Water *topped the UK and US charts simultaneously in March 1970.*

TOP 10 ALBUMS OF THE 1960s IN THE UK

	ALBUM/ARTIST OR GROUP	YEAR RELEASED
1	***Sgt. Pepper's Lonely Hearts Club Band***, The Beatles	1967
2	***The Sound of Music***, Soundtrack	1965
3	***With the Beatles***, The Beatles	1963
4	***Abbey Road***, The Beatles	1969
5	***South Pacific***, Soundtrack	1958
6	***Beatles for Sale***, The Beatles	1964
7	***A Hard Day's Night***, The Beatles, Soundtrack	1964
8	***Rubber Soul***, The Beatles	1965
9	***The Beatles ("The White Album")***, The Beatles	1968
10	***West Side Story***, Soundtrack	1962

Three further albums by The Beatles, *Revolver*, *Please Please Me*, and *Help!*, were the 11th, 12th, and 13th bestselling albums of the decade.

TOP 10 ALBUMS OF EACH YEAR IN THE 1960s IN THE UK

(Year/album/artist or group)

1 1960 ***South Pacific***, Soundtrack **2** 1961 ***G.I. Blues***, Elvis Presley, Soundtrack **3** 1962 ***West Side Story***, Soundtrack **4** 1963 ***With the Beatles***, The Beatles **5** 1964 ***Beatles for Sale***, The Beatles **6** 1965 ***The Sound of Music***, Soundtrack **7** 1966 ***The Sound of Music***, Soundtrack **8** 1967 ***Sgt. Pepper's Lonely Hearts Club Band***, The Beatles **9** 1968 ***The Sound of Music***, Soundtrack **10** 1969 ***Abbey Road***, The Beatles

TOP 10 ALBUMS OF EACH YEAR IN THE 1970s IN THE UK

YEAR	ALBUM/ARTIST OR GROUP
1970	***Bridge over Troubled Water***, Simon and Garfunkel
1971	***Bridge over Troubled Water***, Simon and Garfunkel
1972	***20 Dynamic Hits***, Various artists
1973	***Don't Shoot Me, I'm Only the Piano Player***, Elton John
1974	***The Singles, 1969–1973***, The Carpenters
1975	***The Best of the Stylistics***, The Stylistics
1976	***Greatest Hits***, Abba
1977	***Arrival***, Abba
1978	***Saturday Night Fever***, Soundtrack
1979	***Breakfast in America***, Supertramp

TOP 10 ALBUMS OF THE 1970s IN THE UK

	ALBUM/ARTIST OR GROUP	YEAR RELEASED
1	***Bridge over Troubled Water***, Simon and Garfunkel	1970
2	***Simon and Garfunkel's Greatest Hits***, Simon and Garfunkel	1972
3	***Rumours***, Fleetwood Mac	1977
4	***Dark Side of the Moon***, Pink Floyd	1973
5	***Tubular Bells***, Mike Oldfield	1973
6	***Greatest Hits***, Abba	1976
7	***Bat Out of Hell***, Meat Loaf	1978
8	***Saturday Night Fever***, Soundtrack	1978
9	***And I Love You So***, Perry Como	1973
10	***The Singles, 1969–1973***, The Carpenters	1974

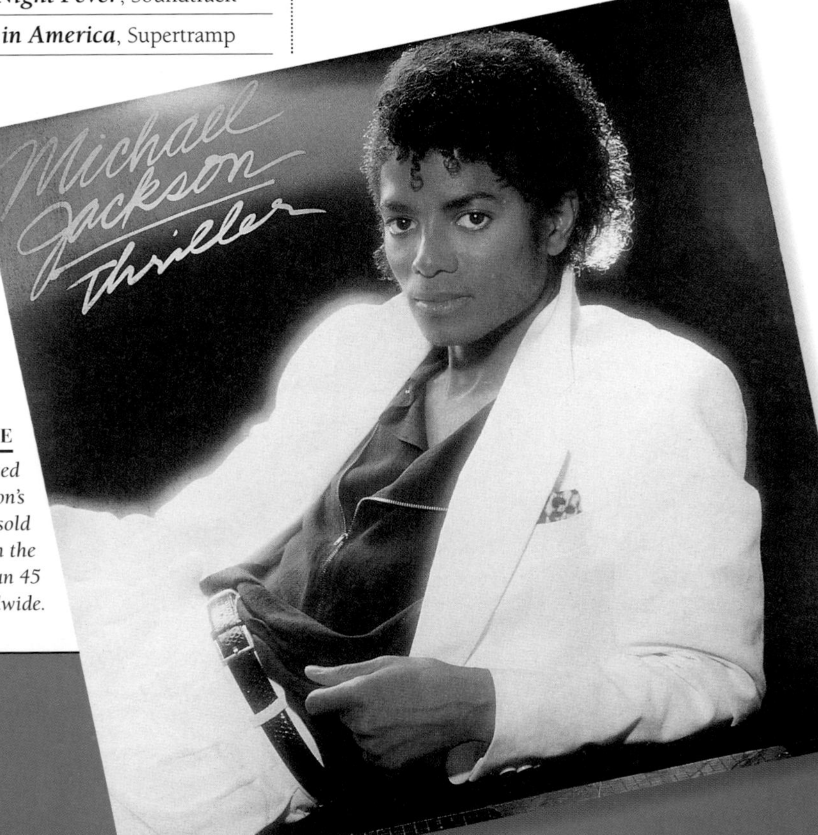

THRILLS GALORE

It has been estimated that Michael Jackson's Thriller *album has sold 25 million copies in the US and more than 45 million worldwide.*

TOP 10 ★ ALBUMS OF EACH YEAR IN THE 1990s IN THE UK

YEAR	ALBUM/ARTIST OR GROUP
1990	*The Immaculate Collection*, Madonna
1991	*Stars*, Simply Red
1992	*The Bodyguard*, Soundtrack
1993	*Bat Out of Hell II – Back into Hell*, Meat Loaf
1994	*Cross Road – The Best of Bon Jovi*, Bon Jovi
1995	*(What's the Story) Morning Glory?*, Oasis
1996	*Spice*, Spice Girls
1997	*Urban Hymns*, The Verve
1998	*Falling into You*, Celine Dion
1999	*Come on Over*, Shania Twain

TOP 10 ★ ALBUMS OF THE 1980s IN THE UK

	ALBUM/ARTIST OR GROUP	YEAR RELEASED
1	*Brothers in Arms*, Dire Straits	1985
2	*Bad*, Michael Jackson	1987
3	*Thriller*, Michael Jackson	1982
4	*Greatest Hits*, Queen	1981
5	*Kylie*, Kylie Minogue	1988
6	*Whitney*, Whitney Houston	1987
7	*Tango in the Night*, Fleetwood Mac	1987
8	*No Jacket Required*, Phil Collins	1985
9	*True Blue*, Madonna	1986
10	*The Joshua Tree*, U2	1987

TOP 10 ALBUMS OF EACH YEAR IN THE 1980s IN THE UK

(Year/album/artist or group)

1 1980 *Super Trouper*, Abba 2 1981 *Kings of the Wild Frontier*, Adam and the Ants 3 1982 *Love Songs*, Barbra Streisand 4 1983 *Thriller*, Michael Jackson 5 1984 *Can't Slow Down*, Lionel Richie 6 1985 *Brothers in Arms*, Dire Straits 7 1986 *True Blue*, Madonna 8 1987 *Bad*, Michael Jackson 9 1988 *Kylie*, Kylie Minogue 10 1989 *Ten Good Reasons*, Jason Donovan

MADONNA V HAMMER

While Madonna's The Immaculate Collection *was the UK's top selling album of 1990, with nine weeks at No. 1, it was held off the top slot in the US by MC Hammer with* Please Hammer Don't Hurt 'Em.

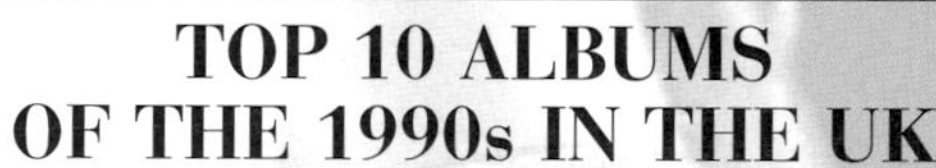

TOP 10 ALBUMS OF THE 1990s IN THE UK

(Album/artist or group/year released)

1 *(What's the Story) Morning Glory?*, Oasis, 1995 2 *Stars*, Simply Red, 1991 3 *Spice*, Spice Girls, 1996 4 *Talk on Corners*, The Corrs, 1997 5 *Jagged Little Pill*, Alanis Morissette, 1996 6 *Robson and Jerome*, Robson and Jerome, 1995 7 *The Immaculate Collection*, Madonna, 1990 8 *Urban Hymns*, The Verve, 1997 9 *Gold - Greatest Hits*, Abba, 1992 10 *Falling into You*, Celine Dion, 1996

Source: *CIN*

Did You Know? The album from the 1992 film *The Bodyguard* became a worldwide bestseller, its 16 million-plus sales in the US making it the country's bestselling soundtrack album ever.

Female Singers

TOP 10 ★ YOUNGEST FEMALE SINGERS TO HAVE A NO. 1 SINGLE IN THE UK

	SINGER/TITLE/YEAR	AGE YEARS	MONTHS	DAYS
1	**Helen Shapiro**, *You Don't Know*, 1961	14	10	13
2	**Billie**, *Because We Want To*, 1998	15	9	20
3	**Tiffany**, *I Think We're Alone Now*, 1988	16	3	28
4	**Nicole**, *A Little Peace*, 1982	17	0	0
5	**Britney Spears**, *...Baby One More Time*, 1999	17	2	25
6	**Sandie Shaw**, *(There's) Always Something There to Remind Me*, 1964	17	7	26
7	**Mary Hopkin**, *Those Were the Days*, 1968	18	4	22
8	**Sonia**, *You'll Never Stop Me Loving You*, 1989	18	5	9
9	**Christina Aguilera**, *Genie in a Bottle*, 1999	18	5	9
10	**Connie Francis**, *Who's Sorry Now*, 1958	19	5	4

The ages shown are those of each artist on the publication date of the chart in which she achieved her first No. 1 single. All ten of these girls were still in their teens when they had their first taste of chart-topping glory.

TOP 10 ★ OLDEST FEMALE SINGERS TO HAVE A NO. 1 SINGLE IN THE UK

	SINGER/TITLE/YEAR	AGE YEARS	MONTHS	DAYS
1	**Cher**, *Believe*, 1998	52	5	12
2	**Barbra Streisand**, *Woman in Love*, 1980	38	6	1
3	**Vera Lynn**, *My Son My Son*, 1954	37	7	25
4	**Tammy Wynette**, *Stand by Your Man*, 1975	33	0	12
5	**Kitty Kallen**, *Little Things Mean a Lot*, 1954	32	3	16
6	**Robin Beck**, *First Time*, 1988	32	2	12
7	**Jo Stafford**, *You Belong to Me*, 1952	32	2	4
8	**Charlene**, *I've Never Been to Me*, 1982	32	0	25
9	**Doris Day**, *Que Sera Sera (Whatever Will Be Will Be)*, 1956	32	0	13
10	**Chaka Khan**, *I Feel for You*, 1984	31	7	18

The ages shown are those of each artist on the publication date of the chart in which her first No. 1 single reached the top.

BRITNEY'S BEST

Her debut single ...Baby One More Time *was a No. 1 hit for Louisiana-born Britney Spears, a former performer on Disney Channel's Mickey Mouse Club.*

TOP 10 SINGLES BY FEMALE SINGERS IN THE US

(Title/artist/year)

1 ***I Will Always Love You***, Whitney Houston, 1992 2 ***How Do I Live***, LeAnn Rimes, 1997 3 ***The Boy Is Mine***, Brandy & Monica, 1998 4 ***Fantasy***, Mariah Carey, 1995 5 ***Vogue***, Madonna, 1990 6 ***Mr. Big Stuff***, Jean Knight, 1971 7 ***You Were Meant for Me/Foolish Games***, Jewel, 1996 8 ***You Light Up My Life***, Debby Boone, 1977 9 ***The Power of Love***, Celine Dion, 1993 10 ***Believe***, Cher, 1999

Source: *The Popular Music Database*

Among these blockbusters, all platinum sellers, it is fitting that Whitney Houston's multiplatinum success from *The Bodyguard Original Soundtrack* was also written by a woman – Dolly Parton.

SINGING PHENOMENON

Born Cherilyn Sarkasian La Pier in El Centro, California, on 20 May 1946, Cher formed the singing double act of Sonny and Cher with her husband Sonny Bono. Their single *I Got You Babe* topped the charts in both the US and UK in 1965, and Cher went on to achieve her first solo million-seller, *Bang Bang (My Baby Shot Me Down)* the following year. Televison work with Sonny (from whom she was divorced in 1974) and later film acting, for which she won an Oscar in 1988 (for *Moonstruck*), have since served as the backdrop to a quite phenomenal singing career that saw her score a No. 1 hit at the age of 52.

SNAP SHOTS

TOP 10 SINGLES BY FEMALE SINGERS IN THE UK

	TITLE/ARTIST	YEAR
1	***Believe***, Cher	1998
2	***I Will Always Love You***, Whitney Houston	1992
3	***The Power of Love***, Jennifer Rush	1985
4	***My Heart Will Go On***, Celine Dion	1998
5	***Think Twice***, Celine Dion	1994
6	***Don't Cry for Me Argentina***, Julie Covington	1977
7	***Fame***, Irene Cara	1982
8	***Anyone Who Had a Heart***, Cilla Black	1964
9	***Feels Like I'm in Love***, Kelly Marie	1980
10	***Woman in Love***, Barbra Streisand	1980

Perhaps the most significant aspect of this list is how comparatively recent most of its entries are. Statistically, a female artist has stood a better chance of major chart success since the 1980s than in any of pop music's earlier eras.

SAILING TO FAME

One of Canada's most successful singers, Celine Dion achieved worldwide fame with My Heart Will Go On *from the film* Titanic.

TOP 10 FEMALE SINGERS WITH THE MOST TOP 10 HITS IN THE UK

	SINGER	TOP 10 HITS
1	**Madonna**	46
2	**Diana Ross** (including duets with Marvin Gaye and Lionel Richie)	18
3=	**Kylie Minogue** (including a duet with Keith Washington)	16
=	**Mariah Carey** (including duets with Boyz II Men, Luther Vandross, and Whitney Houston)	16
5=	**Janet Jackson** (including duets with Michael Jackson, Luther Vandross, and Busta Rhymes)	14
=	**Whitney Houston** (including a duet with Mariah Carey)	14
7	**Celine Dion** (including duets with Peabo Bryson, the Bee Gees, and R. Kelly)	13
8	**Petula Clark**	12
9	**Cher**	11
10=	**Connie Francis**	10
=	**Olivia Newton-John** (including duets with John Travolta and Electric Light Orchestra)	10

Cher's singing career shows remarkable longevity: her first solo Top 10 hit, *All I Really Want to Do*, was released in 1965, 33 years before her single *Believe* became the second bestselling single of the 1990s.

Did You Know? Released in 1915, Romanian soprano Alma Gluck's *Carry Me Back to Old Virginny* was the first recording by a woman to sell over a million copies.

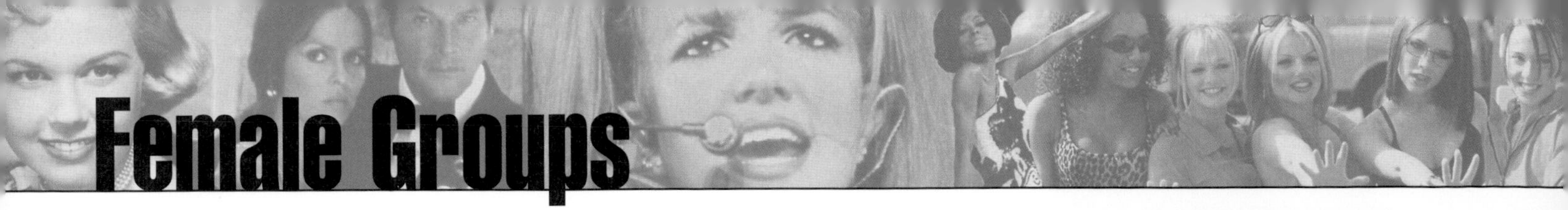

TOP 10

FEMALE GROUPS OF ALL TIME IN THE US

	GROUP	SINGLES AT NO. 1	SINGLES IN TOP 10	SINGLES IN TOP 20
1	The Supremes	12	20	24
2	The Pointer Sisters	–	7	13
3	=Expose	1	8	9
	=The McGuire Sisters	2	4	9
5	The Fontane Sisters	2	2	8
6	=The Shirelles	2	6	7
	=TLC	–	7	7
	=Martha & the Vandellas	–	6	7
	=En Vogue	–	5	7
	=Spice Girls	–	4	7

Source: *The Popular Music Database*

TOP TRIO

The initial letters of the singers' nicknames – "T-Boz", "Left Eye", and "Chilli" – provided the name for the 1990s' singing sensation TLC.

TOP 10

FEMALE GROUPS OF ALL TIME IN THE UK*

	GROUP	SINGLES AT NO. 1	SINGLES IN TOP 10	SINGLES IN TOP 20
1	The Supremes	1	13	18
2	=Eternal	1	13	15
	=Bananarama	–	10	15
4	Spice Girls	8	9	9
5	=The Three Degrees	1	5	7
	=Sister Sledge	1	4	7
	=The Nolans	–	3	7
8	All Saints	3	6	6
9	=The Bangles	1	3	5
	=Salt-n-Pepa	–	4	5

* To 1 January 2000

The Supremes also had three other Top 20 hits, not included here, in partnership with Motown male groups the Four Tops and the Temptations. However, Bananarama's charity revival of *Help!*, shared with Dawn French and Jennifer Saunders, has been included because all the participants are female. The only two groups to have had more than one chart-topper – the Spice Girls and All Saints – had their success in the late '90s.

WORTH THEIR SALT

Formed as a duo in 1985 and joined by Spinderella in 1987, rap girl group Salt-n-Pepa have achieved huge success on both sides of the Atlantic.

TOP 10 SINGLES BY FEMALE GROUPS IN THE US

	TITLE/GROUP	YEAR
1	***Don't Let Go,*** En Vogue	1996
2	***Hold On,*** En Vogue	1990
3	***Wannabe,*** Spice Girls	1997
4	***Whatta Man,*** Salt-n-Pepa	1994
5	***Expressions,*** Salt-n-Pepa	1990
6	***Push It,*** Salt-n-Pepa	1987
7	***Waterfall,*** TLC	1995
8	***Creep,*** TLC	1994
9	***Weak,*** SWV	1993
10	***Baby, Baby, Baby,*** TLC	1992

Source: *The Popular Music Database*

TOP 10 SINGLES BY FEMALE GROUPS IN THE UK

	TITLE/GROUP	YEAR
1	***Wannabe,*** Spice Girls	1996
2	***Say You'll Be There***, Spice Girls	1996
3	***2 Become 1***, Spice Girls	1996
4	***Never Ever***, All Saints	1997
5	***C'Est La Vie***, B*Witched	1998
6	***Goodbye***, Spice Girls	1998
7	***Viva Forever***, Spice Girls	1998
8	***Spice up Your Life***, Spice Girls	1997
9	***Too Much***, Spice Girls	1997
10	***Mama/Who Do You Think You Are***, Spice Girls	1997

Such has been the Spice Girls' impact on popular music that they have totally rewritten the record book as far as successful girl-group singles are concerned, snatching eight of the all-time bestsellers in the UK.

TOP 10 ALBUMS BY FEMALE GROUPS IN THE UK

	TITLE/GROUP	YEAR
1	***Spice***, Spice Girls	1996
2	***Spiceworld***, Spice Girls	1997
3	***All Saints***, All Saints	1997
4	***Always and Forever***, Eternal	1993
5	***Greatest Hits***, Eternal	1997
6	***The Greatest Hits Collection***, Bananarama	1988
7	***Power of a Woman***, Eternal	1995
8	***B*Witched***, B*Witched	1998
9	***Different Light***, The Bangles	1986
10	***Greatest Hits***, The Bangles	1990

All of these albums were released within the last two decades, and the three biggest sellers of all within the last four years. All of these groups are British, except B*Witched, who are Irish, and the Bangles, who are American.

GIRL POWER

The original line-up of five Spice Girls achieved unprecedented dominance of the singles charts during the late 1990s.

Which classical composer is considered the most prolific?

see p.153 for the answer

A Beethoven
B Mozart
C Haydn

Star Singles & Albums

BEAT ALL

In a lifespan of little over 10 years (1960–70), the Beatles revolutionized rock music, achieving 20 US and 17 UK No. 1 singles and worldwide sales of more than 1 billion.

TOP 10 ★

ARTISTS WITH THE MOST ALBUM SALES IN THE US

	ARTIST OR GROUP	TOTAL ALBUM SALES*
1	The Beatles	106,530,000
2	Garth Brooks	92,000,000
3	Led Zeppelin	83,620,000
4	Elvis Presley	77,280,000
5	Eagles	65,000,000
6	Billy Joel	63,250,000
7	Barbra Streisand	62,750,000
8	Elton John	61,620,000
9	Aerosmith	54,370,000
10	Pink Floyd	52,600,000

* *To 1 January 2000*

Source: *RIAA*

The RIAA, which certifies US record sales, has logged over 70 artists who have achieved total album sales of more than 20 million each.

TOP 10 ★

ELVIS PRESLEY SINGLES IN THE UK

	SINGLE	YEAR
1	*It's Now or Never*	1960
2	*Jailhouse Rock*	1958
3	*Are You Lonesome Tonight*	1961
4	*Wooden Heart*	1961
5	*Return to Sender*	1962
6	*Can't Help Falling in Love*	1962
7	*The Wonder of You*	1970
8	*Surrender*	1961
9	*Way Down*	1977
10	*All Shook Up*	1957

Source: *MRIB*

Elvis's sales peak in the UK was not in his 1950s' heyday, but shortly after he left the army in the early 1960s. *It's Now or Never* was his only million-seller on UK sales alone, though all the records in this list registered sales in excess of 600,000.

KING OF ROCK

Elvis Presley's first singles were released in 1954, when he was 19. Baby, Let's Play House, *released in 1955, became his first chart hit in the US.*

TOP 10 ★

BEATLES SINGLES IN THE UK

	SINGLE	YEAR
1	*She Loves You*	1963
2	*I Want to Hold Your Hand*	1963
3	*Can't Buy Me Love*	1964
4	*I Feel Fine*	1964
5	*We Can Work It Out/Day Tripper*	1965
6	*Help!*	1965
7	*Hey Jude*	1968
8	*A Hard Day's Night*	1964
9	*From Me to You*	1963
10	*Hello Goodbye*	1967

The Beatles' two bestselling UK singles, both from the late-1963 "Beatlemania" period, still remain among the UK's all-time Top 15 singles, almost 40 years on.

TOP 10 JOHN LENNON SINGLES IN THE UK

(Single/year)

❶ ***Imagine***, 1975 ❷ ***Woman***, 1981 ❸ ***(Just Like) Starting Over***, 1980 ❹ ***Happy Xmas (War is Over)***, 1972 ❺ ***Give Peace a Chance***, 1969 ❻ ***Instant Karma***, 1970 ❼ ***Power to the People***, 1971 ❽ ***Nobody Told Me***, 1984 ❾ ***Cold Turkey***, 1969 ❿ ***Mind Games***, 1973

Source: *MRIB*

TOP 10 MADONNA ALBUMS IN THE UK

	ALBUM	YEAR
1	*The Immaculate Collection*	1990
2	*True Blue*	1986
3	*Ray of Light*	1998
4	*Like a Virgin*	1984
5	*Like a Prayer*	1989
6	*Something to Remember*	1995
7	*Erotica*	1992
8	*The First Album*	1984
9	*Bedtime Stories*	1994
10	*I'm Breathless*	1990

Source: *The Popular Music Database*

The first five albums in this list hit UK No. 1, *True Blue* becoming the first album by a US female to enter the chart at No. 1 (as did *The Immaculate Collection* and *Ray of Light*), while *Like a Virgin*, although her most successful in the US, took almost a year to attain this position. The rest of those listed failed to make No. 1, although three reached the No. 2 slot.

TOP 10 ELTON JOHN SINGLES IN THE UK

	SINGLE	YEAR
1	*Candle in the Wind (1997)/ Something About the Way You Look Tonight*	1997
2	*Don't Go Breaking My Heart* (with Kiki Dee)	1976
3	*Sacrifice*	1990
4	*Rocket Man*	1972
5	*Nikita*	1985
6	*Crocodile Rock*	1972
7	*Daniel*	1973
8	*Song for Guy*	1978
9	*I Guess That's Why They Call it the Blues*	1983
10	*I'm Still Standing*	1983

Source: *MRIB*

TOP 10 ROLLING STONES ALBUMS IN THE UK

	ALBUM	YEAR
1	*The Rolling Stones No. 2*	1965
2	*Aftermath*	1966
3	*Rolled Gold – The Very Best of The Rolling Stones*	1975
4	*Let it Bleed*	1969
5	*Sticky Fingers*	1971
6	*Some Girls*	1978
7	*Emotional Rescue*	1980
8	*Exile on Main Street*	1972
9	*The Rolling Stones*	1964
10	*Tattoo You*	1981

Source: *MRIB*

ROLLING ON

The Rolling Stones' greatest album successes come from the decades 1960s to 1980s, but they continued to perform live throughout the 1990s.

Did You Know? *Come On*, the Rolling Stones' first single (1963), had to be re-recorded, altering the word "jerk" to "guy" in order to avoid a radio ban.

Pop Stars of the 90s

TOP 10 BLUR SINGLES IN THE UK

	TITLE	YEAR
1	*Country House*	1995
2	*Beetlebum*	1997
3	*Tender*	1999
4	*Song 2*	1997
5	*The Universal*	1995
6	*Girls and Boys*	1994
7	*Charmless Man*	1996
8	*On Your Own*	1997
9	*Stereotypes*	1996
10	*There's No Other Way*	1991

Launched in 1990, Blur rapidly became one of the foremost British bands of the decade. Their second single, *There's No Other Way*, released in 1991, made No. 8, but 1995 smash *Country House* entered at No. 1, the 42nd single ever to do so in British chart history.

TOP 10 PULP SINGLES IN THE UK

	TITLE	YEAR
1	*Common People*	1995
2	*Mis-Shapes/ Sorted For E's and Wizz*	1995
3	*Disco 2000*	1995
4	*Help the Aged*	1997
5	*Something Changed*	1996
6	*This is Hardcore*	1998
7	*The Sisters (EP)*	1994
8	*Party Hard*	1998
9	*A Little Soul*	1998
10	*Do You Remember the First Time*	1994

TOP 10 BOYZONE SINGLES IN THE UK

	TITLE	YEAR
1	*When the Going Gets Tough the Tough Get Going*	1999
2	*No Matter What*	1998
3	*I Love the Way You Love Me*	1998
4	*You Needed Me*	1999
5	*Words*	1996
6	*All That I Need*	1998
7	*A Different Beat*	1996
8	*Father and Son*	1995
9	*Every Day I Love You*	1999
10	*Picture of You*	1999

TOP 10 CHER SINGLES OF THE 1990s IN THE UK

	TITLE	YEAR
1	*Believe*	1998
2	*The Shoop Shoop Song (It's in His Kiss)*	1991
3	*Strong Enough*	1999
4	*One by One*	1996
5	*Love and Understanding*	1991
6	*Walking in Memphis*	1995
7	*All or Nothing*	1999
8	*Just Like Jesse James*	1990
9	*Oh No Not My Baby*	1992
10	*Love Hurts*	1991

With the exception of 1994, Cher had a UK Top 40 single in every year of the 1990s, her 1998 *Believe* becoming the 5th bestselling single of the entire decade.

TOP 10 OASIS SINGLES IN THE UK

	TITLE	YEAR
1	*Don't Look Back in Anger*	1996
2	*D'you Know What I Mean?*	1997
3	*Wonderwall*	1995
4	*Some Might Say*	1995
5	*Stand by Me*	1998
6	*All Around the World*	1998
7	*Roll With It*	1995
8	*Whatever*	1994
9	*Cigarettes and Alcohol*	1994
10	*Live Forever*	1994

TOP 10 MADONNA SINGLES IN THE UK

(Single/year)

1 *Like a Virgin*, 1984 2 *Into the Groove*, 1985 3 *Papa Don't Preach*, 1986 4 *Crazy for You*, 1985 5 *Holiday*, 1984 6 *True Blue*, 1986 7 *Vogue*, 1990 8 *La Isla Bonita*, 1987 9 *Like a Prayer*, 1989 10 *Who's That Girl?*, 1987

Source: *MRIB*

TOP 10 PRODIGY SINGLES IN THE UK

	TITLE	YEAR
1	*Firestarter*	1996
2	*Breathe*	1996
3	*Everybody in the Place (EP)*	1996
4	*Charly*	1991
5	*Out of Space/Ruff in the Jungle*	1996
6	*No Good (Start the Dance)*	1996
7	*Smack My Bitch up*	1997
8	*Wind it up (Rewound)*	1996
9	*Fire/Jericho*	1992
10	*Voodoo People*	1996

TOP 10 SUEDE SINGLES IN THE UK

(Title/year)

1 *Trash*, 1996 2 *Stay Together*, 1994 3 *Electricity*, 1999 4 *Beautiful Ones*, 1996 5 *Animal Nitrate*, 1993 6 *Saturday Night*, 1997 7 *Filmstar*, 1997 8 *Lazy*, 1997 9 *She's in Fashion*, 1999 10 *The Wild Ones*, 1994

GORGEOUS GEORGE

George Michael has achieved bestselling albums across two decades in both the UK and the US.

TOP 10 MANIC STREET PREACHERS SINGLES IN THE UK

	TITLE	YEAR
1	*If You Tolerate This Your Children Will Be Next*	1998
2	*A Design for Life*	1996
3	*Everything Must Go*	1996
4	*Australia*	1996
5	*You Stole the Sun from My Heart*	1999
6	*Theme from M*A*S*H (Suicide Is Painless)*	1992
7	*Kevin Carter*	1996
8	*The Everlasting*	1998
9	*Motorcycle Emptiness*	1992
10	*Tsunami*	1999

The Manic Street Preachers scored a string of hits in the 1990s, their *If You Tolerate This Your Children Will Be Next* entering the chart at No. 1.

TOP 10 TAKE THAT SINGLES IN THE UK

	TITLE	YEAR
1	*Relight My Fire*	1993
2	*Sure*	1994
3	*Back for Good*	1995
4	*How Deep is Your Love*	1996
5	*Babe*	1993
6	*Everything Changes*	1994
7	*Pray*	1993
8	*Never Forget*	1995
9	*Could it be Magic*	1992
10	*Why Can't I Wake up With You*	1993

TOP 10 SPICE GIRLS SINGLES IN THE UK

(*Single/year*)

1 *Wannabe*, 1996 2 *2 Become 1*, 1996 3 *Too Much*, 1997 4 *Goodbye*, 1998 5 *Say You'll Be There*, 1996 6 *Spice up Your Life*, 1997 7 *Viva Forever*, 1998 8 *Mama/Who Do You Think You Are*, 1997 9 *Stop*, 1998 10 *When You're Gone* (Bryan Adams featuring Melanie C), 1998

TOP 10 GEORGE MICHAEL SINGLES OF THE 1990s IN THE UK

(*Title/year*)

1 *Outside*, 1998 2 *Fast Love*, 1996 3 *Jesus to a Child*, 1996 4 *You Have Been Loved/The Strangest Thing '97*, 1997 5 *Star People '97*, 1997 6 *Spinning the Wheel*, 1996 7 *Older/I Can't Make You Love Me*, 1997 8 *Too Funky*, 1992 9 *Praying for Time*, 1990 10 *Freedom*, 1990

Did You Know? The Spice Girls' first six singles all hit UK No. 1, and their first release, *Wannabe*, sold over 1.25 million copies in the UK alone.

DIAMOND FOR HEAVY METAL

In 1999, Joe Elliot, Def Leppard's vocalist, received an RIAA Diamond award (for albums that have sold more than 10 million copies) for the band's 1987 Hysteria.

TOP 10 ★

HEAVY METAL ALBUMS IN THE UK

	ALBUM/ARTIST OR GROUP	YEAR
1	***Bat out of Hell***, Meat Loaf	1978
2	***Bat out of Hell II – Back to Hell***, Meat Loaf	1993
3	***Led Zeppelin II***, Led Zeppelin	1969
4	***Hysteria***, Def Leppard	1987
5	***Led Zeppelin IV***, Led Zeppelin	1971
6	***Cross Road – The Best of Bon Jovi***, Bon Jovi	1994
7	***So Far So Good***, Bryan Adams	1993
8	***Eliminator***, ZZ Top	1983
9	***Appetite for Destruction***, Guns N' Roses	1987
10	***Slippery When Wet***, Bon Jovi	1986

Unlike its 1993 sequel, which made No. 1 in the UK, *Bat out of Hell* only ever peaked at No. 9, but logged an impressive 470-plus weeks on the chart, an achievement split over three decades.

TOP 10 ★

REGGAE ALBUMS IN THE US, 1999

	TITLE	ARTIST
1	***Reggae Gold 1999***	Various
2	***Strictly the Best 21***	Various
3	***Reggae Gold 1998***	Various
4	***Pure Reggae***	Various
5	***The Doctor***	Beenie Man
6	***Reggae Party***	Various
7	***DJ Reggae Mix***	Various
8	***Best of Bob Marley***	Bob Marley
9	***Everyone Falls in Love***	Tantro Metro & Devonte
10	***Labour of Love III***	UB40

Source: Billboard

TOP 10 LATIN POP ALBUMS IN THE US, 1999

	TITLE	ARTIST
1	*Vuelve*	Ricky Martin
2	*Bailamos*	Enrique Iglesias
3	*Donde Estan los Ladrones?*	Shakira
4	*Cosas del Amor*	Enrique Iglesias
5	*MTV Unplugged*	Maná
6	*Trozos de Mi Alma*	Marco Antonio Solis
7	*Marte es Un Placer*	Luis Miguel
8	*Atado a Tu Amor*	Chayanne
9	*Amor, Familia y Respeto*	A. B. Quintanilla y Los Kumbia Kings
10	*Latin Mix USA Vol. 2*	Various Artists

Source: Billboard

TOP 10 INSTRUMENTAL SINGLES IN THE UK

	SINGLE/ARTIST OR GROUP	YEAR
1	***Stranger on the Shore***, Mr. Acker Bilk	1961
2	***Eye Level***, Simon Park Orchestra	1973
3	***Telstar***, The Tornados	1962
4	***The Harry Lime Theme (The Third Man)***, Anton Karas	1950
5	***Amazing Grace***, Royal Scots Dragoon Guards Band	1972
6	***Chi Mai***, Ennio Morricone	1981
7	***Wonderful Land***, The Shadows	1962
8	***Apache***, The Shadows	1960
9	***Albatross***, Fleetwood Mac	1968
10	***Mouldy Old Dough***, Lieutenant Pigeon	1972

If this Top 10 reveals anything, it is that non-vocal hits are more likely to be found in the "middle-of-the-road" sector than in rock 'n' roll. Most of these pieces are the equivalent of ballads, with only *Apache*, possibly *Telstar*, and just possibly *Mouldy Old Dough* – which is really a novelty instrumental – qualifying as rock music. The Acker Bilk and Simon Park entries were both UK million sellers.

Source: *MRIB*

LEGEND

Bob Marley's posthumous compilation Legend *became the all-time bestselling reggae album, residing at UK No. 1 for 12 weeks and in the charts for 129 weeks.*

TOP 10 REGGAE ALBUMS IN THE UK

	TITLE/ARTIST OR GROUP	YEAR
1	***Legend***, Bob Marley and the Wailers	1984
2	***The Best of UB40 Vol. 1***, UB40	1987
3	***Labour of Love II***, UB40	1989
4	***Labour of Love***, UB40	1983
5	***Promises and Lies***, UB40	1993
6	***Present Arms***, UB40	1981
7	***Signing Off***, UB40	1980
8	***Tease Me***, Chaka Demus and Pliers	1993
9	***Labour of Love III***, UB40	1998
10	***Exodus***, Bob Marley and the Wailers	1977

Source: *The Popular Music Database*

TOP 10 IRISH ALBUMS IN THE UK

	TITLE/ARTIST	YEAR
1	***Talk on Corners***, Corrs	1997
2	***By Request***, Boyzone	1999
3	***The Joshua Tree***, U2	1987
4	***Where We Belong***, Boyzone	1998
5	***Watermark***, Enya	1988
6	***Shepherd Moons***, Enya	1991
7	***Rattle and Hum***, U2	1988
8	***Said and Done***, Boyzone	1995
9	***A Different Beat***, Boyzone	1996
10	***Achtung Baby!***, U2	1991

Source: *The Popular Music Database*

THE BOYS IN THE BAND

A string of UK No. 1 albums has secured Boyzone four of the Top 10 Irish albums of all time. The band was formed in Dublin in 1993 as Ireland's answer to Take That.

TOP 10 WORLD MUSIC ALBUMS IN THE US, 1999

	TITLE	ARTIST
1	***Sogno***	Andrea Bocelli
2	***Romanza***	Andrea Bocelli
3	***Buena Vista Social Club***	Buena Vista Social Club
4	***Tears of Stone***	Chieftains
5	***The Book of Secrets***	Loreena McKennitt
6	***Buena Vista Social Club***	Buena Vista Social Club Presents Ibrahim Ferrer
7	***The Irish Tenors***	John McDermott/ Anthony Kearns/Ronan Tynan
8	***Sueno (with Spanish tracks)***	Andrea Bocelli
9	***Romanza (with Spanish tracks)***	Andrea Bocelli
10	***Return To Pride Rock – Songs Inspired by Disney's The Lion King II***	Various Artists

Source: Billboard

TOP 10 JAZZ ALBUMS IN THE UK

	ALBUM/ARTIST OR GROUP	YEAR
1	***We Are in Love***, Harry Connick Jr.	1990
2	***Blue Light, Red Light***, Harry Connick Jr.	1991
3	***Jazz on a Summer's Day***, Various	1992
4	***Morning Dance***, Spyro Gyra	1979
5	***In Flight***, George Benson	1977
6	***Duotones***, Kenny G	1987
7	***Best of Ball, Barber and Bilk***, Kenny Ball, Chris Barber, and Acker Bilk	1962
8	***Sinatra/Basie***, Frank Sinatra and Count Basie	1963
9	***Kenny Ball's Golden Hits***, Kenny Ball	1963
10	***Time Out Featuring Take Five***, Dave Brubeck Quartet	1960

Source: *MRIB*

Despite a solid base of afficionados, jazz has always been a comparatively poor-selling musical genre in the UK.

Did You Know? The first-ever rap album to reach a mass audience and achieve gold status was *Run-D.M.C.*, by the group of that name, on 17 December 1984.

TWAIN MAKES HER MARK

Although it combines rock, pop, and country genres, Canadian-born Shania Twain's Come on Over *ranks as the all-time bestselling country album in the UK.*

TOP 10

RAP SINGLES IN THE UK

	TITLE/ARTIST	YEAR
1	*I'll Be Missing You*, Puff Daddy featuring Faith Evans	1997
2	*Killing Me Softly*, Fugees	1996
3	*Gangsta's Paradise*, Coolio featuring LV	1995
4	*It's Like That*, Run-D.M.C. vs. Jason Nevins	1998
5	*Men in Black*, Will Smith	1997
6	*Ghetto Supastar (That Is What You Are)*, Pras featuring ODB & Mya	1998
7	*Ice Ice Baby*, Vanilla Ice	1990
8	*White Lines (Don't Don't Do It)*, Grandmaster Flash & Melle Mel	1983
9	*Boom! Shake That Room*, Jazzy Jeff & the Fresh Prince	1993
10	*Ready or Not*, Fugees	1996

Grandmaster Flash's anti-cocaine message charted on four separate occasions between 1983 and 1985, making it the longest-charting rap single ever.

TOP 10

COUNTRY ALBUMS IN THE UK

	TITLE/ARTIST	YEAR
1	*Come on Over*, Shania Twain	1998
2	*20 Golden Greats*, Glen Campbell	1976
3	*40 Golden Greats*, Jim Reeves	1975
4	*Images*, Don Williams	1978
5	*Trampoline*, Mavericks	1998
6	*Johnny Cash at San Quentin*, Johnny Cash	1969
7	*Greatest Hits*, Glen Campbell	1971
8	*The Very Best of Slim Whitman*, Slim Whitman	1976
9	*The Best of Tammy Wynette*, Tammy Wynette	1975
10	*Johnny Cash Live at Folsom Prison*, Johnny Cash	1968

Source: *MRIB*

Of Johnny Cash's two celebrated live albums recorded at two of America's most severe penal institutions, the San Quentin release holds the record for the longest-charting Country album in UK chart history, with 114 weeks notched up between 1969 and 1971.

COOL GUY

Coolio (born Artis Ivey, 1963) sold over a million copies of his debut album, It Takes a Thief, *achieving even greater success with his bestselling 1995 album,* Gangsta's Paradise.

Gold & Platinum Albums

COUNTRY GOLD

In a recording career of over 30 years, Kenny Rogers has gained an impressive 28 gold and 44 platinum albums in the US.

TOP 10 MALE ARTISTS WITH THE MOST GOLD ALBUMS IN THE US

	ARTIST	GOLD ALBUMS
1	Elvis Presley	62
2	Neil Diamond	35
3	Elton John	32
4	Kenny Rogers	28
5	Frank Sinatra	26
6	Bob Dylan	24
7	=George Strait	23
	=Willie Nelson	23
9	Hank Williams Jr.	21
10	=Paul McCartney/Wings	20
	=Rod Stewart	20

Source: *RIAA*

TOP 10 MALE ARTISTS WITH THE MOST PLATINUM ALBUMS IN THE UK

	ARTIST	PLATINUM ALBUMS
1	Michael Jackson	38
2	Phil Collins	30
3	George Michael	21
4	Elton John	19
5	Meat Loaf	17
6	=Rod Stewart	14
	=Chris Rea	14
8	=Cliff Richard	13
	=Michael Bolton	13
	=Robbie Williams	13

Source: *BPI*

Platinum albums in the UK are those that have achieved sales of 300,000. Relative to the population of the UK, where it represents approximately one sale per 195 inhabitants, this is a greater attainment than a US platinum award, where the ratio is one per 266. Multi-platinum albums are those that have sold multiples of 300,000: thus a quadruple platinum album denotes sales of 1,200,000.

TOP 10 MALE ARTISTS WITH THE MOST GOLD ALBUMS IN THE UK

	ARTIST	GOLD ALBUMS
1	=Elton John	20
	=Cliff Richard	20
3	Rod Stewart	19
4	=Neil Diamond	17
	=James Last	17
	=Paul McCartney*	17
7	Mike Oldfield	16
8	=David Bowie	15
	=Elvis Presley	15
10	Prince	13

* *Including gold albums with Wings*

Source: *BPI*

TOP 10 GROUPS WITH THE MOST PLATINUM ALBUMS IN THE UK

	GROUP	PLATINUM ALBUMS
1	Simply Red	37
2	Queen	29
3	Dire Straits	27
4	Oasis	26
5	U2	24
6	=Abba	19
	=Fleetwood Mac	19
8	=UB40	17
	=Wet Wet Wet	17
10	R.E.M.	16

Source: *BPI*

TOP 10 GROUPS WITH THE MOST GOLD ALBUMS IN THE UK

	GROUP	GOLD ALBUMS
1	Queen	22
2	Status Quo	19
3	The Rolling Stones	18
4	=Abba	14
	=Genesis	14
	=The Beatles	14
7	Roxy Music	13
8	UB40	12
9	Pink Floyd	11
10	10cc	10

Source: *BPI*

Gold discs have been awarded since 1 April 1973 in the UK. They are presented for sales of 400,000 singles or 100,000 albums, cassettes, and CDs (200,000 for budget-priced products). Although neither "groups" nor "solo artists", there are a number of duos who have received multiple gold albums: two with sufficient to qualify them for a place in this list are brother-and-sister act the Carpenters (14) and Irish pair Foster and Allen (12).

Did You Know? In the US, gold discs are those that have sold 500,000, while platinum are for sales of 1 million. The newer diamond award is for sales of 10 million.

ONE OF THE BEST

With eight gold and 17 platinum albums to her name, Tina Turner has secured a place in the top echelons of UK hit-makers.

TOP 10 FEMALE ARTISTS WITH THE MOST PLATINUM ALBUMS IN THE UK

	ARTIST	PLATINUM ALBUMS
1	Madonna	35
2	Celine Dion	21
3	Whitney Houston	19
4	Tina Turner	17
5	=Enya	12
	=Gloria Estefan	12
7	=Kylie Minogue	10
	=Mariah Carey	10
	=Alanis Morissette	10
10	Kate Bush	9

Source: *BPI*

TOP 10 FEMALE ARTISTS WITH THE MOST PLATINUM ALBUMS IN THE US

	ARTIST	PLATINUM ALBUMS
1	Barbra Streisand	49
2	Madonna	47
3	=Whitney Houston	45
	=Mariah Carey	45
5	Celine Dion	34
6	Reba McEntire	24
7	Linda Ronstadt	23
8	=Janet Jackson	19
	=Shania Twain	19
9	=Sade	18
	=Gloria Estefan	18

Source: *RIAA*

TOP 10 FEMALE ARTISTS WITH THE MOST GOLD ALBUMS IN THE UK

	ARTIST	GOLD ALBUMS
1	Diana Ross	17
2	=Barbra Streisand	12
	=Madonna	12
4	Donna Summer	9
5	=Mariah Carey	8
	=Tina Turner	8
7	=Kate Bush	7
	=Cher	7
	=Celine Dion	7
10	=Joan Armatrading	6
	=Janet Jackson	6

Source: *BPI*

TOP 10 FEMALE ARTISTS WITH THE MOST GOLD ALBUMS IN THE US

	ARTIST	GOLD ALBUMS
1	Barbra Streisand	40
2	Reba McEntire	19
3	Linda Ronstadt	17
4	Olivia Newton-John	15
5	=Aretha Franklin	13
	=Madonna	13
	=Dolly Parton	13
8	=Gloria Estefan*	12
	=Anne Murray	12
	=Tanya Tucker	12

* *Includes hits with Miami Sound Machine*

Source: *RIAA*

GOLDEN SUMMER

Donna Summer has been making hit records for almost 30 years, during which time she has scored nine gold albums in the UK.

Oscar-winning Film Music

THE 10 ★ "BEST SONG" OSCAR WINNERS OF THE 1940s

YEAR	TITLE/FILM
1940	*When You Wish Upon a Star*, Pinocchio
1941	*The Last Time I Saw Paris*, Lady Be Good
1942	*White Christmas*, Holiday Inn
1943	*You'll Never Know*, Hello, Frisco, Hello
1944	*Swinging on a Star*, Going My Way
1945	*It Might as Well Be Spring*, State Fair
1946	*On the Atchison, Topeka and Santa Fe*, The Harvey Girls
1947	*Zip-A-Dee-Doo-Dah*, Song of the South
1948	*Buttons and Bows*, The Pale Face
1949	*Baby, It's Cold Outside*, Neptune's Daughter

THE 10 ★ "BEST SONG" OSCAR WINNERS OF THE 1950s

YEAR	TITLE/FILM
1950	*Mona Lisa*, Captain Carey
1951	*In the Cool, Cool, Cool of the Evening*, Here Comes the Groom
1952	*High Noon (Do Not Forsake Me, Oh My Darling)*, High Noon
1953	*Secret Love*, Calamity Jane
1954	*Three Coins in the Fountain*, Three Coins in the Fountain
1955	*Love Is a Many-Splendored Thing*, Love Is a Many-Splendored Thing
1956	*Whatever Will Be, Will Be (Que Sera, Sera)*, The Man Who Knew Too Much
1957	*All the Way*, The Joker is Wild
1958	*Gigi*, Gigi
1959	*High Hopes*, A Hole in the Head

Doris Day benefited strongly from these Oscars, scoring million-selling singles with *Secret Love* and *Whatever Will Be, Will Be*.

THE 10 ★ "BEST SONG" OSCAR WINNERS OF THE 1960s

YEAR	TITLE/FILM
1960	*Never on Sunday*, Never on Sunday
1961	*Moon River*, Breakfast at Tiffany's
1962	*Days of Wine and Roses*, Days of Wine and Roses
1963	*Call Me Irresponsible*, Papa's Delicate Condition
1964	*Chim Chim Cheree*, Mary Poppins
1965	*The Shadow of Your Smile*, The Sandpiper
1966	*Born Free*, Born Free
1967	*Talk to the Animals*, Dr. Dolittle
1968	*The Windmills of Your Mind*, The Thomas Crown Affair
1969	*Raindrops Keep Fallin' on My Head*, Butch Cassidy and the Sundance Kid

Both *The Windmills of Your Mind* and *Raindrops Keep Fallin' on My Head* hit the US Top 10. Sacha Distel's cover version of the 1969 Oscar winner charted five times in the UK in 1970.

TOP 10 ★ "BEST SONG" OSCAR-WINNING SINGLES IN THE UK

	TITLE/ARTIST OR GROUP	YEAR
1	*I Just Called to Say I Love You*, Stevie Wonder	1984
2	*Fame*, Irene Cara	1980
3	*Take My Breath Away*, Berlin	1986
4	*My Heart Will Go On*, Celine Dion	1997
5	*Flashdance...What a Feeling*, Irene Cara	1983
6	*Evergreen*, Barbra Streisand	1976
7	*Streets of Philadelphia*, Bruce Springsteen	1994
8	*Moon River*, Danny Williams	1961
9	*Whatever Will Be, Will Be (Que Sera, Sera)*, Doris Day	1956
10	*Raindrops Keep Fallin' on My Head*, Sacha Distel	1969

Source: *The Popular Music Database*

ALL IN A DAY'S WORK

Songs by Doris Day (real name Doris Kappelhoff), from films in which she also starred, produced a duo of Oscar winners in the 1950s.

OSCAR-WINNING PRINCE

A new phenomenon is that half the Oscar-winning songs of the past decade are from animated films, such as the 1998 winner The Prince of Egypt.

THE 10 "BEST SONG" OSCAR WINNERS OF THE 1970s

YEAR	TITLE/FILM
1970	***For All We Know***, *Lovers and Other Strangers*
1971	***Theme from "Shaft"***, *Shaft*
1972	***The Morning After***, *The Poseidon Adventure*
1973	***The Way We Were***, *The Way We Were*
1974	***We May Never Love Like This Again***, *The Towering Inferno*
1975	***I'm Easy***, *Nashville*
1976	***Evergreen***, *A Star is Born*
1977	***You Light up My Life***, *You Light up My Life*
1978	***Last Dance***, *Thank God It's Friday*
1979	***It Goes Like It Goes***, *Norma Rae*

THE 10 "BEST SONG" OSCAR WINNERS OF THE 1980s

YEAR	TITLE/FILM
1980	***Fame***, *Fame*
1981	***Up Where We Belong***, *An Officer and a Gentleman*
1982	***Arthur's Theme (Best That You Can Do)***, *Arthur*
1983	***Flashdance... What a Feeling***, *Flashdance*
1984	***I Just Called to Say I Love You***, *The Woman in Red*
1985	***Say You, Say Me***, *White Nights*
1986	***Take My Breath Away***, *Top Gun*
1987	***(I've Had) The Time of My Life***, *Dirty Dancing*
1988	***Let the River Run***, *Working Girl*
1989	***Under the Sea***, *The Little Mermaid*

THE 10 "BEST SONG" OSCAR WINNERS OF THE 1990s

YEAR	TITLE/FILM
1990	***Sooner or Later (I Always Get My Man)***, *Dick Tracy*
1991	***Beauty and the Beast***, *Beauty and the Beast*
1992	***Whole New World***, *Aladdin*
1993	***Streets of Philadelphia***, *Philadelphia*
1994	***Can You Feel the Love Tonight***, *The Lion King*
1995	***Colors of the Wind***, *Pocahontas*
1996	***You Must Love Me***, *Evita*
1997	***My Heart Will Go On***, *Titanic*
1998	***When You Believe***, *The Prince of Egypt*
1999	***You'll Be in My Heart***, *Tarzan*

What is the most popular pop music film?

see p.149 for the answer

A *Purple Rain*
B *La Bamba*
C *The Blues Brothers*

Soundtrack Smashes

TOP 10 ★ MUSICAL FILMS*

	TITLE	YEAR
1	*Grease*	1978
2	*Saturday Night Fever*	1977
3	*The Sound of Music*	1965
4	*Footloose*	1984
5	*American Graffiti*	1973
6	*Mary Poppins*	1964
7	*Flashdance*	1983
8	*The Rocky Horror Picture Show*	1975
9	*Coal Miner's Daughter*	1980
10	*My Fair Lady*	1964

* *Traditional musicals (in which the cast actually sing) and films in which a musical soundtrack is a major component of the film are included*

MUSIC TO THE EARS

Despite being made over 35 years ago, The Sound of Music, *starring British actress Julie Andrews, remains among the Top 10 highest-earning musical films of all time.*

TOP 10 ORIGINAL SOUNDTRACK ALBUMS OF ALL TIME IN THE UK

(Album/year)

❶ ***The Bodyguard***, 1992 ❷ ***Titanic***, 1997 ❸ ***Trainspotting***, 1996 ❹ ***The Commitments***, 1991 ❺ ***Top Gun***, 1986 ❻ ***The Full Monty***, 1997 ❼ ***Evita***, 1996 ❽ ***The Blues Brothers***, 1980 ❾ ***The Sound of Music***, 1965 ❿ ***Saturday Night Fever***, 1978

Source: *MRIB*

TOP 10 ★ JAMES BOND FILM THEMES IN THE UK

	TITLE/ARTIST OR GROUP	YEAR
1	***A View to a Kill***, Duran Duran	1985
2	***We Have All the Time in the World*** (from *On Her Majesty's Secret Service*), Louis Armstrong	1994
3	***The Living Daylights***, a-ha	1987
4	***Licence to Kill***, Gladys Knight	1989
5	***Nobody Does It Better*** (from *The Spy Who Loved Me*), Carly Simon	1977
6	***For Your Eyes Only***, Sheena Easton	1981
7	***Live and Let Die***, Paul McCartney and Wings	1973
8	***GoldenEye***, Tina Turner	1995
9	***You Only Live Twice***, Nancy Sinatra	1967
10	***Tomorrow Never Dies***, Sheryl Crow	1997

All the songs on this list reached the Top 20 but there has never been a Bond-associated UK No. 1. Themes from two films, *The Man with the Golden Gun* and *Moonraker*, failed to chart at all, even though Lulu and Shirley Bassey were involved.

NOBODY DOES IT BETTER

Written by Marvin Hamlisch and Carole Bayer Sager, Carly Simon's song from The Spy Who Loved Me *was a UK and US hit.*

TOP 10

ARTISTS WITH THE MOST "BEST SONG" OSCAR NOMINATIONS

	ARTIST/WINS/YEARS	NOMINATIONS
1	**Sammy Cahn**, 4, 1942–75	26
2	**Johnny Mercer**, 4, 1938–71	18
3	=**Paul Francis Webster**, 3, 1944–76	16
	=**Alan and Marilyn Bergman**, 2, 1968–95	16
5	**James Van Heusen**, 4, 1944–68	14
6	=**Henry Warren**, 3, 1935–57	11
	=**Henry Mancini**, 2, 1961–86	11
	=**Ned Washington**, 1, 1940–61	11
9	=**Alan Menken**, 4, 1986–97	10
	=**Sammy Fain**, 2, 1937–77	10
	=**Leo Robin**, 1, 1934–53	10
	=**Jule Styne**, 1, 1940–68	10

It was not until 1934 that the category of "Best Song" was added to the many accolades bestowed on films. The Awards are often multiple, and include the writers of the music and the lyrics.

THE 10

FIRST DISNEY "BEST SONG" OSCAR WINNERS

YEAR	TITLE/FILM
1940	***When You Wish Upon a Star***, *Pinocchio*
1947	***Zip-a-Dee-Doo-Dah***, *Song of the South*
1964	***Chim Chim Cher-ee***, *Mary Poppins*
1989	***Under the Sea***, *The Little Mermaid*
1990	***Sooner or Later (I Always Get My Man)***, *Dick Tracy*
1991	***Beauty and the Beast***, *Beauty and the Beast*
1992	***Whole New World***, *Aladdin*
1994	***Can You Feel the Love Tonight***, *The Lion King*
1995	***Colors of the Wind***, *Pocahontas*
1996	***You Must Love Me***, *Evita*

TOP 10

POP MUSIC FILMS

	TITLE	YEAR
1	*The Blues Brothers*	1980
2	*Purple Rain*	1984
3	*La Bamba*	1987
4	*The Doors*	1991
5	*What's Love Got to Do With It?*	1993
6	*Xanadu*	1980
7	*The Jazz Singer*	1980
8	*Sgt. Pepper's Lonely Hearts Club Band*	1978
9	*Lady Sings the Blues*	1972
10	*Pink Floyd – The Wall*	1982

RAINING PRINCE

Produced in 1984, Prince's semi-autobiographical film Purple Rain *is one of the most successful pop music films ever released.*

THE 10

LATEST GRAMMY RECORDS OF THE YEAR

YEAR	RECORD/ARTIST
1999	*Smooth*, Santana featuring Rob Thomas
1998	*My Heart Will Go On*, Celine Dion
1997	*Sunny Came Home*, Shawn Colvin
1996	*Change the World*, Eric Clapton
1995	*Kiss from a Rose*, Seal
1994	*All I Wanna Do*, Sheryl Crow
1993	*I Will Always Love You*, Whitney Houston
1992	*Tears in Heaven*, Eric Clapton
1991	*Unforgettable*, Natalie Cole with Nat "King" Cole
1990	*Another Day in Paradise*, Phil Collins

THE 10 LATEST RECIPIENTS OF THE GRAMMY LIFETIME ACHIEVEMENT AWARD

(Year/artist)*

1 2000 Harry Belafonte 2 2000 Woody Guthrie 3 2000 John Lee Hooker 4 2000 Mitch Miller 5 2000 Willie Nelson 6 1999 Johnny Cash 7 2000 Sam Cooke 8 1999 Otis Redding 9 1999 William "Smokey" Robinson 10 1999 Mel Tormé

* *Listed alphabetically by year*

Source: *NARAS*

TOP 10

ARTISTS WITH THE MOST GRAMMY AWARDS

	ARTIST	AWARDS
1	Sir Georg Solti	31
2	Quincy Jones	26
3	Vladimir Horowitz	25
4	Pierre Boulez	23
5	Stevie Wonder	21
6	Henry Mancini	20
7	=John T. Williams	17
	=Leonard Bernstein	17
9	=Aretha Franklin	15
	=Itzhak Perlman	15

The Grammy Awards ceremony has been held annually in the United States since its inauguration on 4 May 1959, and the awards are considered to be the most prestigious in the music industry.

THE 10

FIRST GRAMMY RECORDS OF THE YEAR

YEAR	RECORD/ARTIST OR GROUP
1958	*Nel Blu Dipinto di Blu (Volare)*, Domenico Modugno
1959	*Mack the Knife*, Bobby Darin
1960	*Theme from a Summer Place*, Percy Faith
1961	*Moon River*, Henry Mancini
1962	*I Left My Heart in San Francisco*, Tony Bennett
1963	*The Days of Wine and Roses*, Henry Mancini
1964	*The Girl from Ipanema*, Stan Getz and Astrud Gilberto
1965	*A Taste of Honey*, Herb Alpert and the Tijuana Brass
1966	*Strangers in the Night*, Frank Sinatra
1967	*Up Up and Away*, 5th Dimension

CASHBACK

Johnny Cash was awarded the accolade of a Grammy Lifetime Achievement Award in 1999, 44 years after releasing his first single, Hey Porter/Cry Cry Cry.

TOP 10

COUNTRIES WITH THE MOST WINS AT THE EUROVISION SONG CONTEST

	COUNTRY/YEARS	WINS
1	**Ireland**, 1970, 1980, 1987, 1992, 1993, 1994, 1996	7
2	=**France**, 1958, 1960, 1962, 1969*, 1977	5
	=**Luxembourg**, 1961, 1965, 1972, 1973, 1983	5
	=**UK**, 1967, 1969*, 1976, 1981, 1997	5
5	=**Netherlands**, 1957, 1959, 1969*, 1975	4
	=**Sweden**, 1974, 1984, 1991, 1999	4
7	**Israel**, 1978, 1979, 1998	3
8	=**Italy**, 1964, 1990	2
	=**Norway**, 1984, 1995	2
	=**Spain**, 1968, 1969*	2
	=**Switzerland**, 1956, 1988	2

* *All four countries tied as winners in 1969.*

TOP 10

ARTISTS WITH THE MOST BRIT AWARDS

	ARTIST	AWARDS
1	Annie Lennox	8
2	=Phil Collins	6*
	=Prince	6#
4	=Michael Jackson	5
	=George Michael	5+
6	=Blur	4
	=Bjork	4
	=Oasis	4
	=Dave Stewart	4
	=Spice Girls	4
	=Take That	4
	=U2	4
	=Robbie Williams	4

* *Includes award for "Best Film Soundtrack" (1989, for* Buster *Original Soundtrack)*

\# *Includes award for "Best Film Soundtrack" (1990, for* Batman *Original Soundtrack)*

\+ *Includes two awards with Wham! (1985 and 1986)*

THE 10

LATEST WINNERS OF THE BRIT AWARD FOR BEST SINGLE BY A BRITISH ARTIST

YEAR	SINGLE/ARTIST OR GROUP
2000	*She's the One*, Robbie Williams
1999	*Angels*, Robbie Williams
1998	*Never Ever*, All Saints
1997	*Wannabe*, Spice Girls
1996	*Back for Good*, Take That
1995	*Parklife*, Blur
1994	*Pray*, Take That
1993	*Could It Be Magic*, Take That
1992	*These Are the Days of Our Lives*, Queen
1991	*Enjoy the Silence*, Depeche Mode

THE 10

LATEST WINNERS OF THE BRIT AWARD FOR BEST BRITISH VIDEO*

YEAR	VIDEO/ARTIST OR GROUP
2000	*She's the One*, Robbie Williams
1999	*Millennium*, Robbie Williams
1998	*Never Ever*, All Saints
1997	*Say You'll Be There*, Spice Girls
1996	*Wonderwall*, Oasis
1995	*Parklife*, Blur
1994	*Pray*, Take That
1993	*Stay*, Shakespears Sister
1992	*Killer*, Seal
1991	*A Little Time*, The Beautiful South

* *Formerly "Best Video", open to international acts*

THE 10 LATEST WINNERS OF THE *Q MAGAZINE* AWARD FOR CLASSIC SONGWRITER

1 **1999** Ian Dury and Chas Jankel 2 **1998** Paul Weller 3 **1997** Paul McCartney 4 **1996** Elvis Costello 5 **1995** Van Morrison 6 **1994** Morissey 7 **1993** Neil Finn 8 **1992** U2 9 **1991** Richard Thompson 10 **1990** Prince

THE 10 LATEST WINNERS OF THE *Q MAGAZINE* AWARD FOR BEST NEW ACT

1 **1999** Basement Jaxx 2 **1998** Gomez 3 **1997** Fun Lovin' Criminals 4 **1996** Alanis Morissette 5 **1995** Supergrass 6 **1994** Oasis 7 **1993** Suede 8 **1992** Tori Amos 9 **1991** Seal 10 **1990** They Might Be Giants

THE 10

LATEST WINNERS OF THE *Q MAGAZINE* AWARD FOR BEST ALBUM

YEAR	ALBUM/ARTIST OR GROUP
1999	*Surrender,* Chemical Brothers
1998	*Mezzanine,* Massive Attack
1997	*OK Computer,* Radiohead
1996	*Everything Must Go,* Manic Street Preachers
1995	*The Great Escape,* Blur
1994	*Parklife,* Blur
1993	*Ten Summoner's Tales,* Sting
1992	*Automatic for the People,* R.E.M.
1991	*Out of Time,* R.E.M.
1990	*Goodbye Jumbo,* World Party

THE 10 LATEST WINNERS OF THE *Q MAGAZINE* AWARD FOR BEST LIVE ACT IN THE WORLD TODAY

1 **1999** Blur 2 **1998** Manic Street Preachers 3 **1997** Oasis 4 **1996** Oasis 5 **1995** R.E.M. 6 **1994** R.E.M. 7 **1993** U2 8 **1992** U2 9 **1991** R.E.M. 10 **1990** U2

Did You Know? The first-ever Grammy Record of the Year, *Nel Blu Dipinto di Blu (Volare)*, was revived by David Bowie in the 1986 film *Absolute Beginners*.

TOP 10

OPERAS MOST FREQUENTLY PERFORMED AT THE ROYAL OPERA HOUSE, COVENT GARDEN, 1833–2000

	OPERA	COMPOSER	FIRST PERFORMANCE	TOTAL*
1	*La Bohème*	Giacomo Puccini	2 Oct 1897	526
2	*Carmen*	Georges Bizet	27 May 1882	495
3	*Aïda*	Giuseppe Verdi	22 June 1876	471
4	*Rigoletto*	Giuseppe Verdi	14 May 1853	429
5	*Faust*	Charles Gounod	18 July 1863	428
6	*Tosca*	Giacomo Puccini	12 July 1900	388
7	*Don Giovanni*	Wolfgang Amadeus Mozart	17 Apr 1834	386
8	*La Traviata*	Giuseppe Verdi	25 May 1858	379
9	*Norma*	Vincenzo Bellini	12 July 1833	355
10	*Madama Butterfly*	Giacomo Puccini	10 July 1905	342

* *To 31 December 2000*

Most of the works listed were first performed at Covent Garden within a few years of their world premiers. Although some were considered controversial at the time, all are now regarded as important classical operas.

TOP 10

CLASSICAL ALBUMS OF ALL TIME IN THE US

	TITLE	PERFORMER/ORCHESTRA
1	*The Three Tenors In Concert*	Carreras, Domingo, Pavarotti
2	*Romanza*	Andrea Bocelli
3	*Sogno*	Andrea Bocelli
4	*Chant*	Benedictine Monks of Santo Domingo De Silos
5	*The Three Tenors in Concert 1994*	Carreras, Domingo, Pavarotti
6	*Sacred Arias*	Andrea Bocelli
7	*Tchaikovsky: Piano Concerto No. 1*	Van Cliburn
8	*Fantasia (50th Anniversary Edition)*	Soundtrack (Philadelphia Orchestra)
9	*Perhaps Love*	Placido Domingo
10	*O Holy Night*	Luciano Pavarotti

Classical recordings held far greater sway in the early years of the US album chart, and most notably during the 1950s, than they have in subsequent decades, and this is partly reflected in the vintage nature of much of the Top 10. The two film soundtracks contained short pieces or excerpts by a number of composers, including Bach, Beethoven, and Stravinsky in *Fantasia*, and Richard and Johann Strauss in *2001: A Space Odyssey*. According to some criteria, the soundtrack album of *Titanic* is regarded as a "classical" album; if accepted as such, it would appear at No. 1 in this Top 10.

THE 10

LATEST WINNERS OF THE "BEST CLASSICAL ALBUM" GRAMMY AWARD

YEAR	COMPOSER/TITLE	CONDUCTOR/SOLOIST/ORCHESTRA
1999	Stravinsky, *Firebird; The Right of Spring; Perséphone*	Michael Tilson Thomas, Stuart Neill, San Francisco Symphony Orchestra
1998	Barber, *Prayers of Kierkegaard*/ Vaughan Williams, *Dona Nobis Pacem*/ Bartok, *Cantata Profana*	Robert Shaw, Richard Clement, Nathan Gunn, Atlanta Symphony Orchestra and chorus
1997	Danielpour, Kirchner, Rouse, *Premières – Cello Concertos*	Yo-Yo Ma, David Zinman, Philadelphia Orchestra
1996	Corigliano, *Of Rage and Remembrance*	Leonard Slatkin, National Symphony Orchestra
1995	Claude Debussy, *La Mer*	Pierre Boulez, Cleveland Orchestra
1994	Béla Bartók, *Concerto for Orchestra; Four Orchestral Pieces, Op. 12*	Pierre Boulez, Chicago Symphony Orchestra
1993	Béla Bartók, *The Wooden Prince*	Pierre Boulez, Chicago Symphony Orchestra and Chorus
1992	Gustav Mahler, *Symphony No. 9*	Leonard Bernstein, Berlin Philharmonic Orchestra
1991	Leonard Bernstein, *Candide*	Leonard Bernstein, London Symphony Orchestra
1990	Charles Ives, *Symphony No. 2 (and Three Short Works)*	Leonard Bernstein, New York Philharmonic Orchestra

Source: *NARAS*

TOP 10

CLASSICAL ALBUMS OF ALL TIME IN THE UK

	TITLE	PERFORMER/ORCHESTRA
1	*The Essential Pavarotti*	Luciano Pavarotti
2	*The Three Tenors Concert*	Carreras, Domingo, Pavarotti
3	*Vivaldi: The Four Seasons*	Nigel Kennedy/ English Chamber Orchestra
4	*The Three Tenors – In Mehta Concert 1994*	Carreras, Domingo, Pavarotti
5	*The Essential Pavarotti, 2*	Luciano Pavarotti
6	*The Essential Mozart*	Various
7	*Essential Opera*	Various
8	*The Pavarotti Collection*	Luciano Pavarotti
9	*Sogno*	Andrea Bocelli
10	*Mendelssohn/Bruch Violin Concertos*	Nigel Kennedy/English Chamber Orchestra

NORMAN CONQUEST

One of the world's leading opera divas, Georgia-born Jessye Norman's role on a recording of Bluebeard's Castle contributed to its gaining the 1999 Grammy "Best Opera Recording" award.

TOP 10 MOST PROLIFIC CLASSICAL COMPOSERS

(Composer/nationality/hours of music)

❶ **Joseph Haydn** (1732–1809), Austrian, 340 ❷ **George Handel** (1685–1759), German–English, 303 ❸ **Wolfgang Amadeus Mozart** (1756–91), Austrian, 202 ❹ **Johann Sebastian Bach** (1685–1750), German, 175 ❺ **Franz Schubert** (1797–1828), German, 134 ❻ **Ludwig van Beethoven** (1770–1827), German, 120 ❼ **Henry Purcell** (1659–95), English, 116 ❽ **Giuseppe Verdi** (1813–1901), Italian, 87 ❾ **Anton Dvořák** (1841–1904), Czech, 79 ❿ = **Franz Liszt** (1811–86), Hungarian, 76;· = **Peter Tchaikovsky** (1840–93), Russian, 76

This list is based on a survey conducted by *Classical Music*, which ranked classical composers by the total number of hours of music each composed.

THE 10 LATEST WINNERS OF THE "BEST OPERA RECORDING" GRAMMY AWARD

YEAR	COMPOSER/TITLE	SOLOISTS/ORCHESTRA
1999	Stravinsky, *The Rake's Progress*	Ian Bostridge, Bryn Terfel, Anne Sofie van Otter, Deborah York, Monteverdi Choir, London Symphony Orchestra
1998	Bartok, *Bluebeard's Castle*	Jessye Norman, Laszlo Polgar, Karl-August Naegler, Chicago Symphony Orchestra
1997	Richard Wagner, *Die Meistersinger von Nürnberg*	Ben Heppner, Herbert Lippert, Karita Mattila, Alan Opie, Rene Pape, Jose van Dam, Iris Vermillion, Chicago Symphony Chorus, Chicago Symphony Orchestra
1996	Benjamin Britten, *Peter Grimes*	Philip Langridge, Alan Opie, Janice Watson, Opera London, London Symphony Chorus, City of London Sinfonia
1995	Hector Berlioz, *Les Troyens*	Charles Dutoit, Orchestra Symphonie de Montreal
1994	Carlisle Floyd, *Susannah*	Jerry Hadley, Samuel Ramey, Cheryl Studer, Kenn Chester
1993	George Handel, *Semele*	Kathleen Battle, Marilyn Horne, Samuel Ramey, Sylvia McNair, Michael Chance
1992	Richard Strauss, *Die Frau Ohne Schatten*	Placido Domingo, Jose Van Dam, Hildegard Behrens
1991	Richard Wagner, *Götterdämmerung*	Hildegard Behrens, Ekkehard Wlashiha
1990	Richard Wagner, *Das Rheingold*	James Morris, Kurt Moll, Christa Ludwig

Source: *NARAS*

TOP 10 LARGEST OPERA HOUSES

(Opera house/location/capacity)*

❶ **Arena di Verona**,# Verona, Italy, 16,663 ❷ **Municipal Opera Theater**,# St. Louis, USA, 11,745 ❸ **Music Hall**, Cincinnati, USA, 3,417 ❹ **Teatro alla Scala**, Milan, Italy, 3,600 ❺ **Civic Opera House**, Chicago, USA, 3,563 ❻ = **The Metropolitan**, Lincoln Centre, New York, USA, 3,500; = **Teatro San Carlo**, Naples, Italy, 3,500 ❽ = **Teatro Massimo**, Palermo, Italy, 3,200; = **The Hummingbird Center**, Toronto, Canada, 3,200 ❿ **Halle aux Grains**, Toulouse, France, 3,000

* *For indoor venues, seating capacity given; numbers may be increased by standing capacity* # *Open-air venue*

Although there are many more venues where opera is regularly performed, this list is limited to those venues where the principal performances are opera.

Did You Know? After performing *Otello* at the Vienna Staatsoper on 30 July 1991, Placido Domingo received 101 curtain calls and was applauded for 1 hour 20 minutes.

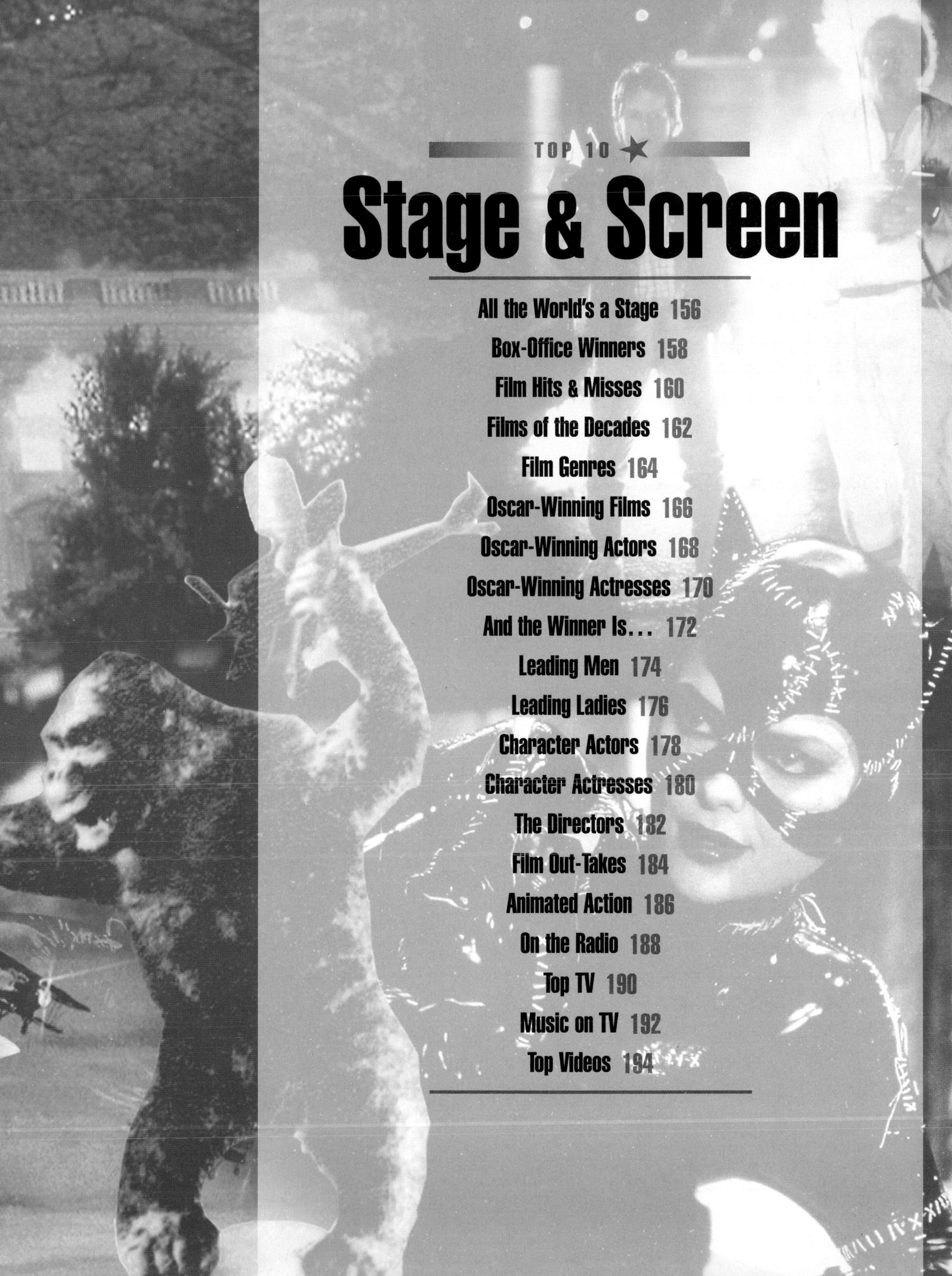

TOP 10 ★

Stage & Screen

All the World's a Stage

MONEY FOR NOTHING

Much Ado About Nothing, starring Emma Thompson and Kenneth Branagh (who also directed it), achieved both critical and commercial success.

THE 10 ★ LATEST WINNERS OF THE LAURENCE OLIVIER AWARD FOR BEST ACTOR

YEAR	ACTOR/PLAY
2000	Henry Goodman, *The Merchant of Venice*
1999	Kevin Spacey, *The Iceman Cometh*
1998	Ian Holm, *King Lear*
1997	Anthony Sher, *Stanley*
1996	Alex Jennings, *Peer Gynt*
1995	David Bamber, *My Night With Reg*
1994	Mark Rylance, *Much Ado About Nothing*
1993	Robert Stephens, *Henry IV, Parts 1 and 2*
1992	Nigel Hawthorne, *The Madness of George III*
1991	Ian McKellen, *Richard III*

THE 10 ★ LATEST WINNERS OF THE LAURENCE OLIVIER AWARD FOR BEST ACTRESS

YEAR	ACTRESS/PLAY
2000	Janie Dee, *Comic Potential*
1999	Eileen Atkins, *The Unexpected Man*
1998	Zoë Wanamaker, *Electra*
1997	Janet McTeer, *A Doll's House*
1996	Judi Dench, *Absolute Hell*
1995	Clare Higgins, *Sweet Bird of Youth*
1994	Fiona Shaw, *Machinal*
1993	Alison Steadman, *The Rise and Fall of Little Voice*
1992	Juliet Stevenson, *Death and the Maiden*
1991	Kathryn Hunter, *The Visit of Sichuan*

TOP 10 ★ FILMS OF SHAKESPEARE PLAYS

	FILM	YEAR
1	*William Shakespeare's Romeo + Juliet*	1996
2	*Romeo and Juliet*	1968
3	*Much Ado About Nothing*	1993
4	*Hamlet*	1990
5	*Henry V*	1989
6	*Hamlet*	1996
7	*Richard III*	1995
8	*Othello*	1995
9	*The Taming of the Shrew*	1967
10	*Hamlet*	1948

TOP 10 ★ MOST PRODUCED PLAYS BY SHAKESPEARE, 1961–99

	PLAY	PRODUCTIONS
1	*A Midsummer Night's Dream*	30
2	=*Macbeth*	26
	=*Twelfth Night*	26
4	*Romeo and Juliet*	25
5	*The Taming of the Shrew*	24
6	=*As You Like It*	23
	=*Richard III*	23
8	*King Lear*	22
9	=*Hamlet*	21
	=*Much Ado About Nothing*	21

TOP 10 MOST-FILMED PLAYS BY SHAKESPEARE

❶ *Hamlet* ❷ *Romeo and Juliet* ❸ *Macbeth* ❹ *A Midsummer Night's Dream* ❺ *Julius Caesar* ❻ *Othello* ❼ *Richard III* ❽ *Henry V* ❾ *The Merchant of Venice* ❿ *Antony and Cleopatra*

Counting modern versions, including those in foreign languages, but discounting made-for-TV films, parodies, and stories derived from the plays, it appears that *Hamlet* is the most-filmed of all Shakespeare's works, with some 70 releases to date, while *Romeo and Juliet* has been made on at least 40 occasions.

TOP 10

LONGEST-RUNNING COMEDIES OF ALL TIME IN THE UK

	COMEDY/YEARS	PERFORMANCES
1	*No Sex, Please – We're British*, 1971–81; 1982–86; 1986–87	6,761
2	*Run for Your Wife*, 1983–91	2,638
3	*There's a Girl in My Soup*, 1966–69; 1969–72	2,547
4	*Pyjama Tops*, 1969–75	2,498
5	*Worm's Eye View*, 1945–51	2,245
6	*Boeing Boeing*, 1962–65; 1965–67	2,035
7	*Blithe Spirit*, 1941–42; 1942; 1942–46	1,997
8	*Dirty Linen*, 1976–80	1,667
9	*Reluctant Heroes*, 1950–54	1,610
10	*Seagulls Over Sorrento*, 1950–54; 1954	1,551

THE 10

LATEST WINNERS OF THE AMERICAN EXPRESS AWARD FOR BEST NEW MUSICAL

YEAR	MUSICAL
2000	*Honk! The Ugly Duckling*
1999	*Kat and the Kings*
1998	*Beauty and the Beast*
1997	*Martin Guerre*
1996	*Jolson*
1995	*Once on This Island*
1994	*City of Angels*
1993	*Crazy for You*
1992	*Carmen Jones*
1991	*Sunday in the Park With George*

The first recipient of the Laurence Olivier "Musical of the Year" Award, in 1976 (since 1991 "The American Express Award for Best Musical") was *A Chorus Line*. In addition to the 1986 win for *The Phantom of the Opera*, musicals by Andrew Lloyd Webber have won on two further occasions – *Evita* in 1978 and *Cats* in 1981.

TOP 10

LONGEST-RUNNING SHOWS IN THE UK

	SHOW/YEARS	PERFORMANCES
1	*The Mousetrap*, 1952–	19,647*
2	*Cats*, 1981–	8,012*
3	*No Sex, Please – We're British*, 1971–81; 1982–86; 1986–87	6,761
4	*Starlight Express*, 1984–	6,674*
5	*Les Misérables*, 1985–	5,882*
6	*The Phantom of the Opera*, 1986–	5,539*
7	*Miss Saigon*, 1989–99	4,263
8	*Oliver!*, 1960–69	4,125
9	*Oh! Calcutta!*, 1970–80	3,918
10	*Jesus Christ, Superstar*, 1972–80	3,357

* Still running; total as at 11 February 2000

All the longest-running shows in the UK have been London productions. *The Mousetrap* opened on 25 November 1952 at the Ambassadors Theatre. After 8,862 performances it transferred to St. Martin's Theatre, where it re-opened on 25 March 1974. It is not the only play in the world to have run continuously since the 1950s – Eugène Ionesco's *La Cantatrice Chauve* was first performed in Paris on 11 May 1950 and ran on a double bill with *La Leçon* (which had its debut on 20 February 1951) after 16 February 1957, clocking up 12,772 performances to 31 December 1996. The two plays were seen by over 920,000 people – despite being staged in la Huchette, a theatre with just 90 seats.

TOP 10

LONGEST-RUNNING MUSICALS IN THE UK

	MUSICAL/YEARS	PERFORMANCES
1	*Cats*, 1981–	8,012*
2	*Starlight Express*, 1984–	6,674*
3	*Les Misérables*, 1985–	5,882*
4	*The Phantom of the Opera*, 1986–	5,539*
5	*Miss Saigon*, 1989–99	4,263
6	*Oliver!*, 1960–69	4,125
7	*Jesus Christ, Superstar*, 1972–80	3,357
8	*Evita*, 1978–86	2,900
9	*The Sound of Music*, 1961–67	2,386
10	*Salad Days*, 1954–60	2,283

* Still running; total as at 11 February 2000

On 12 May 1989 *Cats* became the longest continuously running musical in British theatre history, and on 26 January 1996, with its 6,138th performance, it became the longest-running musical of all time in either the West End or on Broadway. The previous record holder, *A Chorus Line*, ended its Broadway run in 1990 after a total of 6,137 performances.

OUT OF THEIR MISERY

Les Misérables *has achieved the dual feat of being one of the longest-running musicals both in London and on Broadway.*

Box Office Winners

TOP 10 HIGHEST-GROSSING FILMS OF ALL TIME

	FILM	YEAR	GROSS INCOME ($) USA	GROSS INCOME ($) WORLD
1	*Titanic*	1997	600,800,000	1,835,100,000
2	*Star Wars: Episode I – The Phantom Menace*	1999	431,100,000	922,600,000
3	*Jurassic Park*	1993	357,100,000	920,100,000
4	*Independence Day*	1996	306,200,000	811,200,000
5	*Star Wars*	1977/97	461,000,000	798,000,000
6	*The Lion King*	1994	312,900,000	767,900,000
7	*E.T.: The Extra-Terrestrial*	1982	399,800,000	704,800,000
8	*Forrest Gump*	1994	329,700,000	679,700,000
9	*The Lost World: Jurassic Park*	1997	229,100,000	614,400,000
10	*The Sixth Sense*	1999	279,600,000	610,900,000

TOP 10 FILM OPENINGS OF ALL TIME IN THE US

	FILM/RELEASE DATE	OPENING WEEKEND GROSS ($)
1	*The Lost World: Jurassic Park*, 23 May 1997	72,132,785
2	*Star Wars: Episode I – The Phantom Menace*, 21 May 1999	64,820,970
3	*Toy Story 2*, 24 Nov 1999	57,388,839
4	*Austin Powers: The Spy Who Shagged Me*, 11 June 1999	54,917,604
5	*Batman Forever*, 16 June 1995	52,784,433
6	*Men in Black*, 2 July 1997	51,068,455
7	*Independence Day*, 3 July 1996	50,228,264
8	*Jurassic Park*, 11 June 1993	47,059,560
9	*Batman Returns*, 19 June 1992	45,687,711
10	*Mission: Impossible*, 22 May 1996	45,436,830

MONSTER MOVIE

Jurassic Park *set new standards for animatronic action and reigned as the world's highest-earning film for five years, before being toppled by* Titanic.

Did You Know? On 19 May 1999, *Star Wars: Episode I – The Phantom Menace* became the highest-earning film in a single day, taking a total of $28,540,000 at 2,970 box offices across the US.

BEST OF BRITISH

The highest-earning British-made film, The Full Monty, *was successful both in the UK and worldwide, grossing in excess of $250 million.*

TOP 10

HIGHEST-GROSSING FILMS OF ALL TIME IN THE UK

	FILM	YEAR	UK GROSS (£)
1	*Titanic*	1998	68,532,000
2	*The Full Monty*	1997	51,992,000
4	*Star Wars: Episode I – The Phantom Menace*	1999	50,735,000
4	*Jurassic Park*	1993	47,140,000
5	*Toy Story 2*	2000	40,169,000
6	*Independence Day*	1996	36,800,000
7	*Men In Black*	1997	35,400,000
8	*Notting Hill*	1999	30,404,000
9	*The World is Not Enough*	1999	28,367,000
10	*Four Weddings and a Funeral*	1994	27,800,000

Inevitably, because of inflation, the top-grossing films of all time are releases from the 1990s.

BACK FROM THE FUTURE

In the second of the two Terminator *films, Arnold Schwarzenegger is a caring cyborg who protects a boy and his mother from a near-indestructible rival.*

TOP 10

HIGHEST-GROSSING FILMS OF ALL TIME IN THE US

	FILM	YEAR	US GROSS ($)
1	*Titanic*	1997	600,800,000
2	*Star Wars*	1977/97	461,000,000
3	*Star Wars: Episode I – The Phantom Menace*	1999	431,100,000
4	*E.T.: The Extra-Terrestrial*	1982	399,800,000
5	*Jurassic Park*	1993	357,100,000
6	*Forrest Gump*	1994	329,700,000
7	*The Lion King*	1994	312,900,000
8	*Return of the Jedi*	1983/97	309,100,000
9	*Independence Day*	1996	306,200,000
10	*The Empire Strikes Back*	1980/97	290,200,000

Star Wars: Episode I – The Phantom Menace was the fastest film ever to earn over $100 million, in its first five days. Box-office takings reached $102.7 million.

TOP 10

FILM SEQUELS THAT EARNED THE GREATEST AMOUNT MORE THAN THE ORIGINAL*

	ORIGINAL	OUTEARNED BY
1	*The Terminator*	*Terminator 2: Judgment Day*
2	*First Blood*	*Rambo: First Blood Part II / Rambo III*
3	*Lethal Weapon*	*Lethal Weapon 2 / Lethal Weapon 3 / Lethal Weapon 4*
4	*Austin Powers: International Man of Mystery*	*Austin Powers: The Spy Who Shagged Me*
5	*Die Hard*	*Die Hard 2 / Die Hard With a Vengeance*
6	*Rocky*	*Rocky III / Rocky IV*
7	*Raiders of the Lost Ark*	*Indiana Jones and the Last Crusade*
8	*Ace Ventura: Pet Detective*	*Ace Ventura: When Nature Calls*
9	*48 HRS*	*Another 48 HRS*
10	*Patriot Games*	*Clear and Present Danger*

* *Ranked by greatest differential between original and highest-earning sequel*

Film Hits

TOP 10 MOST EXPENSIVE FILMS EVER MADE

	FILM	YEAR	BUDGET ($)
1	*Titanic*	1997	200,000,000
2	=*Waterworld*	1995	175,000,000
	=*Wild Wild West*	1999	175,000,000
4	=*Speed 2: Cruise Control*	1997	150,000,000
	=*Armageddon*	1998	150,000,000
6	*Lethal Weapon 4*	1998	140,000,000
7	=*Batman and Robin*	1997	125,000,000
	=*Godzilla*	1998	125,000,000
9	=*Dante's Peak*	1997	115,000,000
	=*Star Wars: Episode I – The Phantom Menace*	1999	115,000,000
	=*The 13th Warrior*	1999	115,000,000

It is coincidental that several of the most expensive films ever made, including the first two in this Top 10, along with *Speed 2: Cruise Control*, are water-based. Large casts and large-scale special effects, such as those featured in *Titanic*, are major factors in escalating budgets.

HIGH WATER

Produced by and starring Kevin Costner, Waterworld *was one of the most expensive films ever made, being topped only by* Titanic.

TOP 10 BEST-ATTENDED FILMS

	FILM	YEAR	ATTENDANCE
1	*Gone With the Wind*	1939	208,100,000
2	*Star Wars*	1977	198,600,000
3	*The Sound of Music*	1965	170,600,000
4	*E.T.: The Extra-Terrestrial*	1982	151,600,000
5	*The Ten Commandments*	1956	132,800,000
6	*The Jungle Book*	1967	126,300,000
7	*Titanic*	1997	124,300,000
8	*Jaws*	1975	123,300,000
9	*Doctor Zhivago*	1965	122,700,000
10	*101 Dalmations*	1961	119,600,000

This list is based on the actual number of people purchasing tickets at the US box office. Because it takes account of the relatively greater numbers of tickets sold to children and other discounted sales (such as matinees for certain films), it differs both from lists that present total box-office receipts (which, as ticket prices increase, tend to feature more recent films) and those that are adjusted for inflation. However, it is interesting to observe that if inflation were factored in, *Gone With the Wind* would also top the all-time list, outearning even mega-blockbuster *Titanic* – the only film from the 1990s to feature in this list. The 1960s stand out from other decades, contributing four films to this list.

TOP 10  FILM SERIES OF ALL TIME

	FILM SERIES	DATES
1	*Star Wars / The Empire Strikes Back / Return of the Jedi / Star Wars Episode I: The Phantom Menace*	1977–99
2	*Jurassic Park / The Lost World: Jurassic Park*	1993–97
3	*Batman / Batman Returns / Batman Forever / Batman & Robin*	1989–97
4	*Raiders of the Lost Ark / Indiana Jones and the Temple of Doom / Indiana Jones and the Last Crusade*	1981–89
5	*Star Trek: The Motion Picture / II : The Wrath of Khan / III: The Search for Spock / IV: The Voyage Home / V: The Final Frontier / VI: The Undiscovered Country / Generations / First Contact / Insurrection*	1979–98
6	*Back to the Future / II / III*	1985–90
7	*Lethal Weapon / II / III / IV*	1987–98
8	*Home Alone / Home Alone 2: Lost in New York*	1990–92
9	*Jaws / 2 / 3(-D) / : The Revenge*	1975–87
10	*Die Hard / 2 / Die Hard With a Vengeance*	1988–95

Based on total earnings of the original film and all its sequels up to 1998, George Lucas's *Star Wars* series just beats Steven Spielberg's *Jurassic Park* and its sequel *The Lost World: Jurassic Park*, which have grossed $2,806,400,000 and $1,534,500,000 respectively around the world. Each of the other film series in the Top 10 have achieved cumulative global earnings of more than $700 million.

"BLOCKBUSTER"

During World War II, "blockbuster" was air force slang for a bomb heavy enough to flatten an entire city block. Once the word had become widely used in military reports, it was adopted by journalists to describe a book or film that had a great impact. "Blockbuster" has since acquired the specific meaning of a film that has made more than $100 million on its North American release. This was once a rare phenomenon, but now some 200 films have gained this sobriquet.

TOP 10 FILMS OF 1999

	FILM	GROSS INCOME ($) USA	WORLD TOTAL
1	*Star Wars: Episode I – The Phantom Menace*	430,500,000	977,900,000
2	*The Sixth Sense*	276,400,000	470,400,000
3	*The Matrix*	171,400,000	456,400,000
4	*The Mummy*	155,200,000	401,700,000
5	*Tarzan*	170,800,000	391,800,000
6	*Notting Hill*	116,000,000	354,800,000
7	*Austin Powers: The Spy Who Shagged Me*	205,400,000	308,400,000
8	*Runaway Bride*	152,100,000	281,600,000
9	*The World Is Not Enough*	118,600,000	265,200,000
10	*Toy Story 2*	211,200,000	234,700,000

TOP 10

FILMS OF 1999 IN THE UK

	FILM	UK GROSS (£)
1	*Star Wars: Episode I – The Phantom Menace*	50,700,000
2	*Notting Hill*	30,400,000
3	*Austin Powers: The Spy Who Shagged Me*	25,600,000
4	*The World Is Not Enough*	20,500,000
5	*The Sixth Sense*	19,300,000
6	*The Mummy*	17,400,000
7	*Tarzan*	17,200,000
8	*The Matrix*	16,900,000
9	*The Blair Witch Project*	14,900,000
10	*American Pie*	13,800,000

This list features only films released in the UK during 1999. Three films released in 1998 – *A Bug's Life, Shakespeare in Love, and Saving Private Ryan* – continued to earn at the UK box office well into 1999.

NEO CLASSIC

Keanu Reeves as Neo/Thomas A. Anderson shoots to thrill in The Matrix, *one of the sci-fi films that led the world's box office in 1999.*

What do the top four highest-earning films of the 1940s have in common?

see p.162 for the answer

A They are all Disney cartoons
B They all star Humphrey Bogart
C They are all black-and-white

Films of the Decades

TOP 10 FILMS OF THE 1930s

1	*Gone With the Wind**	1939
2	*Snow White and the Seven Dwarfs*	1937
3	*The Wizard of Oz*	1939
4	*The Woman in Red*	1935
5	*King Kong*	1933
6	*San Francisco*	1936
7	=*Hell's Angels*	1930
	=*Lost Horizon*	1937
	=*Mr. Smith Goes to Washington*	1939
10	*Maytime*	1937

* Winner of "Best Picture" Academy Award

Gone With the Wind and *Snow White and the Seven Dwarfs* have generated more income than any other pre-war film. However, if the income of *Gone With the Wind* is adjusted to allow for inflation in the period since its release, it could be regarded as the most successful film ever, earning some $885 million in the US alone.

TOP 10 FILMS OF THE 1940s

1	*Bambi*	1942
2	*Pinocchio*	1940
3	*Fantasia*	1940
4	*Cinderella*	1949
5	*Song of the South*	1946
6	*The Best Years of Our Lives**	1946
7	*The Bells of St. Mary's*	1945
8	*Duel in the Sun*	1946
9	*Mom and Dad*	1948
10	*Samson and Delilah*	1949

* Winner of "Best Picture" Academy Award

With the top four films of the decade classic Disney cartoons, the 1940s may be regarded as the "golden age" of the animated film.

TOP 10 FILMS OF THE 1950s

1	*Lady and the Tramp*	1955
2	*Peter Pan*	1953
3	*Ben-Hur**	1959
4	*The Ten Commandments*	1956
5	*Sleeping Beauty*	1959
6	*Around the World in 80 Days**	1956
7	=*The Robe*	1953
	=*The Greatest Show on Earth**	1952
9	*The Bridge on the River Kwai**	1957
10	*Peyton Place*	1957

* Winner of "Best Picture" Academy Award

While the popularity of animated films continued, the 1950s was outstanding as the decade of the "big" picture (in cast and scale).

TOP 10 FILMS OF THE 1960s

1 *One Hundred and One Dalmatians*, 1961 2 *The Jungle Book*, 1967 3 *The Sound of Music**, 1965 4 *Thunderball*, 1965 5 *Goldfinger*, 1964 6 *Doctor Zhivago*, 1965 7 *You Only Live Twice*, 1967 8 *The Graduate*, 1968 9 *Mary Poppins*, 1964 10 *Butch Cassidy and the Sundance Kid*, 1969

* Winner of "Best Picture" Academy Award

TALL STORY

In one of cinema history's most famous scenes, King Kong fights off his attackers atop the newly opened Empire State Building. The film was one of the 1930s' highest earners.

TOP 10 FILMS OF THE 1990s

	Film	Year
1	*Titanic**	1997
2	*Star Wars: Episode I – The Phantom Menace*	1999
3	*Jurassic Park*	1993
4	*Independence Day*	1996
5	*The Lion King*	1994
6	*Forrest Gump**	1994
7	*The Lost World: Jurassic Park*	1997
8	*Men in Black*	1997
9	*The Sixth Sense*	1999
10	*Armageddon*	1998

* *Winner of "Best Picture" Academy Award*

Each of the Top 10 films of the 1990s has earned more than $550 million around the world.

BRINGING THE HOUSE DOWN

The White House sustains a direct hit from the invading spacecraft in a scene from Independence Day, *one of the top films of the 1990s.*

TOP 10 FILMS OF THE 1980s

❶ *E.T.: The Extra-Terrestrial*, 1982 ❷ *Indiana Jones and the Last Crusade*, 1989 ❸ *Batman*, 1989 ❹ *Rain Man*, 1988 ❺ *Return of the Jedi*, 1983 ❻ *Raiders of the Lost Ark*, 1981 ❼ *The Empire Strikes Back*, 1980 ❽ *Who Framed Roger Rabbit*, 1988 ❾ *Back to the Future*, 1985 ❿ *Top Gun*, 1986

TOP 10 FILMS OF THE 1970s

	Film	Year
1	*Star Wars*	1977/97
2	*Jaws*	1975
3	*Close Encounters of the Third Kind*	1977/80
4	*The Exorcist*	1973/98
5	*Moonraker*	1979
6	*The Spy Who Loved Me*	1977
7	*The Sting**	1973
8	*Grease*	1978
9	*The Godfather**	1972
10	*Saturday Night Fever*	1977

* *Winner of "Best Picture" Academy Award*

In the 1970s, the arrival of Steven Spielberg and George Lucas set the scene for the high-adventure blockbusters whose domination has continued ever since. Lucas wrote and directed *Star Wars*, formerly the highest-earning film of all time.

JAWS OF DEATH

Although it once held the record as the world's highest-earning film, Jaws *was eventually beaten by* Star Wars, *directed by George Lucas.*

Which actress provided the voice of Tzipporah in *The Prince of Egypt*?

see p.176 for the answer

A Julia Roberts
B Demi Moore
C Michelle Pfeiffer

Film Genres

TOP 10 HORROR FILMS

1	*Jurassic Park*	1993
2	*The Lost World: Jurassic Park*	1997
3	*The Sixth Sense*	1999
4	*Jaws*	1975
5	*The Mummy*	1999
6	*Godzilla*	1998
7	*The Exorcist*	1973
8	*The Blair Witch Project*	1999
9	*Interview With the Vampire*	1994
10	*Jaws II*	1978

TOP 10 VAMPIRE FILMS

1	*Interview With the Vampire*	1994
2	*Bram Stoker's Dracula*	1992
3	*Blade*	1998
4	*From Dusk Till Dawn*	1996
5	*Love at First Bite*	1979
6	*The Lost Boys*	1987
7	*Vampires*	1998
8	*Dracula*	1979
9	*Fright Night*	1985
10	*Vampire in Brooklyn*	1995

TOP 10 WESTERNS

1	*Dances With Wolves*	1990
2	*Wild Wild West*	1999
3	*Maverick*	1994
4	*Unforgiven*	1992
5	*Butch Cassidy and the Sundance Kid*	1969
6	*Jeremiah Johnson*	1972
7	*How the West Was Won*	1962
8	*Young Guns*	1988
9	*Young Guns II*	1990
10	*Pale Rider*	1985

TOP 10 GHOST FILMS

1	*The Sixth Sense*	1999
2	*Ghost*	1990
3	*Ghostbusters*	1984
4	*Casper*	1995
5	*Ghostbusters II*	1989
6	*The Haunting*	1999
7	*Sleepy Hollow*	1999
8	*Beetlejuice*	1988
9	*Scrooged*	1988
10	*The House on Haunted Hill*	1999

TOP 10 SCIENCE-FICTION FILMS

1	*Star Wars: Episode I – The Phantom Menace*	1999
2	*Jurassic Park*	1993
3	*Independence Day*	1996
4	*Star Wars*	1977/97
5	*E.T.: The Extra-Terrestrial*	1982
6	*The Lost World: Jurassic Park*	1997
7	*Men in Black*	1997
8	*Return of the Jedi*	1983/97
9	*Armageddon*	1998
10	*Terminator 2: Judgment Day*	1991

TOP 10 WAR FILMS

1	*Saving Private Ryan*	1998
2	*Platoon*	1986
3	*Good Morning, Vietnam*	1987
4	*Apocalypse Now*	1979
5	*The Thin Red Line*	1998
6	*M*A*S*H*	1970
7	*Three Kings*	1999
8	*Patton*	1970
9	*The Deer Hunter*	1978
10	*Full Metal Jacket*	1987

This list excludes successful films that are not technically "war" films but that have military themes, such as *A Few Good Men* (1992), *The Hunt for Red October* (1990), *Crimson Tide* (1995), and *An Officer and a Gentleman* (1982), which would otherwise be placed in the top five, and *Top Gun* (1986), which would feature prominently in the list.

WHO YOU GONNA CALL?

Ghostbusters *starred Bill Murray alongside Dan Aykroyd and Harold Ramis, both of whom also co-wrote the first film and its sequel.*

FUTURE PERFECT

Schoolkid Marty McFly (Michael J. Fox) and scientist Dr. Emmett "Doc" L. Brown (Christopher Lloyd) are dazzled as the Doc's DeLorean zips back to 1955. The first Back to the Future *film earned $350 million.*

TOP 10 TIME TRAVEL FILMS

1	*Terminator 2: Judgment Day*	1991
2	*Back to the Future*	1985
3	*Back to the Future Part III*	1990
4	*Back to the Future Part II*	1989
5	*Timecop*	1994
6	*The Terminator*	1984
7	*Pleasantville*	1998
8	*Time Bandits*	1981
9	*Bill and Ted's Excellent Adventure*	1989
10	*Highlander III: The Sorcerer*	1994

TOP 10 FILMS STARRING ANIMALS

	FILM/YEAR	ANIMAL
1	*Jaws*, 1975	Shark
2	*101 Dalmatians*, 1996	Dogs
3	*Babe*, 1995	Pig
4	*Jaws II*, 1978	Shark
5	*Free Willy*, 1993	Orca whale
6	*Turner & Hooch*, 1989	Dog
7	*Jaws 3-D*, 1983	Shark
8	*Babe: Pig in the City*, 1998	Pig
9	*Beethoven*, 1992	Dog
10	*Homeward Bound II: Lost in San Francisco*, 1996	Dogs

This list is of films where real animals are acknowledged as central rather than secondary characters. Man-eating sharks, dogs, and pigs stand out as the most popular subjects!

TOP 10 COMEDY FILMS

1 *Forrest Gump*, 1994 2 *Home Alone*, 1990 3 *Ghost*, 1990 4 *Pretty Woman*, 1990 5 *Mrs. Doubtfire*, 1993 6 *The Flintstones*, 1994 7 *Notting Hill*, 1999 8 *Who Framed Roger Rabbit*, 1988 9 *There's Something About Mary*, 1998 10 *The Mask*, 1994

TOP 10 COP FILMS

1	*Die Hard With a Vengeance*	1995
2	*The Fugitive*	1993
3	*Basic Instinct*	1992
4	*Se7en*	1995
5	*Lethal Weapon 3*	1992
6	*Beverly Hills Cop*	1984
7	*Beverly Hills Cop II*	1987
8	*Lethal Weapon 4*	1998
9	*Speed*	1994
10	*Lethal Weapon 2*	1989

Although films in which one of the central characters is a police officer have never been among the most successful films of all time, many have earned respectable amounts at the box office. They are divided between those with a comic slant, such as all three *Beverly Hills Cop* films, and darker police thrillers, such as *Basic Instinct*. Films featuring FBI and CIA agents have been excluded here, thus eliminating blockbusters such as *Mission: Impossible* and *The Silence of the Lambs*.

TOP 10 DISASTER FILMS

1	*Titanic*	1997
2	*Armageddon*	1998
3	*Twister*	1996
4	*Die Hard With a Vengeance*	1995
5	*Deep Imapct*	1998
6	*Apollo 13*	1995
7	*Outbreak*	1995
8	*Dante's Peak*	1997
9	*Daylight*	1996
10	*Die Hard*	1988

"LIFE IS LIKE A BOX OF CHOCOLATES ..."

As Forrest Gump, Tom Hanks plays a man whose simple homespun philosophy enables him to succeed against all odds.

Did You Know? The 1980 British film *Raise the Titanic!* itself became a disaster film, losing over $30 million of the $40 million it had cost to make, as it sank without trace at the box office.

Oscar-Winning Films

TOP 10

HIGHEST-EARNING "BEST PICTURE" OSCAR WINNERS

	FILM	YEAR
1	*Titanic*	1997
2	*Forrest Gump*	1994
3	*Dances With Wolves*	1990
4	*Rain Man*	1988
5	*Schindler's List*	1993
6	*Shakespeare in Love*	1999
7	*The English Patient*	1996
8	*American Beauty*	1999
9	*Braveheart*	1995
10	*Gone With the Wind*	1939

THE 10 "BEST PICTURE" OSCAR WINNERS OF THE 1950s

(Year/film)

1 1950 *All About Eve* 2 1951 *An American in Paris* 3 1952 *The Greatest Show on Earth* 4 1953 *From Here to Eternity* 5 1954 *On the Waterfront* 6 1955 *Marty* 7 1956 *Around the World in 80 Days* 8 1957 *The Bridge on the River Kwai* 9 1958 *Gigi* 10 1959 *Ben-Hur*

The first winning film of the 1950s, *All About Eve*, received the most Oscar nominations (14), while the last, *Ben-Hur*, won the most (11).

THE 10 "BEST PICTURE" OSCAR WINNERS OF THE 1960s

(Year/film)

1 1960 *The Apartment* 2 1961 *West Side Story* 3 1962 *Lawrence of Arabia* 4 1963 *Tom Jones* 5 1964 *My Fair Lady* 6 1965 *The Sound of Music* 7 1966 *A Man for All Seasons* 8 1967 *In the Heat of the Night* 9 1968 *Oliver!* 10 1969 *Midnight Cowboy*

The 1960 winner, *The Apartment*, was the last black-and-white winner until *Schindler's List* in 1993.

HEALTHY PATIENT

Nominated for 12 and winner of 9 Oscars, The English Patient is also among the highest-earning of all "Best Picture" winners.

TOP 10 FILMS NOMINATED FOR THE MOST OSCARS*

(Film/year/awards/nominations)

1 = ***All About Eve***, 1950, 6, 14; = ***Titanic***, 1997, 11, 14 3 ***Gone With the Wind***, 1939 ,8#, 13; = ***From Here to Eternity***, 1953, 8, 13; = ***Mary Poppins***, 1964, 5, 13; = ***Who's Afraid of Virginia Woolf?***, 1966, 5, 13; = ***Forrest Gump***, 1994, 6, 13; = ***Shakespeare in Love***, 1998, 7, 13 9 = ***Mrs. Miniver***, 1942, 6, 12; = ***The Song of Bernadette***, 1943, 4, 12; = ***Johnny Belinda***, 1948, 1, 12; = ***A Streetcar Named Desire***, 1951, 4, 12; = ***On the Waterfront***, 1954, 8, 12; = ***Ben-Hur***, 1959, 11, 12; = ***Becket***, 1964, 1, 12; = ***My Fair Lady***, 1964, 8, 12; = ***Reds***, 1981, 3, 12; = ***Dances With Wolves***, 1990, 7, 12; = ***Schindler's List***, 1993, 7, 12; = ***The English Patient***, 1996 , 9, 12

* Oscar® is a Registered Trade Mark

\# Plus two special awards

THE 10

"BEST PICTURE" OSCAR WINNERS OF THE 1970s

YEAR	FILM
1970	*Patton*
1971	*The French Connection*
1972	*The Godfather*
1973	*The Sting*
1974	*The Godfather Part II*
1975	*One Flew Over the Cuckoo's Nest*
1976	*Rocky*
1977	*Annie Hall*
1978	*The Deer Hunter*
1979	*Kramer vs. Kramer*

THE 10

"BEST PICTURE" OSCAR WINNERS OF THE 1980s

YEAR	FILM
1980	*Ordinary People*
1981	*Chariots of Fire*
1982	*Gandhi*
1983	*Terms of Endearment*
1984	*Amadeus*
1985	*Out of Africa*
1986	*Platoon*
1987	*The Last Emperor*
1988	*Rain Man*
1989	*Driving Miss Daisy*

Did You Know? *Who's Afraid of Virginia Woolf?* (1966) was the first film in which the entire cast was nominated for Oscars, with wins for both Elizabeth Taylor and Sandy Dennis.

DRAMATIC ENTRANCE

Career woman (Annette Benning) confronts drop-out husband (Kevin Spacey) in the suburban satire American Beauty, *winner of the 1999 "Best Picture" Oscar.*

THE 10 LATEST "BEST PICTURE" OSCAR WINNERS

YEAR	FILM
1999	*American Beauty*
1998	*Shakespeare in Love*
1997	*Titanic*
1996	*The English Patient*
1995	*Braveheart*
1994	*Forrest Gump*
1993	*Schindler's List*
1992	*Unforgiven*
1991	*The Silence of the Lambs*
1990	*Dances With Wolves*

TOP 10 FILMS TO WIN THE MOST OSCARS

	FILM	YEAR	NOMINATIONS	AWARDS
1	=*Ben-Hur*	1959	12	11
	=*Titanic*	1997	14	11
3	*West Side Story*	1961	11	10
4	=*Gigi*	1958	9	9
	=*The Last Emperor*	1987	9	9
	=*The English Patient*	1996	12	9
7	=*Gone With the Wind*	1939	13	8*
	=*From Here to Eternity*	1953	13	8
	=*On the Waterfront*	1954	12	8
	=*My Fair Lady*	1964	12	8
	=*Cabaret*	1972	10	8
	=*Gandhi*	1982	11	8
	=*Amadeus*	1984	11	8

* *Plus two special awards*

TOP 10 STUDIOS WITH THE MOST "BEST PICTURE" OSCARS

(Studio/awards)

1. United Artists, 13 2. Columbia, 12 3. Paramount, 11 4. MGM, 9 5. Twentieth Century Fox, 7 6. Warner Bros, 6 7. Universal, 5 8. Orion, 4 9. = Miramax, 2; = RKO, 2

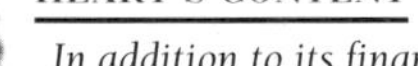

HEART'S CONTENT

In addition to its financial success, Mel Gibson's 1995 film Braveheart *won five Oscars, including "Best Director" and "Best Actor".*

ACTING HIS AGE

Septuagenarian actor John Gielgud secured a "Best Supporting Actor" Oscar for his role as Hobson, the acerbic valet to the lead character star of Arthur.

"OSCAR"

Founded on 4 May 1927, the Hollywood-based Academy of Motion Picture Arts and Sciences proposed improving the image of the film industry by issuing "awards for merit or distinction" in various categories. The award itself, a statuette designed by Cedric Gibbons, was modelled by a young artist, George Stanley. The gold-plated naked male figure holds a sword and stands on a reel of film. It was simply called "the statuette" until 1931, when Academy librarian Margaret Herrick commented, "It looks like my Uncle Oscar!" – and the name stuck.

WHY DO WE SAY?

THE 10 "BEST ACTRESS" OSCAR WINNERS OF THE 1950s

(*Year/actress/film*)

1 1950 Judy Holiday, *Born Yesterday* 2 1951 Vivien Leigh, *A Streetcar Named Desire* 3 1952 Shirley Booth, *Come Back, Little Sheba* 4 1953 Audrey Hepburn, *Roman Holiday* 5 1954 Grace Kelly, *The Country Girl* 6 1955 Anna Magnani, *The Rose Tattoo* 7 1956 Ingrid Bergman, *Anastasia* 8 1957 Joanne Woodward, *The Three Faces of Eve* 9 1958 Susan Hayward, *I Want to Live* 10 1959 Simone Signoret, *Room at the Top*

TOP 10 OLDEST OSCAR-WINNING ACTORS AND ACTRESSES

	ACTOR OR ACTRESS	AWARD/FILM	YEAR	AGE*
1	Jessica Tandy	"Best Actress" (*Driving Miss Daisy*)	1989	80
2	George Burns	"Best Supporting Actor" (*The Sunshine Boys*)	1975	80
3	Melvyn Douglas	"Best Supporting Actor" (*Being There*)	1979	79
4	John Gielgud	"Best Supporting Actor" (*Arthur*)	1981	77
5	Don Ameche	"Best Supporting Actor" (*Cocoon*)	1985	77
6	Peggy Ashcroft	"Best Supporting Actress" (*A Passage to India*)	1984	77
7	Henry Fonda	"Best Actor" (*On Golden Pond*)	1981	76
8	Katharine Hepburn	"Best Actress" (*On Golden Pond*)	1981	74
9	Edmund Gwenn	"Best Supporting Actor" (*Miracle on 34th Street*)	1947	72
10	Ruth Gordon	"Best Supporting Actress" (*Rosemary's Baby*)	1968	72

* *At the time of the Award ceremony; those of apparently identical age have been ranked according to their precise age in days at the time of the ceremony*

THE 10 "BEST ACTOR" OSCAR WINNERS OF THE 1950s

YEAR	ACTOR/FILM
1950	Jose Ferrer, *Cyrano de Bergerac*
1951	Humphrey Bogart, *The African Queen*
1952	Gary Cooper, *High Noon*
1953	William Holden, *Stalag 17*
1954	Marlon Brando, *On the Waterfront**
1955	Ernest Borgnine, *Marty**
1956	Yul Brynner, *The King and I*
1957	Alec Guinness, *The Bridge on the River Kwai**
1958	David Niven, *Separate Tables*
1959	Charlton Heston, *Ben-Hur**

* *Winner of "Best Picture" Oscar*

THE 10 "BEST ACTRESS" OSCAR WINNERS OF THE 1960s

YEAR	ACTRESS/FILM
1960	Elizabeth Taylor, *Butterfield 8*
1961	Sophia Loren, *Two Women*
1962	Anne Bancroft, *The Miracle Worker*
1963	Patricia Neal, *Hud*
1964	Julie Andrews, *Mary Poppins*
1965	Julie Christie, *Darling*
1966	Elizabeth Taylor, *Who's Afraid of Virginia Woolf?*
1967	Katharine Hepburn, *Guess Who's Coming to Dinner*
1968	=Katharine Hepburn*, *The Lion in Winter*
	=Barbra Streisand*, *Funny Girl*
1969	Maggie Smith, *The Prime of Miss Jean Brodie*

* *The only tie for "Best Actress"*

THE 10 "BEST ACTOR" OSCAR WINNERS OF THE 1960s

YEAR	ACTOR/FILM
1960	Burt Lancaster, *Elmer Gantry*
1961	Maximilian Schell, *Judgement at Nuremberg*
1962	Gregory Peck, *To Kill a Mockingbird*
1963	Sidney Poitier, *Lilies of the Field*
1964	Rex Harrison, *My Fair Lady**
1965	Lee Marvin, *Cat Ballou*
1966	Paul Scofield, *A Man for All Seasons**
1967	Rod Steiger, *In the Heat of the Night**
1968	Cliff Robertson, *Charly*
1969	John Wayne, *True Grit*

* *Winner of "Best Picture" Oscar*

THE 10 "BEST ACTOR" OSCAR WINNERS OF THE 1970s

YEAR	ACTOR/FILM
1970	George C. Scott, *Patton**
1971	Gene Hackman, *The French Connection**
1972	Marlon Brando, *The Godfather**
1973	Jack Lemmon, *Save the Tiger*
1974	Art Carney, *Harry and Tonto*
1975	Jack Nicholson, *One Flew Over the Cuckoo's Nest*#*
1976	Peter Finch, *Network*
1977	Richard Dreyfuss, *The Goodbye Girl*
1978	John Voight, *Coming Home*
1979	Dustin Hoffman, *Kramer vs. Kramer**

* *Winner of "Best Picture" Oscar*

\# *Winner of "Best Director", "Best Actress", and "Best Screenplay" Oscars*

THE 10 "BEST ACTRESS" OSCAR WINNERS OF THE 1970s

(Year/actress/film)

1. 1970 Glenda Jackson, *Women in Love*
2. 1971 Jane Fonda, *Klute*
3. 1972 Liza Minnelli, *Cabaret*
4. 1973 Glenda Jackson, *A Touch of Class*
5. 1974 Ellen Burstyn, *Alice Doesn't Live Here Any More*
6. 1975 Louise Fletcher, *One Flew Over the Cuckoo's Nest**#
7. 1976 Faye Dunaway, *Network*
8. 1977 Diane Keaton, *Annie Hall**
9. 1978 Jane Fonda, *Coming Home*
10. 1979 Sally Field, *Norma Rae*

* *Winner of "Best Picture" Oscar*

\# *Winner of "Best Director", "Best Actor", and "Best Screenplay" Oscars*

CABARET STAR

Liza Minnelli won "Best Actress" Oscar for her role as Sally Bowles in Cabaret. The film itself received 10 nominations and eight wins, but lost "Best Picture" to The Godfather.

In which of these films did Leonardo DiCaprio star?

see p.174 for the answer

A *Peggy Sue Got Married*
B *What's Eating Gilbert Grape*
C *Raging Bull*

Oscar-Winning Stars 2

THE 10 "BEST ACTRESS" OSCAR WINNERS OF THE 1980s

YEAR	ACTRESS/FILM
1980	Sissy Spacek, *Coal Miner's Daughter*
1981	Katharine Hepburn, *On Golden Pond**
1982	Meryl Streep, *Sophie's Choice*
1983	Shirley MacLaine, *Terms of Endearment#*
1984	Sally Field, *Places in the Heart*
1985	Geraldine Page, *The Trip to Bountiful*
1986	Marlee Matlin, *Children of a Lesser God*
1987	Cher, *Moonstruck*
1988	Jodie Foster, *The Accused*
1989	Jessica Tandy, *Driving Miss Daisy#*

* *Winner of "Best Actor" Oscar*

\# *Winner of "Best Picture" Oscar*

THE 10 "BEST ACTOR" OSCAR WINNERS OF THE 1980s

YEAR	ACTOR/FILM
1980	Robert De Niro, *Raging Bull*
1981	Henry Fonda, *On Golden Pond**
1982	Ben Kingsley, *Gandhi#*
1983	Robert Duvall, *Tender Mercies*
1984	F. Murray Abraham, *Amadeus#*
1985	William Hurt, *Kiss of the Spider Woman*
1986	Paul Newman, *The Color of Money*
1987	Michael Douglas, *Wall Street*
1988	Dustin Hoffman, *Rain Man#*
1989	Daniel Day-Lewis, *My Left Foot*

* *Winner of "Best Actress" Oscar*

\# *Winner of "Best Picture" Oscar*

GETTING IN ON THE ACT

Jack Nicholson, winner of "Best Actor" Oscar for As Good As It Gets, *confronts Jill, a Brussels Griffon performing the part of Verdell.*

THE 10 LATEST "BEST ACTOR" OSCAR WINNERS

YEAR	ACTOR/FILM
1999	Kevin Spacey, *American Beauty**
1998	Roberto Benigni, *La vita è bella (Life Is Beautiful)*
1997	Jack Nicholson, *As Good as It Gets#*
1996	Geoffrey Rush, *Shine*
1995	Nicolas Cage, *Leaving Las Vegas*
1994	Tom Hanks, *Forrest Gump**
1993	Tom Hanks, *Philadelphia*
1992	Al Pacino, *Scent of a Woman*
1991	Anthony Hopkins, *The Silence of the Lambs*#*
1990	Jeremy Irons, *Reversal of Fortune*

* *Winner of "Best Picture" Oscar*

\# *Winner of "Best Actress" Oscar*

Tom Hanks shares the honour of two consecutive wins with Spencer Tracy (1937: *Captains Courageous* and 1938: *Boys Town*). Only four other actors have won twice: Marlon Brando (1954; 1972), Gary Cooper (1941; 1952), Dustin Hoffman (1977; 1988), and Jack Nicholson (1975; 1997),

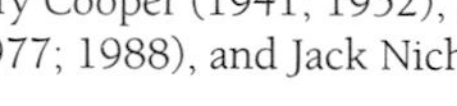

GOLDEN DOUBLE

Katharine Hepburn and Henry Fonda won "Best Actress" and "Best Actor" Academy Awards for On Golden Pond. *It was Hepburn's fourth but Fonda's only Oscar, awarded just four months before his death.*

ROLE REVERSAL

Former television actress Hilary Swank (right) won the 1999 «Best Actress» Oscar for her demanding role as a girl who adopts the persona of a boy.

THE 10

LATEST "BEST ACTRESS" OSCAR WINNERS

YEAR	ACTRESS/FILM
1999	Hilary Swank, *Boys Don't Cry*
1998	Gwyneth Paltrow, *Shakespeare in Love*
1997	Helen Hunt, *As Good as It Gets*
1996	Frances McDormand, *Fargo*
1995	Susan Sarandon, *Dead Man Walking*
1994	Jessica Lange, *Blue Sky*
1993	Holly Hunter, *The Piano*
1992	Emma Thompson, *Howard's End*
1991	Jodie Foster, *The Silence of the Lambs**
1990	Kathy Bates, *Misery*

* *Winner of "Best Picture" and "Best Actor" Oscars*

TOP 10

YOUNGEST OSCAR-WINNING ACTORS AND ACTRESSES

	ACTOR OR ACTRESS	AWARD/FILM (WHERE SPECIFIED)	YEAR	AGE*
1	Shirley Temple	Special Award – outstanding contribution during 1934	1934	6
2	Margaret O' Brien	Special Award (*Meet Me in St Louis*)	1944	8
3	Vincent Winter	Special Award (*The Little Kidnappers*)	1954	8
4	Ivan Jandl	Special Award (*The Search*)	1948	9
5	Jon Whiteley	Special Award (*The Little Kidnappers*)	1954	10
6	Tatum O'Neal	"Best Supporting Actress" (*Paper Moon*)	1973	10
7	Anna Paquin	"Best Supporting Actress" (*The Piano*)	1993	11
8	Claude Jarman, Jr.	Special Award (*The Yearling*)	1946	12
9	Bobby Driscoll	Special Award (*The Window*)	1949	13
10	Hayley Mills	Special Award (*Pollyanna*)	1960	13

* *At the time of the Award ceremony; those of apparently identical age have been ranked according to their precise age in days at the time of the ceremony*

The Academy Awards ceremony usually takes place at the end of March in the year following that in which the film was released in the US, so the winners are generally at least a year older when they receive their Oscars than when they acted in their award-winning films.

Who provided the voice of Woody in *Toy Story* and *Toy Story 2*?

see p.175 for the answer

A Jack Nicholson
B Dustin Hoffman
C Tom Hanks

THE 10 LATEST WINNERS OF THE CANNES PALME D'OR FOR "BEST FILM"

YEAR	FILM/COUNTRY
1999	*Rosetta*, France
1998	*Eternity and a Day*, Greece
1997	*The Eel*, Japan/ *The Taste of Cherries*, Iran
1996	*Secrets and Lies*, UK
1995	*Underground*, Yugoslavia
1994	*Pulp Fiction*, USA
1993	*Farewell My Concubine*, China/ *The Piano*, Australia
1992	*Best Intentions*, Denmark
1991	*Barton Fink*, USA
1990	*Wild at Heart*, USA

RISE OF *SHINE*

Geoffrey Rush received the "Best Actor" BAFTA (and Oscar) for his role in Shine, the multi-award-winning story of the turbulent life of David Helfgott.

THE 10 FIRST WINNERS OF THE BAFTA "BEST ACTRESS" AWARD

YEAR	ACTRESS/FILM/COUNTRY
1968	Katharine Hepburn, *Guess Who's Coming to Dinner*, USA and *The Lion in Winter*, UK
1969	Maggie Smith, *The Pride of Miss Jean Brodie*, UK
1970	Katharine Ross, *Tell Them Willie Boy is Here*, USA and *Butch Cassidy and the Sundance Kid*, USA
1971	Glenda Jackson, *Sunday, Bloody Sunday*, UK
1972	Liza Minnelli, *Cabaret*, USA
1973	Stephane Audrane, *The Discreet Charm of the Bourgeoisie*, France/Spain/Italy and *Just Before Nightfall*, France
1974	Joanne Woodward, *Summer Wishes, Winter Dreams*, USA
1975	Ellen Burstyn, *Alice Doesn't Live Here Anymore*, USA
1976	Louise Fletcher, *One Flew Over the Cuckoo's Nest*, USA
1977	Diane Keaton, *Annie Hall*, USA

THE 10 FIRST WINNERS OF THE BAFTA "BEST ACTOR" AWARD

YEAR	ACTOR/FILM/COUNTRY
1968	Spencer Tracy, *Guess Who's Coming to Dinner*, USA
1969	Dustin Hoffman, *Midnight Cowboy*, (USA) and *John and Mary*, USA
1970	Robert Redford, *Butch Cassidy and the Sundance Kid*, USA, *Tell Them Willie Boy is Here*, USA, and *Downhill Racer*, USA
1971	Peter Finch, *Sunday, Bloody Sunday*, UK
1972	Gene Hackman, *The French Connection*, USA and *The Poseidon Adventure*, USA
1973	Walter Matthau, *Pete 'n Tillie*, USA and *Charley Varrick*, USA
1974	Jack Nicholson, *The Last Detail*, USA and *Chinatown*, USA
1975	Al Pacino, *The Godfather Part II*, USA and *Dog Day Afternoon*, USA
1976	Jack Nicholson, *One Flew Over the Cuckoo's Nest*, USA
1977	Peter Finch, *Network*, USA

THE 10 LATEST WINNERS OF THE BAFTA "BEST ACTOR" AWARD

YEAR	ACTOR/FILM/COUNTRY
1999	Kevin Spacey, *American Beauty*, USA
1998	Roberto Benigni, *La vita è bella (Life Is Beautiful)*, Italy
1997	Robert Carlyle, *The Full Monty*, UK
1996	Geoffrey Rush, *Shine*, Australia
1995	Nigel Hawthorne, *The Madness of King George*, UK
1994	Hugh Grant, *Four Weddings and a Funeral*, UK
1993	Anthony Hopkins, *The Remains of the Day*, UK
1992	Robert Downey Jr., *Chaplin*, UK
1991	Anthony Hopkins, *The Silence of the Lambs*, USA
1990	Philippe Noiret, *Cinema Paradiso*, Italy/France

THE 10 LATEST WINNERS OF THE BAFTA "BEST ACTRESS" AWARD

YEAR	ACTRESS/FILM/COUNTRY
1999	Annette Benning, *American Beauty*, USA
1998	Cate Blanchett, *Elizabeth*, UK
1997	Judi Dench, *Mrs. Brown*, UK
1996	Brenda Blethyn, *Secrets and Lies*, UK
1995	Emma Thompson, *Sense and Sensibility*, UK
1994	Susan Sarandon, *The Client*, USA
1993	Holly Hunter, *The Piano*, Australia
1992	Emma Thompson, *Howards End*, UK
1991	Jodie Foster, *The Silence of the Lambs*, USA
1990	Jessica Tandy, *Driving Miss Daisy*, USA

THE 10 LATEST WINNERS OF THE BAFTA "BEST DIRECTOR" AWARD

YEAR	DIRECTOR/FILM/COUNTRY
1999	Pedro Almodovar, *All About My Mother*, Spain
1998	Peter Weir, *The Truman Show*, USA
1997	Baz Luhrmann, *William Shakespeare's Romeo + Juliet*, USA
1996	Joel Cohen, *Fargo*, USA
1995	Michael Radford, *Il Postino*, Italy
1994	Mike Newell, *Four Weddings and a Funeral*, UK
1993	Steven Spielberg, *Schindler's List*, USA
1992	Robert Altman, *The Player*, USA
1991	Alan Parker, *The Commitments*, USA/UK
1990	Martin Scorsese, *GoodFellas*, USA

TRUE TO FORM

Australian director Peter Weir won his 1998 BAFTA "Best Director" award for The Truman Show, *which starred comic master Jim Carrey.*

THE 10 LATEST WINNERS OF THE BAFTA "BEST FILM" AWARD

(Year/film/country)

1 1999 *American Beauty*, USA 2 1998 *Shakespeare in Love*, USA 3 1997 *The Full Monty*, UK 4 1996 *The English Patient*, UK 5 1995 *Sense and Sensibility*, UK 6 1994 *Four Weddings and a Funeral*, UK 7 1993 *Schindler's List*, USA 8 1992 *Howards End*, UK 9 1991 *The Commitments*, USA/UK 10 1990 *GoodFellas*, USA

THE 10 FIRST WINNERS OF THE BAFTA "BEST DIRECTOR" AWARD

YEAR	DIRECTOR/FILM/COUNTRY
1968	Mike Nichols, *The Graduate*, USA
1969	John Schlesinger, *Midnight Cowboy*, USA
1970	George Roy Hill, *Butch Cassidy and the Sundance Kid*, USA
1971	John Schlesinger, *Sunday, Bloody Sunday*, UK
1972	Bob Fosse, *Cabaret*, USA
1973	François Truffault, *Day for Night* , France
1974	Roman Polanski, *Chinatown*, USA
1975	Stanley Kubrick, *Barry Lyndon*, UK
1976	Milos Forman, *One Flew Over the Cuckoo's Nest*, USA
1977	Woody Allen, *Annie Hall*, USA

THE 10 FIRST WINNERS OF THE BAFTA "BEST FILM" AWARD

(Year/film/country)

1 1947 *The Best Years of Our Lives*, USA 2 1948 *Hamlet*, UK 3 1949 *Bicycle Thieves*, Italy 4 1950 *All About Eve*, USA 5 1951 *La Ronde*, France 6 1952 *The Sound Barrier*, UK 7 1953 *Jeux Interdits*, France 8 1954 *Le Salaire de la Peur*, France 9 1955 *Richard III*, UK 10 1956 *Gervaise*, France

Which actress provides the voice of Marge in *The Simpsons*?

see p.184 for the answer

A Julie Kavner
B Catherine Kenner
C Marie-Louise Parker

Leading Men

TOP 10 ★ LEONARDO DiCAPRIO FILMS

1	*Titanic*	1997
2	*The Man in the Iron Mask*	1998
3	*Romeo + Juliet*	1996
4	*The Beach*	2000
5	*The Quick and the Dead*	1995
6	*Marvin's Room*	1996
7	*What's Eating Gilbert Grape*	1993
8	*Celebrity*	1998
9	*This Boy's Life*	1993
10	*The Basketball Diaries*	1995

TOP 10 ★ NICOLAS CAGE FILMS

1	*The Rock*	1996
2	*Face/Off*	1997
3	*Con Air*	1997
4	*City of Angels*	1998
5	*Snake Eyes*	1998
6	*8MM*	1999
7	*Moonstruck*	1987
8	*Leaving Las Vegas*	1995
9	*Peggy Sue Got Married*	1986
10	*It Could Happen to You*	1994

TOP 10 ★ PIERCE BROSNAN FILMS

1	*Mrs. Doubtfire*	1993
2	*GoldenEye*	1995
3	*Tomorrow Never Dies*	1997
4	*The World Is Not Enough*	1999
5	*Dante's Peak*	1997
6	*The Thomas Crown Affair*	1999
7	*Mars Attacks!*	1996
8	*The Mirror Has Two Faces*	1996
9	*The Lawnmower Man*	1992
10	*Love Affair*	1994

Pierce Brosnan, now best known as James Bond, provided the voice of King Arthur in *Quest for Camelot* (1998). If included, it would be ranked ninth. *The World Is Not Enough*, and six other films in which Brosnan starred, have each earned well over $100 million apiece. His Top 10 total now approaches $2 billion.

PIERCING LOOK

Irish-born Pierce Brosnan took over the role of James Bond with GoldenEye. *This, along with* Tomorrow Never Dies *and* The World Is Not Enough, *are the highest earning of all the Bond series.*

RATTLING THE CAGE

Nicolas Cage stars as FBI biochemist Dr. Stanley Godspeed in the 1996 film The Rock, *which is his highest-earning film to date.*

TOP 10 ★ ARNOLD SCHWARZENEGGER FILMS

1	*Terminator 2: Judgment Day*	1991
2	*True Lies*	1994
3	*Total Recall*	1990
4	*Eraser*	1996
5	*Twins*	1988
6	*Kindergarten Cop*	1990
7	*End of Days*	1999
8	*Jingle All the Way*	1996
9	*Last Action Hero*	1993
10	*Junior*	1994

TOP 10 ★ TOM CRUISE FILMS

1	*Mission: Impossible*	1996
2	*Rain Man*	1988
3	*Top Gun*	1986
4	*Jerry Maguire*	1996
5	*The Firm*	1993
6	*A Few Good Men*	1992
7	*Interview With the Vampire*	1994
8	*Days of Thunder*	1990
9	*Eyes Wide Shut*	1999
10	*Cocktail*	1988

TOP 10 MEL GIBSON FILMS

1	*Lethal Weapon 4*	1998
2	*Lethal Weapon 2*	1989
3	*Lethal Weapon 3*	1992
4	*Braveheart**	1995
5	*Ransom*	1996
6	*Payback*	1999
7	*Conspiracy Theory*	1997
8	*Forever Young*	1992
9	*Maverick*	1994
10	*Bird on a Wire*	1990

* *Academy Award for "Best Director"*

Mel Gibson also provided the voice of John Smith in *Pocahontas* (1995) and appeared uncredited as himself in *Casper* (1995). If included, these would enter in first and third positions respectively. Nine out of Gibson's Top 10 films have earned more than $100 million each at the worldwide box office.

TOP 10 BRAD PITT FILMS

1	*Se7en*	1995
2	*Interview With the Vampire*	1994
3	*Sleepers*	1996
4	*Legends of the Fall*	1994
5	*Twelve Monkeys*	1995
6	*The Devil's Own*	1997
7	*Seven Years in Tibet*	1997
8	*Meet Joe Black*	1998
9	*Fight Club*	1999
10	*Thelma & Louise*	1991

PITT STOPPER

Brad (William Bradley) Pitt plays Detective David Mills in Se7en, *his most successful film to date. Pitt appeared in more than 20 films during the 1990s.*

TOP 10 JACK NICHOLSON FILMS

1	*Batman*	1989
2	*A Few Good Men*	1992
3	*As Good As It Gets**	1997
4	*Terms of Endearment*#	1983
5	*Wolf*	1994
6	*One Flew Over the Cuckoo's Nest**	1975
7	*Mars Attacks!*	1996
8	*The Witches of Eastwick*	1987
9	*The Shining*	1980
10	*Broadcast News*	1987

* *Academy Award for "Best Actor"*

Academy Award for "Best Supporting Actor"

TOP 10 TOM HANKS FILMS

1	*Forrest Gump**	1994
2	*Saving Private Ryan*	1998
3	*Apollo 13*	1995
4	*Sleepless in Seattle*	1993
5	*Philadelphia**	1993
6	*You've Got M@il*	1998
7	*The Green Mile*	1999
8	*Big*	1988
9	*A League of Their Own*	1992
10	*Turner & Hooch*	1989

* *Academy Award for "Best Actor"*

Tom Hanks also appeared in a voice-only part as Woody in *Toy Story 2* (1999) and *Toy Story* (1995). If included, these would be ranked third and fourth.

TOP 10 JOHN TRAVOLTA FILMS

1	*Look Who's Talking*	1989
2	*Face/Off*	1997
3	*Pulp Fiction*	1994
4	*Grease*	1978
5	*The General's Daughter*	1999
6	*Phenomenon*	1996
7	*Saturday Night Fever**	1977
8	*The Thin Red Line*	1998
9	*Get Shorty*	1995
10	*Broken Arrow*	1996

* *Nominated for Academy Award for "Best Actor"*

TOP 10 JOHNNY DEPP FILMS

1 ***Platoon***, 1986 2 ***Donnie Brasco***, 1997 3 ***Sleepy Hollow***, 1999 4 ***Edward Scissorhands***, 1990 5 ***Don Juan DeMarco***, 1995 6 ***Freddy's Dead: The Final Nightmare****, 1991 7 ***A Nightmare on Elm Street***, 1984 8 ***The Astronaut's Wife***, 1999 9 ***Fear and Loathing in Las Vegas***, 1998 10 ***What's Eating Gilbert Grape***, 1993

* *Uncredited appearance*

TOP 10 DENZEL WASHINGTON FILMS

1 ***Philadelphia***, 1993 2 ***The Pelican Brief***, 1993 3 ***Crimson Tide***, 1995 4 ***The Siege***, 1998 5 ***Courage Under Fire***, 1996 6 ***The Bone Collector***, 1999 7 ***The Preacher's Wife***, 1996 8 ***Malcolm X***, 1992 9 ***The Hurricane***, 1999 10 ***Virtuosity***, 1995

What are the characters in *Reservoir Dogs* named after?
see p.179 for the answer

A Dogs
B Colours
C Planets

RYAN'S DAUGHTER

Born Margaret Mary Emily Anne Hyra, Meg Ryan took her mother's maiden name before her film debut in 1981. She has gone on to enjoy huge success in a range of romantic comedies.

TOP 10 MICHELLE PFEIFFER FILMS

1	*Batman Returns*	1992
2	*Dangerous Minds*	1995
3	*Wolf*	1994
4	*Up Close & Personal*	1996
5	*One Fine Day*	1996
6	*The Witches of Eastwick*	1987
7	*Tequila Sunrise*	1988
8	*Scarface*	1983
9	*Dangerous Liaisons*	1988
10	*The Age of Innocence*	1993

Michelle Pfeiffer also provided the voice of Tzipporah in the animated film *The Prince of Egypt* (1998). If this was included in her Top 10, it would feature in second place.

TOP 10 MEG RYAN FILMS

1	*Top Gun*	1986
2	*You've Got M@il*	1998
4	*Sleepless in Seattle*	1993
5	*City of Angels*	1998
5	*French Kiss*	1995
6	*Courage Under Fire*	1996
7	*When Harry Met Sally*	1989
8	*Addicted to Love*	1997
9	*When a Man Loves a Woman*	1994
10	*Joe Versus the Volcano*	1990

Meg Ryan provided the voice of Anastasia in the 1997 film of that title. If included, it would appear in ninth place.

TOP 10 RENE RUSSO FILMS

1	*Lethal Weapon 3*	1992
2	*Ransom*	1996
3	*Lethal Weapon 4*	1998
4	*Outbreak*	1995
5	*In the Line of Fire*	1993
6	*The Thomas Crown Affair*	1999
7	*Get Shorty*	1995
8	*Tin Cup*	1996
9	*Major League II*	1994
10	*Major League*	1989

TOP 10 NICOLE KIDMAN FILMS

1. *Batman Forever*, 1995 2. *Days of Thunder*, 1990 3. *Eyes Wide Shut*, 1999 4. *The Peacemaker*, 1997 5. *Practical Magic*, 1998 6. *Far and Away*, 1992 7. *Malice*, 1993 8. *To Die For*, 1995 9. *My Life*, 1993 10. *Portrait of a Lady*, 1996

TOP 10 SHARON STONE FILMS

1	*Basic Instinct*	1992
2	*Total Recall*	1990
3	*The Specialist*	1995
4	*Last Action Hero*	1993
5	*Sliver*	1993
6	*Sphere*	1998
7	*Casino**	1995
8	*Diabolique*	1996
9	*Police Academy 4: Citizens on Patrol*	1987
10	*Intersection*	1994

** Academy Award nomination for "Best Actress"*

Sharon Stone's part in *Last Action Hero* amounted to no more than a brief cameo. If it was discounted, *Action Jackson* (1988) would occupy 10th place.

CATWOMAN

Batman Returns *is Michelle Pfeiffer's most successful film to date, but half the films in her Top 10 have earned a healthy $100 million-plus.*

PRETTY WOMAN

Former model Julia Roberts, shown here in My Best Friend's Wedding, *became the first Hollywood actress to be paid $10 million (for her role in the 1996 film* Mary Reilly*). She now commands almost $20 million.*

TOP 10

WINONA RYDER FILMS

1	*Bram Stoker's Dracula*	1992
2	*Alien: Resurrection*	1997
3	*Edward Scissorhands*	1990
4	*Beetlejuice*	1988
5	*Little Women*	1994
6	*Mermaids*	1990
7	*The Age of Innocence*	1993
8	*How to Make an American Quilt*	1995
9	*Reality Bites*	1994
10	*The Crucible*	1996

TOP 10 GWYNETH PALTROW FILMS

❶ *Se7en*, 1995 ❷ *Hook*, 1991 ❸ *Shakespeare in Love**, 1998 ❹ *A Perfect Murder*, 1998 ❺ *The Talented Mr. Ripley*, 1999 ❻ *Sliding Doors*, 1998 ❼ *Great Expectations*, 1998 ❽ *Malice*, 1993 ❾ *Emma*, 1996 ❿ *Hush*, 1998

* Academy Award for "Best Actress"

TOP 10

DEMI MOORE FILMS

1	*Ghost*	1990
2	*Indecent Proposal*	1993
3	*A Few Good Men*	1992
4	*Disclosure*	1995
5	*Striptease*	1996
6	*G.I. Jane*	1997
7	*The Juror*	1996
8	*About Last Night...*	1986
9	*St. Elmo's Fire*	1985
10	*Young Doctors in Love*	1982

Demi Moore provided the voice of Esmeralda in *The Hunchback of Notre Dame* (1996). If included in her Top 10, it would be in second place.

TOP 10

JULIA ROBERTS FILMS

1	*Pretty Woman**	1990
2	*Notting Hill*	1999
3	*Hook*	1991
4	*My Best Friend's Wedding*	1997
5	*Runaway Bride*	1999
6	*The Pelican Brief*	1993
7	*Sleeping With the Enemy*	1991
8	*Stepmom*	1998
9	*Conspiracy Theory*	1997
10	*Steel Magnolias*#	1989

* Academy Award nomination for "Best Actress"

Academy Award nomination for "Best Supporting Actress"

Julia Roberts also appeared in a cameo role as herself in *The Player* (1992), which just failed to make her personal Top 10.

TOP 10

DREW BARRYMORE FILMS

1	*E.T.: The Extra-Terrestrial*	1982
2	*Batman Forever*	1995
3	*Scream*	1996
4	*The Wedding Singer*	1998
5	*Never Been Kissed*	1999
6	*Ever After*	1998
7	*Wayne's World 2*	1993
8	*Everyone Says I Love You*	1996
9	*Boys on the Side*	1995
10	*Mad Love*	1995

TOP 10

GEENA DAVIS FILMS

1	*Tootsie*	1982
2	*Stuart Little*	1999
3	*A League of Their Own*	1992
4	*The Long Kiss Goodnight*	1996
5	*Beetlejuice*	1988
6	*Hero*	1992
7	*Fletch*	1985
8	*Thelma & Louise*	1991
9	*The Fly*	1986
10	*The Accidental Tourist*	1988

TOP 10

UMA THURMAN FILMS

1	*Batman & Robin*	1997
2	*Pulp Fiction*	1994
3	*The Truth About Cats & Dogs*	1996
4	*The Avengers*	1998
5	*Dangerous Liaisons*	1988
6	*Final Analysis*	1992
7	*Beautiful Girls*	1996
8	*Les Misérables*	1988
9	*Johnny Be Good*	1997
10	*Gattaca*	1998

In which film remake did Pierce Brosnan star in the title role?
see p.174 for the answer

A *Bullitt*
B *The Thomas Crown Affair*
C *Papillon*

Character Actors

TOP 10 KEVIN SPACEY FILMS

1	*Se7en*	1995
2	*Outbreak*	1995
3	*A Time to Kill*	1996
4	*American Beauty*	1999
5	*L.A. Confidential*	1997
6	*The Negotiator*	1998
7	*The Usual Suspects*	1995
8	*See No Evil, Hear No Evil*	1989
9	*Heartburn*	1986
10	*Midnight in the Garden of Good and Evil*	1997

TOP 10 JAMES CAAN FILMS

❶ ***The Godfather***, 1972 ❷ ***Eraser***, 1996 ❸ ***Dick Tracy***, 1990 ❹ ***The Godfather Part III***, 1990 ❺ ***The Godfather Part II***, 1974 ❻ ***Misery***, 1990 ❼ ***Mickey Blue Eyes***, 1999 ❽ ***Honeymoon in Vegas***, 1992 ❾ ***Alien Nation***, 1988 ❿ ***The Program***, 1993

TOP 10 MORGAN FREEMAN FILMS

❶ ***Robin Hood: Prince of Thieves***, 1991 ❷ ***Deep Impact***, 1998 ❸ ***Se7en***, 1995 ❹ ***Outbreak***, 1995 ❺ ***Unforgiven***, 1992 ❻ ***Driving Miss Daisy***, 1989 ❼ ***Kiss the Girls***, 1997 ❽ ***Amistad***, 1997 ❾ ***The Shawshank Redemption***, 1994 ❿ ***Chain Reaction***, 1996

TOP 10 KEVIN BACON FILMS

1	*Apollo 13*	1995
2	*A Few Good Men*	1992
3	*JFK*	1991
4	*Sleepers*	1996
5	*Animal House*	1978
6	*The River Wild*	1994
7	*Footloose*	1984
8	*Wild Things*	1998
9	*Flatliners*	1990
10	*Planes, Trains & Automobiles*	1987

STRANGE STEVE

Steve Buscemi has carved out a film career playing quirky roles, such as that of Carl Showalter in the Coen Brothers' Fargo.

TOP 10 STEVE BUSCEMI FILMS

❶ ***Armageddon***, 1998 ❷ ***Big Daddy***, 1999 ❸ ***Con Air***, 1997 ❹ ***Pulp Fiction***, 1994 ❺ ***The Wedding Singer****, 1998 ❻ ***Rising Sun***, 1993 ❼ ***Desperado***, 1995 ❽ ***Fargo***, 1996 ❾ ***Escape from L.A.***, 1996 ❿ ***The Big Lebowski***, 1998

* Uncredited

TOP 10 SAMUEL L. JACKSON FILMS

1	*Star Wars: Episode I – The Phantom Menace*	1999
2	*Jurassic Park*	1993
3	*Die Hard With a Vengeance*	1995
4	*Coming to America*	1988
5	*Pulp Fiction*	1994
6	*Patriot Games*	1992
7	*Deep Blue Sea*	1999
8	*A Time to Kill*	1996
9	*Sea of Love*	1989
10	*Jackie Brown*	1997

ACTION JACKSON

Samuel Jackson received a Silver Bear award at the Berlin Film Festival for his role in Jackie Brown*, one of a series of bad-guy roles.*

TOP 10 TIM ROTH FILMS

❶ *Pulp Fiction*, 1994 ❷ *Rob Roy*, 1995 ❸ *Everyone Says I Love You*, 1996 ❹ *Hoodlum*, 1997 ❺ *Reservoir Dogs*, 1992 ❺ *The Cook, the Thief, His Wife & Her Lover*, 1989 ❻ *Gridlock'd*, 1997 ❼ *Four Rooms*, 1995 ❽ *A World Apart*, 1988 ❿ *Vincent & Theo*, 1990

"LET'S GO TO WORK ..."

British actor Tim Roth (second from right) appeared as Mr. Orange in writer–director Quentin Tarantino's cult debut, the violent gangster film Reservoir Dogs.

TOP 10 JOHN MALKOVICH FILMS

1	*In the Line of Fire*	1993
2	*The Man in the Iron Mask*	1998
3	*The Messenger: The Story of Joan of Arc*	1999
4	*Dangerous Liaisons*	1988
5	*Places in the Heart*	1984
6	*The Killing Fields*	1984
7	*Rounders*	1998
8	*Being John Malkovich*	1999
9	*Con Air*	1997
10	*Empire of the Sun*	1987

Although uncredited, John Malkovich was the narrator of the film *Alive* (1993). If included, this would be in fourth place. *Being John Malkovich* (1999), in which a puppeteer enters the mind of the actor, is a newcomer to his personal Top 10.

TOP 10 HARVEY KEITEL FILMS

❶ *Sister Act*, 1992 ❷ *Pulp Fiction*, 1994 ❸ *Get Shorty**, 1995 ❹ *Cop Land*, 1997 ❺ *Rising Sun*, 1993 ❻ *From Dusk Till Dawn*, 1996 ❼ *Bugsy*, 1991 ❽ *Thelma & Louise*, 1991 ❾ *The Piano*, 1993 ❿ *The Assassin*, 1993

* *Uncredited cameo*

TOP 10 JOE PESCI FILMS

1	*Home Alone*	1990
2	*Lethal Weapon 3*	1992
3	*Lethal Weapon 4*	1998
4	*Home Alone 2: Lost in New York*	1992
5	*Lethal Weapon 2*	1989
6	*JFK*	1991
7	*Casino*	1995
8	*My Cousin Vinny*	1992
9	*GoodFellas*	1990
10	*Raging Bull*	1980

TOP 10 GARY BUSEY FILMS

1	*The Firm*	1993
2	*Under Siege*	1992
3	*Lethal Weapon*	1987
4	*Rookie of the Year*	1993
5	*Point Break*	1991
6	*Black Sheep*	1996
7	*Predator 2*	1990
8	*Drop Zone*	1994
9	*The Player*	1992
10	*Soldier*	1998

Did You Know? *Reservoir Dogs* (1992) is not the first film in which the gangsters use colours as names: *The Taking of Pelham 123* (1974) has characters called Blue, Green, Grey, and Brown.

Character Actresses

FAMILY JEWEL

A member of the Fonda film family (daughter of Peter, granddaughter of Henry, niece of Jane) Bridget Fonda – shown here in Jackie Brown *– has built a successful film career since her 1982 debut.*

TOP 10 ★ BRIDGET FONDA FILMS

1	*The Godfather Part III*	1990
2	*Jackie Brown*	1997
3	*The Road to Wellville*	1994
4	*Doc Hollywood*	1991
5	*Single White Female*	1992
6	*It Could Happen to You*	1994
7	*City Hall*	1996
8	*Lake Placid*	1999
9	*The Assassin*	1993
10	*Singles*	1992

TOP 10 ★ ALFRE WOODARD FILMS

1	*Star Trek: First Contact*	1996
2	*Primal Fear*	1996
3	*Scrooged*	1988
4	*Grand Canyon*	1991
5	*How to Make an American Quilt*	1995
6	*Blue Chips*	1994
7	*Heart and Souls*	1993
8	*Crooklyn*	1994
9	*Extremities*	1986
10	*Down in the Delta*	1998

TOP 10 ★ CATHERINE KEENER FILMS

1	*8MM*	1999
2	*Out of Sight*	1998
3	*About Last Night...*	1986
4	*Being John Malkovich*	1999
5	*Switch*	1991
6	*Your Friends & Neighbors*	1998
7	*The Gun in Betty Lou's Handbag*	1992
8	*Walking and Talking*	1996
9	*Living in Oblivion*	1995
10	*Box of Moonlight*	1996

TOP 10 ★ FRANCES McDORMAND FILMS

1	*Primal Fear*	1996
2	*Fargo**	1996
3	*Madeline*	1998
4	*Mississippi Burning*	1988
5	*Darkman*	1990
6	*Raising Arizona*	1987
7	*Lone Star*	1996
8	*Beyond Rangoon*	1995
9	*The Butcher's Wife*	1991
10	*Short Cuts*	1993

* *Academy Award for "Best Actress"*

TOP 10 JENNIFER JASON LEIGH FILMS

❶ *Backdraft*, 1991 ❷ *Single White Female*, 1992 ❸ *Dolores Claiborne*, 1995 ❹ *Miami Blues*, 1990 ❺ *A Thousand Acres*, 1997 ❻ *Rush*, 1991 ❼ *Short Cuts*, 1993 ❽ *Georgia*, 1995 ❾ *The Hudsucker Proxy*, 1994 ❿ *eXistenZ*, 1999

TOP 10 JULIE KAVNER FILMS

1	*Forget Paris*	1995
2	*Awakenings*	1990
3	*Hannah and Her Sisters*	1986
4	*Radio Days*	1987
5	*Deconstructing Harry*	1997
6	*New York Stories*	1989
7	*I'll Do Anything*	1994
8	*Alice*	1990
9	*Surrender*	1987
10	*This Is My Life*	1992

Although an actress with a number of films to her credit, Julie Kavner is best known for providing the voice of Marge Simpson and other characters in the TV series *The Simpsons*. She was also the voice of a pigeon in *Doctor Dolittle* (1998).

TOP 10 EMMA THOMPSON FILMS

1	*Sense and Sensibility*	1995
2	*Junior*	1994
3	*Primary Colors*	1998
4	*Dead Again*	1991
5	*Howards End**	1992
6	*In the Name of the Father*#	1993
7	*The Remains of the Day*#	1993
8	*Much Ado About Nothing*	1993
9	*Henry V*	1989
10=	*Impromptu*	1991
=	*Peter's Friends*	1992

* Academy Award for "Best Actress"
\# Academy Award nomination

TOP 10 MARY-LOUISE PARKER FILMS

❶ *The Client*, 1994 ❷ *Fried Green Tomatoes at the Whistle Stop Cafe*, 1991 ❸ *Boys on the Side*, 1995 ❹ *Grand Canyon*, 1991 ❺ *Portrait of a Lady*, 1996 ❻ *Bullets Over Broadway*, 1994 ❼ *Longtime Companion*, 1990 ❽ *Mr. Wonderful*, 1993 ❾ *Goodbye Lover*, 1999 ❿ *Naked in New York*, 1994

DRIVEN MAD

Kathy Bates has appeared in diverse roles from the psychotic Annie Wilkes in Stephen King's Misery *to "Unsinkable" Molly Brown in* Titanic *– her most successful film.*

FIRM FAVOURITE

Star of mainstream films including The Firm, *Holly Hunter has also taken on offbeat parts such as those in* The Piano *and* Crash.

TOP 10 HOLLY HUNTER FILMS

1	*The Firm**	1993
2	*Copycat*	1995
3	*Always*	1989
4	*Broadcast News*	1987
5	*The Piano*#	1993
6	*Raising Arizona*	1987
7	*Crash*	1996
8	*Home for the Holidays*	1995
9	*Once Around*	1991
10	*Living Out Loud*	1998

* Academy Award nomination
\# Academy Award for "Best Actress"

TOP 10 KATHY BATES FILMS

1	*Titanic*	1997
2	*The Waterboy*	1998
3	*Dick Tracy*	1990
4	*Fried Green Tomatoes at the Whistle Stop Cafe*	1991
5	*A Civil Action**	1998
6	*Misery*	1990
7	*Diabolique*	1996
8	*Dolores Claiborne*	1995
9	*Primary Colors*	1998
10	*The Morning After*	1986

* Uncredited

Which cartoon character made his film debut in 1938?
see p.187 for the answer
A Bugs Bunny
B Popeye
C Yogi Bear

The Directors

TOP 10 FILMS DIRECTED BY ACTORS

	FILM/YEAR	DIRECTOR
1	*Pretty Woman*, 1990	Garry Marshall
2	*Dances With Wolves*, 1990	Kevin Costner
3	*The Bodyguard*, 1992	Kevin Costner
4	*Apollo 13*, 1995	Ron Howard
5	*Ransom*, 1996	Ron Howard
6	*Rocky IV*, 1985	Sylvester Stallone
7	*Doctor Dolittle*, 1998	Betty Thomas
8	*Runaway Bride*, 1999	Garry Marshall
9	*Waterworld*, 1995	Kevin Costner
10	*A Few Good Men*, 1992	Rob Reiner

The role of actor–director has a long cinema tradition, numbering such luminaries as Charlie Chaplin, Buster Keaton, Orson Welles, and John Huston among its ranks. Heading this list, *Pretty Woman* director Garry Marshall is the brother of actress–director Penny Marshall.

WOMAN'S WORLD

The laddish comedy Wayne's World *was directed by a woman, Penelope Spheeris, who also directed* The Beverly Hillbillies *(1993) and* The Little Rascals *(1994).*

TOP 10 FILMS DIRECTED BY WOMEN

	FILM/YEAR	DIRECTOR
1	*Look Who's Talking*, 1989	Amy Heckerling
2	*Doctor Dolittle*, 1998	Betty Thomas
3	*Sleepless in Seattle*, 1993	Nora Ephron
4	*The birdcage*, 1996	Elaine May
5	*You've Got M@il*, 1998	Nora Ephron
6	*Wayne's World*, 1992	Penelope Spheeris
7	*Big*, 1988	Penny Marshall
8	*Michael*, 1996	Nora Ephron
9	*A League of Their Own*, 1992	Penny Marshall
10	*Father of the Bride*, 1991	Nancy Meyers

TOP 10 FILMS DIRECTED BY MARTIN SCORSESE

	FILM	YEAR
1	*Cape Fear*	1991
2	*Casino*	1995
3	*The Color of Money*	1986
4	*GoodFellas*	1990
5	*The Age of Innocence*	1993
6	*Taxi Driver*	1976
7	*Raging Bull*	1980
8	*Bringing Out the Dead*	1999
9	*Alice Doesn't Live Here Anymore*	1975
10	*New York, New York*	1977

RUNAWAY SUCCESS

Actor–director Garry Marshall has achieved outstanding directorial triumphs with box-office smash hits such as Runaway Bride, *in which he appears in an uncredited role.*

TOP 10 FILMS DIRECTED BY STEVEN SPIELBERG

	FILM	YEAR
1	*Jurassic Park*	1993
2	*E.T.: The Extra-Terrestrial*	1982
3	*The Lost World: Jurassic Park*	1997
4	*Indiana Jones and the Last Crusade*	1989
5	*Saving Private Ryan*	1998
6	*Jaws*	1975
7	*Raiders of the Lost Ark*	1981
8	*Indiana Jones and the Temple of Doom*	1984
9	*Schindler's List*	1993
10	*Hook*	1991

Steven Spielberg has directed some of the most successful films of all time: the top five in this list appear among the top 20 films of all time, while the cumulative world box-office gross of his Top 10 amounts to over $5 billion. If his credits as producer are included, further blockbusters, such as *Deep Impact*, *The Mask of Zorro*, *Men in Black*, *The Flintstones*, *Casper*, *Twister*, the *Back to the Future* trilogy, *Gremlins*, *Poltergeist* (which he also wrote), the animated film *An American Tail*, and the part-animated *Who Framed Roger Rabbit* would all score highly.

Did You Know? Hollywood director D. W. Griffith (1875–1948) is considered the most prolific director of all time, with a remarkable 545 films credited to him in the period 1908–36, spanning both the silent and talkie eras.

TOP 10 FILMS DIRECTED BY FRANCIS FORD COPPOLA

1	*The Godfather*	1972
2	*Bram Stoker's Dracula*	1992
3	*The Godfather Part III*	1990
4	*The Godfather Part II*	1974
5	*Jack*	1996
6	*Apocalypse Now*	1979
7	*The Rainmaker*	1997
8	*Peggy Sue Got Married*	1986
9	*The Cotton Club*	1984
10	*The Outsiders*	1983

TOP 10 FILMS DIRECTED BY STANLEY KUBRICK

1	*Eyes Wide Shut*	1999
2	*The Shining*	1980
3	*2001: A Space Odyssey*	1968
4	*Full Metal Jacket*	1987
5	*A Clockwork Orange*	1971
6	*Spartacus*	1960
7	*Barry Lyndon*	1975
8	*Dr. Strangelove or: How I Learned to Stop Worrying and Love the Bomb*	1964
9	*Lolita*	1962
10	*Paths of Glory*	1957

TOP 10 FILMS DIRECTED BY ROBERT ZEMECKIS

❶ *Forrest Gump*, 1994 ❷ *Who Framed Roger Rabbit*, 1988 ❸ *Back to the Future*, 1985 ❹ *Back to the Future Part III*, 1990 ❺ *Back to the Future Part II*, 1989 ❻ *Contact*, 1997 ❼ *Death Becomes Her*, 1992 ❽ *Romancing the Stone*, 1984 ❾ *The House on Haunted Hill*, 1999 ❿ *Used Cars*, 1980

TOP 10 FILMS DIRECTED OR PRODUCED BY GEORGE LUCAS

1	*Star Wars: Episode I – The Phantom Menace* (D/P)	1999
2	*Star Wars* (D)	1977/97
3	*Return of the Jedi* (P)	1983/97
4	*The Empire Strikes Back* (P)	1980/97
5	*Indiana Jones and the Last Crusade* (P)	1989
6	*Raiders of the Lost Ark* (P)	1981
7	*Indiana Jones and the Temple of Doom* (P)	1984
8	*American Graffiti* (D)	1973
9	*Willow* (P)	1988
10	*The Land Before Time* (P)	1988

D = Director; P = Producer

George Lucas made the move from directing to producing after the phenomenal success of *Star Wars*. The first five films on this list rank among the 20 highest-earning films of all time.

TOP 10 FILMS DIRECTED BY JOHN CARPENTER

1	*Halloween*	1978
2	*Escape from L.A.*	1996
3	*Starman*	1984
4	*Escape from New York*	1981
5	*Vampires*	1998
6	*The Fog*	1980
7	*Christine*	1983
8	*Memoirs of an Invisible Man*	1992
9	*Prince of Darkness*	1987
10	*They Live*	1988

GREAT ESCAPES

Kurt Russell stars in Escape from L.A., *the futuristic sequel to* Escape from New York, *both films directed by John Carpenter.*

TOP 10

FILMS WITH THE MOST EXTRAS

	FILM/COUNTRY/YEAR	EXTRAS
1	*Gandhi*, UK, 1982	300,000
2	*Kolberg*, Germany, 1945	187,000
3	*Monster Wang-magwi*, South Korea, 1967	157,000
4	*War and Peace*, USSR, 1967	120,000
5	*Ilya Muromets*, USSR, 1956	106,000
6	*Tonko*, Japan, 1988	100,000
7	*The War of Independence*, Romania, 1912	80,000
8	*Around the World in 80 Days*, USA, 1956	68,894
9	=*Intolerance*, USA, 1916	60,000
	=*Dny Zrady*, Czechoslovakia, 1972	60,000

A CAST OF THOUSANDS

Some 300,000 of Delhi's residents were drafted in as extras on Gandhi for a sequence that occupied just 125 seconds of screen time.

TOP 10 COUNTRIES WITH THE MOST CINEMAS

(Country/cinemas)

1 **China**, 65,000 2 **USA**, 34,186 3 **India**, 12,900 4 **France**, 4,762 5 **Germany**, 4,244 6 **Spain**, 2,968 7 **UK**, 2,638 8 **Italy**, 2,500 9 **Canada**, 2,486 10 **Indonesia**, 2,100

Source: Screen Digest

TOP 10

CINEMA COUNTRIES

	COUNTRY	NO. OF CINEMA SCREENS PER MILLION INHABITANTS
1	Iceland	165.2
2	Sweden	131.3
3	USA	128.3
4	Norway	89.2
5	Australia	86.1
6	Azerbaijan	85.8
7	France	81.1
8	Canada	81.0
9	New Zealand	78.1
10	Switzerland	75.8

Source: Screen Digest

TOP 10

MOST PROLIFIC FILM-PRODUCING COUNTRIES

	COUNTRY	AVERAGE NO. OF FILMS PRODUCED PER ANNUM, 1989–98
1	India	787
2	USA	591
3	Japan	255
4	Philippines	160
5	France	148
6	China	127
7	Russia	124
8	=South Korea	73
	=Thailand	73
10	UK	67

Source: Screen Digest

CHINESE CINEMA-GOERS

Although in relation to its vast population it remains a minor player, China is steadily joining the ranks of the world's foremost makers and watchers of films.

TOP 10 CINEMA-GOING COUNTRIES

(Country/total annual attendance)

1 **India**, 2,860,000,000 2 **USA**, 1,480,700,000 3 **Indonesia**, 222,200,000 4 **France**, 170,110,000 5 **Japan**, 153,100,000 6 **Germany**, 148,880,000 7 **Brazil**, 137,160,000 8 **UK**, 136,500,000 9 **China**, 121,000,000 10 **Italy**, 117,900,000

Source: Screen Digest

TOP 10 COUNTRIES SPENDING THE MOST ON FILM PRODUCTION

(Country/average investment per film in $)

1 **USA**, 14,000,000 2 **UK**, 8,250,000 3 **France**, 5,260,000 4 **Ireland**, 5,140,000 5 **Australia**, 4,370,000 6 **Italy**, 3,930,000 7 **Argentina**, 3,800,000 8 **Japan**, 3,570,000 9 **Spain**, 3,180,000 10 **Canada**, 3,160,000

Source: Screen Digest

TOP 10 COUNTRIES WITH THE BIGGEST INCREASE IN FILM PRODUCTION

(Country/percentage increase in production, 1989–98)

1 **Ireland**, 400.0 2 **Luxembourg**, 200.0 3 **UK**, 117.5 4 **Iceland**, 100.0 5 **New Zealand**, 75.0 6 **Australia**, 72.7 7 **Norway**, 55.6 8 **Venezuela**, 42.9 9 **France**, 33.6 10 = **Austria**, 33.3; = **Brazil**, 33.3

Source: Screen Digest

TOP 10 MOST EXPENSIVE ITEMS OF FILM MEMORABILIA EVER SOLD AT AUCTION

	ITEM/SALE	PRICE (£)*
1	**Vivien Leigh's Oscar for *Gone With the Wind***, Sotheby's, New York, 15 Dec 1993	380,743
2	**Clark Gable's Oscar for *It Happened One Night***, Christie's, Los Angeles, 15 Dec 1996	364,500
3	**Poster for *The Mummy*, 1932**, Sotheby's, New York, 1 Mar 1997	252,109
4	**James Bond's Aston Martin DB5 from *Goldfinger***, Sotheby's, New York, 28 June 1986	179,793
5	**Clark Gable's personal script for *Gone With the Wind***, Christie's, Los Angeles, 15 Dec 1996	146,700
6	**"Rosebud" sled from *Citizen Kane***, Christie's, Los Angeles, 15 Dec 1996	140,000
7	**Herman J. Mankiewicz's scripts for *Citizen Kane* and *The American***, Christie's, New York, 21 June 1989	139,157
8	**Judy Garland's ruby slippers from *The Wizard of Oz***, Christie's, New York, 21 June 1988	104,430
9	**Piano from the Paris scene in *Casablanca***, Sotheby's, New York, 16 Dec 1988	97,469
10	**Charlie Chaplin's hat and cane**, Christie's, London, 11 Dec 1987 (resold at Christie's, London, 17 Dec 1993, for £55,000)	82,500

* *$/£ conversion at rate then prevailing*

TOP 10 LONGEST FILMS EVER SCREENED

	FILM/COUNTRY	YEAR	DURATION HRS	MINS
1	***The Longest and Most Meaningless Movie in the World***, UK	1970	48	0
2	***The Burning of the Red Lotus Temple***, China	1928–31	27	0
3	************, USA	1967	25	0
4	***Heimat***, West Germany	1984	15	40
5	***Berlin Alexanderplatz***, West Germany/Italy	1980	15	21
6	***The Journey***, Sweden	1987	14	33
7	***The Old Testament***, Italy	1922	13	0
8	***Comment Yukong déplace les montagnes***, France	1976	12	43
9	***Out 1: Noli me Tangere***, France	1971	12	40
10	***Ningen No Joken*** *(The Human Condition)*, Japan	1958–60	9	29

The list includes commercially screened films, but not "stunt" films created solely to break endurance records (particularly those of their audiences), among which is the 85-hour *The Cure for Insomnia*.

Which country rents the most videos per household?
see p.194 for the answer
A South Korea
B Mexico
C Iceland

THE 10 ★ FIRST FULL-LENGTH SIMPSONS EPISODES

	EPISODE	FIRST SCREENED
1	*Simpsons Roasting on an Open Fire**	17 Dec 1989
2	*Bart the Genius*	14 Jan 1990
3	*Homer's Odyssey*	21 Jan 1990
4	*There's No Disgrace Like Homer*	28 Jan 1990
5	*Bart the General*	4 Feb 1990
6	*Moaning Lisa*	11 Feb 1990
7	*The Call of the Simpsons*	18 Feb 1990
8	*The Telltale Head*	25 Feb 1990
9	*Life on the Fast Lane*#	18 Mar 1990
10	*Homer's Night Out*	25 Mar 1990

* *a.k.a.* The Simpsons Christmas Special

\# *a.k.a.* Jacques to Be Wild

ON THE COUCH

The infinitely changing couch gag has been an enduring feature of the opening sequence of The Simpsons *– one of the most popular cartoons currently being screened on television.*

TOP 10 ★ ANIMATED FILMS

1	*The Lion King*	1994
2	*Aladdin*	1992
3	*Toy Story 2*	1999
4	*Tarzan*	1999
5	*A Bug's Life*	1998
6	*Toy Story*	1995
7	*Beauty and the Beast*	1991
8	*Who Framed Roger Rabbit**	1988
9	*Pocahontas*	1995
10	*The Hunchback of Notre Dame*	1996

* *Part animated, part live action*

The 1990s provided nine of the 10 most successful animated films of all time, which, in turn, ejected a number of their high-earning predecessors from this Top 10. Animated films stand out among the leading money-makers of each decade: in the 1930s, *Snow White* was the second highest-earning film after *Gone With the Wind*.

THE 10 ★ LATEST OSCAR-WINNING ANIMATED FILMS*

YEAR	FILM	DIRECTOR/COUNTRY
1999	*The Old Man and the Sea*	Aleksandr Petrov, USA
1998	*Bunny*	Chris Wedge, USA
1997	*Geri's Game*	Jan Pinkava, USA
1996	*Quest*	Tyron Montgomery, UK
1995	*A Close Shave*	Nick Park, UK
1994	*Bob's Birthday*	David Fine and Alison Snowden, UK
1993	*The Wrong Trousers*	Nick Park, UK
1992	*Mona Lisa Descending a Staircase*	Joan C. Gratz, USA
1991	*Manipulation*	Daniel Greaves, UK
1990	*Creature Comforts*	Nick Park, UK

* *In the category "Short Subjects (Animated Films)"*

THE 10 ★ FIRST OSCAR-WINNING ANIMATED FILMS*

YEAR	FILM	DIRECTOR#
1932	*Flowers and Trees*	Walt Disney
1934	*The Three Little Pigs*	Walt Disney
1935	*The Tortoise and the Hare*	Walt Disney
1936	*Three Orphan Kittens*	Walt Disney
1937	*The Country Cousin*	Walt Disney
1938	*The Old Mill*	Walt Disney
1939	*Ferdinand the Bull*	Walt Disney
1940	*The Ugly Duckling*	Walt Disney
1941	*The Milky Way*	Rudolf Ising
1942	*Lend a Paw*	Walt Disney

* *In the category "Short Subjects (Cartoons)"*

\# *All from the US*

Oscars were awarded in the category "Short Subjects (Cartoons)" until 1971, when it was altered to "Short Subjects (Animated Films)".

Did You Know? Walt Disney (1901–66) won an unequalled individual total of 26 Oscars and six special Academy Awards for his animated films.

THE 10

FIRST DISNEY ANIMATED FEATURES

1	*Snow White and the Seven Dwarfs*	1937
2	*Pinocchio*	1940
3	*Fantasia*	1940
4	*Dumbo*	1941
5	*Bambi*	1942
6	*Victory Through Air Power*	1943
7	*The Three Caballeros*	1945
8	*Make Mine Music*	1946
9	*Fun and Fancy Free*	1947
10	*Melody Time*	1948

Excluding part-animated films such as *Song of the South* and *Mary Poppins*, and films made specially for television serialization, Disney has made a total of 40 full-length animated feature films up to the end of 1999, when *Fantasia 2000* was released.

TOP 10

PART ANIMATION/PART LIVE-ACTION FILMS

1	*Who Framed Roger Rabbit*	1988
2	*Casper*	1995
3	*Space Jam*	1996
4	*9 to 5*	1980
5	*Mary Poppins*	1964
6	*Small Soldiers*	1999
7	*Song of the South*	1946
8	*James and the Giant Peach*	1976
9	*Pete's Dragon*	1977
10	*Fletch Lives*	1989

With the increasing use of computer animation, the distinction between animation and live action is becoming blurred: even long-dead actors and actresses are now capable of being resurrected on film through sophisticated computer techniques.

THE 10

FIRST BUGS BUNNY CARTOONS

	TITLE	RELEASED
1	*Porky's Hare Hunt*	30 Apr 1938
2	*Hare-um Scare-um*	12 Aug 1939
3	*Elmer's Candid Camera*	2 Mar 1940
4	*A Wild Hare*	27 July 1940
5	*Elmer's Pet Rabbit*	4 Jan 1941
6	*Tortoise Beats Hare*	15 Mar 1941
7	*Hiawatha's Rabbit Hunt*	7 June 1941
8	*The Heckling Hare*	5 July 1941
9	*All This and Rabbit Stew*	13 Sep 1941
10	*Wabbit Twouble*	20 Dec 1941

Bugs Bunny's debut was as a co-star alongside Porky Pig in *Porky's Hare Hunt*. *A Wild Hare* was the first film in which he said the line that became his trademark: "Eh, what's up, Doc?"

TOP 10

NON-DISNEY ANIMATED FEATURE FILMS

1	*The Prince of Egypt*	1998
2	*Antz*	1998
3	*Pokémon the First Movie: Mewtwo Strikes Back*	1999
4	*The Rugrats Movie*	1998
5	*South Park: Bigger, Longer and Uncut*	1999
6	*Pocket Monsters: Revelation Lugia*	1999
7	*The Land Before Time*	1988
8	*An American Tail*	1986
9	*The Lord of the Rings*	1978
10	*All Dogs Go to Heaven*	1989

Such was the success of *Pocket Monsters: Revelation Lugia* in Japan that it earned a place in this list before being released elsewhere.

TOP 10

FIRST TOM AND JERRY CARTOONS

	CARTOON	RELEASE DATE
1	*Puss Gets the Boot**	20 Feb 1940
2	*The Midnight Snack*	19 July 1941
3	*The Night Before Christmas**	6 Dec 1941
4	*Fraidy Cat*	17 Jan 1942
5	*Dog Trouble*	18 Apr 1942
6	*Puss 'N' Toots*	30 May 1942
7	*The Bowling Alley-Cat*	18 July 1942
8	*Fine Feathered Friend*	10 Oct 1942
9	*Sufferin' Cats!*	16 Jan 1943
10	*The Lonesome Mouse*	22 May 1943

* *Academy Award nomination*

CAT AND MOUSE

Tom and Jerry, and their occasional accomplices, have been battling on celluloid for over 60 years. Despite current concern by the politically correct about the level of violence, the cartoons remain firm favourites with children of all ages.

TOP 10

BBC RADIO 1 PROGRAMMES

	SHOW	LISTENERS
1	*Zoë Ball*	6,650,000
2	*Simon Mayo*	6,020,000
3	*Chris Moyles*	5,190,000
4	*Jo Whiley*	4,850,000
5	*Mark Radcliffe*	4,820,000
6	*Dave Pearce* (Mon–Thurs)	3,860,000
7	*UK Top 40*	3,280,000
8	*Chris Moyles* (Saturday)	2,520,000
9	*Mark Goodier* (Saturday)	2,270,000
10	*Mark Goodier Request*	1,990,000

TOP 10

BESTSELLING RADIO COLLECTION CHILDREN'S TITLES

1. *The Lion, the Witch and the Wardrobe*
2. *The Hobbit* (children's version)
3. *Hodgeheg/Martin's Mice*
4. *A Party for Pooh*
5. *Daggie Dogfoot*
6. *Winnie the Pooh*
7. *The House at Pooh Corner*
8. *Fifty Favourite Nursery Rhymes*
9. *Six Adventures of Tintin*
10. *Wallace and Gromit*

Source: *BBC Worldwide*

THE 10

LATEST SONY RADIO AWARDS

YEAR	GOLD AWARD	PERSONALITY/ BROADCASTER OF THE YEAR
1999	Zoë Ball	Tim Hubbard
1998	Chris Evans	Anna Raeburn
1997	Jimmy Young	John Inverdale
1996	Richard Baker	Chris Evans
1995	Alistair Cooke	Neil Fox
1994	Kenny Everett	Henry Kelly
1993	Humphrey Lyttleton	John Peel
1992	Sir James Savile	Danny Baker
1991	Charlie Gillett	James Naughtie
1990	Roy Hudd	Chris Tarrant

TOP 10

BESTSELLING RADIO COLLECTION FICTION AND DRAMA TITLES*

1. *Talking Heads* Vol. 2
2. *Talking Heads* Vol. 1
3. *Captain Corelli's Mandolin*
4. *The Nation's Favourite Poems*
5. *The Murder of Roger Ackroyd*
6. *Murder on the Orient Express*
7. *The Body in the Library*
8. *Woman's Hour Short Stories* Vol. 2
9. *Under Milk Wood*
10. *The Clothes They Stood Up In*

* *Tapes, unless otherwise stated*

Source: *BBC Worldwide*

TOP 10

BESTSELLING RADIO COLLECTION COMEDY TITLES

1. *I'm Sorry I Haven't a Clue* Vol. 4
2. *Hancock's Half Hour* Vol. 10
3. *The Goon Show and Guests* Vol. 16
4. *I'm Sorry I Haven't a Clue* Vol. 1
5. *Hancock's Happy Christmas*
6. *The Goons at Christmas* Vol. 15
7. *Dad's Army* Vol. 9: *A Man of Action*
8. *Hancock: A Celebration*
9. *Only Fools and Horses*
10. *Dad's Army* Vol. 1: *A Jumbo Sized Problem*

Source: *BBC Worldwide*

TOP 10

RADIO STATIONS IN THE UK, 1999

	STATION	LISTENER HOURS*
1	BBC Radio 2	120,495,000
2	BBC Radio 1	104,655,000
3	BBC Radio 4	104,194,000
4	BBC Radio 5 Live	41,450,000
5	Classic FM	40,400,000
6	Capital Radio London (excl. XFM)	37,433,000
7	95.8 Capital FM	27,963,000
8	Virgin Radio (am)	21,405,000
9	Talk Radio 1053/1089 am	14,373,000
10	BBC Radio 3	12,185,000

* *Total number of hours spent by all adults (over 15) listening to the station in an average week, July to Sep 1999*

Source: *RAJAR*

Background image: **EKCO RADIO MODEL AD 65, 1932–34**

TOP 10 RADIO-OWNING COUNTRIES

	COUNTRY	RADIO SETS PER 1,000 POPULATION
1	USA	2,115
2	UK	1,445
3	=Australia	1,385
	=Finland	1,385
5	Denmark	1,146
6	Canada	1,078
7	South Korea	1,037
8	New Zealand	1,027
9	Monaco	1,021
10	Switzerland	969

Source: *UNESCO*

The top nine countries in this list have at least one radio per person. In addition, many small island communities have very high numbers of radios, which enable their small populations to maintain regular contact with the outside world.

TOP 10 LONGEST-RUNNING PROGRAMMES ON BBC RADIO

	PROGRAMME	FIRST BROADCAST
1	*The Week's Good Cause*	24 Jan 1926
2	*The Shipping Forecast*	26 Jan 1926
3	*Choral Evensong*	7 Oct 1926
4	*Daily Service*	2 Jan 1928*
5	*The Week in Westminster*	6 Nov 1929
6	*Sunday Half Hour*	14 July 1940
7	*Desert Island Discs*	29 Jan 1942
8	*Saturday Night Theatre*	3 Apr 1943
9	*Composer of the Week*#	2 Aug 1943
10	*Letter from America*+	24 Mar 1946

* *Experimental broadcast; national transmission began December 1929*

\# *Formerly* This Week's Composer

\+ *Formerly* American Letter

A pilot for *The Archers* was broadcast in the Midland region for a one-week trial from 29 May 1950, but the serial began its national run on 1 January 1951.

SNAPSHOTS

RADIO FOR ALL

London inventor Trevor Bayliss, a former international swimmer and swimming-pool salesman, was inspired to develop his clockwork radio after seeing a television programme about communication problems in Africa. After the necessary financial backing had been secured, his Freeplay® wind-up radio went into production in Cape Town, South Africa, in 1994, and is now available worldwide. Its simple operating mechanism – a coil spring that drives a dynamo, providing 40 minutes of play time, with optional solar cells – is a perfect solution for radio communication in communities without electricity and where batteries are expensive.

Top TV

TOP 10 ★

BBC 1 AUDIENCES, 1999

	PROGRAMME*	DATE	AUDIENCE
1	*EastEnders*	7 Jan	15,717,000
2	*Walking With Dinosaurs*	4 Oct	14,998,000
3	*The Vicar of Dibley*	27 Dec	14,368,000
4	*Casualty*	13 Feb	13,089,000
5	*EastEnders Special*	14 Feb	12,967,000
6	*Mission: Impossible* (film)	26 Dec	12,799,000
7	*Before They Were Famous*	25 Dec	12,251,000
8	*Total Eclipse*	10 Aug	12,187,000
9	*Ground Force*	5 Mar	11,985,000
10	*Changing Rooms Christmas Special*	27 Dec	11,877,000

* *The highest-rated episode only of series shown*

Source: BARB/SPC

TOP 10 ★

ITV AUDIENCES, 1999

	PROGRAMME*	DATE	AUDIENCE#
1	*Coronation Street*	7 Mar	19,817,000
2	*Who Wants to Be a Millionaire?*	7 Mar	19,208,000
3	Champion's League Final: Man. United v Bayern Munich	26 May	18,800,000
4	Euro 2000 Play-off: England v Scotland	17 Nov	17,600,000
5	*Heartbeat*	28 Feb	17,006,000
6	*A Touch of Frost*	26 May	16,849,000
7	*New You've Been Framed*	7 Nov	13,904,000
8	*Emmerdale*	20 Jan	13,352,000
9	*GoldenEye* (film)	10 Mar	13,229,000
10=	Champions League: Manchester United v Inter Milan	3 Mar	13,200,000
=	Champions League: Manchester United v Juventus	21 Apr	13,200,000

* *The highest-rated episode only of series shown*
# *Peak figures given for sports events*

Source: BARB/SPC

TOP 10 ★

CHANNEL 4 AUDIENCES, 1999

	PROGRAMME*	DATE	AUDIENCE
1	*Friends*	9 July	5,808,000
2	*Merlin* (film)	4 Apr	5,372,000
3	*Countdown*	14 Jan	4,795,000
4	*Four Weddings and a Funeral* (film)	30 May	4,570,000
5	*Michael* (film)	12 Dec	4,439,000
6	*Geri*	5 May	4,375,000
7	*Brassed Off* (film)	25 Oct	4,335,000
8	*The Coroner*	16 Feb	4,113,000
9	*Brookside*	21 Dec	3,992,000
10	*The Real Story of Airtours Air Rage*	24 Feb	3,974,000

* *The highest-rated episode only of series shown*

Source: BARB/SPC

TOP 10 ★

TELEVISION-WATCHING COUNTRIES

	COUNTRY	AVERAGE DAILY VIEWING TIME HOURS	MINS
1	USA	3	58
2	Greece	3	39
3=	Italy	3	36
=	UK	3	36
5	Spain	3	31
6=	Canada	3	14
=	Ireland	3	14
8	Germany	3	8
9	France	3	7
10	Belgium	2	57

Source: Screen Digest

A survey of television-viewing habits in Western Europe and North America showed that the number of channels, including new digital channels, is proliferating at a much faster rate than the time spent actually watching them, thus creating, in the jargon of the industry, "audience fragmentation". Viewers in the US watch, on average, 23 per cent more than those in Europe, but this figure is decreasing by about half a per cent per annum.

TOP 10 ★

CARTOONS ON UK TELEVISION WATCHED BY THE MOST CHILDREN, 1999

	CARTOON	CHANNEL	AUDIENCE*
1	*The Mask*	BBC 1	1,429,000
2	*Gadget Boy*	BBC 1	1,341,000
3	*Chipmunks*	BBC 1	1,304,000
4	*Hey Arnold*	ITV	1,163,000
5	*Rugrats*	BBC 1	1,154,000
6	*Pokémon*	ITV	1,131,000
7	*Aladdin*	ITV	1,058,000
8	*Chipmunks at the Movies*	BBC 1	1,024,000
9=	*Cartoon Critters*	BBC 2	1,013,000
=	*Rotten Ralph*	BBC 1	1,013,000

* *Children only*

Source: BARB/SPC

TOP 10 ★

CHILDREN'S PROGRAMMES ON BRITISH TELEVISION, 1999

	PROGRAMME*	DATE	AUDIENCE
1	*Blue Peter*	20 Dec	1,532,000
2	*Smart*	24 Dec	1,452,000
3	*The Mask*	24 Dec	1,429,000
4	*Newsround*	20 Dec	1,411,000
5	*Pig Heart Boy*	21 Dec	1,390,000
6	*The Worst Witch*	28 Jan	1,384,000
7	*Tweenies*	24 Dec	1,375,000
8	*Insides Out*	20 Oct	1,372,000
9	*My Parents Are Aliens*	6 Dec	1,363,000
10	*Gadget Boy*	24 Dec	1,341,000

* *The highest-rated episode only of series shown*

Source: BARB/SPC

Did You Know? The funeral of Diana, Princess of Wales, on 6 September 1997, attracted the biggest television audience of all time, with an estimated 2.5 billion viewers worldwide.

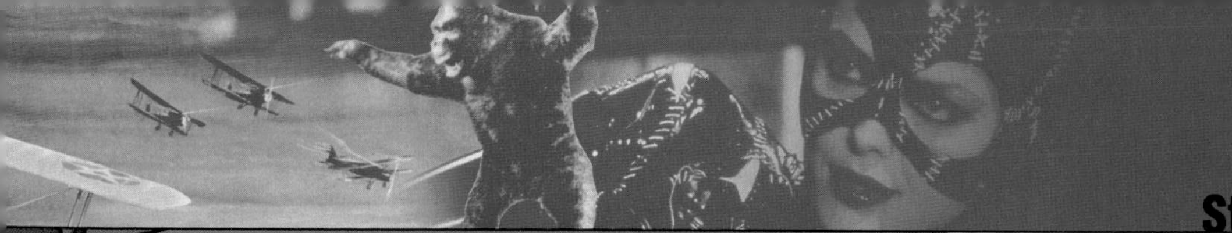

TOP 10 TELEVISION AUDIENCES OF ALL TIME IN THE UK

	PROGRAMME	DATE	AUDIENCE
1	Royal Wedding of HRH Prince Charles to Lady Diana Spencer	29 July 1981	39,000,000
2	1970 World Cup: Brazil v England	10 June 1970	32,500,000
3	=1966 World Cup Final: England v West Germany	30 July 1966	32,000,000
	=Cup Final Replay: Chelsea v Leeds	28 Apr 1970	32,000,000
5	Funeral of Diana, Princess of Wales	6 Sep 1997	31,000,000
6	*EastEnders* Christmas episode	26 Dec 1987	30,000,000
7	*Morecambe and Wise Christmas Show*	25 Dec 1977	28,000,000
8	=World Heavyweight Boxing Championship: Joe Frazier v Muhammad Ali	8 Mar 1971	27,000,000
	=*Dallas*	22 Nov 1980	27,000,000
10	*Only Fools and Horses*	29 Dec 1996	24,350,000

The 22 November 1980 screening of *Dallas* was the most watched because it was the episode that revealed who shot J. R. Ewing. The most-watched film of all time on British television is *Live and Let Die*. Although already seven years old when it was first broadcast on 20 January 1980, it attracted an audience of 23,500,000.

TOP 10 TV PROGRAMMES OF THE 1990s IN THE UK

	PROGRAMME	CHANNEL	BROADCAST	AUDIENCE
1	*Only Fools and Horses*	BBC 1	29 Dec 1996	24,350,000
2	*Panorama* (Diana, Princess of Wales interview)	BBC 1	20 Nov 1995	22,750,000
3	*Only Fools and Horses*	BBC 1	27 Dec 1996	21,350,000
4	*Only Fools and Horses*	BBC 1	25 Dec 1996	21,300,000
5	*Coronation Street*	ITV	22 Mar 1993	20,750,000
6	*Olympic Ice Dancing* (Torvill and Dean)	BBC 1	21 Feb 1994	20,650,000
7	*Coronation Street*	ITV	6 Jan 1993	20,500,000
8	=*Coronation Street*	ITV	25 Nov 1991	20,450,000
	=*Coronation Street*	ITV	22 Jan 1992	20,450,000
10	*Coronation Street*	ITV	11 Jan 1993	20,400,000

Source: *Royal Television Society*

RAT RACE

After attracting a huge following as a television series, Rugrats *was developed into a film –* The Rugrats Movie *– by Nickelodeon Pictures; it became a box-office smash.*

THE 10 ★ LATEST RECIPIENTS OF THE MTV US "VIEWER'S CHOICE" AWARD

YEAR	ARTIST OR GROUP/TITLE
1999	Backstreet Boys, *I Want It That Way*
1998	Puff Daddy & the Family, featuring the Lox, Lil' Kim, the Notorious B.I.G. and fuzzbubble, *It's All About the Benjamins* (Rock Remix)
1997	Prodigy, *Breathe*
1996	Bush, *Glycerine*
1995	TLC, *Waterfalls*
1994	Aerosmith, *Cryin'*
1993	Aerosmith, *Livin' on the Edge*
1992	Red Hot Chili Peppers, *Under the Bridge*
1991	Queensryche, *Silent Lucidity*
1990	Aerosmith, *Janie's Got a Gun*

THE 10 ★ LATEST RECIPIENTS OF THE MTV "BEST VIDEO" AWARD

YEAR	ARTIST OR GROUP/TITLE
1999	Lauryn Hill, *Doo Wop (That Thing)*
1998	Madonna, *Ray of Light*
1997	Jamiroquai, *Virtual Insanity*
1996	The Smashing Pumpkins, *Tonight, Tonight*
1995	TLC, *Waterfalls*
1994	Aerosmith, *Cryin'*
1993	Pearl Jam, *Jeremy*
1992	Van Halen, *Right Now*
1991	R.E.M., *Losing My Religion*
1990	Sinead O'Connor, *Nothing Compares 2 U*

THE 10 ★ LATEST RECIPIENTS OF THE MTV "BEST GROUP VIDEO" AWARD

YEAR	ARTIST OR GROUP/TITLE
1999	TLC, *No Scrubs*
1998	Backstreet Boys, *Everybody (Backstreet's Back)*
1997	No Doubt, *Don't Speak*
1996	Foo Fighters, *Big Me*
1995	TLC, *Waterfalls*
1994	Aerosmith, *Cryin'*
1993	Pearl Jam, *Jeremy*
1992	U2, *Even Better Than the Real Thing*
1991	R.E.M., *Losing My Religion*
1990	The B-52s, *Love Shack*

TOP 10 MUSIC VIDEOS OF THE 20TH CENTURY ON MTV

(Artist or group/title)

1. **Michael Jackson**, *Thriller*
2. **Madonna**, *Vogue*
3. **Nirvana**, *Smells Like Teen Spirit*
4. **Peter Gabriel**, *Sledgehammer*
5. **Run DMC with Aerosmith**, *Walk This Way*
6. **Guns N' Roses**, *Sweet Child O' Mine*
7. **Beastie Boys**, *Sabotage*
8. **Robert Palmer**, *Addicted to Love*
9. **2Pac and Dr. Dre**, *California Love*
10. **Madonna**, *Express Yourself*

PRODIGIOUS SUCCESS

Prodigy, featuring lead singer Keith Flint, won MTV US's "Viewer's Choice" award as well as three MTV Europe Music awards in 1997 for their single Breathe.

THE 10 ★ LATEST RECIPIENTS OF THE MTV "BEST FEMALE VIDEO" AWARD

YEAR	ARTIST/TITLE
1999	Lauryn Hill, *Doo Wop (That Thing)*
1998	Madonna, *Ray of Light*
1997	Jewel, *You Were Meant for Me*
1996	Alanis Morissette, *Ironic*
1995	Madonna, *Take a Bow*
1994	Janet Jackson, *If*
1993	k.d. lang, *Constant Craving*
1992	Annie Lennox, *Why*
1991	Janet Jackson, *Love Will Never Do Without You*
1990	Sinead O'Connor, *Nothing Compares 2 U*

TOP 10

MUSIC PROGRAMMES ON TELEVISION IN THE UK, 1999

	PROGRAMME	CHANNEL	BROADCAST DATE	AUDIENCE
1	*The Abba Story – The Winner Takes It All*	ITV	15 May	11,005,000
2	*Abbamania*	ITV	6 Nov	10,091,000
3	*Record of the Year Results*	ITV	11 Dec	9,122,000
4	*Happy Birthday Tina*	ITV	27 Nov	6,991,000
5	*Boyzone – Just for You*	ITV	29 May	6,257,000
6	*Turn of the Screw*	ITV	26 Dec	6,082,000
7	*Charlotte Church – Voice of an Angel*	BBC1	31 Oct	5,789,000
8	*Top of the Pops Christmas Special*	BBC1	25 Dec	5,611,000
9	*Bay City Rollers – Remember When*	BBC1	5 Apr	5,335,000
10	*S Club 7 Special*	BBC1	12 Dec	5,235,000

Source: *BARB/SPC*

THE 10 FIRST ARTISTS TO APPEAR IN PEPSI-COLA COMMERCIALS

1 Michael Jackson 2 Lionel Richie 3 Glenn Frey 4 Robert Palmer 5 Linda Ronstadt 6 Tina Turner 7 David Bowie 8 Gloria Estefan 9 MC Hammer 10 Ray Charles

TOP 10

SINGLES OF TV THEME TUNES IN THE UK

	ARTIST/TITLE	PROGRAMME
1	**Mr. Acker Bilk,** *Stranger on the Shore*	*Stranger on the Shore*
2	**Simon Park Orchestra,** *Eye Level*	*Van Der Valk*
3	**Wombles,** *The Wombling Song*	*The Wombles*
4	**TV Cast,** *The Army Game*	*The Army Game*
5	**Cilla Black,** *Something Tells Me*	*The Cilla Black Show*
6	**Dennis Waterman,** *I Could Be So Good For You*	*Minder*
7	**Elmer Bernstein,** *Staccato's Theme*	*Johnny Staccato*
8	**Clannad,** *Theme From Harry's Game*	*Harry's Game*
9	**Gheorghe Zamfir,** *Doina De Jale*	*Light of Experience*
10	**Jan Hammer,** *Miami Vice Theme*	*Miami Vice*

These themes, equally divided between instrumentals and vocal, cover more than 30 years of British TV shows. All those listed here were Top 5 hits following exposure on the programme concerned.

ALL IN THE FAMILY

David Cassidy and real-life stepmother Shirley Jones starred in the popular TV series The Partridge Family, *screened from 1970 to 1974.*

TOP 10

HIGHEST-RATED NETWORKED MUSIC TELEVISION SERIES IN THE US, 1950–99

	PROGRAMME	YEAR	PER CENT OF TV AUDIENCE*
1	*Stop the Music*	1951	34.0
2	*Your Hit Parade*	1958	33.6
3	*The Perry Como Show*	1956	32.6
4	*Name That Tune*	1958	26.7
5	*The Dean Martin Show*	1966	24.8
6	*The Sonny & Cher Hour*	1973	23.3
7	*The Partridge Family*	1972	22.6
8	*The Glen Campbell Goodtime Hour*	1968	22.5
9	*The Johnny Cash Show*	1969	21.8
10	*Cher*	1975	21.3

* *Percentage of American households with TV sets watching the broadcast: the total number of households rose from 3.8 million in 1950 to 99.4 million in 1999.*

© 2000, Nielsen Media Research

What was unique about *The Milky Way* cartoon?

see p.186 for the answer

A It was the first non-Disney animation to win an Oscar
B It was the first animated film made in colour
C It was the longest film ever made

TOP 10 DVD TITLES PURCHASED IN THE UK, 1999

1 *The Matrix* 2 *Armageddon* 3 *Blade* 4 *Lock, Stock and Two Smoking Barrels* 5 *A Bug's Life* 6 *Enemy of the State* 7 *Notting Hill* 8 *Lethal Weapon 4* 9 *The Exorcist* 10 *Ronin*

Source: *British Video Association*

TOP 10 DVD-PURCHASING COUNTRIES IN EUROPE

		TOTAL AVERAGE VIDEO SPEND (ECU)*	AVERAGE DVD SPEND PER HOUSEHOLD 1998 (ECU)
1	Iceland	664	615
2	Norway	568	536
3	Germany	452	436
4	France	317	258
5	Denmark	250	198
6	Switzerland	223	196
7	UK	256	189
8	Czech Republic	181	175
9	Ireland	217	174
10	Belgium	199	162

* *Excluding rental* Source: Screen Digest/*IVF*

The countries that spend the most on DVDs do not necessarily purchase the most, because prices vary significantly.

TOP 10 MOST EXPENSIVE EUROPEAN COUNTRIES IN WHICH TO RENT A VIDEO

(Country/average VHS rental cost in $)

1 **Sweden**, 4.28 2 **Switzerland**, 4.14 3 **UK**, 3.90 4 **Iceland**, 3.79 5 **Denmark**, 3.73 6 **France**, 3.72 7 **Norway**, 3.53 8 **Belgium**, 3.29 9 **Netherlands**, 3.17 10 **Austria**, 3.05

In the Czech Republic, the average cost of video rental is 68 cents.

Source: Screen Digest/IVF

TOP 10 VIDEO-RENTING COUNTRIES

	COUNTRY	AVERAGE NO. OF RENTALS PER VHS HOUSEHOLD, 1998
1	South Korea	88.6
2	Taiwan	57.4
3	USA	39.1
4	South Africa	37.7
5	India	37.3
6	Philippines	33.9
7	Australia	31.2
8	Canada	29.3
9	Japan	22.0
10	Pakistan	18.8

This list is at odds with the list of European countries because here only those homes that have a VHS video player are included in the statistics.

Source: Screen Digest

TOP 10 MOST-PURCHASED VIDEO CATEGORIES IN THE UK

	CATEGORY	% OF TOTAL SALES
1	Feature films	51.9
2	TV programmes	16.6
3	Children's animated films	8.9
4	Children's pre-school	7.3
5	Children's school age	4.6
6	Music	4.3
7	Sport	2.8
8	Live comedy	1.8
9	Special interest	1.0
10	Fitness	0.8

Source: *British Video Association*

It is clear that by far the biggest proportion of people who buy tapes do so in order to own copies of feature films and, to a much lesser extent, favourite TV programmes. As the DVD format progressively takes over from video tapes, the desirability of assembling a personal library of popular films is expected to further enhance the predominance of the feature film category.

TOP 10 VIDEO-RENTING COUNTRIES IN EUROPE

	COUNTRY	AVERAGE NO. OF VHS RENTALS PER HOUSEHOLD, 1998
1	Croatia	54.7
2	Ireland	34.2
3	Iceland	33.8
4	Hungary	17.1
5	Norway	11.9
6	Denmark	11.3
7	Czech Republic	10.3
8	UK	9.9
9	Spain	8.7
10	Belgium	8.2

Source: Screen Digest

TOP 10 VIDEO-BUYING COUNTRIES IN EUROPE

	COUNTRY	AVERAGE NO. OF VHS PURCHASES PER HOUSEHOLD, 1998
1	UK	4.8
2	Ireland	3.5
3	=Denmark	3.2
	=France	3.2
5	Belgium	2.8
6	Iceland	2.4
7	Finland	2.3
8	=Italy	2.1
	=Netherlands	2.1
	=Norway	2.1

Source: Screen Digest

TOP 10 VIDEO RENTAL MONTHS IN THE UK

(Month/percentage of total video rental, 1995–98)

1 **April**, 9.0 2 **August**, 8.9 3 = **December**, 8.6; = **July**, 8.6 5 **March**, 8.5 6 **September**, 8.4 7 **February**, 8.3 8 **November**, 8.2 9 **May**, 8.1 10 = **June**, 7.9; = **October**, 7.9

Source: Screen Digest

Background image: **VIDEOS TO RENT**

TOP 10

MOST RENTED VIDEOS IN THE UK, 1999

	TITLE	RENTALS
1	*There's Something About Mary*	2,911,843
2	*Armageddon*	2,670,459
3	*Saving Private Ryan*	2,605,251
4	*Enemy of the State*	2,347,615
5	*Lock, Stock and Two Smoking Barrels*	2,294,711
6	*Blade*	2,229,781
7	*Lethal Weapon 4*	2,015,953
8	*The Truman Show*	1,970,369
9	*Payback*	1,671,970
10	*Dr. Dolittle*	1,524,935

Source: *MRIB*

This annual list traditionally represents the gamut of popular genres, and includes comedies, thrillers, war, and science-fiction films.

MARY, MARY

Blockbuster comedy There's Something About Mary, *starring Cameron Diaz in the title role, became the UK's most rented, and the US's No. 2 video of 1999.*

TOP 10

VIDEOS THAT SPENT LONGEST AT NO. 1 IN THE RENTAL CHART

	TITLE/YEAR	WEEKS AT NO. 1
1	*Raiders of the Lost Ark*, 1983	14
2	*First Blood*, 1983	11
3	*Police Academy*, 1985	13
4=	*An Officer and a Gentleman*, 1984	9
=	*Tightrope*, 1985*	9
=	*Se7en*, 1996	9
7=	*Trading Places*, 1984–85	8
=	*The Goonies*, 1986	8
=	*Aliens*, 1987	8
=	*Big Trouble in Little China*, 1987	8

* Tightrope's *tenure at the top was split into two runs of six weeks and three weeks*

Source: *MRIB*

A film that can hold No. 1 for a full month now is special indeed, such is the urgency with which recent box office successes transfer to video.

TOP 10

BESTSELLING CHILDREN'S VIDEOS IN THE UK*

1	*The Jungle Book*
2	*The Lion King*
3	*Snow White and the Seven Dwarfs*
4	*Toy Story*
5	*Fantasia*
6	*One Hundred and One Dalmatians*#
7	*Lady and the Tramp*
8	*Beauty and the Beast*
9	*Cinderella*
10	*Aladdin*

* *To 1 January 2000* # *Animated version*

TOP 10

CHILDREN'S VIDEOS IN THE UK, 1999

1	*A Bug's Life*
2	*The Lion King 2 – Simba's Pride*
3	*Mulan*
4	*Antz*
5	*Rugrats – The Movie*
6	*The Prince of Egypt*
7	*Tweenies – Song Time*
8	*Tweenies – Ready to Play With*
9	*Mickey's Once Upon a Christmas*
10	*Annabella's Wish*

Source: *British Video Association*

TOP 10 MOST RENTED VIDEOS OF ALL TIME IN THE UK*

1 *Four Weddings and a Funeral* 2 *Dirty Dancing* 3 *Basic Instinct* 4 *Crocodile Dundee* 5 *Sister Act* 6 *Forrest Gump* 7 *Home Alone* 8 *Ghost* 9 *Pretty Woman* 10 *Speed*

* *To 1 January 2000* Source: *MRIB*

Did You Know? The first ever video to top the UK video rental chart (inaugurated in March 1981) was *Jaws* – a film that had been released six years earlier.

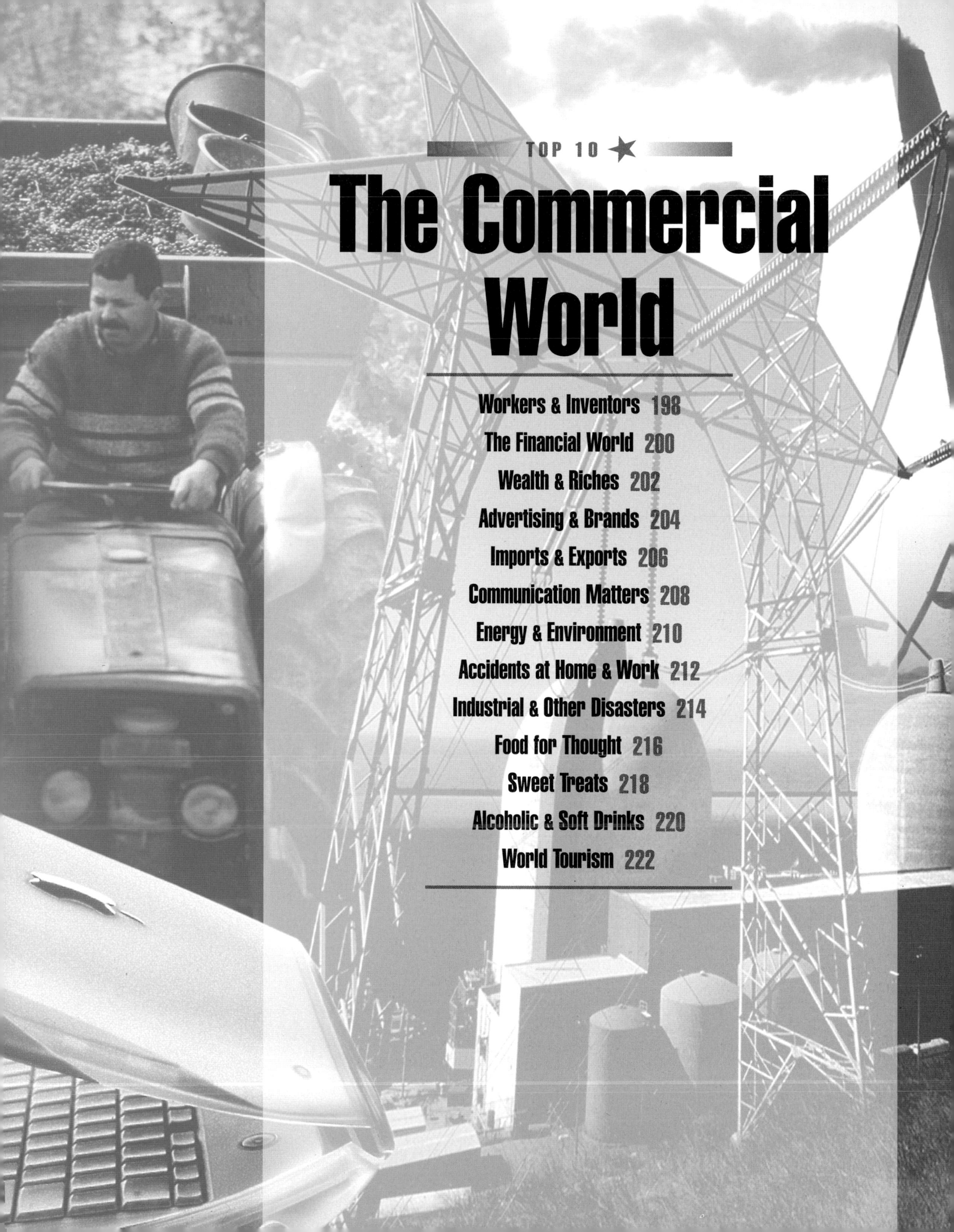

TOP 10 ★

The Commercial World

Workers & Inventors

TOP 10 ★ COUNTRIES WITH THE MOST WORKERS

	COUNTRY	WORKERS*
1	China	736,000,000
2	India	423,000,000
3	USA	136,000,000
4	Indonesia	94,000,000
5	Russia	78,000,000
6	Brazil	75,000,000
7	Japan	68,000,000
8	Bangladesh	63,000,000
9	Pakistan	48,000,000
10	Nigeria	47,000,000

* *Based on people aged 15–64 who are currently employed; unpaid groups are not included*

Source: *World Bank*

TOP 10 ★ COUNTRIES WITH THE HIGHEST PROPORTION OF FEMALE WORKERS*

	COUNTRY	LABOUR FORCE PERCENTAGE
1	Latvia	50
2	=Belarus	49
	=Burundi	49
	=Estonia	49
	=Malawi	49
	=Moldova	49
	=Russia	49
	=Rwanda	49
	=Tanzania	49
	=Ukraine	49
	=Vietnam	49

* *Based on people aged 15–64 who are currently employed; unpaid groups are not included*

Source: *World Bank*

TOP 10 ★ COUNTRIES WITH THE HIGHEST PROPORTION OF FARMERS

	COUNTRY	PERCENTAGE IN AGRICULTURE
1	Bhutan	93.9
2	Nepal	93.3
3	Burkina Faso	92.4
4	Rwanda	91.2
5	Burundi	90.7
6	=Niger	89.2
	=Mali	89.2
8	Ethiopia	85.3
9	Guinea Bissau	84.1
10	Uganda	83.1

Source: *Food and Agriculture Organization of the United Nations*

TOP 10 ★ BRITISH COMPANIES WITH THE MOST EMPLOYEES

	COMPANY	EMPLOYEES
1	Rentokil Initial	138,635
2	HSBC Holdings	132,969
3	Compass Group	130,548
4	British Telecom	129,200
5	Tesco	124,172
6	BTR	110,498
7	J. Sainsbury	107,226
8	Lloyds TSB Group	92,655
9	Boots	85,349
10	Barclays	84,300

HARD LABOUR

India's huge work force relies on traditional manual labour, but the country is increasingly becoming a major centre for computer technology.

TOP 10 OCCUPATIONS IN THE UK

	JOB SECTOR	EMPLOYEES
1	**Manufacturing**	3,984,000
2	**Real estate, renting, and business activities**	3,415,000
3	**Retail** (except motor and repair of personal/household goods)	2,396,000
4	**Transport, storage, and communication**	1,462,000
5	**Hotels and restaurants**	1,326,000
6	**Wholesale and commission trade** (excluding motor)	1,135,000
7	**Construction**	1,092,000
8	**Financial intermediation**	1,036,000
9	**Motor vehicles** (including retail of automotive fuel)	555,000
10	**Agriculture, hunting, and forestry and fishing**	317,000

There were 26.4 million people in the labour force in the UK in 1999 (with a working age population of 35.9 million), compared to a peak of 28.9 million in spring 1990. Among employees, the pattern of industrial employment has changed substantially over the past century. The percentage of the workforce in agriculture declined from 12 per cent in 1901 to 2 per cent, and mining and transport industries' workforces have halved; in contrast, office workers have increased from 18 per cent of the workforce to 40 per cent in 1999.

THE 10 FIRST PATENTS IN THE UK

	PATENTEE	PATENT	DATE*
1	**Nicholas Hillyard**	Engraving and printing the king's head on documents	5 May 1617
2	**John Gason**	Locks, mills, and other river and canal improvements	1 July 1617
3	**John Miller and John Jasper Wolfen**	Oil for suits of armour	3 Nov 1617
4	**Robert Crumpe**	Tunnels and pumps	9 Jan 1618
5	**Aaron Rathburne and Roger Burges**	Making maps of English cities	11 Mar 1618
6	**John Gilbert**	River dredger	16 July 1618
7	**Clement Dawbeney**	Water-powered engine for making nails	11 Dec 1618
8	**Thomas Murray**	Sword blades	11 Jan 1619
9	**Thomas Wildgoose and David Ramsey**	Ploughs, pumps, and ships' engines	17 Jan 1619
10	**Abram Baker**	Smalt (glass) manufacture	16 Feb 1619

** Patents issued prior to 1617 were not codified and are excluded from this list.*

The world's first patent, by which the architect Filippo Brunelleschi was granted the exclusive licence to make a barge crane to transport marble, was issued in Florence in 1421.

FACTORY-MADE

Despite the growth of the service sector, manufacturing remains a vital component of most developed economies, providing employment for countless workers.

THE 10 FIRST WOMEN PATENTEES IN THE US

	PATENTEE	PATENT	DATE
1	**Mary Kies**	Straw weaving with silk or thread	5 May 1809
2	**Mary Brush**	Corset	21 July 1815
3	**Sophia Usher**	Carbonated liquid	11 Sep 1819
4	**Julia Planton**	Foot stove	4 Nov 1822
5	**Lucy Burnap**	Weaving grass hats	16 Feb 1823
6	**Diana H. Tuttle**	Accelerating spinning-wheel heads	17 May 1824
7	**Catharine Elliot**	Manufacturing moccasins	26 Jan 1825
8	**Phoebe Collier**	Sawing wheel-fellies (rims)	20 May 1826
9	**Elizabeth H. Buckley**	Sheet-iron shovel	28 Feb 1828
10	**Henrietta Cooper**	Whitening leghorn straw	12 Nov 1828

THE 10 FIRST TRADEMARKS ISSUED IN THE US

(Issued to/product)

1 **Averill Chemical-Paint Company**, Liquid paint 2 **J. B. Baldy & Co.**, Mustard 3 **Ellis Branson**, Retail coal 4 **Tracy Coit**, Fish 5 **William Lanfair Ellis & Co.**, Oyster packing 6 **Evans, Clow, Dalzell & Co.**, Wrought-iron pipe 7 **W. E. Garrett & Sons**, Snuff 8 **William G. Hamilton**, Cartwheel 9 **John K. Hogg**, Soap 10 **Abraham P. Olzendam**, Woollen hose

All of these trademarks were registered on the same day, 25 October 1870, and are ranked only by the trademark numbers assigned to them.

Did You Know? Thomas Alva Edison (1847–1931) is the world's most prolific inventor, with 1,093 patents issued to him solely or jointly between 1 June 1869 and 16 May 1933.

The Financial World

TOP 10 ★ RETAILERS IN THE UK

	GROUP	SALES 1997/98 (£)
1	Tesco	14,621,000,000
2	J. Sainsbury	12,682,000,000
3	Asda	7,600,800,000
4	Safeway	6,978,700,000
5	Marks & Spencer	6,695,000,000
6	Kingfisher	5,191,800,000
7	The Boots Company	4,574,400,000
8	Somerfield	3,483,600,000
9	John Lewis Partnership	3,117,400,000
10	Kwik Save Group	2,850,200,000

Source: *Based on* The Retail Rankings *(1999) published by Corporate Intelligence on Retailing*

TOP 10 ★ AREAS OF UK GOVERNMENT EXPENDITURE

	DEPARTMENT	ESTIMATED EXPENDITURE, 2000–02 (£)
1	Health	45,500,000,000
2	Department of the Environment, Transport, and the Regions (Local Government)	36,900,000,000
3	Defence	21,400,000,000
4	Education and Employment	16,800,000,000
5	Scotland	13,300,000,000
6	Home Office	7,600,000,000
7	Wales	7,000,000,000
8	Northern Ireland	5,500,000,000
9	Department of the Environment, Transport, and the Regions (Main Programme)	4,800,000,000
10	Social Security Administration	3,400,000,000

TOP 10 ★ SOURCES OF GOVERNMENT INCOME IN THE UK

	SOURCE	ESTIMATED INCOME, 1999–2000 (£)
1	Income Tax	90,800,000,000
2	Social Security contributions	55,700,000,000
3	Value Added Tax	54,000,000,000
4	Corporation Tax	29,900,000,000
5	Fuel duties	23,100,000,000
6	Business rates	15,600,000,000
7	Council Tax	12,800,000,000
8	Tobacco duties	7,000,000,000
9	Alcohol duties	6,100,000,000
10	Stamp duties	5,700,000,000

TOP 10 ★ RICHEST COUNTRIES

	COUNTRY	GDP PER CAPITA, 1998 ($)
1	Liechtenstein	50,000*
2	Luxembourg	43,570
3	Switzerland	40,080
4	Norway	34,330
5	Denmark	33,260
6	Japan	32,380
7	Singapore	30,060
8	USA	29,340
9	Iceland	28,010
10	Austria	26,850
	UK	21,400

* *World Bank estimate for the purpose of ranking*
Source: *World Bank,* World Development Indicators

GDP (Gross Domestic Product) is the total value of all the goods and services produced annually within a country (Gross National Product, or GNP, also includes income from overseas). Dividing GDP by the country's population produces GDP per capita, which is often used as a measure of how "rich" a country is.

EASTERN STAR

Despite recent economic setbacks, the wealth of cities such as Tokyo has helped Japan to maintain its prominent place among the world's richest countries.

TOP 10 ★ US COMPANIES MAKING THE GREATEST PROFIT PER SECOND

	COMPANY	PROFIT PER SEC ($)
1	Ford Motor Company	699
2	General Electric	294
3	AT&T	202
4	Exxon Corporation	201
5	IBM	200
6	Intel Corporation	192
7	Citigroup	184
8	Philip Morris Companies, Inc.	170
9	Merck	166
10	BankAmerica Corporation	163

THE 10 COUNTRIES MOST IN DEBT

	COUNTRY	TOTAL EXTERNAL DEBT ($)
1	Brazil	193,663,000,000
2	Mexico	149,690,000,000
3	China	146,697,000,000
4	South Korea	143,373,000,000
5	Indonesia	136,174,000,000
6	Russia	125,645,000,000
7	Argentina	123,221,000,000
8	India	94,404,000,000
9	Thailand	93,416,000,000
10	Turkey	91,205,000,000

Source: *World Bank*

The World Bank's annual debt calculations estimated the total indebtedness of low- and middle-income countries at 2.177 trillion in 1996.

THE 10 POOREST COUNTRIES

	COUNTRY	GDP PER CAPITA, 1998 ($)
1	Ethiopia	100
2	Dem. Rep. of Congo	110
3	=Sierra Leone	140
	=Burundi	140
5	Guinea-Bissau	160
6	Niger	190
7	=Eritrea	200
	=Malawi	200
9	=Mozambique	210
	=Nepal	210
	=Tanzania	210

Source: *World Bank,* Word Development Indicators

TOP 10 OLDEST ESTABLISHED BUSINESSES IN THE UK

	BUSINESS/LOCATION	FOUNDED
1	**The Royal Mint**, Cardiff (formerly London)	886
2	**Kirkstall Forge** (axles, etc), Kirkstall, Leeds	1200
3	**The Shore Porters Society of Aberdeen**, Aberdeen	1498
4	**Cambridge University Press**, Cambridge	1534
5	**John Brooke and Sons** (property management), Huddersfield	1541
6	**Child's Bank** (now part of Royal Bank of Scotland), London	1559
7	**Whitechapel Bell Foundry**, London	1570
8	**Oxford University Press**, Oxford	1585
9	**Richard Durtnell and Sons** (builders), Brasted, nr. Westerham, Kent	1591
10	**Hays at Guildford** (office services), Guildford (formerly London)	1651

A number of these companies belong to an élite club of "tercentarians" – firms that have been in business for 300 years or more. A few have been controlled by the same family for their entire history.

TOP 10 INTERNATIONAL INDUSTRIAL COMPANIES

	COMPANY/ LOCATION/SECTOR	ANNUAL SALES ($)
1	**General Motors Corp.**, USA, Transport	161,315,000,000
2	**DaimlerChrysler**, Germany, Transport	154,615,000,000
3	**Ford Motor Co.**, USA, Transport	144,416,000,000
4	**Wal-Mart Stores, Inc.**, USA, Retailing	139,208,000,000
5	**Mitsui and Co. Ltd.**, Japan, Trading	109,372,000,000
6	**Itochu Corp.**, Japan, Trading	108,749,100,000
7	**Mitsubishi Corp.**, Japan, Trading	107,184,000,000
8	**Exxon Corp.**, USA, Oil, gas, fuel	100,697,000,000
9	**General Electric**, USA, Electronics, electrical equipment	100,469,000,000
10	**Toyota Motor**, Japan, Transport	99,740,100,000

Source: Fortune Global 500

POVERTY-STRIKEN LAND

Factors including civil wars and severe droughts affecting their rural economies mean that several sub-Saharan African countries are among the world's poorest

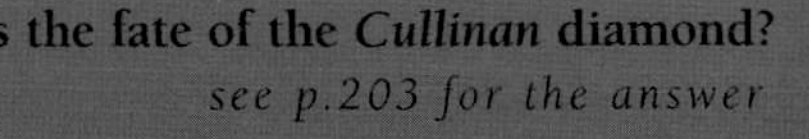

What was the fate of the *Cullinan* diamond?

see p.203 for the answer

A It became part of the British Crown Jewels
B It was stolen and never recovered
C It is owned by Elizabeth Taylor

Wealth & Riches

TAKING A BACK SEAT

Comedian Jerry Seinfeld formerly headed the richest entertainers' list with earnings of $225 million, but dropped out of the Top 10 with the end of his TV series.

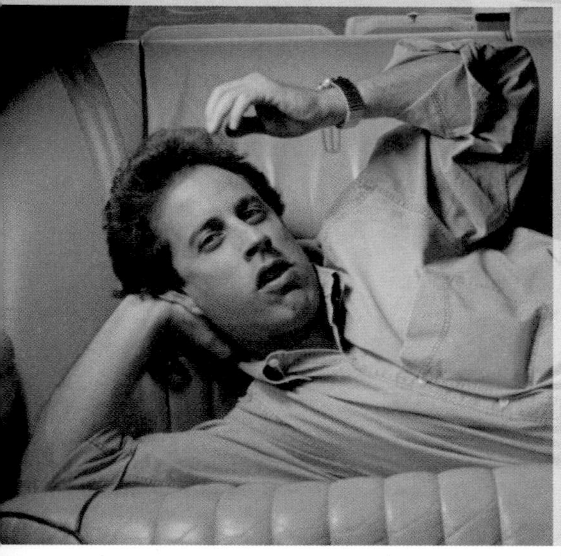

TOP 10 ★ HIGHEST-EARNING ENTERTAINERS

	ENTERTAINER	PROFESSION	1999 INCOME ($)
1	George Lucas	Film producer/director	400,000,000
2	Oprah Winfrey	TV host/producer	150,000,000
3	David Kelley	TV writer/producer (*Ally McBeal* etc.)	118,000,000
4	Tom Hanks	Film actor	71,000,000
5	=Backstreet Boys	Pop band	60,000,000
	=Steven Spielberg	Film producer/director	60,000,000
7	Bruce Willis	Film actor	54,000,000
8	=David Copperfield	Illusionist	50,000,000
	=Julia Roberts	Film actress	50,000,000
	=The Rolling Stones	Rock band	50,000,000

Used by permission of Forbes *magazine*

TOP 10 ★ RICHEST RULERS

	RULER/COUNTRY/ YEAR CAME TO POWER	ESTIMATED WEALTH ($)
1	**Sultan Hassanal Bolkiah**, Brunei, 1967	30,000,000,000
2	**King Fahd bin Abdulaziz Al Saud**, Saudi Arabia, 1982	28,000,000,000
3	**Sheikh Zayed bin Sultan al-Nahyan**, UAE (Abu Dhabi), 1966	20,000,000,000
4	**Amir Jaber al-Ahmed al Jaber Al-Sabah**, Kuwait, 1977	17,000,000,000
5	**Sheikh Maktoum bin Rashid Al Maktoum**, UAE (Dubai), 1990	12,000,000,000
6	**President Saddam Hussein**, Iraq, 1979	6,000,000,000
7	**Queen Beatrix**, Netherlands, 1980	5,200,000,000
8	**Amir Hamad bin Khalifa Al Thani**, Qatar, 1995	5,000,000,000
9	**President Hafez Al-Assad**, Syria, 1971	2,000,000,000
10	**Queen Elizabeth II**, UK, 1952	450,000,000

Based on data published in Forbes *magazine*

TOP 10 ★ RICHEST PEOPLE IN THE UK

	NAME/SOURCE OF WEALTH	ASSETS (£)
1	**Hans Rausing**, Food packaging	3,400,000,000
2	**Lord Sainsbury and family**, Retailing	3,100,000,000
3	**George Soros**, Finance	2,000,000,000
4	**=Joseph Lewis**, Finance	1,750,000,000
	=Duke of Westminster, Land and property	1,750,000,000
6	**=Lady Grantchester and the Moores family**, Stores, mail order, and football pools	1,500,000,000
	=Garfield Weston and family, Food	1,500,000,000
8	**=Sri and Gopi Hinduja**, Trading and finance	1,300,000,000
	=Bruno Schroder and family, Banking	1,300,000,000
10	**=Richard Branson**, Travel, retailing, and entertainment	1,200,000,000
	=Lakshmi Mittal, Steel	1,200,000,000

Based on data published in The Sunday Times

TOP 10 ★ YOUNGEST BILLIONAIRES IN THE US

	NAME/SOURCE OF WEALTH	ASSETS ($)	AGE
1	**Daniel Morton Ziff**, Ziff Brothers Investments	1,200,000,000	27
2	**Jerry Yang**, Yahoo!	3,700,000,000	30
3	**=Pierre M. Omidyar**, eBay	4,900,000,000	31
	=Mark Cuban, Broadcast.com	1,200,000,000	31
5	**=David Filo**, Yahoo!	3,700,000,000	33
	=Robert David Ziff, Ziff Brothers Investments	1,200,000,000	33
7	**Michael Dell**, Dell Computer Corp.	20,000,000,000	34
8	**=Jeffrey P. Bezos**, Amazon.com	7,800,000,000	35
	=Dirk Edward Ziff, Ziff Brothers Investments	1,200,000,000	35
10	**=Theodore W. Waitt**, Gateway 2000 Computers	6,200,000,000	36
	=William Wrigley Jr., Wrigley's Chewing Gum	2,700,000,000	36

Based on data published in Forbes *magazine*

Did You Know? The weight of diamonds is measured in carats (the word derives from the carob bean, which was once used as a measure). There are approximately 142 carats to the ounce.

TOP 10 ★ MOST EXPENSIVE SINGLE DIAMONDS SOLD AT AUCTION

	DIAMOND/SALE	PRICE ($)
1	*Star of the Season*, pear-shaped 100.10-carat "D" flawless diamond, Sotheby's, Geneva, 17 May 1995	16,548,750 (SF19,858,500)
2	*The Mouawad Splendor*, pear-shaped 11-sided 101.84-carat diamond, Sotheby's, Geneva, 14 November 1990	12,760,000 (SF15,950,000)
3	*Star of Happiness*, rectangular-cut 100.36-carat diamond, Sotheby's, Geneva, 17 November 1993	11,882,333 (SF17,823,500)
4	Fancy blue emerald-cut 20.17-carat diamond ring, Sotheby's, New York, 18 October 1994	9,902,500
5	*Eternal Light*, pear-shaped 85.91-carat pendant, Sotheby's, New York, 19 April 1988	9,130,000
6	Rectangular-cut fancy deep blue 13.49-carat diamond ring, Christie's, New York, 13 April 1995	7,482,500
7	Rectangular-cut 52.59-carat diamond ring, Christie's, New York, 20 April 1988	7,480,000
8	Fancy pink rectangular-cut 19.66-carat diamond, Christie's, Geneva, 17 November 1994	7,421,318 (SF9,573,500)
9	*The Jeddah Bride*, rectangular-cut 80.02-carat diamond, Sotheby's, New York, 24 October 1991	7,150,000
10	*The Agra Diamond*, fancy light pink cushion-shaped 32.24-carat diamond, Christie's, London, 20 June 1990	6,959,700 (£4,070,000)

TOP 10 ★ COUNTRIES WITH THE MOST DOLLAR BILLIONAIRES*

	COUNTRY	BILLIONAIRES
1	USA	50
2	Germany	43
3	Japan	30
4	France	15
5	=China (Hong Kong)	13
	=Switzerland	13
7	UK	12
8	Mexico	10
9	=Brazil	8
	=Canada	8

* *Individuals and families with a net worth of $1 billion or more*

Based on data published in Forbes magazine

TOP 10 ★ GOLD-PRODUCING COUNTRIES

	COUNTRY	1998 PRODUCTION IN TONNES
1	South Africa	473.8
2	USA	364.4
3	Australia	313.0
4	Canada	164.0
5	China	161.0
6	Indonesia	139.3
7	Russia	127.3
8	Peru	89.2
9	Uzbekistan	80.6
10	Ghana	73.3

As reported by Gold Fields Mineral Services Ltd., world-dominating gold producer South Africa saw its output fall yet again for the sixth consecutive year, although it has still held on to the top slot as the world's largest gold producer.

TOP 10 ★ LARGEST ROUGH DIAMONDS

DIAMOND/DESCRIPTION — CARATS

1 *Cullinan* — 3,106.00
Measuring roughly 10 x 6.5 x 5 cm (4 x 2½ x 2 in), and weighing 621 g (1 lb 6 oz), the Cullinan was unearthed in 1905, and bought by the Transvaal Government for £150,000. It was presented to King Edward VII, who had it cut; the most important of the separate gems are among the British Crown Jewels.

2 *Excelsior* — 995.20
Found at the Jagersfontein Mine on 30 June 1893, it was cut by the celebrated Amsterdam firm of Asscher in 1903, producing 21 superb stones.

3 *Star of Sierra Leone* — 968.80
Found in Sierra Leone on St. Valentine's Day, 1972, the rough diamond weighed 225 g (8 oz) and measured 63.5 x 38.1 mm (2½ x 1½ in).

4 *Incomparable* — 890.00
Discovered in 1980 at Mbuji-Mayi, Dem. Rep. of Congo (then Zaïre).

5 *Great Mogul* — 787.50
When found in 1650 in the Gani Mine, India, it was presented to Shah Jehan, the builder of the Taj Mahal.

6 *Millennium Star* — 777.00
Recently discovered near the village of Mbuji-Mayi in the Dem. Rep. of Congo, the polished stone cut from it is 203.04 carats and measures 50.06 x 36.56 x 18.5 mm (2 x 1½ x ¾ in).

7 *Woyie River* — 770.00
Found in 1945 beside the Woyie River in Sierra Leone, it was cut into 30 stones. The largest of these, known as Victory and weighing 31.35 carats, was auctioned at Christie's, New York in 1984 for $880,000 (£704,000).

8 *Golden Jubilee* — 755.50
Found in 1986 in the Premier Mine (the home of the Cullinan), the polished diamond cut from it is, at 545.67 carats, the largest in the world.

9 *Presidente Vargas* — 726.60
Discovered in the Antonio River, Brazil, in 1938, it was named after the then President, Getulio Vargas.

10 *Jonker* — 726.00
In 1934 Jacobus Jonker found this massive diamond. Acquired by Harry Winston, it was exhibited in the American Museum of Natural History.

WORTH ITS WEIGHT IN GOLD

International trade in gold is customarily carried out with either 1-kg (32.15-troy ounce) or 12.5-kg (400-troy ounce) gold bars.

Advertising & Brands

TOP 10 ALCOHOL ADVERTISERS IN THE UK

	BRAND/TYPE	ADVERTISING EXPENDITURE (£)
1	Budweiser lager	10,661,000
2	Foster's lager	9,663,000
3	Carling lager	8,956,000
4	Smirnoff vodka	8,924,000
5	Carlsberg lager	7,721,000
6	Heineken lager	7,219,000
7	Bacardi rum	6,727,000
8	Kronenburg 1664 lager	5,172,000
9	Holsten lager	4,997,000
10	Gordons gin	4,844,000

Source: *ACNielsen MMS*

TOP 10 TYPES OF PRODUCT ADVERTISED IN GREAT BRITAIN

	TYPE OF PRODUCT	ADVERTISING SPEND 1998 (£)
1	Retail and mail order	1,093,000,000
2	Motors	631,000,000
3	Food	625,000,000
4	Financial	481,000,000
5	Toiletries and cosmetics	356,000,000
6	Leisure equipment	327,000,000
7	Drink	245,000,000
8	Household stores	244,000,000
9	Holidays, travel, and transport	242,000,000
10	Publishing	217,000,000

Source: *The Advertising Association*

TOP 10 ADVERTISING CAMPAIGNS OF THE 20TH CENTURY*

	CAMPAIGN	COMPANY OR PRODUCT	FIRST YEAR
1	*"Think small"*	Volkswagen	1959
2	*"The pause that refreshes"*	Coca-Cola	1929
3	*The Marlboro Man*	Marlboro	1955
4	*"Just do it"*	Nike	1988
5	*"You deserve a break today"*	McDonald's	1971
6	*"A diamond is forever"*	DeBeers	1948
7	The Absolut bottle	Absolut vodka	1981
8	*"Tastes great, less filling"*	Miller Lite beer	1974
9	*"Does she...or doesn't she?"*	Clairol	1957
10	*"We try harder"*	Avis	1963

* *Based on industry research*

Source: Advertising Age

BIG MAC

Global fast-food company McDonald's is ranked second only to Coca-Cola as one of the world's most valuable food and drink brands.

TOP 10 MOST VALUABLE FOOD AND DRINK BRANDS

(Brand name/industry/brand value in $)*

❶ **Coca-Cola**, Beverages, 83,845,000,000 ❷ **McDonald's**, Food, 26,231,000,000 ❸ **Nescafe**, Switzerland, Beverages, 17,595,000,000 ❹ **Heinz**, Food, 11,806,000,000 ❺ **Budweiser**, Alcohol, 8,510,000,000 ❻ **Kelloggs**, Food, 7,052,000,000 ❼ **Pepsi-Cola**, Beverages, 5,932,000,000 ❽ **Wrigley's**, Food, 4,404,000,000 ❾ **Burger King**, Food, 2,806,000,000 ❿ **Moët & Chandon**, France, Alcohol, 2,804,000,000

* *US is country of origin unless otherwise stated*

Source: *Interbrand*

"SHOPPING MALL"

In 16th-century London, a croquet-like game called pall-mall (from the Italian *pallamaglio*, "ball to mallet") was played in long alleys in two parallel streets called Pall Mall and The Mall, where fashionable London society promenaded. By the 18th century, the game had fallen out of favour and Pall Mall had become renowned for its expensive shops. Later, "mall" became synonymous with any strolling and shopping area – especially the shopping malls of the United States.

WHY DO WE SAY?

Crowd cheers! Coke nears!
Game goes better refreshed.
Coca-Cola, never too sweet,
gives that special zing . . . refreshes best.

TOP 10 ★ BESTSELLING BRANDS IN THE UK, 1999*

	BRAND	BRAND OWNER	SALES (£)
1	Coca-Cola	Coca-Cola GB	395,900,000
2	Nescafe	Nestlé	355,700,000
3	Walkers Crisps	PepsiCo (Walkers Snack Foods)	343,600,000
4	Persil	Unilever (Lever Brothers)	237,800,000
5	Andrex Toilet Tissue	Kimberly-Clark	219,800,000
6	Pampers Nappies	Procter & Gamble	201,200,000
7	Müller Pot Desserts	Müller Dairy (UK)	197,600,000
8	Ariel	Procter & Gamble	182,000,000
9	Robinsons	Britvic Soft Drinks	154,300,000
10	Sunny Delight	Procter & Gamble	150,200,000

* *In year to 7 August 1999*

Source: *ACNielsen MMS*

Persil is not only the most popular washpowder but also the leading non-food brand in the UK. Its closest rival, Ariel, is the only brand in the Top 10 to suffer a drop in sales in 1999, with a 7.3 per cent decrease.

THE REAL THING

Bestselling, most advertised, and most valuable are only three of the many superlatives applied to Coca-Cola's world-beating status.

TOP 10 SOFT DRINK ADVERTISERS IN THE UK

(Drink/advertising expenditure, 1998 in £)

❶ **Coca-Cola**, 28,779,000 ❷ **Pepsi Cola**, 9,260,000 ❸ **Sunny Delight**, 6,820,000 ❹ **Robinsons**, 6,045,000 ❺ **Dr. Pepper**, 5,787,000 ❻ **Ribena**, 5,490,000 ❼ **Fanta**, 5,123,000 ❽ **Sprite**, 3,956,000 ❾ **Tango**, 3,775,000 ❿ **Lilt**, 3,449,000

Source: *ACNielsen MMS*

TOP 10 ★ MOST VALUABLE GLOBAL BRANDS

	BRAND NAME	INDUSTRY	BRAND VALUE ($)
1	Coca-Cola	Beverages	83,845,000,000
2	Microsoft	Software	56,654,000,000
3	IBM	Computers	43,781,000,000
4	General Electric	Diversified	33,502,000,000
5	Ford	Automobiles	33,197,000,000
6	Disney	Entertainment	32,275,000,000
7	Intel	Computers	30,021,000,000
8	McDonald's	Food	26,231,000,000
9	AT&T	Telecommunications	24,181,000,000
10	Marlboro	Tobacco	21,048,000,000

Source: *Interbrand*

Brand consultants Interbrand use a method of estimating value that takes account of the profitability of individual brands within a business (rather than the companies that own them), as well as such factors as their potential for growth. The Top 10 are all US-owned – as, indeed, are some two-thirds of the top 60 – while Germany, followed by the UK, lead the European brands league.

TOP 10 FASTEST GROWING GROCERY BRANDS IN THE UK, 1999*

(Brand/brand owner/percentage increase in sales)

❶ **Sunny Delight,** Procter & Gamble, 210.9 ❷ **Celebrations,** Mars Confectionery, 96.9 ❸ **Ocean Spray,** Ocean Spray Cranberries (UK partners, Gerber Foods), 59.3 ❹ **Chicago Town Pizza**, Schwan's Europe, 53.2 ❺ **Pringles,** Procter & Gamble, 33.0 ❻ **Goodfellas,** Green Isle Foods, 31.5 ❼ **Yoplait pot desserts,** Yoplait, 23.3 ❽ **McCain frozen chips**, McCain Foods, 22.7 ❾ **Tropicana,** PepsiCo (Tropicana UK), 20.5 ❿ **Dairylea,** Kraft Jacob Suchard, 17.8

* *In year to 7 August 1999* Source: *ACNielsen MMS*

Imports & Exports

TOP 10 GOODS EXPORTED FROM THE UK

	PRODUCT	TOTAL VALUE OF 1998 EXPORTS (£)
1	Electrical machinery	34,990,000,000
2	Mechanical machinery	23,267,000,000
3	Road vehicles	14,788,000,000
4	Scientific and photographic equipment	6,837,000,000
5	Petroleum and petroleum products	6,494,000,000
6	Other transport equipment	6,007,000,000
7	Medicinal products	5,917,000,000
8	Organic chemicals	4,960,000,000
9	Metal manufactures	3,630,000,000
10	Clothing and footwear	3,560,000,000
	Total (including goods not in Top 10)	165,387,000,000

Source: *Office for National Statistics*

The value of goods exported from the UK rose from £93.7 billion in 1989 to £165.4 billion in 1998. These figures reflect a rise in every area, with some showing a threefold increase.

TOP 10 GOODS IMPORTED TO THE UK

	PRODUCT	TOTAL VALUE OF 1998 IMPORTS (£)
1	Electrical machinery	38,354,000,000
2	Road vehicles	23,210,000,000
3	Mechanical machinery	17,882,000,000
4	Clothing and footwear	9,910,000,000
5	Scientific and photographic equipment	6,386,000,000
6	Transport equipment	6,240,000,000
7	Textile manufactures	5,071,000,000
8	Organic chemicals	4,724,000,000
9	Paper and paperboard manufactures	4,692,000,000
10	Vegetables and fruit	4,236,000,000
	Total (including goods not in Top 10)	191,278,000,000

Source: *Office for National Statistics*

In 1998, the UK imported machinery and transport equipment worth £85.7 billion; manufactured goods worth £28.7 billion, and chemicals worth £18.1 billion. Food imports amounted to £13.9 billion and beverages to £3.1 billion.

TOP 10 COUNTRIES FOR DUTY-FREE SHOPPING

	COUNTRY	ANNUAL SALES ($)
1	UK	2,480,000,000
2	USA	1,775,000,000
3	Finland	1,046,000,000
4	Germany	885,000,000
5	France	724,000,000
6	South Korea	704,000,000
7	Denmark	652,000,000
8	Sweden	620,000,000
8	US Virgin Islands	601,000,000
10	Japan	491,000,000

Source: *Generation AB*

Duty-free sales began in 1951 with the opening of a small kiosk at Shannon Airport in Ireland, where transatlantic flights stopped for refuelling on the final leg of their journey to New York. This has grown into a huge international business, of which Europe takes almost half (49.8 per cent) of global sales, Asia and Oceania 20.9 per cent, the Americas 28.4 per cent, and the whole of Africa just 1 per cent.

TOP 10 SOURCES OF IMPORTS TO THE UK

	COUNTRY	TOTAL VALUE OF 1998 IMPORTS (£)
1	USA	25,656,000,000
2	Germany	25,516,000,000
3	France	17,913,000,000
4	Netherlands	13,634,000,000
5	Italy	9,900,000,000
6	Belgium and Luxembourg	9,573,000,000
7	Japan	9,549,000,000
8	Ireland	7,920,000,000
9	Spain	5,836,000,000
10	Switzerland	5,042,000,000

Source: *Office for National Statistics*

In 1998 the USA just overtook Germany to become the number one source of imports to the UK.

TOP 10 EXPORT MARKETS FOR GOODS FROM THE UK

	MARKET	TOTAL VALUE OF 1998 EXPORTS (£)
1	USA	20,954,000,000
2	Germany	20,589,000,000
3	France	16,450,000,000
4	Netherlands	12,993,000,000
5	Ireland	9,600,000,000
6	Italy	8,611,000,000
7	Belgium/Luxembourg	8,417,000,000
8	Spain	7,164,000,000
9	Sweden	4,393,000,000
10	Japan	3,238,000,000

Source: *Office for National Statistics*

In 1997 the USA regained its former place as Britain's pre-eminent export market.

TOP 10 DUTY-FREE FERRY OPERATORS

	FERRY OPERATOR/LOCATION	ANNUAL SALES ($)
1	**P & O Stena Line**, UK	320,000,000
2	**Eurotunnel**, UK/France	280,000,000
3	**Silja Ferries**, Finland	260,000,000
4	**Viking Line Ferries**, Finland	210,000,000
5	**Stena Line**, Sweden	185,000,000
6	**Scandlines**, Denmark	*
7	**Color Line**, Norway	114,900,000
8	**Seafrance**, France	89,000,000
9	**Hoverspeed**, UK	75,000,000
10	**Brittany Ferries**, France	*

* *Precise figure confidential*

Source: *Generation AB*

UK and Scandinavian ferry services have long led this sector of the world markets.

CALL OF DUTY

World wide, duty-free sales have virtually doubled during the past decade and now exceed $20 billion. The top 10 countries account for almost half the total.

TOP 10 DUTY-FREE AIRPORTS

	AIRPORT/LOCATION	ANNUAL SALES ($)
1	**London Heathrow**, UK	433,200,000
2	**Amsterdam Schiphol**, Netherlands	361,800,000
3	**Paris Charles De Gaulle**, France	320,700,000
4	**Frankfurt**, Germany	260,500,000
5	**Singapore Changi**, Singapore	250,000,000
6	**Honolulu**, Hawaii, USA	242,500,000
7	**London Gatwick**, UK	208,300,000
8	=**Copenhagen**, Denmark	200,000,000
	=**Tel Aviv Ben Gurion**, Israel	200,000,000
10	**São Paulo**, Brazil	*

* *Precise figure confidential*

Source: *Generation AB*

SCENT OF MONEY

Women's fragrances were once the foremost duty- and tax-free item, but since 1990 they have been overtaken by cigarettes.

TOP 10 DUTY-FREE SHOPS

(Shop/location)

1 **London Heathrow Airport**, UK 2 **Silja Ferries**, Finland 3 **P & O Stena Line**, UK 4 **Amsterdam Schiphol Airport**, Netherlands 5 **Viking Line Ferries**, Finland 6 **Paris Charles De Gaulle Airport**, France 7 **London Gatwick Airport**, UK 8 **Frankfurt Airport**, Germany 9 **Eurotunnel**, UK/France 10 **Stena Line**, Sweden

Source: *Generation AB*

In 1998, total global duty- and tax-free sales were worth $20.5 billion, down 2.2 per cent on 1997 sales. Under recently introduced EC laws, duty-free sales in member countries have been axed since July 1999.

TOP 10 DUTY-FREE PRODUCTS

	PRODUCT	SALES ($)
1	Cigarettes	2,477,000,000
2	Women's fragrances	2,157,000,000
3	Scotch whisky	1,423,000,000
4	Jewellery	1,331,000,000
5	Women's cosmetics	1,267,000,000
6	Confectionery	1,096,000,000
7	Men's fragrances and toiletries	995,000,000
8	Accessories	984,000,000
9	Leather goods (handbags, belts, etc)	890,000,000
10	Cognac	807,000,000

Source: *Generation AB*

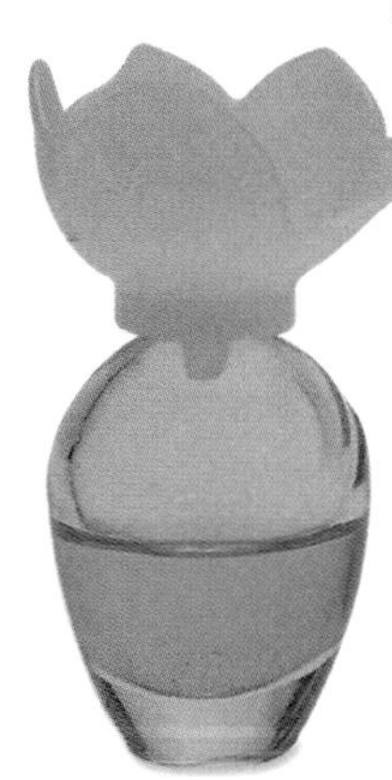

Did You Know? Bestselling perfume Chanel No. 5 was invented in 1921 by Ernest Beaux. It was so-called because it was the fifth sample he submitted to Coco Chanel.

Communication Matters

FIRST PAST THE POST

India's high population and tradition of bureaucracy combine to make it the world leader in number of post offices. The country's postal service employs some 600,000 people.

TOP 10

COUNTRIES WITH THE MOST POST OFFICES

	COUNTRY	POST OFFICES*
1	India	153,021
2	China	112,204
3	Russia	43,900
4	USA	38,159
5	Japan	24,678
6	Indonesia	20,139
7	UK	18,760
8	France	17,038
9	Turkey	16,984
10	Ukraine	15,227

* *1998 or latest year available*

Source: *Universal Postal Union*

TOP 10

COUNTRIES MAKING THE MOST INTERNATIONAL PHONE CALLS

	COUNTRY	MINUTES PER HEAD	TOTAL MINUTES OUTGOING CALLS PER ANNUM
1	USA	90.3	24,593,000,000
2	UK	38.7	5,820,000,000
3	Canada	158.8	4,805,000,000
4	Germany	57.4	4,711,000,000
5	France	56.9	3,400,000,000
6	Italy	47.1	2,705,000,000
7	Switzerland	266.8	1,901,000,000
8	Japan	14.9	1,895,000,000
9	Netherlands	114.6	1,805,000,000
10	Spain	45.7	1,803,000,000

Source: *International Telecommunication Union*

TOP 10

COUNTRIES WITH THE HIGHEST RATIO OF CELLULAR MOBILE PHONE USERS

	COUNTRY	SUBSCRIBERS*	MOBILE PHONES PER 1,000 INHABITANTS*
1	Finland	2,966,000	577.0
2	Sweden	4,527,000	511.5
3	Norway	2,081,000	471.9
4	Italy	20,300,000	352.9
5	Denmark	1,854,000	351.1
6	Australia	6,000,000	323.8
7	Japan	39,786,000	315.7
8	Portugal	3,075,000	311.9
9	South Korea	13,988,000	304.2
10	Austria	2,270,000	281.3
	UK	13,001,000	220.4

* *Figures partly Siemens estimates*

Source: *Siemens AG*

TOP 10

LETTER-SENDING COUNTRIES

	COUNTRY	AVERAGE NO. OF LETTER POST ITEMS SENT PER INHABITANT*
1	Vatican City	6,700.0
2	USA	728.9
3	Norway	554.9
4	Sweden	502.8
5	France	435.9
6	Austria	371.6
7	Belgium	345.7
8	Luxembourg	339.7
9	Denmark	334.7
10	UK	324.9

* *In 1998 or latest year for which data available*

TOP 10

COUNTRIES WITH THE MOST TELEPHONES

	COUNTRY	TELEPHONE LINES PER 100 INHABITANTS*
1	Luxembourg	71.00
2	Sweden	69.64
3	USA	67.66
4	Switzerland	67.41
5	Norway	65.42
6	Denmark	65.38
7	Iceland	62.86
8	Canada	61.51
9	Netherlands	58.45
10	Hong Kong	58.36
	UK	54.92

* *Figures partly Siemens estimates*

Source: *Siemens AG*

The world average "teledensity" is 14.36 phone lines per 100 inhabitants. On a continental basis, Oceania (Australia, New Zealand, and their neighbours) has the highest ratio of telephone lines per 100 people – an average of 41.19 – followed by Europe with 36.74. The Americas as a whole has an average of 32.70, because even the high US figure fails to compensate for the much lower numbers in Central and South America.

Did You Know? In 1876 Elisha Gray attempted to patent the telephone, only to discover that Alexander Graham Bell had beaten him to it by a matter of hours. Undaunted, he invented the telautograph, a pen-driven precursor of the fax machine.

VATICAN POST

The list of the countries sending the most letters per person is headed by the Vatican City, with an average of over 27 per person daily, or almost 10,000 annually. The Vatican's population (which is variable, but seldom exceeds 750) is small, and this statistical anomaly results in part from the large numbers of official missives dispatched via the Holy See's post office and its 32 postboxes, but mainly because Rome's inhabitants have discovered that mail posted there and bearing Vatican stamps is treated as priority and so is delivered more promptly.

SNAP SHOTS

TOP 10

ONLINE LANGUAGES

	LANGUAGE	NUMBER*
1	English	91,969,000
2	Japanese	9,000,000
3	French	7,100,000
4	German	6,900,000
5	Chinese (Mandarin)	5,600,000
6	=Korean	3,300,000
	=Swedish	3,300,000
8	Italian	3,200,000
9	Finnish	1,430,000
10	Russian	1,300,000

* *Of individuals accessing the Internet in this language*

Source: *Headcount.com*

TOP 10

BUSIEST INTERNET SITES

	SITE	HITS*
1	Yahoo	32,263,000
2	AOL.com	30,545,000
3	msn.com	25,579,000
4	geocities.com	23,270,000
5	lycos.com	18,099,000
6	passport.com	17,793,000
7	microsoft.com	16,182,000
8	netscape.com	15,524,000
9	bluemountain.com	14,755,000
10	tripod.com	14,661,000

* *Number of accesses during December 1999*

Source: *PC Data Online*

One of the principal aims of the Internet is the dissemination of information, but information about its own users is rather patchy and erratic.

TOP 10

COUNTRIES WITH THE MOST INTERNET USERS

	COUNTRY	PERCENTAGE OF POPULATION	INTERNET USERS*
1	USA	41	110,825,000
2	Japan	14	18,156,000
3	UK	23	13,975,000
4	Canada	44	13,277,000
5	Germany	15	12,285,000
6	Australia	36	6,837,000
7	Brazil	4	6,790,000
8	China	0.5	6,308,000
9	France	10	5,696,000
10	South Korea	12	5,688,000
	World total	4.2	259,000,000

* *Estimates for weekly usage as at end of 1999*

Source: *Computer Industry Almanac, Inc.*

"CYBERSPACE"

The English word cybernetics – the communication and control of living things or machines – was coined in 1948 by American mathematician Norbert Wiener (1894–1964). He may have derived it from the French word *cybernétique* – the art of governing – created in 1834 by André Marie Ampère. From that, the term "cyberspace" was invented by American science-fiction writer William Gibson in his 1982 short story *Burning Chrome*, and developed in his 1984 novel *Neuromancer*. The term now refers to the ethereal electronic space that the Internet is thought to occupy.

WHY DO WE SAY?

TOP 10 COUNTRIES WITH THE MOST COMPUTERS

(Country/computers)

1 **USA**, 164,100,000 2 **Japan**, 49,900,000 3 **Germany**, 30,600,000 4 **UK**, 26,000,000 5 **France**, 21,800,000 6 **Italy**, 17,500,000 7 **Canada**, 16,000,000 8 **China**, 15,900,000 9 **= Australia**, 10,600,000; **= South Korea**, 10,600,000

Source: *Computer Industry Almanac, Inc.*

Computer industry estimates put the number of computers in the world at 98 million in 1990, 222 million in 1995, and 579 million in 2000 – a sixfold increase over the decade.

LAPTOP OF LUXURY

Ever-increasing power, reducing costs, and the growth of the Internet have resulted in the global explosion of the computer industry.

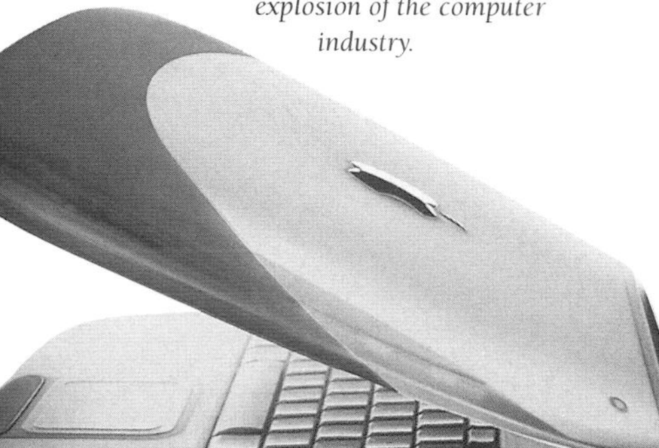

POWER TO THE PEOPLE

In the 20th century the creation of national grids for the transmission of electricity brought power to even the remotest communities.

TOP 10 ELECTRICITY-CONSUMING COUNTRIES

	COUNTRY	CONSUMPTION (KW/HR)
1	USA	3,278,500,000,000
2	China	955,980,000,000
3	Japan	904,600,000,000
4	Russia	712,400,000,000
5	Germany	477,270,000,000
6	Canada	475,120,000,000
7	India	397,280,000,000
8	France	375,550,000,000
9	Brazil	322,650,000,000
10	UK	309,590,000,000

Source: *Energy Information Administration*

TOP 10 ENVIRONMENTAL CONCERNS IN THE UK

	CONCERN	PERCENTAGE OF PEOPLE CONCERNED
1	Traffic (congestion, fumes, noise)	37
2	Global warming/ climate change	32
3	Air pollution	30
4	Pollution of lakes, rivers, and seas	23
5	Depletion of the ozone layer	22
6	Loss of tropical rainforest	15
7	Population growth	14
8	Consumption of natural resources	12
9=	Radioactive wastes	10
=	Toxic waste	10
=	Loss of countryside to urban development	10

Source: *Department of the Environment, Transport and the Regions*

THE 10 COUNTRIES EMITTING THE MOST SULPHUR DIOXIDE

	COUNTRY	ANNUAL SO_2 EMISSIONS PER HEAD KG	LB	OZ
1	Czech Republic	149.4	329	6
2	Former Yugoslavia	138.2	304	11
3	Bulgaria	116.8	257	8
4	Canada	104.0	229	4
5	Hungary	81.4	179	7
6=	Romania	79.2	174	10
=	USA	79.2	174	10
8	Poland	71.1	156	12
9	Slovakia	70.0	154	5
10	Belarus	57.5	126	12

Source: *World Resources Institute*

Sulphur dioxide, the principal cause of acid rain, is produced by fuel combustion in factories and especially by power stations.

THE 10 COUNTRIES EMITTING THE MOST CARBON DIOXIDE

	COUNTRY	ANNUAL CO_2 EMISSIONS PER HEAD (TONNES)
1	Qatar	52.18
2	United Arab Emirates	36.20
3	Kuwait	25.24
4	Luxembourg	20.12
5	USA	19.68
6	Singapore	19.45
7	Bahrain	18.53
8	Trinidad and Tobago	17.14
9	Australia	16.96
10	Brunei	16.89
	UK	9.48

Source: *Carbon Dioxide Information Analysis Center*

CO_2 emissions derive from three principal sources – fossil fuel burning, cement manufacturing, and gas flaring.

TOP 10 COAL-CONSUMING COUNTRIES

	COUNTRY	1998 CONSUMPTION IN TONNES OF OIL EQUIVALENT
1	China	615,400,000
2	USA	533,700,000
3	India	153,600,000
4	Russia	102,800,000
5	Japan	88,400,000
6	South Africa	87,900,000
7	Germany	84,700,000
8	Poland	60,900,000
9	Australia	45,800,000
10	UK	40,700,000

Source: BP Statistical Review of World Energy 1999

POWER PLANT

Opened in 1985–86, Pacific Gas and Electric's Diablo Canyon Nuclear Power Station, California, is one of the US's 104 reactors.

TOP 10 COUNTRIES WITH THE MOST NUCLEAR REACTORS

(Country/reactors)

1 **USA**, 104 2 **France**, 58 3 **Japan**, 53 4 **UK**, 35 5 **Russia**, 29 6 **Germany**, 20 7 **Ukraine**, 16 8 **South Korea**, 15 9 **Canada**, 14 10 **Sweden**, 12

Source: *International Atomic Energy Agency*

There are some 434 nuclear power stations in operation in a total of 32 countries around the world, with a further 36 under construction. Lithuania has the greatest reliance on nuclear power, obtaining 77.2 per cent of its electricity from nuclear sources.

TOP 10 ENERGY-CONSUMING COUNTRIES

	COUNTRY	1998 ENERGY CONSUMPTION* OIL	GAS	COAL	NUCLEAR	HEP#	TOTAL
1	USA	852.4	551.2	533.7	183.0	26.7	2,146.9
2	China	190.3	17.4	615.4	3.9	17.1	844.0
3	Russia	122.3	328.3	102.8	26.9	13.6	593.8
4	Japan	255.0	62.5	88.4	84.0	9.3	499.2
5	Germany	136.6	71.6	84.7	41.7	1.8	336.3
6	India	86.1	20.9	153.6	2.8	7.2	270.6
7	France	94.5	33.7	15.1	100.0	5.7	249.1
8	UK	80.5	79.9	40.7	25.8	0.6	227.5
9	Canada	83.2	63.3	25.9	18.5	28.6	219.3
10	South Korea	93.3	14.1	36.1	23.1	0.5	167.1
	World	3,389.0	2,016.4	2,219.4	626.6	226.4	8,477.4

* *Millions of tonnes of oil equivalent* # *Hydroelectric power*

Source: BP Statistical Review of World Energy 1999

THE 10 MOST DEFORESTING COUNTRIES

(Country/average annual forest loss 1990–95 in sq km/sq miles)

1 **Brazil**, 25,544/9,862 2 **Indonesia**, 10,844/4,186 3 **Dem. Rep. of Congo**, 7,400/2,857 4 **Bolivia**, 5,814/2,244 5 **Mexico**, 5,080/1,961 6 **Venezuela**, 5,034/1,943 7 **Malaysia**, 4,002/1,545 8 **Myanmar**, 3,874/1,495 9 **Sudan**, 3,526/1,361 10 **Thailand**, 3,294/1,271

Source: *Food and Agriculture Organization of the United Nations*

TOP 10 NATURAL GAS-CONSUMING COUNTRIES

	COUNTRY	1998 CONSUMPTION BILLION CU M	BILLION CU FT
1	USA	612.4	24,005.4
2	Russia	364.7	14,297.9
3	UK	88.8	3,479.7
4	Germany	79.6	3,118.3
5	Canada	70.3	2,756.8
6	Japan	69.4	2,722.0
7	Ukraine	68.8	2,695.8
8	Italy	57.2	2,242.9
9	Iran	51.7	2,025.1
10	Saudi Arabia	46.0	1,803.0
	World total	2,240.2	87,816.6

Source: BP Statistical Review of World Energy 1999

TOP 10 OIL-CONSUMING COUNTRIES

	COUNTRY	1998 CONSUMPTION TONNES
1	USA	852,400,000
2	Japan	255,000,000
3	China	190,300,000
4	Germany	136,600,000
5	Russia	122,300,000
6	Italy	94,700,000
7	France	94,500,000
8	South Korea	93,300,000
9	=Brazil	83,200,000
	=Canada	83,200,000
	UK	80,500,000

Source: BP Statistical Review of World Energy 1999

In which year was Coca-Cola introduced?

see p.220 for the answer

A 1886
B 1902
C 1927

Accidents at Home & Work

THE 10 ★ MOST DANGEROUS INDUSTRIES IN GREAT BRITAIN

	INDUSTRY	FATAL/MAJOR INJURIES PER 100,000 EMPLOYEES (1998/99)*
1	Mining and quarrying	508.8
2	Manufacturing wood and wood products	449.4
3	Manufacturing food products, beverages, and tobacco	335.7
4	Manufacturing basic metals and fabricated metal products	329.3
5	Manufacturing rubber and plastic products	287.1
6	Agriculture, hunting, forestry, and fishing	229.9
7	Transport, storage, and communication	209.5
8	Manufacturing chemicals, chemical products, and man-made fibres	206.6
9	Manufacturing transport equipment	194.5
10	Manufacturing machinery and equipment necessary	193.0

* *Provisional*

DANGER ON DECK

Exposure to extreme weather conditions and other hazards places fishing among the world's most dangerous industries.

THE 10 MOST DANGEROUS JOBS IN THE UK

1 **Formula One driver** 2 **Bomb disposal officer** 3 **Test pilot** 4 **SAS employee** 5 **Circus performer** 6 **Film stuntman** 7 **Commercial diver** 8 **Oil rig worker** 9 **Scaffolder** 10 **= Fisherman; = Miner; = Dockworker; = Sailor in Merchant Navy; = Linesman** (electrical industry)

THE 10 ★ MOST COMMON ACCIDENTAL CAUSES OF DEATH FOR THE SELF-EMPLOYED IN GREAT BRITAIN

	ACCIDENT	FATALITIES (1998/99)*
1	Falls from a height	33
2	Struck by a moving vehicle	9
3	Struck by a moving object (including flying or falling)	6
4	=Drowning or asphyxiation	4
	=Trapped by something collapsing/overturning	4
6	Contact with moving machinery	3
7	Injured by an animal	2
8	Exposure to an explosion	1
	=Exposure to fire	1
	=Contact with electricity or electrical discharge	1

* *Provisional figures*

Source: *Health and Safety Executive*

THE 10 ★ MOST COMMON CAUSES OF INJURY TO THE SELF-EMPLOYED IN GREAT BRITAIN

	CAUSE	FATALITIES	INJURIES*
1	Falls from a height	33	430
2	Slip, trip, or fall on same level	–	249
3	Struck by a moving object (including flying or falling object)	6	243
4	Handling, lifting, or carrying	–	211
5	Contact with moving machinery	3	87
6	Struck against something fixed or stationary	–	59
7	Acts of violence	–	52
8	Struck by a moving vehicle	9	44
9	Exposure to or contact with a harmful substance	–	30
10	Animal	2	24

* *1998/99 provisional figures*

Source: *Health and Safety Executive*

THE 10 MOST ACCIDENT-PRONE COUNTRIES

(Country/accidental death rate per 100,000)*

1 **South Korea**, 120.2 2 **Moldova**, 114.0 3 **Russia**, 112.3 4 **South Africa**, 99.4 5 **Lithuania**, 95.0 6 **Estonia**, 94.5 7 **Latvia**, 94.1 8 **Ukraine**, 89.0 9 **Belarus**, 82.0 10 **Slovenia**, 56.5

UK, 20.7

* *Traffic accidents, accidental falls, and other accidents*

Source: UN Demographic Yearbook

DOMESTIC INFERNO

A combination of deliberate and accidental fires, many of which result from avoidable causes, contributes to losses of life and property.

THE 10 MOST COMMON ACCIDENTS IN UK HOMES

	ACCIDENT	NO. PER ANNUM*
1	Unspecified falls	459,000
2	Tripping over	344,000
3	Struck by static object	311,000
4	Cut or tear from sharp object	288,000
5	Fall on or from stairs	268,000
6	Struck by moving object	152,000
7	Foreign body	128,000
8	Struck (unspecified)	107,000
9	Thermal effect	99,000
10	Pinched or crushed by blunt object	85,000

* *National estimates based on actual Home Accident Surveillance System figures for sample population*

Falls are the leading cause of accidents in the home. Total accidents resulting from falls were estimated to be 1,110,000 in 1996.

THE 10 MOST COMMON CAUSES OF DOMESTIC FIRES IN THE UK

	CAUSE	APPROX. NO. OF FIRES PER ANNUM
1	Misuse of equipment or appliances	17,100
2	Malicious (or suspected malicious)	15,500
3	Chip/fat pan fires	12,300
4	Faulty appliances and leads	9,000
5	Careless handling of fire or hot substances	5,400
6	Placing articles too close to heat	4,800
7	Other accidental	4,100
8	Faulty fuel supplies	1,900
9	Playing with fire	1,100
10	Unspecified	900
	UK total	72,200

THE 10 ANIMALS MOST INVOLVED IN ACCIDENTS IN THE UK

(Animal/injuries caused per annum)*

❶ **Dog**, 66,528 ❷ **Cat**, 14,150 ❸ **Bee and wasp**, 14,035 ❹ **Other insect**, 9,658 ❺ **Horse, pony, donkey**, 3,302 ❻ **Rabbit, hamster, etc.**, 2,976 ❼ **Wild creature**, 960 ❽ **Wild bird**, 826 ❾ **Cow, bull, calf**, 730 ❿ **Chicken, swan, duck, etc.**, 653

* *National estimates based on actual Home Accident Surveillance System figures for sample population*

"HAZARD"

Before it came to mean a risk, hazard was a dice game, popular in Europe since the 14th century. It comes from the Arabic word *al* (the) and *zahr* (dice). The uncertainty of casting the dice led to the adoption of *al-zahr* in Spanish as *azahr*, an unexpected accident. In French this became *hasard*, and in the English *hazard*.

WHY DO WE SAY?

Did You Know? In the US, in a single year, a total of 162 people aged 65 and over were treated for skateboarding injuries.

Industrial & Other Disasters

THE 10

WORST DISASTERS AT SPORTS VENUES IN THE 20TH CENTURY

	LOCATION/DATE/TYPE	NO. KILLED
1	**Hong Kong Jockey Club**, 26 Feb 1918, Stand collapse and fire	604
2	**Lenin Stadium**, Moscow, 20 Oct 1982, Crush in football stadium	340
3	**Lima**, Peru, 24 May 1964, Riot in football stadium	320
4	**Sinceljo**, Colombia, 20 Jan 1980, Bullring stand collapse	222
5	**Hillsborough**, Sheffield, UK, 15 Apr 1989, Crush in football stadium	96
6	**Guatemala City**, Guatemala, 16 Oct 1996, Stampede in Mateo Flores National Stadium during World Cup soccer qualifying match, Guatemala v Costa Rica, with 127 injured	83
7	**Le Mans**, France, 11 June 1955, Racing car crash	82
8	**Katmandu**, Nepal, 12 Mar 1988, Stampede in football stadium	80
9	**Buenos Aires**, Argentina, 23 May 1968, Riot in football stadium	74
10	**Ibrox Park**, Glasgow, Scotland, 2 Jan 1971, Barrier collapse in football stadium	66

Before the Ibrox Park disaster, the worst accident at a British stadium was caused by the collapse of a stand at Burnden Park, Bolton, on 9 March 1946, in an FA Cup Tie against Stoke City, which left 33 dead and 400 injured. If stunt-flying is included as a "sport", the worst airshow disaster of all time occurred at the Ramstein US Air Force base, Germany, on 28 August 1988, when three fighters in an Italian aerobatic team collided, one of them crashing into the crowd, leaving 70 dead and 150 injured. Such tragedies are not an exclusively modern phenomenon: during the reign of Roman Emperor Antoninus Pius (AD 138–161), a stand at the Circus Maximus collapsed during a gladiatorial spectacle and 1,162 spectators were killed.

THE 10

WORST MINING DISASTERS

	LOCATION/DATE	NO. KILLED
1	**Hinkeiko**, China, 26 Apr 1942	1,549
2	**Courrières**, France, 10 Mar 1906	1,060
3	**Omuta**, Japan, 9 Nov 1963	447
4	**Senghenydd**, UK, 14 Oct 1913	439
5	**Coalbrook**, South Africa, 21 Jan 1960	437
6	**Wankie**, Rhodesia, 6 June 1972	427
7	**Dhanbad**, India, 28 May 1965	375
8	**Chasnala**, India, 27 Dec 1975	372
9	**Monongah**, USA, 6 Dec 1907	362
10	**Barnsley**, UK, 12 Dec 1866	361*

* *Including 27 killed the following day while searching for survivors*

A mine disaster at the Fushun mines, Manchuria, in February 1931 may have resulted in up to 3,000 deaths, but information was suppressed by the Chinese government. Soviet security was also responsible for obscuring details of an explosion at the East German Johanngeorgendstadt uranium mine on 29 November 1949, when as many as 3,700 may have died. Among the most tragic disasters of this century was a mine disaster at Aberfan, Wales, on 20 October 1966. Waste from the local mine had been building up for many years to become a heap some 244 m (800 ft) in height. Weakened by the presence of a spring, a huge volume of slurry suddenly flowed down and engulfed the local school, killing 116 children.

THE 10

WORST FIRES AT THEATRE AND ENTERTAINMENT VENUES*

	LOCATION/DATE/TYPE	NO. KILLED
1	**Canton**, China, 25 May 1845, Theatre	1,670
2	**Shanghai**, China, June 1871, Theatre	900
3	**Vienna**, Austria, 8 Dec 1881, Ring Theatre	640–850
4	**St. Petersburg**, Russia, 14 Feb 1836, Lehmann Circus	800
5	**Antoung**, China, 13 Feb 1937, Cinema	658
6	**Chicago**, USA, 30 Dec 1903, Iroquois Theater	591
7	**Boston**, USA, 28 Nov 1942, Cocoanut Grove Night Club	491
8	**Abadan**, Iran, 20 Aug 1978, Theatre	422
9	**Niteroi**, Brazil, 17 Dec 1961, Circus	323
10	**Brooklyn Theater**, New York 5 Dec 1876	295

* *19th and 20th centuries, excluding sports stadiums and race tracks*

All the worst theatre disasters have been caused by fire. The figure given for the first entry in this list is a conservative estimate, some sources putting the figure as high as 2,500, but, even in recent times, reports of disasters from China are often unreliable.

THE 10

WORST FIRES OF THE 20TH CENTURY*

	LOCATION/DATE/TYPE	NO. KILLED
1	**Kwanto**, Japan, 1 Sep 1923, Following earthquake	60,000
2	**Chungking**, China, 2 Sep 1949, Docks	1,700
3	**Hakodate**, Japan, 22 Mar 1934, City	1,500
4	**San Francisco**, US, 18 Apr 1906, Following earthquake	600–700
5	**Cloquet**, Minnesota, USA, 12 Oct 1918, Forest	559
6	=**Lagunillas**, Venezuela, 14 Nov 1939, Oil refinery and city	over 500
	=**Mandi Dabwali**, India, 23 Dec 1995, School tent	over 500
8	**Hoboken**, New Jersey, USA, 30 June 1900, Docks	326
9	**Brussels**, Belgium, 22 May 1967 Department store	322
10	**Columbus**, Ohio, USA, 21 Apr 1930, State Penitentiary	320

* *Excluding sports and entertainment venues, mining disasters, and the results of military action*

Did You Know? One of the worst fires in history was that which engulfed the wooden London Bridge on 11 July 1212, with some 3,000 victims burned, crushed, or drowned in the ensuing panic.

TROUBLE IN STORE

Some 1,500 people were inside the Sampoong Department Store, Seoul, when it collapsed, leaving over a third of them dead and as many as 900 injured.

THE 10 WORST COMMERCIAL AND INDUSTRIAL DISASTERS*

	LOCATION/DATE	TYPE	NO. KILLED
1	**Bhopal**, India, 3 Dec 1984	Methyl isocyante gas escape at Union Carbide plant	up to 3,000
2	**Oppau**, Germany, 21 Sep 1921	Chemical plant explosion	561
3	**Mexico City**, Mexico 20 Nov 1984	Explosion at a PEMEX liquified petroleum gas plant	540
4	**Seoul**, Korea, 29 June 1995	Collapse of Sampoong Department Store	501
5	**Brussels**, Belgium 22 May 1967	Fire in l'Innovation department store	322
6	**Novosibirsk**, USSR Apr 1979#	Anthrax infection following accident at biological and chemical warfare plant	up to 300
7	**Guadalajara**, Mexico 22 Apr 1992	Explosions caused by gas leak into sewers	230
8	**Sâo Paulo**, Brazil 1 Feb 1974	Fire in Joelma bank and office building	227
9	**Oakdale**, USA, 18 May 1918	Chemical plant explosion	193
10	**Bangkok**, Thailand, 10 May 1993	Fire engulfed a four-storey doll factory	187

* *Including industrial sites, factories, offices, and stores; excluding military, mining, marine, and other transport disasters* # *Precise date unknown*

THE 10 WORST EXPLOSIONS*

	LOCATION/DATE	TYPE	NO. KILLED
1	**Rhodes**, Greece, 1856#	Lightning strike of gunpowder store	4,000
2	**Brescia**, Italy, 1769#	Arsenal	over 3,000
3	**Salang Tunnel**, Afghanistan, 3 Nov 1982	Petrol tanker collision	over 2,000
4	**Lanchow**, China, 26 Oct 1935	Arsenal	2,000
5	**Halifax**, Nova Scotia, 6 Dec 1917	Ammunition ship *Mont Blanc*	1,963
6	**Memphis**, USA, 27 Apr 1865	*Sultana* boiler explosion	1,547
7	**Bombay**, India, 14 Apr 1944	Ammunition ship *Fort Stikine*	1,376
8	**Cali**, Colombia, 7 Aug 1956	Ammunition trucks	up to 1,200
9	**Chelyabinsk**, USSR, 3 June 1989	Liquid gas beside railway	up to 800
10	**Texas City**, Texas, USA, 16 Apr 1947	Ammonium nitrate on cargo ships	576

* *Excluding mining disasters, terrorist and military bombs, and natural explosions such as volcanoes* # *Precise date unknown*

THE 10 FIRST HEINZ'S "57 VARIETIES"

(Product/year introduced)

1 **Horseradish**, 1869 2 = **Sour gherkins**, 1870; = **Sour mixed pickles**, 1870; = **Chow chow pickle**, 1870; = **Sour onions**, 1870; = **Prepared mustard**, 1870; = **Sauerkraut in crocks**, 1870 8 = **Heinz and Noble catsup**, 1873; = **Vinegar**, 1873 10 **Tomato ketchup**, 1876

LABOUR SAVER

When Heinz was restructured in 1876, its first product was tomato ketchup. Although a staple product in every American household, until then making it involved stirring a huge cauldron over an open fire for a day.

TOP 10

FOOD AND DRINK ITEMS CONSUMED IN THE UK BY WEIGHT*

	PRODUCT	AVERAGE ANNUAL CONSUMPTION PER CAPITA[#] KG	LB	OZ
1	Milk and cream	110.0	242	11
2	Vegetables and vegetable products	104.3	229	15
3	Cereal products	76.8	169	5
4	Fruit and fruit products	56.0	123	7
5	Meat and meat products	48.7	107	5
6	Fats and oils	10.1	22	4
7	Sugar and preserves	8.1	17	13
8	Fish	7.4	16	5
9	Cheese	5.3	11	10
10	Beverages	3.0	6	9

* *Excluding beer and other alcoholic drinks*

[#] *Based on the Ministry of Agriculture, Fisheries, and Food* National Food Survey

TOP 10

HOTTEST CHILLIES

	EXAMPLES OF CHILLIES	SCOVILLE UNITS
1	Datil, Habanero, Scotch Bonnet	100,000–350,000
2	Chiltepin, Santaka, Thai	50,000–100,000
3	Aji, Cayenne, Piquin, Tabasco	30,000–50,000
4	de Arbol	15,000–30,000
5	Serrano, Yellow Wax	5,000–15,000
6	Chipotle, Jalapeno, Mirasol	2,500–5,000
7	Cascabel, Sandia, Rocotillo	1,500–2,500
8	Ancho, Espanola, Pasilla, Poblano	1,000–1,500
9	Anaheim, New Mexico	500–1,000
10	Cherry, Peperoncini	100–500

Hot peppers contain substances called capsaicinoids, which determine how "hot" they are. In 1912 pharmacist Wilbur Scoville pioneered a test, based on which chillies are ranked by Scoville Units. According to this scale, one part of capsaicin (the principal capsaicinoid) per million equals 15,000 Scoville Units.

TOP 10 ★ MEAT-EATING COUNTRIES

	COUNTRY	ANNUAL CONSUMPTION PER CAPITA KG	LB	OZ
1	USA	117.1	258	2
2	Cyprus	109.8	242	1
3	Bahamas	105.0	231	7
4	New Zealand	104.0	229	4
5	Australia	101.0	222	10
6	Austria	100.6	221	12
7	Spain	98.9	218	0
8	Denmark	97.2	214	4
9	Yugoslavia	94.6	208	8
10	Slovenia	93.5	206	2
	UK	73.7	162	7

Source: *Meat and Livestock Commission*

There is a huge range in levels of meat consumption around the world, from the No. 1 meat consumer, the USA, at 117.1 kg (258 lb) per person per year, to India, where the figure may be just 3.4 kg (7 lb).

FISH DISH

The national popularity of sushi (raw fish and rice) and other recipes helps to make Japan one of the world's leading fish consumers.

TOP 10 ★ PORK-CONSUMING COUNTRIES

	COUNTRY	ANNUAL CONSUMPTION PER CAPITA KG	LB	OZ
1	Austria	63.9	140	14
2	Yugoslavia	60.1	132	7
3	Denmark	57.4	126	8
4	Spain	56.2	123	14
5	Hungary	52.8	116	6
6	Cyprus	52.3	115	4
7	Germany	51.9	114	6
8	Slovakia	48.2	106	4
9	Netherlands	47.7	105	2
10	Czech Republic	44.6	98	5
	UK	24.6	54	3

Source: *Meat and Livestock Commission*

TOP 10 ★ FISH-CONSUMING COUNTRIES

	COUNTRY	ANNUAL CONSUMPTION PER CAPITA* KG	LB	OZ
1	Maldives	153.4	338	3
2	Iceland	95.7	211	0
3	Kiribati	78.6	173	4
4	Japan	76.1	167	12
5	Seychelles	60.5	133	6
6	Portugal	58.7	129	7
7	Norway	54.6	120	6
8	Malaysia	54.1	119	4
9	French Polynesia	51.8	114	3
10	South Korea	51.6	113	12
	UK	21.9	48	4

* *Combines sea and freshwater fish totals*

Source: *Food and Agriculture Organization of the United Nations*

TOP 10 ★ BEEF-CONSUMING COUNTRIES

	COUNTRY	ANNUAL CONSUMPTION PER CAPITA KG	LB	OZ
1	Uruguay	58.8	129	10
2	Argentina	50.5	111	5
3	USA	43.3	95	7
4	Paraguay	39.8	87	11
5	Australia	37.5	82	10
6	New Zealand	36.7	80	14
7	Mongolia	35.8	78	14
8	Canada	32.5	71	10
9	Bahamas	32.1	70	12
10	French Polynesia	30.9	68	1
	UK	16.9	37	4

Source: *Meat and Livestock Commission*

TOP 10 ★ POULTRY-CONSUMING COUNTRIES

	COUNTRY	ANNUAL CONSUMPTION PER CAPITA KG	LB	OZ
1	Antigua & Barbuda	69.6	142	6
2	Saint Lucia	54.6	120	5
3	Bahamas	51.5	113	5
4	Brunei	50.6	111	8
5	St. Kitts & Nevis	50.3	110	14
6	USA	45.3	99	13
7	=Israel	44.0	97	0
	=Saint Vincent	44.0	97	0
9	Barbados	43.2	95	3
10	Dominica	40.5	89	4
	UK	25.7	56	10

Source: *Meat and Livestock Commission*

A MARS A DAY ...

Mars's first product, the Milky Way bar, was renamed Mars bar when launched in the UK in 1932. The name did not appear in the US until 1940, when a new bar was introduced.

THE 10 ★

FIRST MARS PRODUCTS

	PRODUCT	YEAR INTRODUCED
1	=Milky Way bar	1923
	=Snickers bar (non-chocolate)	1923
3	Snickers bar (chocolate)	1930
4	3 Musketeers bar	1932
5	Maltesers	1937
6	Kitekat (catfood; now Whiskas)	1939
7	Mars almond bar	1940
8	M&M's plain chocolate candies	1941
9	Uncle Ben's converted brand rice	1942
10	=M&M's peanut chocolate candies	1954
	=Pal (dogfood)	1954

American candy manufacturer Franklin C. Mars set up his first business in Tacoma, Washington, in 1911, and formed the Mar-O-Bar company in Minneapolis in 1922, with the first of its products, the Milky Way bar. The founder's son, Forrest E. Mars, set up in the UK in 1932, merging the firm with its American counterpart in 1964. Strangely, outside the US the Milky Way bar is known as a Mars bar, while in the UK a Milky Way is a rather different product, introduced in 1935.

TOP 10 ★

OLDEST-ESTABLISHED BRITISH CHOCOLATE PRODUCTS

	PRODUCT	YEAR INTRODUCED
1	Fry's Chocolate Cream	1853
2	Fry's Easter Egg	1873
3	Cadbury's Easter Egg	1875
4	Cadbury's Chocolate Drops*	1904
5	Cadbury's Dairy Milk	1905
6	Cadbury's Bournville	1908
7	Fry's Turkish Delight	1915
8	=Cadbury's Milk Tray	1920
	=Cadbury's Milk Chocolate Flake	1920
10	Cadbury's Creme Egg#	1923

* Now Chocolate Buttons

\# Original version

TOP 10 CHOCOLATE BRANDS IN THE UK

(Brand/sales in £)*

1 KitKat, 122,200,000 **2** Mars Bar, 71,400,000 **3** Cadbury's Dairy Milk, 67,600,000 **4** Celebrations, 58,600,000 **5** Twix, 56,500,000 **6** Roses, 56,000,000 **7** Maltesers, 50,300,000 **8** Quality Street, 45,000,000 **9** Galaxy, 40,100,000 **10** Aero, 37,000,000

* In year to 7 August 1999 Source: ACNielsen MMS

TOP 10 SWEET BRANDS IN THE UK*

1 Rowntree Fruit Pastilles **2** Bassett's & Beyond **3** Haribo **4** Chewits **5** Bassett's Jelly Babies **6** Skittles **7** Wrigley's Hubba Bubba **8** Fruit-tella **9** Rowntree's Fruit Gums **10** Jelly Tots

* Excluding chocolate

Source: Cadbury's Confectionery Review 1999

TOP 10 ★

SUGAR-CONSUMING COUNTRIES

	COUNTRY	ANNUAL CONSUMPTION PER CAPITA KG	LB	OZ
1	Israel	100.2	220	14
2	Belize	70.8	156	1
3	Trinidad and Tobago	61.1	134	11
4	Cuba	58.7	129	7
5	Barbados	58.0	127	14
6	Brazil	56.5	124	9
7	Swaziland	54.2	119	8
8	=Costa Rica	53.6	118	3
	=Malta	53.6	118	3
10	Iceland	53.3	117	8
	World average	20.2	44	8
	UK	39.2	86	7

Source: *Food and Agriculture Organization of the United Nations*

Background image: CHOCOLATE SELECTION

TOP 10

CHOCOLATE-CONSUMING NATIONS

	COUNTRY	TOTAL COCOA CONSUMPTION TONNES
1	USA	654,000
2	Germany	289,200
3	UK	192,000
4	France	177,300
5	Japan	124,000
6	Brazil	120,400
7	Russia	119,300
8	Italy	91,200
9	Canada	78,100
10	Spain	69,700
	World	2,722,000

Europe has the highest intake of the continents, with a cocoa consumption of 1,352,000 tonnes; the Americas are next with 1,015,000; then Asia and Oceania with 296,000; and lastly Africa, where only 59,000 tonnes are consumed across the entire continent.

TOP 10

ICE CREAM-CONSUMING COUNTRIES

	COUNTRY	PRODUCTION PER CAPITA PINTS	LITERS
1	New Zealand	46.61	26.48
2	US	38.79	22.04
3	Canada	33.05	18.78
4	Australia	31.50	17.90
5	Belgium	25.88	14.71
6	Sweden	24.69	14.03
7	Finland	24.49	13.92
8	Norway	23.48	13.34
9	Denmark	18.01	10.24
10	Israel	13.26	7.23

Source: *International Dairy Foods Association*

Global statistics for ice cream consumption are hard to come by, but this list presents recent and reliable estimates for per capita production of ice ceam and related products.

TOP 10

SUGAR PRODUCERS, 1999

	COUNTRY	TONNES*
1	Brazil	20,995,000
2	India	16,826,000
3	China	8,958,000
4	USA	7,556,000
5	Australia	5,778,000
6	Mexico	4,985,000
7	France	4,891,000
8	Thailand	4,314,000
9	Germany	4,054,000
10	Pakistan	3,817,000
	UK	1,680,000
	World	133,089,042

* *Raw centrifugal sugar*

Source: *Food and Agriculture Organization of the United Nations*

TOP 10 CONSUMERS OF KELLOGG'S CORNFLAKES*

1 Ireland 2 UK 3 Australia 4 Denmark 5 Sweden 6 Norway 7 Canada 8 USA 9 Mexico 10 Venezuela

* *Based on per capita consumption*

In 1894, the brothers Will Keith Kellogg and Dr. John Harvey Kellogg discovered, by accident, that boiled and rolled wheat dough turned into flakes if left overnight; once baked, they became a tasty cereal. In 1898, they replaced wheat with corn, thereby creating the Cornflakes we know today. Will Keith Kellogg went into business manufacturing Cornflakes, with his distinctive signature on the packet. Today, Cornflakes remain Kellogg's bestselling product.

CEREAL SUCCESS

One of the world's most popular breakfast foods, Kellogg's Cornflakes have a history spanning more than a century.

Alcoholic & Soft Drinks

TOP 10

SOFT DRINK BRANDS IN THE UK, 1999

	BRAND	SALES (£)*
1	Coca-Cola	395,900,000
2	Robinsons	154,300,000
3	Sunny Delight	150,200,000
4	Pepsi	132,500,000
5	Ribena	118,000,000
6	Tropicana	69,300,000
7	Lucozade	61,000,000
8	Tango	58,900,000
9	Schweppes	54,600,000
10	Del Monte fruit juice	47,600,000

* *In 12 months to 7 August 1999*

Source: ACNielsen MMS

TOP 10

SOFT DRINK-CONSUMING COUNTRIES*

	COUNTRY	ANNUAL CONSUMPTION PER CAPITA LITRES	PINTS
1	USA	212	373
2	=Iceland	138	242
	=Mexico	138	242
4	Malta	127	223
5	Norway	121	212
6	Canada	117	205
7	Australia	115	202
8	Israel	110	194
9	Chile	106	186
10	Ireland	103	185

* *Carbonated drinks only*

Source: *Zenith International*

As one might expect, affluent Western countries feature prominently in this list and, despite the spread of the so-called "Coca-Cola culture", former Eastern Bloc and Third World countries rank very low – some African nations recording extremely low consumption figures of less than 1 litre (1.76 pints) per annum.

THE 10 FIRST COCA-COLA PRODUCTS

(Product/date introduced)

1 **Coca-Cola**, May 1886 2 **Fanta**, June 1960 3 **Sprite**, Feb 1961 4 **TAB**, May 1963 5 **Fresca**, Feb 1966 6 **Mr. PiBB***, June 1972 7 **Hi-C Soft Drinks**, Aug 1977 8 **Mello Yello**, Mar 1979 9 **Ramblin' Root Beer**, June 1979 10 **Diet Coke**, July 1982

* *Mr. PiBB without Sugar launched Sep 1974; changed name to Sugar-free Mr. PiBB, 1975*

TOP 10

ALCOHOL-CONSUMING COUNTRIES

	COUNTRY	ANNUAL CONSUMPTION PER CAPITA (100 PER CENT ALCOHOL) LITRES	PINTS
1	Luxembourg	13.3	23.4
2	Portugal	11.2	19.7
3	=France	10.8	19.0
	= Ireland	10.8	19.0
5	Germany	10.6	18.6
6	Czech Republic	10.2	17.9
7	Spain	10.1	17.7
8	=Denmark	9.5	16.7
	=Romania	9.5	16.7
10	Hungary	9.4	16.5
	UK	7.5	13.1

Source: *Productschap voor Gedistilleerde Dranken*

After heading this list for many years, France was overtaken by Luxembourg, now acknowledged as the world's leading alcohol consumer.

TOP 10

WINE-DRINKING COUNTRIES

	COUNTRY	ANNUAL CONSUMPTION PER CAPITA LITRES	PINTS
1	Luxembourg	70.0	123.1
2	France	58.1	102.2
3	Portugal	53.2	93.6
4	Italy	52.0	91.5
5	Switzerland	43.2	76.0
6	Argentina	38.8	68.2
7	Greece	35.9	63.1
8	Spain	35.6	62.6
9	Austria	30.1	52.9
10	Denmark	29.0	51.0
	UK	14.4	25.3

Source: *Productschap voor Gedistilleerde Dranken*

The UK still does not make it into the Top 10, or even Top 20, wine-drinking countries in the world.

TOP 10 MOST COMMON PUB NAMES IN THE UK

1 The Red Lion 2 The Crown 3 The Royal Oak 4 The White Hart 5 The King's Head 6 The Bull 7 The Coach and Horses 8 The George 9 The Plough 10 The Swan

There are said to be over 600 Red Lions in Britain. The name is taken from the heraldic device of John of Gaunt, Duke of Lancaster (1340–99), the son of Edward III.

GRAPE HARVEST

Although Italy's wine production has led the world, it has recently been overtaken by that of France, which produced almost 6 million tonnes in 1999.

TOP 10 BEER-DRINKING COUNTRIES

	COUNTRY	ANNUAL CONSUMPTION PER CAPITA LITRES	PINTS
1	Czech Republic	161.8	284.7
2	Ireland	150.5	264.8
3	Germany	127.4	224.1
4	Luxembourg	110.9	195.1
5	Austria	108.6	191.1
6	Denmark	105.0	184.7
7	UK	99.4	174.9
8	Belgium	98.0	172.4
9	Australia	94.5	166.2
10	Slovak Republic	91.8	161.5

Source: *Productschap voor Gedistilleerde Dranken*

While no African countries appear in this list, or even in the Top 50 countries, many people in Africa do drink a lot of beer. Since bottled beer is often prohibitively expensive, however, they tend to consume home-made beers sold in local markets, which are excluded from national statistics.

HERE FOR THE BEER

During the 1990s, beer consumption in Ireland rose by 20 per cent, elevating the country from eighth to second place among the world's beer consumers.

TOP 10 MILK-DRINKING COUNTRIES*

	COUNTRY	ANNUAL CONSUMPTION PER CAPITA LITRES	PINTS
1	Iceland	149.1	262.4
2	=Finland	139.3	245.1
	=Ireland	139.3	245.1
4	Norway	115.8	203.8
5	UK	114.4	201.4
6	Sweden	113.0	198.8
7	New Zealand	99.4	174.9
8	USA	96.0	168.9
9	Spain	91.5	161.1
10	Switzerland	91.2	160.5

* *Only those reporting to the International Dairy Federation*

Source: *National Dairy Council*

TOP 10 CHAMPAGNE-IMPORTING COUNTRIES

	COUNTRY	BOTTLES IMPORTED (1999)
1	UK	32,261,232
2	USA	23,700,839
3	Germany	17,496,865
4	Belgium	10,753,197
5	Italy	9,431,994
6	Switzerland	8,658,165
7	Japan	3,946,155
8	Canada	2,462,938
9	Spain	1,731,055
10	Australia	1,686,231

In 1998 France consumed 179,004,405 bottles of champagne and exported 113,453,686. In that year Canada increased its imports by a record 45 per cent, entering the Top 10 for the first time.

TOP 10 COFFEE-DRINKING COUNTRIES

	COUNTRY	ANNUAL CONSUMPTION PER CAPITA KG	LB	OZ	CUPS*
1	Finland	11.71	25	13	1,756
2	Denmark	9.57	21	14	1,435
3	Norway	9.52	20	15	1,428
4	Sweden	8.47	18	10	1,270
5	Austria	8.04	17	11	1,206
6	Netherlands	7.82	17	3	1,173
7	Germany	7.07	15	9	1,060
8	Switzerland	6.85	15	1	1,027
9	France	5.39	11	14	808
10	Italy	5.13	11	5	772

* *Based on 150 cups per 1 kg (2 lb 3 oz)*

Source: *International Coffee Organization*

Did You Know? Until the invention of pasteurization, milk-drinkers risked contracting the disease scrofula. It was known as "King's Evil", because it was believed the only cure was to be touched by a king.

World Tourism

TOP 10 TOURIST DESTINATIONS

	COUNTRY	TOTAL VISITORS, 1999
1	France	71,400,000
2	Spain	51,958,000
3	USA	46,983,000
4	China	37,480,000*
5	Italy	35,839,000
6	UK	25,740,000
7	Mexico	20,216,000
8	Canada	19,556,000
9	Poland	17,940,000
10	Austria	17,630,000

* *Includes 10,433,000 vistors to Hong Kong*

Source: *World Tourism Organization*

TOP 10 TOURIST EARNING COUNTRIES

	COUNTRY	TOTAL RECEIPTS ($), 1999
1	USA	73,000,000,000
2	Italy	31,000,000,000
3	Spain	25,179,000,000*
4	France	24,657,000,000*
5	UK	20,972,000,000
6	China	14,099,000,000
7	Austria	11,259,000,000
8	Canada	10,282,000,000
9	Germany	9,570,000,000#
10	Mexico	7,850,000,000

* *Estimates based on first nine months*

Estimates based on first seven months

Source: *World Tourism Organization*

TOP 10 PACKAGE HOLIDAY DESTINATIONS FROM THE UK

(Destination/no. of UK package tourists)

1 **Spain**, 5,800,000 2 **France**, 2,300,000 3 **Greece**, 1,500,000 4 **Turkey**, 830,000 5 **USA**, 800,000 6 **Italy**, 790,000 7 **Portugal**, 720,000 8 **Cyprus**, 660,000 9 **North Africa**, 460,000 10 **Caribbean**, 420,000

Source: *CSFB/ABTA*

"FERRIS WHEEL"

Pennsylvania bridge engineer George W. Ferris gave his name to the Ferris wheels that are popular attractions at many of the world's amusement parks. He invented the first one for the Chicago Columbian Exposition of 1893. It had a diameter of 76 m (250 ft), its 36 wooden cars carried up to 60 people, and its 14-m (45-ft) axle was the largest steel object ever forged. Modern versions, such as the BA London Eye, opened in 2000, have improved on Ferris's original.

WHY DO WE SAY?

TOP 10 OLDEST ROLLERCOASTERS*

	ROLLERCOASTER/LOCATION	YEAR FOUNDED
1	**Leap-the-Dips**, Lakemont Park, Altoona, PA, USA	1902
2	**Scenic Railway**, Luna Park, Melbourne, Australia	1912
3	**Rutschbanen**, Tivoli, Copenhagen, Denmark	1914
4	**Jack Rabbit**, Clementon Amusement Park, Clementon, NJ, USA	1919
5	=**Jack Rabbit**, Sea Breeze Park, Rochester, NY, USA	1920
	=**Scenic Railway**, Dreamland, Margate, UK	1920
7	=**Jack Rabbit**, Kennywood, West Mifflin, PA, USA	1921
	=**Roller Coaster**, Lagoon, Farmington, UT, USA	1921
9	=**Big Dipper**, Blackpool Pleasure Beach, Blackpool, UK	1923
	=**Thunderhawk**, Dorney Park, Aleentown, PA, USA	1923
	=**Zippin Pippin**, Libertyland, Memphis, TN, USA	1923

* *In operation at same location since founded*

Leap-the-Dips at Lakemont Park, Altoona, Pennslyvania, was out of operation from 1985 but was restored and reopened in 1999.

IT JUST KEEPS ROLLING ALONG

In operation since 1914, the Rutschbanen in Copenhagen's Tivoli Gardens is Europe's oldest working rollercoaster. The oldest American one predates this by twelve years.

TOP 10 FASTEST ROLLERCOASTERS IN THE US

	ROLLERCOASTER/ LOCATION/YEAR OPENED	SPEED KM/H	MPH
1	**Superman: The Escape**, Six Flags Magic Mountain, Valencia, CA, 1997	161	100
2	**Millennium Force**, Cedar Point, Sandusky, OH, 2000	148	92
3	**Goliath**, Six Flags Magic Mountain, Valencia, CA, 2000	137	85
4	=**Desperado,** Buffalo Bill's Resort and Casino, Primm, NV, 1994	129	80
	=**Steel Phantom**, Kennywood Park, West Mifflin, PA, 1991	129	80
	=**Superman: The Ride of Steel**, Six Flags, Darien Lake, NY, 1999	129	80
7	**Son of Beast**, Paramount's Kings Island, Cincinnati, OH, 2000	126	78.4
8	=**Mamba**, Worlds of Fun, Kansas City, MO, 1998	121	75
	=**Steel Force**, Dorney Park, Allentown, PA, 1997	121	75
10	**Wild Thing**, Valleyfair!, Skakopee, MN, 1996	119	74

TOP 10 OLDEST AMUSEMENT PARKS

	PARK/LOCATION	YEAR FOUNDED
1	**Bakken**, Klampenborg, Denmark	1583
2	**The Prater**, Vienna, Austria	1766
3	**Blackgang Chine Cliff Top Theme Park**, Ventnor, Isle of Wight, UK	1842
4	**Tivoli**, Copenhagen, Denmark	1843
5	**Lake Compounce Amusement Park**, Bristol, CT, USA	1846
6	**Hanayashiki**, Tokyo, Japan	1853
7	**Grand Pier**, Teignmouth, UK	1865
8	**Blackpool Central Pier**, Blackpool, UK	1868
9	**Cedar Point**, Sandusky, OH, USA	1870
10	**Clacton Pier**, Clacton, UK	1871

TOP 10 AMUSEMENT AND THEME PARKS, 1999*

	PARK/LOCATION	ATTENDANCE
1	**Tokyo Disneyland**, Tokyo, Japan	17,459,000
2	**Disneyland Paris**, Marne-La-Vallée, France	12,500,000
3	**Everland**, Kyonggi-Do, South Korea	8,640,000
4	**Blackpool Pleasure Beach**, Blackpool, UK	6,900,000#
5	**Lotte World**, Seoul, South Korea	6,101,085
6	**Yokohama Hakkeijima Sea Paradise**, Yokohama, Japan	5,667,000
7	**Huis Ten Bosch**, Sasebo, Japan	4,030,000
8	**Nagashima Spa Land**, Kuwana, Japan	4,000,000
9	**Ocean Park, Hong Kong**, China	3,300,000
10	**Suzuka Circuit**, Suzuka, Japan	3,163,000

* *Excluding USA* # *Estimated attendance*

Source: Amusement Business

TOP 10 MUSEUMS AND GALLERIES IN THE UK

	MUSEUM OR GALLERY/LOCATION	VISITS, 1999
1	**British Museum**, London	5,460,537*
2	**National Gallery**, London	4,964,879*
3	**Tate Gallery**, London	1,822,428*
4	**Natural History Museum**, London	1,739,591
5	**Science Museum**, London	1,480,000
6	**Royal Academy**, London	1,390,000
7	**Kelvingrove Art Gallery and Museum**, Glasgow	1,051,020*
8	**National Portrait Gallery**, London	999,842*
9	**Victoria and Albert Museum**, London	945,677
10	**Royal Museum of Scotland**, Edinburgh	759,579

* *Free admission*

Source: *English Tourist Board*

TOP 10 LEISURE PARKS AND PIERS IN THE UK

	LEISURE PARK OR PIER/LOCATION	VISITS, 1999
1	**Blackpool Pleasure Beach**	7,200,000*#
2	**Palace Pier**, Brighton	3,750,000*#
3	**Segaworld**, The Trocadero, London	3,455,000#
4	**Eastbourne Pier**	2,800,000*#
5	**Alton Towers**, Staffordshire	2,650,000
6	**Pleasureland**, Southport	2,500,000*#
7	**Peter Pan's Adventure Island**, Southend	2,000,000*#
8	**Legoland**, Windsor	1,620,000
9	**Chessington World of Adventures**	1,550,000
10	**Pleasure Beach**, Great Yarmouth	1,500,000*#

* *Estimated*

\# *Free admission*

Source: *English Tourist Board*

Did You Know? The first rollercoaster, invented by Lemarcus Adna Thompson in 1884, was installed at Coney Island, New York.

Background image: FRANCE

TOP 10

On the Move

Speed Records

THE 10

FIRST AMERICAN HOLDERS OF THE LAND SPEED RECORD

	DRIVER*/CAR/LOCATION	DATE	KM/H	MPH
1	**William Vanderbilt**, *Mors*, Albis, France	5 Aug 1902	121.72	76.08
2	**Henry Ford**, *Ford Arrow*, Lake St. Clair, USA	12 Jan 1904	146.19	91.37
3	**Fred Marriott**, *Stanley Rocket*, Daytona Beach, USA	23 Jan 1906	195.65	121.57
4	**Barney Oldfield**, *Benz*, Daytona Beach, USA	16 Mar 1910	210.03	131.27
5	**Bob Burman**, *Benz*, Daytona Beach, USA	23 Apr 1911	226.19	141.37
6	**Ralph de Palma**, *Packard*, Daytona Beach, USA	17 Feb 1919	239.79	149.87
7	**Tommy Milton**, *Duesenberg*, Daytona Beach, USA	27 Apr 1920	249.64	156.03
8	**Ray Keech**, *White Triplex*, Daytona Beach, USA	22 Apr 1928	332.08	207.55
9	**Craig Breedlove**, *Spirit of America*, Bonneville Salt Flats, USA	5 Aug 1963	651.92	407.45
10	**Tom Green**, *Wingfoot Express*, Bonneville Salt Flats, USA	2 Oct 1964	661.12	413.20

* *Excluding those who subsequently broke their own records*

ICE RACER

In 1904 Henry Ford set the land speed record – although it was actually achieved on ice – on the frozen Lake St. Clair. A former employee of Thomas Edison, Ford (standing) had established the Ford Motor Company the previous year.

TOP 10

FASTEST PRODUCTION MOTORCYCLES

	MAKE/MODEL	KM/H	MPH
1	**Suzuki GSX1300R Hayabusa**	309	192
2	=**Honda CBR1100XX Blackbird**	291	181
	=**Honda RC45(m)**	291	181
4	=**Harris Yamaha YZR500**	289	180
	=**Kawasaki ZZR1100 D7**	289	180
6	**Bimota YB10 Biposto**	283	176
7	**Suzuki GSX-R1100WP(d)**	280	174
8	**Suzuki GSX-R750-WV**	279	173
9	=**Bimota Furano**	278	173
	=**Kawasaki ZZR1100 C1**	278	173

Since Honda (1940s), Suzuki and Yamaha (1950s), and Kawasaki (1960s) were established as motorcycle manufacturers, their machines have dominated the world's superbike league.

THE 10

LATEST HOLDERS OF THE MOTORCYCLE SPEED RECORD

	RIDER/MOTORCYCLE	YEAR	KM/H	MPH
1	**Dave Campos**, Twin 1,491cc Ruxton Harley-Davidson Easyrider	1990	518.45	322.15
2	**Donald A. Vesco**, Twin 1,016cc Kawasaki Lightning Bolt	1978	512.73	318.60
3	**Donald A. Vesco**, 1,496cc Yamaha Silver Bird	1975	487.50	302.93
4	**Calvin Rayborn**, 1,480cc Harley-Davidson	1970	426.40	264.96
5	**Calvin Rayborn** 1,480cc Harley-Davidson	1970	410.37	254.99
6	**Donald A. Vesco**, 700cc Yamaha	1970	405.25	251.82
7	**Robert Leppan**, 1,298cc Triumph	1966	395.27	245.62
8	**William A. Johnson**, 667cc Triumph	1962	361.40	224.57
9	**Wilhelm Herz**, 499cc NSU	1956	338.08	210.08
10	**Russell Wright**, 998cc Vincent HRD	1955	297.64	184.95

All the records listed here were achieved at the Bonneville Salt Flats, USA, with the exception of No. 10, which was attained at Christchurch, New Zealand. To break a Fédération Internationale Motorcycliste record, the motorcycle has to cover a measured distance, making two runs within one hour and taking the average of the two. American Motorcycling Association records require a turnround within two hours. Although all those listed were specially adapted for their record attempts, the two most recent had two engines and were stretched to 6.4 m (21 ft) and 7 m (23 ft) respectively.

Did You Know? The last steam vehicle to hold the land speed record was the Stanley Rocket, in which Fred Marriott achieved 195.65 km/h (121.57 mph) at Daytona Beach, USA, on 23 January 1906.

THE 10 FIRST HOLDERS OF THE LAND SPEED RECORD

	DRIVER/CAR/LOCATION	DATE	KM/H	MPH
1	**Gaston de Chasseloup-Laubat**, *Jeantaud*, Achères, France	18 Dec 1898	62.78	39.24
2	**Camile Jenatzy**, *Jenatzy*, Achères, France	17 Jan 1899	66.27	41.42
3	**Gaston de Chasseloup-Laubat**, *Jeantaud*, Achères, France	17 Jan 1899	69.90	43.69
4	**Camile Jenatzy**, *Jenatzy*, Achères, France	27 Jan 1899	79.37	49.92
5	**Gaston de Chasseloup-Laubat**, *Jeantaud*, Achères, France	4 Mar 1899	92.16	57.60
6	**Camile Jenatzy**, *Jenatzy*, Achères, France	29 Apr 1899	105.26	65.79
7	**Leon Serpollet**, *Serpollet*, Nice, France	13 Apr 1902	120.09	75.06
8	**William Vanderbilt**, *Mors*, Albis, France	5 Aug 1902	121.72	76.08
9	**Henri Fournier**, *Mors*, Dourdan, France	5 Nov 1902	122.56	76.60
10	**M. Augières**, *Mors*, Dourdan, France	17 Nov 1902	123.40	77.13

The first official land speed records were all broken within three years, the first six of them by rival French racers Comte Gaston de Chasseloup-Laubat and Camile Jenatzy. Both the *Jeantaud* and the *Jenatzy* were electrically powered.

THE 10 LATEST HOLDERS OF THE LAND SPEED RECORD

	DRIVER/CAR	DATE	KM/H	MPH
1	**Andy Green**, *Thrust SSC**	15 Oct 1997	1,227.99	763.04
2	**Richard Noble**, *Thrust 2**	4 Oct 1983	1,013.47	633.47
3	**Gary Gabelich**, *The Blue Flame*	23 Oct 1970	995.85	622.41
4	**Craig Breedlove**, *Spirit of America – Sonic 1*	15 Nov 1965	960.96	600.60
5	**Art Arfons**, *Green Monster*	7 Nov 1965	922.48	576.55
6	**Craig Breedlove**, *Spirit of America – Sonic 1*	2 Nov 1965	888.76	555.48
7	**Art Arfons**, *Green Monster*	27 Oct 1964	858.73	536.71
8	**Craig Breedlove**, *Spirit of America*	15 Oct 1964	842.04	526.28
9	**Craig Breedlove**, *Spirit of America*	13 Oct 1964	749.95	468.72
10	**Art Arfons**, *Green Monster*	5 Oct 1964	694.43	434.02

* *Location, Black Rock Desert, USA. All other speeds were achieved at Bonneville Salt Flats, USA*

TOP 10 FASTEST PRODUCTION CARS

(Model/country of manufacture/top speed in km/h#/mph#)*

❶ **McLaren F1**, UK, 386/240 ❷ **Lister Storm**, UK, 323/201 ❸ **Lamborghini Diablo GT**, Italy, 341/200 ❹ **Ferrari 550 Maranello**, Italy, 320/199 ❺ **Renault Espace F1**, France, 312/194 ❻ = **Ascari Ecosse**, Italy, >305/190; = **Pagani Zonda**, Italy, >305/190 ❽ = **Callaway C12**, USA, 305/190; = **Porsche 911 Turbo**, Germany, 305/190 ❿ **Aston Martin DB7 Vantage**, UK, 297/185

* *Fastest of each manufacturer*

May vary according to specification modifications to meet national legal requirements

Source: Auto Express

TOP 10 PRODUCTION CARS WITH THE FASTEST 0–60MPH TIMES

(Model/country of manufacture/seconds taken#)*

❶ **Renault Espace F1**, France, 2.8 ❷ **McLaren F1**, UK, 3.2 ❸ **Caterham Superlight R500**, UK, 3.5 ❹ **Porsche 911 Turbo**, Germany, 3.6 ❺ **Lamborghini Diablo GT**, Italy, 3.8 ❻ **Westfield FW400**, UK, 4.0 ❼ = **Ascari Ecosse**, Italy, 4.1; = **Marcos Mantis**, UK, 4.1 ❾ = **AC Cobra Superblower**, UK, 4.2; = **Callaway C12**, US, 4.2; = **TVR Tuscan Speed Six**, UK, 4.2

* *Fastest of each manufacturer*

May vary according to specification modifications to meet national legal requirements

Source: Auto Express

RED HOT

One of the fastest cars ever built (with a top speed of 320 km/h/199 mph), the Ferrari 550M (Maranello) has been acclaimed as the best-handling car in the world.

Cars & Road Transport

THE 10 ★

FIRST COUNTRIES TO MAKE SEAT BELTS COMPULSORY

	COUNTRY	INTRODUCED
1	Czechoslovakia	Jan 1969
2	Ivory Coast	Jan 1970
3	Japan	Dec 1971
4	Australia	Jan 1972
5	=Brazil	June 1972
	=New Zealand	June 1972
7	Puerto Rico	Jan 1974
8	Spain	Oct 1974
9	Sweden	Jan 1975
10	=Netherlands	June 1975
	=Belgium	June 1975
	=Luxembourg	June 1975

Seat belts, long in use in aeroplanes, were not designed for use in private cars until the 1950s. Ford was the first manufacturer in Europe to fit anchorage-points, and belts were first fitted as standard equipment in Swedish Volvos from 1959.

TOP 10 ★

MOST COMMON CAUSES OF CAR BREAKDOWN IN THE UK*

	CAUSE	BREAKDOWNS
1	**Battery** (flat or faulty)	680,044
2	**Tyres**	222,999
3	**Keys** (keys/locks/ immobilizers)	179,174
4	**Alternator**	98,117
5	**Starter motor**	89,791
6	**Spark plugs**	83,760
7	**Engine**	77,289
8	**Distributor cap**	68,037
9	**Clutch cable**	65,535
10	**Fuel**	64,051

* *Based on calls to the Automobile Association*

Although most modern car batteries are maintenance-free, they remain the principal cause of breakdowns.

TOP 10 ★

MOST COMMON TYPES OF PROPERTY LOST ON LONDON TRANSPORT, 1998–99

	TYPE	ITEMS FOUND
1	**Books, cheque books, and credit cards**	21,604
2	**Clothing**	19,305
3	**"Value items"** (handbags, purses, wallets, etc.)	18,630
4	**Cases and bags**	12,627
5	**Umbrellas**	11,072
6	**Cameras, electronic articles, and jewellery**	8,998
7	**Keys**	7,603
8	**Spectacles**	5,885
9	**Gloves** (pairs)	3,272
10	**Mobile phones**	2,717
	Total items in Top 10	111,713

Source: *London Transport*

TOP 10 ★

MOTOR VEHICLE-OWNING COUNTRIES

	COUNTRY	CARS	COMMERCIAL VEHICLES	TOTAL
1	USA	134,981,000	65,465,000	200,446,000
2	Japan	44,680,000	22,173,463	66,853,463
3	Germany	40,499,442	3,061,874	43,561,316
4	Italy	30,000,000	2,806,500	32,806,500
5	France	25,100,000	5,195,000	30,295,000
6	UK	24,306,781	3,635,176	27,941,957
7	Russia	13,638,600	9,856,000	23,494,600
8	Spain	14,212,259	3,071,621	17,283,880
9	Canada	13,182,996	3,484,616	16,667,612
10	Brazil	12,000,000	3,160,689	15,160,689
	World total	477,010,289	169,748,819	646,759,108

FRENCH JAM

France has one of the world's highest ratios of cars to people and can claim a record traffic jam of 176 km (190 miles), which occurred between Paris and Lyons.

A CAR IS BORN

Japan's car production, which places increasing reliance on advanced robotic technology, closely rivals that of world leader the USA.

TOP 10

COUNTRIES PRODUCING THE MOST MOTOR VEHICLES

	COUNTRY	CARS	COMMERCIAL VEHICLES	TOTAL
1	USA	5,554,390	6,451,689	12,006,079
2	Japan	8,055,736	1,994,029	10,049,792
3	Germany	5,348,115	378,673	5,726,788
4	France	2,603,021	351,139	2,954,160
5	Spain	2,216,571	609,492	2,826,063
6	Canada	1,122,287	1,050,375	2,172,662
7	UK	1,748,277	232,793	1,981,070
8	South Korea	1,625,125	329,369	1,954,494
9	Italy	1,402,382	290,355	1,692,737
10	China	507,103	1,120,726	1,627,829

Source: *Ward's Motor Vehicle Facts and Figures*

TOP 10 BESTSELLING CARS OF ALL TIME

	MANUFACTURER/MODEL	FIRST YEAR PRODUCED	ESTIMATED NO. MADE
1	Toyota Corolla	1966	23,000,000
2	Volkswagen Beetle	1937*	21,376,331
3	Lada Riva	1972	19,000,000
4	Volkswagen Golf	1974	18,453,646
5	Ford Model T	1908	16,536,075
6	Nissan Sunny/Pulsar	1966	13,571,100
7	= Ford Escort/Orion	1967	12,000,000
	= Honda Civic	1972	12,000,000
9	Mazda 323	1977	9,500,000
10	Renault 4	1961	8,100,000

* *Original model still produced in Mexico and Brazil*

Estimates of manufacturers' output of their bestselling models vary from the vague to the unusually precise: 16,536,075 of the Model T Ford, with 15,007,033 produced in the US and the rest in Canada and the UK in 1908–27.

TOP 10

BESTSELLING CARS IN THE UK

	MODEL	1999 SALES
1	Ford Focus	103,228
2	Ford Fiesta	99,830
3	Vauxhall Astra	92,050
4	Vauxhall Corsa	86,779
5	Vauxhall Vectra	77,479
6	Ford Mondeo	77,183
7	Renault Mégane	65,127
8	Renault Clio	63,991
9	Volkswagen Golf	63,715
10	Peugeot 206	58,788

Source: *The Society of Motor Manufacturers and Traders Ltd.*

THE CAR IN FRONT ...

The Toyota Motor Company was started in 1937, in Koromo, Japan, by Kiichiro Toyoda. Its Corolla model became the world's bestselling car.

Road Accidents & Disasters

THE 10 ★ COUNTRIES WITH THE HIGHEST NUMBER OF ROAD DEATHS

	COUNTRY	TOTAL DEATHS*
1	USA	41,967
2	Thailand	15,176
3	South Korea	13,343
4	Japan	11,254
5	Germany	8,549
6	France	8,444
7	Poland	7,310
8	Brazil	6,759
9	Turkey	6,735
10	Italy	6,724
	UK	3,743

* *In latest year for which figures are available*

Based on the ratio of fatalities to distance travelled, road deaths in the US have declined markedly since 1921, the first year they were recorded.

DRIVEN TO DESTRUCTION

In an average year in the US, over 6 million motor vehicle accidents are reported, 4 million involving property and 3 million resulting in injuries.

THE 10 ★ COUNTRIES WITH THE MOST DEATHS BY MOTOR ACCIDENTS

	COUNTRY	DEATH RATE PER 100,000 POPULATION
1	South Korea	38.4
2	Latvia	27.7
3	Greece	24.2
4	=Portugal	22.5
	=Venezuela	22.5
6	=El Salvador	20.3
	=Kuwait	20.3
8	Lithuania	19.7
9	Russia	19.5
10	Cuba	18.3
	UK	6.4

Source: *United Nations*

THE 10 MOST ACCIDENT-PRONE CAR COLOURS

(Colour/accidents per 10,000 cars of each colour)

❶ **Black**, 179 ❷ **White**, 160 ❸ **Red**, 157 ❹ **Blue**, 149 ❺ **Grey**, 147 ❻ **Gold**, 145 ❼ **Silver**, 142 ❽ **Beige**, 137 ❾ **Green**, 134 ❿ = **Brown**, 133; = **Yellow**, 133

THE 10 ★ OBJECTS MOST FREQUENTLY INVOLVED IN MOTOR ACCIDENTS IN THE UK

	OBJECT	ACCIDENTS (1998)
1	No object involved	54,191
2	Various permanent objects	7,663
3	Trees	3,084
4	Lamp posts	2,417
5	Crash barriers	2,048
6	Ditches	1,917
7	Road signs and traffic signals	1,407
8	Telegraph/electricity poles	889
9	Bus stops and shelters	126
10	Submerged (rivers, canals, etc.)	20

ACCIDENT BLACKSPOT

Black cars are reputed to be the least safe because they are less visible at night, but types of vehicle and age and experience of drivers are equally salient factors.

SEARCHING FOR SURVIVORS

The 1995 underground gas explosion at Taegu, South Korea, destroyed scores of vehicles, leaving 110 dead and 250 injured.

THE 10 WORST MOTOR VEHICLE AND ROAD DISASTERS

	LOCATION/DATE/INCIDENT	NO. KILLED
1	**Afghanistan**, 3 Nov 1982 *Following a collision with a Soviet army truck, a petrol tanker exploded in the 2.7-km (1.7-mile) Salang Tunnel. Some authorities have put the death toll from the explosion, fire, and fumes as high as 3,000.*	over 2,000
2	**Colombia**, 7 Aug 1956 *Seven army ammunition trucks exploded at night in the centre of Cali, destroying eight city blocks, including a barracks where 500 soldiers were sleeping.*	1,200
3	**Thailand**, 15 Feb 1990 *A dynamite truck exploded.*	over 150
4	**Nepal**, 23 Nov 1974 *Hindu pilgrims were killed when a suspension bridge over the River Mahahali collapsed.*	148
5	**Egypt**, 9 Aug 1973 *A bus drove into an irrigation canal.*	127
6	**Togo**, 6 Dec 1965 *Two lorries collided with dancers during a festival at Sotouboua.*	over 125
7	**Spain**, 11 July 1978 *A liquid gas tanker exploded in a camping site at San Carlos de la Rapita.*	over 120
8	**South Korea**, 28 Apr 1995 *An undergound explosion destroyed vehicles and caused about 100 cars and buses to plunge into the pit it created.*	110
9	=**The Gambia**, 12 Nov 1992 *After brake failure, a bus ferrying passengers to a dock plunged into a river.*	c.100
	=**Kenya**, early Dec 1992 *A bus carrying 112 people skidded, hit a bridge, and plunged into a river.*	c.100

The worst-ever motor racing accident occurred on 13 June 1955, at Le Mans, France, when Pierre Levegh's Mercedes-Benz 300 SLR went out of control, hit a wall, and exploded in mid-air, showering wreckage into the crowd and killing 82. The worst-ever accident involving a single car was on 17 Dec 1956: 12 people were killed when their car was hit by a train near Phoenix, Arizona.

THE 10 WORST YEARS FOR ROAD FATALITIES IN GREAT BRITAIN

(Year/no. killed)

1 **1941**, 9,169 2 **1940**, 8,609 3 **1939**, 8,272 4 **1966**, 7,985 5 **1965**, 7,952 6 **1964**, 7,820 7 **1972**, 7,763 8 **1971**, 7,699 9 **1970**, 7,499 10 **1973**, 7,406

THE 10 AGE GROUPS MOST VULNERABLE TO ROAD ACCIDENTS IN GREAT BRITAIN

	AGE GROUP	NO. KILLED OR INJURED (1998)
1	20–24	40,511
2	15–19	40,386
3	25–29	40,092
4	30–34	35,633
5	35–39	27,531
6	40–44	20,822
7	10–14	19,331
8	45–49	16,776
9	50–54	15,660
10	5–9	13,987

The most vulnerable single age is 18, with 11,368 accidents and fatalities, which is more than double the figure for any age below 15.

THE 10 MANOEUVRES MOST FREQUENTLY CAUSING MOTOR ACCIDENTS IN THE UK*

	MANOEUVRE	ACCIDENTS (1998)
1	Going ahead (various)	189,521
2	Turning right, or waiting to do so	49,373
3	Held up while waiting to go ahead	34,674
4	Going ahead on a bend	32,143
5	Stopping	18,818
6	Parked	15,261
7	Overtaking	14,247
8	Turning left, or waiting to do so	13,657
9	Changing lane	6,447
10	Starting	5,875

* *Vehicles other than two-wheeled*

On what did Henry Ford set the land speed record in 1904?

see p.226 for the answer

A A beach
B A racetrack
C A frozen lake

TOP 10

LONGEST RAIL NETWORKS

	LOCATION	TOTAL RAIL LENGTH KM	MILES
1	USA	240,000	149,129
2	Russia	150,000	93,205
3	Canada	67,773	42,112
4	China	64,900	40,327
5	India	62,915	39,093
6	Germany	46,300	28,769
7	Australia	38,563	23,962
8	Argentina	37,830	23,506
9	France	32,027	19,901
10	Mexico	31,048	19,292

RAILROAD

Although the USA still has the longest rail network in the world, US rail mileage has declined considerably since its 1916 peak of 408,773 km (254,000 miles).

THE 10

WORST RAIL DISASTERS IN THE UK

LOCATION/DATE/INCIDENT — NO. KILLED

1 Quintinshill, near Gretna Green, Scotland, 22 May 1915 — 227
A troop train carrying 500 soldiers from Larbert to Liverpool collided head-on with a local passenger train. Barely a minute later, the Scottish express, drawn by two engines and weighing a total of 600 tons, ploughed into the wreckage. The 15 coaches of the troop train, 195 m (640 ft) long, were so crushed that they ended up just 61 m (200 ft) long. The gas-lit troop train then caught fire. Since their records were destroyed in the fire, the actual number of soldiers killed was never established, but it was probably 215, as well as two members of the train's crew, eight in the express and two in the local train. In addition to the deaths, 246 people were injured, many very seriously.

2 Harrow and Wealdstone Station, Middlesex, 8 Oct 1952 — 122
In patchy fog, Robert Jones, the relief driver of the Perth to Euston sleeping-car express, pulled by the City of Glasgow, failed to see a series of signal lights warning him of danger, and at 8.19 a.m. collided with the waiting Watford to Euston train. Seconds later, the Euston to Liverpool and Manchester express hit the wreckage of the two trains. The casualties were 112 killed instantly, 10 who died later, and 349 injured.

3 Lewisham, South London, 4 Dec 1957 — 90
A steam and an electric train were in collision in fog. The disaster was made worse by the collapse of a bridge on to the wreckage, leaving 90 dead and 109 seriously injured.

4 Tay Bridge, Scotland, 28 Dec 1879 — 80
As the North British mail train passed over it during a storm, the bridge collapsed, killing all 75 passengers and the crew of five. The bridge – the longest in the world at that time – had only been opened on 31 May the previous year, and Queen Victoria had crossed it in a train soon afterwards.

5 Armagh, Northern Ireland, 12 June 1889 — 78
A Sunday school excursion train with 940 passengers stalled on a hill. When 10 carriages were uncoupled, they ran backwards and collided with a passenger train, killing 78 and leaving 250 injured.

6 Hither Green, South London, 5 Nov 1967 — 49
The Hastings to Charing Cross train was derailed by a broken track. As well as those killed, 78 were injured, 27 of them very seriously.

7=Bourne End, Hertfordshire, 30 Sep 1945 — 43
Travelling at about 80 km/h (50 mph), the Perth to Euston express sped through a crossover with a 32-km/h (20-mph) speed restriction imposed during engineering works. The train was derailed and the coaches plunged down an embankment.

=Moorgate Station, London, 28 Feb 1975 — 43
The Drayton Park to Moorgate tube ran into the wall at the end of a tunnel, killing 43 and injuring 74 in London Transport's worst rail disaster.

9 Castlecary, Scotland 10 Dec 1937 — 35
In heavy snow the Edinburgh to Glasgow train ran into a stationary Dundee to Glasgow train and rode over the top of it, leaving 179 injured and 35 dead.

10=Shipton, near Oxford, 24 Dec 1874 — 34
The Paddington to Birkenhead train plunged over the embankment after a carriage wheel broke, killing 34 and badly injuring 65.

=Clapham Junction, London, 12 Dec 1988 — 34
The 7.18 Basingstoke to Waterloo train, carrying 906 passengers, stopped at signals outside Clapham Junction; the 6.30 train from Bournemouth ran into its rear, and an empty train from Waterloo hit the wreckage, leaving 33 dead (and one who died later) and 111 injured.

Did You Know? The world's first passenger rail fatality occurred on the Stockton and Darlington Railway on 19 March 1828, when a boiler explosion killed the driver, John Gillespie.

TOP 10 ★ FASTEST RAIL JOURNEYS*

	JOURNEY/COUNTRY/TRAIN	DISTANCE KM	DISTANCE MILES	SPEED KM/H	SPEED MPH
1	**Hiroshima–Kokura**, Japan, Nozomi 500	192.0	119.3	261.8	162.7
2	**Massy–St. Pierre des Corps**, France, 7 TGV	206.9	128.5	253.3	157.4
3	**Brussels–Paris**, Belgium/France, Thalys 9342	313.4	194.7	226.5	140.7
4	**Madrid–Seville**, Spain, 5 AVE	470.5	292.4	209.1	129.9
5	**Karlsruhe–Mannheim**, Germany, 2 trains	71.0	44.1	193.8	120.4
6	**London–York**, UK, 1 IC225	303.4	188.5	180.2	112.0
7	**Skövde–Södertälje**, Sweden, 3 X2000	277.0	172.1	171.3	106.4
8	**Piacenza–Parma**, Italy, ES 9325	57.0	35.4	171.0	106.2
9	**North Philadelphia–Newark Penn**, USA, 1 NE Direct	122.4	76.0	153.0	95.0
10	**Salo–Karjaa**, Finland, S220 132	53.1	33.0	151.7	94.3

* *Fastest journey for each country; all those in the Top 10 have other similarly or equally fast services*

Source: Railway Gazette International

THE 10 FIRST UNDERGROUND RAILWAY LINES IN LONDON

(Line/date first section opened)

❶ **Metropolitan**, 10 Jan 1863 ❷ **District**, 24 Dec 1868 ❸ **Circle**, 6 Oct 1884 ❹ **Waterloo & City**, 8 Aug 1898 ❺ **Central**, 30 July 1900 ❻ **Bakerloo**, 10 Mar 1906 ❼ **Piccadilly**, 15 Dec 1906 ❽ **Northern**, 22 June 1907 ❾ **Victoria**, 7 Mar 1969 ❿ **Jubilee**, 1 May 1979

TOP 10 ★ BUSIEST UNDERGROUND RAILWAY NETWORKS

	CITY	YEAR OPENED	TRACK LENGTH KM	TRACK LENGTH MILES	STATIONS	PASSENGERS PER ANNUM
1	**Moscow**	1935	243.6	153	150	3,183,900,000
2	**Tokyo**	1927	169.1	106	154	2,112,700,000
3	**Mexico City**	1969	177.7	112	154	1,422,600,000
4	**Seoul**	1974	133.0	84	112	1,354,000,000
5	**Paris**	1900	201.4	127	372	1,170,000,000
6	**New York**	1867	398.0	249	469	1,100,000,000
7	**Osaka**	1933	105.8	66	99	988,600,000
8	**St. Petersburg**	1955	91.7	58	50	850,000,000
9	**Hong Kong**	1979	43.2	27	38	804,000,000
10	**London**	1863	392.0	247	245	784,000,000

THE 10 ★ WORST RAIL DISASTERS

LOCATION/DATE/INCIDENT — NO. KILLED

1 Bagmati River, India, 6 June 1981 — *c.*800
The carriages of a train travelling from Samastipur to Banmukhi in Bihar plunged off a bridge over the River Bagmati near Mansi, when the driver braked, apparently to avoid hitting a sacred cow. Although the official death toll was said to have been 268, many authorities have claimed that the train was so massively overcrowded that the actual figure was in excess of 800, making it probably the worst rail disaster of all time.

2 Chelyabinsk, Russia, 3 June 1989 — up to 800
Two passenger trains, laden with holidaymakers heading to and from Black Sea resorts, were destroyed when liquid gas from a nearby pipeline exploded.

3 Guadalajara, Mexico, 18 Jan 1915 — over 600
A train derailed on a steep incline, but political strife in the country meant that full details of the disaster were suppressed.

4 Modane, France, 12 Dec 1917 — 573
A troop-carrying train ran out of control and was derailed. It has been claimed that the train was overloaded and that as many as 1,000 may have died.

5 Balvano, Italy, 2 Mar 1944 — 521
A heavily laden train stalled in the Armi Tunnel, and many passengers were asphyxiated. Like the disaster at Torre (No. 6), wartime secrecy prevented full details from being published.

6 Torre, Spain, 3 Jan 1944 — over 500
A double collision and fire in a tunnel resulted in many deaths – some have put the total as high as 800.

7 Awash, Ethiopia, 13 Jan 1985 — 428
A derailment hurled a train laden with some 1,000 passengers into a ravine.

8 Cireau, Romania, 7 Jan 1917 — 374
An overcrowded passenger train crashed into a military train and was derailed.

9 Quipungo, Angola, 31 May 1993 — 355
A trail was derailed by UNITA guerrilla action.

10 Sangi, Pakistan, 4 Jan 1990 — 306
A train was diverted on to the wrong line, resulting in a fatal collision.

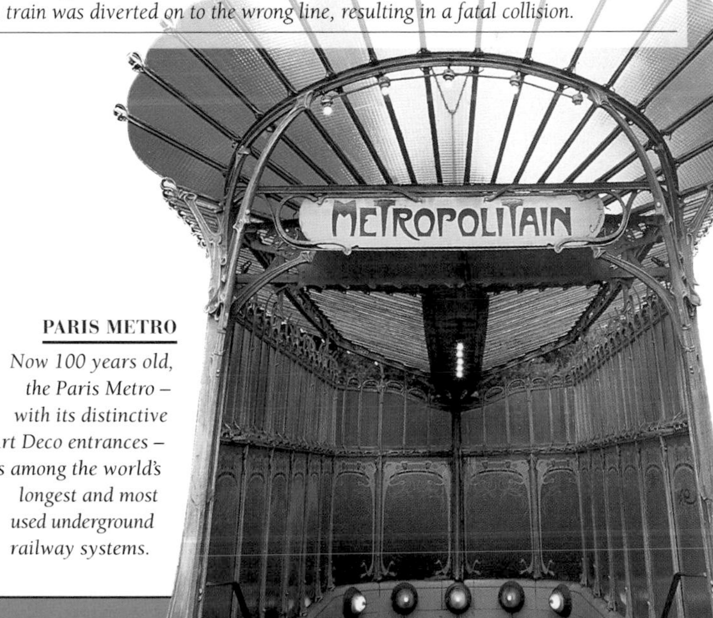

PARIS METRO

Now 100 years old, the Paris Metro – with its distinctive Art Deco entrances – is among the world's longest and most used underground railway systems.

Water Transport

TOP 10

BUSIEST PORTS*

	PORT/LOCATION
1	**Hong Kong**, China
2	**Singapore**
3	**Kaohsiung**, Taiwan
4	**Rotterdam**, Netherlands
5	**Pusan**, South Korea
6	**New York/New Jersey**, USA
7	**Long Beach**, USA
8	**Hamburg**, Germany
9	**Antwerp**, Belgium
10	**Los Angeles**, USA

* *Handling the most TEUs (Twenty-ft Equivalent Units)*

Source: *International Association of Ports & Harbors*

TOP 10

LARGEST CRUISE SHIPS

	SHIP/YEAR BUILT/ COUNTRY	PASSENGER CAPACITY	GROSS TONNAGE
1	=*Explorer of the Seas*, 2000, Finland	3,840	142,000
	=*Voyager of the Seas*, 1999, Finland	3,840	142,000
3	*Grand Princess*, 1998, Italy	3,300	108,806
4	*Carnival Triumph*, 1999, Italy	3,473	101,672
5	*Carnival Destiny*, 1996, Italy	3,336	101,353
6	*Disney Magic*, 1998, Italy	2,500	83,338
7	*Disney Wonder*, 1999, Italy	6,000	83,308
8	*Rhapsody of the Seas*, 1997, France	2,416	78,491
9	*Vision of the Seas*, 1995, Italy	2,416	78,340
10	*Sun Princess*, 1995, Italy	2,272	77,441

Source: *Lloyd's Register of Shipping, MIPG/PPMS*

PORT OF CALL

Its substantial and well-protected harbour has contributed to Singapore's becoming the most important commercial centre in Southeast Asia.

"WOMEN AND CHILDREN FIRST"

The film *Titanic* brought home to many the significance of a ship built with insufficient lifeboats, whereby choices had to be made as to who would have a seat to safety and who would have to take their chances in the sea. The first such incident involved the sinking of the *Birkenhead* off South Africa in 1852. The 20 women and children on board were placed in the only three lifeboats that were serviceable, while the British soldiers remained on deck, 445 of them drowning in the incident. This subsequently became a naval tradition known to all as the "Birkenhead Drill".

WHY DO WE SAY?

FLOATING GIANT

One of the world's largest cruise ships, the 1997 French-built Rhapsody of the Seas *is also one of the longest afloat, at 278.94 m (915 ft 2 in).*

THE 10

WORST PASSENGER FERRY DISASTERS OF THE 20TH CENTURY

	FERRY/LOCATION/DATE	NO. KILLED
1	***Dona Paz***, Philippines, 20 Dec 1987	up to 3,000
2	***Neptune***, Haiti, 17 Feb 1992	1,800
3	***Toya Maru***, Japan, 26 Sep 1954	1,172
4	***Don Juan***, Philippines, 22 Apr 1980	over 1,000
5	***Estonia***, Baltic Sea, 28 Sep 1994	909
6	***Samia***, Bangladesh, 25 May 1986	600
7	***MV Bukoba***, Lake Victoria, Tanzania, 21 May 1996	549
8	***Salem Express***, Egypt, 14 Dec 1991	480
9	***Tampomas II***, Indonesia, 27 Jan 1981	431
10	***Nam Yung Ho***, South Korea, 15 Dec 1970	323

The *Dona Paz* sank in the Tabias Strait, Philippines, after the ferry was struck by the oil tanker *MV Victor*. The loss of life may have been much higher than the official figure (up to 4,386 has been suggested by some authorities).

THE 10 WORST MARINE DISASTERS OF THE 20TH CENTURY

	LOCATION/DATE/INCIDENT	APPROX. NO. KILLED
1	**Off Gdansk**, Poland, 30 Jan 1945 *The German liner* Wilhelm Gustloff, *laden with refugees, was torpedoed by a Soviet submarine S-13. The precise death toll remains uncertain, but is in the range of 5,348 to 7,800.*	up to 7,800
2	**Off Cape Rixhöft** (Rozeewie), Poland, 16 Apr 1945 *The German ship Goya, carrying evacuees from Gdansk, was torpedoed in the Baltic.*	6,800
3	**Off Yingkow**, China, Nov 1947 *The boilers of an unidentified Chinese troop ship, carrying Nationalist soldiers from Manchuria, exploded, detonating ammunition.*	over 6,000
4	**Lübeck**, Germany, 3 May 1945 *The German ship* Cap Arcona, *carrying concentration camp survivors, was bombed and sunk by British aircraft.*	5,000
5	**Off St. Nazaire**, France, 17 June 1940 *The British troop ship* Lancastria *sank.*	3,050
6	**Off Stolpmünde** (Ustka), Poland, 9 Feb 1945 *German war-wounded and refugees were lost when the* Steuben *was torpedoed by the same Russian submarine that had sunk the* Wilhelm Gustloff.	3,000
7	**Tabias Strait**, Philippines, 20 Dec 1987 *The ferry* Dona Paz *was struck by oil tanker* MV Victor.	up to 3,000
8	**Woosung**, China, 3 Dec 1948 *The overloaded steamship* Kiangya, *carrying refugees, struck a Japanese mine.*	over 2,750
9	**Lübeck**, Germany, 3 May 1945 *The refugee ship* Thielbeck *sank during the British bombardment of Lübeck harbour in the closing weeks of World War II.*	2,750
10	**South Atlantic**, 12 Sep 1942 *The British passenger vessel* Laconia, *carrying Italian prisoners-of-war, was sunk by German U-boat* U-156.	2,279

Other disasters occurring during wartime and resulting in losses of more than 1,000 include the explosion of *Mont Blanc*, a French ammunition ship, following its collision with the Belgian steamer *Imo* on 6 December 1917, with 1,635 lost; the sinking of the British cruiser *HMS Hood* by the German battleship *Bismarck* on 24 May 1941, with 1,418 killed; and the torpedoing by German submarine *U-20* of the *Lusitania*, a British passenger liner, on 7 May 1915, with the loss of 1,198 civilians.

THE 10 WORST OIL TANKER SPILLS

	TANKER(S)/LOCATION/DATE	APPROX. SPILLAGE TONNES
1	***Atlantic Empress*** and ***Aegean Captain***, Trinidad, 19 July 1979	300,000
2	***Castillio de Bellver***, Cape Town, South Africa, 6 Aug 1983	255,000
3	***Olympic Bravery***, Ushant, France, 24 Jan 1976	250,000
4	***Showa-Maru***, Malacca, Malaya, 7 June 1975	237,000
5	***Amoco Cadiz***, Finistère, France, 16 Mar 1978	223,000
6	***Odyssey***, Atlantic, off Canada, 10 Nov 1988	140,000
7	***Torrey Canyon***, Isles of Scilly, UK, 18 Mar 1967	120,000
8	***Sea Star***, Gulf of Oman, 19 Dec 1972	115,000
9	***Irenes Serenada***, Pilos, Greece, 23 Feb 1980	102,000
10	***Urquiola***, Corunna, Spain, 12 May 1976	101,000

ENVIRONMENTAL DISASTER

The 1979 collision of the Atlantic Empress *and the* Aegean Captain *off Trinidad resulted in the worst oil spill of all time.*

THE 10

FIRST TRANSATLANTIC FLIGHTS

	AIRCRAFT/CREW/COUNTRY	CROSSING	DATE*
1	**US Navy/Curtiss flying boat *NC-4*,** Lt.-Cdr. Albert Cushing Read and crew of five, USA	Trepassy Harbor, Newfoundland, to Lisbon, Portugal	16–27 May 1919
2	**Twin Rolls-Royce-engined converted Vickers Vimy bomber#,** Capt. John Alcock and Lt. Arthur Whitten Brown, UK	St John's, Newfoundland, to Galway, Ireland	14–15 June 1919
3	**British *R-34* airship+,** Maj. George Herbert Scott and crew of 30, UK	East Fortune, Scotland, to Roosevelt Field, New York	2–6 July 1919
4	**Fairey IIID seaplane *Santa Cruz*,** Adm. Gago Coutinho and Cdr. Sacadura Cabral, Portugal	Lisbon, Portugal, to Recife, Brazil	30 Mar–5 June 1922
5	**Two Douglas seaplanes, *Chicago* and *New Orleans*,** Lt. Lowell H. Smith and Leslie P. Arnold/ Erik Nelson and John Harding, USA	Orkneys, Scotland, to Labrador, Canada	2–31 Aug 1924
6	***Los Angeles*, a renamed German-built *ZR 3* airship,** Dr. Hugo Eckener, with 31 passengers and crew, Germany	Friedrichshafen, Germany, to Lakehurst, New Jersey	12–15 Oct 1924
7	***Plus Ultra*, a Dornier Wal twin-engined flying boat,** Capt. Julio Ruiz and crew, Spain	Huelva, Spain, to Recife, Brazil	22 Jan–10 Feb 1926
8	***Santa Maria*, a Savoia-Marchetti S.55 flying boat,** Francesco Marquis de Pinedo, Capt. Carlo del Prete, and Lt. Vitale Zacchetti, Italy	Cagliari, Sardinia, to Recife, Brazil	8–24 Feb 1927
9	**Dornier Wal flying boat,** Sarmento de Beires and Jorge de Castilho, Portugal	Lisbon, Portugal, to Natal, Brazil	16–17 Mar 1927
10	**Savoia-Marchetti flying boat,** João De Barros and crew, Brazil	Genoa, Italy, to Natal, Brazil	28 Apr–14 May 1927

** All dates refer to the actual Atlantic legs of the journeys; some started earlier and ended beyond their first transatlantic landfalls # First non-stop flight + First east–west flight*

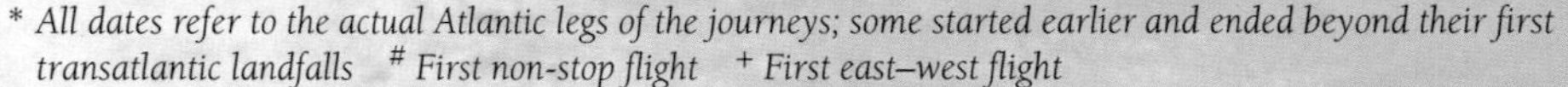

THE 10

FIRST PEOPLE TO FLY IN HEAVIER-THAN-AIR AIRCRAFT

	PILOT/COUNTRY/AIRCRAFT	DATE
1	**Orville Wright**, USA, *Wright Flyer I*	17 Dec 1903
2	**Wilbur Wright**, USA, *Wright Flyer I*	17 Dec 1903
3	**Alberto Santos-Dumont**, Brazil, *No. 14-bis*	23 Oct 1906
4	**Charles Voisin**, France, *Voisin-Delagrange I*	30 Mar 1907
5	**Henri Farman**, UK, later France, *Voisin-Farman I-bis*	7 Oct 1907
6	**Léon Delagrange**, France, *Voisin-Delagrange I*	5 Nov 1907
7	**Robert Esnault-Pelterie**, France, *REP No. 1*	16 Nov 1907
8	**Charles W. Furnas***, USA, *Wright Flyer III*	14 May 1908
9	**Louis Blériot**, France, *Blériot VIII*	29 June 1908
10	**Glenn Hammond Curtiss**, USA, *AEA June Bug*	4 July 1908

** As a passenger in a plane piloted by Wilbur Wright, Furnas was the first aeroplane passenger in the US.*

"MACH NUMBER"

A Mach number is a unit of speed, related to the speed of sound, that varies according to such factors as altitude and the moisture content of the air. In dry air at sea level, Mach 1 is 1,229 km/h (763.67 mph). The land speed record set in 1997 was undertaken early in the morning, when high humidity and a cool temperature lower the speed of sound. The word Mach derives from the name of Ernst Mach (1838–1916), an Austrian physicist and philosopher.

WHY DO WE SAY?

COAST TO COAST

A previous transatlantic crossing had been made as a series of "hops", but Alcock and Brown's Vickers Vimy flight of 1919 was the first non-stop crossing.

TOP 10

FASTEST X-15 FLIGHTS

	PILOT/DATE	MACH*	SPEED KM/H	SPEED MPH
1	**William J. Knight**, 3 Oct 1967	6.70	7,274	4,520
2	**William J. Knight**, 18 Nov 1966	6.33	6,857	4,261
3	**Joseph A. Walker**, 27 June 1962	5.92	6,606	4,105
4	**Robert M. White**, 9 Nov 1961	6.04	6,589	4,094
5	**Robert A. Rushworth**, 5 Dec 1963	6.06	6,466	4,018
6	**Neil A. Armstrong**, 26 June 1962	5.74	6,420	3,989
7	**John B. McKay**, 22 June 1965	5.64	6,388	3,938
8	**Robert A. Rushworth**, 18 July 1963	5.63	6,317	3,925
9	**Joseph A. Walker**, 25 June 1963	5.51	6,294	3,911
10	**William H. Dana**, 4 Oct 1967	5.53	6,293	3,910

* *Mach no. varies with altitude – the list is ranked on actual speed*

THE 10

FIRST ROCKET AND JET AIRCRAFT

	AIRCRAFT/COUNTRY	FIRST FLIGHT
1	**Heinkel He 176***, Germany	20 June 1939
2	**Heinkel He 178**, Germany	27 Aug 1939
3	**DFS 194***, Germany	Aug 1940#
4	**Caproni-Campini N-1**, Italy	28 Aug 1940
5	**Heinkel He 280V-1**, Germany	2 Apr 1941
6	**Gloster E.28/39**, UK	15 May 1941
7	**Messerschmitt Me 163 Komet***, Germany	13 Aug 1941
8	**Messerschmitt Me 262V-3**, Germany	18 July 1942
9	**Bell XP-59A Airacomet**, USA	1 Oct 1942
10	**Gloster Meteor F Mk 1**, UK	5 Mar 1943

* *Rocket-powered* # *Precise date unknown*

FASTEST AIRCRAFT

The speeds attained by the rocket-powered X-15 and X-15A-2 aircraft remain the greatest by piloted vehicles in the Earth's atmosphere. They were air-launched by being released from B-52 bombers, and so do not qualify for the official air speed record, for which aircraft must take off and land under their own power. An X-15 also set an unofficial altitude record when, on 22 August 1963, Joseph A. Walker piloted one to 107,960 m (354,200 ft) – some 108 km (67 miles) high. The pioneering work of the pilots of the X-15s laid the foundations of US spaceflight.

THE 10

FIRST FLIGHTS OF MORE THAN ONE HOUR

	PILOT	DURATION	DATE
1	**Orville Wright**	1:2:15	9 Sep 1908
2	**Orville Wright**	1:5:52	10 Sep 1908
3	**Orville Wright**	1:10:0	11 Sep 1908
4	**Orville Wright**	1:15:20	12 Sep 1908
5	**Wilbur Wright**	1:31:25	21 Sep 1908
6	**Wilbur Wright**	1:7:24	28 Sep 1908
7	**Wilbur Wright***	1:4:26	6 Oct 1908
8	**Wilbur Wright**	1:9:45	10 Oct 1908
9	**Wilbur Wright**	1:54:53	18 Dec 1908
10	**Wilbur Wright**	2:20:23	31 Dec 1908

* *First ever flight of more than one hour with a passenger (M. A. Fordyce)*

TOP 10

BIGGEST AIRSHIPS EVER BUILT

	AIRSHIP	COUNTRY	YEAR	VOLUME CU M	VOLUME CU FT	LENGTH M	LENGTH FT
1	=***Hindenburg***	Germany	1936	200,000	7,062,934	245	804
	=***Graf Zeppelin II***	Germany	1938	200,000	7,062,934	245	804
3	=***Akron***	USA	1931	184,060	6,500,000	239	785
	=***Macon***	USA	1933	184,060	6,500,000	239	785
5	***R101***	UK	1930	155,744	5,500,000	237	777
6	***Graf Zeppelin***	Germany	1928	105,000	3,708,040	237	776
7	***L72***	Germany	1920	68,500	2,419,055	226	743
8	***R100***	UK	1929	155,743	5,500,000	216	709
9	***R38***	UK*	1921	77,136	2,724,000	213	699
10	=***L70***	Germany	1918	62,200	2,418,700	212	694
	=***L71***	Germany	1918	62,200	2,418,700	212	694

* *UK-built, but sold to US Navy*

The giant airships in this list ultimately suffered unfortunate fates: the *Hindenburg*, *Akron*, *Macon*, *R101*, *L72*, and *R38* crashed, the *L70* was shot down, and the remainder were broken up for scrap.

Background image: HEINKEL HE 178

In which incident did 36 people die in the US in 1937?
see p.238 for the answer

A *Hindenburg* explosion
B Airplane crash
C Baseball stand collapse

THE 10 WORST AIRSHIP DISASTERS

LOCATION/DATE/INCIDENT	NO. KILLED
1 Off the Atlantic coast, USA, 4 Apr 1933 *US Navy airship* Akron *crashed into the sea in a storm, leaving only three survivors in the world's worst airship tragedy.*	73
2 Over the Mediterranean, 21 Dec 1923 *French airship* Dixmude *is assumed to have been struck by lightning and to have broken up and crashed into the sea. Wreckage, believed to be from the airship, was found off Sicily 10 years later.*	52
3 Near Beauvais, France, 5 Oct 1930 *British airship R101 crashed into a hillside leaving 48 dead, with two dying later, and six survivors.*	50
4 Off the coast near Hull, UK, 24 Aug 1921 *Airship R38, sold by the British Government to the US and renamed USN ZR-2, broke in two on a training and test flight.*	44
5 Lakehurst, New Jersey, USA, 6 May 1937 *German Zeppelin* Hindenburg *caught fire when mooring.*	36
6 Hampton Roads, Virginia, USA, 21 Feb 1922 Roma, *an Italian airship bought by the US Army, crashed, killing all but 11 men on board.*	34
7 Berlin, Germany, 17 Oct 1913 *German airship LZ18 crashed after engine failure during a test flight at Berlin-Johannisthal.*	28
8 Baltic Sea, 30 Mar 1917 *German airship SL9 was struck by lightning on a flight from Seerappen to Seddin and crashed into the sea.*	23
9 Mouth of the River Elbe, Germany, 3 Sep 1915 *German airship L10 was struck by lightning and plunged into the sea.*	19
10=Off Heligoland, 9 Sep 1913 *German Navy airship L1 crashed into the sea, leaving six survivors.*	14
=Caldwell, Ohio, USA, 3 Sep 1925 *US dirigible* Shenandoah, *the first airship built in the US and the first to use safe helium instead of inflammable hydrogen, broke up in a storm, scattering sections over a large area of the Ohio countryside.*	14

THE 10 WORST AIR DISASTERS CAUSED BY HIJACKINGS AND BOMBS

LOCATION/DATE/INCIDENT	NO. KILLED
1 Off the Irish coast, 23 June 1985 *An Air India Boeing 747, on a flight from Vancouver to Delhi, exploded in mid-air, perhaps as a result of a terrorist bomb, resulting in the worst-ever air disaster over water.*	329
2 Lockerbie, Scotland, 21 Dec 1988 *(See Worst Air Disasters, No. 10)*	270
3 Tenere Desert, Niger, 19 Sep 1989 *A Union de Transports Ariens DC-10, flying out of Ndjamena, Chad, exploded over Niger. French investigators implicated Libyan and Syrian terrorists.*	170
4 Baiyun Airport, China, 2 Oct 1990 *A Xiamen Airlines Boeing 737 was hijacked in flight and, during an enforced landing, crashed into a taxiing 757.*	132
5 Comoro Islands, Indian Ocean, 23 Nov 1996 *An Ethiopian Airlines Boeing 767 was hijacked and ditched in the sea when it ran out of fuel.*	127
6 Andaman Sea, off Myanmar, 29 Nov 1987 *A Korean Air Boeing 707 exploded in mid-air. Two North Korean terrorists were captured, one of whom committed suicide, while the other was sentenced to death but later pardoned.*	115
7 Near Abu Dhabi, United Arab Emirates, 23 Sep 1983 *A Gulf Air Boeing 737 exploded as it prepared to land. Evidence indicated that the explosion had been caused by a bomb in the cargo hold.*	111
8 Near El Dorado Airport, Bogota, Colombia, 27 Nov 1989 *An AVIANCA Boeing 727 exploded soon after take-off in a drug cartel-related bombing.*	110
9 Near Johor Baharu, Malaysia, 4 Dec 1977 *A Malaysian Airline System Boeing 737 plunged to earth and exploded. Investigators concluded that the pilots had been shot.*	100
10 Near Kefallinia, Greece, 8 Sep 1974 *A Trans World Airlines Boeing 707 plunged into the Ionian Sea after an explosion resulted in loss of control.*	88

"BLACK BOX"

During World War II, the slang term for the radar apparatus that aided British Royal Air Force navigators and bomb-aimers was "black box", the mystery and secrecy surrounding this invention emphasized by its colour. The name was later applied to the flight data recorder on a modern airliner, the device that records all the aircraft's principal actions. In fact, to make them easier to find after a crash, black boxes are now customarily painted a luminous orange.

WHY DO WE SAY?

FIERY FINALE

Astonishingly, 61 of the 97 people on board the Hindenburg *survived its explosion, but the awesome and terrible images of the catastrophe ended the airship era.*

Background image: **CHARLES DE GAULLE AIRPORT, PARIS, FRANCE**

SIFTING THROUGH THE WRECKAGE

Military personnel inspect the wreckage of the airliner and cargo aircraft that collided at Charkhi Dadri, India, in 1996, leaving no survivors.

THE 10

WORST AIR DISASTERS

LOCATION/DATE/INCIDENT	NO. KILLED
1 **Tenerife**, Canary Islands, 27 Mar 1977 *Two Boeing 747s (Pan Am and KLM, carrying 364 passengers and 16 crew and 230 passengers and 11 crew respectively) collided and caught fire on the runway of Los Rodeos airport after the pilots received incorrect control-tower instructions.*	583
2 **Mt. Ogura**, Japan, 12 Aug 1985 *A JAL Boeing 747 on an internal flight from Tokyo to Osaka crashed, killing all but four on board in the worst-ever disaster involving a single aircraft.*	520
3 **Charkhi Dadri**, India, 12 Nov 1996 *Soon after taking off from New Delhi's Indira Gandhi International Airport, a Saudi Airways Boeing 747 collided with a Kazakh Airlines Ilyushin IL76 cargo aircraft on its descent and exploded, killing all 312 on the Boeing and 37 on the Ilyushin in the world's worst mid-air crash.*	349
4 **Paris**, France, 3 Mar 1974 *A Turkish Airlines DC-10 crashed at Ermenonville, north of Paris, immediately after take-off for London, with many English rugby supporters among the dead.*	346
5 **Off the Irish coast**, 23 June 1985 *An Air India Boeing 747 on a flight from Vancouver to Delhi exploded in mid-air, perhaps as a result of a terrorist bomb.*	329
6 **Riyadh**, Saudi Arabia, 19 Aug 1980 *A Saudia (Saudi Arabian) Airlines Lockheed Tristar caught fire during an emergency landing.*	301
7 **Kinshasa, Zaïre**, 8 Jan 1996 *A Zaïrean Antonov-32 cargo plane crashed shortly after take-off, killing shoppers in a market.*	298
8 **Off the Iranian coast**, 3 July 1988 *An Iran Air A300 airbus was shot down in error by a missile fired by the USS Vincennes.*	290
9 **Chicago**, USA, 25 May 1979 *An engine fell off an American Airlines DC-10 as it took off from Chicago O'Hare airport; the plane plunged out of control, killing all 271 on board and two on the ground, in the US's worst-ever air disaster.*	273
10 **Lockerbie**, Scotland, 21 Dec 1988 *Pan Am Flight 103 from London Heathrow to New York exploded in mid-air as a result of a terrorist bomb, killing 243 passengers, 16 crew, and 11 on the ground in the UK's worst-ever air disaster.*	270

TOP 10 AIRLINE-USING COUNTRIES

(Country/passenger km per annum/passenger miles per annum*)*

1 **USA**, 964.533 billion/599.332 billion 2 **UK**, 157.895 billion/98.111 billion 3 **Japan**, 151.048 billion/93.856 billion 4 **Germany**, 86.189 billion/53.555 billion 5 **France**, 84.675 billion/52.614 billion 6 **Australia**, 75.873 billion/47.145 billion 7 **China**, 72.964 billion/45.337 billion 8 **Netherlands**, 66.666 billion/41.424 billion 9 **Canada**, 61.862 billion/38.439 billion 10 **South Korea**, 59.372 billion/36.892 billion

* *Total distance travelled by scheduled aircraft of national airlines multiplied by number of passengers carried*

Source: *International Civil Aviation Organization*

TOP 10

BUSIEST INTERNATIONAL AIRPORTS

	AIRPORT/LOCATION	PASSENGERS PER ANNUM
1	**London Heathrow**, London, UK	50,612,000
2	**Frankfurt**, Frankfurt, Germany	32,333,000
3	**Charles de Gaulle**, Paris, France	31,549,000
4	**Schiphol**, Amsterdam, Netherlands	30,832,000
5	**Hong Kong**, Hong Kong, China	28,316,000
6	**London Gatwick**, Gatwick, UK	24,835,000
7	**Singapore International**, Singapore	23,799,000
8	**New Tokyo International (Narita)**, Tokyo, Japan	22,941,000
9	**J. F. Kennedy International**, New York, USA	17,378,000
10	**Zurich**, Zurich, Switzerland	16,747,000

Source: *International Civil Aviation Organization*

In addition to New York's JFK, only five airports in the US handle more than 5 million international passengers a year: notably Miami, Los Angeles, Chicago O'Hare, Honolulu, and San Francisco.

TOP 10 COUNTRIES WITH THE MOST AIRPORTS

(Country/airports)

1 **USA**, 14,459 2 **Brazil**, 3,265 3 **Russia**, 2,517 4 **Mexico**, 1,805 5 **Argentina**, 1,374 6 **Canada**, 1,395 7 **Bolivia**, 1,130 8 **Colombia**, 1,120 9 **Paraguay**, 941 10 **South Africa**, 749

Source: *Central Intelligence Agency*

Airports, as defined by the CIA, range in size from those with paved runways over 3,048 m (10,000 ft) in length to those with only short landing strips. Among European countries those with the most airports are Germany (618), France (474), and the UK (387).

Which country has the world's fastest scheduled rail service?

see p.232 for the answer

A France
B USA
C Japan

TOP 10 ★

Sports

SYDNEY 2000

Indigenous Australian creatures welcome the world to the 27th Olympiad, held in Sydney from 15 September to 1 October 2000.

TOP 10

LONGEST-STANDING CURRENT OLYMPIC TRACK AND FIELD RECORDS

	EVENT	WINNING DISTANCE, TIME OR SCORE	COMPETITOR/ COUNTRY	DATE SET
1	Men's long jump	8.90 m	Bob Beamon, USA	18 Oct 1968
2	Women's shot put	22.41 m	Ilona Slupianek, East Germany	24 July 1980
3	Women's 800 metres	1 min 53.43 sec	Nadezhda Olizarenko, USSR	27 July 1980
4	=Women's 4 x 100 metres	41.60 sec	East Germany	1 Aug 1980
	=Men's 1500 metres	3 min 32.53 sec	Sebastian Coe, GB	1 Aug 1980
6	Women's marathon	2 hr 24 min 52 sec	Joan Benoit, USA	5 Aug 1984
7	Decathlon	8,847 points	Daley Thompson, GB	9 Aug 1984
8	Men's 5,000 metres	13 min 05.59 sec	Said Aouita, Morocco	11 Aug 1984
9	Men's marathon	2 hr 9 min 21 sec	Carlos Lopes, Portugal	12 Aug 1984
10	=Men's shot put	22.47 m	Ulf Timmermann, East Germany	23 Sep 1988
	=Men's 20-km walk	1 hr 19 min 57 sec	Jozef Pribilinec, Czechoslovakia	23 Sep 1988

Bob Beamon's record-breaking jump in 1968 is regarded as one of the greatest achievements in athletics. He was aided by Mexico City's rarefied atmosphere, but to add a staggering 55.25 cm (21¾ in) to the old record, and win the competition by 72.39 cm (28½ in), was no mean feat. Beamon's jump of 8.90 m (29 ft 2½ in) was the first beyond both 8.53 and 8.84 m (28 and 29 ft). The next 8.53-m (28-ft) jump in the Olympics was not until 1980, 12 years after Beamon's leap.

THE 10 OLYMPIC DECATHLON EVENTS

1 100 metres 2 Long jump 3 Shot put 4 High jump 5 400 metres 6 110 metres hurdles 7 Discus 8 Pole vault 9 Javelin 10 1500 metres

TOP 10

OLYMPIC SPORTS IN WHICH GREAT BRITAIN HAS WON THE MOST MEDALS

	SPORT	MEDALS GOLD	SILVER	BRONZE	TOTAL
1	Athletics	47	79	57	183
2	Swimming	18	23	30	71
3	=Cycling	9	21	16	46
	=Tennis	16	14	16	46
5	Shooting	13	14	18	45
6	Boxing	12	10	21	43
7	Rowing	19	15	7	41
8	Yachting	14	12	9	35
9	Equestrianism	5	7	9	21
10	Wrestling	3	4	10	17

TOP 10

OLYMPIC SPORTS IN WHICH THE US HAS WON THE MOST MEDALS

	SPORT	MEDALS GOLD	SILVER	BRONZE	TOTAL
1	Athletics	299	216	177	692
2	Swimming	230	176	137	543
3	Diving	46	40	41	127
4	Wrestling	46	38	25	109
5	Boxing	47	21	34	102
6	Shooting	45	26	21	92
7	Gymnastics	26	23	28	77
8	Rowing	29	28	19	76
9	Yachting	16	19	16	51
10	Speed skating	22	16	10	48

Background image: THE OLYMPIC STADIUM IN SYDNEY

TOP 10

COUNTRIES WITH THE MOST SUMMER OLYMPICS MEDALS, 1896–1996

	COUNTRY	MEDALS GOLD	SILVER	BRONZE	TOTAL
1	USA	833	634	548	2,015
2	Soviet Union*	485	395	354	1,234
3	Great Britain	177	233	225	635
4	France	176	181	205	562
5	Germany#	151	181	184	516
6	Sweden	134	152	173	459
7	Italy	166	136	142	444
8	Hungary	142	128	155	425
9	East Germany	153	130	127	410
10	Australia	87	85	122	294

* *Includes Unified Team of 1992; does not include Russia since this date*

\# *Not including West/East Germany 1968–88*

The medals table was led by the host nations at the first three Games: Greece in 1896, France in 1900, and the USA in 1904. Germany led at the 1936 Games, after which the USA and the Soviet Union vied for pre-eminence.

TOP 10 SUMMER OLYMPICS ATTENDED BY THE MOST COMPETITORS, 1896–1996

(City/year/competitors)

1 **Atlanta**, 1996, 10,310 2 **Barcelona**, 1992, 9,364 3 **Seoul**, 1988, 9,101 4 **Munich**, 1972, 7,156 5 **Los Angeles**, 1984, 7,058 6 **Montreal**, 1976, 6,085 7 **Mexico City**, 1968, 5,530 8 **Rome**, 1960, 5,346 9 **Moscow**, 1980, 5,326 10 **Tokyo**, 1964, 5,140

The first Games in 1896 were attended by just 311 competitors, all men, representing 13 countries. Women took part for the first time four years later at the Paris Games.

TOP 10

MEDAL WINNERS IN A SUMMER OLYMPICS CAREER

	MEDALLIST	COUNTRY	SPORT	YEARS	MEDALS GOLD	SILVER	BRONZE	TOTAL
1	Larissa Latynina	USSR	Gymnastics	1956–64	9	5	4	18
2	Nikolay Andrianov	USSR	Gymnastics	1972–80	7	5	3	15
3	=Edoardo Mangiarotti	Italy	Fencing	1936–60	6	5	2	13
	=Takashi Ono	Japan	Gymnastics	1952–64	5	4	4	13
	=Boris Shakhlin	USSR	Gymnastics	1956–64	7	4	2	13
6	=Sawao Kato	Japan	Gymnastics	1968–76	8	3	1	12
	=Paavo Nurmi	Finland	Athletics	1920–28	9	3	0	12
8	=Viktor Chukarin	USSR	Gymnastics	1952–56	7	3	1	11
	=Vera Cáslavská	Czechoslovakia	Gymnastics	1964–68	7	4	0	11
	=Carl Osborn	USA	Shooting	1912–24	5	4	2	11
	=Mark Spitz	USA	Swimming	1968–72	9	1	1	11
	=Matt Biondi	USA	Swimming	1984–92	8	2	1	11

"OLYMPICS"

What we call the Olympics is a modern revival of games that took place at Olympia in Greece from as early as 1370 BC, as part of a religious festival held every four years. Originally foot races were the only events, and the earliest record is that of Coroibis of Olis, winner of a 170-m (186-yd) race in 776 BC. New sports were progressively added, but the Games were banned in AD 393 by Emperor Theodosius I. The Olympics were reborn with the first modern games held in Athens in 1896.

WHY DO WE SAY?

MEDAL WINNER

Russian gymnast Nikolay Andrianov's tally of 15 individual and team medals won in three Olympics makes him the most decorated male athlete of all time.

Did You Know? Several unusual Olympic events have been discontinued, including underwater swimming, long jump and high jump on horseback, club-swinging, and stone-throwing.

Sporting Heroes

TOP 10 ★ MOST POINTS SCORED BY MICHAEL JORDAN IN A GAME

	TEAM	DATE	POINTS
1	Cleveland Cavaliers	28 Mar 1990	69
2	Orlando Magic	16 Jan 1993	64
3	Boston Celtics	20 Apr 1986	63
4	=Detroit Pistons	4 Mar 1987	61
	=Atlanta Hawks	16 Apr 1987	61
6	Detroit Pistons	3 Mar 1988	59
7	New Jersey Nets	6 Feb 1987	58
8	Washington Bullets	23 Dec 1992	57
9	=Philadelphia 76ers	24 Mar 1987	56
	=Miami Heat	29 Apr 1992	56

Source: *NBA*

TOP 10 ★ SEASONS BY WAYNE GRETZKY

	SEASON	GOALS	ASSISTS	POINTS
1	1985–86	52	163	215
2	1981–82	92	120	212
3	1984–85	73	135	208
4	1983–84	87	118	205
5	1982–83	71	125	196
6	1986–87	62	121	183
7	1988–89	54	114	168
8	1980–81	55	109	164
9	1990–91	41	122	163
10	1987–88	40	109	149

Wayne Gretzky, who retired in 1999 after 20 seasons in the NHL, is considered to be the greatest ice-hockey player of all time. He gained more records than any player in history, including the most goals, assists, and points in a career.

ICE MAN

Wayne Gretzky (pictured here during his 1984–85 season with the Edmonton Oilers) holds more career records than any player in ice-hockey history.

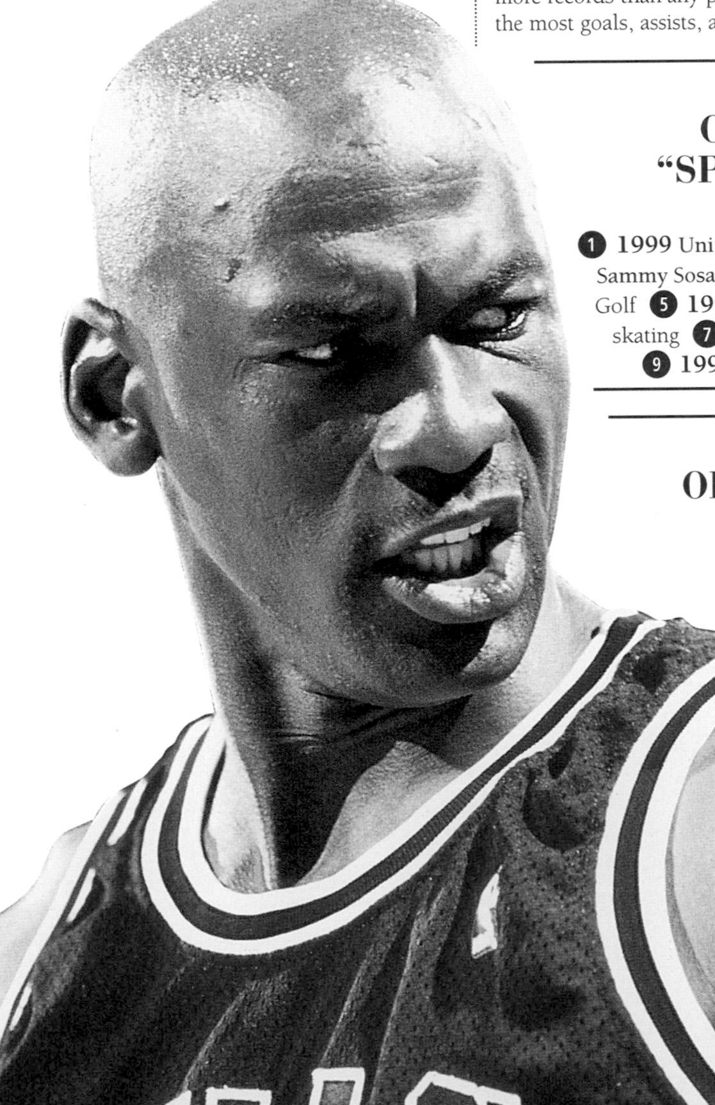

THE 10 LATEST WINNERS OF THE *SPORTS ILLUSTRATED* "SPORTSMAN OF THE YEAR" AWARD

(Year/winner(s)/sport)

❶ **1999** United States Women's World Cup Squad, Soccer ❷ **1998** Mark McGwire and Sammy Sosa, Baseball ❸ **1997** Dean Smith, Basketball coach ❹ **1996** Tiger Woods, Golf ❺ **1995** Cal Ripken Jr., Baseball ❻ **1994** Johan Olav Koss and Bonnie Blair, Ice skating ❼ **1993** Don Shula, American football coach ❽ **1992** Arthur Ashe, Tennis ❾ **1991** Michael Jordan, Basketball ❿ **1990** Joe Montana, American football

THE 10 LATEST WINNERS OF THE BBC "SPORTS PERSONALITY OF THE YEAR" AWARD

(Year/winner/sport)

❶ **1999** Lennox Lewis, Boxing ❷ **1998** Michael Owen, Football ❸ **1997** Greg Rusedski, Tennis ❹ **1996** Damon Hill, Motor racing ❺ **1995** Jonathan Edwards, Athletics ❻ **1994** Damon Hill, Motor racing ❼ **1993** Linford Christie, Athletics ❽ **1992** Nigel Mansell, Motor racing ❾ **1991** Liz McColgan, Athletics ❿ **1990** Paul Gascoigne, Football

This annual award is based on a poll of BBC television viewers.

ON THE BALL

In many seasons during his exceptional career, Michael Jordan achieved an average of over 30 points per game, with those listed above standing out as his highest-scoring ones.

THE 10 ★
LATEST EVANDER HOLYFIELD WINS BY KNOCKOUT

	OPPONENT	ROUND	DATE
1	**Michael Moorer**	8	8 Nov 1997
2	**Mike Tyson**	11*	9 Nov 1996
3	**Bobby Czyz**	5	10 May 1996
4	**Riddick Bowe**	8*	4 Nov 1995
5	**Bert Cooper**	7	23 Nov 1991
6	**Buster Douglas**	3	25 Oct 1990
7	**Seamus McDonagh**	4*	1 June 1990
8	**Alex Stewart**	8*	4 Nov 1989
9	**Adilson Rodrigues**	2	15 July 1989
10	**Michael Dokes**	10*	11 Mar 1989

** Technical knockout*

Born 19 October 1962, boxer Evander Holyfield won his first undisputed heavyweight title in 1990 when he defeated Buster Douglas. His 1993 defeat of Riddick Bowe (when Holyfield won on points) and his 1996 victory over Mike Tyson established him as the only fighter, apart from Muhammad Ali, to win the heavyweight title on three occasions.

TOP 10 ★
FASTEST 100-METRE RUNS BY LINFORD CHRISTIE

	STADIUM/LOCATION	DATE	TIME SECS
1	**Stuttgart**, Germany	15 Aug 1993	9.87
2	**Victoria**, Canada	23 Aug 1994	9.91
3	**Tokyo**, Japan	25 Aug 1991	9.92
4	**Barcelona**, Spain	1 Aug 1992	9.96
5	=**Seoul**, Korea	24 Sep 1988	9.97
	=**Stuttgart**, Germany	15 Aug 1993	9.97
	=**Johannesburg**, SA	23 Sep 1995	9.97
8	**Victoria**, Canada	23 Aug 1994	9.98
9	**Tokyo**, Japan	25 Aug 1991	9.99
10	=**Barcelona**, Spain	1 Aug 1992	10.00
	=**Stuttgart**, Germany	14 Aug 1993	10.00

Christie made his international debut for Great Britain in 1980, became the fastest runner outside the USA in 1986, and won Olympic gold in 1992.

TOP 10 ★
LONGEST LONG JUMPS BY CARL LEWIS

	STADIUM/LOCATION	DATE	DISTANCE M
1	**Tokyo**, Japan	30 Aug 1991	8.87
2	=**Indianapolis**, USA	19 June 1983	8.79
	=**New York**, USA*	27 Jan 1984	8.79
4	=**Indianapolis**, USA	24 July 1982	8.76
	=**Indianapolis**, USA	18 July 1988	8.76
6	**Indianapolis**, USA	16 Aug 1987	8.75
7	**Seoul**, Korea	26 Sep 1988	8.72
8	=**Westwood**, USA	13 May 1984	8.71
	=**Los Angeles**, USA	19 June 1984	8.71
10	**Barcelona**, Spain	5 Aug 1992	8.68

** Indoor performance*

All-round athlete Lewis won four gold medals at the 1984 Olympics, two in 1988, two in 1992, and his ninth in 1996.

THE 10 ★
LATEST WINNERS OF THE JESSE OWENS INTERNATIONAL TROPHY

YEAR	WINNER	SPORT
2000	Lance Armstrong	Cycling
1999	Marion Jones	Athletics
1998	Haile Gebrselassie	Athletics
1997	Michael Johnson	Athletics
1996	Michael Johnson	Athletics
1995	Johann Olav Koss	Speed skating
1994	Wang Junxia	Athletics
1993	Vitaly Scherbo	Gymnastics
1992	Mike Powell	Athletics
1991	Greg LeMond	Cycling

The Jesse Owens International Trophy, named in honour of American Olympic athlete Jesse (James Cleveland) Owens (1913–80), has been presented by the Amateur Athletic Association since 1981, when it was won by speed skater Eric Heiden. Michael Johnson is the only sportsperson to have won on two occasions, while Marion Jones, the 1999 winner, is only the fourth woman to receive the award.

POLES APART

Ukrainian pole-vaulter Sergei Bubka (b. 1963) has ruled his sport since winning the 1983 World Championship. He has set 35 world records, which is more than any other athlete in sports history.

TOP 10 ★
HIGHEST POLE VAULTS BY SERGEI BUBKA

	STADIUM/LOCATION	DATE	HEIGHT M
1	**Donetsk**, Ukraine*	21 Feb 1993	6.15
2	=**Lievin**, France*	13 Feb 1993	6.14
	=**Sestriere**, Italy	31 July 1994	6.14
4	=**Berlin**, Germany*	21 Feb 1992	6:13
	=**Tokyo**, Japan	19 Sep 1992	6.13
6	=**Grenoble**, France*	23 Mar 1991	6.12
	=**Padua**, Italy	30 Aug 1992	6.12
8	=**Donetsk**, Ukraine*	19 Mar 1991	6.11
	=**Dijon**, France	13 June 1992	6.11
10	=**San Sebastian**, Spain*	15 Mar 1991	6.10
	=**Malmo**, Sweden	5 Aug 1991	6.10

** Indoor performance*

Did You Know? In little over a century, the world pole-vaulting record leaped from 3.62 m (achieved by Raymond Clapp of the US in 1898) to today's 6.14-m outdoor record.

American Football

TOP 10 ★ LARGEST NFL STADIUMS

	STADIUM/HOME TEAM	CAPACITY
1	**Pontiac Silverdome**, Detroit Lions	80,311
2	**FedExField**, Washington Redskins	80,116
3	**Giants Stadium**, New York Giants*	79,469
4	**Arrowhead Stadium**, Kansas City Chiefs	79,409
5	**Mile High Stadium**, Denver Broncos	76,082
6	**Ralph Wilson Stadium**, Buffalo Bills	75,339
7	**Pro Player Stadium**, Miami Dolphins	74,916
8	**Sun Devil Stadium**, Arizona Cardinals	73,273
9	**Alltel Stadium**, Jacksonville Jaguars	73,000
10	**Ericsson Stadium**, Carolina Panthers	72,250

* *Seating reduced to 77,803 for New York Jets games*

Source: *National Football League*

The roof of the octagonal Pontiac Silverdome is the world's largest air-supported structure.

TOP 10 ★ BIGGEST WINNING MARGINS IN THE SUPER BOWL

	GAME*	YEAR	MARGIN
1	**San Francisco 49ers v Denver Broncos**	1990	45
2	**Chicago Bears v New England Patriots**	1986	36
3	**Dallas Cowboys v Buffalo Bills**	1993	35
4	**Washington Redskins v Denver Broncos**	1988	32
5	**Los Angeles Raiders v Washington Redskins**	1984	29
6	**Green Bay Packers v Kansas City Chiefs**	1967	25
7	**San Francisco 49ers v San Diego Chargers**	1995	23
8	**San Francisco 49ers v Miami Dolphins**	1985	22
9	**Dallas Cowboys v Miami Dolphins**	1972	21
10=	**Green Bay Packers v Oakland Raiders**	1968	19
=	**New York Giants v Denver Broncos**	1987	19

* *Winners first*

TOP 10 ★ MOST SUCCESSFUL TEAMS*

	TEAM	WINS	LOSSES	PTS
1	**Dallas Cowboys**	5	3	13
2	**San Francisco 49ers**	5	0	10
3	**Pittsburgh Steelers**	4	1	10
4	**Washington Redskins**	3	2	8
5	**Denver Broncos**	2	4	8
6=	**Green Bay Packers**	3	1	7
=	**Oakland/L.A. Raiders**	3	1	7
8	**Miami Dolphins**	2	3	7
9	**New York Giants**	2	0	4
10=	**Buffalo Bills**	0	4	4
=	**Minnesota Vikings**	0	4	4

* *Based on two points for a Super Bowl win and one for a loss; wins take precedence over losses in determining ranking*

Source: *National Football League*

TOP 10 ★ MOST SUCCESSFUL COACHES IN AN NFL CAREER

	COACH	GAMES WON
1	**Don Shula**	347
2	**George Halas**	324
3	**Tom Landry**	270
4	**Curly Lambeau**	229
5	**Chuck Noll**	209
6	**Chuck Knox**	193
7	**Dan Reeves***	175
8	**Paul Brown**	170
9	**Bud Grant**	168
10	**Marv Levy**	154

* *Still active*

Source: *National Football League*

TOP COACH

Don Shula retired at the end of the 1995 season, having achieved an NFL record of coaching his team, the Miami Dolphins, to 347 wins.

Background image: **PONTIAC SILVERDOME**

PASSING GREAT

Jerry Rice, who joined the San Francisco 49ers in 1985, is one of the greatest-ever pass catchers and the player with the most career touchdowns.

TOP 10

PLAYERS WITH THE MOST CAREER POINTS

	PLAYER	POINTS
1	George Blanda	2,002
2	Gary Anderson*	1,948
3	Morten Andersen*	1,840
4	Norm Johnson*	1,736
5	Nick Lowery	1,711
6	Jan Stenerud	1,699
7	Eddie Murray*	1,549
8	Pat Leahy	1,470
9	Jim Turner	1,439
10	Matt Bahr	1,422

** Still active 1999 season*

Source: *National Football League*

TOP 10

LONGEST CAREERS OF CURRENT NFL PLAYERS

	PLAYER	TEAM	YEARS
1	Wade Wilson	Oakland Raiders	19
2	=Morten Andersen	Atlanta Falcons	18
	=Gary Anderson	Minnesota Vikings	18
	=Norm Johnson	Philadelphia Eagles	18
5	=Darrell Green	Washington Redskins	17
	=Trey Junkin	Arizona Cardinals	17
	=Dan Marino	Miami Dolphins	17
	=Bruce Matthews	Tennessee Titans	17
	=Eddie Murray	Dallas Cowboys	17
	=Mike Horan	St. Louis Rams	17

Source: *National Football League*

TOP 10

PLAYERS WITH THE MOST CAREER TOUCHDOWNS

	PLAYER	TOUCHDOWNS
1	Jerry Rice*	179
2	Emmitt Smith*	147
3	Marcus Allen	145
4	Jim Brown	126
5	Walter Payton	125
6	John Riggins	116
7	Lenny Moore	113
8	Don Hutson	105
9	Steve Largent	101
10	Franco Harris	100

** Still active*

Source: *National Football League*

TOP 10

PLAYERS WITH THE MOST PASSING YARDS IN AN NFL CAREER

	PLAYER	PASSING YARDS
1	Dan Marino*	61,243
2	John Elway	51,475
3	Warren Moon*	49,117
4	Fran Tarkenton	47,003
5	Dan Fouts	43,040
6	Joe Montana	40,551
7	Johnny Unitas	40,239
8	Dave Krieg	37,946
9	Boomer Esiason	37,920
10	Jim Kelly	35,467

** Still active 1999 season*

Source: *National Football League*

TOP 10

POINT SCORERS IN AN NFL SEASON

	PLAYER/TEAM/YEAR	GAMES WON
1	**Paul Hornung**, Green Bay Packers, 1960	176
2	**Gary Anderson**, Minnesota Vikings, 1998	164
3	**Mark Moseley**, Washington Redskins,1983	161
4	**Gino Cappelletti**, Boston Patriots, 1964	155*
5	**Emmitt Smith**, Dallas Cowboys, 1995	150
6	**Chip Lohmiller**, Washington Redskins, 1991	149
7	**Gino Cappelletti**, Boston Patriots, 1961	147
8	**Paul Hornung**, Green Bay Packers, 1961	146
9	**=Jim Turner**, New York Jets, 1968	145
	=John Kasay, Carolina Panthers, 1996	145
	=Mike Vanderjagt, Indianapolis Colts, 1999	145

** Including a two-point conversion*

Source: *National Football League*

THE 10 LATEST ATTENDANCES OF NFL TEAMS*

(Year/attendance)

1 **1999** 16,206,640 2 **1998** 16,187,758 3 **1997** 15,769,193 4 **1996** 15,381,727 5 **1995** 15,834,468 6 **1994** 14,810,173 7 **1993** 14,781,450 8 **1992** 14,644,797 9 **1991** 14,654,706 10 **1990** 14,807,439

** Regular season only* Source: NFL

What sort of baskets were originally used in basketball?

see p.250 for the answer

A Fish
B Peach
C Bread

Athletic Achievements

TOP 10 ★

FASTEST WINNING TIMES IN THE NEW YORK CITY MARATHON

MEN

	RUNNER/COUNTRY	YEAR	TIME*
1	**Juma Ikangaa**, Tanzania	1989	2.08.01
2	**John Kagwe**, Kenya	1997	2.08.12
3	**Alberto Salazar**, USA	1981	2.08.13
4	**Steve Jones**, UK	1988	2.08.20
5	**John Kagwe**, Kenya	1998	2.08.45
6	**Rod Dixon**, New Zealand	1983	2.08.59
7	**Joseph Chebet**, Kenya	1999	2.09.14
8	**Salvador Garcia**, Mexico	1991	2.09.28
9	=**Alberto Salazar**, USA	1982	2.09.29
	=**Willie Mtolo**, South Africa	1992	2.09.29

WOMEN

	RUNNER/COUNTRY	YEAR	TIME*
1	**Lisa Ondieki**, Australia	1992	2.24.40
2	**Adriana Fernandez**, Mexico	1999	2.25.06
3	**Franca Fiacconi**, Italy	1998	2.25.17
4	**Allison Roe**, New Zealand	1981	2.25.29
5	**Ingrid Kristiansen**, Norway	1989	2.25.30
6	**Grete Waitz**, Norway	1980	2.25.41
7	**Uta Pippig**, Germany	1993	2.26.24
8	**Grete Waitz**, Norway	1983	2.27.00
9	**Grete Waitz**, Norway	1982	2.27.14
10	**Liz McColgan**, Scotland	1991	2.27.23

** In 1981–83 the circuit was 155 m (170 yd) shorter.*

JUMPING AHEAD

US athlete Mike Powell's long-jump record of 8.95 m, set at Tokyo on 30 August 1991, broke Bob Beamon's record, which had stood for 23 years.

TOP 10 LONGEST LONG JUMPS*

(Athlete/country/year/distance in metres)

1 **Mike Powell**, USA, 1991, 8.95 2 **Bob Beamon**, USA, 1968, 8.90 3 **Carl Lewis**, USA, 1991, 8.87 4 **Robert Emmiyan**, USSR, 1987, 8.86 5 = **Larry Myricks**, USA, 1988, 8.74; = **Eric Walder**, USA, 1994, 8.74 7 **Ivan Pedroso**, Cuba, 1995, 8.71 8 **Kareem Streete-Thompson**, USA, 1994, 8.63 9 **James Beckford**, Jamaica, 1997, 8.62 10 **Yago Lamela**#, Spain, 1999, 8.56

** Longest by each athlete only # Indoor*

TOP 10 ★

HIGHEST POLE VAULTS*

	ATHLETE/COUNTRY	YEAR	HEIGHT METRES
1	**Sergey Bubka**#, Ukraine	1993	6.15
2	**Maxin Tarasov**, Russia	1999	6.05
3	**Okkert Brits**, South Africa	1995	6.03
4	=**Rodion Gataullin**#, USSR	1989	6.02
	=**Jeff Hartwig**, USA	1999	6.02
6	**Igor Trandenkov**, Russia	1996	6.01
7	=**Jeane Galfione**, France	1999	6.00
	=**Tim Lobinger**, Germany	1997	6.00
	=**Dmitri Markov**, Belarus	1998	6.00
10	**Lawrence Johnson**, USA	1996	5.98

** Highest by each athlete only*
 # Indoor

THE 10 ★

FIRST ATHLETES TO RUN A MILE IN UNDER FOUR MINUTES

	ATHLETE/COUNTRY	LOCATION	MIN:SEC	DATE
1	**Roger Bannister**, UK	Oxford	3:59.4	6 May 1954
2	**John Landy**, Australia	Turku, Finland	3:57.9	21 June 1954
3	**Laszlo Tabori**, Hungary	London	3:59.0	28 May 1955
4	=**Chris Chataway**, UK	London	3:59.8	28 May 1955
	=**Brian Hewson**, UK	London	3:59.8	28 May 1955
6	**Jim Bailey**, Australia	Los Angeles	3:58.6	5 May 1956
7	**Gunnar Nielsen**, Denmark	Compton, USA	3:59.1	1 June 1956
8	**Ron Delany**, Ireland	Compton, USA	3:59.4	1 June 1956
9	**Derek Ibbotson**, UK	London	3:59.4	6 Aug 1956
10	**István Rózsavölgyi**, Hungary	Budapest	3:59.0	26 Aug 1956

Within a little over two years of Roger Bannister's capturing the imagination of the world by shattering the four-minute-mile barrier, the number of athletes to do so had risen to 10.

TOP 10

FASTEST WOMEN EVER*

	ATHLETE/COUNTRY	YEAR	TIME
1	**Florence Griffith-Joyner**, USA	1988	10.49
2	**Marion Jones**, USA	1998	10.65
3	**Christine Arron**, France	1998	10.73
4	**Merlene Ottey**, Jamaica	1996	10.74
5	**Evelyn Ashford**, USA	1984	10.76
6	**Irina Privalova**, Russia	1994	10.77
7	**Dawn Sowell**, USA	1989	10.78
8	**Inger Miller**, USA	1999	10.79
9	**Marlies Göhr**, East Germany	1983	10.81
10	=**Gail Devers**, USA	1992	10.82
	=**Gwen Torrence**, USA	1994	10.82

* *Based on fastest time for the 100 metres*

TOP 10

FASTEST MEN EVER*

	ATHLETE/COUNTRY	YEAR	TIME
1	**Maurice Green**, USA	1999	9.79
2	=**Donovan Bailey**, Canada	1996	9.84
	=**Bruny Surin**, Canada	1999	9.84
4	**Leroy Burrell**, USA	1994	9.85
5	=**Ato Boldon**, Trinidad	1998	9.86
	=**Frank Fredericks**, Namibia	1996	9.86
	=**Carl Lewis**, USA	1991	9.86
8	=**Linford Christie**, UK	1993	9.87
	=**Obadele Thompson**, Barbados	1998	9.87
10	**Dennis Mitchell**, USA	1991	9.91

* *Based on fastest time for the 100 metres*

TOP 10 HIGHEST HIGH JUMPS*

(Athlete/country/year/height in metres)

❶ **Javier Sotomayor**, Cuba, 1993, 2.45 ❷ = **Patrik Sjöberg**, Sweden, 1987, 2.42; = **Carlo Thränhardt**#, West Germany, 1988, 2.42 ❹ **Igor Paklin**, USSR, 1985, 2.41 ❺ = **Rudolf Povarnitsyn**, USSR, 1985, 2.40; = **Sorin Matei**, Romania, 1990, 2.40; = **Charles Austin**, USA, 1991, 2.40; = **Hollis Conway**#, USA, 1991, 2.40 ❾ = **Zhu Jianhua**, China, 1984, 2.39; = **Hollis Conway**, USA, 1989, 2.39; = **Dietmar Mögenburg**#, West Germany, 1985, 2.39; = **Ralph Sonn**#, Germany, 1991, 2.39

* *Highest by each athlete only* # *Indoor*

TOP 10

FASTEST TIMES IN THE LONDON MARATHON

MEN

	RUNNER/COUNTRY	YEAR	TIME
1	Antonio Pinto, Portugal	2000	2:06:36
2	**Antonio Pinto**, Portugal	1997	2:07:55
3	=**Abel Anton**, Spain	1998	2:07:57
	=**Abel Kader El Mouaziz**, Morocco	1999	2:07:57
5	**Steve Jones**, UK	1985	2:08:16
6	**Dionicio Ceron**, Mexico	1995	2:08:30
7	**Dionicio Ceron**, Mexico	1994	2:08:53
8	**Douglas Wakiihuri**, Kenya	1989	2:09:03
9	**Yakov Tolstikov**, USSR	1991	2:09:17
10	**Hugh Jones**, UK	1982	2:09:24

WOMEN

	RUNNER/COUNTRY	YEAR	TIME
1	**Ingrid Kristiansen**, Norway	1985	2:21:06
2	**Ingrid Kristiansen**, Norway	1987	2:22:48
3	**Joyce Chepchumba**, Kenya	1999	2:23:22
4	**Ingrid Kristiansen**, Norway	1984	2:24:26
5	**Tegla Loroupe**, Kenya	2000	2:24:33
6	**Grete Waitz**, Norway	1986	2:24:54
7	**Grete Waitz**, Norway	1983	2:25:29
8	**Ingrid Kristiansen**, Norway	1988	2:25:41
9	**Veronique Marot**, UK	1989	2:25:56
10	**Rosa Mota**, Portugal	1991	2:26:14

FASTEST MAN ON EARTH

US sprinter Maurice Green broke the world 100-m record on 16 June 1999, trimming 5/100ths of a second off Donovan Bailey's record.

Did You Know? The marathon distance was established at the Olympics in London in 1908. It was to have been 26 miles, but 385 yards were added to ensure that the race started beneath the Royal Nursery at Windsor Castle.

Basketball Bests

TOP 10 BIGGEST ARENAS IN THE NBA

	ARENA/LOCATION	HOME TEAM	CAPACITY
1	**The Alamodome**, San Antonio, Texas	San Antonio Spurs	34,215
2	**Charlotte Coliseum**, Charlotte, North Carolina	Charlotte Hornets	23,799
3	**The Palace of Auburn Hills**, Auburn Hills, Michigan	Detroit Pistons	22,076
4	**United Center**, Chicago, Illinois	Chicago Bulls	21,711
5	**MCI Center**, Washington, DC	Washington Wizards	20,674
6	**Gund Arena**, Cleveland, Ohio	Cleveland Cavaliers	20,562
7	**First Union Center**, Philadelphia, Pennsylvania	Philadelphia 76ers	20,444
8	**Continental Airlines Arena**, East Rutherford, New Jersey	New Jersey Nets	20,049
9	**The Rose Garden**, Portland, Oregon	Portland Trailblazers	19,980
10	**Delta Center**, Salt Lake City, Utah	Utah Jazz	19,911

The smallest arena in the NBA is the 15,200 capacity Miami Arena, home of the Miami Heat team. The largest ever NBA stadium was the Louisiana Superdome, used by Utah Jazz from 1975 to 1979, which was capable of holding crowds of 47,284.

Source: *NBA*

TOP 10 NBA COACHES

	COACH	GAMES WON*
1	**Lenny Wilkens**#	1,179
2	**Pat Riley**#	999
3	**Bill Fitch**	944
4	**Red Auerbach**	938
5	**Dick Motta**	935
6	**Don Nelson**#	926
7	**Jack Ramsay**	864
8	**Cotton Fitzsimmons**	832
9	**Gene Shue**	784
10	**John MacLeod**	707

* *Regular season games only*

\# *Still active 1999–2000 season*

Source: *NBA*

TOP 10 NCAA COACHES

(Coach/wins)

1 **Dean Smith**, 879 2 **Adolph Rupp**, 876 3 **Jim Phelan***, 803 4 **Henry Iba**, 767 5 **Bob Knight***, 762 6 **Ed Diddle**, 759 7 **Phog Allen**, 746 8 **Norm Stewart**, 731 9 **Ray Meyer**, 724 10 **Don Haskins**, 719

* *Still active 1999–2000 season* Source: *NCAA*

TOP 10 MOST SUCCESSFUL DIVISION 1 NCAA TEAMS

	COLLEGE	DIVISION 1 WINS
1	**Kentucky**	1,765
2	**North Carolina**	1,753
3	**Kansas**	1,708
4	**Duke**	1,606
5	**St. John's**	1,602
6	**Temple**	1,542
7	**Syracuse**	1,522
8	**Pennsylvania**	1,495
9	**Oregon State**	1,481
10	**Indiana**	1,472

Source: *NCAA*

TOP 10 POINT SCORERS IN AN NBA CAREER*

	PLAYER	TOTAL POINTS
1	**Kareem Abdul-Jabbar**	38,387
2	**Wilt Chamberlain**	31,419
3	**Karl Malone**#	31,041
4	**Michael Jordan**	29,277
5	**Moses Malone**	27,409
6	**Elvin Hayes**	27,313
7	**Oscar Robertson**	26,710
8	**Dominique Wilkins**	26,534
9	**John Havlicek**	26,395
10	**Hakeem Olajuwon**#	25,822

* *Regular season games only*

\# *Still active at end of 1999–2000 season*

Source: *NBA*

TOP 10 POINTS AVERAGES IN AN NBA SEASON

	PLAYER/TEAM	SEASON	AVERAGE
1	**Wilt Chamberlain**, Philadelphia 76ers	1961–62	50.4
2	**Wilt Chamberlain**, San Francisco Warriors	1962–63	44.8
3	**Wilt Chamberlain**, Philadelphia 76ers	1960–61	38.4
4	**Elgin Baylor**, Los Angeles Lakers	1961–62	38.3
5	**Wilt Chamberlain**, Philadelphia 76ers	1959–60	37.6
6	**Michael Jordan**, Chicago Bulls	1986–87	37.1
7	**Wilt Chamberlain**, San Francisco Warriors	1963–64	36.9
8	**Rick Barry**, San Francisco Warriors	1966–67	35.6
9	**Michael Jordan**, Chicago Bulls	1987–88	35.0
10=	**Elgin Baylor**, Los Angeles Lakers	1960–61	34.8
=	**Kareem Abdul-Jabbar**, Milwaukee Bucks	1971–72	34.8

Source: *NBA*

Did You Know? When basketball was invented in 1891, the peach baskets that were originally used had bases, and the balls had to be retrieved by ladder.

TOP 10 AVERAGE ATTENDANCES IN THE 1990s

(Years/attendance)

1 **1997–8** 20,373,079 **2** **1995–6** 20,513,218 **3** **1996–7** 20,304,629 **4** **1999–2000** 20,058,536 **5** **1994–5** 18,516,484 **6** **1993–4** 17,984,014 **7** **1992–3** 17,778,295 **8** **1989–90** 17,368,659 **9** **1991–2** 17,367,240 **10** **1990–1** 16,876,125

Source: *NBA*

TOP 10 ★ POINTS SCORED IN THE WNBA

	PLAYER/GAME	DATE	PTS
1	**Cynthia Cooper**, Houston v Sacramento	25 July 1997	44
2	**Cynthia Cooper**, Houston v Charlotte	11 Aug 1997	39
3	**Jennifer Gillom**, Phoenix v Cleveland	10 Aug 1998	36
4	=**Cynthia Cooper**, Houston v Los Angeles	1 Aug 1997	34
	=**Cynthia Cooper**, Houston v Phoenix	7 Aug 1997	34
	=**Ruthie Bolton-Holifield**, Sacramento v Utah	8 Aug 1997	34
	=**Ruthie Bolton-Holifield**, Sacramento v Cleveland	12 Aug 1997	34
	=**Cynthia Cooper**, Houston v Sacramento	3 July 1998	34
	=**Cynthia Cooper**, Houston at Detroit	7 Aug 1998	34
10	**Linda Burgess**, Sacramento v Utah	15 Aug 1998	33

Source: *WNBA*

TOP 10 ★ FREE THROW PERCENTAGES

	PLAYER	ATTEMPTS	BASKETS	%
1	**Mark Price**	2,362	2,135	90.4
2	**Rick Barry**	4,243	3,818	90.0
3	**Calvin Murphy**	3,864	3,445	89.2
4	**Scott Skiles**	1,741	1,548	88.9
5	**Larry Bird**	4,471	3,960	88.6
6	**Bill Sharman**	3,559	3,143	88.3
7	**Reggie Miller***	5,690	5,015	88.1
8	**Ricky Pierce**	3,871	3,389	87.5
9	**Kiki Vandeweghe**	3,997	3,484	87.2
10	**Jeff Malone**	3,383	2,947	87.1

* *Still active at end of 1999–2000 season*

Source: *NBA*

TOP 10 PLAYERS WITH THE MOST CAREER ASSISTS

(Player/assists)

1 **John Stockton***, 13,790 **2** **Magic Johnson**, 10,141 **3** **Oscar Robertson**, 9,887 **4** **Isiah Thomas**, 9,061 **5** **Mark Jackson***, 8,574 **6** **Maurice Cheeks**, 7,392 **7** **Lenny Wilkens**, 7,211 **8** **Bob Cousy**, 6,995 **9** **Guy Rodgers**, 6,917 **10** **Nate Archibald**, 6,476

* *Still active at end of 1999–2000 season*

Source: *NBA*

MAGIC TOUCH

Magic (Earvin) Johnson turned professional in 1979, becoming one of the NBA's most legendary players.

TOP 10 ★ PLAYERS TO HAVE PLAYED MOST GAMES IN THE NBA AND ABA

	PLAYER	GAMES PLAYED*
1	**Robert Parish**	1,611
2	**Kareem Abdul-Jabbar**	1,560
3	**Moses Malone**	1,455
4	**Buck Williams**	1,348
5	**Artis Gilmore**	1,329
6	**Elvin Hayes**	1,303
7	**Caldwell Jones**	1,299
8	**John Havlicek**	1,270
9	**John Stockton**#	1,258
10	**Paul Silas**	1,254

* *Regular season only*

\# *Still active at end of 1999–2000 season*

Source: *NBA*

TOP 10 OLYMPIC JUDO COUNTRIES

(Country/medals)

1 **Japan**, 40 2 **Soviet Union***, 27 3 **France**, 26 4 **South Korea**, 25 5 = **Cuba**, 15; = **Great Britain**, 15 7 **Netherlands**, 10 8 = **Germany** #, 9; = **East Germany**, 9 10 = **USA**, 8; = **Poland**, 8; = **West Germany**, 8; = **Hungary**, 8; = **Brazil**, 8

* *Including United Team of 1992; excludes Russia since this date*

Not including West Germany or East Germany 1968–88

FIGHTING FIT

Judo was first introduced as an Olympic sport for men at the 1964 Tokyo Games, and for women in 1992. Min Soo Kim, from South Korea, here wins bronze at the Olympic Games, Atlanta, 1996.

TOP 10 ★ OLYMPIC WRESTLING COUNTRIES/ GRECO-ROMAN

	COUNTRY	GOLD	SILVER	BRONZE	TOTAL
			MEDALS		
1	Soviet Union*	37	19	13	69
2	Finland	19	21	18	58
3	Sweden	19	16	19	54
4	Hungary	15	9	11	35
5	Bulgaria	8	14	7	29
6	Romania	6	8	13	27
7	Germany	4	13	8	25
8	Poland	5	8	6	19
9	Italy	5	4	9	18
10	Turkey	10	4	3	17

* *Including United Team of 1992; excludes Russia since this date*

Great Britain, Australia, and Canada have never won a Greco-Roman medal.

TOP 10 ★ OLYMPIC WRESTLING COUNTRIES/FREESTYLE

	COUNTRY	GOLD	SILVER	BRONZE	TOTAL
			MEDALS		
1	USA	44	33	22	99
2	Soviet Union*	31	17	15	63
3	Turkey	16	11	6	33
4	=Japan	16	9	7	32
	=Bulgaria	7	16	9	32
6	Sweden	8	10	8	26
7	=Finland	8	7	10	25
	=Iran	4	9	12	25
9	=Great Britain	3	4	10	17
	=Hungary	4	7	6	17

* *Including United Team of 1992; excludes Russia since this date*

TOP 10 WRESTLING WEIGHT DIVISIONS

(Weight/limit in kg/lb)

1 **Heavyweight plus**, over 100/over 220 2 **Heavyweight**, 100/220 3 **Light-heavyweight**, 90/198 4 **Middleweight**, 82/181 5 **Welterweight**, 74/163 6 **Lightweight**, 68/150 7 **Featherweight**, 62/137 8 **Bantamweight**, 57/126 9 **Flyweight**, 52/115 10 **Light-flyweight**, 48/106

TOP 10

HEAVIEST BOXING WEIGHT DIVISIONS

	WEIGHT	LIMIT KG	LB
1	Heavyweight	over 86	over 190
2	Cruiserweight	86	190
3	Light-heavyweight	79	175
4	Super-middleweight	76	168
5	Middleweight	73	160
6	Junior-middleweight/ Super-welterweight	70	154
7	Welterweight	67	147
8	Junior-welterweight/ Super-lightweight	65	140
9	Lightweight	61	135
10	Junior-lightweight/ Super-featherweight	59	130

TOP 10

BOXERS WITH THE MOST KNOCKOUTS IN A CAREER

	BOXER*	CAREER	KOS
1	Archie Moore	1936–63	129
2	Young Stribling	1921–63	126
3	Billy Bird	1920–48	125
4	Sam Langford	1902–26	116
5	George Odwell	1930–45	114
6	Sugar Ray Robinson	1940–65	110
7	Sandy Saddler	1944–65	103
8	Henry Armstrong	1931–45	100
9	Jimmy Wilde	1911–23	99
10	Len Wickwar	1928–47	93

* *All from the US except Jimmy Wilde, who was Welsh*

TOP 10

OLYMPIC FENCING COUNTRIES

	COUNTRY	MEDALS GOLD	SILVER	BRONZE	TOTAL
1	France	38	34	32	104
2	Italy	37	36	24	97
3	Hungary	32	20	26	78
4	Soviet Union*	19	17	18	54
5	=Poland	4	7	9	19
	=USA	2	6	11	19
7	Germany	6	6	6	18
8	West Germany#	7	8	1	16
9	Belgium	5	3	5	13
10	Romania	2	3	6	11
	Great Britain	1	9	0	10

* *Including United Team of 1992; excludes Russia since this date*

Not including West Germany or East Germany 1968–88

THE 10 LATEST WORLD HEAVYWEIGHT BOXING CHAMPIONS*

(Years/boxer)

1 1999–, Lennox Lewis 2 1997–99, Evander Holyfield 3 1996–97, Mike Tyson 4 1995–96, Bruce Seldon 5 1994–95, George Foreman 6 1994, Michael Moorer 7 1993–94, Evander Holyfield 8 1992–93, Riddick Bowe 9 1990–92, Evander Holyfield 10 1990, James Douglas

* *WBA only*

TOP 10

FASTEST KNOCKOUTS IN WORLD TITLE FIGHTS

	FIGHT (WINNERS FIRST)	WEIGHT	DATE	SEC*
1	Gerald McClellan v Jay Bell	Middleweight	7 Aug 1993	20
2	James Warring v James Pritchard	Cruiserweight	6 Sep 1991	24
3	Lloyd Honeyghan v Gene Hatcher	Welterweight	30 Aug 1987	45
4	Mark Breland v Lee Seung-soon	Welterweight	4 Feb 1989	54
5	Emile Pladner v Frankie Genaro	Flyweight	2 Mar 1929	58
6	=Jackie Paterson v Peter Kane	Flyweight	19 June 1943	61
	=Bobby Czyz v David Sears	Light-heavyweight	26 Dec 1986	61
8	Michael Dokes v Mike Weaver	Heavyweight	10 Dec 1982	63
9	Tony Canzoneri v Al Singer	Lightweight	14 Nov 1930	66
10	Marvin Hagler v Caveman Lee	Middleweight	7 Mar 1982	67

* *Duration of fight*

WORLD CHAMPION

After a much-disputed previous contest, Lennox Lewis finally defeated Evander Holyfield at Las Vegas on 12 December 1999 to take the World Heavyweight title.

Cricket Tests

TOP 10 MOST CAPPED CRICKETERS

	NAME/COUNTRY	CAPS
1	**Allan Border**, Australia	156
2	**Kapil Dev**, India	131
3	**Sunil Gavaskar**, India	125
4	**Javed Miandad**, Pakistan	124
5	**Viv Richards**, West Indies	121
6	**Graham Gooch**, England	118
7	**David Gower**, England	117
8	=**Desmond Haynes**, West Indies	116
	=**Dilip Vengsarkar**, India	116
10	**Ian A. Healy**, Australia	115

TOP 10 LOWEST COMPLETED INNINGS IN TEST CRICKET*

	MATCH/VENUE/YEAR	TOTAL
1	**New Zealand v England**, Auckland, 1954–55	26
2	=**South Africa v England**, Port Elizabeth, 1895–96	30
	=**South Africa v England**, Birmingham, 1924	30
4	**South Africa v England**, Cape Town, 1898–99	35
5	=**Australia v England**, Birmingham, 1902	36
	=**South Africa v Australia**, Melbourne, 1931–32	36
7	=**Australia v England**, Sydney, 1887–88	42
	=**New Zealand v Australia**, Wellington, 1945–46	42
	=**India# v England**, Lord's, 1974	42
10	**South Africa v England**, Cape Town, 1888–89	43

** Completed by first team listed*

 # India batted one man short

England's lowest total is 45, when dismissed by Australia at Sydney in 1886–87.

TOP 10 HIGHEST INDIVIDUAL TEST INNINGS

	BATSMAN*	MATCH/VENUE	YEAR	RUNS
1	**Brian Lara**	West Indies v England, St. John's	1993–94	375
2	**Gary Sobers**	West Indies v Pakistan, Kingston	1957–58	365#
3	**Len Hutton**	England v Australia, The Oval	1938	364
4	**Sanath Jayasuriya**	Sri Lanka v India, Colombo	1997–98	340
5	**Hanif Mohammad**	Pakistan v West Indies, Bridgetown	1957–58	337
6	**Walter Hammond**	England v New Zealand, Auckland	1932–33	336#
7	=**Don Bradman**	Australia v England, Leeds	1930	334
	=**Mark Taylor**	Australia v Pakistan, Peshawar	1998–99	334#
9	**Graham Gooch**	England v India, Lord's	1990	333
10	**Andrew Sandham**	England v West Indies, Kingston	1929–30	325

** From first listed team # Not out*

TOP 10 RUN-MAKERS OF ALL TIME IN TEST CRICKET

	PLAYER/COUNTRY/YEARS	TESTS	RUNS
1	**Allan Border**, Australia, 1978-94	156	11,174
2	**Sunil Gavaskar**, India, 1971-87	125	10,122
3	**Graham Gooch**, England, 1975-95	118	8,900
4	**Javed Miandad**, Pakistan, 1976-94	124	8,832
5	**Viv Richards**, West Indies, 1974-91	121	8,540
6	**David Gower**, England, 1978-92	117	8,231
7	**Geoff Boycott**, England, 1964-82	108	8,114
8	**Gary Sobers**, West Indies, 1954-74	93	8,032
9	**Colin Cowdrey**, England, 1954-75	114	7,624
10	**S. R. Waugh**, Australia, 1985–99	115	7,622

TOP 10 HIGHEST INDIVIDUAL INNINGS IN A TEST DEBUT

	PLAYER*	MATCH/VENUE	YEAR	SCORE
1	**Reginald Foster**	England v Australia, Sydney	1903–04	287
2	**Lawrence Rowe**	West Indies v New Zealand, Kingston	1971–72	214
3	**Brendon Kuruppu**	Sri Lanka v New Zealand, Colombo	1986–87	201*
4	**George Headley**	West Indies v England, Bridgetown	1929–30	176
5	**Khalid Ibadulla**	Pakistan v Australia, Karachi	1964–65	166
6	**Charles Bannerman**	Australia v England, Melbourne	1876–77	165#
7	**Archie Jackson**	Australia v England, Adelaide	1928–29	164
8	=**Javed Miandad**	Pakistan v New Zealand, Lahore	1976–77	163
	=**Andrew Hudson**	South Africa v West Indies, Bridgetown	1991–92	163
10	**Kepler Wessels**	Australia v England, Brisbane	1982–83	162

** From first listed team # Not out*

Did You Know? The first known women's cricket match was held on 26 July 1745, when "11 maids from Hambledon" beat "11 maids from Bramley" at Gosden Common, Surrey.

TOP 10 WICKET TAKERS OF ALL TIME IN TEST CRICKET

	PLAYER/COUNTRY/YEARS	TESTS	WICKETS
1	**Kapil Dev**, India, 1978–94	131	434
2	**Richard Hadlee**, New Zealand, 1973–90	86	431
3	**Courtney Walsh**, West Indies, 1984–98	107	404
4	**Ian Botham**, England, 1977–92	102	383
5	**Wasim Akram**, Pakistan, 1985–99	88	378
6	**Malcolm Marshall**, West Indies, 1978–91	81	376
7	**Curtly Ambrose**, West Indies, 1988–99	88	369
8	**Imran Khan**, Pakistan, 1971–92	88	362
9	**Dennis Lillee**, Australia, 1971–84	70	355
10	**Bob Willis**, England, 1971–84	90	325

TOP 10 HIGHEST TEAM TOTALS IN TEST CRICKET*

(Match/venue/year/score)

❶ **Sri Lanka v India**, Colombo (1997–98), 952–6 dec ❷ **England v Australia**, The Oval (1938), 903–7 dec ❸ **England v West Indies**, Kingston (1929–30), 849 ❹ **West Indies v Pakistan**, Kingston (1957–58), 790–3 dec ❺ **Australia v West Indies**, Kingston (1954–55), 758–8 dec ❻ **Australia v England**, Lord's (1930), 729–6 dec ❼ **Pakistan v England**, The Oval (1987), 708 ❽ **Australia v England**, The Oval (1934), 701 ❾ **Pakistan v India**, Lahore (1989–90), 699–5 dec ❿ **Australia v England**, The Oval (1930), 695

* *Scored by first team listed*

TOP 10 PARTNERSHIPS IN TEST CRICKET

	BATSMEN*	MATCH	YEAR	RUNS
1	**Sanath Jayasuriya/Roshan Mahanama**	Sri Lanka v India	1997–98	576
2	**Andrew Jones/Martin Crowe**	New Zealand v Sri Lanka	1990–91	467
3	=**Bill Ponsford/Don Bradman**	Australia v England	1934	451
	=**Mudasser Nazar/Javed Miandad**	Pakistan v India	1982–83	451
5	**Conrad Hunte/Gary Sobers**	West Indies v Pakistan	1957–58	446
6	**Vinoo Mankad/Pankaj Roy**	India v New Zealand	1955–56	413
7	**Peter May/Colin Cowdrey**	England v West Indies	1957	411
8	**Sidney Barnes/Don Bradman**	Australia v England	1946–47	405
9	**Gary Sobers/Frank Worrell**	West Indies v England	1959–60	399
10	**Qasim Omar/Javed Miandad**	Pakistan v Sri Lanka	1985–86	397

* *From first listed team*

Gundappa Viswanath, Yashpal Sharma, and Dilip Vengsarkar put on 415 runs for India's third wicket against England at Madras in 1981–82; Vengsarkar retired hurt when the partnership was on 99.

TOP 10 RUN MAKERS IN A TEST SERIES

	BATSMAN*	SERIES/TESTS	YEAR	RUNS
1	**Don Bradman**	Australia v England, 5	1930	974
2	**Walter Hammond**	England v Australia, 5	1928–29	905
3	**Mark Taylor**	Australia v England, 6	1989	839
4	**Neil Harvey**	Australia v South Africa, 5	1952–53	834
5	**Viv Richards**	West Indies v England, 4	1976	829
6	**Clyde Walcott**	West Indies v Australia, 5	1954–55	827
7	**Gary Sobers**	West Indies v Pakistan, 5	1957–58	824
8	**Don Bradman**	Australia v England, 5	1936–37	810
9	**Don Bradman**	Australia v South Africa, 5	1931–32	806
10	**Brian Lara**	West Indies v England, 5	1993–94	798

* *From first listed team*

Don Bradman's remarkable tally in Australia's Test series against England in 1930 came only a year after Walter Hammond had become the first man to score 900 runs in a series. Bradman, who was making his debut on English soil, scored his runs in just seven innings, at an average of 139 per innings. He scored just eight runs in the first innings of the opening Test, but then came the first of his centuries when he went on to score 131 in the second innings.

TOP 10 BATSMEN WITH THE MOST TEST CENTURIES

(Batsman/country/centuries)

❶ **Sunil Gavaskar**, India, 34 ❷ **Don Bradman**, Australia, 29 ❸ **Allan Border**, Australia, 27 ❹ **Gary Sobers**, West Indies, 26 ❺ = **Greg Chappell**, Australia, 24; = **Viv Richards**, West Indies, 24 ❼ **Javed Miandad**, Pakistan, 23 ❽ = **Walter Hammond**, England, 22; = **Geoff Boycott**, England, 22; = **Colin Cowdrey**, England, 22

Football Stars

TOP 10 ★ TRANSFER FEES BETWEEN ENGLISH CLUBS

	PLAYER	FROM	TO	YEAR	FEE (£)
1	Alan Shearer	Blackburn Rovers	Newcastle United	1996	15,000,000
2	Dwight Yorke	Aston Villa	Manchester United	1998	12,600,000
3	Chris Sutton	Blackburn Rovers	Chelsea	1999	10,000,000
4	Stan Collymore	Nottingham Forest	Liverpool	1995	8,500,000
5	=Kevin Davies	Southampton	Blackburn Rovers	1998	7,500,000
	=John Hartson	West Ham United	Wimbledon	1999	7,500,000
7	=Stan Collymore	Liverpool	Aston Villa	1997	7,000,000
	=Duncan Ferguson	Everton	Newcastle United	1998	7,000,000
9	Paul Merson	Middlesbrough	Aston Villa	1998	6,750,000
10	Andy Cole	Newcastle United	Manchester United	1995	6,250,000

Transfer fees appear to have spiralled in recent years, but it was a similar story in 1979, when Trevor Francis became Britain's first million-pound footballer. In 1962, Manchester United made Denis Law Britain's first £100,000 player when they bought him from Italian club Torino. The first four-figure transfer fee came in 1905, when Middlesbrough paid Sunderland £1,000 for Alf Common, and the first £100 deal was clinched way back in 1892, when Aston Villa bought Willie Grives from West Bromwich. When Bill Nicholson signed Jimmy Greaves for Spurs from Milan in 1961, he paid £99,999, but would not pay the other £1 because he did not want Greaves to have to be Britain's first £100,000 footballer.

TOP 10 ★ ENGLAND GOAL SCORERS IN FULL INTERNATIONALS*

	PLAYER	GOALS
1	Bobby Charlton	49
2	Gary Lineker	48
3	Jimmy Greaves	44
4	=Tom Finney	30
	=Nat Lofthouse	30
6	Vivian Woodward	29
7	=Steve Bloomer	28
	=Alan Shearer	28
9	David Platt	27
10	Bryan Robson	26

* *At 1 January 2000*

Had Gary Lineker not been substituted in his final game, against Sweden in 1992, he may well have gone on to equal or beat Bobby Charlton's record.

TOP 10 ★ TRANSFER FEES

	PLAYER/COUNTRY	FROM	TO	YEAR	FEE (£)
1	**Christian Vieri**, Italy	Lazio, Italy	Inter Milan	1999	24,000,000*
2	**Micholas Anelka**, France	Arsenal, England	Real Madrid, Spain	1999	23,500,000
3	**Denilson**, Brazil	São Paulo, Brazil	Real Betis, Spain	1998	21,400,000
4	=**Christian Vieri**, Italy	Atletico Madrid, Spain	Lazio, Italy	1998	18,000,000
	=**Marco Amoroso**, Brazil	Udinese, Italy	Parma, Italy	1999	18,000,000
6	**Juan Sebastian Veron**, Argentina	Parma, Italy	Lazio, Italy	1999	17,500,000
7	**Rivaldo**, Brazil	Deportivo la Coruna, Spain	Barcelona, Spain	1997	17,000,000
8	**Ronaldo**, Brazil	Barcelona, Spain	Inter Milan, Italy	1997	16,800,000
[illegible]	**Andriy Sche[illegible]henko**, Uk[illegible]ine	Dynamo Ki[illegible], Ukraine	AC Milan, Italy	1999	15,[illegible]00,000
[illegible]	**Vincenz[illegible] Montella**, Italy	Sampdori[illegible]	Roma, [illegible]	1999	[illegible]300,000

* *[illegible]i's transfer was part of [illegible] package deal with [illegible]icola Ventola, who was value[illegible] at £7 million. [illegible]ri was [illegible]lued at £2[illegible] million.*

T[illegible]e world's first £100,000 player [illegible] Omar Siv[illegible] when he [illegible] to Juventus ([illegible]) from River Pl[illegible] (A[illegible]ntina) in [illegible]; the wor[illegible] first [illegible] player was Gi[illegible]ppe Savol[illegible] when he moved from Bolo[illegible]na (Italy) to [illegible] (Ita[illegible]); a[illegible] the world's first [illegible]-million player was Gianluigi Lentini when he moved from To[illegible] (Italy) to AC Milan (Italy) in [illegible] 1992.

TOP 10 ★ SIGNINGS TO MANCHESTER UNITED

	PLAYER/SIGNED FROM	YEAR	FEE (£)
1	**Dwight Yorke**, Aston Villa	1998	12,600,000
2	**Jaap Stam**, PSV Eindhoven (Holland)	1998	10,750,000
3	**Andy Cole**, Newcastle United	1995	6,250,000
4	**Henning Berg**, Blackburn Rovers	1997	5,000,000
5	**Massimi Taibi**, Venezia (Italy)	1999	4,500,000
6	**Jesper Blomqvist**, Palma (Italy)	1998	4,4[illegible]00
7	**Roy Keane**, [illegible]ottingham [illegible]orest	[illegible]993	3,750,000
[illegible]	**Teddy [illegible]heringham**, [illegible]otten[illegible]am Hotspur	1997	3,500,000
[illegible]	**[illegible]ickha[illegible] Si[illegible]es[illegible]**, [illegible] (Fra[illegible]e)	1[illegible]99	3,300,000
[illegible]	**Ga[illegible]llister**, Midd[illegible]broug[illegible]	1989	2,[illegible]00,000

Did You Know? Hungarian footballer Alfred Schaffer played for a total of 21 clubs during his career (1910–25), setting a world record that still remains unbroken.

TOP 10

GOAL SCORERS IN THE FINAL STAGES OF THE WORLD CUP

	PLAYER/COUNTRY	YEARS	GOALS
1	**Gerd Müller**, W. Germany	1970–74	14
2	**Just Fontaine**, France	1958	13
3	**Pelé**, Brazil	1958–70	12
4	=**Sandor Kocsis**, Hungary	1954	11
	=**Jürgen Klinsman**, Germany	1990–98	11
6	=**Helmut Rahn**, W. Germany	1954–58	10
	=**Teófilio Cubillas**, Peru	1970–78	10
	=**Grzegorz Lato**, Poland	1974–82	10
	=**Gary Lineker**, England	1986–90	10
10	=**Leónidas da Silva**, Brazil	1934–38	9
	=**Ademir Marques de Menezes**, Brazil	1950	9
	=**Vavà**, Brazil	1958–62	9
	=**Uwe Seeler**, W. Germany	1958–70	9
	=**Eusébio**, Portugal	1966	9
	=**Jairzinho**, Brazil	1970–74	9
	=**Paolo Rossi**, Italy	1978–82	9
	=**Karl-Heinz Rummenigge**, W. Germany	1978–86	9
	=**Roberto Baggio**, Italy	1990–98	9
	=**Gabriel Batistuta**, Argentina	1994–98	9

THE 10

LATEST ENGLAND PLAYERS TO SCORE A HAT-TRICK

	PLAYER	SCORED AGAINST	VENUE	YEAR
1	**Alan Shearer**	Luxembourg	Wembley	1999
2	**Paul Scholes**	Poland	Wembley	1999
3	**Ian Wright***	San Marino	Bologna	1993
4	**David Platt***	San Marino	Wembley	1993
5	**Gary Lineker***	Malaysia	Kuala Lumpur	1991
6	**Gary Lineker***	Spain	Madrid	1987
7	**Gary Lineker**	Turkey	Wembley	1987
8	**Gary Lineker**	Poland	Monterrey	1986
9	**Gary Lineker**	Turkey	Wembley	1985
10	**Bryan Robson**	Turkey	Istanbul	1985

* *Scored four goals*

THE 10

LATEST WINNERS OF THE "FOOTBALLER OF THE YEAR" AWARD

YEAR	PLAYER/TEAM
1999	**David Ginola**, Tottenham Hotspur
1998	**Dennis Bergkamp**, Arsenal
1997	**Gianfranco Zola**, Chelsea
1996	**Eric Cantona**, Manchester United
1995	**Jürgen Klinsman**, Tottenham Hotspur
1994	**Alan Shearer**, Blackburn Rovers
1993	**Chris Waddle**, Sheffield Wednesday
1992	**Gary Lineker**, Tottenham Hotspur
1991	**Gordon Strachan**, Leeds United
1990	**John Barnes**, Liverpool

The award is presented by the Football Writers' Association. All players in the English League are eligible, irresepective of country of origin.

TOP 10

GOAL SCORERS IN INTERNATIONAL FOOTBALL

	PLAYER	COUNTRY	YEARS	MATCHES	GOALS
1	Ferenc Puskás	Hungary/Spain	1956–56	84	[illegible]
2	Pelé	Brazil	1957–71	92	77
3	Sándor K[illegible]sis	Hungary	1948–56	68	75
4	Gerd Müller	West Germany	1966–74	62	68
5	Imre [illegible]osser	Hungary	1906–27	68	[illegible]
6	Kaz[illegible] Miura	Japan	[illegible]	[illegible]	54
7	Joachi[illegible] Streich	East Germany	[illegible]	[illegible]	[illegible]
8	=Jass[illegible] Al[illegible]uwad[illegible]	Kuwait	1992–[illegible]	[illegible]	52
	=Poul Ni[illegible]	[illegible]	[illegible]–25	38	52
10	Kunishige [illegible]amamoto	[illegible]	1964–77	59	51

TOP 10

MOST CAPPED ENGLAND PLAYERS

	PLAYER	YEARS	APPEARANCES
1	Peter Shilton	1970–90	[illegible]
2	Bobby Moore	19[illegible]2–73	[illegible]
3	Bobby Charlton	19[illegible]–70	106
4	Billy Wright	1946–59	105
5	Bryan Robson	1980–91	[illegible]
6	Kenny Sansom	1979–88	[illegible]
7	Ray Wilkins	1976–86	[illegible]
8	Gary Lineker	1984–92	80
9	John Barnes	198[illegible]–95	78
10	Terry Butcher	1980–90	77

BRAZIL'S 100TH GOAL

Pelé celebrates not only the first goal of the 1970 World Cup Final against Italy, but also his country's 100th World Cup goal.

TOP 10 HIGHEST-SCORING WORLD CUP FINALS

	YEAR	GAMES	GOALS	AVERAGE PER GAME
1	1954	26	140	5.38
2	1938	18	84	4.66
3	1934	17	70	4.11
4	1950	22	88	4.00
5	1930	18	70	3.88
6	1958	35	126	3.60
7	1970	32	95	2.96
8	1982	52	146	2.81
9	=1962	32	89	2.78
	=1966	32	89	2.78

The lowest-scoring World Cup was Italia '90, which produced just 115 goals from 52 matches at an average of 2.21 per game. The 1994 final between Brazil and Italy was the first World Cup final to fail to produce a goal, with Brazil wining 3–2 on penalties.

TOP 10 COUNTRIES WITH THE MOST PLAYERS SENT OFF IN THE FINAL STAGES OF THE WORLD CUP

(Country/dismissals)

1 = **Brazil**, 8; = **Argentina**, 8 **3** = **Uruguay**, 6; = **Cameroon**, 6 **5** = **Germany/West Germany**, 5; = **Hungary**, 5 **7** = **Czechoslovakia**, 4; = **Holland**, 4; = **Italy**, 4; = **Mexico**, 4

A total of 97 players have received their marching orders in the final stages of the World Cup since 1930. The South American nations account for 27 of them. Brazil, Czechoslovakia, Denmark, Hungary, and South Africa have each had three players sent off in a single game – Brazil twice (1938 and 1954).

TOP 10 WORLD CUP ATTENDANCES

	MATCH (WINNERS FIRST)	VENUE	YEAR	ATTENDANCE
1	Brazil v Uruguay	Rio de Janeiro*	1950	199,854
2	Brazil v Spain	Rio de Janeiro	1950	152,772
3	Brazil v Yugoslavia	Rio de Janeiro	1950	142,409
4	Brazil v Sweden	Rio de Janeiro	1950	138,886
5	Mexico v Paraguay	Mexico City	1986	114,600
6	Argentina v West Germany	Mexico City*	1986	114,590
7	=Mexico v Bulgaria	Mexico City	1986	114,580
	=Argentina v England	Mexico City	1986	114,580
9	Argentina v Belgium	Mexico City	1986	110,420
10	Mexico v Belgium	Mexico City	1986	110,000

*Final tie

The biggest crowd outside Mexico or Brazil was that of 98,270 at Wembley Stadium in 1966 for England's game against France. The attendance for the Brazil–Uruguay final in 1950 is the world's highest for a soccer match.

TOP 10 COUNTRIES IN THE WORLD CUP*

	COUNTRY	WIN	R/U	3RD	4TH	TOTAL
1	Brazil	4	2	2	1	27
2	Germany/West Germany	3	3	2	1	26
3	Italy	3	2	1	1	21
4	Argentina	2	2	–	–	14
5	Uruguay	2	–	–	2	10
6	France	1	–	2	1	9
7	Sweden	–	1	2	1	8
8	Holland	–	2	–	1	7
9	=Czechoslovakia	–	2	–	–	6
	=Hungary	–	2	–	–	6
	England	1	–	–	1	5

* *Based on 4 points for winning the tournament, 3 points for runner-up, 2 points for 3rd place and 1 point for 4th; up to and including the 1998 World Cup*

Did You Know? When Daniel Xuereb of France played in the 1986 finals, it meant that every letter of the alphabet had been used in players' surnames in the World Cup.

TOP 10 ★ EUROPEAN CUP WINNERS

	COUNTRY	YEARS*	WINS
1	=England	1968–99	9
	=Italy	1961–96	9
3	Spain	1956–98	8
4	Holland	1970–95	6
5	Germany	1974–97	5
6	Portugal	1961–87	3
7	=France	1993	1
	=Romania	1986	1
	=Scotland	1967	1
	=Yugoslavia	1991	1

* *Of first and last win*

The European Cup, now known as the European Champions' League Cup, has been competed for annually since 1956. It was won in that year, and the next four, by Real Madrid (who also won it in 1966 and 1998), a total of seven times. Italy's AC Milan is their only close competitor, with five wins, while Ajax and Liverpool have each won the Cup on four occasions.

TOP 10 ★ RICHEST FOOTBALL CLUBS

	CLUB/COUNTRY	INCOME (£)
1	**Manchester United,** England	87,939,000
2	**Barcelona,** Spain	58,862,000
3	**Real Madrid,** Spain	55,659,000
4	**Juventus,** Italy	53,223,000
5	**Bayern Munich,** Germany	51,619,000
6	**AC Milan,** Italy	47,480,000
7	**Borussia Dortmund,** Germany	42,199,000
8	**Newcastle United,** England	41,134,000
9	**Liverpool,** England	39,153,000
10	**Inter Milan,** Italy	39,071,000

A survey conducted by accountants Deloitte & Touche and football magazine *FourFourTwo* compared incomes of the world's top football clubs during the 1997/8 season. It revealed the extent to which soccer has become a major business enterprise, with many clubs generating considerably more revenue from commercial activities, such as the sale of merchandise and income from TV rights, than they receive from admissions to matches.

TOP 10 ★ EUROPEAN CLUB SIDES WITH THE MOST DOMESTIC LEAGUE TITLES

	CLUB/COUNTRY	TITLES
1	**Glasgow Rangers**, Scotland	48
2	**Linfield**, Northern Ireland	42
3	**Glasgow Celtic**, Scotland	36
4	**Rapid Vienna**, Austria*	31
5	**Benfica**, Portugal	30
6	=**CSKA Sofia**, Bulgaria	28
	=**Olympiakos**, Greece	28
8	=**Ajax**, Holland	27
	=**Real Madrid**, Spain	27
10	=**Ferencvaros**, Hungary	26
	=**Jeunesse Esch**, Luxembourg	26

* *Rapid Vienna also won one German League title, in 1941*

UNITED EFFORT

Manchester United confirmed their status as the world's richest club in 1999, and also captured the unique treble of League, Cup, and European Champions' League.

INTERNATIONAL STAR

Lothar Matthäus, Germany's World Cup-winning captain and European Footballer of the Year in 1990, has played for his country on 143 occasions. As a still-active player, he may yet improve on this figure.

TOP 10 ★ MOST CAPPED INTERNATIONAL PLAYERS

	PLAYER/COUNTRY	YEARS	CAPS
1	=**Thomas Ravelli**, Sweden	1981–97	143
	=**Lothar Matthäus***, West Germany/Germany	1980–99	143
3	**Majed Abdullah**, Saudi Arabia	1978–94	140
4	**Claudio Suarez***, Mexico	1982-99	131
5	**Marcelo Balboa***, USA	1988–98	127
6	**Andoni Zubizarreta**, Spain	1985–98	126
7	**Peter Shilton**, England	1970–90	125
8	**Masami Ihara***, Japan	1988–99	123
9	=**Pat Jennings**, Northern Ireland	1964–86	119
	=**Gheorghe Hagi***, Romania	1983-99	119
	=**Cobi Jones***, USA	1982-99	119

* *Still active in 1999*

TOP 10

FASTEST WORLD CHAMPIONSHIP RACES OF ALL TIME

	RIDER/COUNTRY	BIKE*	YEAR	AVERAGE SPEED KM/H	AVERAGE SPEED MPH
1	**Barry Sheene**, UK	Suzuki	1977	217.37	135.07
2	**John Williams**, UK	Suzuki	1976	214.83	133.49
3	**Phil Read**, UK	MV Agusta	1975	214.40	133.22
4	**Wil Hartog**, Holland	Suzuki	1978	213.88	132.90
5	**Phil Read**, UK	MV Agusta	1974	212.41	131.98
6	**Giacomo Agostini**, Italy	MV Agusta	1973	206.81	128.51
7	**Walter Villa**, Italy	Harley-Davidson	1977	204.43	127.03
8	**Walter Villa**, Italy	Harley-Davidson	1976	202.90	126.08
9	**Giacomo Agostini**, Italy	MV Agusta	1969	202.53	125.85
10	**Kevin Schwartz**, USA	Suzuki	1991	201.72	125.34

* *500cc except for Nos. 7 and 8, which were 250cc*

All races except for No. 10 were during the Belgian Grand Prix at the Spa-Francorchamps circuit. No. 10 was during the German Grand Prix at Hockenheim. The World Championships were first held in 1949, under the aegis of the Fédération Internationale Motorcycliste, when R. Leslie Graham (UK) won the 500cc class on an AJS.

TOP 10

FASTEST WINNING SPEEDS OF THE DAYTONA 200

	RIDER/COUNTRY*	BIKE	YEAR	AVERAGE SPEED KM/H	AVERAGE SPEED MPH
1	**Miguel Duhamel**, Canada	Honda	1999	182.61	113.46
2	**Kenny Roberts**	Yamaha	1984	182.09	113.84
3	**Kenny Roberts**	Yamaha	1983	178.52	110.93
4	**Graeme Crosby**, New Zealand	Yamaha	1982	175.58	109.10
5	**Steve Baker**	Yamaha	1977	175.18	108.85
6	**Johnny Cecotto**, Venezuela	Yamaha	1976	175.05	108.77
7	**Dale Singleton**	Yamaha	1981	174.65	108.52
8	**Kenny Roberts**	Yamaha	1978	174.41	108.37
9	**Kevin Schwartz**	Suzuki	1988	173.49	107.80
10	**Dale Singleton**	Yamaha	1979	173.31	107.69

* *From the US unless otherwise stated*

The Daytona 200, which was first held in 1937, forms a round in the AMA (American Motorcyclist Association) Grand National Dirt Track series. It is raced over 57 laps of the 5.73-km (3.56-mile) Daytona International Speedway. The other non-US winners have been: Billy Matthews (Canada), Jaarno Saarinen (Finland), Giacomo Agostini (Italy), and Patrick Pons (France) .

TOP 10

MOTORCYCLISTS WITH THE MOST WORLD TITLES

	RIDER/COUNTRY	YEARS	TITLES
1	**Giacomo Agostini**, Italy	1966–75	15
2	**Angel Nieto**, Spain	1969–84	13
3	=**Carlo Ubbiali**, Italy	1951–60	9
	=**Mike Hailwood**, UK	1961–67	9
5	=**John Surtees**, UK	1956–60	7
	=**Phil Read**, UK	1964–74	7
7	=**Geoff Duke**, UK	1951–55	6
	=**Jim Redman**, Southern Rhodesia	1962–65	6
	=**Klaus Enders**, W. Germany	1967–74	6
10	**Anton Mang**, W. Germany	1980–87	5

THE 10

LATEST WORLD CHAMPION SUPERBIKE RIDERS

YEAR	RIDER/COUNTRY	BIKE
1999	**Carl Fogarty**, UK	Ducati
1998	**Carl Fogarty**, UK	Ducati
1997	**John Kocinski**, USA	Honda
1996	**Troy Corser**, Australia	Ducati
1995	**Carl Fogarty**, UK	Ducati
1994	**Carl Fogarty**, UK	Ducati
1993	**Scott Russell**, USA	Kawasaki
1992	**Doug Polen**, USA	Ducati
1991	**Doug Polen**, USA	Ducati
1990	**Raymond Roche**, France	Ducati

SUPERBIKE CHAMPION

British motorcycle legend Carl Fogarty (b. 1966) won his first Grand Prix in 1986. Up to the 2000 season, he had won a record 59 Superbike events.

TOP 10 500cc WORLD CHAMPIONSHIPS RIDERS, 1999

(Rider/country/points)

1 **Alex Criville**, Spain, 267 2 **Kenny Roberts**, USA, 220 3 **Tadayuki Okada**, Japan, 211 4 **Max Biaggi**, Italy, 194 5 **Sete Gibernau**, Spain, 165 6 **Norick Abe**, Japan, 136 7 **Carlos Checa**, Spain, 125 8 **John Kocinski**, USA, 115 9 **Alex Barros**, Brazil, 110 10 **Tetsuya Harada**, Japan, 104

TOP 10

TOUR DE FRANCE WINNERS

	RIDER/COUNTRY	WINS
1	=**Jacques Anquetil**, France	5
	=**Eddy Merckx**, Belgium	5
	=**Bernard Hinault**, France	5
	=**Miguel Indurain**, Spain	5
5	=**Philippe Thys**, Belgium	3
	=**Louison Bobet**, France	3
	=**Greg LeMond**, USA	3
8	=**Lucien Petit-Breton**, France	2
	=**Firmin Lambot**, Belgium	2
	=**Ottavio Bottecchia**, Italy	2
	=**Nicholas Frantz**, Luxembourg	2
	=**André Leducq**, France	2
	=**Antonin Magne**, France	2
	=**Gino Bartali**, Italy	2
	=**Sylvere Maës**, Belgium	2
	=**Fausto Coppi**, Italy	2
	=**Bernard Thevenet**, France	2
	=**Laurent Fignon**, France	2

TOUR DE FORCE

The 1999 Tour de France approaches the Eiffel Tower. The world's foremost cycle event, the Tour de France was first contested in 1903.

TOP 10

RIDERS WITH THE MOST GRAND PRIX RACE WINS

	RIDER/COUNTRY	YEARS	RACE WINS
1	**Giacomo Agostini**, Italy	1965–76	122
2	**Angel Nieto**, Spain	1969–85	90
3	**Mike Hailwood**, UK	1959–67	76
4	**Rolf Biland**, Switzerland	1975–90	56
5	**Mick Doohan**, Australia	1990–98	54
6	**Phil Read**, UK	1961–75	52
7	**Jim Redman**, Southern Rhodesia	1961–66	45
8	**Anton Mang**, West Germany	1976–88	42
9	**Carlo Ubbiali**, Italy	1950–60	39
10	**John Surtees**, UK	1955–60	38

TOP 10

OLYMPIC CYCLING COUNTRIES

		MEDALS			
	COUNTRY	GOLD	SILVER	BRONZE	TOTAL
1	**France**	32	19	22	73
2	**Italy**	32	15	6	53
3	**Great Britain**	9	21	16	46
4	**USA**	11	13	16	40
5	**Netherlands**	10	14	7	31
6	**Germany***	8	9	9	26
7	**Australia**	6	11	8	25
8	**Soviet Union**#	11	4	9	24
9	**Belgium**	6	6	10	22
10	**Denmark**	6	6	10	21

* *Not including West Germany or East Germany 1968–88*

\# *Including United Team of 1992, exludes Russia since*

TOP 10 ★ DRIVERS IN THE WORLD RALLY CHAMPIONSHIPS*

	DRIVER/COUNTRY	WINS
1	**Tommi Mäkinen**, Finland	62
2	**Richard Burns**, UK	55
3	**Didier Auriol**, France	52
4	=**Juha Kankkunen**, Finland	44
	=**Carlos Sainz**, Spain	44
6	**Colin McRae**, UK	23
7	**Philippe Bugalski**, France	20
8	**Freddy Loix**, Belgium	14
9	**Harri Rovanpera**, Finland	10
10	=**Gilles Panizzi**, France	6
	=**Jesús Puras**, Spain	6
	=**Tero Gardemeister**, Finland	6
	=**Thomas Radström**, Sweden	6
	=**Bruno Thiry**, Belgium	6

* *As at 1 January 2000*

Launched in 1971 under the aegis of the Féderation International de l'Automobile (FIA), the World Rally Championship begins each year in January with the Monte Carlo Rally, after which a further 13 rallies are held across the world. All of Jesús Puras's wins have been in Corsica, where he was beaten in 1999 by Philippe Bugalski (10 times winner in Catalunya, 10 in Corsica), both competing in Citroën kit-cars.

TOP 10 MONTE CARLO RALLY-WINNING CARS*

(Car /wins)

❶ **Lancia**, 12 ❷ = **Hotchkiss**, 6; = **Renault**, 6 ❹ **Ford**, 5 ❺ **Porsche**, 4 ❻ = **Mini-Cooper**, 3; = **Subaru**, 3; = **Toyota**, 3 ❾ = **Citroën**, 2; = **Delahaye**, 2; = **Fiat**, 2; = **Mitsubishi**, 2; = **Opel**, 2; = **Saab**, 2

* *Up to and including 2000*

The Monte Carlo Rally has been run since 1911 (with breaks in 1913–23, 1940–48, 1957, and 1974). The appearance of Hotchkiss in 2nd place is perhaps surprising, but it won the rally six times between 1932 and 1950.

TOP 10 ★ DRIVERS IN THE FORMULA ONE WORLD CHAMPIONSHIP, 1999

	DRIVER/COUNTRY	WINS
1	**Mika Hakkinen**, Finland	76
2	**Eddie Irvine**, Ireland	74
3	**Heinz-Harald Frentzen**, Germany	54
4	**David Coulthard**, UK	48
5	**Michael Schumacher**, Germany	44
6	**Ralf Schumacher**, Germany	35
7	**Rubens Barrichello**, Brazil	21
8	**Johnny Herbert**, UK	15
9	**Giancarlo Fisichella**, Italy	13
10	**Mika Salo**, Finland	10

TOP 10 ★ FORMULA ONE DRIVERS WHO HAVE RACED THE MOST KMS

	DRIVER/COUNTRY	KMS RACED*
1	**Riccardo Patrese**, Italy	52,119
2	**Alain Prost**, France	48,966
3	**Gerhard Berger**, Austria	45,649
4	**Nelson Piquet**, France	45,461
5	**Graham Hill**, UK	44,046
6	**Nigel Mansell**, UK	39,930
7	**Michele Alboreto**, Italy	39,868
8	**Ayrton Senna**, Brazil	37,940
9	**Niki Lauda**, Austria	37,500
10	**Jean Alesi**, France	37,463

* *As at January 2000*

TOP 10 DRIVERS WITH THE MOST FORMULA ONE WORLD CHAMPIONSHIP TITLES

(Driver/country/titles)

❶ **Juan Manuel Fangio**, Argentina, 5 ❷ **Alain Prost**, France, 4 ❸ = **Jack Brabham**, Australia, 3; = **Jackie Stewart**, UK, 3; = **Niki Lauda**, Austria, 3; = **Nelson Piquet**, Brazil, 3; = **Ayrton Senna**, Brazil, 3 ❽ = **Alberto Ascari**, Italy, 2; = **Graham Hill**, UK, 2; = **Jim Clark**, UK, 2; = **Emerson Fittipaldi**, Brazil, 2; = **Michael Schumacher**, Germany, 2; = **Mika Hakkinen**, Finland, 2

THE 10 ★ FORMULA ONE WORLD CHAMPIONS OF THE 1990s

DRIVER/COUNTRY	POINTS	YEAR	POINTS	CONSTRUCTOR/COUNTRY
Mika Hakkinen, Finland	76	**1999**	128	**Ferrari**, Italy
Mika Hakkinen, Finland	100	**1998**	156	**McLaren/Mercedes**, UK/Germany
Jacques Villeneuve, Canada	81	**1997**	123	**Williams/Renault**, UK/France
Damon Hill, UK	97	**1996**	175	**Williams/Renault**, UK/France
Michael Schumacher, Germany	102	**1995**	137	**Benetton/Renault**, Italy/France
Michael Schumacher, Germany	92	**1994**	118	**Williams/Renault**, UK/France
Alain Prost, France	99	**1993**	168	**Williams/Renault**, UK/France
Nigel Mansell, UK	108	**1992**	164	**Williams/Renault**, UK/France
Ayrton Senna, Brazil	96	**1991**	139	**McLaren/Honda**, UK/Japan
Ayrton Senna, Brazil	78	**1990**	121	**McLaren/Honda**, UK/Japan

TOP 10 ★ FASTEST GRAND PRIX RACES, 1999

	GRAND PRIX	CIRCUIT	WINNER'S SPEED KM/H	MPH
1	Italy	Monza	237.939	147.848
2	Germany	Hockenheim	224.724	139.638
3	Belgium	Spa-Francorchamps	214.596	133.343
4	Austria	Al-Ring	208.587	129.609
5	Japan	Suzuka	204.086	126.813
6	Great Britain	Silverstone	199.971	124.256
7	Spain	Catalunya	195.609	121.546
8	San Marino	Enzo e Dino Ferrari	195.481	121.467
9	Brazil	Interlagos	192.994	119.922
10	Malaysia	Sepang	192.682	119.728

TOP 10 COUNTRIES WITH THE MOST GRAND PRIX WINS*

(Country/wins)

1 **Great Britain**, 182 **2** **=Brazil**, 79; = **France**, 79 **4** = **Austria**, 41; = **Germany**, 41 **6** **Italy**, 39 **7** **Argentina**, 36 **8** **USA**, 33 **9** **Australia**, 26 **10** **Finland**, 19

* *As at January 2000*

TOP 10 ★ FORMULA ONE SUPER-CHAMPIONSHIP DRIVERS*

	DRIVER/COUNTRY	WORLD CHAMPIONSHIP PLACINGS 1ST	2ND	3RD	4TH	5TH	6TH	SUPER POINTS#
1	**Alain Prost**, France	4	4	-	2	2	-	74
2	**Juan Manuel Fangio**, Argentina	5	2	-	-	-	-	62
3	**Ayrton Senna**, Brazil	3	2	1	3	-	-	55
4	=**Jackie Stewart**, UK	3	2	1	-	1	-	48
	=**Nelson Piquet**, Brazil	3	1	2	-	1	2	48
6	**Niki Lauda**, Austria	3	1	-	2	1	-	44
7	**Graham Hill**, UK	2	3	-	-	1	-	40
8	**Michael Schumacher**, Germany	2	1	2	1	1	-	39
9	**Jack Brabham**, UK	3	1	-	-	1	-	38
10	**Stirling Moss**, UK	-	4	3	-	-	-	36

* *As at January 2000*

\# *1st = 10 pts; 2nd = 6 pts; 3rd = 4 pts; 4th = 3 pts; 5th = 2 pts; 6th = 1 pt*

TOP 10 ★ YOUNGEST FORMULA ONE WORLD CHAMPIONS OF ALL TIME

	DRIVER/COUNTRY	YEAR	AGE* YRS	MTHS
1	**Emerson Fittipaldi**, Brazil	1972	25	9
2	**Michael Schumacher**, Germany	1994	25	10
3	**Jacques Villeneuve**, Canada	1997	26	5
4	**Niki Lauda**, Austria	1975	26	7
5	**Jim Clark**, UK	1963	27	7
6	**Jochen Rindt**, Austria	1970	28	6
7	**Ayrton Senna**, Brazil	1988	28	7
8	=**James Hunt**, UK	1976	29	2
	=**Nelson Piquet**, Brazil	1981	29	2
10	**Mike Hawthorn**, UK	1958	29	6

* *If a driver is eligible on more than one occasion, only his youngest age is considered.*

TOP 10 ★ FASTEST LE MANS 24-HOUR RACES

	DRIVERS/COUNTRY	CAR	YEAR	AVERAGE SPEED KM/H	MPH
1	**Helmut Marko**, Austria, **Gijs van Lennep**, Holland	Porsche	1971	222.304	138.133
2	**Jan Lammers**, Holland, **Johnny Dumfries**, **Andy Wallace**, UK	Jaguar	1988	221.665	137.737
3	**Jochen Mass, Manuel Reuter**, West Germany, **Stanley Dickens**, Sweden	Mercedes	1989	219.990	136.696
4	**Dan Gurney, A. J. Foyt**, USA	Ford	1967	218.038	135.483
5	**Geoff Brabham**, Australia, **Christophe Bouchot**, **Eric Hélary**, France	Peugeot	1993	213.358	132.574
6	**Klaus Ludwig, "John Winter" (Louis Krager)**, West Germany, **Paulo Barilla**, Italy	Porsche	1985	212.021	131.744
7	**Chris Amon, Bruce McLaren** New Zealand,	Ford	1966	210.795	130.983
8	**Vern Schuppan**, Austria, **Hurley Haywood**, **Al Holbert**, USA	Porsche	1983	210.330	130.693
9	**Jean-Pierre Jassaud**, **Didier Pironi**, France	Renault Alpine	1978	210.189	130.606
10	**Jacky Ickx**, Belgium **Jackie Oliver**, UK	Ford	1969	208.250	129.401

What type of sport did the highest-earning sportsman of 1999 make his fortune in?

see p278 for the answer

A Boxing
B Motor racing
C Basketball

TOP 10 PLAYERS TO WIN THE MOST MAJORS IN A CAREER

	PLAYER/COUNTRY*	BRITISH OPEN	US OPEN	MASTERS	PGA	TOTAL
1	Jack Nicklaus	3	4	6	5	18
2	Walter Hagen	4	2	0	5	11
3	=Ben Hogan	1	4	2	2	9
	=Gary Player, South Africa	3	1	3	2	9
5	Tom Watson	5	1	2	0	8
6	=Harry Vardon, UK	6	1	0	0	7
	=Gene Sarazen	1	2	1	3	7
	=Bobby Jones	3	4	0	0	7
	=Sam Snead	1	0	3	3	7
	=Arnold Palmer	2	1	4	0	7

** From the US unless otherwise stated*

TOP 10

LOWEST WINNING SCORES IN THE US MASTERS

	PLAYER/COUNTRY*	YEAR	SCORE
1	Tiger Woods	1997	270
2	=Jack Nicklaus	1965	271
	=Raymond Floyd	1976	271
4	=Ben Hogan	1953	274
	=Ben Crenshaw	1995	274
6	=Severiano Ballesteros, Spain	1980	275
	=Fred Couples	1992	275
8	=Arnold Palmer	1964	276
	=Jack Nicklaus	1975	276
	=Tom Watson	1977	276
	=Nick Faldo, England	1996	276

** From the US unless otherwise stated*

The US Masters is the only major played on the same course each year, at Augusta, Georgia. The course was built on the site of an old nursery, and the abundance of flowers, shrubs, and plants is a reminder of its former days, with each of the holes named after the plants growing adjacent to it.

TOP 10

WINNERS OF WOMEN'S MAJORS

	PLAYER*	TITLES
1	Patty Berg	16
2	=Mickey Wright	13
	=Louise Suggs	13
4	Babe Zaharias	12
5	Betsy Rawls	8
6	JoAnne Carner	7
7	=Kathy Whitworth	6
	=Pat Bradley	6
	=Julie Inkster	6
	=Glenna Collett Vare	6

** All from the US*

Women's majors once numbered six, but today comprise the US Open (first staged 1946), LPGA Championship (1955), Du Maurier Classic (1973; major status since 1979), and Dinah Shore Tournament (1972).

TOP 10

LOWEST FOUR-ROUND TOTALS IN THE BRITISH OPEN

	PLAYER/COUNTRY/VENUE	YEAR	TOTAL
1	Greg Norman, Australia, Sandwich	1993	267
2	=Tom Watson, USA, Turnberry	1977	268
	=Nick Price, Zimbabwe, Turnberry	1994	268
4	=Jack Nicklaus, USA, Turnberry	1977	269
	=Nick Faldo, UK, Sandwich	1993	269
	=Jesper Parnevik, Sweden, Turnberry	1994	269
7	=Nick Faldo, UK, St. Andrews	1990	270
	=Bernhard Langer, Germany, Sandwich	1993	270
9	=Tom Watson, USA, Muirfield	1980	271
	=Fuzzy Zoeller, USA, Turnberry	1994	271
	=Tom Lehman, USA, Lytham	1996	271

IRON LADY

US golfer Kathy Whitworth (b. 1939) scored a total of 88 tour wins, achieving victories in six majors, and was voted Player of the Year on seven occasions.

Did You Know? Mary, Queen of Scots (1542–87) is regarded as the first female golfer. In 1567, she was criticized for playing within two weeks of her husband Darnley's murder.

TOP 10 LOWEST WINNING TOTALS IN THE US OPEN

	PLAYER/COUNTRY*/VENUE	YEAR	SCORE
1	=**Jack Nicklaus**, Baltusrol	1980	272
	=**Lee Janzen**, Baltusrol	1993	272
3	**David Graham**, Australia, Merion	1981	273
4	=**Jack Nicklaus**, Baltusrol	1967	275
	=**Lee Trevino**, Oak Hill	1968	275
6	=**Ben Hogan**, Riviera	1948	276
	=**Fuzzy Zoeller**, Winged Foot	1984	276
	=**Ernie Els**, South Africa, Congressional	1997	276
9	=**Jerry Pate**, Atlanta	1976	277
	=**Scott Simpson**, Olympic Club	1987	277

* From the US unless otherwise stated

TOP 10 PLAYERS WITH THE MOST CAREER WINS ON THE US TOUR

	PLAYER*	TOUR WINS
1	**Sam Snead**	81
2	**Jack Nicklaus**	71
3	**Ben Hogan**	63
4	**Arnold Palmer**	60
5	**Byron Nelson**	52
6	**Billy Casper**	51
7	=**Walter Hagen**	40
	=**Cary Midlecoff**	40
9	**Gene Sarazen**	38
10	**Lloyd Mangrum**	36

* All from the US

For many years Sam Snead's total of wins was held to be 84, but the PGA Tour amended his figure in 1990 after discrepancies had been found in their previous lists. They deducted 11 wins from his total, but added eight others that should have been included, giving a revised total of 81.

TOP 10 MONEY-WINNING GOLFERS, 1999

	PLAYER/COUNTRY*	WINNINGS ($)
1	**Tiger Woods**	6,981,836
2	**David Duval**	3,641,906
3	**Davis Love III**	2,475,328
4	**Vijay Singh**, Fiji	2,473,372
5	**Colin Montgomerie**, Scotland	2,281,884
6	**Ernie Els**, South Africa	2,151,574
7	**Chris Perry**	2,145,707
8	**Hal Sutton**	2,127,578
9	**Payne Stewart**	2,077,950
10	**Justin Leonard**	2,020,991

* From the US unless otherwise stated

This list is based on winnings of the world's five top tours: US PGA Tour, European PGA Tour, PGA Tour of Japan, Australasian PGA Tour, and FNB Tour of South Africa.

TOP 10 GOLFERS TO PLAY MOST STROKES AT ONE HOLE*

	PLAYER/COUNTRY#/YEAR/EVENT	STROKES
1	**Tommy Armour**, 1927, Shawnee Open	23
2	**Philippe Porquier**, France, 1978, French Open	21
3	**Ray Ainsley**, 1938, US Open	19
4	=**John Daly**, 1998, Bay Hill Invitational	18
	=**Willie Chisolm**, 1919, US Open	18
6	=**Porky Oliver**, 1953, Bing Crosby	16
	=**Ian Woosnam**, Wales, 1986, French Open	16
8	**Hermann Tissies**, Germany, 1950, British Open	15
9	=**Greg Norman**, Australia, 1982, Martini International	14
	=**Orrin Vincent**, 1992, Austrian Open	14

* In a leading professional tournament
\# From the US unless otherwise stated

TOP 10 MONEY-WINNING GOLFERS OF ALL TIME

(Player/country/career winnings in $#)*

❶ **Greg Norman**, Australia, 12,507,322 ❷ **Davis Love III**, 12,487,463 ❸ **Payne Stewart**, 11,737,008 ❹ **Nick Price**, Zimbabwe, 11,386,236 ❺ **Tiger Woods**, 11,315,128 ❻ **Fred Couples**, 11,305,069 ❼ **Mark O'Meara**, 11,162,269 ❽ **Tom Kite**, 10,533,102 ❾ **Scott Hoch**, 10,308,995 ❿ **David Duval**, 10,047,947

* From the US unless otherwise stated # As at 6 December 1999

DEATH OF A LEGEND

Payne Stewart (1957–99), one of the top professional golfers of the late 20th century, won 18 tournaments, including three major championships. In June 1999 he won his second US Open, by a single shot, with a 4.57 m (15-ft) putt. He was a leading money-winner and noted for his adherence to traditional golfing clothing of plus-fours and cap. On 25 October 1999, he was killed in a bizarre plane accident, when the Lear jet in which he was flying from Orlando, Florida, became depressurized and its pilots and passengers fell unconscious. The plane, shadowed by an F-16 fighter, flew on autopilot for some 2,250 km (1,400 miles) before crashing.

SNAP SHOTS

Background image: THE CLUBHOUSE AT AUGUSTA, GEORGIA, USA

Horse Racing

TOP 10 JOCKEYS IN THE 2,000 GUINEAS

	JOCKEY	YEARS	WINS
1	Jem Robinson	1825–48	9
2	John Osborne	1857–88	6
3	=Frank Buckle	1810–27	5
	=Charlie Elliott	1923–49	5
	=Lester Piggott	1957–92	5
6	=John Day	1826–41	4
	=Fred Archer	1874–85	4
	=Tom Cannon	1878–89	4
	=Herbert Jones	1900–09	4
	=Willie Carson	1972–89	4

TOP 10 JOCKEYS IN THE 1,000 GUINEAS

	JOCKEY	YEARS	WINS
1	George Fordham	1859–83	7
2	Frank Buckle	1818–27	6
3	=Jem Robinson	1824–44	5
	=John Day	1826–40	5
5	=Jack Watts	1886–97	4
	=Fred Rickaby Jr.	1913–17	4
	=Charlie Elliott	1924–44	4
8	=Bill Arnull	1817–32	3
	=Nat Flatman	1835–57	3
	=Tom Cannon	1866–84	3
	=Charlie Wood	1880–87	3
	=Dick Perryman	1926–41	3
	=Harry Wragg	1934–45	3
	=Rae Johnstone	1935–50	3
	=Gordon Richards	1942–51	3
	=Walter Swinburn	1989–93	3

Raced at Newmarket, the 1,000 Guineas, for three-year-old fillies, was first run in 1814. As well as his wins in this race, jockey George "The Demon" Fordham (1837–87) achieved a further 2,580 victories in his career.

TOP 10 JOCKEYS IN THE ENGLISH CLASSICS

	JOCKEY	YEARS	1,000 GUINEAS	2,000 GUINEAS	DERBY	OAKS	ST. LEGER	WINS
1	Lester Piggott	1954–92	2	5	9	6	8	30
2	Frank Buckle	1792–1827	6	5	5	9	2	27
3	Jem Robinson	1817–48	5	9	6	2	2	24
4	Fred Archer	1874–86	2	4	5	4	6	21
5	=Bill Scott	1821–46	0	3	4	3	9	19
	=Jack Watts	1883–97	4	2	4	4	5	19
7	Willie Carson	1972–94	2	4	4	4	3	17
8	=John Day	1826–41	5	4	0	5	2	16
	=George Fordham	1859–83	7	3	1	5	0	16
10	Joe Childs	1912–33	2	2	3	4	4	15

TOP 10 JOCKEYS IN THE PRIX DE L'ARC DE TRIOMPHE

(Jockey/wins)

1 =Jacko Doyasbère, 4; = Pat Eddery, 4; = Freddy Head, 4; = Yves Saint-Martin, 4
5 = Enrico Camici, 3; = Charlie Elliott, 3; = Olivier Peslier, 3;
= Lester Piggot, 3; = Roger Poincelet, 3; = Charles Semblat, 3

TOP 10 FASTEST WINNING TIMES OF THE EPSOM DERBY

	HORSE	YEAR	TIME MINS	SECS
1	Lammtarra	1995	2	32.31
2	Mahmoud	1936	2	33.80
3	Kahyasi	1988	2	33.84
4	High-Rise	1998	2	33.88
5	Reference Point	1987	2	33.90
6	=Hyperion	1933	2	34.00
	=Windsor Lad	1934	2	34.00
	=Generous	1991	2	34.00
9	Erhaab	1994	2	34.16
10	Golden Fleece	1982	2	34.27

Barely two seconds separates the times of the current record-holder and the 10th-ranked horse in this list of Epsom winners.

TOP 10 JOCKEYS OF ALL TIME IN THE UK

	JOCKEY	CAREER	CAREER FLAT WINNERS
1	Gordon Richards	1921–54	4,870
2	Lester Piggott	1948–95	4,513
3	Pat Eddery	1969–99	4,105
4	Willie Carson	1962–96	3,828
5	Doug Smith	1931–67	3,111
6	Joe Mercer	1950–85	2,810
7	Fred Archer	1870–86	2,748
8	Edward Hide	1951–85	2,591
9	George Fordham	1850–84	2,587
10	Eph Smith	1930–65	2,313

When Pat Eddery rode Silver Patriarch to victory in the St. Leger at Doncaster on 13 Sep 1997, he became the third member of the elite "4,000 club" – jockeys who have won more than 4,000 races. Gordon Richards was champion jockey 26 times and held the record for best season with 269 wins.

TOP 10 FASTEST WINNING TIMES OF THE GRAND NATIONAL

	HORSE	YEAR	TIME MINS	SECS
1	Mr. Frisk	1990	8	47.8
2	Rough Quest	1996	9	00.8
3	Red Rum	1973	9	01.9
4	Royal Athlete	1995	9	04.6
5	Lord Gwyllene	1997	9	05.8
6	Party Politics	1992	9	06.3
7	Grittar	1982	9	12.6
8	Bobbyjo	1999	9	14.0
9	Maori Venture	1987	9	19.3
10	Reynoldstown	1935	9	20.0

TOP 10 MONEY-WINNING TRAINERS, 1999

	TRAINER	WINS	PRIZE MONEY (£)
1	Saeed bin Suroor	43	3,320,084
2	Henry Cecil	68	2,728,907
3	Aiden O'Brien	112	2,213,429
4	Barry Hills	110	1,687,907
5	Richard Hannon	123	1,676,006
6	John Dunlop	123	1,560,660
7	Sir Michael Stoute	83	1,502,758
8	John Gosden	74	1,137,354
9	Mark Johnston	111	1,068,526
10	Luca Cumani	36	965,827

Source: Racing Post

TOP 10 MONEY-WINNING JOCKEYS, 1999

	JOCKEY	WINS	PRIZE MONEY (£)
1	Frankie Dettori	138	3,905,340
2	Kieren Fallon	206	3,902,442
3	Michael Kinane	113	2,047,601
4	Richard Quinn	151	1,993,741
5	Pat Eddery	105	1,657,265
6	Gary Stevens	47	1,480,905
7	Michael Hills	92	1,422,433
8	Richard Hills	77	1,313,343
9	Richard Hughes	97	1,178,526
10	Jimmy Fortune	95	1,138,334

Source: Racing Post

TOP 10 JOCKEYS IN THE GRAND NATIONAL

	JOCKEY*	YEARS	WINS
1	George Stevens	1856–70	5
2	Tom Oliver	1838–53	4
3	=Mr. Tommy Pickernell	1860–75	3
	=Mr. Tommy Beasley	1880–89	3
	=Arthur Nightingall	1890–1901	3
	=Ernie Piggott	1912–19	3
	=Mr. Jack Anthony	1911–20	3
	=Brian Fletcher	1968–74	3
9	=Mr. Alec Goodman	1852–66	2
	=John Page	1867–72	2
	=Mr. Maunsell Richardson	1873–74	2
	=Mr. Ted Wilson	1884–85	2
	=Percy Woodland	1903–13	2
	=Arthur Thompson	1948–52	2
	=Bryan Marshall	1953–54	2
	=Fred Winter	1957–62	2
	=Richard Dunwoody	1986–94	2
	=Carl Llewellyn	1992–98	2

* *Amateur riders are traditionally indicated by the prefix "Mr."*

TOP 10 NATIONAL HUNT JOCKEYS, 1999

	JOCKEY	PERCENTAGE WON	RACES	WINS
1	Tony McCoy	31	579	184
2	Richard Johnson	15	618	95
3	Norman Williamson	22	387	87
4	Mick Fitzgerald	20	363	73
5	Carl Llewellyn	16	312	50
6	=Tony Dobbin	17	267	48
	=Joe Tizzard	18	259	48
8	Andrew Thornton	12	371	47
9	Adrian Maguire	13	339	46
10	Seamus Durack	14	306	43

Source: Racing Post

TOP 10 NATIONAL HUNT JOCKEYS WITH THE MOST CAREER WINS*

	JOCKEY	YEARS	WINS
1	Richard Dunwoody	1983–99	1,679
2	Peter Scudamore	1978–95	1,678
3	John Francome	1970–85	1,138
4	Stan Mellor	1952–72	1,035
5	Tony McCoy	1994–99	1,000
6	Peter Niven	1984–99	974
7	Fred Winter	1939–64	923
8	Graham McCourt	1975–96	921
9	Bob Davies	1966–82	911
10	Terry Biddlecombe	1958–74	908

**As at 1 January 2000*

TOP 10 JOCKEYS IN A FLAT RACING SEASON

(*Jockey/year/wins*)

1 **Gordon Richards**, 1947, 269 2 **Gordon Richards**, 1949, 261 3 **Gordon Richards**, 1933, 259 4 **Fred Archer**, 1885, 246 5 **Fred Archer**, 1884, 241 6 **Fred Archer**, 1883, 232 7 **Gordon Richards**, 1952, 231 8 **Fred Archer**, 1878, 229 9 **Gordon Richards**, 1951, 227 10 **Gordon Richards**, 1948, 224

Richards rode over 200 winners in a season 12 times, while Archer did so on eight occasions.

Which sport was originally called "sphairistike"?
see p.271 for the answer

A Lawn tennis
B Polo
C Croquet

Rugby Records

TOP 10 POINT SCORERS IN THE SUPER LEAGUE*

	CLUB	TOTAL POINTS
1	St. Helens	3,249
2	Wigan Warriors	3,224
3	Bradford Bulls	2,931
4	Leeds Rhinos	2,671
5	Halifax Blue Sox	2,422
6	London Broncos	2,286
7	Warrington Wolves	2,117
8	Castleford Tigers	2,040
9	Sheffield Eagles	2,027
10	Salford City Reds	1,273

* *Over the four seasons up to and including 1999*

TOP 10 WINNERS OF THE CHALLENGE CUP

	CLUB	YEARS	WINS
1	Wigan Warriors	1924–95	16
2	Leeds Rhinos	1910–99	11
3=	Widnes Vikings	1930–84	7
=	St. Helens	1956–97	7
5	Huddersfield-Sheffield Giants	1913–53	6
6=	Wakefield Trinity Wildcats	1909–63	5
=	Warrington Wolves	1905–74	5
=	Halifax Blue Sox	1903–87	5
9=	Bradford Bulls	1906–49	4
=	Castleford Tigers	1935–86	4

The first Challenge Cup final, then known as the Northern Union Cup, was held at Headingley, Leeds, on 24 April 1897.

TOP 10 TRY SCORERS IN THE 1999 SUPER LEAGUE*

	PLAYER/CLUB	TRIES
1=	**Matt Daylight**, Gateshead Thunder	25
=	**Toa Kohe-Love**, Warrington Wolves	25
3	**Anthony Sullivan**, St. Helens	24
4=	**Francis Cummins**, Leeds Rhinos	23
=	**Greg Fleming**, London Broncos	23
6	**Sean Long**, St. Helens	20
7=	**Jason Robinson**, Wigan Warriors	19
=	**Darren Rogers**, Castleford Tigers	19
9=	**Iestyn Harris**, Leeds Rhinos	17
=	**Alan Hunte**, Warrington Wolves	17
=	**Kris Radlinski**, Wigan Warriors	17

* *League matches only; excluding play-offs*

TOP 10 SCORING TEAMS IN CHALLENGE CUP FINALS*

	TEAM	POINTS
1	Wigan Warriors	414
2	Leeds Rhinos	291
3	St. Helens	211
4	Widnes Vikings	158
5	Huddersfield–Sheffield Giants	130
6	Warrington Wolves	129
7	Hull FC	128
8	Wakefield Trinity Wildcats	118
9	Bradford Bulls	113
10	Halifax Blue Sox	110

* *Including the two-stage finals during World War II*

TOP 10 INDIVIDUAL POINT SCORERS IN A WORLD CUP TOURNAMENT

	PLAYER/COUNTRY	YEAR	POINTS
1	**Grant Fox**, New Zealand	1987	126
2	**Gavin Hastings**, Scotland	1995	104
3	**Thierry Lacroix**, France	1995	103
4	**Gozalo Quesada**, Argentina	1999	102
5	**Andrew Mehrtens**, New Zealand	1995	84
6	**Michael Lynagh**, Australia	1987	82
7	**Rob Andrew**, England	1995	70
8	**Ralph Keyes**, Ireland	1991	68
9	**Michael Lynagh**, Australia	1991	66
10	**Gavin Hastings**, Scotland	1987	62

TOP 10 HIGHEST-SCORING VARSITY MATCHES*

	WINNERS	SEASON	SCORE
1	Oxford	1909–10	35–3
2	Cambridge	1975–76	34–12
3	Cambridge	1935–36	33–3
4	Cambridge	1984–85	32–6
5	Cambridge	1926–27	30–5
6	Cambridge	1934–35	29–4
7	Oxford	1988–89	27–7
8	Cambridge	1978–79	25–7
9	Oxford	1910–11	23–18
10=	Cambridge	1989–90	22–13
=	Cambridge	1927–28	22–14

* *Ranked by score of winning team*

The first Varsity Match was played at Oxford in 1871–72, when the home side won by one goal and a try to nil. The following year Cambridge played host and duly won. From 1873–74 to 1879–80 the match was played at the Oval, before a seven-year spell at Blackheath. Queen's Club was its home between 1887–88 and 1920–21, and it then moved to Twickenham. To date, Cambridge have won 49 times, Oxford 46 times, and 13 matches have been drawn.

TOP 10 AUSTRALIAN RUGBY TEAMS

(Team/Grand Final wins)

1 **South Sydney**, 20 2 **St. George**, 15 3 = **Balmain** 11; = **Eastern Suburbs**, 11
5 = **Canterbury-Bankstown**, 6; = **Manly-Warringah**, 6 7 = **Parramatta**, 4;
= **Western Suburbs**, 4 9 = **Brisbane Broncos**, 3; = **Canberra**, 3

In 1998 the rivalry that had existed since 1995 between the News' Super League and Australian Rugby League was put to an end with the unification of the two leagues in the new National Rugby League.

TOP 10 MOST-CAPPED RUGBY UNION PLAYERS

	PLAYER	COUNTRY	YEARS	CAPS
1	Philippe Sella	France	1982–95	111
2	D. I. Campese	Australia	1982–96	101
3	Serge Blanco	France	1980–91	93
4	S. B. T. Fitzpatrick	New Zealand	1986–97	92
5	R. Underwood	England/British Lions	1984–96	91
6	Mike Gibson	Ireland/British Lions	1964–79	81
7	Willie John McBride	Ireland/British Lions	1962–75	80
8	I. C. Evans	Wales/British Lions	1985–97	79
9	=C. R. Andrew	England/British Lions	1985–97	76
	=I. D. Jones	New Zealand	1990–98	76

TOP 10 HIGHEST-SCORING INTERNATIONAL RUGBY UNION MATCHES, 1993–99*

	MATCH (WINNERS FIRST)	DATE	SCORE
1	Hong Kong v Singapore	27 Oct 1994	164–13
2	New Zealand v Japan	4 June 1995	145–17
3	Japan v Thailand	4 Nov 1996	141–10
4	England v Holland	14 Nov 1998	110–0
5	Hong Kong v Taiwan	9 Nov 1996	114–12
6	South Korea v Malaysia	5 Nov 1996	112–5
7	Italy v Poland	26 May 1996	107–19
8	Italy v Czech Republic	18 May 1994	104–8
9	Hong Kong v Malaysia	3 Nov 1996	103–5
10	=Japan v Malaysia	26 Oct 1994	103–9
	=Argentina v Paraguay	24 Sep 1995	103–9

** 1 March 1993 to 1 January 2000*

TOP 10 RANKED RUGBY UNION COUNTRIES*

1 Australia 2 New Zealand 3 South Africa 4 Wales 5 England 6 France 7 Argentina 8 Scotland 9 Ireland 10 Samoa

** As at 1 February 2000*

THE 10 FIRST PLAYERS INDUCTED INTO THE RUGBY UNION HALL OF FAME*

1 Serge Blanco 2 Graham Mourie 3 Peter Dixon 4 Gareth Edwards 5 Simon Poidevin 6 Grant Fox 7 Jo Maso 8 Hugo Porta 9 Mike Gibson 10 Andy Irvine

** In November 1996* Rugby News *magazine launched its own Hall of Fame and each month thereafter nominated a new inductee.*

TOP 10 BIGGEST WINS IN THE INTERNATIONAL CHAMPIONSHIP

	MATCH (WINNERS FIRST)	VENUE	YEAR	SCORE
1	England v Wales	Twickenham	1998	60–26
2	France v Wales	Wembley	1998	51–0
3	France v Scotland	Murrayfield	1998	51–16
4	Wales v France	Swansea	1910	49–14
5	France v Scotland	Paris	1997	47–20
6	England v Ireland	Twickenham	1997	46–6
7	France v Ireland	Paris	1996	45–10
8	France v Ireland	Paris	1992	44–12
9	England v Scotland	Twickenham	1997	41–13
10	England v France	Paris	1914	39–13

This Top 10 is based on the winning team's scores, not the margin of victory. However, where two nations share the highest score, then margin of victory is used to separate them. The biggest victory by margin is France's 51–0 win over Wales at Wembley in 1998.

TOP 10 POINT SCORERS IN MAJOR INTERNATIONALS*

	PLAYER	COUNTRY	YEARS	POINTS
1	Neil Jenkins	Wales	1991–2000	939
2	Michael Lynagh	Australia	1984–95	911
3	Diego Dominguez	Italy	1991–2000	787
4	Gavin Hastings	Scotland	1986–95	733
5	Grant Fox	New Zealand	1985–93	645
6	Andrew Mehrtens	New Zealand	1995–99	594
7	Matthew Burke	Australia	1993–99	509
8	Gareth Rees	Canada	1986–99	492
9	Stefano Bettarello	Italy	1979–88	483
10	Hugo Porta	Argentina	1973–80	408

** Full International Board countries and British Lions*

What were once used as targets in Olympic archery events?

see p.273 for the answer

A Rabbits
B Birds
C Goats

Tennis Triumphs

TOP 10

MEN WITH THE MOST WIMBLEDON TITLES

	PLAYER/COUNTRY	YEARS	TITLES S	D	M	TOTAL
1	**William Renshaw**, UK	1880–89	7	7	0	14
2	**Lawrence Doherty**, UK	1897–1905	5	8	0	13
3	**Reginald Doherty**, UK	1897–1905	4	8	0	12
4	**John Newcombe**, Australia	1965–74	3	6	0	9
5	=**Ernest Renshaw**, UK	1880–89	1	7	0	8
	=**Tony Wilding**, New Zealand	1907–14	4	4	0	8
7	=**Wilfred Baddeley**, UK	1891–96	3	4	0	7
	=**Bob Hewitt**, Australia/S. Africa	1962–79	0	5	2	7
	=**Rod Laver**, Australia	1959–69	4	1	2	7
	=**John McEnroe**, USA	1979–84	3	4	0	7

S – singles; D – doubles; M – mixed

TOP 10 TOURNAMENT WINNERS, MALE*

(Player/country/tournament wins)

1 **Jimmy Connors**, USA, 109 2 **Ivan Lendl**, Czechoslovakia, 94 3 **John McEnroe**, USA, 77 4 = **Bjorn Borg**, Sweden, 62; = **Guillermo Vilas**, Argentina, 62 6 **Ilie Nastase**, Romania, 57 7 **Pete Sampras**, USA, 56 8 **Boris Becker**, Germany, 49 9 **Rod Laver**, Australia, 47 10 **Thomas Muster**, Austria, 44

** Tournament leaders since Open Tennis introduced in 1968. Totals include ATP tour, Grand Prix, and WCT tournaments.*

TOP 10

WINNERS OF MEN'S GRAND SLAM SINGLES TITLES

	PLAYER/COUNTRY	TITLES A	F	W	US	TOTAL
1	**Roy Emerson**, Australia	6	2	2	2	12
2	=**Björn Borg**, Sweden	0	6	5	0	11
	=**Rod Laver**, Australia	3	2	4	2	11
	=**Pete Sampras**, USA	2	0	5	4	11
5	**Bill Tilden**, USA	0	0	3	7	10
6	=**Jimmy Connors**, USA	1	0	2	5	8
	=**Ivan Lendl**, Czechoslovakia	2	3	0	3	8
	=**Fred Perry**, UK	1	1	3	3	8
	=**Ken Rosewall**, Australia	4	2	0	2	8
10	=**Henri Cochet**, France	0	4	2	1	7
	=**René Lacoste**, France	0	3	2	2	7
	=**William Larned**, USA	0	0	0	7	7
	=**John McEnroe**, USA	0	0	3	4	7
	=**John Newcombe**, Australia	2	0	3	2	7
	=**William Renshaw**, UK	0	0	7	0	7
	=**Richard Sears**, USA	0	0	0	7	7
	=**Mats Wilander**, Sweden	3	3	0	1	7

A – Australian Open; F – French Open; W – Wimbledon; US – US Open

THE 10 LATEST WINNERS OF THE US OPEN MEN'S CHAMPIONSHIP

(Year/winner/country)

1 **1999**, Andre Agassi, USA 2 **1998**, Patrick Rafter, Australia 3 **1997**, Patrick Rafter, Australia 4 **1996**, Pete Sampras, USA 5 **1995**, Pete Sampras, USA 6 **1994**, Andre Agassi, USA 7 **1993**, Pete Sampras, USA 8 **1992**, Stefan Edberg, Sweden 9 **1991**, Stefan Edberg, Sweden 10 **1990**, Pete Sampras, USA

TOP 10 MALE PLAYERS*

(Player/country/weeks at No. 1)

1 **Pete Sampras**, USA, 276 2 **Ivan Lendl**, Czechoslovakia, 270 3 **Jimmy Connors**, USA, 268 4 **John McEnroe**, USA, 170 5 **Bjorn Borg**, Sweden, 109 6 **Stefan Edberg**, Sweden, 72 7 **Jim Courier**, USA, 58 8 **Andre Agassi**, USA, 47 9 **Ilie Nastase**, Romania, 40 10 **Mats Wilander**, Sweden, 20

** Based on weeks at No. 1 in ATP rankings (1973 to 1999)*

TOP 10 WINNERS OF WOMEN'S GRAND SLAM SINGLES TITLES

	PLAYER/COUNTRY	A	F	W	US	TOTAL
1	**Margaret Court**, Australia	11	5	3	5	24
2	**Steffi Graf**, Germany	4	5	7	5	21
3	**Helen Wills-Moody**, USA	0	4	8	7	19
4	=**Chris Evert-Lloyd**, USA	2	7	3	6	18
	=**Martina Navratilova**, USA	3	2	9	4	18
6	=**Billie Jean King**, USA	1	1	6	4	12
	=**Suzanne Lenglen**, France	0	6	6	0	12
8	=**Maureen Connolly**, USA	1	2	3	3	9
	=**Monica Seles**, USA	4	3	0	2	9
10	**Molla Mallory**, USA	0	0	0	8	8

A – Australian Open; F – French Open; W – Wimbledon; US – US Open

TOP 10 TOURNAMENT WINNERS, FEMALE*

	PLAYER/COUNTRY	TOURNAMENT WINS
1	**Martina Navratilova**, USA	167
2	**Chris Evert-Lloyd**, USA	154
3	**Steffi Graf**, Germany	106
4	**Margaret Court**, Australia	92
5	**Billie Jean King**, USA	67
6	**Evonne Goolagong Cawley**, Australia	65
7	**Virginia Wade**, UK	55
8	**Monica Seles**, USA	43
9	**Conchita Martinez**, Spain	30
10	**Tracy Austin**, USA	29

** Tournament leaders since Open Tennis introduced in 1968*

TOP 10 DAVIS CUP WINNING TEAMS

	COUNTRY	WINS
1	United States	31
2	Australia	21
3	France	8
4	Sweden	7
5	Australasia	6
6	British Isles	5
7	Great Britain	4
8	West Germany	2
9	=Germany	1
	=Czechoslovakia	1
	=Italy	1
	=South Africa	1

South Africa's sole win was gained when, for political reasons, India refused to meet them in the 1974 final.

TOP 10 CAREER MONEY-WINNING WOMEN*

(Player/country/winnings in $)

1. **Steffi Graf**, Germany, 20,646,410 2. **Martina Navratilova**, USA, 20,344,061 3. **Arantxa Sanchez-Vicario**, Spain, 14,119,642 4. **Monica Seles**, USA, 10,928,640 5. **Jana Novotna**, Czech Republic, 10,507,680 6. **Chris Evert-Lloyd**, USA, 8,896,195 7. **Gabriela Sabatini**, Argentina, 8,785,850 8. **Martina Hingis**, Switzerland, 8,331,496 9. **Conchita Martinez**, Spain, 7,780,941 10. **Natasha Zvereva**, Belarus, 7,036,143

** To end of 1999 season*

GOLDEN GIRL

German-born Steffi Graf was one of the youngest players ever ranked, aged just 13 in 1982. As her career progressed, she was first ranked No. 1 in 1987, and held the No. 1 ranking for a record 374 weeks. Aged just 19 in 1988, she became the youngest-ever winner of the Grand Slam, and also won Olympic gold at Seoul. She continued to win at least one Grand Slam title a year for the next 10 years, until knee injuries prevented her from competing. In 1999, after winning her sixth French Open championship, and her 22nd Grand Slam title, Steffi Graf announced her decision to retire. In 2000, her romantic involvement with Andre Agassi made press headlines.

SNAP SHOTS

BRILLIANT CAREER

In 1995, Andre Agassi was the 12th player to be ranked world No. 1. In 1999, he became only the fifth male player to complete a Grand Slam.

Did You Know? Lawn tennis was patented in 1874 by Major Walter Clopton Wingfield, who originally called it "sphairistike" (from *sphaira*, Greek for ball).

TOP 10 ★

WINNERS OF THE TABLE TENNIS WORLD CHAMPIONSHIP

	COUNTRY	MEN'S	WOMEN'S	TOTAL
1	China	13	13	26
2	Japan	7	8	15
3	Hungary	12	–	12
4	Czechoslovakia	6	3	9
5	Romania	–	5	5
6	Sweden	4	–	4
7	=England	1	2	3
	=USA	1	2	3
9	Germany	–	2	2
10	=Austria	1	–	1
	=North Korea	–	1	1
	=South Korea	–	1	1
	=USSR	–	1	1

Originally a European event, it was later extended to a world championship.

TOP 10 POLO TEAMS WITH THE MOST BRITISH OPEN CHAMPIONSHIP WINS

(Team/wins)

1 = **Stowell Park**, 5; = **Tramontana**, 5
3 = **Ellerston**, 3; = **Cowdray Park**, 3;
= **Pimms**, 3; = **Windsor Park**, 3
7 = **Casarejo**, 2; = **Jersey Lillies**, 2;
= **Woolmer's Park**, 2; = **Falcons**, 2;
= **Southfield**, 2

TOP 10 COUNTIES WITH THE MOST WINS IN THE ALL-IRELAND HURLING CHAMPIONSHIPS

(County/wins)

1 **Cork**, 28 2 **Kilkenny**, 25
3 **Tipperary**, 24 4 **Limerick**, 7
5 = **Dublin**, 6; = **Wexford**, 6
7 = **Galway**, 4; = **Offaly**, 4 9 **Clare**, 3
10 **Waterford**, 2

EYE ON THE BALL

Table tennis is believed to have originated in England in the 1880s, with cigar box lids used as bats and books as nets. Now a world sport, it is dominated by Chinese players like Song Ding, 1997 World Champion.

THE 10

LATEST WINNERS OF THE ROLLER HOCKEY WORLD CHAMPIONSHIP

YEAR	WINNER
1999	Argentina
1997	Italy
1995	Argentina
1993	Portugal
1991	Portugal
1989	Spain
1988	Spain
1986	Spain
1984	Argentina
1982	Portugal

Roller hockey, a five-a-side game formerly called rink hockey, has been played for more than 100 years. The first international tournament was held in Paris in 1910, the first European Championships in Britain in 1926, and the men's World Championship biennially since 1936 (odd-numbered years since 1989). Portugal is the overall winner, with 14 titles to its credit.

TOP 10

OLYMPIC HOCKEY COUNTRIES

	COUNTRY	MEDALS GOLD	SILVER	BRONZE	TOTAL
1	India	8	1	2	11
2	Great Britain*	3	2	5	10
3	Netherlands	2	2	5	9
4	Pakistan	3	3	2	8
5	Australia	2	3	2	7
6	Germany #	1	2	2	5
7	=Spain	1	2	1	4
	=West Germany	1	3	–	4
9	=South Korea	–	2	–	2
	=USA	–	–	2	2
	=Soviet Union	–	–	2	2

* *Including England, Ireland, Scotland, and Wales, which competed separately in the 1908 Olympics*

Not including West Germany or East Germany 1968–88

TOP 10

OLYMPIC ARCHERY COUNTRIES

	COUNTRY	MEDALS GOLD	SILVER	BRONZE	TOTAL
1	USA	13	7	7	27
2	France	6	10	6	22
3	South Korea	10	6	3	19
4	Soviet Union	1	3	5	9
5	Great Britain	2	2	4	8
6	Finland	1	1	2	4
7	=China	0	3	0	3
	=Italy	0	0	3	3
9	=Sweden	0	2	0	2
	=Japan	0	1	1	2
	=Poland	0	1	1	2

Archery was introduced as an Olympic sport at the second Modern Olympics, held in Paris in 1900. The format has changed considerably over succeeding Games, with events such as shooting live birds being discontinued in favour of target shooting. Individual and team events for men and women are now included in the programme.

TOP 10

OLYMPIC VOLLEYBALL COUNTRIES

	COUNTRY	MEDALS GOLD	SILVER	BRONZE	TOTAL
1	Soviet Union*	7	5	1	13
2	Japan	3	3	2	8
3	USA	2	1	2	5
4	=Cuba	2	–	1	3
	=Brazil	1	1	1	3
	=China	1	1	1	3
	=Poland	1	–	2	3
8	=Netherlands	1	1	–	2
	=East Germany	–	2	–	2
	=Bulgaria	–	1	1	2
	=Czechoslovakia	–	1	1	2
	=Italy	–	1	1	2

* *Includes United Team of 1992; excludes Russia since this date*

UP AND OVER DOWN UNDER

Matther Allan (Carlton) and Steven King (Geelong) battle for possession in an Australian football match.

TOP 10 AUSTRALIAN FOOTBALL LEAGUE TEAMS

(Team/Grand Final wins)

1 Carlton Blues, 16 **2** Essendon Bombers, 15 **3** Collingwood Magpies, 14 **4** Melbourne Demons, 12 **5** Richmond Tigers, 10 **6** Hawthorn Hawks, 9 **7** Fitzroy Lions, 8 **8** Geelong Cats, 6 **9** Kangaroos (North Melbourne), 4 **10** South Melbourne, 3

TOP 10

OLYMPIC SHOOTING COUNTRIES

	COUNTRY	MEDALS GOLD	SILVER	BRONZE	TOTAL
1	USA	45	26	21	92
2	Soviet Union	22	17	81	57
3	Sweden	13	23	19	55
4	Great Britain	13	14	18	45
5	France	13	16	13	42
6	Norway	16	9	11	36
7	Switzerland	11	11	12	34
8	Italy	8	5	10	23
9	Greece	5	7	7	19
10	=China	7	5	5	17
	=Finland	3	5	9	17

Did You Know? At the 1932 Los Angeles Olympics, India's hockey team beat the USA by a record 24–1 (with 12 of the goals scored by one player, Roop Singh), and Japan by 11–1.

TOP 10

WINNERS OF MEN'S WORLD WATER-SKIING TITLES

	SKIER/COUNTRY	OVERALL	SLALOM	TRICKS	JUMP	TOTAL
1	**Patrice Martin**, France	6	0	4	0	10
2	**Sammy Duvall**, USA	4	0	0	2	6
3	=**Alfredo Mendoza**, USA	2	1	0	2	5
	=**Mike Suyderhoud**, USA	2	1	0	2	5
	=**Bob La Point**, USA	0	4	1	0	5
	=**Andy Mapple**, UK	0	5	0	0	5
7	=**George Athans**, Canada	2	1	0	0	3
	=**Guy de Clercq**, Belgium	1	0	0	2	3
	=**Wayne Grimditch**, USA	0	0	2	1	3
	=**Mike Hazelwood**, UK	1	0	0	2	3
	=**Ricky McCormick**, USA	0	0	1	2	3
	=**Billy Spencer**, USA	1	1	1	0	3

TOP 10

WINNERS OF WOMEN'S WORLD WATER-SKIING TITLES

	SKIER/COUNTRY	OVERALL	SLALOM	TRICKS	JUMP	TOTAL
1	**Liz Shetter** , USA	3	3	1	4	11
2	**Willa McGuire**, USA	3	2	1	2	8
3	**Cindy Todd**, USA	2	3	0	2	7
4	**Deena Mapple**, USA	2	0	0	4	6
5	=**Marina Doria**, Switzerland	1	1	2	0	4
	=**Tawn Hahn**, USA	0	0	4	0	4
	=**Helena Kjellander**, Sweden	0	4	0	0	4
	=**Natalya Ponomaryeva**, USSR	1	0	3	0	4
9	=**Maria Victoria Carrasco**, Venezuela	0	0	3	0	3
	=**Yelena Milakova**, Russia	2	0	0	1	3

TOP 10 POWERBOAT DRIVERS WITH MOST RACE WINS

(Owner/country/wins)

1 **Bill Seebold**, USA, 912 2 **Jumbo McConnell**, USA, 217 3 **Chip Hanuer**, USA, 203 4 **Steve Curtis**, UK, 184 5 **Mikeal Frode**, Sweden, 152 6 **Neil Holmes**, UK, 147 7 **Peter Bloomfield**, UK, 126 8 **Renato Molinari**, Italy, 113 9 **Cees Van der Valden**, Netherlands, 98 10 **Bill Muney**, USA, 96

Source: Raceboat International

TOP 10 FASTEST WINNING TIMES OF THE OXFORD AND CAMBRIDGE BOAT RACE

(Winner/year/minutes)

1 **Cambridge**, 1998, 16.19 2 **Cambridge**, 1999, 16.41 3 **Oxford**, 1984, 16.45 4 **Cambridge**, 1996, 16.58 5 **Oxford**, 1991, 16.59 6 **Cambridge**, 1993, 17.00 7 **Oxford**, 1985, 17.11 8 **Oxford**, 1990, 17.15 9 = **Oxford**, 1974, 17.35; = **Oxford**, 1988, 17.35

TOP 10

OLYMPIC YACHTING COUNTRIES

	COUNTRY	MEDALS GOLD	SILVER	BRONZE	TOTAL
1	USA	16	19	16	51
2	Great Britain	14	12	9	35
3	Sweden	9	12	9	30
4	Norway	16	11	2	29
5	France	12	6	9	27
6	Denmark	10	8	4	22
7	Germany/West Germany	6	5	6	17
8	Netherlands	4	5	6	15
9	New Zealand	6	4	3	13
10	=Australia	3	2	7	12
	=Soviet Union*	4	5	3	12
	=Spain	9	2	1	12

* *Includes United Team of 1992; excludes Russia since this date*

TOP 10

OLYMPIC ROWING COUNTRIES

	COUNTRY	MEDALS GOLD	SILVER	BRONZE	TOTAL
1	USA	29	28	19	76
2	East Germany	33	7	8	48
3	Soviet Union*	12	20	11	43
4	Germany#	19	12	11	42
5	Great Britain	19	15	7	41
6	=Italy	12	11	9	32
	=Canada	8	12	12	32
8	France	4	14	12	30
9	Romania	12	10	7	29
10	Switzerland	6	7	9	22

* *Includes United Team of 1992; excludes Russia since this date*

\# *Not including West or East Germany 1968–88*

Did You Know? John B. Kelly (1891–1960), father of actress Grace Kelly, later Princess Grace of Monaco, won three rowing gold medals at the 1920 and 1924 Olympics.

TOP 10 ★ OLYMPIC SWIMMING COUNTRIES

	COUNTRY	GOLD	MEDALS SILVER	BRONZE	TOTAL
1	USA	230	176	137	543
2	Australia	41	37	47	125
3	East Germany	40	34	25	99
4	Soviet Union*	24	32	38	94
5	Germany#	19	33	34	86
6	=Great Britain	18	23	30	71
	=Hungary	29	23	19	71
8	Sweden	13	21	21	55
9	Japan	15	18	19	52
10	Canada	11	17	20	48

* *Includes United Team of 1992; excludes Russia since this date*

Not including West Germany or East Germany 1968–88

The medal table includes medals for the synchronized swimming, diving, and water polo events that form part of the Olympic swimming programme. Swimming has been part of the Olympics since the first modern Games in 1896, at which only members of the Greek navy were eligible for one event – the 100-m (328-ft) swimming race for sailors. Events were held in the sea until 1908, when specially built pools were introduced.

TOP 10 ★ OLYMPIC CANOEING COUNTRIES

	COUNTRY	GOLD	MEDALS SILVER	BRONZE	TOTAL
1	=Hungary	10	23	20	53
	=Soviet Union*	30	13	10	53
3	Germany#	18	15	12	45
4	Romania	9	10	12	31
5	East Germany	14	7	9	30
6	Sweden	14	10	4	28
7	France	2	6	14	22
8	=Bulgaria	4	3	8	15
	=USA	5	4	6	15
10	Canada	3	7	4	14

* *Includes United Team of 1992; excludes Russia since this date*

Not including West or East Germany 1968–88

PADDLE POWER

Canoeing has been an Olympic sport since 1936. Six of Sweden's golds were won by one contestant, Gert Fredriksson, who also gained a silver and a bronze, in Games from 1948–60.

SWISS ROLL

The bobsleigh event has been part of the Winter Olympics since 1924. Switzerland has won more medals than any other country.

TOP 10 MEN'S WORLD AND OLYMPIC FIGURE SKATING TITLES

	SKATER/COUNTRY	YEARS	TITLES
1	**Ulrich Salchow**, Sweden	1901–11	11
2	**Karl Schäfer**, Austria	1930–36	9
3	**Richard Button**, USA	1948–52	7
4	**Gillis Grafstrom**, Sweden	1920–29	6
5	=**Hayes Jenkins**, USA	1953–56	5
	=**Scott Hamilton**, USA	1981–84	5
7	=**Willy Bockl**, Austria	1925–28	4
	=**David Jenkins**, USA	1957–60	4
	=**Ondrej Nepela**, Czechoslovakia	1971–73	4
	=**Kurt Browning**, Canada	1989–93	4

TOP 10 OLYMPIC BOBSLEIGHING COUNTRIES

(Country/medals)

❶ **Switzerland**, 26 ❷ **USA**, 14 ❸ **East Germany**, 13 ❹ = **Germany***, 11; = **Italy**, 11 ❻ **West Germany**, 6 ❼ **GB**, 4 ❽ = **Austria**, 3; = **Soviet Union**#, 3 ❿ = **Canada**, 2; = **Belgium**, 2

* *Not including West or East Germany 1968–88*

\# *Includes United Team of 1992; excludes Russia since then*

TOP 10 SKIERS WITH THE MOST ALPINE SKIING WORLD CUP TITLES (MALE)

	SKIER/COUNTRY	YEARS	TOTAL
1	**Ingemar Stenmark**, Sweden	1976–84	18
2	**Pirmin Zurbriggen**, Switzerland	1984–90	15
3	**Marc Girardelli**, Luxembourg	1984–94	11
4	=**Gustavo Thoeni**, Italy	1971–74	9
	=**Alberto Tomba**, Italy	1988–95	9
6	**Hermann Maier**, Austria	1998–2000	8
7	=**Jean-Claude Killy**, France	1967–68	6
	=**Phil Mahre**, USA	1981–83	6
9	=**Luc Alphand**, France	1997	5
	=**Franz Klammer**, Austria	1975–83	5

TOP 10 SKIERS WITH THE MOST ALPINE SKIING WORLD CUP TITLES (FEMALE)

	SKIER/COUNTRY	YEARS	TOTAL
1	**Annemarie Moser-Pröll**, Austria	1971–79	16
2	**Vreni Schneider**, Switzerland	1986–95	14
3	**Katia Seizinger**, Germany	1992–98	11
4	**Erika Hess**, Switzerland	1981–84	8
5	**Michela Figini**, Switzerland	1985–89	7
6	**Lise-Marie Morerod**, Switzerland	1975–78	6
7	=**Maria Walliser**, Switzerland	1986–87	5
	=**Hanni Wenzel**, Liechtenstein	1974–80	5
9	=**Renate Goetschl**, Germany	1997–2000	4
	=**Nancy Greene**, Canada	1967–68	4
	=**Petra Kronberger**, Austria	1990–92	4
	=**Tamara McKinney**, USA	1981–84	4
	=**Carole Merle**, France	1989–92	4

The Alpine Skiing World Cup was launched as an annual event in 1967, with the addition of the super-giant slaloom in 1986. Points are awarded for performances over a series of selected races during the winter months at meetings worldwide. In addition to her 16 titles, Annemarie Moser-Pröll won a record 62 individual events in the period 1970–79, and went on to win gold for the Downhill event in the 1980 Olympic Games.

Did You Know? At the third Winter Olympics, at Lake Placid, USA, in 1932, an early thaw meant that snow had to be taken to the venue from Canada by a fleet of trucks.

TOP 10 ★ WOMEN'S WORLD AND OLYMPIC FIGURE SKATING TITLES

	SKATER/COUNTRY/YEARS	TITLES
1	**Sonja Henie**, Norway, 1927–36	13
2=	**Carol Heiss**, USA, 1956–60	6
=	**Herma Planck Szabo**, Austria, 1922–26	6
=	**Katarina Witt**, E. Germany, 1984–88	6
5=	**Lily Kronberger**, Hungary, 1908–11	4
=	**Sjoukje Dijkstra**, Holland, 1962–64	4
=	**Peggy Fleming**, USA, 1966–68	4
8=	**Meray Horvath**, Hungary, 1912–14	3
=	**Tenley Albright**, USA, 1953–56	3
=	**Michelle Kwan**, USA, 1996–2000	3
=	**Annett Poetzsch**, E. Gemany, 1978–80	3
=	**Beatrix Schuba**, Austria, 1971–72	3
=	**Barbara Ann Scott**, Canada, 1947–48	3
=	**Kristi Yamaguchi**, USA, 1991–92	3
=	**Madge Syers**, GB, 1906–08	3

TOP 10 ★ OLYMPIC FIGURE SKATING COUNTRIES

		MEDALS			
	COUNTRY	GOLD	SILVER	BRONZE	TOTAL
1	USA	12	13	14	39
2	Soviet Union*	13	10	6	29
3	Austria	7	9	4	20
4	Canada	2	7	9	18
5	Great Britain	5	3	7	15
6	France	2	2	7	11
7=	Sweden	5	3	2	10
=	East Germany	3	3	4	10
9	Germany#	4	4	1	9
10=	Norway	3	2	1	6
=	Hungary	0	2	4	6

* *Includes United Team of 1992; excludes Russia since then*

\# *Not including West Germany or East Germany 1968–88*

Figure skating was part of the Summer Olympics in 1908 and 1920, becoming part of the Winter programme in 1924.

TOP 10 ★ WINTER OLYMPIC MEDAL-WINNING COUNTRIES, 1908–98

		MEDALS			
	COUNTRY	GOLD	SILVER	BRONZE	TOTAL
1	Norway	83	87	69	239
2	Soviet Union*	87	63	67	217
3	USA	59	59	41	159
4	Austria	39	53	53	145
5	Finland	38	49	48	135
6	Germany#	66	38	32	116
7	East Germany	39	36	35	110
8	Sweden	39	28	35	102
9	Switzerland	29	31	32	92
10	Canada	25	25	28	79

* *Includes United Team of 1992; excludes Russia since then*

\# *Not including West or East Germany 1968–88*

Only skating and ice hockey were featured in the 1908 and 1920 Summer Olympics. The first Winter Olympics was held at Chamonix, France, in 1924.

TOP 10 ★ FASTEST WINNING TIMES OF THE IDITAROD DOG SLED RACE

			TIME			
	WINNER	YEAR	DAY	HR	MIN	SEC
1	Doug Swingley	2000	9	0	58	6
2	Doug Swingley	1995	9	2	42	19
3	Jeff King	1996	9	5	43	19
4	Jeff King	1998	9	5	52	26
5	Martin Buser	1997	9	8	30	45
6	Doug Swingley	1999	9	14	31	7
7	Martin Buser	1994	10	13	2	39
8	Jeff King	1993	10	15	38	15
9	Martin Buser	1992	10	19	17	15
10	Susan Butcher	1990	11	1	53	28

Source: *Iditarod Trail Committee*

TOP DOUG

Doug Swingley from Simms, Montana, is one of the few non-Alaskans to win the gruelling 1,864-km (1,158-mile) Anchorage-to-Nome Iditarod dog sled race.

Background image: **IDITAROD DOG SLED RACE, 1999**

Sporting Miscellany

TOP 10 PARTICIPATION SPORTS, GAMES, AND PHYSICAL ACTIVITIES IN THE UK

	ACTIVITY	PERCENTAGE PARTICIPATING*
1	Walking	44.5
2	Swimming	14.8
3	Keep fit/yoga	12.3
4	Cue sports	11.3
5	Cycling	11.0
6	Weight training	5.6
7	Football	4.8
8	Golf	4.7
9	Running, jogging, etc.	4.5
10	Weight lifting	1.3

* *Based on the percentage of people over age 16 participating in each activity in the four weeks before interview*

TOP 10 MOST COMMON SPORTING INJURIES

	COMMON NAME	MEDICAL TERM
1	Bruise	A soft tissue contusion
2	Sprained ankle	Sprain of the lateral ligament
3	Sprained knee	Sprain of the medial collateral ligament
4	Low back strain	Lumbar joint dysfunction
5	Hamstring tear	Muscle tear of the hamstrings
6	Jumper's knee	Patella tendinitis
7	Achilles tendinitis	Tendinitis of the Achilles tendon
8	Shin splints	Medial periostitis of the tibia
9	Tennis elbow	Lateral epicondylitis
10	Shoulder strain	Rotator cuff tendinitis

WINGS WINNER

Soviet-born Detroit Red Wings star Sergei Federov is one of the highest scoring and highest earning of all sports personalities.

TOP 10 SPORTING EVENTS WITH THE LARGEST TV AUDIENCES IN THE UK, 1999*

	PROGRAMME	DATE	CHANNEL	AUDIENCE
1	Canadian Grand Prix	13 June	ITV	11,500,000
2	Grand National	10 Apr	BBC1	10,100,000
3	World Athletics Championships 1999 (including women's and men's 400m finals)	26 Aug	BBC1	8,600,000
4	Wimbledon Men's Singles Final	4 July	BBC1	8,100,000
5	=Brazilian Grand Prix	11 Apr	ITV	7,900,000
	=World Athletics Championships 1999 (including men's triple jump final; men's 100m hurdles final; and decathlon)	6 Aug	BBC1	7,900,000
7	=Davis Cup: Great Britain v USA	4 Apr	BBC1	7,800,000
	=Rugby World Cup: England v New Zealand	9 Oct	ITV	7,800,000
9	Embassy Snooker Final	3 May	BBC2	7,600,000
10	World Athletics Championships 1999 (including 400m semi-finals)	24 Aug	BBC1	7,500,000

* *Excluding football*

Source: *BARB*

TOP 10 HIGHEST-EARNING SPORTSMEN

	SPORTSMAN*	SPORT	1999 INCOME ($)
1	Michael Shumacher, Germany	Motor racing	49,000,000
2	Tiger Woods	Golf	47,000,000
3	Oscar De La Hoya	Boxing	43,500,000
4	Michael Jordan	Basketball	40,000,000
5	Evander Holyfield	Boxing	35,500,000
6	Mike Tyson	Boxing	33,000,000
7	Shaquille O'Neal	Basketball	31,000,000
8	Lennox Lewis, UK	Boxing	29,000,000
9	Dale Earnhardt	Stock car racing	26,500,000
10	Grant Hill	Basketball	23,000,000

* *From the US unless otherwise stated*

Source: Forbes *magazine*

TOP 10 SPECTATOR SPORTS IN THE UK

(Sport/percentage of adults who pay to watch)

1 **Football**, 13.1 **2** **Cricket**, 4.5 **3** = **Horse racing**, 3.8; = **Rugby Union**, 3.8 **5** **Motor racing**, 3.3 **6** = **Greyhound racing**, 2.5; = **Stock car racing**, 2.5 **8** **Rugby league**, 2.4 **9** **Motor cycle racing**, 2.1 **10** **Tennis**, 1.8

Source: *The Sports Council*

Did You Know? The Tour de France cycle race is believed to be watched by more spectators than any other sport, with some 10 million people lining the route during the three-week event.

THE 10

LATEST TRIATHLON WORLD CHAMPIONS

MAN/COUNTRY	TIME	YEAR	TIME	WOMAN/COUNTRY
Dimitry Gaag, Kazahkstan	1:45:25	**1999**	1:55:28	**Loretta Harrop**, Australia
Simon Lessing, UK	1:55:31	**1998**	2:07:25	**Joanne King**, Australia
Chris McCormack, Australia	1:48:29	**1997**	1:59:22	**Emma Carney**, Australia
Simon Lessing, UK	1:39:50	**1996**	1:50:52	**Jackie Gallagher**, Australia
Simon Lessing, UK	1:48:29	**1995**	2:04:58	**Karen Smyers**, USA
Spencer Smith, UK	1:51:04	**1994**	2:03:19	**Emma Carney**, Australia
Spencer Smith, UK	1:51:20	**1993**	2:07:41	**Michellie Jones**, Australia
Simon Lessing, UK	1:49:04	**1992**	2:02:08	**Michellie Jones**, Australia
Miles Stewart, Australia	1:48:20	**1991**	2:02:04	**Joanne Ritchie**, Canada
Greg Welch, Australia	1:51:37	**1990**	2:03:33	**Karen Smyers**, USA

The Triathlon World Championship has been contested since 1989 and consists of a 1.5-km (1-mile) swim, a 40-km (25-mile) bike ride, and a 10-km (6¼-mile) run.

TOP 10

ALL-ROUND CHAMPION COWBOYS

	COWBOY	YEARS	WINS
1	**Ty Murray**	1989–98	7
2	**=Tom Ferguson**	1974–79	6
	=Larry Mahan	1966–73	6
4	**Jim Shoulders**	1949–59	5
5	**=Lewis Feild**	1985–87	3
	=Dean Oliver	1963–65	3
7	**=Joe Beaver**	1995–96	2
	=Everett Bowman	1935–37	2
	=Louis Brooks	1943–44	2
	=Clay Carr	1930–33	2
	=Bill Linderman	1950–53	2
	=Phil Lyne	1971–72	2
	=Gerald Roberts	1942–48	2
	=Casey Tibbs	1951–55	2
	=Harry Tompkins	1952–60	2

The All-Around World Champion Cowboy title is presented by the Professional Rodeo Cowboys Association (PRCA) each year. The winner is the rodeo athlete who wins the most prize money in a single year in two or more events, with minimum earnings of $2,000 per event. During the 1990s, several winners earned more than $250,000 a year.

TOP 10

FASTEST WINNING TIMES FOR THE HAWAII IRONMAN

	WINNER/COUNTRY*	YEAR	TIME HR:MIN:SEC
1	**Luc Van Lierde**, Belgium	1996	8:04:08
2	**Mark Allen**	1993	8:07:45
3	**Mark Allen**	1992	8:09:08
4	**Mark Allen**	1989	8:09:16
5	**Luc Van Lierde**	1999	8:17:17
6	**Mark Allen**	1991	8:18:32
7	**Greg Welch**, Australia	1994	8:20:27
8	**Mark Allen**	1995	8:20:34
9	**Peter Reid**, Canada	1998	8:24:20
10	**Mark Allen**	1990	8:28:17

* *From the US unless otherwise stated*

In perhaps one of the most gruelling sporting contests, competitors engage in a 3.86-km (2½-mile) swim, a 180-km (112-mile) cycle race, and a 42.195-km (26¼ mile) run.

TOP 10

MOST DANGEROUS AMATEUR SPORTS

	SPORT	RISK FACTOR*
1	**Powerboat racing**	15
2	**Ocean yacht racing**	10
3	**Cave diving**	7
4	**Potholing**	6
5	**=Drag racing**	5
	=Karting	5
7	**Microlyte**	4
8	**=Hang gliding**	3
	=Motor racing	3
	=Mountaineering	3

* *Risk factor refers to the premium that insurance companies place on insuring someone for that activity – the higher the risk factor, the higher the premium*

Source: *General Accident*

DANGER BELOW

The risk of injury or becoming trapped underground has resulted in potholing being ranked among the world's most hazardous sports.

Index

A

B

top10

N

O

P

UK research assistants:
Harriet Hart, Lucy Hemming

Special US research: Dafydd Rees

Thanks to the individuals, organizations, and publications listed below who kindly supplied information to enable me to prepare many of the lists.

Caroline Ash, Mark Atterton, John Bardsley, Richard Braddish, Steve Butler, Henry Button, Lesley Coldham, Stanley Coren, Sidney S. Culbert, François Curiel, Louise Firth, Christopher Forbes, Raymond Fletcher, Professor Ken Fox, Darryl Francis, Simon Gilbert, Russell E. Gough, Monica Grady, Stan Greenberg, Max Hanna, Peter Harland, Andrew Hemming, Duncan Hislop, Andreas Hoerstemeier, Michael A. Hutson, Tony Hutson, Alan Jeffreys, Robert Lamb, Dr Jaquie Lavin, Jo Littmoden, Dr Benjamin Lucas, John Malam, Professor Richard Moody, Ian Morrison, Vincent Nasso, Sarah Owen, Adrian Room, Bill Rudman, Robert Senior, Lisa E. Smith, Mitchell Symons, Tony Waltham, Professor Edward O. Wilson, Peter Wynne-Thomas

Academy of Motion Picture Arts and Sciences, *Advertising Age*, Advertising Association, Amateur Athletic Association, American Forestry Association, *Amusement Business*, *Annual Abstract of Statistics*, *Art Newspaper*, Art Sales Index, Associated Examining Board, Associated Press, Association of Tennis Professionals (ATP), Audit Bureau of Circulations Ltd., Automobile Association, BAFTA, BARB/SPC, BBC Radio 1, BBC Worldwide, *Billboard*, Booker Prize, *Bookseller*, Book Trust, Bookwatch Ltd., BPI, *BP Statistical Review of World Energy*, BRIT Awards, British Association of Toy Retailers, British Broadcasting Corporation, British Cave Research Association, British Columbia Vital Statistics Agency, British Film Academy, British Library, British Museum (Natural History), British Video Association, Cadbury Schweppes Group, Cannes Film Festival, Carbon Dioxide Information Analysis Center, Center for Disease Control, Central Intelligence Agency, Central Statistics Office/An Príomh-Oifig Staidrimh, Ireland, Champagne Bureau, Channel Swimming Association, Christian Research, Christie's, CIN, *Classical Music*, Coca-Cola, Columbia University/Pulitzer Prizes, Computer Industry Almanac, Inc., Corporate Intelligence on Retailing Ltd., *Crime in the United States*, *Criminal Statistics England & Wales*, Dateline International, De Beers, Deloitte & Touche, Department of the Environment, Transport and the Regions, Department of Trade and Industry, *Economist*, Electoral Reform Society, Energy Information Administration, English Tourist Board, Euromonitor, *FBI Uniform Crime Reports*, Feste Catalogue Index Database/Alan Somerset, *Financial Times*, *Flight International*, Food and Agriculture Organization of the United Nations, Football Writers' Association, *Forbes*, Forestry Commission, *Fortune*, Gemstone Publishing, Inc., General Accident, Generation AB, Geologists' Ass., Gold Fields Mineral Services Ltd., Governing Council of the Cat Fancy, Headcount.com, Health and Safety Executive, H. J. Heinz, Home Accident Surveillance System (HASS), Home Office, Iditarod Trail Committee, Interbrand, International Association of Ports and Harbors, International Atomic Energy Agency, International Civil Aviation Organization, International Cocoa Organization, International Coffee Organization, International Commission on Large Dams, International Dairy Foods Association, International Game Fish Association, International Tea Committee, International Union for the Conservation of Nature, Inter-Parliamentary Union, Interpol, Kellogg's, Kennel Club, Korbel Champagne Cellars, Library Association, Lloyds Register of Shipping/MIPG/PPMS, London Theatre Record, London Transport Lost Property, Cameron Mackintosh Ltd., *Marketing*, Mars, Inc., Meat and Livestock Commission, *Melody Maker*, Ministry of Agriculture, Meteorological Office, MRIB, MTV, Museum of Rugby, NASA, National Academy of Recording Arts and Sciences (NARAS), National Basketball Association (NBA), National Book Foundation, National Collegiate Athletic Association (NCAA), National Dairy Council, National Football League (NFL), National Hurricane Center, *New Musical Express*, New South Wales Registry of Births, Deaths and Marriages, New York Road Runners Club, Niagara Falls Museum, ACNielsen MMS, Nielsen Media Research, Nobel Foundation, NOP, Northern Ireland Statistics and Research Agency, NPD Group Worldwide, Nua Ltd., Office for National Statistics, Patent Office, PC Data Online, Pet Food Manufacturers' Association, PetPlan Pet Insurance, Phobics Society, Popular Music Database, Produktschap voor Gedistilleerde Dranken, Professional Rodeo Cowboys Association (PRCA), Project Feeder Watch/Cornell Lab of Ornithology, Public Lending Right, *Q Magazine*, *Raceboat International*, *Racing Post*, *Railway Gazette International*, RAJAR, Really Useful Group, Recording Industry Association of America (RIAA), *Regional Trends*, Royal Aeronautical Society, Royal College of General Practitioners, Royal College of Music, Royal Opera House, Covent Garden, Royal Society for the Protection of Birds, Royal Television Society, *Rugby News*, Scottish Office, *Screen Digest*, Shakespeare Birthplace Trust, Siemens AG, Sightseeing Research, *Slimming World*, W.H. Smith Ltd., *Social Trends*, Society of Motor Manufacturers and Traders Ltd., Society of West End Theatre (SWET) Awards, Sony Radio Awards, Sotheby's, *Spaceflight*, *Sports Illustrated*, *Statistical Abstract of the United States*, Statistics Norway, STATS Inc., Stockholm International Peace Research Institute, *Sunday Times*, Trebor Bassett Ltd., Tree Register of the British Isles, Ty Inc., UNESCO, United Nations, Universal Postal Union, University of Westminster, US Board on Geographic Names, US Bureau of the Census, US Department of Justice, US Geological Survey, US Patent Office, US Social Security Administration, *Variety*, Ward's Automotive, Whitbread Literary Awards, Women's National Basketball Association (WNBA), World Association of Newspapers, World Bank, World Health Organization, World Meteorological Organization, World Resources Institute, World Tourism Organization, Zenith International.

Index
Patrica Coward

DK Picture Librarians
Denise O'Brien, Melanie Simmonds

Packager's acknowledgments:
Cooling Brown would like to thank the following: Pauline Clarke for design assistance; Peter Cooling for technical support; Carolyn MacKenzie for proof reading; Chris and Eleanor Bolus for the loan of the Beanie Babies.

Picture Credits

Advertising Archives: 205tl, 218tl
Allsport: 243br, 244tr, 248tr, 259bl, 264br; Al Bello 253br; Hamish Blair 273tr; Sean Botterill 276tl, 249r; Clive Brunskill 271br; Simon Bruty 252l; David Cannon 246–247, 264–265; Michael Cooper 260tr; Tim Defrisco 244bl; Stephen Dunn 251r; Stu Forster 270b; John Gichigi 272; Otto Greule 247tl; Elsa Hasch 278tr; Tom Herbert 266–267; Mike Hewitt 245tr; Harry How 265br; Doug Pensinger 246bl, 260–261; Gary M Prior 259tr; Pascal Rondeau 274–275; Ezra Shaw 276–277
Apple Computers: 209br
Austin Brown/Aviation Picture Library: 236bl, 236–237, 237tr
British Museum: 97bc
Camera Press: 69tr, 76–77, 103; Richard Open 114bl; R Stonehouse 194; Brian Snyder 77br
Capital Pictures: Phil Loftus 143tl
Christie's Images Ltd: 102bl, 112tr, 113br; Edward S. Curtis 117tr; *Kiss II*, 1962 by Roy Lichtenstein © DACS 115br
Bruce Coleman Ltd: John Cancalosi 42bl; Geoff Dore 43b; Jeff Foott 40l; Earl Kowall 50bl; Fritz Prenzel 48b
Colorsport: John Varley 258tl.
Corbis UK Ltd: 75tr; Paul Almasy 114tr; Yann Arthus–Bertrand 92–93, 238–239; Bettmann 9tl, 29bl, 63, 67tr, 130tl, 146bl, 162br, 226; Jonathan Blair 14–15b; Ralph A Clevenger 40–41; Sheldan Collins 99, 198–199; Dean Conger 26br; Jonathan Smith/Cordaiy Photo Library 23tr; Philip James Corwin 72–73; Jay Dickman 213; Henry Diltz 126tl; Wayne Lawler/Ecoscene 22–23; Trisha Rafferty/Eye Ubiquitous 204; Jack Fields 58t, 79br; Kevin Fleming 50–51; Natalie Fobes 212bl; Stephen Frink 41br; Marc Garanger 230bl; Mitchell Gerber 128l; Mark Gibson 230t; Dallas and John Heaton 242tl, 242–243; Robert Holmes 100tl; Jeremy Horner 59r, 208tl; Hulton Deutsch Collection 125t, 127tl; Kelly–Mooney Photography 185tl; Earl Kowall 93br; Daniel Laine 84t; Jean–Pierre Lescourret 228bl; James Marshall 21tr; C Moore 89; Kevin R Morris 234–235t; David A Northcott 38tr; Richard T Nowitz 24t, 71br; Neal Preston 129tr, 133bl; Bob Rowan/Progressive Image 199tr, 210–211; Neil Rabinowitz 51tr; Steve Raymer 82r; Jim Richardson 28bl; Kevin Schafer 42–43; Lee Snider 9br; Paul A Souders 90–91t, 210tl; Keren Su 8–9; Chase Swift 37r; Liba Taylor 201br; Peter Turnley 74–75; David Turnley 202; Underwood and Underwood 124b; UPI 77tl; Nik Wheeler 27tr; Staffan Widstrand 83br; Michael S Yamashita 157br, 229tl
China Photo Library: 92b
DC Comics: 119tr
Ferrari UK: 227
Galaxy Picture Library: Gordan Garradd 12tr
Ronald Grant Archive: *Purple Rain* 149; *The Spy Who Loved Me* © 1977 EON Productions 148br; *Back to the Future* ©1985 Universal UIP 165tl; *Misery* ©1990 Columbia 181bl; *Terminator II* ©1991 Columbia Tristar 159br; *Wayne's World* ©1992 Paramount (UIP) 182tr; *Batman Returns* ©1992 Warner Bros 176br; *Independence Day* ©1996 20th Century Fox 162–163t; *The Rock* ©1996 Buena Vista 174tr; *Escape from LA* ©1996 Paramount; photo Robert Zuckerman 183; *Jackie Brown* ©1997 Buena Vista 180t; *Tomorrow Never Dies* ©1997 EON Productions; photo Keith Hamshere 174bl; *The Prince of Egypt* ©1998 Dreamworks 147t; *You Got Mail* ©1998 Warner Bros 176tl; 20th Century Fox 186t; MGM 187br
Mike Griggs Photography: 67br
H J Heinz: 216; **Chris Howes:** 279br
Johnson Space Centre: 18t
Kobal Collection: *Cabaret* ©1972 ABC/Allied Artists 169tl; *Jaws* ©1975 Universal (UIP) 163br; *Arthur* ©1981 Orion 168tl; *On Golden Pond* ©1981 Universal 170bl; *Gandhi* ©1984 Indo-British/International Film Investors 184l; *Ghostbusters* ©1989 Columbia 164bl; *Reservoir Dogs* ©1992 Live Entertainment 179; *Jurassic Park* ©1993 Amblin/Universal (UIP) 158; *Much Ado About Nothing* ©1993 Sam Goldwyn/ Renaissance Films/BBC 156tr; *Forest Gump* ©1994 Paramount (UIP) 165br; *Braveheart* ©1995 Icon/Ladd Co/Paramount 167br; *The Full Monty* ©1995 20th Century Fox 159tl; *Seven* ©1995 New Line Cinema/Entertainment Film 175tr; *Waterworld* ©1995 Universal, photo Ben Glass 160b; *Copycat* ©1995 WB Monarchy Enterprises 181tr; *Shine* ©1996 Momentum Films 172tr; *Fargo* ©1996 Polygram Filmed Entertainment/ Gramercy Pictures; photo James Bridges 178tr; *The English Patient* ©1996 Tigermoth/Miramax 166tr; *Jackie Brown* ©1997 Buena Vista 178bl; *My Best Friend's Wedding* ©1997 Columbia Tristar 177; *As Good As It Gets* ©1997 Tristar/Gracie Films 170tr; ©1999 Paramount Pictures and Touchstone Pictures Company; photo Ron Batzdorff 182bl; *The Matrix* ©1999 Warner Bros; photo Jasin Boland 161l; *The Truman Show* © 1997 Paramount Pictures Corp., photograph Melinda Sue Gordon 173; 193tr; *There's Something About Mary* © 1998 20th Century Fox, photograph Glenn Watson 195tr
Lebrecht Collection: Peter Mares 153tl
London Features International: 139r, 192bl; Jen Lowery 132; *The Sound of Music* © 1965 Argyle Enterprises, Inc./Twentieth Century Fox 148tl; David Fisher 62bl
Moviestore Collection: *American Beauty* ©1999 Dreamworks 167tl; *Boys Don't Cry* ©1999 Fox Searchlight 171t
NASA: 15tr, 16–17, 25br; Finley Holiday Films 13t
Natural History Museum, London: 35b
Network Photographers Ltd: Greg Smith/SABA 70t; Homer Sykes 207tr
© Newspapers International Newspapers Limited, 1st January 2000: *The Sun*, London 107tr
Nickelodeon International Ltd: 190–191
Nordfoto: Liselotte Sabroe 222bl
Oxford Scientific Films: G I Bernard 47tl; Alastair MacEwan 34tl; Rob Nunnington 49t
Panos Pictures: Caroline Penn 100br
PetExcellence, Florida USA: 277br
Photodisc: 24–25, 79, 254–255, 256–257
Popperfoto: 238bl; Reuter 30bl, 64tr, 214–215, 231tr, 239tl
Redferns: 130br; Fin Costello 145br; Kieran Doherty 135b; Paul Hampartsoumian 134tr; Mick Hutson 133tr, 140–141l; Jm Enternational 142b; Michel Linssen 131r,145tl; Keith Morris 137; Michael Ochs Archive 123bl, 136br; Rb Collection 127br; David Redfern 123tr, 136tl; Ebet Roberts 134bl, 141tl, 144tl; Barbara Steinwehe 150bl; Gai Terrell 122bl; Des Willie 143r
Royal Caribbean Cruises Ltd: 234bl
Royal Geographical Society: Ranulph Fiennes 66tr
Science & Society Picture Library: Science Museum 188br
Science Photo Library: 54l; GJLP 55br; Laguna Design 29tr; Johnson Matthey 203br; Hank Morgan 54tr; NASA 19b; Novosti 17br; Dr Linda Stannard 31; Peter Thorne
Sotheby's Picture Library, London: 116, 118–119
Frank Spooner Pictures: De Kerle/Gamma 106bl; Peter Orme/Gamma 105r; Frederic Reglain/Gamma 104bl
Still Pictures: 68bl; Fritz Polking 39r
The Stock Market: Charles Gupton 221tr; M Smith 20–21; Ken Straiton 200
Tony Stone Images: Thierry Cazabon 110–111; Paul Chesley 78tl; Will and Deni McIntyre 20br; Nicholas Parfitt 26–27; Peter Pearson 90–91; Antonia Reeve 98tl; Ron Sherman 100–101
Sveriges Riksdag: 65bc; **Sygma:** Corbis 235br
Toyota (GB) PLC: 229br
Jerry Young: 46